THE OXFORD HISTORY OF
ENGLISH LITERATURE

General Editors

JOHN BUXTON *and* NORMAN DAVIS

ENGLISH LITERATURE
1832–1890
EXCLUDING THE NOVEL

PAUL TURNER

CLARENDON PRESS · OXFORD
1989

Oxford University Press, Walton Street, Oxford OX2 6DP
Oxford New York Toronto
Delhi Bombay Calcutta Madras Karachi
Petaling Jaya Singapore Hong Kong Tokyo
Nairobi Dar es Salaam Cape Town
Melbourne Auckland
and associated companies in
Berlin Ibadan

Oxford is a trade mark of Oxford University Press

Published in the United States
by Oxford University Press, New York

British Library Cataloguing in Publication Data
Turner, Paul
English literature 1832–1890 excluding
the novel.
1. English literature—1800–1900
Critical studies.
I. Title
820.9'007
ISBN 0–19–812217–9

Library of Congress Cataloging in Publication Data
Turner, Paul, 1917–
English literature, 1832–1890 : excluding the novel / Paul Turner.
(The Oxford history of English literature)
Bibliography. Includes index.
1. English literature—19th century—History and criticism.
I. Title. II. Series.
PR461.T87   1989   820'.9'008—dc 19   88–19501
ISBN 0–19–812217–9

Set by Latimer Trend & Co Ltd, Plymouth
Printed in Great Britain
at the University Printing House, Oxford
by David Stanford
Printer to The University

To Jane

Preface

IT has often seemed unlikely, over the past fourteen years, that this book would ever get written. That it has done so is largely due to help from many people, whom I now wish to thank. In 1975 Professor Kathleen Tillotson let me see the comprehensive bibliography prepared before his untimely death by Geoffrey Tillotson, who was originally responsible for this volume. I have had unfailing support and encouragement from the General Editors, John Buxton and Norman Davis, and from Jon Stallworthy, John Bell, and Kim Scott Walwyn at the Clarendon Press. I was also encouraged by James Sutherland and Ian Jack, the more effectually as they were walking proofs that such a book could be finished, though I could hardly hope to equal their performances. My friend Park Honan was a cheering example of the same kind, and a mine of information on several of my authors. To get the books I needed, I shamelessly exploited the kindness of many College and Faculty librarians in Oxford, of Sheila Gordon-Rae at the Bodleian, and especially of Margaret Weedon, Eileen Davies, and Gwen Hampshire in the English Faculty Library. The English Faculty Board made it easier for me to haunt that library, by generously allowing me to keep my nearby teaching-room for three years after retirement. During the long process of research and writing, I owed much to the special knowledge of friends at Linacre College; to John Bamborough, who raised my sagging spirits at many a lunch-time there; to my wife Jane, for help of every kind; and to our rough collie, Georgy, who kept me fit, and acted as my Muse.

Contents

1. The Spirit of the Age

'REFORM, that you may preserve', Macaulay urged the House of Commons in 1831. The alternative was to 'persist in a hopeless struggle against the spirit of the age'. John Stuart Mill thought so too. His articles on 'The Spirit of the Age', published the same year, described the age as one of 'transition', in which 'worldly power' must cease to be monopolized by 'the landed gentry, and the monied class'. Thirty years later another student of the *Zeitgeist*, Matthew Arnold announced: 'Democracy is trying *to affirm its own essence*; to live, to enjoy, to possess the world, as aristocracy has tried, and successfully tried, before it.' The affirmation was most explicit in a series of Reform Acts, which enfranchised first the industrial middle class (1832), then some working men in towns (1867), and finally agricultural labourers (1884); but democratic feeling was shown in many other ways, and drew strength from sources not purely political. One was the fear that, without some degree of reform, the horrors of the French Revolution would be re-enacted in England. Another was the social conscience cultivated by the Evangelicals, which became increasingly sensitive to working-class suffering. A third was the Utilitarian philosophy developed by James and John Mill from Bentham's principle: 'It is the greatest happiness of the greatest number that is the measure of right and wrong.'

Until the mid-century the greatest number were conspicuously unhappy. 'A feeling very generally exists', wrote Carlyle in 1839, 'that the condition and disposition of the Working Classes is a rather ominous matter at present; that something ought to be said, something ought to be done, in regard to it.' Their condition was the product of many factors. The most obvious one was a population explosion, accompanied by rapid industrialization and urbanization. Between 1801 and 1881 the population of England and Wales rose from nearly nine to nearly twenty-six millions. The mechanization of industry attracted labour to manufacturing towns, and by 1851 more than half the people were living in urban areas. Working and living conditions for factory hands grew worse and worse, as industrialists, encouraged by Ricardo's economic theory to think market forces immutable and irresistible, competed to exploit new technology for instant profit, while over-production caused periodic slumps, and mass unemployment. The increase in population, accelerated by immigration from Ireland, especially after the potato famine of 1845, produced the 'poverty and misery . . . among the lower classes of people' which Malthus had predicted. A typical passage in Henry Mayhew's social survey, *London Labour and the London Poor* (1851) was a report on those who earned their living by searching for objects of value in rat-infested sewers.

The 'condition of England', as this huge social problem was commonly called, was first brought to the consciousness of the middle class by government reports published in the thirties and forties. In one of them a section on the effects of disease among the working classes was drily headed: 'Misery not a check to the pressure of population on subsistence'. Malthusians, of course,, and Utilitarians realized that population-growth was a large part of the problem: J. S. Mill had been arrested at seventeen for distributing leaflets on birth control, after finding a strangled baby in St James's Park. If society as a whole was dimly aware of it too, the Victorian prejudice against sex was more rational than is generally thought. The prejudice was strongly supported by public opinion, and even given scientific authority by doctors like William Acton, who claimed in a medical textbook of 1857 that 'every sexual indulgence' in youth was an 'unmitigated evil'. As a 'check to population', however, prudery proved ineffective. Pornography flourished, the number of prostitutes in London alone was put at eighty thousand in 1862, and what Tennyson once called 'the torrent of babies' continued to flow.

The fear of revolution had been increased by Chartism (1837–48), a largely working-class movement which campaigned for political rights by massive demonstrations. Carlyle saw Chartism as an inarticulate plea for authoritarian government, but to most thoughtful minds the threat of mob violence seemed to confirm the need for further reform. It also encouraged the belief that, as J. S. Mill later expressed it, 'the higher classes . . . had more to fear from the poor when uneducated, than when educated.' For Tennyson one of the two great social questions of the day was 'the housing and education of the poor man before making him our master'. Thus education was initially conceived as a charm to soothe the savage breasts of the poor, and eventually make them fit for democratic power; but it developed into one of the period's chief preoccupations. Though belief in *laissez-faire* and rivalries between religious organizations delayed until 1870 the establishment of any system of state education, the work of educating the poorer classes had been started long before then, by a variety of agencies, religious, philanthropic, and commercial. The percentage of literate males and females was recorded in 1841 as 67.3 and 51.1 respectively: the figures for 1891 were 93.6 and 92.7. This growth of literacy in a growing population created a vast new demand for reading-matter, at a time when technological improvements were making all forms of publication cheaper. The result was a huge expansion of the book trade, and the proliferation of newspapers and periodicals. It thus became much easier to earn a living by writing, and periodical journalism offered a convenient approach to full-time authorship. The period's literature was notably enriched by the increased variety of its authors' backgrounds, yet most authors shared a tendency to didacticism, as if conscious of a duty to educate readers who might be comparative newcomers to the written word.

As illiteracy was gradually reduced, concern shifted to the quality and content of education. At first the main object had been to teach religion or 'useful knowledge'. The latter continued to be emphasized by Herbert Spencer and others who thought science the subject 'most worth knowing'; but broader ideas of education were diffused, first by Newman and then by Matthew Arnold, who as an Inspector of Schools complained in 1860 that the pupil had, 'except his Bible, no literature, no *humanizing* instruction at all'. In 1871 'English literature' was added to the elementary school syllabus, and in 1880 Huxley, while rejecting Arnold's version of 'culture', admitted that an 'exclusively scientific training [would] bring about a mental twist as surely as an exclusively literary training.'

The interest in education was just one of the ways in which the reforming spirit spread from Parliamentary representation to every sphere of social life. In trade and industry, for instance, the rights of capital were gradually reduced by a series of Factory Acts, and by the growth of trade-union power, from Robert Owen's Grand National Consolidated Trades Union (1834) to the first Trades Union Congress in 1868, and the successful dock-strike of 1889. The idea of socialism, which Owen had also pioneered in England, was slow to gain wide acceptance; but J. S. Mill discussed it quite sympathetically in his *Principles of Political Economy* (1848), the year of the *Communist Manifesto*, and by the end of the period Morris was preaching Marxism.

A type of social reform more congenial to the spirit of the age was one that drew strong words in 1870 from Queen Victoria:

The Queen is most anxious to enlist every one who can speak or write to join in checking this mad, wicked folly of 'Women's Rights', with all its attendant horrors, on which the poor feeble sex is bent, forgetting every sense of womanly feeling and propriety. Lady — ought to get a good *whipping*. It is a subject which makes the Queen so furious that she cannot contain herself. God created men and women different—then let them remain each in their own position.

The cause of feminism had not been helped by the association of its first English exponent, Mary Wollstonecraft, with the French Revolution; but the Owenite William Thompson had argued the case more cogently in 1825, and poems like *The Princess* (1847) and *Aurora Leigh* (1857) gave feminism greater emotional appeal. The Queen's fury was a tribute to the effectiveness of Mill's *On the Subjection of Women* (1869), and to his recent efforts in Parliament to make the 1867 Reform Act the logical climax of the series, by amending the word 'man' to read 'person'.

Mill typified his period not only in wanting to be a 'reformer of the world' but also in defending personal freedom, since reforming zeal bulked no larger in the *Zeitgeist* than individualism. This, though partly inherited from the Romantics, was probably intensified by a new sense of overcrowding, especially in large towns. Ethologists say that every animal needs a specific amount of living-space, and there was perhaps something analogous in Mill's claim that

there is a sphere of action in which society, as distinguished from the individual, has, if any, only an indirect interest; comprehending all that portion of a person's life and conduct which affects only himself . . . This, then, is the appropriate region of human liberty.

Apart from the physical overcrowding, the mere feeling that there were growing numbers of people about must have challenged some individuals to assert their own uniqueness, on Mill's uncompromising principle:

If all mankind minus one were of one opinion, and only one person were of the contrary opinion, mankind would be no more justified in silencing that one person, than he, if he had the power, would be justified in silencing mankind.

Carlyle's taste for speaking in a 'minority of one' exemplified the same attitude; and the obstinacy of the solitary dissident doubtless grew, as the period's interest in travel and history made the human majority seem greater, and science extended in both space and time the apparent dimensions of the universe.

In poetry individualism was protean. The philosophy of *In Memoriam* was based on individual feeling: 'And like a man in wrath the heart | Stood up and answered "I have felt."' It thus illustrated Mill's distinction between eighteenth- and nineteenth-century thinking: 'For the apotheosis of Reason we have substituted that of Instinct; and we call everything instinct which we find in ourselves and for which we cannot trace any rational foundation.' Browning's dramatic monologues centred on the discrepancies between the individual's 'conceit of truth' and other people's view of it. Clough's *Dipsychus* was about something that Matthew Arnold thought typically 'modern': 'the dialogue of the mind with itself'; and his own *Empedocles* was about an endogenous psychological state: ''Tis not the times, 'tis not the sophists vex him; | There is some root of suffering in himself.' The egocentricity of the Spasmodics went to absurd lengths, but was defended by one reviewer on the assumption that 'a true allegory of the state of one's own mind . . . is perhaps the highest thing that one can attempt in the way of fictitious art'; and this theory closely resembled the practice of the Pre-Raphaelites. Hopkins developed a whole new language and prosody to express his own sense of individuality: 'Nothing else in nature comes near this unspeakable stress of pitch, distinctiveness, and selving, this selfbeing of my own.'

Pater's first principle of criticism was equally self-orientated: 'What is this song or picture . . . to *me*?' His theory of style demanded a precise correspondence between wording and 'the true nature of one's own impression': 'what might seem mere details of form' had the function of 'bringing to the surface,

sincerely and in their integrity, certain strong personal intuitions'.
A similar view was implied by translations from the Classics.
Where Pope had been content to make Homer sound like Pope,
Clough and many other translators felt obliged to imitate Homer's
hexameters, as if these were an integral part of the poet's
personality. Francis Newman's *Iliad* was only an extreme example
of a general anxiety to reproduce the 'surface' of an original.
Working 'on the principles rather of a daguerrotypist than of a
fashionable portrait-painter', he tried to show 'what the true
Homer really was', with all his 'oddities and peculiarities'. But this
concern with personality was naturally strongest when the personality in question was the writer's own, as in the autobiographies
of Ruskin or Harriet Martineau. It expressed itself less formally in
the delightful letters of Jane Welsh Carlyle, and more aggressively
in her husband's eccentric prose. To his style, as to Browning's,
the words of Hopkins may be applied with special force: '*myself* it
speaks and spells; | Crying *What I do is me: for that I came.*'

In life, individualism was seen at its best in the spirit of self-help
celebrated by Samuel Smiles and the large number of eminent
people who were self-made and self-educated. Faraday began his
career as an errand-boy. Livingstone was a factory-hand at the age
of ten, but taught himself enough Latin in the evenings to read
Virgil and Horace, and then studied botany, zoology, and geology.
During working hours, which began at 6 a.m., he put his book on
the spinning-jenny, so as to catch a sentence every time his work
took him past it. Another sign of the age's faith in the individual
was the cult of the great man. 'The History of the World', wrote
Carlyle, 'is but the Biography of great men', and the attitudes
recommended in *Heroes and Hero-Worship* were duly directed
both to him and to several other sages. Hence the wooden bridge
that Tennyson had to have built, to escape his worshippers at
Farringford, and the tea-party given by the Newnham Browning
Society, at which the poet was said to have sat, 'bland and ruddy,
and slightly buttery from the muffins, with [a] crown of pink roses
laid upon his white locks, and looking like a lamb decked for
sacrifice.'

If such eminent Victorians were the victims of individualism, its
beneficiaries were children. Arguing in 1850 that each person's
individuality should be allowed to develop 'without limit, save for
the like individualities of others', Herbert Spencer specifically

included children, and condemned parental 'coercion'. At the start of the century, Samuel Butler recalled, it had been 'universally admitted that to spare the rod was to spoil the child', and a father's duty was thought to consist in

checking the first signs of self-will while his children were too young to offer serious resistance. If their wills were 'well broken' in childhood, to use an expression then much in vogue, they would acquire habits of obedience which they would not venture to break through till they were over twenty-one years old.

By 1869, however, Lecky could write:

there is a method of education which was never more prevalent than in the present day, which exhausts its efforts in making virtue attractive, in associating it with all the charms of imagination and of prosperity, and in thus insensibly drawing the desires in the wished-for direction.

The gradual change in attitudes to children, though partly due to writers like Wordsworth and Rousseau, was also connected with a growing interest in psychology (the backwardness of which had been deplored by Mill in 1843 as a 'blot on the face of science'), and with the growth of humane feeling for all types of underdog, from slaves, factory-workers, and convicts to actual dogs, horses, and other animals. The psychological and humanitarian components of the new approach to upbringing were both shown, in the year of Lecky's comment, by Florence Montgomery's popular novel, *Misunderstood*; and the period's increasing concern to understand and sympathize with the child's point of view is clear from the unprecedented volume and variety of its children's books.

The spirit of reform and the spirit of individualism soon began to seem incompatible. As Democracy affirmed its essence, injustice to the 'greatest number' threatened to turn into the 'tyranny of the majority'.

Protection, therefore, against the tyranny of the magistrate is not enough: there needs protection also against the tyranny of the prevailing opinion and feeling; against the tendency of society to impose, by other means than civil penalties, its own ideas and practices as rules of conduct on those who dissent from them; to fetter the development, and, if possible, prevent the formation, of any individuality not in harmony with its ways, and compel all characters to fashion themselves upon the model of its own.

So warned Mill in 1859, and the next year Spencer published an article, of which he would write in *The Man versus the State* (1884):

the thesis maintained was that, unless due precautions were taken, increase of freedom in form would be followed by decrease of freedom in fact ... The drift of legislation since that time has been of the kind anticipated. Dictatorial measures, rapidly multiplied, have tended continually to narrow the liberties of individuals

Despite such apparent contradictions between intentions and results, there was a general feeling that progress was being made; and Darwin's theory of evolution, as first propounded in the year of Mill's warning, seemed almost to suggest that progress was inevitable: 'as natural selection works solely by and for the good of each being, all corporeal and mental endowments will tend to progress towards perfection.' Five years later a Benthamite politician thought perfection had already been reached:

I look round me and ask what is the state of England? Is not property safe? Is not every man able to say what he likes? Can you not walk from one end of England to the other in perfect security? I ask you whether, the world over or in past history, there is anything like it? Nothing. I pray that our unrivalled happiness may last.

Matthew Arnold was just one of many authors who ridiculed such complacency; but in spite of 'Wragg, poor thing!' the period had good reason to congratulate itself. It had survived, without a revolution, social tensions never experienced before. It had improvised, within a few decades, the framework of a modern industrial democracy. It was inventing or rapidly developing much that might now be classed among the bare essentials of any civilized life, such as drainage, water-supplies, gas-lighting, a railway-network, a police force, local authorities responsible for public health, and cheap postal services. Towards civilization in a less material sense it contributed a great variety of humane legislation, and a general improvement of public opinion, even if at the cost of making it rather puritanical and hypocritical. It is easy to laugh at Victorian moralizing, and the Victorians laughed at it too. 'We know no spectacle so ridiculous', wrote Macaulay, 'as the British public in one of its periodical fits of morality.' But he still insisted

that a 'great moral change' had taken place. Having listed some
atrocities tolerated in 1685, he continued:

But on all this misery society looked with profound indifference.
Nowhere could be found that sensitive and restless compassion which
has, in our time, extended a powerful protection to the factory child, to
the Hindoo widow, to the negro slave . . . which winces at every lash laid
on the back of a drunken soldier, which will not suffer the thief in the
hulks to be ill fed or overworked, and which has repeatedly endeavoured
to save the life even of the murderer . . . But the more we study the annals
of the past the more shall we rejoice that we live in a merciful age, in an
age in which cruelty is abhorred, and in which pain, even when deserved,
is inflicted reluctantly and from a sense of duty.

Now that 'Victorian' has become a popular term of abuse, the
word 'merciful' may seem as inapt as the name of Pecksniff's
younger daughter, and the last phrase may remind one of Butler's
Theobald Pontifex; but in relation to the past, Macaulay's boast
was justified.

   The sense of progress was celebrated by Tennyson in 1830 with
a line composed after travelling on the first train from Liverpool to
Manchester: 'Let the great world spin for ever down the ringing
grooves of change.' He was wrong to assume, not having seen the
train's wheels, that they ran in grooves, but the railway was then
exactly the right image to express the contemporary feeling of
advancing at high speed. 'Better fifty years of Europe than a cycle
of Cathay', Tennyson added, and his poem 'On the Jubilee of
Queen Victoria' (1887) summarized, more prosaically, what those
fifty years had brought to England:

>   Fifty years of ever-broadening Commerce!
>   Fifty years of ever-brightening Science!
>   Fifty years of ever-widening Empire!

The triumph of English commerce, which had helped to avert
revolution in the 1840s, was proclaimed to the world by the Great
Exhibition of 1851. The growth of the British Empire needed no
such advertisement, but was given both religious and academic
status by J. R. Seeley in 1883, when he attributed it to 'the God
who is revealed in history', and made it the basis of a new historical
approach. Science, however, was the period's chief source of pride,
and its prime example of progress. 'Philosophy', wrote one of its
historians, G. H. Lewes, in 1857,

has been ever in movement, but the movement has been circular; and this fact is thrown into stronger relief by contrast with the linear progress of Science. Instead of perpetually finding itself, after years of gigantic endeavour, returned to the precise point from which it started, Science finds itself year by year, and almost day by day, advancing step by step, each accumulation of power adding to the momentum of its progress . . .

In the year of Tennyson's first train-journey from Liverpool, that city's MP was run over and killed by an engine. Three years later Tennyson's image for progress was used by Carlyle to suggest blind destruction: 'To me the Universe was all void of Life, of Purpose, of Volition, even of Hostility: it was one huge dead, immeasurable Steam-Engine, rolling on, in its dead indifference, to grind me limb from limb.' This was more than an early expression of the age's protest against machinery, a protest that would be voiced most loudly by Ruskin and Morris. The two uses of the railway-image marked a duality in the period's mood: the sense of progress was balanced by a sense of loss, and the enthusiasm for ranging 'Forward, forward' was somewhat damped by 'Tears, idle tears' for 'the days that are no more.'

Having said (1856) that 'faithlessness' was 'the most startling fault of the age', Ruskin went on: 'another notable weakness of the age is its habit of looking back, in a romantic and passionate idleness, to the past ages, not understanding them all the while, nor really desiring to understand them'. This was hardly true of the period's historians, who tried much harder than their predecessors to understand the past; but even Macaulay once confessed that his interest in historical facts was due to his 'love of castle-building. The past is in my mind soon constructed into a romance.' When walking through the streets, he preferred imagining himself 'in Greece, in Rome, in the midst of the French Revolution' to 'gazing vacantly at the shop windows'. Among non-historians there was certainly much nostalgia for an earlier world, pictured as simpler and more beautiful than the modern one. The feeling was expressed in many different ways, including the medievalism of Carlyle and the Pre-Raphaelites, the Hellenism of Matthew Arnold, Morris, and Pater, the Oxford movement, and Pugin's revival of Gothic architecture. Ruskin explained it as a reaction to the Renaissance, which had

banished beauty, so far as human effort could succeed in doing so, from the face of the earth, and the form of man. To powder the hair, to patch the cheek, to hoop the body, to buckle the foot, were all part and parcel of the same system which reduced streets to brick walls, and pictures to brown stains. One desert of Ugliness was extended before the eyes of mankind; and their pursuit of the beautiful, so recklessly continued, received unexpected consummation in high-heeled shoes and periwigs, Gower Street, and Gaspar Poussin.

The ugliness of urban life made people 'steal out ... to the fields and mountains', and this part at least of Ruskin's diagnosis was confirmed by the age's literature and painting, which expressed a new delight in natural scenery, and a special feeling for landscape, as in the work of Turner. As towns and factories devoured the countryside, the need for conservation began to be realized. 'Towards what ultimate point', asked J. S. Mill in 1848,

is society tending by its industrial progress? ... solitude in the presence of natural beauty and grandeur, is the cradle of thoughts and aspirations which are not only good for the individual, but which society could ill do without. Nor is there much satisfaction in contemplating the world with nothing left to the spontaneous activity of nature.

'Long live the weeds and the wilderness yet', wrote Hopkins; but this aspect of the period's sense of loss was best epitomized in his 'Binsey Poplars' (1879): 'Aftercomers cannot guess the beauty been.'

The loss, however, that troubled his contemporaries most was one from which he did not suffer: the loss of religious faith. It was lost for a variety of reasons, among which the moral sense of an increasingly 'merciful age' was more important than is often assumed. Darwin found the Old Testament untrustworthy, not just for its 'manifestly false history of the world', but also for 'attributing to God the feelings of a revengeful tyrant'. As for the New Testament:

I can indeed hardly see how anyone ought to wish Christianity to be true; for if so, the plain language of the text seems to show that the men who do not believe, and this would include my Father, Brother and almost all my best friends, will be everlastingly punished. And this is damnable doctrine.

J. S. Mill quoted his father as saying 'a hundred times' that

all ages and nations have represented their gods as wicked, in a constantly increasing progression; that mankind have gone on adding trait after trait till they reached the most perfect conception of wickedness which the human mind could devise, and have called this God, and prostrated themselves before it. This *ne plus ultra* of wickedness he considered to be embodied in what is commonly presented to mankind as the creed of Christianity. Think (he used to say) of a being who could make a Hell— who could create the human race with the infallible foreknowledge, and therefore with the intention, that the great majority of them would be consigned to horrible and everlasting torment.

To such moral objections Biblical criticism added rational ones, as in Strauss's *Das Leben Jesu*, which George Eliot translated in 1846; and the findings of science, especially in geology and zoology, combined to discredit the Genesis account of the creation. The final blow to traditional belief was delivered by Darwin's *The Origin of Species* in 1859, which seemed to prove that the element of design in organic life, thought by Paley to demonstrate God's wisdom and benevolence, was in fact the result of a mechanism propelled by random variations. Man was merely an animal, and God a quite unnecessary hypothesis.

That loss of faith might then seem an earth-shaking experience, is confirmed by the type of imagery used to describe it. To Tennyson it was like the erosion of which he had read in Lyell's *Principles of Geology*:

> If e'er when faith had fallen asleep,
>   I heard a voice 'believe no more'
>   And heard an ever-breaking shore
> That tumbled in the Godless deep . . .

Matthew Arnold's images had the same geological flavour: the 'charred, blackened, melancholy waste' around the crater of a volcano, and the ebb-tide, with at least a hint of technical denudation:

> The Sea of Faith
> Was once, too, at the full, and round earth's shore
> Lay like the folds of a bright girdle furled.
> But now I only hear
> Its melancholy, long, withdrawing roar,
> Retreating, to the breath
> Of the night-wind, down the vast edges drear
> And naked shingles of the world.

His *Empedocles* was a study of deep depression associated by

Arnold with 'refusal of limitation by the religious sentiment', and a similar state of mind was presented in James Thomson's *The City of Dreadful Night* (1874), most explicitly in a cathedral-sermon on the text: 'There is no God'.

But the spirit of the age, like Tennyson's in 'The Two Voices', was too resourceful to be 'brought to anchor by one gloomy thought'. Its chief resource was to transfer from politics to religion the principle of 'Reform, that you may preserve.'

Science moves, but slowly slowly, creeping on from point to point:

Slowly comes a hungry people, as a lion creeping nigher,
Glares at one that nods and winks behind a slowly-dying fire.

Though Tennyson did not here envisage science as a threat to religion, both slow advances evoked the same response: that of throwing sops to Cerberus. Religion, like the electoral system, was adapted to satisfy its critics. This Broad-Church policy was exemplified by *Essays and Reviews* (1860), an attempt by seven Anglicans to purge religion of what science could not swallow. Thus of the 'Mosaic Cosmogony':

No one contends that it can be used as a basis of astronomical or geological teaching, and those who profess to see in it an accordance with facts, only do this *sub modo* [subject to conditions or restrictions], and by processes which despoil it of its consistency and grandeur, both which may be preserved if we recognise in it, not an authentic utterance of Divine Knowledge, but a human utterance, which it has pleased Providence to use in a special way for the education of mankind.

The argument was made even more palatable to scientists, by applying to religion their idea of 'progressive development' or evolution. Though the Bishops condemned the book, its method became popular, and Matthew Arnold's *Literature and Dogma* (1874) would sell over 100,000 copies. 'The thing is,' he wrote there, 'to recast religion.' By jettisoning miracles, the after-life, and the supernatural generally, he tried to keep Christianity afloat on the strange seas of modern thought, as a system of '*morality touched by emotion*' which was, above all, experimentally verifiable: 'It is so; try it!'

The scientific challenge to religion was met in many other ways. One was simply to say, with Newman, that theology was itself a science, 'more certain' than mathematics, 'far wider and more

noble' than any other branch of knowledge. Another was to adopt
a synthetic substitute like Comte's Religion of Humanity. 'The
idealization of our earthly life', wrote Mill,

the cultivation of a high conception of what *it* may be made, is . . . capable
of supplying a poetry, and, in the best sense of the word, a religion,
equally fitted to exalt the feelings, and . . . still better calculated to
ennoble the conduct, than any belief respecting the unseen powers.

A third was to invent, like Carlyle, a cloudy religion of one's own,
on the principle that 'Belief is great, life-giving', or, as Browning's
Bishop Blougram put it, 'Come, come, it's best believing, if we
can.' Religious belief of some kind was still widely thought to be
indispensable, and Carroll's White Queen was perhaps not the
only one who conscientiously practised believing 'impossible
things' for half an hour before breakfast.

The high valuation of faith was partly based on the assumption
that, without it, public and private morality would collapse. The
Agnostics took the opposite view. 'It is wrong', wrote Huxley, 'for
a man to say that he is certain of the objective truth of any
proposition unless he can produce evidence which logically justifies that certainty', and 'Surely, the attempt to cast out Beelzebub
by the aid of Beelzebub is a hopeful procedure as compared with
that of preserving morality by the aid of immorality.' Thus the
finer moral sense of the period changed sides in the conflict
between science and religion, rather as science itself had changed
from an ally of religion, in Paley's *Natural Theology* and the
Bridgewater Treatises, into an enemy, with Darwin's *The Origin*.
Of course, the growth of scepticism, which both these changes
accelerated, was felt by some as a liberation rather than a loss; but
the outlook for humanity described just after the end of the period
by Huxley's *Evolution and Ethics* was not a cheering one, and, as
Galton pointed out, the individual needed a special kind of
stoicism to face the facts of life without the consolations of
religion. The age deserves considerable respect for having pioneered this type of practical philosophy.

'The time for levity, insincerity, and idle babble and play-acting,
in all kinds, is gone by; it is a serious, grave time.' So said Carlyle
(1843) in a book with this epigraph from Schiller: '*Ernst ist das
Leben.*' For once he was not exaggerating. The formidable prob-

lems then confronting society required to be taken seriously, and
could hardly have been solved otherwise. The following year a
reviewer honoured Dr Arnold's memory 'above all' for his
'*earnestness*':

Life, in his view of it, was no pilgrimage of pleasure, but a scene of toil, of
effort, of appointed work—of grand purposes to be striven for—of vast
ends to be achieved—of fearful evils to be uprooted or trampled down—
of sacred and mighty principles to be asserted and carried out.

While headmaster of Rugby (1828–42) he had impressed this
attitude deeply on his pupils; but as one of them, Clough,
observed, Arnold was here just expressing 'the spirit of the time':
'The real cause ... was, I take it, the religious movement of the
last century, beginning with Wesleyanism, and culminating at last
in Puseyism.' In one form or another, earnestness was preached by
Evangelicals, Utilitarians, Tractarians, and Agnostics. One of
Newman's *Parochial Sermons* (1834) prescribed 'Self-denial' as
the 'Test of Religious Earnestness':

Rise up then in the morning with the purpose that (please God) the day
shall not pass without its self-denial, with a self-denial in innocent
pleasures and tastes, if none occurs to mortify sin. Let your very rising
from your bed be a self-denial; let your meals be self-denials.

On the secular side, Morley was equally stern forty years later:

Our comfort and the delight of the religious imagination are no better
than forms of self-indulgence, when they are secured at the cost of that
love of truth on which, more than anything else, the increase of light and
happiness among men must depend. We have to fight and do lifelong
battle against the forces of darkness, and anything that turns the edge of
reason blunts the surest and most potent of our weapons.

The view of life as a battlefield, epitomized in Clough's poem,
'Say not the struggle nought availeth', went with the more prosaic
one of life as a place of work. 'A steady application to work', wrote
Samuel Smiles, 'is the healthiest training for every individual, so is
it the best discipline of a state.' 'Produce! Produce!' urged Carlyle.
'Were it but the pitifullest infinitesimal fraction of a Product,
produce it, in God's name!' The advice was followed. In industry,
technology, architecture, and art the period was hugely produc-
tive; and one reason why its literature was so voluminous was that
much of it was written (as Macaulay said pain was inflicted) 'from

a sense of duty'. For that 'Stern Daughter of the Voice of God' survived the doubts cast on other aspects of the deity. The 'human spirit' commended in Clough's poem of 1844 spoke for many other agnostics when it said: 'I know not, I will do my duty'. So did Matthew Arnold when he wrote, a quarter of a century later: 'For my part, the deeper I go in my own consciousness, and the more simply I abandon myself to it, the more it seems to tell me that I have no rights at all, only duties . . .'.

'Why, Uncle Matthew, Oh why, will not you be always wholly serious?' That was the caption (spoken by Mrs Humphry Ward as a small girl) of a caricature by Max Beerbohm, portraying Arnold as a tall, lounging figure with a wicked smile. The *Zeitgeist* was not always wholly serious either. Just as *Literature and Dogma* originally contained 'an abominable illustration' comparing the Holy Trinity to three Lord Shaftesburys, so *The Ring and the Book* included comic monologues by the lawyers. While writing *In Memoriam*, Tennyson versified an anecdote about a kidnapped sow. His fellow-Arthurian poet, Hawker, had once, for a joke, let all the pigs in Boscastle out of their sties. On another occasion he had sat naked three nights running on a rock near Bude, pretending to be a mermaid. Some of Newman's lectures at Birmingham sent his audience into 'peals of laughter'. Carlyle, the proscriber of 'levity', boarded a Chelsea bus still roaring with laughter at a story he had just been telling for perhaps the twentieth time, about a Scotch gentleman who remarked, towards the end of a 'three days' bout of steady drinking', that one of his companions looked 'unco gash [*very dismal*]'. 'Gash!' said his neighbour, 'he may weel look gash, as he has been deid these two days.' And Hopkins, not five years before writing 'The Wreck of the Deutschland', thus described the effects of vaccination:

My shoulder is like a shoulder of beef. I dare not speak above a whisper for fear of bellowing—there now, I was going to say I am obliged to speak low for fear of lowing . . . my left forequarter is swollen and painful (I meant to have written arm but I cowld not).

The official view, as worded by Carroll, was that

> The Good and Great must ever shun
> That reckless and abandoned one
> Who stoops to perpetrate a pun

but punning was endemic. In the theatre farce, pantomime,

burlesque, and extravaganza were, with melodrama, the most popular forms. In the streets, a Punch and Judy showman told Mayhew: 'Everybody's funny now-a-days, and they like comic business. They won't listen to anything sensible or sentimental, but they wants foolishness.' In journalism, the demand for 'fun' was supplied, not just by the magazine of that name, but by more than a hundred and fifty other comic journals. In literature it stimulated a vast output of comic verse and parodies, and the development of a new sub-genre: Nonsense.

The cruder manifestations of humour were doubtless an instinctive form of safety-valve, which helped the Victorians to survive the new stresses and strains of their situation. More 'thoughtful laughter' was given a higher function by Meredith's conception of the *Comic Spirit* (1877), as an expression of civilization which registered any imbalance in human behaviour:

Men's future upon earth does not attract it; their honesty and shapeliness in the present does; and whenever they wax out of proportion, over-blown, affected, pretentious, bombastical, hypocritical, pedantic, fantastically delicate . . . false in humility or mined with conceit, individually or in the bulk—the Spirit overhead will look humanely malign and cast an oblique light on them, followed by volleys of silvery laughter. That is the Comic Spirit.

Walter Pater would probably not have found Carlyle's story very funny, but in theory even he broke the ban on levity:

There is a certain shade of levity and unconcern, the perfect manner of the eighteenth century, which marks complete culture in the handling of abstract questions . . . A kind of humour is one of the conditions of the true mental attitude in the criticism of past stages of thought. Humanity cannot afford to be too serious about them, any more than a man of sense can afford to be too serious in looking back upon his own childhood.

But the *Zeitgeist* could see the funny side of the present as well as the past. In one point at least Swinburne was representative—that he wrote a splendid parody of himself; nor was Samuel Butler wholly out of tune with his time when he said: 'The one serious conviction that a man should have is that nothing is to be taken too seriously.'

2. Tennyson

'A HORRIBLE thing has happened to me', wrote Hopkins after reading *Enoch Arden*. 'I have begun to *doubt* Tennyson.'[1] He had previously thought of Tennyson as 'always new, *touching*, beyond other poets, not pressed with human ailments, never using Parnassian.' But now, it appeared, he did use Parnassian, the kind of verse that a poetical genius could produce 'without further effort of inspiration.' That same year Tennyson commented in 'The Flower' on the reception of his poetry: despised at first, it had then been so widely imitated, that his 'flower' had come to seem as commonplace as a weed. Both Hopkins and Tennyson were right. Tennyson's later work does suffer from self-plagiarism, and other plagiarists have damaged his reputation; but the original flowering of his poetry was indeed a marvellous phenomenon. Though its special power is more easily felt than analysed, it clearly springs from a rare gift for verbal music, and for suggesting, by imagery, sound-effects and word-connotations, the flavour of subjective experience.

The flavours suggested by the early poems were evidently related to the poet's situation in childhood. The son of a talented but depressive village parson, with a grudge against the world and a weakness for alcohol, Tennyson grew up in an atmosphere of gloomy isolation, which made life endurable only by recourse to fantasy, and by extracting pleasure from such negative states of mind as boredom, frustration, and melancholy. A typical product of this predicament is a picture in 'The Palace of Art':

> One seemed all dark and red—a tract of sand,
>   And some one pacing there alone,
> Who paced for ever in a glimmering land,
>   Lit with a low large moon.

[1] Alfred, first baron Tennyson, 1809–92, was born at Somersby, Lincolnshire, the fourth son of the rector. He went to Louth Grammar School and Trinity College, Cambridge. There he joined the Apostles, and met Arthur Hallam, who died suddenly, 1833. Derisively reviewed in the *Quarterly* five months earlier, he was generally unrecognized as a poet until 1850, when he published *In Memoriam A.H.H.* and became Poet Laureate. That year he married Emily Sellwood, to whom he had first been engaged in 1838. They lived from 1853 at Farringford, Isle of Wight, and in 1868 had a second home built, Aldworth, near Haslemere. He turned playwright, 1875, and accepted a barony, 1883.

The need to escape into subjectivity tended to inspire poetry about sleep, dream, vision, madness, intoxication, and other states of heightened sensation and lowered intellectual control; about things distant in time or space, remembered or imagined; and with such physical correlatives as dimness of light or vision (perhaps connected with Tennyson's myopia), faintness of sound or hearing, echoes or reflections in mirrors or water. Thus everything is seen through a haze, which softens outlines while increasing glamour, like the 'vinous mist' through which Will Waterproof's 'college friendships glimmer.' In fact Will speaks for his creator generally when he says: 'I look at all things as they are, | But through a kind of glory.'

Enjoying a negative mood meant deliberately prolonging it, so these poems were full of refrains and repetitions, which also served to hypnotize the reader, just as Tennyson had always been able to induce in himself what he called 'a kind of waking trance' by silently repeating his own name. This type of emotional immobility was often reflected in the landscape: Oenone's environment, for instance, is as static as her feelings:

> For now the noonday quiet holds the hill:
> The grasshopper is silent in the grass:
> The lizard, with his shadow on the stone,
> Rests like a shadow, and the winds are dead.

As he matured, however, Tennyson began to feel that such static concentration on subjective sensation was morbid, ineffectual, anti-social, and suicidal. Real life, he felt, was dangerous, but it had to be faced. So the Lady of Shalott emerges from her island-fortress to face a world that she used to experience only indirectly—and it kills her. Lady Godiva descends from her 'inmost bower' in a castle, to brave the world naked—and survives.

Tennyson, too, survived. From an isolated childhood he grew up so shy that he is said to have fled in panic from his first sight of Hall crowded for dinner at Trinity College, Cambridge. But he exposed his intensely private poetry to the public, overcame their initial hostility, and ended up as one of the greatest public figures of his age, a bestselling Poet Laureate, friend of the most distinguished authors, artists, and politicians, a London playwright, and a member of the House of Lords. As his range of human contacts increased, his interests broadened, and his sense of social responsibility grew stronger. All this was reflected in the subjects of his poems, but the essential character of his poetry remained unchanged. The general pattern of his poetic development was a process of adapting techniques evolved from an almost solipsistic state of mind to themes and purposes that concerned society as a whole. That the adaptation was not always perfect is less surprising than its usual success.

Tennyson's *juvenilia* began at the age of four, when on stormy days he would spread his arms to the blast and declaim: 'I hear a voice that's speaking in the wind'—characteristically expressing an objective fact as a subjective sensation, and prefiguring the 'infant' poet of *In Memoriam*, 'with no language but a cry.' At fourteen he wrote an amusing pastiche of Elizabethan comedy, *The Devil and the Lady*, in which boredom and frustration are personified by the Lady (the young wife of an octogenarian wizard) and melancholy by the Devil employed to keep her out of mischief. The first firm evidence, however, of Tennyson's originality appeared in *Poems, Chiefly Lyrical* (1830). Published during his second year at Cambridge, it contained such striking images of introversion as 'The Owl' ('Alone and warming his five wits, The white owl in the belfry sits'), 'The Sleeping Beauty', and 'The Kraken', a magnificent monster who sleeps 'His ancient, dreamless, uninvaded sleep' on the ocean-bed, until forced to surface and die. The title of the volume was justified by a great variety of irregular and experimental metres, and by a tendency, conspicuous on the first page with 'Claribel: A Melody', to use words more for musical and suggestive than for strictly semantic purposes. The two finest poems in the collection make brilliant use of scenery to convey tedium and claustrophobia. 'A Spirit haunts the year's last hours' makes the sights, sounds, and smells of autumn in the garden of Somersby Rectory express the death-bed atmosphere (presented to the ear in the panting aspirates of 'Heavily hangs the hollyhock, Heavily hangs the tiger-lily') that oppressed the poet's adolescence. 'Mariana' builds up from a circular rhyme-scheme, a tautological refrain, details of neglect and dilapidation, and a flat, featureless landscape like the Lincolnshire Fens, a living picture of utter dejection, beside which even Millais' splendid painting seems a bare diagram.

Mariana is a poetical figure of a type first popularized by Ovid's *Heroides*: the betrayed, deserted, or otherwise ill-used female. In *Poems* (1833) this type, already an apt vehicle for Tennyson's early feelings, was further adapted to express a growing conviction, probably encouraged by Shelley's *Alastor*, that the inner life might become a prison or a tomb instead of a refuge, and that duty to oneself as well as to society demanded an escape from it. 'The Lady of Shalott', shut up in a beautifully symmetrical piece of architecture on an island, seeing life only in a mirror, and weaving what she sees there into a 'magic web', clearly suggests 'the Poet's self-centred seclusion' condemned in the Preface to *Alastor*. The dreamlike monotony of her existence, stressed by the incantatory rhyme-scheme, eventually disgusts her: 'I am half sick of shadows'—and, even at the cost of her death, she escapes from art into life. In 'The Palace of Art' the Ovidian 'heroine' is explicitly the poet's Soul, imprisoned, like many a Victorian wife, in a perfectly equipped, gas-lighted Ideal Home, and expected to be happy there with her music, her books, and her pictures. After three years of aesthetic hedonism she has a nervous breakdown. The only cure is to come down to earth, and live in a cottage among ordinary people. Though rambling in structure and too heavily allegorical, the poem contains, in its catalogue of artefacts, some marvels of impressionistic epigram.

Other poems of 1833 show the gradual shifting of Tennyson's attitudes. 'The Dream of Fair Women' starts with a purely subjective experience, but instead of using individual 'heroines' to voice his personal problems, Tennyson touches on the wider social issue of women's oppression by men. 'The Miller's Daughter', like the Lady of Shalott, is heard singing from a building beside a stream; but here 'the wave that runs for ever' is used to grind corn, the whole context is modern and realistic, and the lady survives to enjoy a long and happy marriage. In two notable poems the conflict between the inner and outer worlds is very differently presented. 'The Hesperides' takes its image for the poetic imagination partly from the Greek myth, and partly from a reference by a Carthaginian explorer of the fifth century BC to a mysterious island in a lake in an island, from which music was heard. This doubly insulated music is identified with the magic spells and songs by which the Hesperides guard their golden apples against 'one from the East', i.e. from the modern world. Yet those songs are associated with autumn, sunset, and old age, while the destined thief of the apples is Heracles, the traditional personification of real human achievement.

Similarly in 'The Lotos-Eaters', based on an episode in the *Odyssey*, the heroic ideal of action, struggle, and endurance in the real world is epitomized by the opening words of Odysseus: '"Courage!" he said, and pointed toward the land, | "This mounting wave will roll us shoreward soon."' The opposite ideal is then voiced by his drugged companions, who see no point in 'ever climbing up the climbing wave', no hope of the triumphant home-coming that Odysseus will actually achieve. They prefer to enjoy a perpetual siesta in an 'afternoon' land where 'all things always seemed the same':

> How sweet it were, hearing the downward stream,
> With half-shut eyes ever to seem
> Falling asleep in a half-dream!

The attractions of such regression are so convincingly expressed that critics in the tranquillizer age, ignoring the Homeric context, have attributed the regression to Tennyson. In fact, the poem marks his determination to emerge from the brooding dreams that had fostered his early poetry, and grapple with real life.

This meant exchanging a static for a moving world; and the heterogeneous contents of *Poems* (1842), apart from much-improved versions of pieces published earlier, are unified by the theme of time and change. Some poems deal directly with the political implications of the 1832 Reform Act, denouncing 'the falsehood of extremes' and advocating gradual democratization. Others deal, more regrettably, with such symptoms of social change as inter-class marriages. The best attempt to tackle the question of Reform is 'Godiva', a story told to show that social concern is not a modern invention like the railway, but an element in a long historical process which should not be artificially accelerated. The tale itself gives scope for Tennyson's characteristic dream-technique in a cinematic shot of empty streets weirdly anthropomorphized by Godiva's terror.

Time and change presented Tennyson with a special literary problem. He had always, he said, been possessed by 'the passion of the past', inspired by the remote ('it is the distance that charms me in the landscape, the picture and the past, and not the immediate today in which I move'), and deeply responsive from childhood to classical literature. How was such a mind to produce 'contemporary' poetry in the 1830s? One solution was to adapt ancient genres to the treatment of modern subjects. In an up-to-date conversation poem, 'The Epic', he tentatively defended the anachronism of using that form, and then used it with supreme individuality in 'Morte d'Arthur'. Based on Malory, with tacit allusions to Homer and Virgil, it was epic and yet topical in its implicit theme, the collapse of political, intellectual, and religious orthodoxy. It was highly personal, Sir Bedivere's despair at the loss of King Arthur reflecting Tennyson's own at the sudden death of his Cambridge friend, Arthur Hallam, in the year that he started writing the poem. And the bleak consolation offered by the King ('The old order changeth, yielding place to new, And God fulfils himself in many ways') was the principle on which Tennyson was then struggling to rebuild his life. For this aspect of his subject Tennyson's early techniques were particularly suitable; the translation, for instance, of feeling into landscape (the nightmarish, frozen ridges across which Arthur is carried to the lake), and the trance-like prolongation of a desolate mood:

> . . . and from them rose
> A cry that shivered to the tingling stars,
> And, as it were one voice, an agony
> Of lamentation, like a wind that shrills
> All night in a waste land, where no one comes,
> Or hath come, since the making of the world.

The other classical genre to be freely modernized was the Pastoral. Thus 'Audley Court' ingeniously transposes the autumn picnic with a poet-friend described by Theocritus in *Idyll* VII into a Victorian setting at Torquay, with topical allusions to the Corn Laws and the current interest in fossils, and with Francis Hale, as Lycidas, probably carrying memories of Arthur Hallam. It ends with a landscape expressing, not the usual melancholy, but the quiet satisfaction of the star-gazing shepherd at the end of *Iliad* VIII:

> . . . and as we sank
> From rock to rock upon the glooming quay,
> The town was hushed beneath us: lower down
> The bay was oily calm; the harbour-buoy,
> Sole star of phosphorescence in the calm,
> With one green sparkle ever and anon
> Dipt by itself, and we were glad at heart.

The oddest modernization of Theocritus is 'Walking to the Mail'.
Based on *Idyll* IV, a desultory bucolic dialogue made up of gossip,
anecdote, comic incident, and jocular obscenity, it presents, in a
flat, prosaic style recalling Southey's 'English Eclogues', a rambling conversation between James and John. They mention the
Reform Act and Chartism, but mostly discuss the problems of a
local neurotic who

> Vexed with a morbid devil in his blood
> That veiled the world with jaundice, hid his face
> From all men, and commercing with himself,
> He lost the sense that handles daily life . . .

The poem ends with a significant burlesque of Tennyson's high-
altitude 'Heroines': the story of a sow, imprisoned for a joke at the
top of a 'college tower', and bereft of her piglets one by one, 'till
she was left alone Upon her tower, the Niobe of swine.'

The collection also included specimens of a modern form, the
dramatic monologue. When the setting was also modern, they
were not very good. 'Locksley Hall', a tirade against the commercial ethic of the age by a young man whose girl has let him down,
has no delicacy of music or meaning, only an insistent rhythm and
an interesting enthusiasm for contemporary science. 'Will Waterproof's Lyrical Monologue' is chiefly remarkable for its unexpected blend of melancholy, humour, and self-satire—for its solitary
port-drinker seems to voice Tennyson's own sense of failure as a
poet. Two monologues, however, set in the chronological 'distance', are among his finest work.

Both 'St Simeon Stylites' and 'Ulysses' are about the use of
time. Simeon has wasted thirty years making himself miserable in
the hope that 'a time may come' when people will worship him as a
saint. Ulysses has packed his life with vivid experiences, and is
determined to make the most of what little time remains: 'every
hour is saved from that eternal silence'. Simeon remains in doubt
whether his self-torment will actually pay off. Ulysses can always
chalk up the past on the credit side, and his only doubt now is
about the possibility of a bonus: 'It may be we shall touch the
Happy Isles, And see the great Achilles, whom we knew.' The two
old men may be regarded as negative and positive examples.
Simeon's perverted pride and sordid practices are grimly ridiculed, though he is allowed some pathos in his final uncertainty.

Perhaps he caricatured some impulse in Tennyson to let his friend's death ruin his own life. 'Ulysses', also written soon after Hallam's death, expressed, according to the poet, his 'feeling about the need of going forward and braving the struggle of life'.

Since the plain meaning of 'Ulysses' has been somewhat obscured by critics, the reader may usefully be warned against certain misunderstandings. That one of the poem's sources is the *Inferno* (XXVI. 90 ff.) need not imply that Tennyson shared Dante's disapproval of Ulysses. There is nothing disparaging in the words of Ulysses about Telemachus. 'Blameless' is a stock Homeric epithet for heroes, applied by Nestor, for instance, to his own 'dear son'. 'Common duties' mean service to the community. 'Decent' means that Telemachus can be trusted to do the right thing, as in the '*nobilis et decens*' of Horace, whose *Odes* the poet had learnt by heart before he went to school. And 'slow prudence' merely recognizes the fact that Telemachus has what Ulysses does not have: time to attempt the long, slow process of civilizing a primitive society. Nor should the discrepancy between vigorous sentiments and enervated rhythms be thought an artistic failure: it subtly suggests the natural contradiction between an old man's spiritual and physical powers. Paradoxically, both studies of ageing characters draw on aspects of Tennyson's youthful sensibility: his absorption in private fantasies more vivid than the world around him (like Ulysses' glorious memories and Simeon's heavenly visions), his sense of restriction, his melancholy yearning, his unfocused sense-perceptions, and even the type of 'voice' that spoke to him in the wind:

> The lights begin to twinkle from the rocks:
> The long day wanes: the slow moon climbs: the deep
> Moans round with many voices. Come, my friends,
> 'Tis not too late to seek a newer world.

Two other poems in the 1842 volumes are notable for opposite reasons: 'The Two Voices' not for its rather pedestrian form or its anticlimactic final tableau, but for its moral content, its determined resistance to suicidal impulses; 'The Vision of Sin', not for its exaggerated horror of sex, but for its powerful allegory. Though suggested by a painting, it uses two dynamic images, an orgiastic dance and a dance of death, to imply the change by time of a young sensualist into an elderly cynic. It exploits, with touches of

macabre humour, Tennyson's special talent for visionary impreci-
sion.

Vision and humour figured largely in Tennyson's strategy for
handling, in *The Princess* (1847), the controversial and emotive
issue of feminism. Turning his taste for 'the distance' to diplomatic uses, he distanced the issue by treating it in a fantastic tale
improvised as a party-game by students during the vacation.
Having thus created a playful, imaginary world in which passionate prejudice could hardly survive, he then used humour to
mediate between the sexual factions: first placating male readers
by reactionary ridicule of feminists, then ridiculing male chauvinism in the views of the Prince's father, and subtly making fun of
male complacency in the character of the Prince. His final verdict,
serious if guarded, was in favour of feminism. Moving, as he said
in a 'strange diagonal' between opposing forces, he expressed the
view that women should be free to develop their own potential but,
being essentially different from men, should not model themselves
on them, though the two sexes would ultimately grow more like
one another; that equality between the sexes was as meaningless as
between the ventricles of the heart; that inter-sex warfare was
therefore absurd; and that the abolition of marriage would disin-
tegrate society and damage future generations. This last fear was
epitomized in a kind of recurrent pun about 'losing the child'.
Women were right, it implied, to disdain the status of children,
but they would be wrong to frustrate their own maternal instincts,
or to injure children by neglect.

The poem was cleverly structured to present two simultaneous
views of 'the woman-question': as it looked in 1839, when the
poem was first planned (thirty years before J. S. Mill thought it
prudent to publish *On the Subjection of Women*), and as it might
look in a conspectus of human history, from the most distant past
to the most distant future. The contemporary perspective was
established in the Prologue, describing the annual festival of a
Mechanics' Institute in the grounds of a country house. This
emphasized the modernity of the working-class movement, and of
the science demonstrated by the side-shows, which included
railways, paddle-steamers, fire-balloons, telegraphic and electrical
apparatus. The long-term perspective was suggested by the house
itself, its contents and its setting. Greek and Gothic architecture,
geological, archaeological, and anthropological specimens, the

family's ancestral armour, and a medieval chronicle—all these implied that the nineteenth century was 'A Medley' (the poem's subtitle) of past and present.

A quotation from the chronicle paraphrased a reference in Froissart to the militant feminism of the Countess of Montfort. The Princess was accordingly named after another mountain, Ida, and presented as a character too far removed from ordinary human life, like the Soul in 'The Palace of Art'. She has to be brought down to earth by sexual love, as in the pastoral idyll, 'Come down, O maid, from yonder mountain height.' In its narrative form this descent from idealistic reformer to wife now seems depressingly reactionary; but the reader's revulsion against such a conclusion stems partly from the poet's own obvious sympathy with her bitter frustration, and his admiration for her as a heroic personality. Certainly her strength is underlined by the Prince's feebleness, which is further stressed (in passages added, like the Songs on the child-theme, after the first edition) by his susceptibility to 'weird seizures'. They have two other functions: to mark the points in the plot where feminism, male chauvinism, or sex-antagonism are pushed to ludicrous lengths, and to hint that against the eternal realities, as against Plato's Ideas, the temporal world is shadowy and unreal—although, as Ida says, one must 'work' in it.

Feminism in *The Princess* is a hopeful symptom of evolution, which will end in human perfection and complete harmony between the sexes. This cheerful view, encouraged by *Vestiges of Creation*, gives significance to the geological expedition, and to Psyche's lecture, which like Mill's Essay identifies the subjection of women with primitive barbarism. But evolution can have losses as well as gains, and nostalgia for 'the days that are no more' (voiced by a student who evidently regrets the loss of contact with the opposite sex) finds perfect expression in the blank-verse lyric, 'Tears, idle tears'. Like Ida, Tennyson had grown impatient with such 'moans about the retrospect'; but here, as in describing the 'weird seizures', he turned his early talent for suggesting a negative mood to appropriate use in a very different context.

It is for such incidental lyrics that *The Princess* is usually now admired; but it deserves admiration for the versatility of its narrative blank verse, for its highly ingenious structure, and for the variety of its comic drama. This last is best seen in the sequence where the Princess, 'blind with rage', falls into a river; is

rescued by the 'woman-vested' Prince in a parody of Cassius
rescuing Caesar, 'Oaring one arm, and bearing in my left | The
weight of all the hopes of half the world'; superbly dominates a
quasi-operatic scene of panic in the crowded hall of the women's
College, and finally has the Prince and his friends thrown out by
'Eight mighty daughters of the plough', thus provoking a 'weird
seizure':

> I seemed to move among a world of ghosts;
> The Princess with her monstrous woman-guard,
> The jest and earnest working side by side,
> The cataract and the tumult and the kings
> Were shadows; and the long fantastic night
> With all its doings had and had not been,
> And all things were and were not.

'Let us be serious over the grave', wrote Dr Johnson. Tennyson
clearly agreed, for *In Memoriam A.H.H.* (1850) is his only major
work without a trace of humour. The exclusion, however, of this
vital element in his personality may be felt to impoverish the
poem, making it seem, as it did to his friend Fitzgerald, 'monotonous'. For this reason it should not, perhaps, be considered his
greatest work, only the purest and most perfect expression of a
poetic sensibility that he had partly outgrown. As an anthology of
short lyrics it is still irresistible. As a continuous poem it lacks
sufficient variety of atmosphere and tempo.

Its composition began as a kind of self-therapy for the trauma of
losing an intimate friend and a great source of moral support.
Arthur Hallam had warmly reviewed Tennyson's first volume of
poems, found a publisher for the second and seen it personally
through the press, helped him to act as paterfamilias after his
father's death, and become his sister Emily's fiancé. Within a
month of Hallam's death (September 1833) Tennyson started
giving vent to his feelings in isolated lyrics. As these accumulated
over the next sixteen years, he gradually arranged them into a
sequence, recording his psychological recovery from despair, and
his religious recovery from scientific atheism to an intuitive faith in
Providence and the immortality of the soul. In the first phase of
semi-automatic writing, forms, themes and images were evidently
suggested by various literary models, notably Horace's *Odes*, the
pastoral elegy from Theocritus to Shelley, and the love-sonnets of

Petrarch and Shakespeare. The more deliberate structuring of the composite poem was doubtless influenced by the convention of pastoral elegy that grief is turned into joy at the deification of the dead person. Another influence was Dante, whose *Vita Nuova* traced the growth of his love for Beatrice and his sorrow at her death, and whose *Divina Commedia* related his slow ascent from Hell, culminating in a reunion with Beatrice, and a vision of the Divine Love that governs the universe. In the corresponding section of *In Memoriam* (XCV) Tennyson makes mystical contact with the dead man after reading his letters, and also with 'that which is,' at the heart of the whole creation.

The religious thought of the poem, much vaguer than Dante's, is ultimately based on subjective feeling:

> A warmth within the breast would melt
> The freezing reason's colder part,
> And like a man in wrath the heart
> Stood up and answered 'I have felt.'

This feeling results in a synthesis of two scarcely compatible theories of evolution, a scientific and a spiritual one. Such a synthesis had been hinted at by Goethe, and cheerfully expounded in *Vestiges of Creation* (1844), where 'Progressive Development' was organized by a 'Divine Mind', perhaps with 'a system of mercy and grace behind the screen of nature'. A gloomier view, more powerfully expressed in the poem, but dismissed by a tentative act of faith, came from the evidence of constant, apparently aimless destruction of species in Lyell's *Principles of Geology*.

In Memoriam was welcomed by its first readers because it tried to solve a problem that haunted them, the conflict between science and religion. That problem has now been generally shelved, if not solved, and the poem is valued less as theology than as literature, for its verbal music and its human interest as a convincing study of bereavement. It is closely related to the earlier poems. The singer or intoner, occasionally compared to a widow, a neglected wife, or a poor girl in love with a social superior, is at first obsessed with the past, like Mariana; but the opening stanza asserts a faith in progress, and the theme of 'going forward' against the backward pull of the past is suggested throughout the poem by the implicit image (originally adopted after a railway-journey in 1830) of a turning wheel. Like Dante's 'great wheels' which 'direct each seed to some end', like 'the great world' in 'Locksley Hall', spinning along the 'grooves of change', like the clock in Section II that shows the passage of time by its revolving hands, so the grief that seems merely to 'circle moaning in the air' is actually moving forwards. This idea of progress by revolution round a fixed point is stressed by a series of annual returns (Christmases, seasons, birthdays, anniversaries), by the repetition of certain themes or incidents after intervals of time, and especially by a rhyme-scheme which ends where it began, yet by accumulation hints at growth:

> Let knowledge grow from more to more,
>   But more of reverence in us dwell;
>   That mind and soul, according well,
> May make one music as before,
>
> But vaster.

The theme of progress so slow as to be almost imperceptible allowed the use of techniques originally evolved to express emotional stasis. In 'Calm is the morn without a sound' (XI) hypnotic repetition gives the sense of a mind paralysed by grief. In Section XCV reiterated images of silence, semi-darkness, solitude and immobility suggest a state of visionary trance. Phases of subjective feeling are often shown refracted through dreams; and dimness and vagueness of sensation, understanding, and belief are characteristic features of the whole poem's texture. When the poet tries to visualize his dead friend's face, 'the hues are faint | And mix with hollow masks of might;' baffled by the apparent contradiction between his own sense of God and the evidence of science, he falls 'Upon the great world's altar-stairs | That slope through darkness up to God', and 'faintly' trusts 'the larger hope.' Death is blurred into a waiting 'Shadow', and the entire argument of the poem, however precisely conceived, is presented in such shadowy terms that the intellectual meaning is sometimes hard to grasp.

This type of expression was partly designed to convey a delicate balance of feeling, which would be falsified by any rigid formulation. Partly it reflected a distrust of language itself: 'For words, like Nature, half reveal | And half conceal the Soul within', and 'matter-moulded forms of speech' cannot accurately describe spiritual experiences. So Tennyson gave both his grief and his philosophical consolations 'in outline and no more', leaving the answers to all specific questions 'behind the veil'. Disclaiming any attempt to 'part and prove' intellectually, he aimed merely to suggest his personal intuitions in 'short swallow-flights of song'.

Song, the self-justifying feature of *Poems, Chiefly Lyrical*, is here more functional. It serves, for instance, to reproduce the feeling of past happiness viewed nostalgically through 'the haze of grief': a golden world where 'all the lavish hills would hum | The murmur of a happy Pan', and 'all the thicket rang | To many a flute of Arcady.' In religious contexts it also serves as an inarticulate language for blind faith:

> So runs my dream: but what am I?
> An infant crying in the night:
> An infant crying for the light:
> And with no language but a cry.

Another feature of the early poems, the translation of inner emotion into natural description, contributes to *In Memoriam* some splendid passages in a running dialogue between inner mood and weather:

> Risest thou thus, dim dawn, again,
> And howlest, issuing out of night,
> With blasts that blow the poplar white,
> And lash with storm the streaming pane?

Finally *In Memoriam* allowed Tennyson to indulge his early passion for 'the distance': to contemplate two remote objects, 'a life removed', and 'one far-off divine event, | To which the whole creation moves'—even to focus on both images simultaneously, by making Arthur Hallam 'a noble type' of future human perfection.

The speaker of the 'monodrama', *Maud* (1855) has no such faith in humanity. Obsessed by the idea that his father was ruined and driven to suicide by a fraudulent business-partner, he distrusts the whole human race. So he lives 'alone in an empty house', infested, like Mariana's, with mice 'shrieking' in the wainscot, and broods over subjective images of universal dishonesty, of chivalrous warfare, of a 'still strong man', of a *femme fatale*. Fearing to be lured outside his imaginary world, he tries to cultivate the 'passionless peace' of a philosopher, and resists his attraction to Maud, who is the daughter of his father's partner. Finally, however, he accepts the 'madness' of love, causes Maud's death by

killing her brother in a duel, goes literally mad with remorse, and
ultimately recovers as much sanity as his psychopathic temperament will allow, by going off to fight against that 'giant liar', the
Czar of Russia. Thus the theme of 'The Lady of Shalott', the
dangerous need to escape from subjectivity, was developed into a
realistic study of mental instability; and here Tennyson drew on
the theories of a former friend, the psychiatrist Dr Matthew Allen.

Originally entitled *Maud or the Madness*, the poem was described by Tennyson as 'a little Hamlet'. More recently than
Shakespeare, the poetic possibilities of madness had been
exploited in Sydney Dobell's *Balder*. For Tennyson the use
of a half-mad persona had two special advantages: it allowed a
heightening of subjective feelings, and vivid hyperboles in social
criticism. Thus the speaker, when elated, sees 'a livelier emerald'
in the grass, and his social maladjustment intensifies the triumph
and the pathos of his passion: his 'love' is indeed his 'only friend'.
Thus the poet could highlight the horrors of slums and the
adulteration of food without suggesting, as his persona did, that
society as a whole was equally horrible. The deliberately ambiguous technique of making serious points through the mouth of
a madman was as old as Horace's Satire II. iii. On the question of
the Crimean War, it enabled him to suggest both sides of the
current controversy, without committing himself to either. In a
private letter disowning his persona's preference of war to peace,
and insisting that *Maud* was 'dramatic', he concluded: 'I do not
mean to say that the madman does not speak truth too.'

The writing of *Maud*, as of *In Memoriam*, began in 1833, as a
reaction to Hallam's death. In the dramatic lyric, 'Oh that 'twere
possible', a dead girl's lover is haunted by her ghost. In 1853
Tennyson started work on a narrative context for this lyric,
making the ghost a hallucination caused by guilt as well as grief.
The bellicose peroration about 'the blood-red blossom of war' was
written just before the Crimean War started; but it was made to
seem less outrageous by six lines added in 1856, to imply that the
speaker was still, as Tennyson put it, 'not quite sane', but had at
least been cured of his original problem, total alienation from
society: 'It is better to fight for the good than to rail at the ill; | I
have felt with my native land, I am one with my kind.'

Maud was at first disliked, not only for its apparent jingoism but
also for its initially puzzling form. It told its story obliquely

through a series of heterogeneous lyrics, each expressing a phase in the experience of a single consciousness. Reality was thus shown distorted by pure subjectivity. No form could have better suited Tennyson's poetic gifts; but the reader was left to infer, from a number of subtle hints, the objective facts behind the speaker's words. One small example is the brother's nickname, 'the Sultan'. In the context of the Crimean War this implied that he, not the querulous speaker, was the victim of aggression by 'a giant liar'. Far from being the monster that he was painted, he was really a tall, handsome young man, 'rough but kind', and fundamentally generous. Even the sneering comparison to an Assyrian Bull served to associate him, via contemporary cartoons of Layard, and his work for the soldiers at the front, with that admirable character, John Bull.

The ingenuity shown by such pointers to the objective facts of the story was matched by the artistry that translated it into an intricate pattern of imagery. The most obvious feature of this is the red–white symbolism. White is the colour of 'passionless peace', which the speaker comes to feel a mere negation of life, like the 'chalk and alum and plaster' used to whiten bread. But he is at first frightened of red, the colour of blood, which he associates with his father's violent death. As the colour of love, however, typified in Maud's roses, he finds red irresistible, from the moment of Maud's blush in church. Thereafter his whole world reddens, even (as he puts it in a moment of wild euphoria) 'Till the red man dance by his red cedar-tree'. But the roses of love lead to the blood of war, private and public; and the conflict between erotic and aggressive instincts is only resolved when Maud, in a dream, points encouragingly to the 'ruddy shield' of Mars.

The abundant evidence of intellectual and artistic planning makes nonsense of the suggestion by some critics that *Maud* is a piece of undigested autobiography, shrill and hysterical in tone because the poet was still obsessed by old resentments. Certainly the poem draws plot material from personal experience: from the character of Tennyson's father, from family grievances against the wealthier Tennysons living at Bayons Manor, from an abortive love-affair in 1834 with Rosa Baring, an heiress living at Harrington Hall near Somersby. By 1853, however, he was a very successful, happily married man, and the many reflections in the text of his pleasant life at Farringford hardly suggest that he was

still nursing resentments twenty years old. Nor did his plot
material come wholly from his own experience. He also drew on
such literary sources as Scott's *The Bride of Lammermoor* and
Kingsley's *Alton Locke*.

Maud was Tennyson's favourite poem, especially for reading
aloud, and it contains some of his most powerful writing, in passages of social satire, love-lyrics (notably the one beginning, 'I have
led her home, my love, my only friend'), and the delirious ravings
of Section II. v. As a whole, it surpasses *In Memoriam* by its variety
of tone (the persona's instability justifying constant changes of
mood), and by its sardonic humour. Dr Allen had observed the
dire consequences of frustrating a convalescent patient's attempts
to be sociable. Here is the patient describing such frustration:

> Who shall call me ungentle, unfair,
> I longed so heartily then and there
> To give him the grasp of fellowship;
> But while I past he was humming an air,
> Stopt, and then with a riding-whip
> Leisurely tapping a glossy boot,
> And curving a contumelious lip,
> Gorgonised me from head to foot
> With a stony British stare.

Ever since 1833, when he started work on 'Morte d'Arthur',
Tennyson had wanted to write 'a whole great poem' on King
Arthur, but it was only in the year of *Maud* that he finalized his
plan for *Idylls of the King*. It was published by instalments
between 1859 and 1885, when 'Balin and Balan' was added to the
series. Balin 'the Savage' epitomizes the theme of the whole poem.
Temporarily redeemed from savagery by the influence of King
Arthur, he exchanges the 'rough beast' on his shield for Queen
Guinevere's crown-royal; but relapsing into his old nature, he
ends by killing his own brother. So, in the general movement of
the *Idylls*, Arthur tries to turn 'beasts' into 'men' by making his
knights swear obedience to an ideal code of behaviour, only to see
them finally 'reel back into the beast', and so destroy the
'brotherhood' of the Round Table.

Balin's relapse is caused by the contrast between his idealized
picture of Guinevere and the adulterous reality. Such clashes
between fantasy and fact occur throughout the *Idylls*. Elaine lives
'in fantasy' up in a tower, but when she comes down to earth she

finds that Lancelot does not return her love. Pelleas projects 'the young beauty of his own soul' on to Ettarre, and goes mad when he finds her sleeping with Gawain. Arthur marries Guinevere, thinking, 'lo mine helpmate, one to feel | My purpose and rejoicing in my joy.' But she is not like that.

Though the shattering of illusion is a leitmotiv of the poem, it does not imply that all subjective vision is illusory. Of the many dreams and nightmares described, several are veridical, like Tristram's 'red dream', which frames and symbolizes the ultimate degradation of Arthur's knights in the massacre at the Red Knight's castle. The validity of subjective vision is questioned rather than denied. In 'The Holy Grail' most of the knights 'follow wandering fires' with disastrous results; but the Grail does exist, and those who see it are not deluded. Like Tennyson, King Arthur has experience of visionary trances, but thinks it wrong to concentrate on such inward things, until the job has been done of righting 'human wrongs' in the world outside:

> ... but, being done
> Let visions of the night or of the day
> Come, as they will; and many a time they come,
> Until the earth he walks on seems not earth,
> The light that strikes his eyeball is not light,
> This air that strikes his forehead is not air
> But vision—yea, his very hand and foot—
> In moments when he feels he cannot die,
> And knows himself no vision to himself,
> Nor the high God a vision, nor that One
> Who rose again: ye have seen what ye have seen.

Tennyson defined 'the general drift' of the *Idylls* as 'the dream of man coming into practical life and ruined by one sin' (i.e. adultery, as the type of all sexual licence). Happily the poem's significance is not determined by its sexual ethic. It raises the far larger question: is failure to implement one's vision enough to invalidate it? The poet says: No, humanity progresses by the individual's effort to realize the best that he has 'seen', and what is good in his vision is never finally lost—Arthur will 'come again'. The answer is based purely on faith; and the recurrent image of mist suggests that certainty in such things is unattainable. Gareth's first glimpse of Camelot is through a mist, and when Arthur is last seen, his mind is 'clouded with a doubt'.

Though based on prolonged research into Arthurian literature, and often close to the text of Malory, the poem is intensely personal. Besides exploring Tennyson's old subject, the vulnerability of 'the dream' in real life, it also reflected his growing disillusionment with contemporary trends. After the progress celebrated in 'Locksley Hall', he felt the age to be one of spiritual decline, in which science ousted religion, traditional morality was eroded by rationalism, materialism, and individualism, and sexual permissiveness, in life and literature, defied common decency. His negative reactions were voiced in 'Locksley Hall Sixty Years After', but a more positive attempt to see the rise and fall of civilized values in his lifetime as a cycle in history, contributing wheel-like to long-term progress, was imaged in the *Idylls* by the rise and fall of Arthur and of Camelot. The application to Victorian England was hinted at by certain parallels with topical events. Thus the parting of husband and wife in 'Guinevere' was published two years after the Divorce Courts were set up.

Aristotle praised Homer for keeping himself out of his poems, and epic may seem the wrong form for personal self-expression; but the *Idylls* were not really modelled on Homer or Virgil. Of course there are some 'faint Homeric echoes', such as the 'cryings for the light' in the last, mist-shrouded battle, which echo the famous prayer of Ajax. Like the *Iliad* and the *Aeneid*, the *Idylls* relate the fall of a great civilization, and Guinevere like Dido is a threat to the hero's 'purpose'. The effective model, however, was Theocritus, three of whose *Idylls* told stories in the life of Heracles, and were probably meant to form parts of a *Heracleid*. This Alexandrian type of epic, literary, picturesque, and psychological, did not exclude the poet's personality. It also suggested a method of writing a long poem piecemeal.

A work composed by instalments over forty years might well lack unity, but Tennyson took many steps to unify structure and style. The image of the Wheel of Fortune, applied by Malory to Arthur's rise and fall, was here adapted to suggest the ultimately progressive wheels of change, and to determine the external pattern of the poem, an implicitly revolving 'Round Table' of ten Idylls, framed by the 'Coming' and the 'Passing' of Arthur. The first three 'Round Table' idylls carry Arthur up to his zenith. The next three show the beginnings of a downward swing, caused by Balin's ineradicable savagery, Vivien's cynical spite, and Lan-

celot's adulterous obsession. In the next three the fall is accelerated by perverted piety, sexual infatuation, and open defiance of
morality. Finally 'Guinevere' sees Camelot 'topple into the abyss
and be no more' (as Tennyson had put it in a prose summary of
1833). The poem is further unified by its tone, style, and
versification; by repeated lines or phrases which mimic Homeric
formulas, while implying significant contrasts between the contexts in which they occur; and by various chains of imagery, of
which the most important relates to music.

Characteristically, Tennyson still employed verbal melody as an
inarticulate language, interspersing the blank-verse narrative with
rhyming songs. Like those in *The Princess* these songs served to
stress symbolic themes. Thus Enid's song introduces the Wheel of
Fortune, and Vivien's, 'the little rift within the lute' which finally
'makes the music mute'. 'Arthur's music', which is likewise to be
silenced, represents his attempt to create harmonious beauty out of
discordant human life, and the image aptly suggests the precar-
iousness of all human civilization. Its transient, almost illusory
character is well conveyed by the paradox that Camelot is 'built to
music, therefore never built at all, | And therefore built for ever.'
Adapting the Shakespearian pun, Tennyson makes Arthur's music
'broken', that is, music for several parts; but the part-singers find
it too difficult, and it becomes 'broken' in another sense. The last
Idyll differs from the rest in containing no song at all, except for
Arthur's swan-song, the 'wailing' from the barge.

Tennyson's own music was not silenced until just before his
death at eighty-three, and his large output after the age of fifty
showed great technical skill (especially in his imitations of classical
metres), intellectual vitality, and a continuing urge to experiment.
He was still at his best, however, when handling subjective
experience, and that is one reason why his plays, though not total
failures on the stage, are very dull to read. He found more scope in
a dramatic monologue like 'Lucretius'. This ingenious cento of
ideas and phrases from the *De Rerum Natura* combated materialism by stressing inconsistencies in its first great exponent; but its
interest as a poem arises from its picture of a mind confused by a
drug-induced obsession with sex. 'Rizpah', a powerful protest
against barbarous penal codes and the doctrine of Eternal Punishment, is spoken by a working-class mother in a state of semi-
delirium. Even 'Northern Farmer, Old Style', the first of several

humorously realistic monologues in the Lincolnshire dialect, is spoken by a dying man who, though lucid, is totally self-absorbed.

The emphasis on inner experience contributes largely to the success of the narrative poem, *Enoch Arden*, based on a story passed on to the poet by his sculptor friend, Thomas Woolner. Its hero, associated in the poem with both Ulysses and Christ, returns after many years from a voyage undertaken to save his wife and children from beggary, to find her happily remarried. Rather than 'shatter all the happiness of the hearth', he conceals his return and lives in solitude until his death. The most memorable passages describe his sense of literal as well as symbolic isolation, when shipwrecked on a lonely island; and his moment of renunciation after seeing the new family through a window. The foolishly ridiculed final reference to Enoch's 'costly funeral' underlines, with superb irony, the irrelevance of social values to private experience.

The spirit of Ulysses figures again in the culminating lyric, 'Crossing the Bar', written three years before Tennyson's death, though the vessel about to sail 'the dark broad seas' was actually the Solent-ferry:

> . . . Twilight and evening bell,
>   And after that the dark!
> And may there be no sadness of farewell,
>   When I embark . . .

3. Browning

'I CLING', said Henry James, 'to the dear old tradition that Browning is "difficult".' The tradition arose from Browning's unusual syntax, and from his habit of alluding to odd facts picked up in his polymath father's library, as if they were familiar to everyone. At first this difficulty put his readers off. Later they took it as a sign of profundity. An early commentator described him as a 'Buddha' rather than a 'mere man', and the Browning Society was founded to explain the meaning of his prophetic books.[1] No one is likely now to think his utterances the voice of God (as a 'lady patient' did in 1873), or even to value him primarily as a teacher; but there is still something to be learned from the central insight to which he was led by a subtle and agile intellect, and a special instinct for empathy. This was that, as Oscar Wilde would put it, 'The truth is rarely pure and never simple.' Browning's favourite image for it, the inseparability of black and white, is often used to sum up the essential ambiguities of religious belief, of human happiness, or of moral character. In *The Ring and the Book* only Pompilia is 'perfect in whiteness'. Guido, though seen by the Pope as a 'midmost blotch of black', is presented by the poet as likely to baffle any 'sentence absolute for shine or shade'. Absolute judgements Browning does make; but his characteristic attitude is one of reluctance to make them.

J. S. Mill found a 'medicine' for his depression in the poetry of Wordsworth. An effective anti-depressant may also be extracted from Browning's, though many people are allergic to it. This is commonly called his 'optimism', and exemplified in the lines: 'God's in his heaven— | All's right with the world!' But in their context these words are sadly ironical. They merely express the

[1] Robert Browning, 1812–89, was born in Camberwell, London. His father was a clerk in the Bank of England, his mother of German-Scottish descent. He went to school in Peckham and spent one term at London University, but was largely self-educated in his father's library. He had no success as a playwright, 1836–46, or with *Sordello*, 1840. Even *Men and Women*, the first-fruit of his marriage to Elizabeth Barrett, 1846, and his life with her in Italy, was poorly reviewed. His fame came only after her death, 1861, and his return to London, with *The Ring and the Book*, 1868–9. The Browning Society was founded in 1881.

holiday euphoria of an overworked mill-hand, who is quite
unaware of the crime and misery round her. 'All's wrong with the
world!' would come closer to Browning's view of human existence,
and his faith in a future life was largely based on dissatisfaction
with this one. At sixty-five he wrote in *La Saisiaz*: 'I must say—or
choke in silence—"Howsoever came my fate, | Sorrow did and joy
did nowise,—life well weighed—preponderate."' What makes
Browning's poetry exhilarating is not optimism, but strenuous
vitality. Life is presented as a challenge, to be met with positive
effort, even if the contest seems as desperate and pointless as it
does to Childe Roland. Failure is inevitable but unimportant, so
long as the fight goes on. The murdered Pompilia, refusing on her
deathbed to admit 'one faint fleck of failure' in Caponsacchi's
attempt to save her life, expresses almost too literally this never-
say-die spirit. And even Andrea del Sarto, the most depressed and
defeatist of all Browning's characters, is last heard planning to
paint a vast mural in heaven, and stressing ('as I choose') that he is
still, in a way, the master of his fate.

   This sense of irrepressible vitality is conveyed, not just through
character, action, or explicit statement, but more immediately by
language, versification, and poetic texture. Browning's very individual style was evidently developed to satisfy the special feeling for
'fact' that he shared with Carlyle, and that drew him towards
historical subjects. His momentous choice of 'the world' rather
than heaven in *Easter-Day* epitomized his preoccupation with real
life. Real people, speaking naturally, were seldom quite coherent
or grammatical, so Browning adapted syntax and word-order to
simulate the way people actually talked. Life was more real than
literature, so he often used aggressively non-literary and non-
poetic diction. The physical was more real than the mental, so he
contrived, by bunching accented syllables together, or awkwardly
juxtaposing consonants, to suggest, through the muscular effort
needed to pronounce his words,that the words themselves were
virtually physical objects. The use of comic rhymes in the manner
of Thomas Hood was another device to exchange the solemnity of
conventional poetry for the jocular element commonly found in
real-life conversation.

   Such stylistic independence, however, does not appear in the
first two poems he published. The blank verse, influenced by
Shelley, has a certain windy eloquence, but the main point of

interest is the introspective subject-matter. This seems to reflect a
conflict in the young poet, between a narcissistic sense of his own
genius, and a religious upbringing that made him feel ashamed of
his egotism. *Pauline* (1833) is 'A Fragment of a Confession'
spoken in the close embrace, part-amorous and part-maternal, of
an almost uncharacterized female. The confessor, who relates his
gradual recovery from a state of atheistic selfishness, was part of
what Browning called later

a foolish plan ... to assume and realize I know not how many different
characters;—meanwhile the world was never to guess that ... the
respective authors of this poem, the other novel, such an opera, such a
speech, etc. etc. were no other than one and the same individual. The
present abortion was the first work of the *Poet* of the batch, who would
have been more legitimately *myself* than most of the others; but I
surrounded him with all manner of (to my then notion) poetical
accessories, and had planned quite a delightful life for him.

When J. S. Mill was sent *Pauline* for review, he realized that it was
autobiographical, and commented: '... the writer seems to me
possessed with a more intense and morbid self-consciousness than
I ever knew in any sane human being.' No doubt this upset
Browning; but the 'plan' suggests that his use of dramatic personae
was not originally a defence-mechanism for a sensitive soul. It was,
as the poem implies, more like an assertion of universal genius:

> I cannot chain my soul: it will not rest
> In its clay prison, this most narrow sphere:
> It has strange impulse, tendency, desire,
> Which nowise I account for nor explain,
> But cannot stifle, being bound to trust
> All feelings equally, to hear all sides:
> How can my life indulge them?

He indulged them by writing poems described in a Preface of 1868
as 'always dramatic in principle, and so many utterances of so
many imaginary persons, not mine.'

Paracelsus (1835) is dramatic in external form, but scarcely
otherwise. It has next to no action, and virtually only one
character, Paracelsus. His friends, Festus and Michal, have no
function but to listen to his speeches, and be told why he ignores
their good advice. Aprile, a Shelleyan poet, merely personifies
what Paracelsus lacks, the capacity to love. Browning was growing

more self-critical, and Paracelsus, i.e. the sixteenth-century scientist, alchemist, magician, and astrologer, Bombastus ab Hohenheim, may have seemed an appropriate persona, because he was an egotist of vast pretensions, who hovered on the borderline between a genius and a quack. He could also be made to resemble the poet in *Alastor*, as a man who failed because his 'wolfish hunger after knowledge' was not tempered by altruistic love of humanity. In tracing the course of that failure, Browning first outlined his own philosophy of failure as an earnest of success. In a deathbed lecture Paracelsus expounds an evolutionary theory not unlike Tennyson's in *In Memoriam*, casting himself in the role of Arthur Hallam, as a 'type' of a future 'dim splendour'. This was the theory that underlay Browning's constant concern with evil or unsuccessful characters. He had learned, as Paracelsus puts it,

> To trace love's faint beginnings in mankind,
> To know even hate is but a mask of love's,
> To see a good in evil, and a hope
> In ill-success; to sympathize, be proud
> Of their half-reasons, faint aspirings, dim
> Struggles for truth, their poorest fallacies,
> Their prejudice and fears and cares and doubts;
> All with a touch of nobleness, despite
> Their error, upward tending all though weak,
> Like plants in mines which never saw the sun,
> But dream of him, and guess where he may be,
> And do their best to climb and get to him.

In *Sordello* (1840), his first strikingly original poem, Browning again used a historical figure (the Provençal poet often mentioned by Dante) as a pretext for writing about himself; but this time he took pains to fill in the historical background in the allusive manner of Carlyle's recently published *French Revolution*. He thus swamped his professed theme, 'incidents in the development of a soul', by cryptic references to incidents in the struggle between the Guelphs and the Ghibellines. Sordello is a troubadour (etymologically 'a finder'), and his story, told in nearly six thousand lines of enjambed couplets, is a series of 'discoveries'. As an isolated child at Goito, he discovers the beauty of nature, and the pleasures of imagination. At Mantua he discovers 'real men and women', and the excitement of literary success, but finds it difficult to satisfy conventional tastes while trying to write a new type of poetry. His most important discovery is the truth about himself. He is not, as he thought, a divine Apollo, or 'Monarch of the World', but a feeble egotist, intent on self-display rather than service to mankind; and even when finally impelled to relieve human suffering, incapable, as a mere poet, of doing anything about it. He tries to convert the Ghibelline leader to the more democratic cause of the Guelphs, and preaches to him on the text: 'A poet must be earth's essential king'. But the man of action merely yawns. Then, half-contemptuously, he offers Sordello a position of real power in his own party, which needs, he says,

> a youth to bustle, stalk,
> And attitudinize—some fight, more talk,
> Most flaunting badges . . .

Faced with the choice of remaining powerless, or gaining immoral power, Sordello opts for impotence; but the conflict is so intense that it kills him. Thus his story ends ineffectually, with nothing to show for his great gifts and aspirations, but a few of his 'unintelligible words', sung centuries later by a boy near Asolo. The ironic 'unintelligible', like Browning's comparison of himself to Don Quixote in the opening lines of the poem, confirms the impression that *Sordello* was to some extent a satire on its author: on his delusions of grandeur, his selfishness, his experimental poetry, and his uneasy relationship with readers and critics. The poem was also an attempt to explain his developing moral philosophy, and the thinking behind his revolutionary style. On the first score, here is the rationale of his 'apologies' for indefensible characters:

> . . . ask moreover, when they prate
> Of evil men past hope, 'Don't each contrive,
> Despite the evil you abuse, to live?—
> Keeping, each losel, through a maze of lies,
> His own conceit of truth? to which he hies
> By obscure windings, tortuous, if you will,
> But to himself not inaccessible;
> He sees truth, and his lies are for the crowd
> Who cannot see; some fancied right allowed
> His vilest wrong . . .

On the second, a long passage (II. 562 ff.) describes Sordello's gropings after a new poetic language. He fails in his attempt to express 'perceptions whole', because language is essentially analytical. How, then, can 'the simultaneous and the sole' be conveyed by 'the successive and the many?' This was a problem that Browning tried to solve, in the style of the whole poem, by substituting a continuum of emotional metaphor for the series of separate statements that a reader would normally expect. In the Preface to *Paracelsus* Browning had promised the public 'other productions . . . in a more popular, and perhaps less difficult form.' *Sordello* hardly lived up to this description. It was generally found unreadable, except by such enthusiasts as Rossetti and Swinburne, and for many years ruined Browning's reputation. It is still very hard to read, and as a complete poem remains a fiasco. As a poet's working notebook, it shows much psychological and critical insight, and contains many splendid passages of impressionistic narrative.

Its second paragraph issues the curious 'warning' that Browning would rather have told his story dramatically. His instincts led him to the theatre and, encouraged by the actor-manager, Macready, he had already embarked on a ten-year course of writing stage-plays. These are interesting only as milestones on the road to his mature dramatic monologues, and all except one are very dull. The exception, an attempt at popular melodrama called *A Blot in the 'Scutcheon* (1843), is bad enough to be quite entertaining. The 'tragedy' arises from the premarital intercourse of an engaged couple. The lady pleads mitigating circumstances, in words that Dickens found incomparably 'affecting': 'I was so young—I loved him so—I had | No mother—God forgot me—and I fell.' Her pedigree-proud brother is less soft-hearted. He curses her, gives her lover a mortal wound and then, belatedly contrite, asks the dying man, 'Can you stay here till I return with help?' He can, but the help is ineffectual, and his death is promptly followed by his fiancée's (from a broken heart), and her brother's (from poison), while plagiarizing from the Ghost in *Hamlet*. The best immediate result of Browning's efforts as a playwright was a cross between drama and lyric, *Pippa Passes* (1841). Pippa, an embodiment of youthful innocence introduced in a rapturous dawn-soliloquy, is a mill-hand at Asolo, which Browning had visited while working on *Sordello*. Eager to make the most of her one day off a year, she wanders round the little town, singing to herself, and vicariously enjoying the imagined happiness of certain people who live there.

To her they represent four satisfying types of love: romantic, nuptial, parental, and religious; but four dramatic scenes reveal their real situations. The romantic lover is an adulterous murderer, consumed with guilt. The bride and bridegroom are the victims of a cruel practical joke. The mother is trying to dissuade her son from risking his life to do what he thinks his duty. The man of God is being tempted to defraud Pippa herself of her inheritance, and have her sent off to Rome as a prostitute. Pippa knows nothing of all this; but her songs, as she 'passes', reactivate the consciences of her unseen listeners. The murderer rejects the domination that made him commit his crime. The bridegroom accepts responsibility for the bride that he has been tricked into marrying. The son does what he feels to be his duty. The bishop overcomes temptation. Thus Shelley's poet-nightingale, who 'sings to cheer its own solitude with sweet sounds', became an agent of what Matthew Arnold would call 'a power which makes for righteousness'. The structure of *Pippa Passes*, however unrealistic, has great aesthetic charm. It cleverly expresses faith both in Providence and in the poetic imagination—even when the latter is factually wrong. The irregular verse and wildly inventive imagery of the opening soliloquy well convey Pippa's sense of liberation, and the scene tracing the disintegration, under pressure of guilt, of the Sebald-Ottima relationship is dramatically powerful, and psychologically acute.

Pippa Passes may be seen as a long dramatic monologue, in which subjective illusions are corrected by objective interludes. Five years earlier Browning had published two short dramatic monologues, 'Johannes Agricola in Meditation' and 'Porphyria's Lover', where the correction was suggested by the speaker's own words. Both men feel exempt from morality, one as an Antinomian and the other, less confidently, on the strength of his proprietorial instincts. Agricola's 'conceit of truth' invites contradiction by the crude egotism of its language, and his contempt for the deserving; the lover's, by his admission to having strangled Porphyria, by indications of her contrasting altruism, and by the hinted parallel between him and the 'sullen' wind, which 'tears the elm-tops down for spite' and does 'its worst to vex the lake'.

In this, Browning's simplest type of 'evil man' monologue, the main concern is criminal psychology, and the contrast between the speaker's 'conceit of truth' and the normal reader's. The next stage

was to replace the mere soliloquist by a more fully realized
character, addressing a specific interlocutor in a live, dramatic
situation. 'My Last Duchess' (1842) is spoken by a man who has
probably murdered his first wife, and is negotiating for a second
with the emissary of a potential father-in-law. Various aspects of
his character are economically implied: his stiff formality by the
rhyming couplets, and by his punctilious courtesy in escorting his
guest downstairs; his lack of feeling for his first wife, except as an
art-object, by his admiration of her portrait and equal interest in a
bronze of 'Neptune taming a sea-horse', a subject symbolic of the
way he treated her. In 'Soliloquy of the Spanish Cloister' (1842)
and 'The Bishop Orders his Tomb at St Praxed's Church' (1845)
the speakers are handled too humorously to seem really evil,
though the monk is obsessed with sex and consumed by jealousy,
while the bishop has stolen Church property and fathered several
bastards. Both poems focus on the contrast between Christian
preaching and pagan practice: the monk hates his neighbour, and
the dying bishop thinks of nothing but worldly wealth and carnal
joys. His specification for the bas-relief on his tomb includes:

> The Saviour at his sermon on the mount,
> Saint Praxed in a glory, and one Pan
> Ready to twitch the Nymph's last garment off . . .

This comic treatment of inconsistency, which shows an affectionate tolerance for the Bishop, and also points out, as Ruskin
observed, a curious feature of Renaissance art, leads to a broaden-
ing vision and interest in Browning's richest collection of dramatic
monologues, *Men and Women* (1855). Here the concern is not with
criminal psychology, or the contrast between subjective and
objective, but with larger elements in human life like religion, love,
art, music, and the dificult choice between possible attitudes
towards them. Thus 'Bishop Blougram's Apology' is not just a
satire on a hypocrite who feigns religious belief for material ends:
it leaves the Bishop's sincerity a half-open question, and challenges the reader to rethink the whole issue of religion in modern
life. 'Cleon' and 'Karshish' were not just plausible reconstructions
of historical reactions to Christianity in the first century AD. They
also implied the question, how far were Victorians inhibited by
intellectual snobbery or scientific prejudice from satisfying their
emotional need for religious faith.

In *Men and Women* the dramatic monologue, a perfect vehicle for a dual or multiple vision, was used to express the new insight into sexual relations which Browning's recent marriage to Elizabeth Barrett had given him. With delicate and moving accuracy he charted the minefield through which the truest lovers have to advance: the desolation caused by a 'hasty word' ('A Lovers' Quarrel'), the peril of intellectual argument ('A Woman's Last Word'), the fear of infidelity ('Any Wife to any Husband'), or of falling out of love ('Two in the Campagna'). 'The Statue and the Bust', a narrative poem that reads like a dramatic monologue by the poet's *alter ego*, challenges convention in a faint echo of Blake's protest against the 'pale religious letchery' that 'wishes but acts not'. But his most effective attack on contemporary sexual ethics and his saddest picture of marriage occur in poems ostensibly concerned with art, and inspired, partly by pictures at Florence, where the Brownings were now living, and partly by Vasari's *Lives of the Painters*. 'Fra Lippo Lippi', an exuberant 'apology' for a religious painter with an irregular sex-life, implicitly made fun of Victorian prudery; and 'Andrea del Sarto', a lament for artistic failure caused by uxoriousness, gave little support to the current idealization of home.

The monologues on music (about which Browning possessed a great deal of technical knowledge) are equally full of meaning outside their apparent subject. 'Master Hugues of Saxe-Gotha', a brilliant verbal equivalent for the structure and effect of an organ fugue, is also a warning that intellectual ingenuity can blind one to obvious religious truths. 'A Toccata of Galuppi's' parodies, by its prosaic language and pedestrian metre, the symmetrical formality of the eighteenth-century composer's idiom, then translates his harmonic progressions into intimations of mortality, and finally turns the satire back on to the insular, complacent, puritanical, and science-fixated English, of whom the speaker is a caricature.

The most powerful, if the least typical, poem in the collection, '"Childe Roland to the Dark Tower Came"', has a vast range of possible meaning. Browning said that it 'came upon' him 'as a kind of dream', and he did not know what it meant. Superficially it is a monologue by a young knight on a quest, with literary echoes of *King Lear*, *The Pilgrim's Progress*, and Malory, and a nightmarish, *Waste Land* setting. It probably expressed elements in

Browning's unconscious, at which one can merely guess; but many readers will always value it as a memorable image of stubborn perseverance, against a sense of failure and futility.

Men and Women was the product of a happy marriage in Italy. *Dramatis Personae* (1864) was mostly written by a widower in London. Grief was obliquely expressed in monologues like 'James Lee's Wife', enacting the pain of broken marriages; gratitude for fifteen precious years, in poems like 'Youth and Art', imagining missed chances of similar fulfilment. Music, to which he now turned for consolation, was celebrated in 'Abt Vogler', as something more miraculous than art or poetry, even as evidence for the existence of God and a future life.

Some of the religious poems may have been written or started in Florence, but they related to a controversy stirred up, especially in London, by such publications as Strauss's *Das Leben Jesu*, *Essays and Reviews*, Darwin's *The Origin*, and Renan's *Vie de Jésus*. 'A Death in the Desert' answers Renan's doubts about the authenticity of the fourth gospel with a long, dull sermon by the evangelist himself; but its theory of progressive religious enlightenment is delightfully dramatized in 'Caliban on Setebos'. There a creature scarcely above the level of an anthropoid ape reflects on the nature of the deity, projecting on to It all his own moral qualities, and oddly anticipating the Greek notion of *hubris*, the Platonic Ideas, the Epicurean gods, and the Augustinian doctrine of Election. 'Mr Sludge, "The Medium"' is an entertaining but seemingly endless impostor-monologue. Based on Mrs Browning's admiration, and the poet's own angry contempt, for the spiritualist, D. D. Home, it satirizes middle-class gullibility and anachronistic attempts to defend Christianity by an appeal to miracles. Veiled allusions to the meaning of Browning's surname, as implying literary 'muck', and hints that Sludge is himself a kind of poet seem to indicate that the whole piece expresses, among other things, a mood of self-contempt. Artistically, *Dramatis Personae* was certainly inferior to its predecessor, being less concerned with people than with ideas, suggestion than statement, form than content. But Browning had already started writing his *magnum opus*.

According to *Pippa Passes*, the poetic imagination could be of value, even when it got its facts wrong. 'Mr Sludge' hinted that poetry might not be far from imposture. But *The Ring and the Book* (1868–9) showed a return of confidence. It fully endorsed

Carlyle's claim that the 'sacred Poet' is a more truthful historian than 'Dryasdust', and implied as much by giving precedence to the 'Ring' in the title. The 'Book' was a collection of legal documents that Browning had found on a Florence bookstall in 1860. They related to the trial in Rome in 1698 of Count Guido Franceschini for the brutal murder of his wife Pompilia, on the pretext of her alleged adultery with a priest called Caponsacchi. The 'Ring' was a metaphor for the poem itself, suggested by a gold ring that Mrs Browning had worn, inscribed with the word, '*aei*' (for ever). This probably reminded the poet of Thucydides' use of the word, when he hoped that his history, being factual not fabulous, would retain its value for ever. The metaphor was complicated by reference to the goldsmith's technique of alloying gold to make it workable, and later applying acid to remove the inferior metal from the surface of the finished artefact. The application of that idea has been variously interpreted; but to put it most simply, the 'Book' is the pure gold of 'fanciless fact'. The poet alloys it with his subjective imagination, and shapes the mixture into the 'Ring' or poem. But the added ingredient, far from being inferior to crude facts, is 'something else surpassing that', a quasi-divine power of 'mimic creation', capable of bringing dead truth to life, and making it 'of force' in the modern world. The acid that removes the subjective element from the surface of the ring-poem, the 'renovating wash | O' the water' that restores the appearance of gold-fact, is simply the adoption of the dramatic mode after Book I. Here the poet ceases to act as compère. He lets 'the old woe step on the stage again! Act itself o'er anew for men to judge', through ten dramatic monologues. In Book XII he returns to the stage himself, to conclude and comment on the whole performance. Thus Browning got the best of both worlds—the narrative poet's freedom to speak in his own person, and the playwright's apparent objectivity, in letting his characters speak for themselves. And instead of the original duet between a 'conceit of truth' and reality, he composed a whole symphony of 'conceits', as discordant with one another as the 'voices' in Master Hugues's fugue.

The ring-image also implied the artistry of the poem's structure, which suggested a series of circles, all centred on 'truth'. The entire drama is ringed by the poet's personality (Books I, XII). Within the authorial circumference, and encircling the murder at a distance, stands public opinion (II–IV). Closer in come the people

most directly concerned, Guido (addressing his judges), Caponsacchi, and Pompilia (v–vii). Still closer, in theory at least, to the
central truth are Society's official 'truth-extractors', the lawyers:
the counsels for the defence and prosecution, and the Pope, as
appeal judge (viii–x). But the inner truth of Guido's character,
though intuitively recognized by the Pope, is not revealed until his
second monologue, spoken in the condemned cell (xi).

At first sight *The Ring and the Book* looks like a relativist poem,
but its centripetal structure suggests otherwise. It implies that
absolute truth does exist, but in real life is almost undiscoverable.
In *The Cenci* (also based on a controversial Roman murder-trial)
the 'restless and anatomizing casuistry' of Beatrice's excusers did
not, for Shelley, alter the fact of her guilt. For Browning, similarly,
Guido was absolutely evil, and Pompilia (despite documentary
evidence to the contrary) was absolutely good. Having made this
clear enough in Book i, the poet then offers his readers an exercise
in moral judgement, under conditions that simulate those of real
life:

> No dose of purer truth than man digests,
> But truth with falsehood, milk that feeds him now,
> Not strong meat he may get to bear some day ...

By such oblique didacticism ('do the thing shall breed the
thought') Browning hoped to avoid the counter-productiveness of
'telling truth' directly. Fortunately the reader's reactions are not
too rigidly determined by the educational purpose. The answers
may be found at the front of the book, but the pupil is left free to
work out the details of the sum himself. Certain interesting
questions, too, are raised but left unanswered. How far, for
instance, is Guido responsible for his own character? As Pompilia
says, 'So was he made; he nowise made himself ...'.

The final 'lesson' of this massive poem may seem a *ridiculus mus*
in its negativity:

> ... that our human speech is naught,
> Our human testimony false, our fame
> And human estimation words and wind.

But the total effect of the poem itself is supremely positive. The
style and versification is full of Browning's ebullient vitality, and
contains much of his wittiest and most dramatic writing. The work

succeeds, where *Sordello* failed, in convincingly recreating a whole historical context, and individual characters are brilliantly presented. Guido's horrible mixture of intelligence, self-pitying misanthropy, and half-conscious sadism is precisely reflected in his use of language, with its subtle rhetoric, repulsive imagery, and corrosive sarcasm; and if some characters sound a little too like Browning, Pompilia talks with a touching simplicity that seems entirely her own. The Pope, whose verdict comes closest to Browning's, is independently interesting, both as a character and as a thinker. His statement of Christian faith shows no grounds for condemning the pagan philosophy of Euripides, which is later travestied in Guido's 'primitive religion'; and his personality, with its anxious and weary dignity, is conveyed through a style as individual as his ideas.

Comic relief, thematically functional and also very funny, is supplied by the other two representatives of Law. In these monologues Browning satirized the lawyers' indifference to truth, perhaps with bitter memories of the breach-of-promise case in which his father's love-letters, like those attributed to Pompilia and Caponsacchi, were the subject of legal argument. In giving his nastier lawyer a son with a precocious knowledge of Latin, Browning may have had in mind his son's apparent inability to learn Greek; but the most obviously personal feature of *The Ring and the Book* was the idealized relationship between Caponsacchi and Pompilia, whose secret flight from Arezzo neatly paralleled the Brownings' elopement from Wimpole Street.

Mrs Browning had greatly admired Euripides, in whose *Alcestis* Admetus the husband exclaims: 'May I die if I betray her, even though she is dead!' This was Browning's own dominant feeling ten years after his wife's death—a feeling possibly intensified by remorse for having even thought, two years before, of marrying Lady Ashburton. In *Balaustion's Adventure* (1871) he adapted the *Alcestis* to suit his own state of mind. Balaustion is a girl on a voyage from Rhodes to Athens during the Peloponnesian War. When the ship is pursued by pirates, she earns the protection of the anti-Athenian Syracusans, by describing from memory a performance of Euripides' play, 'Just as I saw it; what the actors said, | And what I saw, or thought I saw the while ...'. The original speeches and dialogue are translated quite faithfully, but Balaustion's subjective commentary lays anachronistic stress on the altruism of Herakles, and the 'selfishness' of Admetus, in allowing his wife to die instead of him. She then produces an improved version of the story, in which the husband's behaviour is more creditable; and concludes, rather strangely, with a quotation from one of Mrs Browning's poems, and an allusion to a picture by Frederic Leighton, first exhibited in 1871.

Written at high speed, as 'the most delightful of May-month amusements', the poem is easy to read, and proved very popular; but, compared with *The Ring and the Book*, it now seems bland and flat. Like his later, less readable excursions into Greek drama, *Aristophanes' Apology* (containing a translation of Euripides' *Herakles*) and the ruthlessly literal version of Aeschylus' *Agamemnon*, it says more for Browning's classical scholarship than for his creativity.

Prince Hohenstiel-Schwangau, however, published the same year, was not very far from being what Browning thought it, a sample of his 'very best work'. The epigraph from Euripides' *Herakles* implied that Napoleon III, the real speaker of the monologue, was potentially a 'Helper' of humanity like the Herakles of *Alcestis*, but had actually been more like Herakles madly murdering his own children, when he precipitated the Franco-Prussian war. His potential had been recognized by Mrs Browning, mistaken for his actual character, and extolled in her 'Napoleon III in Italy'; but Browning thought him an unscrupulous opportunist, and here, as in 'Mr Sludge', he gave expression to his wife's view as well as his own. Like Rossetti's 'Jenny', published the previous year, the monologue is addressed to a London prostitute, and the first line suggests that speaker and listener are two of a kind: 'You have seen better days, dear? So have I ...'. Offering to explain the riddle of his personality, he defends, between puffs at his cigar, his political career. If he failed, once in power, to keep his earlier promises, it was from motives of realistic philanthropy: since the average human lifetime was no more than twenty years, he knew that few of his subjects would live to enjoy the benefits of revolution, but all would suffer from its immediate effects. He therefore preferred to concentrate on relieving 'bodily want', providing food and employment, rather than freedom and long-term reforms. The defence is very plausible, with echoes of Burke and of Browning's own evolutionary philosophy; but when the poor girl, like Jenny, has fallen asleep, the Prince admits to himself that he has whitewashed his own character, and rewrites his own history to show what he 'never was, but might have been'. He thus fulfils, if only in imagination, Mrs Browning's expectations.

The introduction of the seedy adventurer, accosted by his own image 'Under a pork-pie hat and crinoline' is in Browning's liveliest vein of dramatic satire. The subsequent apologia is a wonderful mixture of sound and specious argument, and shows great virtuosity in translating abstract ideas into graphic metaphors. But the ratio of conceits to thoughts is much too high: the poet often seems to be producing more and more ways of saying the same thing. And the speaker's personality is too apt to disappear into a cloud of impersonal reasoning. Both faults threaten tedium, and were to recur in Browning's later poetry.

Like its predecessor, *Fifine at the Fair* (1872) is both fascinating and disappointing. The monologue, which mentions Euripides' presentation of Helen as a model wife, is a defence of the equally famous adulterer, Don Juan. A quotation on the manuscript from Aristophanes' *Acharnians* implies that Browning felt he was speaking with his head upon a block. To offer Victorian readers a defence of sexual misconduct was certainly a risky undertaking, and his sense of daring is confirmed by his remark to a friend that *Fifine* was 'the most metaphysical and boldest he had written since *Sordello*', and that 'he was very doubtful as to its reception by the public'. It was indeed badly received, and he added to his manuscript Euripides' complaint in Aristophanes, that intellectual novelties were wasted on stupid barbarians.

His readers must have been confused, not only by the subtleties of the argument, but by the resemblances between the poet and his persona. After Tennyson's detached condemnation of Tristram and Gawain, it was puzzling to find Don Juan expressing some of Browning's characteristic ideas, and parading his knowledge of music and classical literature. To prevent misunderstanding, Browning had tried to indicate, by his epigraph from Molière's *Dom Juan*, that the speaker was essentially Molière's callous hypocrite, with a special gift (as his valet observes) for 'turning things in such a way' that he 'seems to be right' though he is really wrong. To differentiate between Don Juan and himself, he had enclosed the monologue by a lyrical Prologue and Epilogue, both spoken in his own person, and implying fidelity to his dead wife.

But the 'stupid barbarians may well have been misled by thematic
links between these lyrics and the monologue. Thus both Browning and Don Juan use the 'Amphibian' image of the swimmer,
though they mean very different things by it; and Don Juan's
pretence to his wife that he will become a respectable, married
'householder' is ironically echoed in the Epilogue, where 'The
Householder' is the bereaved poet's soul, impatient to leave the
dilapidated 'house' of the body, and join his dead wife 'up there'.
There were also some excuses in the text for Rossetti's otherwise
paranoiac assumption that *Fifine* was a satire on 'Jenny' and
himself. But the poem was no more a lampoon than a serious
defence of promiscuity. It seems to have been designed as an
objective analysis of a life-style that Browning found both repellent and faintly attractive. It therefore brought out quite clearly
the restrictions imposed by monogamy, not merely on sexual
instinct but also on spiritual development: 'one chamber must not
coop Man's life in, though it boasts a marvel like my prize.'

For all its intellectual acrobatics, *Fifine* suffers from lack of
movement. 'Once fairly on the wing', says Don Juan, 'let me flap
far and wide'; but his flappings leave him precisely where he
started. Only at the end does the poem itself take off, with broader
visions of human life, first as a carnival, then as a range of
collapsing and dissolving buildings, and finally as a prehistoric
monolith imaging permanence in the midst of change, but also
implicitly identified by Juan as a phallic symbol, laid flat by order
of the local Curé, yet biding 'Its time to rise again!'

The Curé figured next as the villain of *Red Cotton Night-Cap
Country* (1873), a narrative poem attacking anachronistic theology,
masochistic ethics, and ecclesiastical dishonesty. 'Suppose I could
change the pen with which I write this into a pen-wiper', Matthew
Arnold had just argued in *Literature and Dogma*, 'I should not thus
make what I write any the truer or more convincing.' He claimed
that Christianity was verifiable, not by miracles, but by scientific
experiment: 'Disbelieve it, and you will find out your mistake as
surely as, if you disbelieve that fire burns and put your hand into
the fire, you will find out your mistake!' Browning's poem told
how a devout but stupid believer had burnt off both his hands to
expiate the sin of living with the woman he loved, and finally
jumped off a tower in the hope that the Virgin would 'suspend the
law of gravity', thus confirming his and his country's faith, and

making Renan burn his book. Browning thought 'the poor fellow' should have formed 'some better theory of how God operates'; but, not having done so, he was quite right to 'put faith to proof' rather than go on believing, half in the Virgin Mary, and half in the 'unrobed Venus'. The gruesome story, based on incidents that led to a lawsuit at Caen in 1870, was told to disprove Anne Thackeray's idea that the district around St Aubin in Normandy was sleepy enough to be called 'White Cotton Night-Cap Country'. Browning's emendation was finally justified when a gardener, planting geraniums at the bottom of the tower, is suddenly joined by his master's body: '"Ugh—the Red Night-cap!" (as he raised the head)'.

The subtitle, *Turf and Towers*, refers to Browning's symbolic interpretation of the story. 'Towers', i.e. church-steeples and the belvedere from which the miracle-seeker falls, represent his religious aspirations. 'Turf' is the sensual life that he actually leads, and the awkward distance between them is the cause of the tragedy. Apt as it is, this symbolism is made too explicit: 'our image, bear in mind', the poet keeps saying, and the reader feels treated like a backward child. Equally crude is the treatment of sensational incident. One is never allowed to forget the hands held in the fire: 'There was no washing hands of him (alack, You take me?—in the figurative sense!)'. Instead of Browning's usual subtlety, there is only a kind of black humour. The introductory monologue, spoken to the poet's friend, Anne Thackeray, has a certain rambling charm, and there is one moving soliloquy by the hero's mistress; but the poem as a whole suggests declining powers. The handling of the hero's thoughts before he jumps is especially symptomatic. How could such a stupid man talk coherent theology? Browning had solved a similar problem when he dramatized the thought-processes of Caliban. Now he evaded it by offering a mere translation instead of trying to enact the original: 'He said, then, probably no word at all, But thought as follows . . .'.

As if to redeem this lapse from drama, *The Inn Album* (1875) was at first conceived as a play, but transformed (at the news that Tennyson was turning playwright) into a dramatic poem with versified stage-directions. Its preposterous plot was based, Browning said, on a true story that he had heard thirty years before. It concerns a wicked aristocrat, a virtuous young lady, and a plebeian but honest young millionaire. It ends with the hero, in righteous wrath, strangling the villain, and the heroine poisoning herself. 'As she dies' the news arrives, in baffling defiance of chronology, that the hero has been acquitted of murder. The hero's diction is resolutely contemporary, ranging from 'Do let a fellow speak a moment!' to the terser, 'Shut up!' Various big names in the politics, art, and literature of the day are mentioned, including the poet himself: 'That bard's a Browning; he neglects the form | But ah, the sense, ye gods, the weighty sense!' Certain topical issues are reflected in the text; but all these up-to-date features fail to disguise an old-fashioned melodrama, as absurd, despite some flashes of ironic wit, as *A Blot in the 'Scutcheon*. The only interesting passage describes the '*Inferno*' of being married to a country parson:

> My husband, bent
> On saving his own soul by saving theirs,—
> They, bent on being saved if saving soul
> Included body's getting bread and cheese
> Somehow in life and somehow after death ...

From now on Browning's best work was done in much shorter poems, and the richest of the later collections was *Pacchiarotto and How He Worked in Distemper: With Other Poems* (1876). The title-poem gave vent to Browning's exasperation, accumulated over forty years, against his critics. The chief target was the minor or minimal poet, Alfred Austin, who had, Browning said, been 'flea-biting' him for several years. In a savagely comic story, versified in fantastically rhymed doggerel, Austin figured as a mediocre, sixteenth-century painter, whose political activities led him to share a tomb with a putrefying corpse. In several other poems Browning asserted his superiority to his conventional critics, even casting himself, in 'At the Mermaid', as a Victorian Shakespeare. But there is more in the volume than amusing polemics and embarrassing self-panegyric. 'Pisgah Sights' compresses into lyrical epigram a mature philosophy of life. 'Fears and Scruples' neatly allegorizes the poet's refusal to let critics of the Bible destroy his faith. 'Numpholeptos' and 'St Martin's Summer' hint delicately at a conflict between genuine devotion to the memory of his wife, and need for a live sexual relationship. Finally, 'A Forgiveness', a tense dramatic monologue spoken by a wife-murderer just before killing his wife's monk-lover, makes up for a melodramatic plot by its clever construction and perceptive analysis of obsessional jealousy.

After this macabre flight of fancy Browning turned to a real, personal experience. *La Saisiaz* (1878) was his own *In Memoriam* for his friend Anne Egerton Smith, who had suddenly died while they were on holiday together. Written in the marching rhythms of 'Locksley Hall' (not unsuitable for 'One who never turned his back but marched breast forward'), it reached something like Tennyson's conclusion about God and the afterlife: though nothing could be proved, Browning relied on intuitive 'hope'. As poetry, however, *La Saisiaz* cannot be compared to *In Memoriam*. Verbose and rather tedious in its abstract arguments, the poem is moving only when it expresses Browning's emotional shock at the overnight transformation of a lively and congenial companion into a corpse.

Of his other publications, *Dramatic Idyls* (1879–80) contained stories of violence or paradox, vividly and vigorously told, often in long, shambling lines almost indistinguishable from prose. *Parleyings with Certain People of Importance in their Day* (1887) appeal to Browning specialists because they deal directly, if not clearly, with his own thoughts and attitudes in later life, and with his intellectual background; but they can hardly be read for pleasure. Only *Asolando: Fancies and Facts*, written during the last three years of Browning's life and published the day he died (1889), suggested that he was still a great poet. The title came from a verb coined by Cardinal Bembo, with a pun on the name of Browning's old favourite, Asolo, to mean 'disport in the open air, amuse oneself at random'. Certainly the tone of the poems is one of relaxed enjoyment, but they are much more pithy and concise than relaxed writing tends to be. Nor are they assembled wholly at random: the subtitle points to a central concern of the volume, the acceptance of 'fanciless fact' without discounting the deeper realities glimpsed by imagination. 'Beatrice Signorini', which Browning thought the best in the book, tells how a husband's fancy of his wife's placidity is exploded by an outburst of her passionate temperament. More impressive, however, than this, or the other anecdotal poems, are a few samples of dramatic monologue. 'Bad dreams' is an interesting experiment, which shows the emotional tensions between a man and a woman by making them tell each other their dreams. 'Imperante Augusto Natus Est', like 'Karshish' and 'Cleon', ironically reconstructs the attitude of a contemporary pagan towards the Nativity. 'Development' epitomizes Browning's theory of progressive religious enlightenment under the image of the Homeric Question. Wolf plays Strauss, Homer God, the tale of Troy represents the gospel-story, and the replacement of the *Iliad* by Aristotle's *Ethics* may possibly have satirized Arnold's reduction of religion to 'morality touched by emotion'. Browning's lifelong preference for the dynamic imperfection of real human life to any static ideal of perfection was finally expressed in 'Rephan'. And the famous Epilogue, written in all sincerity, though he knew it sounded 'like bragging', was probably more truthful than most obituaries, and undoubtedly good propaganda for an admirable, and very practical, attitude to life.

4. Clough

SHORTLY before writing his first major poem, Clough addressed himself in his journal as 'a portentously deluded Johanna Southcote, lying-in of a Messiah that is flatulence—hiding thyself five months to listen to thine own belly-rumbling, & interpreting into the leaping of a babe in thy womb.'[1] Certainly his unpublished manuscripts contain much versified borborygmus, but there was nothing false about the pregnancies that resulted in *The Bothie of Toper-na-fuosich*, *Amours de Voyage*, 'Adam and Eve', or 'Dipsychus'. The journal entry was provoked by four hours of trying and failing to write, for lack of 'that electric spark' to 'metamorphose into lustrous shapeliness, solidify, vitrify, crystallize this muddly mess within'. In his efforts to articulate confused feelings about religion, society, and sex, Clough spoke for his whole period; but, since his ideas and forms of expression were unorthodox, he was not recognized as a great Victorian poet, until later writers had tuned us in to poetry like his, which attempts psychological realism, often uses the words and rhythms of ordinary speech, and allows contradictions to float unresolved in an element of wry humour.

His poetry was largely the product of a brilliant mind and an over-active conscience. The former brought him all the prizes at Rugby, a scholarship at Balliol College, Oxford (which Jowett called 'the highest honour that a schoolboy could obtain'), and a Fellowship at Oriel. The latter was mostly due to his mother, who taught him to feel like an outpost of English culture during his early childhood in America, and to Dr Arnold, his headmaster and proxy-father, who taught him to feel like an outpost of Christian morality in an otherwise wicked world. Such a sense of responsibility

---

[1] Arthur Hugh Clough, 1819–61, was born in Liverpool, the son of a cotton-merchant. He went to Rugby under Dr Arnold, where he became a friend of Matthew Arnold, and Balliol College, Oxford, where he won a fellowship at Oriel. He resigned it, 1848, rather than subscribe to the Thirty-nine Articles. He visited Paris, Rome, and Venice during that revolutionary period, and worked in various capacities in London and Cambridge, Massachusetts. In 1854 he married Florence Nightingale's cousin, Blanche Smith. Advised, 1861, to travel for his health, he visited Greece, Turkey, the Pyrenees, and Italy, where he died in Florence, probably of a stroke after malaria. Much of his poetry was unpublished during his lifetime.

demanded constant attempts to identify and eradicate his moral
failings. So at sixteen he started a journal, of which the first entry,
made on Shrove Tuesday, is representative:

Another morning of prayer—too little & too little thought of afterwards.
Another day of Carelessness—Display—Uncharitableness—and idleness. After dinner (of which the pancakes perhaps tempted to too large a
partaking)—lemon-shying—I did not feel it wrong at the time, doing it
from fun (? & love of old custom?) but I think there was a little attempt at
popularity in the business.

The sin of lemon-shying was joined, during his schooldays, by
many others, including 'my worst sin' (presumably masturba-
tion); and at Oxford by *areskeia* (the wish to please) and *dipsychia*
(ambivalence). There his self-castigation was intensified by the
influence of Newman and the Tractarians, focused on him at
short range by his Balliol tutor, W. G. Ward, who apparently
developed a passionate devotion to him. Clough's sense of
'wickedness' even made him contemplate some equivalent of
'floggings &c.', to 'bring home to one's prudential part the real
wrongness of things.' Fortunately his natural instincts proved too
strong for total suppression; but desperate inner conflicts seem to
have made him incapable, for all his brilliance and charm, of
enjoying his years at Oxford. As a second-year undergraduate he
wrote: 'This evening I let myself drink too much & enjoy myself
too much at Congreve's.'

   That year, however, he realized that conflict was inevitable: 'It
struck me that I have three strong Impulses. One of Voluptuousness, one of Love of Praise, & one of Worship.' Ten years later he
had reached a *modus vivendi*. He had stopped being disgusted, and
begun to be faintly amused by his own inconsistencies. No longer
identifying exclusively with his 'best self', as his friend Matthew
Arnold would term it, he was at last free to write his best poetry.

   Most of his earliest poems had been quite impersonal. At eleven
he had tried to 'paint the British heart's distress' at the death of
George IV, on whom *The Times* commented: 'There never was an
individual less regretted by his fellow-creatures than this deceased
King.' At sixteen, he had denounced eighteenth-century wickedness ('Ho sensual Monarch, sensual Noble ho!') in the style of
Childe Harold. At eighteen, in 'The Longest Day', he cleverly
extracted a religious moral from the Greek, Latin and English

terms for the summer solstice. Dr Arnold had set the theme, and was 'immensely taken' by the poem; but the aura of scholarship makes it less appealing than the simple expression of Clough's own homesickness in 'I watched them from the window'. Although such direct self-expression is rare in the juvenilia, some literary imitations give glimpses of the poet's personality. His flippancy comes out for once in a rollicking cross between *Peter Bell* and the ballads of Thomas Hood, 'The Poacher of Dead Man's Corner'. More serious feelings about Nature emerge from adaptations of Wordsworth and Coleridge, coloured by the adapter's sense of guilt. Thus the non-moral theme of the 'Dejection' and 'Immortality' odes, loss of power to respond to natural beauty, is moralized in 'Lines': 'Though nought was wrong that I did know, I thought I must have done some sin.' A pastiche of 'Christabel' called 'Rosabel's Dream' dramatizes the schoolboy's anxiety about sex, and pleasure generally. After 'a day of pleasure', Rosabel purifies herself, by 'penitence and prayer', before she goes to bed. But, once asleep, she has an erotic dream, from which she wakes with 'panting heart' and 'flushed cheek'. She prays for strength, only to be tempted, in another dream, to plunge a knife into a sleeping 'maiden'. Then, transformed into a male knight 'pricking onward to the fight', she 'finds before her eyes a naked breast'. At last her conscience, vigilant even in sleep, dispels the visions called up by 'grosser instincts', and she is in a 'dreamless slumber' at 7 a.m. Her creator was not always so lucky, as he recorded the following year: 'I was as nearly as possible committing my worst sin this morning. I was not *quite* roused fr. sleep, but fully conscious.'

Besides this conflict between Voluptuousness and Worship, there was soon a conflict of religious beliefs and loyalties induced by his Oxford environment. He was torn between Dr Arnold's Christianity, based on dutiful action rather than abstract theology, and Newman's, based on Church authority and personal holiness; between faith in the historical truth of the Bible and Strauss's argument that the Gospels were largely mythical; between wanting to stay in Oxford and not wanting to sign the Thirty-nine Articles, which was a condition of retaining his Fellowship; between conservative instincts and an intellectual conviction from studying current affairs and political economy that radical social changes must be made; between a yearning for solidarity, which tempted him to conform, and a stern resolve never to betray his own view of truth—such was 'the muddly mess' behind Clough's contributions to *Ambarvalia* (1849), published jointly with his friend, Thomas Burbidge.

The title implied that the poems in the volume were offered as victims for slaughter, like the animals sacrificed by two brothers at the Roman festival of that name. In the same spirit Clough called his pieces 'the casualties of at least ten years'. More seriously, the title suggested 'beating the bounds' of the mind, i.e. surveying certain fields of thought (notably love and religion), checking accepted definitions, and purifying ideas, by eliminating merely conventional elements. Such is the theme of Clough's opening poem, 'The Questioning Spirit', where to every question comes the stock response, 'We know not, let us do as we are doing.' The satire on intellectual inertia was almost prophetic of the reply that Clough was given, when he confided his religious doubts to the Provost of Oriel: 'we are sent into this world not so much to speculate as to serve God and serve man. The grand principles of Religions and of our Duty are not so very difficult.' Though this type of attitude ('I know not, I will do my duty') was finally commended in that poem, another one, 'Duty—that's to say complying', sardonically stressed the distinction between real duty and mere social conformity.

Surveying the 'field' of love, Clough examined, in 'When panting sighs the bosom fill', the problems that faced a young man in a strictly monogamous society. The physical aspect of the sex-drive was handled by Burbidge melodramatically: 'Dragging her to shameful shade, | Shall I let forth the battle of my blood | On those white plains?' With contrasting delicacy Clough conveyed, in 'Natura Naturans', the sensation of sexual attraction, defining it as something shared with the lowest grades of organic life. In a splendidly bizarre passage, he fused the spirit of Lucretius' invocation to Venus with the theory of *Vestiges of Creation*, to celebrate the excitement felt by two strangers sitting next to one another in a train:

> In me and her—sensation strange! . . .
> Their shells did slow crustacea build
>   Their gilded skins did snakes renew,
> While mightier spines for loftier kind
>   Their types in amplest limbs outgrew;
> Yea, close comprest in human breast,

What moss, and tree, and livelier thing,
What Earth, Sun, Star of force possest,
Lay budding, burgeoning forth for Spring.

Clough's survey of love concluded with an implied contrast
between Endymion's intercourse with a cloudy goddess on a
mountain, as a type of erotic dream, and a real-life marriage to a
'Highland lassie' in 'some black bothie'.

'A Christian poet am I, or would be', wrote Burbidge, but
confessed that 'the observances' had been 'stripped of their sweet
meanings'. Clough's poems on religion expressed more imaginatively the same sort of wishful thinking. 'The New Sinai' dismissed scientific atheism as a mere cloud of darkness, hiding the
divine truth:

No God, it saith; ah, wait in faith
God's self-completing plan;
Receive it not, but leave it not,
And wait it out, O man!

The Prologue of *In Memoriam*, written in the year that *Ambarvalia*
was published, similarly recommended faith as 'A beam in
darkness', and Tennyson admired another poem in the volume,
'Qui laborat, orat', which claimed that God was not revealed by
intellectual efforts, but only by 'hours of mortal moral strife'.
Unlike Tennyson, however, Clough was particularly concerned
that majority-pressures should not obscure his own insights. The
liveliest poem on this theme, 'Why should I say I see the things I
see not', expresses his resistance to such forces under the image of
two musics. He refuses to dance to worldly music which he cannot
hear, preferring to concentrate on something 'Painfully heard, and
easily forgot', that sounds intermittently in his soul.

Almost more interesting than the pieces on love and religion was
a sequence of ten poems, written at intervals over his time as an
undergraduate, called 'Blank Misgivings of a Creature moving
about in Worlds not realised'. Taking his title, and perhaps his
retrospective method from Wordsworth, Clough gloomily
recorded his own lack of spiritual progress. Looking back over his
'strange distorted youth', he failed to find 'One feeling based on
truth'. In a passage reminiscent of Matthew Arnold's 'The Buried
Life', he stressed the difficulty of verbalizing the unconscious, 'the
buried world below'; but the main trouble, as he saw it, was his

own 'Sin, cowardice, and falsehood', in pretending to form human relationships, when his real loyalties had been pre-empted by God. He was thus guilty of betraying his God-given 'sight and sense of truth', and also of cheating his friends and relations, by enjoying 'the moment's sympathy' under false pretences. Before finally urging himself to do his duty, and hope for better things in heaven, the poet summed up his personality as a dreary landscape, marked by 'unaltering impotence', 'sovereign dulness', and a 'disheartening' lack, both of natural vegetation, and of artificial cultivation. To complete the picture, Clough compared it, doubtless with memories of his American childhood, to 'some half-settled colony'. The general effect of his *Ambarvalia* poems, though much less depressing, is not wholly unlike this internal scenery. They are slightly colourless and dull, suggesting no special aptitude for poetry, natural or acquired; only some tough intellectual pioneering, with a faint promise of something better to come.

Clough's titles can be misleading. *Ambarvalia* ('round the fields') proves claustrophobic, but *The Bothie of Toper-na-fuosich* (1848) gives a wonderful sense of liberation. Subtitled 'A Long-Vacation Pastoral', it captured the holiday spirit of Clough's reading parties with his students in Scotland and the Lake District, and his own sense of release at resigning his Fellowship at Oriel. Like the man in Matthew Arnold's 'A Summer Night', he had escaped from 'a brazen prison' of 'taskwork' (and in his case of inner conflict) and embarked 'on the wide ocean of life anew'. He dramatized his euphoria in the story of Philip Hewson, Oxford undergraduate, poet, and advocate of social reform, who falls in love with a 'Highland lassie' called Elspie, marries her, and, like Clough's best friend, Tom Arnold, emigrates to New Zealand.

The poem was written in two months, after Clough had spent five weeks in Paris, observing with great satisfaction the effects of the February revolution. Several other factors contributed to the work's production. Current interest in the use of hexameters for Homeric translation had started Clough rereading the *Iliad*, with a view to translating it into hexameters himself (a project on which he worked intermittently for the rest of his life). At this point Longfellow's *Evangeline* showed the metre's possibilities for original narrative poetry, and also challenged Clough to make his own hexameters less monotonous than Longfellow's. He did it by using more spondees, especially in the fifth foot, and contriving, as Virgil and other classical poets seemed to have done, a deliberate counterpoint between metrical ictus and natural speech-accent. Another factor was Tennyson's recent *The Princess*, which approached its social theme via the light-hearted conversation of students down for the Long Vacation, thus suggesting a reading-party as a good context for the discussion of similar topics.

A passage in Clough's journal for 1848 seems to indicate that the word 'Pastoral' in the subtitle had for him a more than literary meaning:

For lowly shepherd's life is best. Better is it idly to follow one's own fancy, the leading of one's heart & the instinct of the inner sense than in a seeming industry be respectable & fill one's purse, do one's duty & eat, drink & be drunken ... Only, should one wish to marry, and should one wish for children ... Desolate old Age is sad, and spiritual relation precarious, and 'male & female created *He* them'.

The pastoral life meant freedom from professional commitments, but it raised the problem, how else to earn a living; and that was connected with the problem of sex: how to turn 'the celled-up dishonour of boyhood', as Philip Hewson called it, into 'a relation, oh bliss! unto others'. The first problem Philip solved by emigrating and starting a farm, but before that he had to solve the second, to 'Study the question of sex in the Bothie of What-did-he-call-it'. Clough had found 'Toper-na-fuosich' on a map, and was doubtless glad to adopt such a ready-made ending for a hexameter. When told, after publication, that the name referred in Gaelic to the female genitals, he changed it to 'Tober-na-vuolich'; but, as the text of the first edition makes clear, the original title was quite appropriate to the poem's theme.

Philip studies sex in three stages, each with its own social theory. As a Chartist and 'radical hot', he starts with a preference for the working classes, and is first attracted by a girl that he sees 'uprooting potatoes'. This makes him apply Pugin's *'great principle of decorating utility'* to women, and insist that feminine beauty is inseparable from useful work. So he falls in love with a farmer's daughter called Kate. He then falls in love with the completely non-functional beauty of Lady Maria, and is prepared to condone social injustice, as necessary for the production of a few 'fleeting flowers' like her. His third love is for Elspie, the self-educating and independent-minded daughter of an ex-blacksmith, ex-soldier, and ex-schoolmaster, who now lives in a bothie raising potatoes, among other things, on his 'pittance of soil'. The theory implied is that personality matters more than class, that socially useful work is not always manual, and that everyone should do the work that comes naturally to him, his 'ergon'.

The source of this technical term, Aristotle's *Ethics*, was both a set book for the reading-party, and the model for Philip's sexual and social education. Aristotle's concern, unlike Plato's, was not absolute 'good', but what is good 'for us'. What is good for Philip is Elspie; and his 'ergon', as his surname suggests, is to 'hew and dig' on a farm. His progress from the plebeian Katie to the aristocratic Lady Maria, and then to the enlightened middle-class Elspie (a nice blend of flowers and potatoes) follows what Aristotle called the 'easiest' route to 'the Mean and the Good'—'leaning first to one extreme and then to the other'.

Philip remains a radical, but not quite such a hot one. This results from a running argument between him and the middle-aged, clerical, rather conservative Tutor. One issue between them, left finally undecided, is the demarcation-line between 'Circumstance' and 'Providence'. In the Tutor's view the social system is Providential, so one should do one's duty 'in that state of life to which it has pleased God to call' one. Philip thinks it merely Circumstantial, so one should try to improve it. Urged by the Tutor to fight at the post assigned him by the 'great Field-Marshal', Philip bows to 'the duty of order' but mistrusts the Field-Marshal. He can see no divine strategy, nor even a clear distinction between friend and foe:

> Neither battle I see, nor arraying, nor King in Israel,
> Only infinite jumble and mess and dislocation,
> Backed by a solemn appeal, 'For God's sake do not stir there!'

The argument expressed a conflict in Clough's own political thinking. It was clearly Philip who had written Clough's letters to *The Balance* on political economy (1846), and his pamphlet on 'retrenchment' (1847), urging Oxford students not to spend money on 'champagne and claret', when thousands of Irish were starving. But the Tutor had a hand in the later letter on socialism, which doubted 'the assumed identity of Socialism and Christianity', and satirized egalitarianism: '"Hurrah for the masses", if you like, but let me assure you that all the same there *are* "Upper

Classes", who know a thing or two somehow or other, which you and I don't.'

The poetic form of *The Bothie* was no less original than its thought, and this originality was paradoxically connected with classical imitation. Clough's hexameters, though based on scholarly analysis of ancient prosody, were actually quite unsuitable for translating Homer; but for this modern poem they had the great advantage of accommodating colloquial rhythms and prosaic words that could not have been fitted into iambics. For instance, the modern flavour of the last quotation from the poem is largely a by-product of the metre. The mock-Homeric accounts of the sports and the dinner are amusing in themselves, and strike the note of gaiety that makes the whole work so attractive; but the burlesque of epic also serves to highlight the topical references and the Oxford slang, while contributing to the social satire. It hints that a society must be absurdly archaic, if its upper classes behave like 'gods of Olympus'; if the tables for 'Chairman and Croupier, and gentry fit to be with them' are 'a little up-raised from the level', on which 'keeper and gillie and peasant' are seated; and if Sir Hector is chiefly famous, not even for taming horses like his Trojan namesake, but for stalking deer and preserving game.

In mixing mock-heroic with pastoral, Clough followed the lead of Theocritus, who turned Polyphemus into a semi-comic lover. Such lovers in pastoral are conventionally faithful, unsuccessful, and inconsolable; and this implicit background acted as a foil to Clough's realistic picture of adolescent sexuality. Philip's rapid switches from girl to girl seemed all the more lifelike when superimposed on the image of Polyphemus sitting alone on his rock, obsessed and suicidal. The reader was reminded of such pastoral images by quotations from Virgil's *Eclogues*, used as epigraphs to individual episodes, with subtle changes of meaning. Thus the magic spell that brings Daphnis 'home from town' to the girl who loves him in *Eclogue* VIII became the passing glance from Elspie that detached Philip from Lady Maria and 'Slowly drew me, conducted me, home, to herself.'

The Bothie contains an exhilarating description of bathing in the mountains. Swimming was one of Clough's greatest pleasures, and diving (like the incoming tide) featured prominently in the poem's symbolism. His idealized namesake, Arthur Audley—'Arthur, the shapely, the tranquil, the strength-and-contentment-diffusing'—

is also 'the bather par excellence, glory of headers'. The personal
meaning seems clear when Arthur prepares to dive, 'Eying one
moment the beauty, the life, ere he flung himself in it.' Arnold's
'Thyrsis' presents Clough's exodus from Oxford as a negative
step, a needless self-banishment from Eden. His own poem
presents it in its positive aspect, as a glorious header into life, and
real poetry.

Clough had already started a blank-verse drama about Adam
and Eve. He seems to have worked at it between 1848 and 1850,
and he left it unfinished at his death, a fascinating reflection of his
intellectual growth, though artistically unadventurous: he needed
newer bottles for his wine. Matthew Arnold disliked what he saw
of the poem, but admitted its 'sincerity'. He found in it 'the
spectacle of a writer striving evidently to get breast to breast with
reality.' Clough was, it seems, trying to clarify his persistent sense
of guilt. With her constant cry of 'guilt, guilt, guilt!' Eve typifies
the nagging, Evangelical conscience. To every rational argument
she opposes her blind conviction of sin: 'O Adam, some way, some
time, we have done wrong.' Adam assures her, in Straussian terms,
that 'the mighty mythus of the Fall' is merely a creation of her own
terror; but inwardly he shares her feelings, and the conflict
between superstition and common sense produces an almost comic
alternation of styles:

> My God, my God, that I were back with Thee!
> O fool! O fool! O irretrievable act!
> Irretrievable what, I should like to know?
> What act, I wonder? What is it I mean?

Groundless guilt in the first generation leads to justified guilt in
the second, when Cain murders Abel; and the nearest approach to
solving the problem of guilt is Cain's almost existentialist refusal
either to forget or to be forgiven for his crime:

> That which I did, I did, I who am here:
> There is no safety but in this; and when
> I shall deny the thing that I have done,
> I am a dream.

In a speech that might be used to characterize Clough's poetry
generally, Adam says that even in his 'utmost impotence' he is
aware of 'A living, central, and more inmost I', perpetually

analysing and criticizing his own thoughts and feelings. In *Amours de Voyage* (drafted in 1849, though not published until 1858) the habit of self-observation is a cause of 'impotence' rather than a consolation for it. Claude, the unheroic hero of this epistolary verse-novel, cancels out all his positive feelings about love, politics, and religion by negative afterthoughts. He thus reduces everything to zero. He does not fight for the democratic cause that he believes in. He rejects a much-needed sense of religious 'comfort', because he thinks it 'factitious'. And he loses Mary Trevellyn, whom he genuinely loves, because he doubts the validity of his emotions.

The poem was drafted in Rome during the siege by the French, which led to the fall of the Roman Republic set up by the previous year's revolution. This disappointment of Clough's political hopes was one stimulus to composition. Another was his disappointment with Rome itself, as a home of classical culture. He disliked its Baroque architecture and sculpture, and all signs of Jesuit influence: 'A bomb I am thankful to say has left its mark on the facade of the Gesù. I wish it had stirred up old Ignatius.' There was also an artistic stimulus, from Michelangelo's ceiling in the Sistine Chapel. According to a rejected epilogue, he began the poem when 'Laid on the Sistine boards under the Angeline roof.' The supine spectator was personified in Claude, who always prefers to see life through the medium of art. At the end of the poem, he finds it easier to visualize 'Michael Angelo's figures' than Mary Trevellyn. Earlier, he is doubtless thinking of the *Creation of Adam* and the *Creation of Eve*, as well as himself when he writes, 'But for Adam,—alas, poor critical coxcomb Adam! | But for Adam there is not found an help-meet for him.'

Claude was clearly a caricature of Clough—he was Clough criticizing himself for constantly criticizing himself. The name implied the character. In his efforts to be truthful, Claude falsifies his picture of life. So Ruskin had written of Claude the painter (1853): 'I know of no other instance of a man's working from nature continually with the desire of being true, and never attaining the power of drawing so much as a bough of a tree rightly.' Etymologically the name suggests a self-enclosed character, who is lame and wavering, and therefore unable to solve his problems by the method of the epigraph: '*Solvitur ambulando*'. In contrast, his correspondent, a healthy, outgoing type, who believes in doing the best one can, and leaving the rest to Providence, is called Eustace ('well standing'). Claude was further condemned in two rejected epigraphs. One, from Thucydides, implied that Claude's intellect blinded him to obvious facts. The other, from a comic epic attributed to Homer, dismissed him as a fool. The text of the poem, however, associates him with Odysseus, and leaves it possible to see him as a real, if faintly comic, hero clinging to the 'hard, naked rock' of truth, as he sees it, and resolutely resisting all temptations to self-deception.

In this ambiguity, as in its realistic psychology, and unromantic treatment of love and patriotism, the poem seems curiously modern; but the modernity is again mediated by classical allusion. Horace's *'dulce et decorum'* is handled with something like Wilfred Owen's sarcasm: 'Sweet it may be and decorous, perhaps, for the country to die; but | On the whole we conclude the Romans won't do it, and I sha'n't.'

Here, too, the hexameter, as the metre of epic warfare, adds irony to the debunking of modern war-fever:

> So it stands, you perceive; the labial muscles, that swelled with
> Vehement evolution of yesterday Marseillaises,
> Articulations sublime of defiance and scorning, today col-
> Lapse and languidly mumble, while men and women and papers
> Scream and re-scream to each other the chorus of Victory . . .

Even Claude's name has a classical implication. It recalls the word used in Ovid's *Sad Poems* of exile for elegiacs, and suggests that the *Amours* record an equally sad banishment from the uninhibited joys of the *Amores*. Clough's own elegiacs, which serve as Prologue, Epilogue, and introductions to cantos, have several functions. Sometimes they seem to voice the poet's personal feelings, sometimes his attitude towards his poem, and sometimes Claude's suppressed emotions, otherwise glimpsed only indirectly through the wit of the hexameter-letters. The Prologue tacitly employs a Horatian epigram to demolish Byron's claim, in the opening lines of *The Corsair*, that travel is liberating. The Epilogue, as published, merely states that the poem expresses the problems of contemporary youth; but a tougher, rejected version defends the story's lack of poetic justice on the grounds that it reflects reality: 'There!—thou world! Look, there! is the vile dirty face that you show me . . .'.

Emerson reproached his friend for 'the baulking end or no end' of *Amours de Voyage*. But the final anticlimax is an integral part of the whole design. Nor is there any lack of artistry in the scrambled sequence of letters in Canto IV, as Claude scuttles desperately round Switzerland and Italy, trying to locate Mary. His feverish activity intensifies the flatness of the conclusion, and ironically parodies the conventions of the ancient Greek novel, in which lovers chase one another all over the Mediterranean, before finally falling into each other's arms—a convention revived by Longfellow's *Evangeline*.

Artistically, indeed, *Amours de Voyage* was Clough's finest work. Intellectually gifted but emotionally handicapped, Claude is a wholly convincing character. His speaking voice and dry humour are brilliantly captured in verse of great originality; and the story obliquely told does more than bring out his personal peculiarities. It also delicately questions a general axiom of the period, formulated by Goethe and popularized by Carlyle, that the best cure for doubt is action. '*Action will furnish belief,*—but will that belief be the true one?' Claude wonders. It seems the right question to ask, although Claude's ineffectuality suggests otherwise. Matthew Arnold was still working on the dilemma nearly twenty years later, under the terms, 'Hebraism and Hellenism'.

> Irritability unnatural
> By slow, sure poisons wrought God's
> death's work, God's doom.

This cryptic fragment in a notebook (1839–42) seems to ascribe Clough's loss of religious faith to an 'irrational, almost animal irritability of conscience', caused by an 'over-excitation of the religious sense' in his period, 'beginning with Wesleyanism, and culminating at last in Puseyism.' The more explicit diagnosis comes from the prose epilogue to *Dipsychus*, a tragicomic drama begun in Venice in 1850, but not published until 1865. It traced the gradual transformation of morbid religiosity into atheism. The bells of *In Memoriam* (1850) were told to 'Ring in the Christ that is to be'; but the bells of *Dipsychus* sounded more like the 'ou-boum' echo in *A Passage to India*:

> Ting, ting, there is no God; ting, ting,—
> Dong, there is no God; dong,
> There is no God; dong, dong!

What form the poem might have taken, if Clough had lived to complete it, can only be guessed from a chaos of alternative drafts, but its basic pattern is a debate between Dipsychus and a Spirit (originally Faustulus and Mephisto), leading to a bargain by which Dipsychus sells his soul for worldly success. Apart from this skeleton plot and the original names, the influence of Marlowe and Goethe was minimal. The real source was an internal dialogue that Clough had been conducting since at least 1838. That year he wrote in his journal about 'God's hatred of sin, the sinfulness & Godlessness' of the world, the 'absolute necessity of giving up' worldly things, and 'seeking God only, i.e. the utter uselessness and absurdity of διψυχία [double-mindedness].' 'I am not', he concluded, 'an innocent sufferer, but am rather a sinful and silly δίψυχος.' The ideas and terminology come from the epistle of James, which suggests that the *dipsychos* cannot resist temptation, and the Epistle to the Ephesians, which tells them to put on 'the whole armour of God', to 'stand against the wiles of the devil', and to wrestle with the '*kosmokratoras* [world-rulers] of this darkness'. 'Cosmocrator' is a name that the Spirit suggests for himself, and Dipsychus proves unable to withstand the wiles of the devil; but, as the poet explains to his uncle in the epilogue:

perhaps he wasn't a devil after all. That's the beauty of the poem; nobody can say. You see, my dear sir, the thing which it is attempted to represent is the conflict between the tender conscience and the world. Now, the over-tender conscience will, of course, exaggerate the wickedness of the world . . .

The Spirit's temptations relate chiefly to sex, aggression, and egotism. Dipsychus is urged to pick up a prostitute, to challenge a German officer to a duel, to enjoy travelling in a gondola, without thought of 'Our slaving brother set behind'. The Spirit's common-sense arguments are those that a psychiatrist might well use, if confronted by a patient like Dipsychus. They depreciate his 'better feelings', his religious aspirations, his Wordsworthian love of Nature, even his passion for sea-bathing. His habit of scribbling verses is made to seem absurd, and his poetic technique is mocked for its obliquity: 'You think half-showing, half-concealing | Is God's own method of revealing.' Convinced at last that his moral inhibitions are making him totally ineffectual, Dipsychus submits to the world, the flesh, and the devil, as the only way in which he can do God's work. As the Spirit aptly remarks, 'Could there be a finer special pleading?'

Dipsychus was a frank piece of self-analysis (so frank that Clough asked his fiancée not to read it) which accurately defined points of conflict between orthodox morals and psychological facts. These points were neatly dramatized in short scenes set in appropriate parts of Venice, with relevant alternations of style and metre. Thus earnest, romantic, blank verse was contrasted with flippant, colloquial, rhymed satire, reminiscent of Swift's octosyllabic pieces, and of Byron's *Don Juan*. The Spirit's subversive contributions are highly entertaining and, if often savage in tone, can also be rather endearing:

> They may talk as they please about what they call pelf,
> And how one ought never to think of one's self,
> And how pleasures of thought surpass eating and drinking—
> My pleasure of thought is the pleasure of thinking
>> How pleasant it is to have money, heigh ho!
>> How pleasant it is to have money.

After such exuberance, the sketchy, humourless, and melodramatic sequel, 'Dipsychus Continued' comes as a disappointment. Here Dipsychus, now a highly respected judge, is visited by a woman that he seduced thirty years before. The episode crudely allegorizes a text that follows the condemnation of the *dipsychos* in James: 'Then when lust hath conceived, it bringeth forth sin: and sin, when it is finished, bringeth forth death.' The relapse into orthodoxy is redeemed only by a flash of psychological insight: even after he ceased to be 'a moral sort of prig', Dipsychus remained maladjusted: 'He never entered into life as most men. | That is the reason why he fails so soon.'

Clough, too, failed rather soon as a poet. After *Dipsychus* he was distracted from poetry by a trip to America, by problems connected with his engagement, by a job in the Education Office, and by editorial help that he gave Florence Nightingale. His revision of the Langhorne translation of Plutarch (1770) was a time-consuming but unrewarding pot-boiler; and the most notable result of all his efforts to translate the *Iliad* was that he seems to have ghosted for Matthew Arnold in one or two of the hexameter-specimens that discredited *On Translating Homer*.

Clough returned to original poetry during the last few months of his life, while travelling to recover his health. His last poem, *Mari Magno*, was a series of stories told on a ship crossing the Atlantic. Apart from its literal meaning (on the great sea), the title referred to a famous passage in Lucretius, which described the pleasure of watching, from dry land, other people in danger of shipwreck. This detached, philosophical attitude towards human problems was hardly calculated to produce exciting poetry; and though interesting in its psychological and moral attitudes, *Mari Magno* is generally rather dull, resembling Patmore's recent *Faithful for Ever* much more than its remoter models, the *Tales* of Chaucer and Crabbe.

The two short poems for which Clough is most widely known epitomize the contradictions of his poetic character. The destructive satire of 'The Latest Decalogue' is hardly more central to him than the earnest idealism of 'Say not the struggle nought availeth', an inspired and inspiring expression of a positive approach to life. For a synoptic view of such conflicting aspects, one might quote some famous lines from an unfinished poem:

> The contradictions of the expanding soul,
> These questionings of the manhood of our race,
> These views, these feelings like opposing tides
> Swaying and rolling, and beating against each other,
> Who does not feel them? Happy who (strong ships
> Well steered) maintain a steadfast course across
> Obeying but to use them, happy too
> O'er whom like rocks they break in idle foam
> And vex, but stir not from their base. For me
> I am a log of driftwood tost about
> And moving ever with the stronger stream . . .

The driftwood temperament was rare among Victorian poets, but for poetic purposes it was, perhaps, the happiest of the three.

5. Matthew Arnold

LIKE Lucretius in a famous passage on the joys of philosophy, Matthew Arnold liked looking down at things from a height.[1] While at Rugby, he wrote a Latin Poem about climbing in search of knowledge until 'the works and fields of men' lay far below. *The Strayed Reveller* presents two panoramic views of human life, one seen from Mount Olympus by the gods, and one more painfully imagined by poets. In 'Resignation' the poet is a detached observer, who 'looks down' on a 'populous town' from 'some high station'. *Empedocles* contemplates human life from the top of Mount Etna, the 'Author of "Obermann"', from high up in the Alps. In his prose, too, Arnold tends to adopt some form of elevation from which to survey his subject, as if on Newman's principle that 'we must ascend; we cannot gain real knowledge on a level'. He judges contemporary poetry from the standpoint of those 'highest models of expression', classical authors. He judges Homeric translations by the axiom that Homer is never 'low'. 'Criticism' takes its stand on 'the best that is known and thought in the world', 'Culture', on 'the best which has been thought and said in the world'. Literature, society, and religion are all viewed from higher ground—'high seriousness', 'a high standard', 'high ideals'. Where he finds no 'elevation', as in America, he can find nothing '*interesting*'.

In the earlier poems the angle of vision is often vertical, into the experience of the individual, even into his unconscious, the 'deep-buried self'. Such a view seems implied when Empedocles, on the summit of Etna, sympathizes with Typho, groaning far beneath. Later a horizontal component is added. In 'Sohrab and Rustum' huge crowd scenes alternate with duologues, and when father and son are finally left alone, and the poet's eye travels along the Oxus

---

[1] Matthew Arnold, 1822–88, was born at Laleham, Thames Valley, the eldest son of Thomas Arnold. He went to Winchester, Rugby, while his father was headmaster, and Balliol College, Oxford, where he won a fellowship at Oriel. In 1851 he married the daughter of a judge, and became a school-inspector. This remained his profession until 1886. In his spare time he established himself, first as a poet, and then, once professor of poetry at Oxford, 1857, as a critic of literature, society, and religion. After lecturing in America, 1883–4, he extended his field of criticism to American civilization.

river, individual tragedy is lost in a vast, symbolic landscape of human life. Taking an extensive view is an explicit policy of the prose, with its protests against 'provincialism', and its preference for comparisons between different literatures. Trying to offer guidance over immense fields of thought, Arnold resorts to large generalizations, which can be misleading, and resonant slogans, which seem to clinch arguments, but prove on closer scrutiny to beg questions, or conceal ambiguities. But the reader's sense of enlightenment is enjoyable, even when deceptive.

The tone of the poetry is usually elegiac, implying stoical acceptance of regrettable facts. That of the prose is much more buoyant—sardonic, amused, and often very amusing. In both media the language is clear, but seldom richly evocative. Its characteristic strength is precise statement, not vague suggestion. As a prosodist Arnold was skilful and versatile. He experimented effectively with unrhymed lyric metres; but he had no special talent for verbal music. In all, he defined the character of his poetry quite accurately, when he wrote to his mother in 1869:

It might be fairly argued that I have less poetical sentiment than Tennyson, and less intellectual vigour and abundance than Browning; yet, because I have perhaps more of a fusion of the two than either of them, and have more regularly applied that fusion to the main line of modern development, I am likely to have my turn, as they have had theirs.

Certainly his poems relate, more closely than those of his contemporaries, to the problems of modern man, his bewilderment at living in an apparently pointless universe, his sense of isolation in urban society, his frustration under industrial or bureaucratic conditions of work. The prose is even more concerned with 'modern development'. It stresses the need to keep up with the 'Zeitgeist', 'the essential movement of the world', 'the way the human race is going'. And some of its targets are all too relevant to the twentieth century: doctrinaire ferocity, mob-violence sanctified by democracy, Philistinism no longer confined to the middle classes, and a culture dominated by commercial advertising and the media.

In *The Strayed Reveller, and Other Poems* (1849) the revelry is mixed with stern morality. 'Mycerinus', told by an oracle that he will die in six years, as a punishment for his good deeds, spends the interval revelling round the clock; but inwardly he may be 'calmed, ennobled, comforted, sustained' by his own strength of soul. 'The New Sirens', who represent the ethic of romantic emotion, are rejected because they detract from the spiritual life, and lead only to ennui. The Strayed Reveller himself resembles Tennyson's Lotos Eaters; his drugged passivity is implicitly condemned by contrast with the strenuous ordeals of Ulysses and the poets, and also by the presumption that Circe's wine has made him less than human. The whole volume might almost be seen as a debate between Stoicism and Epicureanism. Stoicism wins. In a sonnet beginning with a line that no hedonist could enjoy ('Who prop, thou ask'st, in these bad days, my mind?') Epictetus is one of the three props. The other two are men of broad vision, Homer, who 'Saw The Wide Prospect' (a translation of the Greek word, *Europe*), and Sophocles, 'Who saw life steadily, and saw it whole'.

The Greeks gave literary as well as moral support. 'The Strayed Reveller' and 'The New Sirens' were based on the *Odyssey*, the story of 'Mycerinus' came from Herodotus, there were two imitations of a Sophoclean chorus, and one of an ode by Sappho. Another literary influence was Wordsworth, a family friend of the Arnolds who lived near their holiday-house in the Lake District; but Wordsworth like the Greeks was used eclectically. His view of Nature as a moral influence is bluntly contradicted in a sonnet ending, 'Fool, if thou canst not pass her, rest her slave!' Though 'Resignation' resembles 'Tintern Abbey' in describing reactions to a landscape revisited after some years, it answers that poem's claim that joy can be found in Nature, by the statement that natural objects 'Seem to bear rather than rejoice.' Wordsworth's 'Immortality' ode is answered even more sadly by 'To a Gipsy Child by the Sea-shore', where the strongest feeling is one of degradation, 'Of the soiled glory and the trailing wing.'

Shakespeare figured in the volume, not as an influence, but as the subject of a grand but slightly incoherent sonnet, in which the 'self-schooled' dramatist was compared to a mountain with its head above the clouds. Arnold's own equivalent for the cryptic autobiography of Shakespeare's *Sonnets* was the first of a series of lyrics about an abortive love-affair with a certain 'Marguerite'. Who she was is not known, but there is reason to suspect that she was Mary Claude, a French girl born in Germany, who had been a neighbour of the Arnolds in the Lake District.

Nearly all the poems in the book strike an individual note, and are interesting intellectually; but their emotional impact is small, chiefly because they seem to have been constructed rather than spontaneously produced. The one exception is 'The Forsaken Merman'. Based on the story of a Danish ballad, the poem creates an enchanting submarine world, in the manner of Tennyson's 'Merman' and 'Mermaid', but it also seems to have a psychological meaning. 'You must plunge yourself down,' Arnold had written in a notebook, 'to the depths of the sea of intuition; all other men are trying as far as lies in them to keep you at the barren surface.' 'The Forsaken Merman' appears to dramatize a similar conflict between organized society and individual feeling. Margaret cannot be content in either element. In 'the kind sea-caves' she longs for human relations. In 'the humming town' her 'joy' is punctuated by nostalgia:

> She steals to the window, and looks at the sand,
> And over the sand at the sea;
> And her eyes are set in a stare;
> And anon there breaks a sigh,
> And anon there drops a tear,
> From a sorrow-clouded eye,
> And a heart sorrow-laden,
> A long, long sigh;
> For the cold strange eyes of a little Mermaiden
> And the gleam of her golden hair.

The sea-image is used differently in Sophocles' *Trachiniae*. There it is a 'sea of troubles'; and the consoling thought is suggested, that joy and sorrow come to all men in rotation. This was the theme of Arnold's 'Consolation', the earliest of the *Other Poems* published with *Empedocles on Etna* (1852). It was followed by five other lyrics in which, perhaps to console himself for the loss of 'Marguerite', Arnold reconstructed the whole experience, in generalized terms, to form a narrative sequence. Under the title of 'Switzerland' it would contain six poems in 1853, and eight in 1857. The clearest part of the story was that the poet felt obliged to part from Marguerite, because their 'different past' made the lovers incompatible. The biographical questions raised by the sequence have possibly brought it more attention than it deserves; but of the 1852 instalments at least two are interesting as poems. In 'Parting' the conflict between the attractions of Marguerite and of Nature in the mountains is effectively conveyed by an alternation of rhythms. Paradoxically, the hurrying anapaests, instead of representing the urgency of sexual passion, express the impulse to disengagement. Linked to the winds that go 'rushing' past the window towards the 'vast seas of snow', they sweep the poet away from the human love to dispassionate communion with Nature. The other notable poem insists on the isolation of the individual:

> Yes! in the sea of life enisled,
> With echoing straits between us thrown,
> Dotting the shoreless watery wild,
> We mortal millions live *alone*.

After picturing love as a hopeless longing aroused by music from another island, the poem concludes, with a fine phrase adapted from Horace, that the impediments to the marriage of true minds are insuperable:

> Who renders vain their deep desire?—
> A God, a God their severance ruled!
> And bade betwixt their shores to be
> The unplumbed, salt, estranging sea.

But for Arnold isolation had a value. He was praising Senancour, the author of *Obermann*, when he called him 'of all writers ... the most perfectly isolated'. He found in time a special understanding of modern life, and in the 'Stanzas' to his memory Arnold classed Senancour with Goethe and Wordsworth as one of the three men who had managed 'to see their way' in the contemporary world. All three 'props', however, had now let him down. Goethe's 'wide and luminous view' was not possible in the 'hopeless tangle of our age'; 'Wordsworth's eyes avert their ken From half of human fate'; and Senancour was too depressed to give any real support. The 'Stanzas' throw useful light on Arnold's spiritual history, but as poetry they are unimpressive, especially when they lapse into abstract epigram:

> Ah! two desires toss about
> The poet's feverish blood.
> One drives him to the world without,
> And one to solitude.

Arnold opted for the world, not as a source of external support, but as a place of work. He bade a pitying farewell to his last prop, and his determination to stand on his own legs in future produced the inspiriting poem, 'Self-Dependence', in which he tried to model himself on the stars:

> Bounded by themselves, and unregardful
> In what state God's other works may be,
> In their own tasks all their powers pouring,
> These attain the mighty life you see.

Solitude, and the type of depression that courage and self-dependence could not cure were the subject of the volume's title-poem, *Empedocles on Etna*. It was based on a study, not only of the Greek philosopher, but also of Lucretius, about whom Arnold had once meant to write a tragedy. It incorporated ideas drawn from Epictetus, Marcus Aurelius, Spinoza, Goethe, Carlyle, and Senan-cour; but the main source was evidently the poet's own experience. 'I have been in a kind of spiritual lethargy', he wrote to his sister Jane in 1850, and he was putting it mildly when he told his friend Clough in 1852, 'I am sometimes in bad spirits, but generally in better than I used to be.' In diagnosing a case of suicidal depression from the fifth century BC, he was perhaps attempting self-therapy.

His diagnosis indicated a loss of contact with the unconscious self, due to an imbalance between 'flesh' and 'mind', the instinc-tive and the intellectual. Recalling past happiness, Empedocles explains:

> We had not lost our balance then, nor grown
> Thought's slaves, and dead to every natural joy.

Nor does he hope to do better in the 'sad probation' of another incarnation,

> To see if we will poise our life at last,
> To see if we will now at last be true
> To our own only true, deep-buried selves,
> Being one with which we are one with the whole world;
> Or whether we will once more fall away
> Into some bondage of the flesh or mind,
> Some slough of sense, or some fantastic maze
> Forged by the imperious lonely thinking-power.

Another part of his problem is lack of flexibility. His 'settled trouble' and 'settled gloom' are explained when he calls himself one 'Whose habit of thought is fixed, who will not change'.

The three scenes of the drama symbolize, by the mountain-climbing image, a progression from 'the world without' to total isolation; from a dinner-party in Catana to a forest high up Etna (where Empedocles gives his doctor-friend Pausanias a Stoic prescription for a moderately happy life), and finally to the 'charred, blackened, melancholy waste' at the top of the volcano. Here, feeling estranged from Nature as well as Mankind, Empedocles uses a moment of renewed vitality to commit suicide, wishing, as Arnold put it in his notes, 'to be reunited with the universe, before by exaggerating his human side he has become utterly estranged from it.'

The external form of *Empedocles* owed something to Byron's *Manfred* (about another sufferer from 'barrenness of spirit', who tried to end it all by jumping off the Jungfrau) and more to Aeschylus' *Prometheus*. Callicles, for instance, takes the part of the chorus of sea-nymphs who comfort Prometheus in his sufferings on a mountain, and his songs, like any tragic chorus, comment obliquely on the action. Two such comments have a special interest. The song about Typho, while offering a striking image for the repression of the 'buried self', also allowed Empedocles to voice Arnold's protest against a contemporary trend: the oppression of individual greatness by collective mediocrity. The song about the flaying of Marsyas expressed Arnold's sense of the painfulness of writing poetry, and partly explains why he later stopped doing so. As he told his sister Jane in 1858, it 'demands not merely an effort and a labour, but an actual tearing of oneself to pieces, which one does not readily consent to ...'.

As a symbolic character, Callicles embodies all that Empedocles has lost: youth, vitality, enjoyment of life, and poetic inspiration. His songs, representing a classical ideal of poetry in contrast with Empedocles' romantic egotism, are among the most attractive features of the work, which also includes many delightful, as well as some ghastly landscapes. The only passage that is not a pleasure to read is the long lecture to Pausanias, though even here the stiff formality of the style, and the plodding versification have a certain appropriateness. The style was doubtless meant to imitate the pontifical manner of Empedocles' surviving fragments, and the metre, which may be resolved into groups of three iambic hexameters, was conceivably meant to simulate the dactylic hexameter used by Empedocles. The difficulty of getting through this

section is also appropriate to its content—a philosophy of reason
and will-power, which has nothing easy or natural about it, and is
no help to the lecturer himself. But the poem as a whole needs no
such theoretical defence. Its main strength lies in its powerful
expression of a state of mind in which life is not worth living; but
its total effect is to give quite the opposite impression.

The other long poem in the volume, 'Tristram and Iseult', was
similarly concerned with the loss of 'natural joy' through 'some
bondage of the flesh or mind'. When the two obsessive lovers are
dead, the narrator reflects that any obsessive passion, whether
'ambition, or remorse, or love', can have the effect of 'drying up
our joy in everything'. Arnold was probably thinking of his own
passion for 'Marguerite'; but he illustrated his generalization by
making Tristram's widow tell her children the story of Merlin,
imprisoned for ever because of his passion for Vivian. Since the
whole poem is about such imprisonment within the confines of
'some tyrannous thought, some fit | Of passion, which subdues our
souls to it', its pleasantest passages describe distant views from
windows. A child, still chasing butterflies in his sleep, is invited to
look out over the moonlit moors, 'far, far away | Into the heart of
Brittany.' A Huntsman, chasing a wild boar in a tapestry, finds
himself somehow sharing a room with the two dead lovers. His
eye, at least, escapes from the prison of passion into a wider
prospect:

> How comes it here, this chamber bright,
> Through whose mullioned windows clear
> The castle-court all wet with rain,
> The drawbridge and the moat appear,
> And then the beach, and, marked with spray,
> The sunken reefs, and far away
> The unquiet bright Atlantic plain?

The Huntsman forms part of a generally resourceful narrative
technique. At first the story is told, in a variety of verse-forms,
through dramatic dialogue and monologue, the latter including
Tristram's delirious mutterings, as he dreams of his past life.
Versified stage-directions and a running commentary on the action
are supplied by an unnamed speaker who, when the lovers freeze
into a final tableau, projects himself into the tapestry figure on the
wall. This almost surrealist device equates an apparently human

figure that only 'flaps' in the draught with the two once passionate human beings, now merely pictorial.

Three other poems in the 1852 volume, written in irregular verse-forms of Arnold's own invention, show him at his most original. 'The Future' uses the image of Man's voyage down the river of Time to protest against increasing urbanization. 'A Summer Night' laments, among other things, the fate of the individual in industrial society:

> For most men in a brazen prison live,
> Where, in the sun's hot eye,
> With heads bent o'er their toil, they languidly
> Their lives to some unmeaning taskwork give,
> Dreaming of nought beyond their prison-wall.
> And as, year after year,
> Fresh products of their barren labour fall
> From their tired hands, and rest
> Never yet comes more near,
> Gloom settles slowly down over their breast;
> And while they try to stem
> The waves of mournful thought by which they are pressed,
> Death in their prison reaches them,
> Unfreed, having seen nothing, still unblest.

'The Buried Life' gives imaginative reality, under the metaphor of a buried stream, to the concept of the unconscious self. The concept may well have been suggested by Newman's 'Implicit Reason', and the metaphor by a passage in Wordsworth's *Prelude*, but the convincing application to individual experience was Arnold's own.

Though not published until 1867, his best-known poem, 'Dover Beach', was probably written about the same time as these poems in the 1852 volume. The beauty of a calm sea, as seen by the poet and his wife soon after their wedding, leads here to the 'melancholy' sound of the waves on the beach, and thence to Sophocles' association of waves with 'human misery'. Arnold was probably thinking of a chorus in the *Oedipus Coloneus* that Clough had translated, ending with the phrase, 'The ceaseless tide of misery.' The misery then becomes specifically modern—the low tide of the sea of 'Faith':

> But now I only hear
> Its melancholy, long, withdrawing roar,

> Retreating, to the breath
> Of the night-wind, down the vast edges drear
> And naked shingles of the world.

'Faith' then shifts meaning from 'religious belief' to 'fidelity', and the sea-image develops, perhaps via the image of dark, swirling water, into a symbolic picture of a night-battle, drawn from a passage in Thucydides, which Clough had used as a metaphor in *The Bothie*:

> And we are here as on a darkling plain
> Swept with confused alarms of struggle and flight,
> Where ignorant armies clash by night.

The poem's train of thought, which proceeds by associative rather than logical links, is not in Arnold's usual manner; but its movement is entirely appropriate to its theme: an appeal, in a world of total confusion and uncertainty, for a secure relationship between individuals. The uneasiness of the transitions reflects the sense that everything is in a state of flux.

When the poet turned to criticism, all trace of uncertainty disappeared. In the Preface to *Poems* (1853) he admitted that the 'confusion of the present times' was great, but confidently offered 'a hand to guide' the young poet through that confusion. Taking some of his ideas from Aristotle, Horace, Goethe and Words-worth, he laid down a number of principles. Poets should not, as Clough and others believed, choose their subjects from contemporary life. They should choose 'great actions', which appealed to 'the great primary human affections, to those elementary feelings which subsist permanently in the race, and which are independent of time.' They should not write about themselves, but about the actions of other people. They should not (like the Spasmodics) model themselves on Shakespeare and Keats, but on the ancient Greeks, who would teach them three vital things: 'the all-importance of the choice of a subject; the necessity of accurate construction; and the subordinate character of expression.' The Preface first demonstrated Arnold's special gift for over-simplification so lucidly expressed as to seem undeniable. Its immediate significance was that it announced a change in Arnold's own policy as a poet. He would now be more like Callicles than Empedocles, more a classical than a romantic poet, more objective than subjective. He therefore decided not to republish *Empedocles*, ostensibly on the grounds that it was too depressing. The business of poetry was to 'inspirit and rejoice the reader', but a picture of prolonged 'suffering' which found 'no vent in action' could not possibly do so.

The new policy was amply justified by the epic 'episode', 'Sohrab and Rustum'. Though the story was taken from the Persian poet Firdausi, it had certain parallels with the *Iliad*, and precisely conformed to Aristotle's prescriptions for a tragic plot. The killing of Sohrab by his father Rustum clearly satisfied Aristotle's demand for a killing 'within a close relationship'; and Rustum's belated recognition of his son offered an ideal combination of *anagnorisis* and *peripeteia*. Arnold imitated the simplicity of Homer's style and syntax, incorporated various features of the *Iliad*, like the fighting in the fog, and used many long similes resembling, or actually drawn from those of Homer and Virgil. His 'construction' was based, not on Epic but on Tragedy (Aristotle's chief concern). It followed a five-act pattern, which simulated the alternation of dialogue and choruses in Greek tragedy by an alternation of private conversations and crowd-scenes. The Oxus-coda, which suggests a human progress towards death by that of a river towards the sea, functioned like the final chorus of the *Oedipus Tyrannus*: 'Call no man happy, until he has reached the end of his life without suffering pain.' The product of this fidelity to the Greeks has been disparaged (even by academics) as an academic exercise; but the unprejudiced reader is likely to find it a moving and often beautiful poem. The supposed incongruity of the simile of the lady lying in bed on a frosty morning while a servant lights her fire may be paralleled in Homer, where one function of the simile is to open windows on contrasting areas of life. The poem reads quite naturally, and certainly leaves in the mind, as the Preface prescribes, 'one moral impression' close to the heart of all human experience—the horror of the irretrievable mistake.

The other major poem in the 1853 volume, 'The Scholar-Gipsy', was curiously at odds with the Preface. Though it began with a distant echo of Theocritus, and ended with an allusion to Herodotus, it was modelled, not on the Greeks, but on the Odes of Keats, both in its stanza and in its sensuous natural description. It was also far from objective. Inspired by nostalgia for the poet's youth at Oxford, and for his walks in the surrounding countryside, it personified his sense of freedom at that time in a figure drawn from Joseph Glanvill's *The Vanity of Dogmatizing*. This was an Oxford student who joined some vagrant gipsies, hoping to learn the secret of their mesmeric powers. The Scholar-Gipsy was given several meanings. He was 'glad perennial youth' close to Nature. He was also the solitary, introspective poet, seeking what Arnold was later to call 'natural magic'. More generally, he was unquestioning faith and single-minded dedication, as opposed to the 'languid doubt' and feeble 'fluctuation' of Victorian 'half-believers'. His mental health was similarly opposed to 'this strange disease of modern life, With its sick hurry, its divided aims, | Its heads o'ertaxed, its palsied hearts . . .'.

So far the Scholar-Gipsy seems to express a positive ideal; but two classical allusions imply that this ideal, though eternally attractive, is incompatible with effective action in the modern world. When compared to Dido in the *Aeneid*, he is characterized as an emotional element that must be sacrificed to more important issues. When compared, in the conclusion, to the 'grave Tyrian trader' who refuses to come to terms with a new civilization, he becomes, for all his gravity, faintly comic. Far from enjoying, like the young Empedocles, 'the delightful commerce of the world', he can do business only in Spain, where, according to Herodotus, he does not have to face his customers. Opting out of society was not Arnold's solution to the problem of modern life; but this poem showed the ambivalence of his feelings. And perhaps, despite the beauty of its scenery and the glamour that it lent to the drop-out, Arnold was right when he wrote to Clough: 'I am glad you like the Gipsy Scholar—but what does it *do* for you? Homer *animates*— Shakespeare *animates*—the Gipsy Scholar at best awakens a pleasing melancholy.'

In 'Stanzas from the Grande Chartreuse' (1855) Arnold described himself as 'Wandering between two worlds, one dead, | The other powerless to be born'. That was his religious position. Christianity, as practised by the Carthusian monks, seemed to him a thing of the past; but he mourned its passing, and had no other faith to put in its place. In a literary sense he was also between two worlds. He had written his best poetry, but not yet started his second career as a writer of prose. The comparative deadness of his poetic powers was demonstrated by *Merope* (1858), a scholarly attempt to reproduce in English the form of ancient Greek tragedy. The Preface explained that his purpose was educational: to teach an 'ill-informed' public what 'classical beauty' was really like. If *Merope* failed to do that, it certainly served another purpose that Arnold mentioned in a letter—'to inaugurate . . . with dignity' his Professorship of Poetry at Oxford.

This appointment encouraged him to become a critic, first of literature, then of politics and society, and finally of religion. He developed a conversational prose-style, equally suitable for simplifying complex issues, ridiculing those who thought differently, and otherwise amusing his readers. He had called *Empedocles* 'painful', because it described a situation where there was 'everything to be endured, nothing to be done'. Now his tone was brisk and urgent, conveying a pleasant sense that there was plenty to be done. His inaugural lecture, 'On the Modern Element in Literature' (1857), argued that the 'copious and complex present' could best be understood by studying the literature of an equally copious and complex past. Arnold flicked through literary history to find a period analogous to the modern age, with a literature that 'adequately' represented it. He settled on fifth-century Athens, after a series of summary judgements on individual authors. Some of these might be questioned. Sophocles, who thought it 'best not to be born at all, and second-best to die as quickly as possible', was praised for his 'cheerfulness', and Lucretius, despite his sunny invocation to Venus as the source of everything 'joyful', was condemned for 'depression and *ennui*'. In such ways the lecture was absurdly dogmatic; but the dogmatism was flavoured with humour (especially in the proof that Sir Walter Ralegh was less 'modern' than Thucydides) and Arnold soon learned to modify that too professorial style. Turning with equal confidence though rather less knowledge to European politics, Arnold first formulated, in *England and the Italian Question* (1859), some of his characteristic axioms. The French were accessible to 'ideas', especially 'the ideas of 1789', and the English were not. The English aristocracy was especially ill-qualified to survive in 'the modern world of ideas'. His view of the nobility as personally admirable but politically obtuse doubtless dated from 1847, when he became private secretary to Lord Lansdowne.

Returning to a field that he knew better, though not so well as is often assumed, he gave a course of lectures *On Translating Homer* (1861). Homer and Homeric translation were having a great vogue, and the epigraph from Juvenal ('Am I never to get my word in?') was almost too apt; for the work was more like satire than criticism, and clearly designed to raise a laugh from what he called 'a wooden Oxford audience'. His main butt, Francis Newman, was actually a man of great knowledge and originality, with a sense of humour of his own. His admittedly repellent translation of the *Iliad* had been offered less as a poem than as a historical document, intended to stress the remoteness of the original from Victorian conceptions of poetry. Arnold rejected such realism, and insisted on a traditional idealization of Homer, as always 'eminently rapid', 'eminently plain and direct', and 'eminently noble'. In his public controversy with Newman, Arnold was often in the wrong, and 'eminently' ungenerous; but Newman had his revenge when, after dismissing other metres as unsuitable for Homeric translation, Arnold opted for the English hexameter, and volunteered some samples of it himself. 'I sincerely thought,' wrote Newman, 'this was meant for prose'.

On Translating Homer was most persuasively written, and sound enough in its negative criticism, as when explaining what was wrong with the *Iliads* of Chapman, Pope, and Cowper; but his theory of translation showed a curious indifference to the character of the original text. Thus he claimed the right to expurgate the Homeric epithet for women, 'trailing-robed', because it 'brings to one's mind long petticoats sweeping a dirty pavement'. 'Whose mind?' Newman might well have asked.

In the same year as these lectures, Arnold published his report for a Royal Commission on *The Popular Education of France*. The Introduction, later entitled 'Democracy', formed the nucleus of all his social criticism. The English aristocracy, he argued, had been like Homer in 'the grand style', and they had raised the tone of English society by their example. What was to perform that function when Aristocracy was, inevitably, replaced by Democracy? What could then save England from the ghastly fate of becoming 'Americanised'? The only answer was 'the action of the State', especially in education.

Without waiting for the State to do it, Arnold would soon take on the job of educating society himself; but first he made a final attempt, in 'Last Words' (1862) to educate Professor Newman. There he made a brave attempt to define the 'grand style' in poetry, and paid tribute to Clough, who had long been translating

Homer into hexameters. This he followed up with 'Thyrsis' (1866), a pastoral elegy on his friend, forming a sequel to 'The Scholar-Gipsy', and 'Rugby Chapel' (1867), a somewhat belated elegy on his father, who had died in 1842. Both poems implied a new sense of purpose in his own life, and the second, an ambition to become, like Dr Arnold, a teacher and guide of his generation. The first step in this direction had already been taken in *Essays in Criticism* (1865), a collection of Oxford lectures and magazine articles on literature, philosophy, and religion. In a semi-jocular Preface he declared war on the 'Philistines', i.e. on the 'earnest, prosaic, practical, severely literal' attitudes of 'the great English middle-class', ending with an apostrophe to the 'adorable dreamer', Oxford, as an age-old campaigner against them. The meaning of 'Philistinism' was explained in an essay on Heine, and illustrated by such things as Colenso's literal-minded approach to the Pentateuch in 'The Bishop and the Philosopher'. The other essays ranged over many subjects and literatures, but the principles of the whole book were summed up in 'The Function of Criticism at the Present Time.' Here the primary meaning of 'Criticism' was objective perception, seeing 'the object as in itself it really is.' Judgement, however, would form itself 'insensibly . . . along with fresh knowledge', and was also implied by Criticism's tendency 'to establish an order of ideas, if not absolutely true, yet true by comparison with that which it displaces; to make the best ideas prevail.' Though the 'critical power' was inferior to the creative, Criticism could stimulate literary creation. By getting to know, and making known, 'the best that is known and thought in the world,' it could produce raw material for 'literary genius' to synthesize and expound, an 'intellectual and spiritual atmosphere', as in Pericles' Athens, Goethe's Germany, and Elizabethan England, conducive to original literature. But since Englishmen were such political animals, English Criticism should aim above all at disinterested curiosity. It should also look for 'the best', not only in England, but in the whole of Europe, as 'one great confederation . . . whose members have, for their proper outfit, a knowledge of Greek, Roman and Eastern antiquity, and of one another.'

While contributing to the self-importance of critics, this essay has been effective in raising standards of criticism, and its form exemplifies Arnold's new propaganda technique, designed, as he told his sister, to counter 'the risk . . . if I cannot charm the wild beast of Philistinism while I am trying to convert him, of being torn to pieces by him.' First delivered as an Oxford lecture, it has the charm of an improvised talk, full of humorous asides and exclamations, and apt quotations from newspapers. Here, in a typical transition from a politician's eulogy of England's 'unrivalled happiness' to a reported case of infanticide by a workhouse-girl 'named Wragg', Arnold blends aesthetic and social criticism:

... what a touch of grossness in our race, what an original shortcoming in the more delicate spiritual perceptions, is shown by the natural growth amongst us of such hideous names—Higginbottom, Stiggins, Bugg! In Ionia and Attica they were luckier in this respect than 'the best race in the world;' by the Ilissus there was no Wragg, poor thing! And our 'unrivalled happiness;'—what an element of grimness, bareness, and hideousness mixes with it and blurs it; the workhouse, the dismal Mapperly Hills,—how dismal those who have seen them will remember;—the gloom, the smoke, the cold, the strangled illegitimate child!

Arnold's finest effort to convert the wild beast of Philistinism, *Culture and Anarchy* (1869), was written between two instalments of his funniest one, *Friendship's Garland* (1871). This elegant volume, with its gilt wreath, black border, and epigraph from Virgil's lament for the untimely death of Marcellus, was a tribute to the memory of an imaginary Prussian called Arminius, Baron von Thunder-ten-Tronckh, and contained a series of letters about him, mostly republished from the Pall Mall Gazette. As a namesake of a German rebel against the Roman Empire, Arminius stood for opposition to the Establishment. His surname, from Voltaire's *Candide*, implied dissent from the Pangloss view that this is the best of all possible worlds. Arnold used him as a mouthpiece for his own slashing criticisms of English society, which he in his own person, as Arminius's 'poor friend', ironically defended. Arminius was supported by a cast of satirical personifications, like Bottles, the vulgar industrialist, and Adolescens Leo, Esq., the cheap journalist on the *Daily Telegraph*. This first of the penny newspapers was a favourite target, and responded by calling Arnold 'the high-priest of the kid-gloved persuasion'. Other targets were the worshippers of technology (the Atlantic cable was 'that great rope, with a Philistine at each end of it talking inutilities!'), and the campaign to legalize marriage with a deceased wife's sister. In a farcical scene at Mrs Bottles's deathbed, Leo suggests that Bottles should marry, first his sister-in-law and then his much prettier niece; and that all obstacles to the 'sexual insurrection of our race' should be removed, except 'the prohibition which forbids a man to marry his grandmother.'

Culture and Anarchy was also produced by instalments, mostly in reply to critics of his controversial pronouncements. It developed from his last Professorial lecture at Oxford, 'Culture and Its Enemies', and five articles in the *Cornhill Magazine* on 'Anarchy and Authority'. The 'enemies' were those who, like John Bright, Frederic Harrison, and the *Daily Telegraph*, dismissed culture as of no practical value. The 'anarchy' referred especially to recent incidents: the Hyde Park riot precipitated by the Reform League in 1866, and a military parade in central London (1867), at which the Colonel in charge thought it imprudent to interfere with gangs of muggers attacking the spectators. The purpose of the book was to prove the practical value of culture, as the only source of authority capable of preventing anarchy, by contradicting the cult of individual freedom, the Englishman's supposed 'right to do what he likes . . . march where he likes, meet where he likes, enter where he likes, hoot as he likes, threaten as he likes, smash as he likes.'

For this purpose Arnold defined culture as an effort to improve oneself and others, to perfect human nature, not one-sidedly but 'harmoniously', not selfishly but for the benefit of the whole 'human family', not outwardly but inwardly. Culture, so defined, was badly needed by the English. Inward perfection would oppose 'a mechanical and material civilisation', general perfection, the obsession with individual freedom, and harmonious perfection, 'our want of flexibility, our inaptitude for seeing more than one side of a thing'. As for the great objects of current interest, such as railways, religious organizations, material wealth, and physical exercise, they were merely 'machinery'. What mattered was 'a perfection in which the characters of beauty and intelligence are both present'; or as Swift's bee had put it, 'sweetness and light'. By such criteria culture would condemn the 'hideousness' of London, with its contrasts of poverty and riches, the Philistines generally, the Puritans ('what intolerable company Shakespeare and Virgil would have found them!'), the *Daily Telegraph*, the Dissenters, John Bright, and Frederic Harrison—the latter because of his ideological ferocity.

So much for culture. As for anarchy, it could only be averted by a government representing, not a class-interest, but the 'best self' of the nation. How this was to be arranged in practice, Arnold did not say. But the book is fascinating chiefly for its theoretical ideas, and for their memorable and persuasive presentation. Of the ideas themselves, perhaps the most suggestive is the distinction between 'Hebraism', or 'strictness of conscience', and 'Hellenism' or 'spontaneity of consciousness'. Arnold attributed the deplorable state of England to a Hebraistic preference for doing to thinking, energy to intelligence, 'conduct and obedience' to 'seeing things as they really are'. More Hellenism was therefore needed to restore a balance lost since the time of the Puritans. So political, social, and religious questions should be answered, not by obedience to 'stock notions', but by letting the mind 'play freely around' the issues involved.

The success of the presentation is largely due to its schematic and almost pedagogic character, with its main points emphasized by striking phrases constantly repeated; to vivid satirical devices like nicknaming the upper, middle, and lower classes Barbarians, Philistines, and Populace respectively; and to a prose-style always lively and often witty. The book is also remarkable for its humorous polemics. To those, for instance, who argued that marrying a deceased wife's sister was nowhere forbidden in Leviticus, he replied with a fine rhetorical flourish: was the last word really said on the subject of love and marriage by 'an oriental and polygamous nation . . . whose wisest king had seven hundred wives and three hundred concubines?'

Arminius, as he died, sent a message to his 'poor friend': 'Tell him . . . to let his Dissenters go to the devil their own way!' The advice came too late. Arnold had just been trying, in *St. Paul and Protestantism* (1870) to turn Dissenters back into Anglicans, by first demolishing their theology, and then showing them that Christianity could best develop within a national church. Their theology, he argued, was unscientific, because it made unverifiable assertions about 'God and his proceedings' as if he were 'a man in the next street'. It was also based on a misunderstanding of St Paul's writings. For such anthropomorphism Arnold substituted his own definition of God (derived from Wordsworth and Spinoza): '*That stream of tendency by which all things seek to fulfil the law of their being*'. For a literal-minded reading of St Paul's 'figurative and poetic language' he offered his own version of what the Apostle 'really thought and meant to say'. Treating the Epistles as a literary text, he decided that St Paul was not really interested in 'election' or 'justification', only in 'righteousness', human '*solidarity*', and a sense that 'in conformity to the *will of God*, as we religiously name the moral order, is our peace and happiness.' By 'faith' he meant that love of Jesus, like 'being in love' with a human being, can change one's whole 'spiritual atmosphere'; by 'resurrection', 'a rising, in this visible earthly existence, from the death of obedience to blind selfish impulse, to the life of obedience to the eternal moral order'. That at least was his unconscious meaning—and here, with a fragment of verse recalling 'The Buried Life', Arnold founded, for better or worse, the psychoanalytical school of literary criticism.

Arnold's last major work, *Literature and Dogma* (1873), extended the method of *St. Paul and Protestantism* to the whole Bible. It was, the Preface explained, an attempt to give the Bible 'a real experimental basis' and so make it interesting to 'the masses', who now demanded '*reason* and *authority* for the things they [had] been taught to believe'. Since the language of the Bible was 'fluid, passing, and literary, not rigid, fixed, and scientific', its meaning was utterly distorted by 'our mechanical and materializing theology, with its insane licence of affirmation about God' and 'a future state'. Arnold now defined religion as '*morality touched by emotion*', and God as 'the *not ourselves* by which we get the sense for *righteousness*, and whence we find the help to *do right*.' In both Testaments he found an original religious insight overlaid by accretions of '*Aberglaube*', or superstition, in which he included miracles, the fulfilment of prophecies, and the idea of a literal resurrection. In the Old Testament the insight was simply an 'intuition' of God and of righteousness. In the New, it was the teaching by Jesus of 'a method', 'a secret', and 'a temper'. The method was that of conscience, the secret was dying to one's 'lower and apparent self' and living to one's 'higher and real self', and the temper was *epieikeia* or 'sweet reasonableness'. This translation of the Bible into Arnoldian formulas had the merit, he claimed, of being verifiable, 'as you can verify that fire burns—by experience! It is so; try it!' Whatever the truth of this claim, the book sold over 100,000 copies, and was important in pioneering the metaphorical type of Christianity that now may satisfy an Anglican bishop. It showed a shift of interest in Arnold from Hellenism to Hebraism (now said to be concerned with 'three-fourths' of human life). As literature, however, it is disappointing. Clotted, inevitably, with biblical texts, it is also diffuse and repetitive in style, and monotonously earnest in tone. Only rarely does the old 'vivacity' appear, as in describing the 'popular conception of a future state of bliss . . . with many, it is that of a kind of perfected middle-class home, with labour ended, the table spread, goodness all round, the lost ones restored, hymnody incessant.'

The Preface ended with some advice on making the best use of one's time. 'Some of us waste all of it, most of us waste much, but all of us waste some.' Arnold wasted remarkably little. All his voluminous writing on a wide range of subjects was done in the intervals of his job as a School Inspector, from which he retired only two years before his sudden death from heart-failure in 1888. Of the many articles, introductions, and lectures produced in his last ten years the most interesting are those on English literature and American society.

In 1879 he judged Wordsworth the third-greatest English poet, on the strength of this definition: '. . . poetry is at bottom a criticism of life . . . the greatness of a poet lies in his powerful and beautiful application of ideas to life,—to the question: How to live.' This was expanded, but hardly clarified, in 'The Study of Poetry' (1880), where Arnold predicted that poetry would super-sede religion as something to 'interpret life for us, to console us, to sustain us.' For this, only 'the best poetry' would do, so a method was needed of forming a 'real estimate', as opposed to a 'historic' or 'personal' one. The method suggested, using brief extracts from 'the great masters' as 'touchstones', has obvious weaknesses; but it might at least serve to make 'personal estimates' consistent. Subtly distorting the meaning of a statement in the *Poetics*, Arnold claimed Aristotle's authority for requiring 'a great classic' to show 'high seriousness', and so for depreciating Chaucer and Burns. While dealing rather rough justice to several other authors, he marked down Dryden and Pope as 'classics of our prose'. Later assessments of romantic poets, unduly influenced by moral judge-ments of their lives, have become famous less for their critical acumen than for their phrasing. Shelley, for instance, was absurdly dismissed as 'a beautiful and ineffectual angel, beating in the void his luminous wings in vain.' The romantic poets might well retort on their critic his earlier charge that they 'did not know enough.'

Arnold's last few writings showed that he was still much better at scanning large areas from a height, than accurately assessing single features of the landscape. 'Literature and Science' was an entertaining lecture first delivered at Cambridge and then so popular in America that he gave it twenty-nine times there, and confessed to getting bored with it. It argued plausibly, against Huxley's 'Science and Culture' (1881) for the greater importance of literary than of scientific education; but it was based on a confessed ignorance of science, and few scientists would find the argument convincing. Arnold's arbitrary judgements, however, were camouflaged with incidental humour, as when he said he would 'rather have a young person ignorant of the moon's diameter', than unaware that 'Can you not wait upon the lunatic?' was a poor paraphrase of a famous line in *Macbeth*. The question-begging statement that the human 'instinct for beauty' would always 'keep Greek as a part of our culture' was similarly protected by a jocular reference to Darwin's description of Man's 'hairy ancestor'.

Arnold's three accounts of American civilization (1882, 1885, 1888) were witty and full of interest; but they were also full of personal prejudice, and based on inadequate knowledge. The first, which assumed that America was 'just ourselves, with the Barbarians quite left out, and the Populace nearly', was written before he had ever been there. The second, which drew on his experience during an arduous lecture-tour of less than six months, reached the airy conclusion that America had solved her political and social problems, but not 'the human problem', since many English 'gentlemen' would rather live in almost any country 'calling itself civilized ... than in the United States'. According to the third, American civilization suffered from 'the want of the *interesting*, a want chiefly due to the want of those two great elements of the interesting, which are elevation and beauty.' On his way to this final judgement, Arnold complained that names like Briggsville, Higginsville, and Jacksonville acted 'upon a cultivated person like the incessant pricking of pins', and was shocked to find that Americans seemed quite satisfied with their own pronunciation:

Far from admitting that the American accent, as the pressure of their climate and of their average man has made it, is a thing to be striven against, they assure one another that it is the right accent, the standard English speech of the future.

It says much for transatlantic *epieikeia* that some of the best work on Matthew Arnold has been done by American scholars.

6. Four Lesser Poets

THOUGH soon to be eclipsed by Tennyson and her husband, Mrs Browning might reasonably have become Poet Laureate, as the *Athenaeum* proposed in June 1850, had she published by then her two best poems, *Sonnets from the Portuguese* and *Aurora Leigh*.[1] But the quality of *Poems* (1844) was no higher than one could expect from her own account of herself in 1831:

... how could I write a diary without throwing upon paper my thoughts, all my thoughts—the thoughts of my heart as well as of my head?—and then how could I bear to look on *them* after they were written? Adam made fig leaves necessary for the mind, as well as for the body. And such *a* mind as I have!—So very exacting & exclusive & eager & headlong—& *strong*—& so very very often *wrong*!

These poems, too, seemed thrown upon paper, and were apt to be rather gushing. The thoughts of her heart included passionate feelings about God, Nature, poetry, love, her spaniel Flush, and all victims of oppression. 'Lady Geraldine's Courtship' was an unhappy cross between the verse of 'Locksley Hall' and the subject of 'Lady Clara Vere de Vere'. It celebrated, with now embarrassing fervour, the love of a poor poet for a rich 'Earl's daughter'. 'The Cry of the Children' protested, more effectively, against the conditions of child-labour described in a recent Government report.

The title of this poem comes from Euripides' *Medea*, where the children are heard crying off-stage that they are being murdered; and the Greek epigraph points to an earlier moment in the tragedy where the murderess is still capable of responding to the appeal in her children's eyes. The aptness of the allusion reminds us that Mrs Browning was not only a fine classical scholar but also, for all

---

[1] Elizabeth Barrett Browning, 1806–61, was born at Coxhoe Hall, near Durham, the eldest child of the heir to a fortune made in Jamaica. The family then moved to Hope End, Herefordshire, where she was educated privately, becoming an omnivorous reader, especially of Greek poetry. Her chronic ill health, probably tubercular in origin, eventually confined her to her room in her father's house in Wimpole Street, London, until she married Robert Browning, 1846, and went off with him to Italy. Their only child, 'Pen' Browning, was born, 1849. She died in Florence.

her emotionalism, a very intellectual poet. At twelve she delighted in studying metaphysics. At thirteen she started reading 'all modern authors who have any claim to superior merit and poetic excellence'. She became a remarkable linguist, with a special interest in Greek. This showed itself in an accurate and readable verse translation of the *Prometheus Vinctus*, and two early imitations of Greek tragic form, but more generally in a precise syntax that mitigated her characteristic diffuseness. Two interesting effects of her intellectualism on her poetry were a fondness for prosodic experiments, including the use of assonantal rhymes, and for highly ingenious, almost metaphysical, imagery.

Despite the efforts of some modern biographers to demythologize the Brownings' love-affair, it remains a historic fact of great human and poetic significance. It did transform Elizabeth from a house-bound invalid into a tolerably healthy and active woman. It gave her and Robert nearly sixteen years of what, by average standards, must be called a very happy marriage. And it made them both much better poets than they had been before. Written in 1845–6, completed two days before their secret wedding (12 September 1846), and first shown to Browning in 1849, *Sonnets from the Portuguese* were not published until they appeared in *Poems* (1850). The title was meant to conceal their autobiographical character, and the ruse was surprisingly successful. Only one reviewer seemed to sense that they were more than translations.

The sequence told, however, in a delicately contrived form, the story of the poet's feelings towards Browning. It began with her scruples about saddling him with such an unequal partner, a dreary invalid six years older than he was. It ended in a mood of wonder, delight, and gratitude, interspersed with persistent doubts and anxieties. It hinted, by an allusion to Sophocles' *Electra*, at the traumatic shock of her brother's death by drowning (Sonnet v). It asked a question especially relevant to the circumstances of the elopement from Wimpole Street, whether a husband's love could wholly compensate for the loss of a home and of family relationships. The complete experience was presented as a movement from suicidal gloom to new life, and the two sonnets that framed the implied narrative reinforced the idea allegorically, as a triumph of Love over Death. The opening sonnet announced this theme, by veiled allusions to the resurrection of Adonis in Theocritus' *Idyll* xv, to the saving of Agamemnon's life by Athene in *Iliad* I, and to a children's guessing-game (an image also used in 'A Child's Thought of God'). The closing sonnet employed the flowers that Browning had brought to 'this close room' throughout the winter as another symbol of miraculous survival. As pastoral gifts such as Polyphemus brought Galatea in *Idyll* XI, they echoed the initial reference to Theocritus, whose Polyphemus had just been turned (Sonnet XL) into a foil for Browning's patience as a lover.

Such complexity of allusion, while contributing to the artistic form and the dignity of the poem, in no way interfered with its expression of simple and genuine feelings. Browning called the *Sonnets* 'a strange, heavy crown', feeling, no doubt, unworthy of such near-idolatry. But the general effect of the work is wonderfully light and happy, despite the almost tragic intensity of its realistic moments:

> But I look on thee ... on thee ...
> Beholding, besides love, the end of love,
> Hearing oblivion beyond memory ...
> As one who sits and gazes, from above,
> Over the rivers to the bitter sea.

Gazing from the windows of her home in Florence, Mrs Browning was less far-sighted. *Casa Guidi Windows* (1851) hailed with wild enthusiasm the new era of liberal reform and Italian freedom that she thought would follow the election of Pope Pius IX in 1846; and then lamented the situation in 1851, when Pius had turned reactionary, and an Austrian army had occupied Florence. Shapeless in structure, the poem seems equally unsatisfactory in sentiment. Its contempt for Italian cowardice (however amusingly expressed), and its call for heroic patriotism would have come rather better from someone not watching, in almost Lucretian security, the troubles of other people. Her gift for satire and her passion for heroism were much more happily employed in *Aurora Leigh* (1857), where the heroism was of a kind that she herself had shown, the courage of a woman taking an independent line in a male-dominated society.

The striking originality of this novel in blank verse did not lie in its rather improbable plot which, apart from some touches of autobiography, was mostly taken from other novels. Its slum scenes seem to have come from *Bleak House* and *Alton Locke*, its

innocent, unmarried mother, Marian Erle, from Mrs Gaskell's
Ruth, its 'principle of good surviving through every adverse
circumstance' from *Oliver Twist*, and Aurora's predicament, as an
Anglo-Italian orphan brought up in England, from Madame de
Staël's *Corinne*. But the greatest debt was to *Jane Eyre*. Aurora's
refusal to become a mere 'helpmate' to the social reformer Romney
Leigh was very like Jane's response to St John Rivers's proposal to
make her 'a missionary's wife'. And the blinding of Romney in a
fire, to bring the lovers finally together, differed from the blinding
of Rochester only by the extra irony that the arson at Leigh Hall
(where Romney had established a socialist community) was aided
and abetted by the very people that he had taken into his home.

The poem's message, however, was far from derivative. It
included, according to the poet, her 'highest convictions upon Life
and Art'. Those on Life assert the special value of the way women
think. The Brownings held different views about their son's
upbringing, but here Aurora has the last word: fathers may love
their children as much as mothers do,

> but still with heavier brains,
> And wills more consciously responsible,
> And not as wisely, since less foolishly.

Women are wiser, too, about social questions. Romney, a typical
male, 'lives by diagrams', generalizations, and statistics, and with
what he ultimately calls 'disastrous arrogance' thinks he can put
the world right by making it conform to 'a pattern on his nail',
designed to satisfy people's bodily needs. Aurora, as a woman,
cares more for the individual, the soul, God's plan for the world,
and poetry, which she considers the most effective agent of social
reform, since 'poets get directlier at the soul | Than any of your
oeconomists'. The spirited apologia for female thought-processes
is prefaced by a delightful piece of satire:

> I read a score of books on womanhood
> To prove, if women do not think at all,
> They may teach thinking (to a maiden aunt
> Or else the author),—books that boldly assert
> Their right of comprehending husband's talk
> When not too deep, and even of answering
> With pretty 'may it please you,' or 'so it is,'—
> Their rapid insight and fine aptitude,

> Particular worth and general missionariness,
> As long as they keep quiet by the fire
> And never say 'no' when the world says 'ay,'
> For that is fatal,—their angelic reach
> Of virtue, chiefly used to sit and darn,
> And fatten household sinners,—their, in brief,
> Potential faculty in everything
> Of abdicating power in it . . .

The convictions on Art relate chiefly to poetry, and implicitly contradict Arnold's 1853 Preface. Form is relatively unimportant: 'Trust the spirit, | As sovran nature does, to make the form'. As for subject, a poet should not 'trundle back his soul five hundred years'. His 'sole work is to represent the age', his own age and 'not Charlemagne's' nor, presumably, that of Pericles or Homer. As a Victorian epic, about 'this live, throbbing age, | That brawls, cheats, maddens, calculates, aspires', *Aurora Leigh* is surprisingly successful. Its blank-verse dialogue between educated people sounds quite authentic. This does not apply to the incredible Marian Erle, whose only education came from 'odd volumes' tossed down to her from a pedlar's cart, but all the other characters are tolerably convincing. Those outside Mrs Browning's range of experience were, wisely, not often quoted verbatim. Slum scenes were quite effectively handled by an impressionistic technique like Carlyle's in the *French Revolution*. Thus, at the wedding of Romney and Marian (called off at the last moment), the friends of the bride 'oozed into the church | In a dark slow stream, like blood'. The friends of the bridegroom were visually caricatured almost in the manner of Hogarth, and made further grotesque by disconnected snippets of their spiteful gossip. The mounting suspense in this wildly heterogeneous congregation terminated in a riot sketched, like the panic in the College hall of Tennyson's *The Princess*, with broad strokes of humour and melodrama.

On the principle of letting 'the spirit make the form', the poem is often allowed to ramble, especially when 'convictions' interrupt the narrative. But it has a fairly firm thematic structure, beginning and ending with motherhood in Florence, and unobtrusively unified, like the *Oedipus* plays of Sophocles, by the theme of blindness, mental and physical. Though immediately popular with the reading public, *Aurora Leigh* was generally condemned by its reviewers, and it was only poetic justice that a work which called

Daphnis and Chloe an 'obscene text' should itself be charged with indecency. Today it seems more open to criticism for its implausible plot, its over-emotional tone, and its prolixity. But this last was caused by the very richness of the poet's imagination. The style seems like a spontaneous chain-reaction of vivid and ingenious images, which carry the thought along by a series of intellectual explosions. Certainly one often wishes that the process could be halted; but the pyrotechnics are always worth watching. In retrospect the poem's faults are glaring: at the time of reading it one is more conscious of its immense vitality.

That was not, however, the feeling of Tennyson's friend Fitzgerald, who made himself Browning's enemy by writing (in a posthumously published private letter): 'Mrs Browning's Death is rather a relief to me, I must say: no more Aurora Leighs, thank God!' Fitzgerald never claimed to be a poet. 'I have not', he confessed, 'the strong inward call, nor cruel-sweet pangs of parturition, that prove the birth of anything bigger than a mouse.' But he thought himself a good judge of poetry and art. As such, he did not 'care for' *In Memoriam*, classed *The Ring and the Book* 'among the absurdest books ever written by a gifted Man', and called it 'a national Absurdity' to devote a whole room in the National Gallery to pictures by Turner. With such self-confidence in criticism, he became a bold improver of other people's poetry. He 'distilled many pretty little poems out of long ones' written by his friend Bernard Barton (1849), and having 'sunk, reduced, altered, and replaced' what he found unsatisfactory in *Six Dramas of Calderon* (1853), he applied similar treatment to the work of three Persian poets, Jámí, Attár, and Omar Khayyám (1856–9), and to Aeschylus' *Agamemnon* (1865).[2]

Fitzgerald's approach to translation was in keeping with his hatred of photographs, and his irreverence towards old masters:

But what do you think of my Impudence in actually rubbing down my Titian Landscape! which Mr. C. was frightened to think of my doing, but says it is certainly improved, now it's done. I will not have green skies at any Price . . .

---

[2] Edward Fitzgerald, 1809–83, was born near Woodbridge, Suffolk, the son of a rich landowner from Dublin. He went to the grammar school at Bury St Edmunds and Trinity College, Cambridge, where he met Tennyson and Thackeray, and took a pass degree. In 1856 he chivalrously married the daughter of his dead poet friend Bernard Barton, whose poems he had edited; but they parted with relief a year later. He spent the rest of his life in or near Woodbridge.

The supreme justification of his impudence was the *Rubáiyát of Omar Khayyám* (1859). Virtually an original poem, it became the Bible of Victorian agnosticism, having developed from a favourite of the Pre-Raphaelites, into 'a little *Craze*' (as Fitzgerald put it) of the Americans, and finally into a piece of world literature.

His first book, *Euphranor: A Dialogue on Youth* (1851) spoke only to the rather smaller world of early-Victorian Cambridge. In a form derived from Plato, Lucian, and Peacock, with numerous quotations, and specific allusions to the *Phaedrus* and the *Clouds*, it described a day's outing from Cambridge to an inn at Chesterton. The speakers included Lexilogus, a plodding undergraduate, Phidippus, modelled on Fitzgerald's horseman-friend Kenworthy Browne, who had never been at a University, and Euphranor himself, an idealistic graduate interested in art and literature. The central theme of the book was a protest against the Cambridge syllabus, as being too exclusively academic. It called for an education better designed to produce 'Locke's "*totus, teres,*" and—except in the matter of waistband—"*rotundus*" man, sufficiently accoutred for the campaign of ordinary Life.' Tennyson had made the same point concisely in 'Lines on Cambridge' of 1830, but the dialogue is lively and pleasant enough, as its title seems to promise. If less interesting intellectually than Hopkins's Oxford equivalent, 'On the Origin of Beauty' (1865), it gives a more attractive impression of University life.

Late in 1853, encouraged by his friend Edward Cowell, a polymath Ipswich brewer, Fitzgerald started learning Persian from a grammar and a dictionary. Next summer he read Jámí's *Salámán and Absál*, thought it inferior to 'almost a single *Line* of the *Agamemnon*', but liked it enough to make what he called 'a metrical Abstract' of it, which he published in 1856. Jámí's poem was a rather confusing allegory about a Sage (the divine First Intelligence), a King (the Tenth Intelligence which governs the universe), his son Salámán (the human Soul), and Absál, Salámán's nurse, with whom he has a passionate love-affair. The story had a certain idyllic charm, but was told in a very ornate and pleonastic style, preceded by several tedious panegyrics and a catalogue of the poet's geriatric symptoms, and often interrupted by parabolic anecdotes. Though some of these were quite funny, like the tale of the Kurd who tied a gourd to his foot so as not to lose himself in a big city, the general effect was, by European

standards, extremely tiresome. So Fitzgerald cut the work ruthlessly. He eliminated boring elements, made the parables seem
shorter and more easily skipped, by putting them into Hiawathan
trochaics, instead of the grander blank verse used for the main
story, and everywhere tightened the style. He also freely trans-
posed passages, as he told Cowell, 'so as to compact the narrative'.
His treatment of the allegory, which he judged 'imperfect' but of
'general and ever-vital significance', was equally unscrupulous: 'I
shall bundle up the Celestial and Earthly Shah so neatly that
neither can be displeased & no Reader know which is which. Trust
an Irishman where any confusion is wanted.' At first he thought it
his duty to 'rub off' as little as possible of Jámí's 'Oriental Colour',
and to imitate the Authorized Version in preferring to be 'Orien-
tally obscure than Europeanly clear'. But in practice, as he
admitted, he took the opposite line: 'I had to choose between being
readably English, or unreadably Oriental.' Though his version
attracted few contemporary readers, it certainly succeeded in
making an otherwise unapproachable work enjoyable in England,
and it is still entertaining, especially in its satire on marriage,
where Fitzgerald expressed strong feelings of his own:

> Clothe her a hundred Years in Gold and Jewel,
> Her Garment with Brocade of Susa braided,
> Her very Night-gear wrought in Cloth of Gold,
> Dangle her Ears with Ruby and with Pearl,
> Her House with Golden Vessels all a-blaze,
> Her Tables loaded with the Fruit of Kings,
> Ispahan Apples, Pomegranates of Yazd;
> And, be she thirsty, from a Jewell'd Cup
> Drinking the Water of the Well of Life—
> One little twist of Temper,—all you've done
> Goes all for Nothing. 'Torment of my life!'
> She cries, 'What have you ever done for me!'

With Jámí, however, and with Attár, of whose *Bird-Parliament*
(*Mantik ut-tair*) he produced 'a bird's eye view' in English
couplets, Fitzgerald did little more than translate, cut, and rewrite.
It was only when Cowell introduced him (1856) to Omar
Khayyám that he became a kind of poet. Cowell later felt guilty at
having exposed his friend to such a bad influence: 'I admire Omar
as I admire Lucretius, but I cannot take him as a *guide*.' Fitzgerald
felt very differently. 'You see all [his] Beauty,' he wrote to Cowell,

'but you don't feel *with* him in some respects as I do.' The Omar
with whom he felt such an affinity was essentially 'Infidel and
Epicurean ... as Savage against Destiny etc. as Manfred'. For his
own epitaph he chose a text from the Psalms, 'It is He that hath
made us and not we ourselves', which could be read in the spirit of
Omar's protest (as literally translated by an Iranian academic in
1975):

When the All-Possessor arranged the composition of (different) natures,
why did he cast them meager and wanting? if they turned out well, what
was this breaking for? And who is at fault if these images did not turn out
well?

Fitzgerald has been accused of taking Omar's mystical metaphors too literally, and so turning a Sufi into a blasphemous,
atheistic, anti-Sufic hedonist. He seems, however, to have summarized quite fairly the surface meaning, at least, of the 179 *rubáis*
included in the prose translation of 1975. During his lifetime in the
eleventh century, Omar was known, not as a poet, but as a
scientific thinker who wrote on mathematics, physics, astronomy,
climatology, ethics, and metaphysics. His poems were written for
his own satisfaction, and he took care to prevent their circulation.
Each *rubái* was a self-contained epigram, which formed no part of
any larger pattern; but a recurrent theme was that of *carpe diem*,
with distrust of an after-life, and a preference for the 'cash' of
present pleasure to a 'credit-paradise'. Such scepticism was developed into total agnosticism: all that can be known for certain is
that 'We came out of the dust and went with the wind.' The
hypothesis of a Creator was mentioned only in criticism of his
injustice and irrationality, and in one *rubái* the nihilism became
suicidal: 'O, I wish I could find a door to nonexistence.' But the
characteristic mood was one of sardonic cheerfulness, with touches
of irreverent humour, like this pun on a word that means both
'constantly' and 'wine': 'The Quran, which is called the Holy
Word, is read from time to time and not always. [But] around the
cup there dwells a verse which is read constantly everywhere.'

To the form of the *rubái* (four hemistichs rhyming AABA or
AAAA), as well as to Omar's apparent meaning, Fitzgerald tried to
be moderately faithful. Looking first for a vaguely analogous
verse-form not too far from Omar's period, he adapted the rhymes
and rhythms of the mediaeval hymn, '*Dies irae*' to produce *rubáis*
like this one:

Si cerebri cerealis esset apud me sinceri
Panis, esset et cruoris Amphora repleta Meri,
Esse[s]atque dulce Carmen dulce canens in Deserto—
Tum non esset unocuique Sultanorum invideri.

Here the thought was derived from two different *rubáis* of Omar, and in the English version the 'paradise' of the one replaced the 'Sultan' of the other, while the bread and wine, metaphorical in the Latin, reverted to their literal status in both originals:

> Here with a Loaf of Bread beneath the Bough,
> A flask of Wine, A Book of Verse—and Thou
>   Beside me singing in the Wilderness—
> And Wilderness is Paradise enow.

The two quotations exemplify Fitzgerald's admitted policy of 'mashing Quatrains together', and playing freely with his author's ideas and images. His purpose was to impose an artistic pattern upon the *disjecta membra poetae*. 'I see,' he wrote to Cowell in 1856, 'how a very pretty Eclogue might be tesselated out of his scattered Quatrains.' He was thinking, perhaps, of Virgil's *Eclogue* I, which begins with Tityrus singing happily about Amaryllis, and ends with Meliboeus going sadly away, as the shadows lengthen and the evening falls. His own pattern, however, as explained to his publishers later, is less reminiscent of Virgil than of Tennyson's 'Will Waterproof': 'He begins with Dawn pretty sober and contemplative: then as he thinks and drinks, grows savage, blasphemous, &c., and then again sobers down into melancholy at nightfall.'

In thus arranging *rubáis* to form a sequence, Fizgerald was not infringing literary convention, for one of Omar's contemporaries had done so too, though the immediate source of the idea was probably *In Memoriam*. For using an earlier poet's verses as tesserae for his own mosaic, he might, on modern theories of oral composition, have claimed the authority of Homer. But the best defence of his methods is the unexpected beauty and power of his *Rubáiyát* as an independent creation. It is always faithful, not to Omar, but to real human feeling. In a letter of 1842, Fitzgerald mentioned his love for 'the common chords, those truisms of music, like other truisms so little understood in the full.' The *Rubáiyát* is full of such truisms, in what seems their definitive form. In this quatrain, for instance, the central image comes from

Omar, and the 'piety' from Horace, but the total effect is of something expressed by the *rerum natura*:

> The Moving Finger writes; and, having writ,
> Moves on: nor all your Piety nor Wit
>   Shall lure it back to cancel half a Line,
> Nor all your Tears wash out a Word of it.

Just such an attempt, by a singular blend of piety and wit, to arrest the movement of time was made by Tennyson's younger friend, Coventry Patmore.[3] 'Alas, and is not mine a language dead?' he asked ironically in *The Unknown Eros*; and though his ideas were often highly original, his general attitudes were reactionary. Shortly before J. S. Mill thought public opinion sufficiently advanced to sympathize with his great protest against the 'Subjection of Women', Patmore wrote *The Angel in the House* (1854–63) to celebrate a view of marriage in which the husband is 'unconditionally lord' of his wife, and 'all the wisdom that she has | Is to love him for being wise.' In an age of political reform, he denounced 1867 as 'the year of the great crime', and 1884 as marking 'the final destruction of the liberties of England'. His religious philosophy was almost medieval in character. If he did not ask how many angels could stand on the point of a needle, he at least tried to explain, in *The Rod, The Root and The Flower* (1895), how two Divine Messengers could share a house. The house was the body, the 'House of God', which was 'expressly formed' for the 'cohabitation and communion of two Persons (whose union is a third)'. The two Persons were Woman, 'the *visible* glory of God' or 'the word made Woman'; and Man, who 'interprets woman to herself,' just as 'God interprets man'.

Though Patmore's theory of sexual love as an internal relationship between the two halves of the 'homo' recalls the humorous fable of Aristophanes in the *Symposium*, it also has points of resemblance to modern psychology: 'The external man and woman are each the projected *simulacrum* of the latent half of the other, and they do but love themselves in thus loving their opposed likenesses.' The main subject, however, of Patmore's

---

[3] Coventry Kersey Dighton Patmore, 1823–96, was born at Woodford, Essex, the son of a free-thinking journalist-friend of Hazlitt and Lamb. Privately educated, he worked from 1846 in the British Museum. His first wife, the daughter of a congregational minister, died in 1862, leaving him with six children. His second wife was a Roman Catholic, and he became one himself, 1864. On her death, 1880, he married his children's governess.

thought was neither ancient nor modern, but of permanent human interest: the conditions and effects of successful relations between the sexes. And his poetic language was very far from 'dead'. While clearly influenced by Donne, Herbert, Herrick, Crabbe, and Tennyson, his style was an idiosyncratic blend of romantic lyric and satirical epigram.

The Angel in the House was originally designed as a tribute, under the title of 'The Happy Wedding', to Patmore's first wife Emily, who died in 1862. It was presented half-humorously as a kind of didactic epic, on 'The first of themes, sung last of all', i.e. conjugal love. As such, it was never completed, but four instalments appeared. The first two, *The Betrothal* and *The Espousals* (1854–6) described the love, courtship, and marriage of the poet narrator, Felix Vaughan, in the unromantic setting of a cathedral close, like that of Trollope's *The Warden* (1855). The last two, *Faithful for Ever* and *The Victories of Love* (1860–2) told how an apparently hopeless marriage between a naval officer called Frederick Graham and 'A dear, good girl' called Jane was eventually turned into a happy one, by the wife's genuine love for her husband, and his valiant efforts to do his duty by her.

The narrative abounds in touches of comic realism, such as Felix's initial dismay at finding his love returned: 'I found, and felt with strange alarm, | I stood committed to my bliss.' There is irony, too, in his delight at having to pay the bill for his new wife's sand-shoes, and in the contrast between Jane's and Frederick's reactions to sitting together in amicable silence. As a quasi-Ovidian *Ars Matrimonii*, *The Angel* gives much sound advice on the maintenance of love within marriage, stressing the need for distance, respect, and non-possessiveness, the danger of fault-finding, the folly of trying to 'mend' one's partner, and the usefulness of 'praise that is not quite deserved'. But the poem is more remarkable for the almost Metaphysical form into which such advice is often put. Praise, for instance, is 'Beauty's elixir vitae', and fault-finding inspires a conceit both witty and profound: 'The eye which magnifies her charms | Is microscopic for defect.' 'The most ardent love,' wrote Patmore in his last book, 'is more epigrammatic than lyrical. The Saints, above all St. Augustine, abound in epigrams.' So does *The Angel*, and readers who expect the poem to be merely sentimental will be surprised at the essentially intellectual character of its style as well as its content.

This quality is most apparent in the versification. In 'An Essay on English Metrical law' (1856) he stressed the importance of rhyme and of the two verse-forms used in *The Angel*:

Rhyme is so far from being extra-metrical and merely 'ornamental', as most persons imagine it to be, that it is the quality to which nearly all our metres owe their very existence. The octo-syllabic couplet and quatrain, two of the most important measures we have, are measures only by virtue of the indication, supplied by rhyme, of the limits of the verse; for they have no catalectic pause, without which 'blank verse' in English is impossible.

These 'inflexibly rigid, and as they are commonly thought, difficult metres' suited in many ways the poem's theme. As being 'difficult', they implied that marriage was a taxing art: 'The death of nuptial joy is sloth'. As commonplace and unpretentious, they were appropriate to a story of ordinary domestic life. As imposing strict limits, they suggested the religious belief that Man, Woman, the Body, and the whole physical world were forces of 'The Infinite' compressed by 'God's limits' into intelligible form, and also the ethical view that 'virtues are nothing but ordered passions ... vices nothing but passions in disorder', and that the best way of ordering sexual passion was marriage. The regular rhymes, like the 'Cathedral chimes', came to symbolize not only 'order'd freedom sweet and fair' but even the music of the spheres. Thus they echoed the poem's central thesis that 'nuptial contrasts are the poles | On which the heavenly spheres revolve,' and that 'This germ of nuptial love' is the root 'Of all our love to man and God.'

Felix, the supposed author of the first two books, claims to be 'An ancient bard of simple mind', and makes fun of learned commentators who will find in his poem 'Outlines occult of abstract scope'. Its religious philosophy, however, is quite clearly outlined in the 'Preludes' between sections of narrative, and there are five obvious allusions to the development of the human soul or psyche, through the ancient allegory of the butterfly. Elsewhere 'Christ's marriage with the Church' is explicitly described as 'more ... than a metaphor', and directly associated with the fable of Cupid and Psyche. The conception of sexual union as 'more than a metaphor' for religious experience was elaborated in *The Unknown Eros* (1877), under an image derived from the fable in Apuleius, and a title alluding to St Paul's sermon on the Areopagus: 'Whom therefore ye ignorantly worship, him I declare unto you.'

The Angel had been a tale of domestic life which showed that the lover's 'familiar thoughts embrace | Unfathomable mystery.' For this attempt to go deeper into the mystery he invented a new verse-form. This was a lyrical ode, iambic in rhythm and retaining such hints of symmetry as assonance and irregular rhyme, but without stanzas or other predictable patterns, and with lines varying in length from two to sixteen syllables. While owing something to the prosodic experiments of Spenser, Milton, and Wordsworth, the form was substantially Patmore's creation, and, when not used for such incongruous purposes as political propaganda, proved highly effective. Of the theory behind it, the most important feature was the doctrine, first formulated in a review of *In Memoriam* (1850), of 'isochronous intervals': '. . . each line, however many syllables it may contain, ought to occupy the same time in reading, according to the analogy of bars in music.' In practice Patmore's prosodic theory, which received qualified approval from Bridges and Hopkins, was chiefly of value for emphasizing the management of significant pauses in verse.

The title-poem of the volume, 'To the Unknown Eros', appears to express the experience of a mystic in terms at least intelligible to an agnostic, and with undeniable artistry, both rhythmic and phonetic:

> What rumour'd heavens are these
> Which not a poet sings,
> O, Unknown Eros? What this breeze
> Of sudden wings
> Speeding at far returns of time from interstellar space
> To fan my very face,
> And gone as fleet,
> Through delicatest ether feathering soft their solitary beat . . .

The other specifically religious poems, which appear in the second Book of the collection, have much less appeal for unbelievers, and even believers might find the 'De Natura Deorum' rather tasteless. In this dialogue between Psyche and the Pythoness (strangely like Corinna's conversation with an old bawd in Ovid's *Amores*) the Soul is ridiculed for her excessive reverence towards the god who has visited her 'incognito':

> Child, any one, to hear you speak,
> Would take you for a Protestant,
> (Such fish I do foresee
> When the charm'd fume comes strong on me).

Patmore had become a Roman Catholic in 1864, and in 1873 had bought up and burnt his publisher's stock of the *Angel*, apparently fearing that it contradicted Catholic doctrine. In 1887 he also burnt the unpublished manuscript of *Sponsa Dei*, a prose-work on the relations between God and the soul. This was in response to some doubts expressed by Hopkins, and perhaps it was, as Gosse described it, 'a distinct loss to literature'. But the poems on the same subject in *The Unknown Eros* are not, for the general reader, the best things in the volume. The most successful pieces appear in Book I, and are concerned, not with mystic revelations, but with ordinary human experience. Of several moving poems inspired by the death of Patmore's first wife, 'Departure' may serve as an example, which amply justifies the theory of 'isochronous intervals':

> It was not like your great and gracious ways!
> Do you, that have nought other to lament,
> Never, my Love, repent
> Of how, that July afternoon,
> You went,
> With sudden, unintelligible phrase,
> And frighten'd eye,
> Upon your journey of so many days,
> Without a single kiss, or a good-bye?

Meredith, like Patmore, wrote philosophical poetry, but was better at human themes. If Patmore was above all the poet of nuptial happiness and grief, Meredith was the poet of the broken marriage, in a work inspired, like Patmore's, by experience, *Modern Love*.[4] A reviewer of this poem called Meredith 'a clever man, without literary genius, taste, or judgment'. The absurdity of this assessment was promptly pointed out by his friend Swinburne, but in one respect it was right. Cleverness was always a threat to Meredith's style, whether in poetry, novels, or criticism.

---

[4] George Meredith, 1828–1909, was born in Portsmouth, the only child of a spendthrift tailor. He went to local schools, then to a Moravian one at Neuwied, Germany, but was mainly self-educated. In 1849 he married T. L. Peacock's widowed daughter. In 1857 she went off with Henry Wallis, for whose *Death of Chatterton* Meredith had modelled. His novels will be discussed in another volume.

Though his ideas were fresh and often profound, his constant efforts to produce cryptic epigram and ingenious metaphor made much of his writing needlessly indigestible.

Poems (1851) were free from this fault, but had no remarkable virtues. Apart from some pleasant 'songs' recalling the early lyrics of Tennyson, only two pieces stood out. 'South-West Wind in the Woodland' was an experimental attempt to convey, in blank octosyllabics, Meredith's 'impression of the reckless rushing rapidity, and sweeping sound of the great wind among the foliage.' 'Love in the Valley' was a lyrical monologue by the lover of a village girl. The title probably came from the pastoral 'idyl' in Tennyson's *The Princess*, the trochaic-dactylic metre from a poem by George Darley, and the picture of 'my young love sleeping in the shade' from a similar episode in *Daphnis and Chloe*, which may also have suggested the engagingly innocent treatment of adolescent sexuality. But such literary elements were fused in a glow of personal feeling. Meredith was possibly translating into pastoral terms his own love for T. L. Peacock's widowed daughter, Mary Nicolls, whom he had recently married, at the age of twenty-one.

By the time he published *Modern Love . . . with Poems and Ballads* (1862), everything had changed. The marriage had failed, Mary was dead, and with *The Ordeal of Richard Feverel* and *Evan Harrington* (1859, 1861) Meredith had become a novelist. Of the minor poems in the volume, the best was 'Ode to the Spirit of Earth in Autumn'. This returned to the theme of 'South-West Wind in the Woodland', but made the description more dramatic, the interpretation more specific, and the versification more varied. The increased anthropomorphism which compared the tree, for instance, to 'frail white-bodied girls in fear' developed into an almost literal acceptance of Greek mythology, with a full cast of Dryads, Satyrs, and Fauns, and a final appeal to 'green bounteous Earth! Bacchante Mother!' The wind became the voice of 'Nature', and its philosophical message became, as in Swinburne's later 'Hertha', pantheistic. Conventional religion should be replaced by filial love and worship of Earth, 'our only visible friend'. This meant that Man, like all other creatures, should live life 'thoroughly', 'without regrets', and with a

> faith that forward sets
> But feeds the living fire.
> Faith that never frets
> For vagueness in the form.

Death should be cheerfully accepted as simply falling back into 'the breast that gives the rose', and all human loss endured in the same spirit.

Thus the poem recommended a faith, admittedly 'vague', in the type of evolution that had just been described in Darwin's *The Origin of Species*. The lovers in *Modern Love* had no such faith, and when love died between them, they made the great mistake of looking, not 'forward', but backward:

> But they fed not on the advancing hours:
> Their hearts held cravings for the buried day.
> Then each applied to each that fatal knife,
> Deep questioning, which probes to endless dole.
> Ah, what a dusty answer gets the soul
> When hot for certainties in this our life!

The story of *Modern Love*, told in fifty sonnet-like sections of sixteen lines, is about a married couple, once passionately in love, who have started to drift apart. The wife is having an affair with another man, and the jealous husband tries to console himself with another woman. Unable to resist the pull of the past, they attempt a reconciliation, only to make it clearer that they no longer love each other. Finally the wife commits suicide, apparently to set her husband free to marry the other woman. Meredith's own marriage had been equally disastrous. After a period of bitter quarrelling, Mary had gone off with the Pre-Raphaelite painter, Henry Wallis, who left her soon afterwards. Meredith refused, not only to take her back, but even to let her see her young son, or to visit her when she was dying in 1861.

The poem reads like an attempt to exorcize this memory, to set the unhappy experience in perspective, and perhaps to express remorse for Meredith's own contribution to it. Certainly, his implacable self-righteousness in real life gave place in the poem to a much more tolerant and sympathetic attitude:

> I see no sin:
> The wrong is mixed. In tragic life, God wot,
> No villain need be! Passions spin the plot:
> We are betrayed by what is false within.

The narrative method, too, suggests an effort by Meredith, not always successful, to detach himself from an overwhelming experience. Though the husband is the angle-character, the story is begun by an external narrator, using the third person and the past tense. In section III, however, the narrator shifts into the present tense, as if commenting on a stage performance. Then suddenly, as if sucked back into a situation from which he has been trying to extricate himself, he starts acting the part of the husband: 'See that I am drawn to her even now!' From then on, despite some returns to third-person narrative, the action is chiefly presented through dramatic monologue by the husband. Only in a final attempt to distance, and partially explain, the tragic past does the philosophical narrator come to the fore:

> Thus piteously Love closed what he begat:
> The union of this ever-diverse pair!
> These two were rapid falcons in a snare,
> Condemned to do the flitting of the bat ...

Whatever the poem may have meant to Meredith, his picture of marital disharmony still seems strikingly accurate. It dramatizes neatly and vividly the stormy feelings that may underlie domestic calm, the extreme difficulty of verbal communication, the lethal effect of 'rational' discussion, and the ironies of keeping up appearances:

> At dinner, she is hostess, I am host.
> Went the feast ever cheerfuller? She keeps
> The Topic over intellectual deeps
> In buoyancy afloat. They see no ghost ...
> But here's the greater wonder; in that we
> Enamoured of an acting nought can tire,
> Each other, like true hypocrites, admire;
> Warm-lighted looks, Love's ephemerioe,
> Shoot gaily o'er the dishes and the wine.
> We waken envy of our happy lot.
> Fast, sweet, and golden, shows the marriage-knot.
> Dear guests, you now have seen Love's corpse-light shine.

The sarcastic wit of the style is often brilliantly concise, and the tendency to melodramatic imagery is justified by its function: to mark the contrast between the savagery of unspoken feeling and the flatness of civilized behaviour. Apart, perhaps, from the wife's suicide, the characterization is psychologically realistic, and the total effect profoundly moving. Nor does the poem lack variety. Though its general movement is like that of a Greek tragedy, and its tone often bitterly satirical, the momentary happiness of the reconciliation is marvellously conveyed through landscape, symbolic image, and phonetic harmony:

> Love that had robbed us of immortal things,
> This little moment mercifully gave,
> Where I have seen across the twilight waves
> The swan sail with her young beneath her wings.

Two years after writing *Modern Love*, Meredith married again, and by 1877 he was taking a less tragic view of marriage. In his lecture (later published as an Essay) *On the Idea of Comedy and the Uses of the Comic Spirit*, he advised 'affectionate couples' who quarrelled to realize that they were in 'a comic situation'. The work itself has been called 'one of the pre-eminent critical essays of the Victorian age', and it certainly broke new ground in distinguishing between different types of humorous writing. It began with a rather airy survey of English, European, Classical, and Oriental Comedy, and concluded that in England only Shakespeare and some bits of Congreve would do, while in world literature Menander and Molière 'stand alone specially as comic poets of the feelings and the ideas'. Considering how little of his original work survives, the tribute to Menander is unconvincing; and the comments on 'fun in Bagdad' are interesting mainly for their feminism: 'there will never be civilization where Comedy is not possible; and that comes of some degree of social equality of the sexes.' The definition of Comedy as provocative of 'thoughtful laughter' was not very far from Fielding's statement that comic writing and painting gave 'a more rational and useful pleasure' than burlesque. The real originality of the essay lay in its conception of the Comic Spirit as a kind of censor, part-moral, part-aesthetic, and part-rational, hovering over human behaviour, and detecting every departure from the 'common sense' on which 'civilization' was founded. The conception was realized in a memorable portrait:

It has the sage's brows, and the sunny malice of a faun lurks at the corners of the half-closed lips drawn in an idle wariness of half-tension. That slim feasting smile, shaped like the long-bow, was once a big round satyr's laugh, that flung up the brows like a fortress lifted by gunpowder. That laugh will come again, but it will be of the order of the smile, finely-tempered, showing sunlight of the mind, mental richness rather than noisy enormity.

Such criticism, with its surprising images and vaguely evolutionary perspective, may be recognized as a kind of Meredithian
poetry, and in *Poems and Lyrics of the Joy of Earth* (1883) he
produced two other kinds. The more attractive one is found in
'The Lark Ascending', an imitation of the bird's song that makes
the efforts of Shelley and Hopkins seem relatively laborious. The
almost unbroken chain of octosyllabic couplets embodies what it
describes:

> . . . simple singing of delight,
> Shrill, irreflective, unrestrained,
> Rapt, ringing, on the jet sustained
> Without a break, without a fall,
> Sweet-silvery, sheer lyrical . . .

The other kind appears in 'The Woods of Westermain', a didactic
allegory of the 'Earth' philosophy, full of tangled thickets of
expression, hardly penetrable without extra-textual guidance. The
basic metre, that of the Witches in *Macbeth*, is used for gnomic
rather than musical purposes, and the toil and trouble of getting
through nearly three hundred lines of cryptic aphorisms are not
adequately rewarded. The Woods, suggested by some real ones
near the home of the poet's second wife, are the *selva oscura* of
human life, a tract of beauty and terror which cannot be traversed
safely without cheerfulness and courage. To make the most of life,
one also needs a sense of kinship with animals, a feeling of
reverence, gratitude, and trust towards 'Earth', and freedom from
egotism. Earth, as 'the Nurse of seed' who governs evolutionary
'Change', is a frightening and puzzling but ultimately benevolent
goddess, the reality behind the pagan Venus and Diana, and the
source of all that is spiritual. As a 'footway' or stairway to 'the God
of Gods', she personifies a 'Triad' of successively evolved forces,
'Blood and brain and spirit', which each human being must 'Join
for true felicity'. The only real menace in the Woods is 'the scaly
Dragon-fowl', Self.

This odd conflation of Darwinism, Christian ethics, pagan
religion, and practical psychology hardly justifies the complexity
of its expression; but the reader may well admire, and even enjoy,
the pyrotechnics of metaphor, and the compression of huge
volumes of thought into tiny lumps of language, as in this ox's-eye
view of prehistory:

> Or, where old-eyed oxen chew
> Speculation with the cud,
> Read their pool of vision through,
> Back to hours when mind was mud;
> Nigh the knot, which did untwine
> Timelessly to drowsy suns;
> Seeing Earth a slimy spine,
> Heaven a space for winging tons.

Also included in the 1883 volume was a fine sonnet, 'Lucifer in Starlight', which pilloried in a cosmetic setting the 'distempered devil of Self'. 'Phaéthôn' (1887) did something similar with the Greek myth, while emulating Tennyson's successful handling of the difficult Galliambic metre in 'Boädicea'. Of other late poems, 'The Nuptials of Attila' (also 1887) made a sensational murder-mystery out of an episode in Gibbon, and four lyrics in *A Reading of Earth* (1888) applied the consolations of the 'Earth' philosophy to such human problems as loss, old age, and death. They all contain vivid touches of natural description; but three of them, 'Seed-Time', 'Hard Weather', and 'The Thrush in February', are so full of condensed ideas as to be rather stiff in their movement. The fourth, 'Dirge in Woods', admirably combines meaning with melody, though it seems a little too like Goethe's '*Über allen Gipfeln*' to be considered wholly original. The independence, however, of Meredith's creativity was still clear enough in the 1892 volume, with a new departure into comic narrative. 'Jump-to-Glory Jane' was a satire on religious fanatics like Mrs Girling (1827–86). The heroine of the piece, Meredith explained, 'founds in our advanced community a sect inflated by the idea that by jumping high and high we take the best way of getting to HIM'. Happily the 'Earth' philosopher was content for once to be simply funny. He did not insist in this poem on the greater wisdom of getting down to HER.

7. The Pre-Raphaelites

'I NEVER do anything I don't like', Rossetti told a friend.[1] He wanted to be a painter, but did not like studying art at the Royal Academy Schools. So at twenty he stopped doing so, and with Holman Hunt and Millais founded the Pre-Raphaelite Brotherhood (1848). This was a gesture of revolt, in a year of political revolutions, against the academic principle that a young artist should begin by imitating the old masters, instead of obeying his own individual impulse, and acting upon his own perception of Nature. The PRB was much influenced by literature, especially the poems of Keats and Tennyson, Ruskin's *Modern Painters*, and Blake's scathing comments on the *Discourses* of Sir Joshua Reynolds. Its literary organ, *The Germ* (1850), was designed by Rossetti to be, not only an artistic manifesto, but also an outlet for poetry, particularly his own. The individual impulses of the brethren sent them off in too many directions to be listed here, though they included medievalism and vague social concern. Rossetti himself developed into a highly original and commercially successful painter; but his strongest natural impulse was to write poems.

His earliest pieces, published in *The Germ*, were conceived pictorially. 'My Sister's Sleep', which exploited in Tennysonian verse the irony of a death on Christmas Eve, was like a genre-painting of a sick-room, lit by candle, fire, and moon, and by dim reflections in a mirror. 'The Blessed Damozel', though not translated into paint before 1875, was a carefully composed portrait of a dead girl, waiting Mariana-like for the arrival of her earthly lover, whose parenthetical interjections paralleled his final

[1] Dante Gabriel Rossetti, 1818–82, was born in London, the son of a political refugee from Naples. From King's College School he went to the Academy Schools, where with Millais and Holman Hunt he founded the Pre-Raphaelite Brotherhood (PRB), 1848. In 1850 he met and eventually married Elizabeth Siddal, who died, 1862, of a laudanum overdose, possibly intentional. He then took a house in Chelsea, where he was joined for some months by Swinburne and Meredith. Having worked with Morris on the Oxford Union frescos, 1857, he shared Kelmscott Manor with him, 1871. He was now in love with Mrs Morris. Soon afterwards he had a nervous breakdown, precipitated by chloral, alcohol, and Buchanan's 'Fleshly School of Poetry', and from then on his health continued to decline.

appearance on a small predella below the main picture. Though the contrived simplicity of the style makes the poem hard to take seriously, it is characteristic of Rossetti in its curious blend of religiosity and eroticism: 'her bosom's pressure must have made | The bar she leaned on warm'.

Also published in *The Germ* was a short story called 'Hand and Soul', about a mysterious picture which appears to have been a portrait of his own soul, in female form, by a thirteenth-century (i.e. Pre-Raphaelite) artist. The story may serve to introduce and partially explain the centrality of the female figure in all Rossetti's poetry and painting. The ubiquitous woman-image takes many forms, ranging from the Virgin Mary to Jenny the prostitute, from Dante's Beatrice to such snake-women as Lilith and Medusa. Beatrice was clearly the prototype of the Blessed Damozel herself, and Dante was a pervasive influence on all Rossetti's poetry and art. His Italian father had worked obsessively to prove that the *Divina Commedia* was full of secret anti-Papal propaganda, and had christened him after the subject of his own research. Dante Gabriel responded by translating the *Vita Nuova* (1861), painting such pictures as *Dantis Amor* and *Beata Beatrix*, specializing in the sonnet-form, and developing a habit of symbolic personification.

Between 1847 and 1854, when the PRB broke up, Rossetti wrote, or started to write, many lyrical, narrative, and dramatic pieces which were first published in *Poems* (1870). This meant exhuming the manuscripts from the coffin of his wife, Elizabeth Siddal, where he had buried them with her at her death (possibly suicide) in 1862. Of these, 'Troy Town' and 'Eden Bower' are typical of Rossetti's fondness for the almost meaningless refrain, and for hints of sexuality. 'Ave' features the fundamentalist piety, derived from his Anglo-Italian mother, that inspired the early paintings, *The Girlhood of Mary Virgin*, and *Ecce Ancilla Domini*. 'Dante at Verona', perhaps partly modelled on his father, presents the poet as a resentful and self-pitying political refugee. 'Stratton Water' is a pseudo-ballad, showing a vein of boisterous humour more familiar to Rossetti's friends than to his readers. And 'The Card-dealer' invites comparison with such paintings as *Astarte Syriaca* as a sensational portrait of a sinister symbolic female. More interesting, though still disappointing, is 'Jenny', a dramatic monologue spoken by an intellectual, but not very intelligent, young man in a prostitute's bedroom at night, while she sleeps undisturbed. It resembles Hunt's PRB painting, *The Awakening Conscience* in its symbolic use of décor and rather vapid moralizing. As dawn breaks, and the final tableau is reflected in a mirror, the young man sees himself and Jenny from another angle; but even his concluding view of prostitution seems astonishingly naïve, nor is there any clear indication that the speaker himself is an object of satire. In this respect 'Jenny' fails to exploit the ironic possibilities of the dramatic monologue.

The most effective of the early poems are 'A Last Confession' (1849) and 'Sister Helen' (1851). The first is a dramatic monologue spoken by a dying member of the Italian resistance movement who has killed the girl he loved. Byron's *Giaour* and Browning's 'The Italian in England' are among the obvious influences, but in its dramatic intensity and psychological emphasis the poem is much closer to Browning's later monologue, 'A Forgiveness' (1876). The murderer keeps approaching, then shying off the confession of his crime, until the series of evasions ends in a climactic release of accumulated tension, subtly prepared for, throughout the poem, by images of a knife, of redness, and of blood:

> 'Take it,' I said to her the second time,
> 'Take it and keep it.' And then came a fire
> That burnt my hand; and then the fire was blood,
> And sea and sky were blood and fire, and all
> The day was one red blindness; till it seemed
> Within the whirling brain's entanglement,
> That she or I or all things bled to death.
> And then I found her laid against my feet
> And knew that I had stabbed her . . .

'Sister Helen', a weird cross between Theocritus' *Idyll* II and such bloodthirsty ballads as 'Edward, Edward' or Tennyson's 'The Sisters', dramatizes the slow killing of an unfaithful lover by burning a wax image of him. The grim story is suggested by a dialogue between the implacable Helen, crouched over the fire, and her innocent small brother, who reports, without comprehension, the effects of her witchcraft. A chorus-like refrain implies a Christian comment on her cold vindictiveness, which is reflected in the icy moonlight outside. Here too, a gradual accumulation of tension leads to a spine-chilling climax.

So far, however, Rossetti's poetry was mostly a matter of

external contrivance and literary adaptation. It began to acquire substance when it became an outlet for his personal feelings. 'Even so' (1859), for instance, movingly records, in laconic, almost conversational language, and highly individual imagery, his sadness at the loss of his original feeling for Elizabeth Siddal. 'The Stream's Secret' (1869–70) delicately alludes, through verse that simulates water flowing softly through darkness to his secret, frustrated love for the wife of his friend, William Morris. In a still more cryptic sonnet, 'The Monochord' (1870), he professes to find a piece of music symbolic of his own emotional history; but the single string seems to imply, not so much a musical instrument, as a line of development, from the 'flame' of his first love for Elizabeth Siddal, through the 'cloud' of their alienation, to the new 'flame' of his passion for Jane Morris:

> Oh! what is this that knows the road I came,
> The flame turned cloud, the cloud returned to flame
>   The lifted shifted steeps and all the way? —
> That draws round me at last this wind-warm space,
> And in regenerate rapture turns my face
> Upon the devious coverts of dismay?

To chart this 'road' was the purpose of Rossetti's most important poem, a sonnet-sequence called *The House of Life*.

It was published by instalments. Sixteen sonnets appeared in the *Fortnightly Review* for March 1869 under the title, 'Of life, love, and death'. Fifty sonnets 'towards a work to be called "The House of Life"' appeared in *Poems* (1870); and in *Ballads and Sonnets* (1881) the number was raised to a hundred and one, while 'Nuptial Sleep' was expurgated. This was a quite unnecessary response to Robert Buchanan's prurient criticisms in 'The Fleshly School of Poetry' (1871), which Rossetti had sufficiently answered at the time in 'The Stealthy School of Criticism'.

The best of the 1869 sonnets are four on 'Willowwood', where the poet and his second 'flame' wander hopelessly, with other frustrated lovers. Willowwood was clearly derived from the *selva oscura* in which Dante lost his way, the *selva* of souls suspended in Limbo, and the barren *bosco* of suicides in the *Inferno*. The fifty sonnets of the 1870 *The House of Life* fall into two groups. The first twenty-eight, which end with 'Willowwood', hint with doubtless deliberate obscurity at a love-story, partly fictitious and partly autobiographical, which begins with rapture and ends in separation and frustration. The last twenty-two reflect generally on the poet's past life and present misery. In the absence of any clear narrative, the reader can only react to individual sonnets, and may well get more pleasure from the eleven 'Songs', which give readier access to feelings rather ponderously analysed in the sonnets themselves. 'The Woodspurge', for instance, instantly conveys a sense of utter misery, without any attempt to explain it.

In the 1881 version the plan, at least, of the whole work is clarified. The introductory sonnet, tacitly alluding to the 'image and superscription' of Luke 20: 24, implies that each sonnet is an 'image' of some critical moment of experience, with a 'superscription' defining its significance. 'Inclusiveness' (LXIII) suggests that every such 'image' is a 'room' in the House of Life. The whole edifice is divided into two parts. The first, 'Youth and Change', is a 'transfigured' account of the poet's love-life, representing the 'image'. The second, 'Change and Fate', is the 'superscription', designed to interpret his own experience in a wider human context. The proportion between these two parts (59: 42) is not very far from that between octave and sestet, so the whole sequence may be seen as a kind of macro-sonnet.

The architectural plan of *The House*, like the splendid decorations of many of its 'rooms', displays plenty of that 'fundamental brainwork' that Rossetti thought essential in poetry. But the total effect is disappointing. Though the poem shows a capacity for acute, if rather self-pitying, self-analysis, and certainly arouses human sympathy for the poet's sense of having somehow wasted his life, it is unsatisfactory as a work of art. This is chiefly due to the pretentious turgidity of its style. As a young man, Rossetti carefully collected what he called 'stunning words for poetry' from 'old romaunts' at the British Museum. In these sonnets he still relied too much on ostentatiously fine phrases, equally studied, and perorations that seem to invite applause:

> So it happeneth
> When Work and Will awake too late, to gaze
> After their life sailed by, and hold their breath.
> Ah! who shall dare to search through what sad maze
> Thenceforth their incommunicable ways
> Follow the desultory feet of Death?

The work of his sister Christina was altogether different.[2] Simple and unpretentious in language and versification, it seems neither cerebral nor calculated, but totally spontaneous. Her range of themes was narrow, and ill-health, abortive love-affairs, a puritanical outlook, and an other-worldly religion combined to make her characteristic tone monotonously gloomy. But strong human feelings, concentrated by frustration, and released only through verse, often produced poetry far purer than any of her brother's.

'Dreamland', the best of her seven poems published in *The Germ*, at one point recalls *The Blind Girl* of Millais:

> She cannot see the grain
> Ripening on hill and plain;
> She cannot feel the rain
> Upon her hand . . .

The general effect, however, is musical rather than pictorial, and more in the manner of Tennyson, whom Christina greatly admired, than of Pre-Raphaelite painting. Other notable influences upon her writings were Coleridge, Shelley, and the Bible, especially Proverbs and Ecclesiastes. Most of the short poems written between 1847 and 1859 were concerned with the desolation of disappointed love, in the spirit of Proverbs 13: 12, 'Hope deferred maketh the heart sick.' The death of a woman whose love was not returned was a theme (1848–9) for several subtle variations. The graceful symmetry of the Song, 'When I am dead, my dearest', culminates in the mildly vindictive statement that she may forget all about him. 'Looking Forward', despite its Tennysonian echoes, makes highly individual music of a suicidal mood. The most moving of the group, because free from self-pity or resentment, is the sonnet, 'Remember', which arrives, by a kind of logical progression, at a climax of altruism that still carries conviction: 'Better by far you should forget and smile | Than that you should remember and be sad.'

---

[2] Christina Georgina Rossetti, 1830–94, was born in London, the younger sister of D. G. Rossetti. She was educated at home and, apart from one trip to Italy and one to France, spent her life there. A devout Anglican, she broke off her engagement to James Collinson, a member of the PRB, when he reverted to Roman Catholicism, 1850, and refused to marry C. B. Cayley, although she loved him 'deeply and permanently', according to her brother William, because she found his religious views unsatisfactory. After her childhood she never enjoyed good health.

The details of Christina's emotional history are not known; but in 1855 some traumatic experience appears to have changed her mood from sad resignation to almost Byronic savagery and gloom. 'My Dream', which seems like Byron's 'The Dream' to reflect some bitter disillusionment in love, is a satiric fantasy, puzzling but powerful, about an exceptionally handsome crocodile, who ruthlessly exploits his fellows:

> He battened on them, crunched, and sucked them in.
> He knew no law, he feared no binding law,
> But ground them with inexorable jaw.
> The luscious fat distilled upon his chin,
> Exuded from his nostrils and his eyes,
> While still like hungry death he fed his maw.

At the approach of retribution, 'The prudent crocodile rose on his feet, | And shed appropriate tears and wrung his hands.' 'Cobwebs', written seven months later, echoed Byron's 'Darkness' and anticipated Thomson's *The City of Dreadful Night* in a nightmarish externalization of hopeless depression. In 1857, for reasons again unknown, Christina's mood changed into its opposite. 'A Birthday' is a rapturous cry of joy, because 'the birthday of my life | Is come, my love is come to me.' Whoever her love may have been, one of her exuberant images was in keeping with her favourite Proverb: 'Hope deferred maketh the heart sick: but when the desire cometh, it is a tree of life.'

> My heart is like a singing bird
>   Whose nest is in a watered shoot:
> My heart is like an apple-tree
>   Whose boughs are bent with thickset fruit . . .

Another seven months, and she produced the far more characteristic 'Up-hill'. This 'lively little Song of the Tomb', as Dante Gabriel called it, was Christina's first public success, when published in *Macmillan's Magazine* (February 1861).

Of her longer poems, 'From House to Home' (1858), which her other brother, William Michael, thought one of her 'most manifest masterpieces', was an allegory implying that her sufferings were an earthly martyrdom that qualified her for heaven. The 'house' of the title was a glass castle reminiscent of Tennyson's 'Palace of Art' and Coleridge's 'Kubla Khan'. As a 'house of lies' it represented the deceptive nature of earthly happiness. Its most interesting feature was an adjoining 'heath', which served as a kind of conservation-area for small animals, of which the poet was very fond. When 'one like an angel' urges her, 'Come home, O love, from banishment: | Come to the distant land', all the animals disappear, and she is left desolate:

> Then with a cry like famine I arose,
>   I lit my candle, searched from room to room,
> Searched up and down; a war of winds that froze
> Swept through the blank of gloom.

The traumatic frustration of animal instinct was again to be the theme of Christina's most remarkable poem, written five months later, *Goblin Market* (1862). She insisted that 'she did not mean anything profound by this fairy tale', but William was right to call it 'suggestive' of some meaning, and it is hard to resist the impression that the 'fruit forbidden' forced upon Laura and Lizzie by the animal-like goblins represents the sexual instinct. The rest of the story, however, is not easy to interpret in such terms. That sexual indulgence was dangerous and addictive would have seemed in the period a reasonable doctrine; but how, in such an interpretation, Lizzie could save her addicted sister's life by fetching her another dose of fruit-juice, without ingesting any of it herself, seems less intelligible. The ostensible moral, 'there is no friend like a sister', and the dedication to Christina's sister Maria, who later became a nun, suggest a private allusion to some incident in their relationship. Whatever it was, one may guess that the poem reflected a switch of interest from sexual love to family affection, a sense of release from obsession with unsatisfactory love-affairs. When first given the 'fiery antidote', Laura is 'like a caged thing freed'; and perhaps it was a new sense of freedom in Christina that made her throw off the restrictions of traditional verse-forms, and adopt an irregular, almost Skeltonic, metre and rhyme-scheme. That *Goblin Market* has always been so popular, despite the tantalizing obscurity of its meaning, is possibly due to its expression, in the spontaneous rhythms of nursery rhymes, of a suddenly rediscovered *joie de vivre*. It is also fascinating as a symbolic creation, especially where an ambivalent attitude towards instinctive feeling is implied by a subtle change in the character of the goblins. At first they are nice, cuddly, rather funny little animals: by the end they are frighteningly evil.

In *The Prince's Progress* (1866) Christina reverted to her usual melancholy. The nucleus of the poem was the final lyric, 'Too late for love, too late for joy, | Too late, too late!' The Prince, like the one in Tennyson's *The Princess*, is told by a 'voice' to go off and claim his bride; but he is so dilatory, and so unable to resist distractions on his journey, that he arrives only to see her carried out feet-first, and to hear, by way of 'bride-song', 'Too late for love . . .'. As the Bunyanesque title implies, the story may be taken as a religious allegory of delay in preparing for the next world; but one is tempted to take it also as a protest against Christina's disappointments in earthly love. Certainly the characterization of the Prince contains many touches of sarcasm, which suggest exasperation, if not with any particular man, then at least with men in general. This apparent confusion of personal and doctrinal elements in the poem interferes with the reader's enjoyment. Still, the story is vividly told, with striking glimpses of symbolic landscape, in a stanza that suggests by its rhyme-scheme an appropriate lack of progress.

Christina Rossetti wrote a great deal of religious verse, including the carol, 'In the bleak mid-winter', and some pleasant pieces for children. Her last important work, however, was a sonnet-sequence called 'Monna Innominata', possibly begun as early as 1866, but not published until 1881. The title implied a mild protest against the tradition that the woman's role in love-poetry was to be quite anonymous, as in the sonnets of early Italian poets, or, like Petrarch's Laura or Dante's Beatrice, to have a name but no personality or 'attractiveness', although they were possibly just as good poets as the men. This faintly feminist flourish introduced a sequence that William called an 'intensely personal' utterance. The personal experience referred to is still a matter of dispute, but, as in Dante and Petrarch (who supply the epigraphs), the general theme is a progress from human love towards *il Primo Amore*. The sequence consists of fourteen sonnets, and the subtitle, 'A Sonnet of Sonnets', suggests that, like *The House of Life*, the whole poem is meant to parallel the sonnet-structure. Thus the first eight sonnets are mainly concerned with the poet's human feelings, and end with a wish that she possessed the physical attractions of Esther. The last six are more concerned with her relationship to God, and end with her acceptance of *la Sua Volontade*. The lines in which she sums up what that Will seems to be for her epitomize her inexplicable gift for making moving poetry out of the unpromising material of self-pity:

> Youth gone and beauty gone, what doth remain?
> The longing of a heart pent up forlorn,
>   A silent heart whose silence loves and longs;
>   The silence of a heart which sang its songs
> While youth and beauty made a summer morn,
> Silence of love that cannot sing again.

After the introverted, and sometimes claustrophobic, poetry of the two Rossettis, the work of William Morris seems like a breath of fresh air.[3] A close friend of D. G. Rossetti and Burne-Jones, he helped to start the second Pre-Raphaelite journal, *The Oxford and Cambridge Magazine* (1856), painted one of the equally short-lived Pre-Raphaelite frescos in the Oxford Union (1857), married Jane Burden, who came to be the type of Pre-Raphaelite beauty, and produced a picture of her as *Queen Guinevere* (1858). But he was much more than a Pre-Raphaelite poet-painter. He was also an influential critic of architecture, who founded the Society for the Preservation of Ancient Buildings. He was a designer of almost everything, from furniture and wallpaper to stained-glass windows and printed books (not to mention a suit of armour in which he got stuck). He was a practical expert in dyeing and weaving, who pioneered the Arts and Crafts movement, and ran a commercial firm which successfully marketed such products. He was finally a Marxist agitator and propagandist, preaching Revolution while still designing flowered chintzes. In literature, his prose was as important as his verse. It included short stories, some very long romances, lectures on art, society, and politics, a satirical play, and a Utopian novel, *News from Nowhere* (1890).

His central impulse had always been Utopian, an urge to live in a better world than his own, or at least in a different one. 'Apart

---

[3] William Morris, 1834-96, was born in Walthamstow, the eldest son of a rich stockbroker. He went to Marlborough and Exeter College, Oxford, where he met Burne-Jones. He studied architecture under G. E. Street, and worked with Rossetti on the Oxford Union frescos, 1857-8. In 1859 he married Jane Burden, a groom's daughter who had modelled for the frescos, and had the Red House built as their home. In 1861 he founded Morris, Marshall, Faulkner, and Co., which marketed his designs, and, 1871 took a joint lease of Kelmscott Manor with Rossetti, and first visited Iceland. From 1877 he was active in the Society for the Protection of Ancient Buildings, and next year moved into his last London home at Hammersmith. He joined the Social Democratic Federation, 1883, and headed the breakaway Socialist League, 1884. He founded the Kelmscott Press, 1890.

from the desire to produce beautiful things,' he wrote in 1894, 'the leading passion of my life has been and is hatred of modern civilization.' All his practical, commercial, and political activities were attempts to improve the existing environment, and the constant search for better worlds to inhabit, if only in imagination, led to the medievalism of his early fiction and poetry, the romantic Hellenism of *Jason*, the Utopian theme of *The Earthly Paradise*, the effort to recreate the world of the sagas in *Sigurd the Volsung*, and the final rejection of paradise in *The Story of the Glittering Plain*.

His attitude to poetry reflected his concern with applied art. In a lecture on 'Pattern-designing' (1881) he seemed to imply that both art and literature were a kind of wallpaper, to clothe 'the bare walls' of a man's life, and make them 'pleasant and helpful to him'. For such ordinary purposes one needed not 'the best art' but the more restful 'lesser art' of 'ornament that reminds us of the outward face of the earth, of the innocent love of animals, or of man passing his days between work and rest as he does.' Most of his own poetry was equally unassuming, and his approach to writing it correspondingly casual: 'if a chap can't compose an epic poem while he's weaving tapestry', said Morris, 'he had better shut up.'

The earliest poems, written under the influence of Tennyson, Browning, and Rossetti, and published in the *Oxford and Cambridge Magazine*, are less interesting than the accompanying short stories. The setting is usually medieval, and the quasi-archaic simplicity of style shows Morris's passion for Malory and Froissart. The environment is pictorially described, with much stress on primary colours. The action is mostly presented by a first-person narrator, so that Morris can project himself psychologically, physically, and emotionally into the period. The main themes are loving and fighting, the latter bloodthirsty, and sometimes savage to the point of sadism. Dreams, nightmares, and confused states of consciousness abound. Despite much juvenile ardour, the stories tend to be too long, too slow, and too shapeless to give much pleasure, but there are two exceptions. 'The Story of the Unknown Church', told by a thirteenth-century master-mason, convincingly relates his emotional experience to his architecture and sculpture. 'Lindenborg Pool', based on a Danish legend of a castle miraculously destroyed for the wickedness of its inmates, is remarkable for its nightmarish atmosphere, and still more for its dramatic-monologue form. This vividly enacts the process of a weird personality change, by which Morris suddenly finds himself a thirteenth-century priest, riding through the darkness with a drunken jester. 'I watched him in my proper nineteenth-century character, with insatiable curiosity and intense amusement; but as a quiet priest of a long past age, with contempt and disgust enough, not unmixed with fear and anxiety.'

The medieval world of *The Defence of Guenevere and Other Poems* (1858) was shown in the same double perspective, both from inside and from outside the characters concerned. Besides pieces based on Malory and Froissart, and one, 'Rapunzel', on a Grimm fairy-tale, there were some drawn almost entirely from Morris's imagination, quasi-surrealist fantasies, part-musical, part-pictorial. Two of these, 'The Blue Closet' and 'The Tune of Seven Towers', were suggested by pictures of Rossetti, to whom the volume was dedicated. The most effective of the Malory-pieces was the title-poem, a Browning-type 'apology' in *terza rima*. Unlike Tennyson's 'Guinevere' (1859), Guenevere is quite impenitent. Instead of trying to refute the charge of adultery, she glories in her physical passion for Lancelot, and in her own physical beauty: 'say no rash word | Against me, being so beautiful'. Morris had recently been Rossetti's model for a Tennyson-illustration of Lancelot, and he seems to have written the poem in that character. Its compelling rhetoric of language, imagery, and bodily movement suggests the intense sympathy of a lover, rather than the probable feelings of the lady herself.

Of the Froissart-pieces, 'Sir Peter Harpdon's End' is a gripping drama that stresses the brutality of medieval warfare; but the best of the group is 'The Haystack in the Floods'. Possibly inspired by Froissart's account of the atrocities committed by the Jacquerie, the story ends with a girl seeing her lover's head cut off and beaten to pieces on the ground. The impact of the poem results not merely from its horrific content but also from its simple and neutral style, almost free from archaisms, its severely detached tone, its meteorological symbolism, and its ironic structure, by which the opening lines are echoed with new meaning at the close. 'Rapunzel' is a kind of operetta, with metrical variety for music, which transforms a disturbing original into a picturesque image, recalling both 'The Blessed Damozel' and 'The Lady of Shalott', of a maiden on a tower. Even the bleeding corpse below her is registered aesthetically: 'Some crimson thing had changed the grass from bright | Pure green I love so.' The Prince, who has hitherto spent most of his time dreaming, seems to confirm Morris's remark of 1856: 'My work is the embodiment of dreams in one form or another', and the fourth type of poem in the volume is particularly dreamlike. In some, the musical but meaningless refrain contributes to this effect. In others, like 'The Wind', harshly irrational imagery produces the sense of nightmare, and in 'Golden Wings' an initially Tennysonian castle-paradise comes to a deliberately jarring end:

> The draggled swans most eagerly eat
>   The green weeds trailing in the moat;
>   Inside the rotting leaky boat
> You see a slain man's stiffen'd feet.

The 1858 volume has appealed to the modern taste for violence, obscurity, and surrealistic effects. It certainly shows great originality and imaginative exuberance, with a grasp of metrical and dramatic techniques surprising in a poet of twenty-four. But for Morris such poetry was a dead end: the way ahead was the mass-production of much simpler and less concentrated narrative verse, as in *The Life and Death of Jason* (1867). Mostly written at night, as a relaxation from the practical work of the Firm, it became instantly popular, and is still his most attractive major poem. Though based on a Greek myth, *Jason* shows little influence of any classical author that handled it; and though Morris calls Chaucer his 'master', he seems much closer to the Keats of *Endymion* in the rambling fluency of his couplets, and the incidental felicities that decorate the narrative. These take the form of pictures, sharp in focus though seen through a mist of dream or distance in time, with a characteristic emphasis on primary colours and on weather conditions. But there is no emotional detachment. The reader is made to share the characters' feelings, and every exciting moment in the story, like the nocturnal escape from Æa, is exploited to the full. The reader is also made aware of Morris's own non-literary interests. Architecture, art-processes, and artefacts are given prominence, while the Argonauts' practical problems are solved quite inventively. Instead of carrying their ship for twelve days and nights on their shoulders, as in Apollonius Rhodius, they

construct 'a stage with broad wheels' for it, and, working in shifts
of twenty men at a time, pull it along with cables.

Predictably, Guenevere's advocate does all he can to exculpate
Medea, clearing her, for instance, from the charge, in Kingsley's
Heroes (1856), of cruelly murdering her brother. For the heroism
of the Argonauts themselves Morris shows some boyish enthusiasm; but the general tone of the poem is not epic, but elegiac. The
pervasive theme is the irony of human life, the vanity of human
wishes. The final comment on Jason is that 'he had hoped that
hope in vain', and the final message of the poem, perhaps
suggested by the failure of Morris's marriage, is that all hopes are
disappointed. The message is often put in the form that all Utopias
are false. Æa seems at first 'an earthly Paradise', but proves a
death-trap; and the process of disillusionment continues with a
series of quasi-Utopias: the 'happy summer isle' that Phrixus
thinks of, the 'happy place' beneath the water where Hylas
drowns, the 'dream' of the Golden Age, the 'lovely land' of Circe
with its garden 'Paradise', the 'glorious land' of the Sirens, the
'lovely' land of the Hesperides, the 'golden age, free from all fear
and pain' that Pelias promises himself, before being killed by his
equally deluded daughters.

The false Utopia of *The Earthly Paradise* (1868–70), like that
imagined by Pelias, is free from death. The twenty-four tales in
this four-volume, composite poem are supposed to be told in a
slightly more realistic Utopia, 'A nameless city in a distant sea',
where mortality is not evaded, but only made easier to bear. The
framing story, mostly related in the Prologue, but continued in
short passages between the tales, and concluded in the Epilogue, is
set in the time of Chaucer. In a desperate attempt to escape death
during a plague, some Norwegians set off in search of a legendary
paradise where no one dies. They never find it, but after wasting
the best years of their lives looking for it, have to make do with the
'nameless city'. There they become resigned to the human condition, and try to enjoy what is still left to them: the beauty of
seasonal changes, the kindness of their Greek-speaking hosts,
and the imaginative delights of mythology, both Greek and
Northern—for two stories are told every month, one by a Greek
and one by a Norwegian.

In the Preface the future revolutionary poses as an 'idle singer of
an empty day', a 'dreamer of dreams', unable to put things right in

the real world, and merely trying to 'build a shadowy isle of bliss |
Midmost the beating of the steely sea'. But the poem's philosophy
is not exactly escapist, since it insists on facing facts and making
the best of them. The structure, though clearly suggested by *The
Canterbury Tales*, is highly original and subtly integrated. Each
tale, for instance, is related in spirit to the month in which it is
told, and the whole series forms a seasonal cycle of moods,
beginning and ending with the cheerfulness of Spring. The tales
themselves are well chosen and well told but, as fiction, they now
seem to move much too slowly, and as poetry, to be too reliant on
stock Romantic phraseology. For the modern reader, the best of
The Earthly Paradise is probably to be found in the Prologue, in
the personal poems that introduce each monthly story-telling, and
seem to reflect Morris's unhappiness about his wife, and in the
bleakest of the individual tales, appropriately told in late
November, 'The Lovers of Gudrun', from the *Laxdaela Saga*.

When Morris wrote this tale, he had never been to Iceland,
though he had started learning Old Norse. But in 1871 he saw the
place where Gudrun was said to have lived, in the course of a six-
weeks' exploration of Iceland on horseback, graphically recorded
in his journal. He returned to Reykjavik lousy but exhilarated, and
the whole experience combined with the Sagas to change his
attitude towards his personal problems from one of romantic
melancholy to one of courage and vitality. The theme of *Love is
Enough* (1872) was still superficially romantic: the quest, as in
Shelley's *Alastor*, for a woman loved in a dream. But King
Pharamond's love is in conflict with his social responsibilities; and
his final decision that 'love is enough' is justified by the fact that
during the three-years' quest his people have turned against him.
He feels there is no point now in trying to win back 'the semblance
of love that they have not to give me'. One is tempted to see here a
reversed image of Morris's own situation. Pharamond settles for
love, after failing in public life: Morris has failed in love, but now
finds public success 'enough' to compensate. The intricate form of
the poem, a play within a play within a play, with a Rossetti-type
personified Love acting as compère, and lyrical interludes of
'Music' serving as Chorus, suggests an attempt to distance private
emotion. Apart from the charm of the dactylic 'Music', and the
interest of the experiments in alliterative verse, the poem is
impressive chiefly as a piece of book-production, half-way between

poetry and decorative art. Its ingenious structure has almost the
same effect as the pattern of interlacing willow-leaves that the poet
designed for its green-and-gold binding.

The same year, he started writing what he called his 'abortive
novel'. The plot, in which two brothers are in love with the same
girl, was clearly based on his own situation with his wife and
Rossetti. One brother is a 'dreamy' type, but the character of the
other, 'whistling in sturdy resolution to keep his heart up', reflects
Morris's new feeling for the cheerful stoicism of the Sagas. With
his Icelandic friend Magnússon he had already published a prose
translation of the *Volsunga Saga*, and after translating the *Aeneid*
in the metre of Chapman's Homer (1875) he now produced his
own Northern epic, *Sigurd the Volsung* (1876). He thought it his
highest achievement in literature, and some critics have agreed.
But only Wagnerians and old Norse specialists are likely to enjoy
its plot, the pseudo-archaic diction is tiresome, and the versification awkward—though the regular hiccup in the third foot of
its six-foot, iambic-anapaestic line might theoretically be
defended, as simulating the caesura in a classical hexameter. The
poem contains, however, some striking scenes, such as the battles
and fires in Siggeir's and Atli's halls, the tipping of the whole
Niblung treasure into a lake (an improvement on the original Saga
prefiguring Morris's later attitude to private property), and the
richly symbolic picture of Gunnar, singing a song of triumph
while awaiting death in a snake-pit: 'And I fought and was glad in
the morning, and I sing in the night and the end . . .'.

From then on Morris himself virtually stopped singing, and did
his best work in prose. But he started fighting, almost in Gunnar's
spirit, first for a less hideous world, and then for a juster society.
As he put it in 'Art and Socialism' (1884), 'These, I say, are the
days of combat, when there is no external peace possible to an
honest man'. The satisfying combustion of Siggeir's and Atli's
halls was translated into artistic, and then political, terms. 'The
Art of the People' (1879) called for most of the furnishings of 'any
rich man's house' to be thrown on a 'bonfire', and 'Art, Wealth
and Riches' (1883) recommended the same treatment for the
'pestilential rubbish' in the 'fair house' of England, 'lest some day
there be no way of getting rid of it but by burning it up inside with
the goods and house and all.' The transformation of the art-critic
into the socialist agitator was a process initiated by Ruskin's 'The

Nature of Gothic'[4] and confirmed by the study of Marx from 1883 onwards. The underlying train of thought can be traced through a series of highly persuasive lectures given between 1877 and 1894. It began with a protest against the destruction of natural beauty by industrialization, and against the ugliness of so-called manu-factured goods. It ended with the conviction that 'the beauty of life' could never be restored without a radical change of the eco-nomic system. Whatever may be thought of Morris's political prescriptions, his criticisms of modern civilization are undeniably sound; and his propagandist purpose had a splendid effect on his prose style. In the effort to communicate with 'those whom the stupidity of language forces me to call the lower classes', he learned to express himself with admirable simplicity and vigour.

Another literary by-product of his political campaign was a new type of imaginative fiction, in which the 'dreamer of dreams' joined forces with the more realistic author of the 'abortive novel'. The first of two such works published in the Socialist League's magazine (which Morris edited), *The Commonweal*, was *A Dream of John Ball* (1886–7). The opening is relaxed and humorous. Morris dreams that he is addressing a large open-air audience in his night-shirt, 'reinforced . . . by a pair of braceless trousers.' He then drifts convincingly into an earlier phase of Marx's 'history of class struggles', the Peasants' Revolt of 1381. The heart of the work, both as propaganda and as fiction, is the conversation in a moonlit church between the medieval priest and the Victorian author. Sharing a social ideal, they have very different attitudes to life and death, and Ball can hardly grasp the idea of a tyranny not feudal but economic. The imaginative power shown in this weird confrontation of period-dreams ('thou hast been a dream to me as I to thee', says John Ball) is considerable; but the effect is partly spoilt by the pseudo-medieval jargon into which Marxist theory is incongruously translated.

In the later prose romances this type of language became almost habitual; but *News from Nowhere*, by far the best of Morris's contributions to *Commonweal* (1890), was mercifully free of it. Here he imagined, again in the form of a dream, a world that would satisfy his socialist aspirations, his tastes in art and architec-

---

[4] See Chap. 12.

ture, and his interest in handicrafts. He goes to sleep one night, after a meeting of the Socialist League, and dreams of waking up in the twenty-first century, to a post-Revolution England, purged of the evils of capitalism, industrialization, and urbanization. His *Nowhere*, named after More's *Utopia*, resembled it in its communism, but made far more allowance for individual impulse, for the aesthetic sense, and for the sexual instinct. Its substitution of anarchy for regimentation, in society, politics, and morality, was a reaction not only against More, but also against Edward Bellamy, whose version of a socialist Utopia in *Looking Backward: 2000–1887* (1888) had conscripted every individual into an 'industrial army'. For Bellamy's urban paradise, enriched by such blessings of technology as piped music in every home, Morris presented an England where everyone could do what he liked, where 'immensely improved machinery' was used only for jobs 'which would be irksome to do by hand', and where everything was beautiful, because everyone worked in the spirit of an artist, and the environment was almost entirely rural.

That communism is enough in itself to bring out the best in human nature, and create a heaven on earth, has not been confirmed by twentieth-century experience, and *News from Nowhere* is full of other improbabilities, e.g. 'Most children, seeing books lying about, manage to read by the time they are four years old.' But it has one great advantage over the vast majority of Utopian novels: it creates a world that would really be pleasant to live in. It is also unusually successful in giving that world the reality of a personal experience. This is done largely by dramatizing the author's emotional involvement with his ideal society, notably in his relationship with Ellen. The closing passage, where all consciousness of his existence gradually fades from her face, transforms Morris's sad feelings about his wife into a moving image for the transition from Utopia to reality.

The relative value of these two worlds was finally reassessed in *The Story of the Glittering Plain* (1891). The *Plain* is a kind of earthly paradise that the hero, Hallblithe, does not find satisfactory. Like Odysseus, when he prefers his less beautiful human wife to Calypso, Hallblithe prefers his own betrothed (whose name implies that she is 'a hostage to fortune') to the daughter of the Undying King. He rejects the passive 'bliss' of the Plain, and opts for a heroic struggle with the fortunes of human life, aided by an enigmatic 'big red man', who reminds one of Sir Gawain's Green Knight.

Morris produced five other prose romances. Written in his own brand of Wardour Street English, at great length and with little variety of tempo, they told vaguely allegorical tales of fantastic quests and adventures. Some modern readers have found them irresistible, and in a paperback reprint of 1975 *The Well at the World's End* (1896) was described as 'Morris's masterpiece'. Those who like structural economy will find *The Glittering Plain* more rewarding than its successors. Relatively brief, it tells an exciting story, and its symbolic drift suggests a healthy conclusion to Morris's quest for Utopia. When Hallblithe turns his back on the 'land of lies', and goes off to fight for a real human being, he is accused of 'still seeking a dream'. 'I seek no dream,' he replies, 'but rather the end of dreams.'

'Now we are four and not *three*', Burne-Jones had said at Oxford in 1857, when Swinburne was first introduced to him and Morris and Rossetti. Sure enough, Swinburne soon formed close links with the second group of Pre-Raphaelites.[5] He modelled for Rossetti, who liked his red hair. He imitated Morris in a poem called 'Queen Yseult'. Later, he dedicated his *Poems and Ballads* to Burne-Jones, enthusiastically reviewed Rossetti's *Poems* (1870), and shared with him Robert Buchanan's abuse in 'The Fleshly School of Poetry'. But Swinburne was a Pre-Raphaelite by friendship and association only, not by the character of his work. This, whether in poetry, prose-fiction, or criticism, was essentially *sui generis*, whatever features it owed to Tennyson, Shakespeare, Shelley, Baudelaire, the Bible or the Marquis de Sade.

As a poet he showed a remarkable gift for verbal and rhythmical spell-binding, a taste for sensational subjects, and a lack of interest in structure. 'What a mess little Swinburne would have made of this!' said Tennyson, pleased with his own treatment of eroticism in 'Lucretius'. Swinburne did make a mess of such things, by his

---

[5] Algernon Charles Swinburne, 1837–1909, was born in London, the son of a naval captain from an old Northumbrian family. After Eton he went to Balliol College, Oxford, where he met Morris, Burne-Jones, and Rossetti. His other friends included Whistler and Burton, and his heroes, Mazzini, Victor Hugo, and Baudelaire. His odd personality contributed to the Aesthetic movement, and his criticism was also influential. His health broke down, 1879, after which he lived with his friend Watts-Dunton at No. 2, The Pines, Putney. There he ceased to be an alcoholic and became a respectable and very prolific author.

obsession with sexual perversion. Paid £10 by Rossetti to 'make a man' of Swinburne, a girl aptly named Dolores had to confess failure: she 'couldn't make him understand that biting's no use'. Nor, for most readers, is flagellation, or any other form of sado-masochism. So this element in his poetry, when not merely monotonous, seems repellent or ridiculous. His form can be as messy as his content. Even his best poems tend to ramble. Brilliant in parts, and in their continuous hypnotic effect, they are disappointing wholes.

In this respect his first great success, *Atalanta in Calydon* (1865), was exceptional. Its structure was determined by that of Greek tragedy, but, unlike Arnold's *Merope*, it had an air of spontaneity. Swinburne's handling of the myth suggested a concern with family tensions, as in his novel, *Love's Cross-Currents*: his Althaea kills her son, not just to avenge her brothers, but also from jealousy of the girl he loves. Like Euripides as well as Shelley, Swinburne attacked orthodox religion, notably in a chorus denouncing the 'supreme evil, God'. He effectively exploited the myth's dramatic possibilities, developing Althaea into a powerful character, part Clytemnestra and part Iago, who stoically accepts herself and her destiny: 'I did this and I say this and I die.' There is equal strength and dignity in much of the blank-verse dialogue; but Swinburne's greatest gifts are most evident in the choral lyrics, where wonderfully fluent and inventive rhythms combine with constant alliteration to induce a mood of great intensity, enjoyable but almost devoid of intellectual meaning.

> When the hounds of spring are on winter's traces,
>   The mother of months in meadow or plain
> Fills the shadows and windy places
>   With lisp of leaves and ripple of rain;
> And the brown bright nightingale amorous
> Is half assuaged for Itylus,
> For the Thracian ships and the foreign faces,
>   The tongueless vigil, and all the pain.

In *Poems and Ballads* (1866) the same vague mood was created by the same stylistic and prosodic virtuosity, but the choice of subjects was deliberately shocking. Of numerous variations on the theme of unnatural sex, 'The Leper' was typical: a thirty-five-stanza monologue by a necrophile, whose loved one has died of leprosy. To outrage religious as well as moral conventions, this kind of material was often treated in the language of Christianity. Thus 'Dolores (Notre-Dame des Sept Douleurs)' parodied a hymn to the Virgin Mary, in a spirit described by the poet as 'half-humorous'. There was indeed a touch of Byronic wit, when 'Our Lady of Pain' turned 'Our loves into corpses or wives'; and few poems in the volume deserve to be taken seriously, except 'The Triumph of Time' and 'A Leave-taking', which seems to reflect a real personal experience; 'Itylus', a convincing expression of grief in a verbal simulation of bird-song; and 'The Garden of Proserpine', a memorable image for a state of emotional inertia.

Swinburne went on to write political poems in support of the *Risorgimento*, a pantheistic verse-sermon called 'Hertha', some quasi-Elizabethan blank-verse tragedies, and a long, slow, narrative poem in couplets, *Tristram of Lyonesse* (1882). The last poem, however, to show his special gifts with a minimum of dilution was 'A Forsaken Garden' (1878). Here a haunting symbol of human transience develops into a wider vision of geological change, and ends (like *Tristram*) with an apocalyptic glimpse of a world obliterated by the sea.

If the best of Swinburne's poetry can be found in *Atalanta* and a few short lyrics, his best work as a novelist was done in *Love's Cross-Currents: A Year's Letters*. The fragments of *Lesbia Brandon* have little to offer readers not fascinated by incest, lesbianism, and flagellation. Written in 1862, though not published in full until 1974, *Love's Cross-Currents* was preceded by an amusing parody of a publisher's rejection-letter, which tacitly acknowledged a debt to such authors as Stendhal and Choderlos de Laclos. An epistolary novel, it describes the adulterous love-affairs that develop between two pairs of aristocratic cousins. The plot is dominated, and the lovers manipulated, by a grandmother-cum-aunt called Lady Midhurst. She is a splendidly vital character: cruelly witty and psychologically acute; stoical, sceptical, rational, realistic, and ruthless in defence of the family reputation. 'I wish to heaven', she writes, 'there were some surgical process discoverable by which one could annihilate or amputate sentiment.' By delicate blackmail she finally frustrates her grandson's 'first love', and complacently plans his future: 'I shall simply reconquer the boy, and hold him in hand till I find a woman fit to have charge of him.' His treatment may be based on some early experience of Swinburne's but, if so, bitterness was transmuted into satirical comedy. The whole novel was a brilliant performance, economically structured and entertainingly, even epigrammatically written. Except for one unpleasant passage about floggings, one would hardly believe it was written by the author of *Poems and Ballads*.

Swinburne the critic was both like and unlike the poet. In criticism, too, he never knew when to stop, and, anxious 'to do homage wherever it may be due', tended to go into rhapsodies, full of superlatives and hyperboles, but empty of specific judgements. He showed, however, intellectual acuteness, objectivity, and a surprisingly catholic taste. Defending *Les Fleurs du Mal* in 1862, he claimed that 'a poet's business is presumably to write good verses, and by no means to redeem the age and remould society'; but in discussing 'the doctrine of art for art' (1872) he was tolerant of authors who had a didactic aim. He was thus prepared to forgive Aeschylus, Dante, Milton, and Shelley for having a message, and thought Dickens 'the greatest Englishman of his generation'. Despite such breadth of sympathy, his finest critical work was done on an author with whom he could instinctively identify, as a heretic in both religion and sexual ethics. *William Blake: A Critical Essay* (1868) was a pioneering study. Rejecting the excuse for ignoring the Prophetic Books that Blake was mad when he wrote them, Swinburne took 'a blind header into the midst of the whirling foam and rolling weed of this sea of words'. Though only *The Marriage of Heaven and Hell* was interpreted in detail, he made the investigation of Blake's meaning seem an exciting project, and offered at least a helpful outline of his philosophy. Even so, his enthusiasm was tempered with realism: 'Seriously, one cannot imagine that people will ever read through this vast poem [*Jerusalem*] with pleasure enough to warrant them in having patience with it.'

His most enjoyable criticism took the form of parody. Praising Arnold's *Empedocles* for its atheism, he burlesqued the theology of *In Memorian* in an amusing quotation from a non-existent 'French critic' (1875). Satirizing the absurdities of certain French novels with an English setting, he wrote (1860) a hilarious imitation, 'La Fille du Policeman', about a *coup d'état* attempted by Prince Albert. And *Specimens of Modern Poets: The Heptalogia, or, The Seven Against Sense* (1880) included some of the best and funniest verse-parody of the period. Inevitably, the *Specimen* of Browning contains a comic rhyme for 'flagellate'. But much can be forgiven the author of the superb self-parody, 'Nephelidia': 'From the depth of the dreamy decline of the dawn through a notable nimbus of nebulous moonshine . . .'.

8. Hopkins

'TUNCKS is a good name. Gerard Manley Tuncks.' So wrote Hopkins in his diary (1864) when an undergraduate at Balliol College, Oxford.[1] He confessed elsewhere to feeling 'mortified' by the ugliness of his surname, and here he was evidently trying out an alternative. He had possibly been to a lecture on 'The Function of Criticism at the Present Time', and was remembering Matthew Arnold's list of 'hideous names,—Higginbottom, Stiggins, Bugg!' But whatever made him think of calling himself 'Tuncks', the thought was curiously characteristic. The sound of words and the concept of identity would together form the nucleus of his mature poetry.

His early interest in the relation between verbal sound and meaning is shown by many philological notes in the diary, including one on 'euphonic concord' in an African language. It also appears in the frequent word-play of the letters, which reminds us that Thomas Hood was a friend of the poet's father. The theme of vaccination inspires a fine cadenza of puns. The effects of catarrh are carefully transliterated: 'Bay our negst beeting be berry and birthful.' And an Italian preaching on Faith is quoted *con amore*: 'He zat has no face cannot be shaved.'

In his lectures on verse-rhetoric (1873–4) Hopkins stressed such sound-effects as rhythm, metre, alliteration, assonance, and rhyme. He defined poetry as 'speech framed for contemplation of the mind by the way of hearing or speech framed to be heard for its own sake and interest even over and above its interest of meaning.' He enjoyed the Nonsense of Lear and observed that, though nonsense-verse could not itself be poetry, 'it might be part of a poem.' He wanted his own poems read 'with the ears', not

---

[1] Gerard Manley Hopkins, 1844–89, was born at Stratford, Essex, the son of a marine insurance adjuster. He went to Highgate Grammar School and Balliol College, Oxford, where he was tutored by Jowett and Pater, and met Robert Bridges. In 1866 he became a Roman Catholic, and taught at Newman's Oratory school near Birmingham. He entered the Jesuit novitiate at Roehampton, where he later taught rhetoric. Having studied at Stonyhurst and St Beuno's College, Wales, he was ordained priest, 1877, and did parish work at Oxford, Bedford Leigh, Liverpool, and Glasgow. He became professor of Greek and Latin literature at University College, Dublin, 1884, where he died of typhoid.

'slovenly' with the eyes, and in his last years told Patmore: 'such verse as I do compose is oral, made away from paper, and I put it down with repugnance.' Towards the end he composed little but music.

Concern with his own identity took visual form in a drawing, shortly before the Tuncks entry in the diary, of 'Gerard Hopkins, reflected in a lake'. In a sonnet written two months before his death, he saw himself once more reflected—in 'smooth spoons'. Both self-portraits were more satirical than narcissistic, but he was always fascinated by the sense of his own uniqueness. In some notes (1880) on the *Spiritual Exercises* of St Ignatius, he appealed to this sense as evidence of his creation by a higher power:

And this is much more true when ... I consider my selfbeing, my consciousness and feeling of myself, that taste of myself, of *I* and *me* above and in all things, which is more distinctive than the taste of ale or alum, more distinctive than the smell of walnutleaf or camphor, and is incommunicable by any means to another man (as when I was a child I used to ask myself: What must it be to be someone else?). Nothing else in nature comes near this unspeakable stress of pitch, distinctiveness, and selving, this selfbeing of my own. Nothing explains it or resembles it, except so far as this, that other men to themselves have the same feeling. But this only multiplies the phenomena to be explained so far as the cases are like and do resemble. But to me there is no resemblance: searching nature I taste *self* but at one tankard, that of my own being.

The distinctiveness of this taste, whether palatable or 'bitter', as it became in a late sonnet, led Hopkins to assume that everything in creation was equally individual. For the outward signs by which a creature's inner identity could be grasped, he coined the word 'inscape'. For the emotional force with which 'inscape' impressed itself on his consciousness, he coined the correlative 'instress'. Though the terms were original, the concepts had been partly anticipated by Ruskin and Pater. Ruskin, in whom Hopkins found 'the insight of a dozen critics', had used Turner's *Rietz near Saumur* to show how every detail of 'a great composition' expressed 'its leading emotional purpose, technically called its motive'. That was virtually the principle of 'inscape', in art if not in nature. And he came near to defining 'instress' when he wrote of the 'true impression' which the great artist 'instantly' and 'strongly' received from a natural landscape. By comparing Turner's *Pass of Faido* with a 'Simple Topography' of the scene, he emphasized the subjective element in the 'true impression', by which the artist presented, 'not so much the image of the place itself, as the spirit of the place'. Hopkins cited this passage when explaining 'running instress', i.e. the modification of one 'instress' by relics of a previous one in the mind of the observer.

Pater, who tutored Hopkins at Oxford, adumbrated the two concepts in *The Renaissance*, when he wrote of the 'special, unique impression of pleasure' that an object in art, nature, or human life might give, and called it the function of an 'aesthetic critic' to identify the peculiar 'virtue' of such objects. Hopkins, however, laid greater emphasis on the design or pattern of the object, and on the divine origin of its 'virtue'. He also felt it his function, as poet rather than critic, to do more than identify. It was not enough to 'catch an inscape'. He had to convey the experience of doing so, in language appropriate both to the inscape and to his own 'selfbeing'. If that language seemed rather odd, especially in vocabulary, syntax, and word-order, it would at least be faithful to his 'taste' of himself: 'every true poet … must be original,' he wrote, 'and originality a condition of poetic genius; so that each poet is like a species in nature (not an *individuum genericum* or *specificum*) and can never recur.'

Few of the early poems (1860–75) were so startlingly original. Most were written in fairly traditional verse, and were clearly influenced by such poets as Milton, Herbert, Byron, Shelley, and Keats. They included imitations of Christina Rossetti and Swinburne, and showed signs of admiration for the Pre-Raphaelites. Hopkins wanted at first to be a poet-painter like D. G. Rossetti, and 'A Vision of the Mermaids' was pictorial in conception. It began as a highly-coloured word-painting in the manner of a Turner sunset. The colour-scheme was unified by various shades of red, and the composition by a series of circular figures, ranging from 'Cyclads' to 'globes', all subsumed by the roundness of the poet's illustrative drawing. The second of two sonnets 'To Oxford' expressed an artist's concern with a question of visual perspective, and repeated the paradox in Rossetti's sonnet, 'Inclusiveness', that a single place may be remembered by countless individuals as a unique part of their private experience.

The 'distinctiveness' of the early verse lay chiefly in its religious content. The publication of the *Apologia* during the poet's first year at Oxford greatly increased Newman's reputation there, and also that of his fellow-Tractarian, Pusey. Hopkins made Pusey's close friend Liddon his confessor, and in 1866 was received by Newman into the Roman Catholic Church. The intensity of the feelings that led to his conversion, and then decided him to become a priest and a Jesuit, was reflected in these poems by certain recurrent themes: death, renunciation, martyrdom, crucifixion, spiritual drouth and self-condemnation, self-flagellation, and a sense of God not only as a loving Saviour but also as a terrible opponent to be 'battled' with.

Two poems on monasticism, however, were strikingly original not in content but in style. The subject of 'Heaven-Haven' was very like that of the Pre-Raphaelite painting, *Convent Thoughts*, by C. A. Collins. But the unbroken continuity of the monastic life was suggested by the repetition, with minimal variations, of certain consonants and vowel-sounds, while the contrast between turbulent world and peaceful cloister was expressed as one between disturbed and regulated rhythm:

> I have desired to go
>   Where springs not fail,
> To fields where flies no sharp and sided hail
>   And a few lilies blow.
>
> And I have asked to be
>   Where no storms come,
> Where the green swell is in the havens dumb,
>   And out of the swing of the sea.

In 'The Habit of Perfection' the rhythm was no less symmetrical than the theme: a balancing of profit against loss, of spiritual joys against the sacrifice of sensuous pleasures. Here, with alliteration and assonance even more prominent, the diction was almost aggressively individual:

> Palate, the hutch of tasty lust,
> Desire not to be rinsed with wine:
> The can must be so sweet, the crust
> So fresh that come in fasts divine!

Hopkins thought contemporary poets too 'voluminous', and was aiming at compression by making his words do more than one thing at a time. 'Hutch', for example, was more than an ugly sound to chime in with the pejorative 'lust'. It also implied animality and humiliating restriction. By another form of compression, all the pleasures of touch were summed up in the strangely evocative phrase 'feel-of-primrose hands'. In the last stanza, however, where allusions to two different Gospel-passages were further complicated by ambiguous syntax, the pursuit of brevity surely went too far.

Nearly nine years later (1875) Hopkins wrote his longest, if not his most attractive, poem, 'The Wreck of the Deutschland'. The ideas that went into it may be seen developing in the earlier prose. In an entertaining 'Platonic Dialogue' on 'The Origin of Beauty', written at Balliol, he had outlined an aesthetic theory to cover visual art, music, and poetry. The speakers were a Professor of Aesthetics (who sounds like Ruskin), an undergraduate, and a Pre-Raphaelite painter. An examination of chestnut-leaves led to the conclusion that 'All beauty may by a metaphor be called rhyme', i.e. a mixture of likeness and unlikeliness, symmetry and asymmetry, uniformity and variety. The principle took in assonance and alliteration, rhythm and metre, metaphor, simile, and antithesis. Poetry was defined unromantically ('let me spell *poet* with a little *p* and perish') as 'differing from prose by having a continuous and regular artificial structure'; but the artifice might be 'almost spontaneous', on the assumption that a poet's 'idea rose in the forms of expression which we read in the poem in his mind, thought and expression indistinguishable.' Patmore queried later whether the extreme artifice of his friend's poetry could possibly be spontaneous. Hopkins assured him that it was.

How he came to link aesthetics with religion can be traced in his Journal (1866–75). In the Dialogue he had called 'composition' 'the pith of the matter', so the Journal was full of attempts to record, in words, sketches, or diagrams, the characteristic composition or inscape of things that appealed to his aesthetic taste. 'All the world is full of inscape', he wrote, and he 'caught' inscapes everywhere: in leaves, flowers, trees, bird-song, bird-flight, horses, and distant sheep; in waves, waterfalls, clouds, sunsets, and stars; in spectators at an academic ceremony, hands playing Musical Glasses, hot chocolate evaporating; in patterns made by drying ink, by ice on a 'tadpole basin', by frost on the slate slabs of urinals. He sought inscape, not always successfully, in picture-galleries, found it 'strong and noble' in the Gothic arch, and, when an ashtree was lopped, 'wished to die and not to see the inscapes of the world destroyed any more'. To him such destruction seemed blasphemy, because natural beauty expressed that of God; 'I do not think I have ever seen anything more beautiful than the bluebell I have been looking at. I know the beauty of our Lord by it.' For this intuitive feeling he found a theological basis in the *Scriptum Oxoniense super Sententiis* of Duns Scotus, which at first reading made Hopkins 'flush with a new stroke of enthusiasm. It may come to nothing, or it may be a mercy from God. But just then when I took in any inscape of the sky or sea I thought of Scotus.' As a Jesuit, he was already familiar with St Ignatius' doctrine that everything had been created to help Man 'praise, reverence, and serve God', on which he later commented: 'This world then is word, expression, news of God.' Scotus, like other Franciscans, saw God reflected in the whole creation, but his special appeal to Hopkins lay in his theory of individuality. Unlike Aquinas, the philosopher normally recommended to Jesuits, Scotus taught that everything in the world was differentiated from everything else of its kind, not just spatially but qualitatively, by a determining factor that he called '*haecceitas*' ('thisness'). Hopkins was struck by two other things about Scotus: his support for the doctrine of the Immaculate Conception, and his theory that the Incarnation would have taken place, even if there had been no Fall. From the latter Hopkins developed a view, scarcely intelligible to non-theologians, that both Incarnation and Creation were inevitable expressions of God's 'selfbeing'. 'Why,' he wrote in 1881,

did the Son of God go thus forth from the Father . . . ? To give God glory and that by sacrifice . . . This sacrifice and this outward procession is a consequence and shadow of the procession of the Trinity, from which mystery sacrifice takes its rise . . . It is as if the blissful agony or stress of selving in God had forced out drops of sweat or blood, which drops were the world . . .

Thus the world might almost be seen as the inscape of God.

Besides reflecting such aesthetic and religious ideas, 'The Wreck of the Deutschland' demonstrated 'a new rhythm' which Hopkins said had long been haunting his ear. The evolution of Sprung Rhythm, as he called it, and of other new types of sound effect in that poem can be traced both in the Journal and in the lectures that he gave as Professor of Rhetoric in the Jesuit novitiate

at Roehampton. The first entry in the Journal (1866) recorded a
song that he had heard some little girls singing under his window:

> Violante
> In the pantry
> Gnawing at a mutton bone,
> How she gnawed it,
> How she clawed it,
> When she felt herself alone.

It probably interested him as a type of verse more easily scanned
by counting stresses than syllables, and rhyming more for the ear
than for the eye. The Journal also contained a number of
philological notes, which show his belief, despite Max Müller's
ridicule of the '*Bow-wow* theory', that many words were onomato-
poeic in origin. In the 'Deutschland', however, he used words to
exploit, not only their imitative power, but also their potential for
music, or what he called in the lectures, 'Rhyme in a wide sense'.

This included, as well as rhyme proper, alliteration, assonance,
and all forms of what he called 'lettering'. Without alliteration, he
doubted if any 'modern English verse' would satisfy 'a good ear',
and his interest in the device was deepened when, while studying
theology at St Beuno's College near St Asaph, he learned some
Welsh, and found out about *cynghanedd* in Welsh poetry. Under
this intricate system, which he occasionally imitated in the
'Deutschland', not only the first but all the consonants in alliterat-
ing words have to be the same, and in the same order. For
assonance ('sameness of vowel in syllables') he merely invented a
new term, '*vowelling on*'; but he also introduced the new concept of
'*vowelling off*' or changing of vowel down some scale or strain or
keeping, as in '*So*ftly now are si*f*ting . . .' He borrowed the example
from a philological textbook, and later adapted it for his own
poem: 'I am soft sift | In an hourglass . . .'. About rhyme in the
ordinary sense, his main point was that it should satisfy the ear,
not the eye.

Under the heading of 'Rhythm', the lectures outlined his own
new prosody. He illustrated accentual verse from Saturnian verse
in Latin, from Langland, and from the Witches in *Macbeth* ('Toad
that under cold stone'), and defined its 'essential principle' in
words that adequately summarize his theory of Sprung Rhythm:
'beat is measured by stress or strength, not number, so that one
strong may be equal not only to two weak, but to less or more.' He

explained to R. W. Dixon (1880) how Sprung Rhythm differed
from 'Common Rhythm':

Its principle is that all rhythm and all verse consists of feet and each foot
must contain one stress or verse-accent: so far is common to it and
Common Rhythm; to this it adds that the stress alone is essential to a foot
and that therefore even one stressed syllable may make a foot and
consequently two or more stresses may come running, which in common
rhythm can, regularly speaking, never happen. But there may and mostly
there does belong to a foot an unaccented portion or 'slack': now in
common rhythm, in which less is made of stress, in which less stress is
laid, the slack must be always one or else two syllables, never less than
one and never more than two, and in most measures fixedly one or fixedly
two, but in sprung rhythm, the stress being more *of* a stress, being more
important, allows of greater variation in the slack and this latter may
range from three syllables to none at all—*regularly*, so that paeons (three
short syllables and one long or three slack and one stressy) are regular in
sprung rhythm, but in common rhythm can occur only by licence ...
Regularly then the feet in sprung rhythm consist of one, two, three, or
four syllables and no more ... But for particular rhythmic effects it is
allowed, and more freely than in common rhythm, to use any number of
slack syllables, limited only by ear.

The last sentence is rather surprising, since Hopkins was trying to
correct his friend's impression that Sprung Rhythm was 'a matter
of ear rather than of formal rule', and to prove that it was 'as strict
as the other rhythm.' But he had a way of bending his own
prosodic rules, while insisting on their rigidity. The strangest
loophole built into his legal system would be '*hangers* or *outrides*,
that is one, two, or three slack syllables added to a foot and not
counting in the nominal scanning.' In the 'Deutschland', however,
this licence did not occur. The poem was strictly versified in
thirty-five eight-line stanzas, rhyming ababcbca, and conforming
to a regular number of stress-feet in each line, i.e. 23435546 in Part
I and 33435546 in Part II.

The opening stanza, for all its strength and dignity, shows the
great drawback of Sprung Rhythm, its ambiguity. According to
Hopkins, it was 'the nearest to the rhythm of prose, that is the
native and natural rhythm of speech, the least forced, the most
rhetorical and emphatic of all possible rhythms, combining ...
markedness of rhythm—that is rhythm's self—and naturalness of
expression ...'. But the stanza cannot be scanned by the light of
nature. 'Thou mastering me | God!' is not natural English. It may

well have been modelled on a Greek quotation from Sophocles in the 1864 diary, which might be literally translated: 'O mastering, ruling all things Zeus . . .'. But whatever the source of the opening words, the reader does not know instinctively what their rhythm is. And the last line, naturally read, will not scan: 'Over again I feel thy finger and find thee.' In prose this would be given only five stresses, the last on 'find'. To recognize the climactic stress on 'thee', one needs to know intellectually that the eighth line of each stanza contains six feet. The difficulty recurs throughout the poem. The style is undeniably 'rhetorical and emphatic', but its expressions are often too unnatural for the 'rhythm of speech' to be known, and that uncertainty makes 'markedness of rhythm' impossible.

Apart from this element of doubt, the poem triumphantly vindicates the new system, which results in a variety of rhythmical effects, many wonderfully adapted to meaning. Concentrations of 'stressy' syllables, for instance, are used to mimic such ideas as the relentless pressure of mortality ('The sóur scýthe crínge, and the bléar sháre cóme'), or the final compression of all emotional and intellectual values into the image of Christ: 'Our héarts' charity's héarth's fíre, our thóught's chivalry's thróng's Lórd.' A contrasting dilution with unusual numbers of 'slack' syllables is used even more brilliantly to suggest the extreme lightness of touch with which God may influence human behaviour:

Nó, not uncómforted: lóvely-felícitous Próvidence
Fínger of a ténder of, O of a feáthery délicacy, the breást of the
    Maíden could obéy so, be a béll to, ríng of it, and
Stártle the poor sheep báck . . .

Of 'Rhyme in a wide sense' the poem was almost too full. Some of its ubiquitous 'lettering' reinforced the thought, as when God was pictured as 'throned behind | Death with a sovereignty that heeds but hides, bodes but abides', or when the nun's resounding cry was imitated by resonant vowel-sounds:

        she rears herself to divine
    Ears, and the call of the tall nun
To the men in the tops and the tackle rode over the storm's brawling.

A rather Keatsian image for sudden religious enlightenment is perhaps brought closer to physical sensation by the ingenuity of its phonetic patterning:

How a lush-kept plush-capped sloe
    Will, mouthed to flesh-burst,
Gush!—flush the man, the being with it, sour or sweet,
    Brim, in a flash, full!

But it is hard to see how this complicated piece of alliteration is relevant to the Nativity: 'Warm-laid grave of a womb-life grey'. One is tempted to apply to it what Hopkins said of a slightly later poem: 'It was written in my Welsh days, in my salad days, when I was fascinated with *cynghanedd* or consonant-chime, and, as in Welsh *englyns*, "the sense", as one of themselves said, "gets the worst of it".'

It was sense, however, not sound, that inspired the poem, as Hopkins explained to Dixon (1878):

You ask, do I write verse myself. What I had written I burnt before I became a Jesuit and resolved to write no more, as not belonging to my profession, unless it were by the wish of my superiors; so for seven years I wrote nothing but two or three little presentation pieces which occasion called for. But when in the winter of '75 the Deutschland was wrecked in the mouth of the Thames and five Franciscan nuns, exiles from Germany by the Falck laws, aboard of her were drowned I was affected by the account and happening to say so to my rector he said that he wished someone would write a poem on the subject. On this hint I set to work . . .

The report of the wreck in *The Times* contained several points that would have struck him. First there was the irony that Catholics trying to escape persecution in one Protestant country should be drowned off the coast of another. Then there was the picture of the five Franciscan nuns clasping hands and dying together, as if to symbolize their founder's stigmata. There was the vain heroism of the sailor, decapitated while trying to save a woman's life, and the prolonged 'scene of horror', during which two passengers tried to kill themselves to avoid a more painful death, and, whether or not from the same motive, 'the chief sister, a gaunt woman 6 ft. high', kept 'calling out loudly and often "O Christ, come quickly!"' There were also verbal suggestions of national guilt. Bismarck's anti-Catholicism had wrecked his own country ('O Deutschland, double a desperate name!'), and the Church of England stood condemned by a shameful fact noted in the report, that 'a wreck could be stranded off the English coast, appealing to English sailors for aid, and for thirty hours should be left without that aid.' But, once the survivors had been taken off, a crowd of 'salvors' instantly arrived in search of loot. Such, it might seem, was the English idea of salvation.

Several things were blamed for the disaster, including negligence on the captain's part, and the absence of a lifeboat at Harwich. The coroner's verdict, however, was 'uncontrollable circumstances'. For Hopkins it was an Act of God, which demonstrated His irresistible power to 'master' Man for his own good. That was the simplest part of the poem's message, most powerfully expressed in the terrifying narrative of the storm:

> They fought with God's cold—
> And they could not and fell to the deck
> (Crushed them) or water (and drowned them) or rolled
> With the sea-romp over the wreck.

More obscurely, the poem alluded to Scotan theology, and the poet's own religious history and speculations. The nuns became emblems, via the stigmata of St Francis, of Christ's 'Lovescape crucified', and their leader, by seeing Christ in a vision and thus 'conceiving' Him, played the part of the Virgin Mary. The Providential (and Scotan) character of the whole event was happily confirmed by the Church-calendar: the tall nun had her vision on the eve of the 'Feast of the one woman without stain', i.e. that of the Immaculate Conception (8 December).

Perhaps the date determined the number of lines in the poem's stanza. Certainly, its fluctuating development from two stress-feet to six suggests organic growth, and the same is true of the poem's overall structure. Part I moves from God's 'mastery' of the poet to a prayer for His 'Mastery' of 'us all'. Part II begins with His mastery of the Deutschland, with its 'two hundred souls' on board, and ends with a prayer for Christ's return as 'King' of a Catholic England. Thus the poem, like its opening stanza, begins and ends with God, the Alpha and the Omega, but the whole work is a slow crescendo.

As '*a figure of spoken sound*' (the definition of verse in the Lectures) 'The Wreck of the Deutschland' was a fascinating creation. As for what it was actually saying, Hopkins admitted to not being anxious 'that the meaning of all should be quite clear, at least unmistakeable.' Far from being so, it is still quite hard to extract from the text, and, once extracted, it may well disappoint many readers, not only by its emphasis on rarefied dogma, but also by its sectarianism. Luther, for instance, is dismissed as a 'beast of the waste wood'. It is odd that modern tastes in poetic style should have been so much influenced by a man whose ideas were otherwise so often at variance with modern thought. In some respects, however, such as his feeling for nature and its conservation, the mind of Hopkins was more in tune with present trends, which doubtless accounts for the popularity of later poems on these themes.

The 'Deutschland' was written at St Beuno's and during the rest of his time there (1875-7) Hopkins adapted the principles of Sprung Rhythm to the sonnet form in several delightful pieces. Though the Jesuit journal, *The Month*, refused to publish the 'Deutschland', he had been encouraged to think that poetry might, after all, 'belong to his profession', and these sonnets were both personal and 'professional' in feeling. 'In the Valley of the Elwy' he felt as he would feel again when a parish priest at Oxford: 'every prospect pleases and only man is vile, I mean unsatisfactory to a Catholic missioner.'

> Lovely the woods, waters, meadows, combes, vales,
> All the air things wear that build this world of Wales;
>   Only the inmate does not correspond . . .

The contrast between habitat and inhabitants inspired three other sonnets. 'God's Grandeur' lamented that the world, though 'charged' with that grandeur, had been desecrated:

> And all is seared with trade; bleared, smeared with toil;
> And wears man's smudge and shares man's smell: the soil
> Is bare now, nor can foot feel, being shod.

The 'pure' natural voices of 'The Sea and the Skylark' similarly put to shame 'our sordid turbid time'. And in 'Spring' a rapturous evocation of the season's beauty ended with the fear that its human analogue, 'Innocent mind and Mayday in girl and boy', might 'sour with sinning'.

The founder of the Jesuit order had prescribed it as Man's first function to praise God, so a poem like 'Glory be to God for dappled things' (i.e. for visual 'rhyme' in the creation) might seem perfectly 'professional'. But St Ignatius also said that one must be 'indifferent to all created things', so far as they interfered with one's other functions, to 'reverence and serve God Our Lord, and by so doing to save [one's] soul.' In two sonnets, therefore, Hopkins tried to define the right attutude to natural beauty. 'The Starlight Night' first demanded an aesthetic reaction to the wonder of the night sky, then explained that the stars were merely a 'piece-bright paling' that 'shuts' in, at the risk of shutting one out from, all that really matters, 'Christ and his mother and all his hallows'. 'Hurrahing in Harvest' was a shout of joy at the beauty of the fields, clouds, and 'azurous hung hills' that insisted on the need 'Down all that glory in the heavens to glean our Saviour'. At such a spectacle the heart, like the soul in Plato's *Phaedrus*, begins to sprout wings, but its failure to take off completely marks the delicate balance between legitimate delight in created things and 'necessary indifference' to them: 'The heart rears wings bold and bolder | And hurls for him, O half hurls earth for him off under his feet.' The image of frustrated flight was again applied to 'Man's mounting spirit' in 'The Caged Skylark'; but it was bird-flight utterly uninhibited that inspired the most remarkable sonnet of the series, 'The Windhover'.

Two years after composing this tribute to a kestrel's aerobatics, Hopkins called it, perhaps rightly, the best thing he ever wrote. Since it has also been a favourite with contradictory explicators, no account of its argument can claim to be more than conjectural; but it appears to move from an 'instress' of half-envious wonder at the beauty of the bird's movements, empathically enacted in words, to an affirmation that the humility and self-sacrifice of Christ are infinitely more beautiful. The transition from 'Brute beauty' to spiritual beauty is mediated by tacit allusion to the *Georgics* (I. 45–6): 'Now let my bull begin to groan over the down-forced plough, and the share to shine from friction in the furrow.' As Virgil makes his bull submit to the yoke, as Bacon's Reason 'doth buckle and bowe the mind unto the nature of things', so Hopkins subordinates his animal instincts, which make him identify with the bird's 'pride', to a higher ideal:

> Brute beauty and valour and act, oh, air, pride, plume here
>   Buckle! AND the fire that breaks from thee then, a billion
> Times told lovelier, more dangerous, O my chevalier!
>
> No wonder of it: shéer plόd makes plough down sillion
> Shine, and blue-bleak embers, ah my dear,
>   Fall, gall themselves, and gash gold-vermilion.

If there still seems to be a gap in the train of thought from the kestrel to Christ, one may, perhaps, suggest a visual link. Hopkins often noticed suggestive shapes and drew them in his Journal, like that of a crucifix in the Rhone valley: 'it looks', he observed, 'like a beacon at sea.' In 1874 he saw, but did not draw, a 'hawk hanging on the hover'; and when he 'caught' the kestrel in the same attitude, he was possibly struck by its resemblance, clear enough in ornithological photographs, to a body hanging with arms outstretched, and head fallen upon its breast.

The kestrel's apparent blend of ecstatic freedom with technical control ('the achieve of, the mastery of the thing!') was reflected in the versification which, as in the other post-'Deutschland' poems written at St Beuno's, was less rigidly systematic. In its pure form, Sprung Rhythm excluded 'Counterpoint', the 'super-inducing or *mounting* of a new rhythm upon the old', because no 'old' rhythm was assumed. By experimenting with the traditional sonnet form, Hopkins regained scope for counterpoint, and used a 'twirl' to 'mark reversed or counterpointed rhythm'. But neither the twirl nor the other marks and accents added to the text made it entirely clear how certain lines were meant to be read, and the element of doubt was increased when he tried mixing 'the two systems', i.e. Sprung and Standard Rhythm. He realized that this was 'the most delicate and difficult business of all', and the results were often confusing. The sestet, for instance, of 'The Starlight Night' began with the line: 'Buy then! bid then!—What?—Prayer, patience, alms, vows.' How this should be scanned on either system was a problem made no less baffling by the musical marking, '*rallentando*'. One is tempted, indeed, to question whether the complicated prosodic theory that underlay both these and the later poems has ever contributed greatly to the reader's enjoyment of them. Certainly they have become widely popular with a public that approaches them as a kind of free verse; and perhaps the main function of Sprung Rhythm was its liberating effect on Hopkins. Like the hexameter with Clough, it enabled an original mind to break away from the formulas of contemporary poetry, and develop a voice of its own.

For Hopkins Wales had been, as he said, 'the mother of the muses', and when he left St Beuno's in 1877, to become first a parish priest in various places, and finally a Professor of Greek at Dublin, the immediate effect was a deterioration in his poetry.

'The Loss of the Eurydice', for instance, reads like a poor imitation of the 'Deutschland', though the verse-form is simpler, and the rhymes more ingenious. But as new interests developed and old ones revived, he went on to write much more creatively in areas connected with conservation, music, visual art, and his own pastoral work. While a priest at St Aloysius' at Oxford (1878–9) he was distressed, not only by the apathy of his parishioners, but also by the destruction of the natural environment. In a sonnet on 'Duns Scotus's Oxford' and a lyrical elegy, 'Binsey Poplars', he protested against the damage being done even then to the character of the city and its surrounding countryside. If the final stress on the Immaculate Conception now seems to blur the effect of the sonnet, the lyric's imaginative appeal against thoughtless damage to nature is today more moving than ever: 'After-comers cannot guess the beauty been.' Hopkins appears to speak even more for our time in 'Inversnaid', where he extended the principle to cover less obvious natural beauty: 'Long live the weeds and the wilderness yet.'

It was also at Oxford that Hopkins became particularly interested in music. He had started learning to play the violin in 1868, had then taught himself to play the piano, and would later compose several settings for songs; but now he wrote 'Henry Purcell', a tribute to his favourite composer, here praised for his individuality: 'it is the rehearsal | Of own, of abrúpt sélf there so thrusts on, so throngs the ear.' This sonnet in Alexandrines showed signs of the poet's abrupt self also, in the obscurity of its language, which had to be carefully construed for his first editor, Robert Bridges, and its curious anxiety that Purcell should not have been damned for the sin of being a Protestant. A more rewarding result of interest in music was 'The Leaden Echo and the Golden Echo' (1882), a song for 'maidens' constructed, rather like a Greek chorus, in two long strophes. The first lamented the transience of human beauty, the second suggested the only remedy: to give it back to God. Hopkins called it 'the most musical' poem he had written, and this quality appears not only in the cadenza-like proliferation of echoes between vowels and consonants, but also in the method of modulation from the first to the second key. It is done by the equivalent of an enharmonic note. Thus the last syllable of 'despair', the key-note of the first strophe, introduces, as 'Spare!', the more cheerful key of the second.

A renewed interest in pictures was reflected in 'Andromeda', written the same year as 'Henry Purcell' (1879). Superficially, it was modelled on Rossetti's 'Sonnets for Pictures', especially those on the *Ruggiero and Angelica* of Ingres. It also shared its subject with Burne-Jones's more recent painting, *Perseus Slaying the Sea Serpent* (*c*.1875–7). But Pre-Raphaelite eroticism was here replaced by religious allegory. Andromeda was evidently the Church of Rome, exposed on the 'rock rude' of Protestant England, and menaced by the 'wilder beast' of the new paganism. Aiming at 'a more Miltonic plainness and severity' than elsewhere, Hopkins thought the sonnet at least 'almost free from quaintness'. That could hardly be said of the much better poem, 'Spring and Fall' (1880), on a theme as old as the *Iliad*, the analogy between leaves and human lives. A more immediate source must surely have been Millais. The 'young child' to whom the poem was addressed seems almost indistinguishable from the smallest girl in *Autumn Leaves* (1856). The pictorial concern was still evident in 1887, when Hopkins wrote 'Harry Ploughman'. He called it 'a direct picture of a ploughman, without afterthought'. The last two words may be questioned, for the apparent theme of the poem is the cooperation of every muscle in the body to perform a single task. But even this theme had its pictorial, as well as social and religious, application, since it paralleled Ruskin's account of 'composition'. 'I want Harry Ploughman', wrote Hopkins, 'to be a vivid figure before the mind's eye; if he is not that the sonnet fails.' That it does not so fail is remarkable, because the syntax is as tangled as Harry's 'wind-lilylocks-laced', and the train of thought obscured by what the poet termed 'burden-lines (they might be recited by a chorus)' interrupting the nominal sonnet form. In spite of such difficulties, the poem does convey not only a clear visual picture but also, by its concentration of heavy stressed and awkward consonant-groups, an almost physical sensation of muscular effort.

Of the poems inspired by the work of a parish priest, few have much appeal for the non-clerical reader. 'The Bugler's First Communion' (made to rhyme with 'boon he on') is described as a 'treat' for a 'youngster', and leads to the hope that the youngster may prove 'God's own Galahad'. 'The Candle Indoors', also written at Oxford in 1879, has at least the attraction of ingenuity, in its punning use of the 'beam in the eye', to suggest that the priest should perhaps worry less about his parishioners' spiritual

welfare, and more about his own. But the most widely appealing
poem in this group is probably 'Felix Randal' (1880). Its theme, a
decline from the strength of manhood to a childlike weakness just
before death, is expressed movingly enough in human terms, and
strikingly imaged in the final transformation of the iron horseshoe;
while natural pity is more in evidence than religious doctrine:

How far from then forethought of, all thy more boisterous years,
When thou at the random grim forge, powerful amidst peers,
Didst fettle for the great grey drayhorse his bright and battering sandal!

'Come you indoors, come home ...', Hopkins had urged
himself in 'The Candle Indoors', and the rest of his greatest poetry
was directly concerned with his own state of mind. The appeal to
'Peace' at Oxford (1879) showed that he could still smile a little at
his own unhappiness, but most of the last poems, written in
Dublin (1884–9), expressed unrelieved gloom. He had fallen into
what mystics might regard as a 'dark night of the soul', and
psychiatrists, as a deep depression. Though the real causes can
only be guessed, his external circumstances were hardly cheering.
Cut off from his family and friends, he was further isolated by the
fact that Irish Catholics were apt to be anti-English, not only in
feeling, but even in political manœuvring. His academic work,
which involved teaching Latin and Greek to rude and inattentive
students, and conducting six gruelling examinations a year, left
him no time or energy for any work of his own. This led to a sense
of total unproductiveness. As he wrote in the last spring of his life:

See, banks and brakes
Now leavèd how thick! lacèd they are again
With fretty chervil, look, and fresh wind shakes

Them; birds build—but not I build; no, but strain,
Time's eunuch, and not breed one work that wakes.

He was wrong there. This was the time when he produced some
of his most powerful and durable poems. 'Spelt from Sibyl's
Leaves' (1884–5) was perhaps not quite in this category, though its
form was markedly creative. With its eight stresses to the line,
Hopkins called it 'the longest sonnet ever made', and insisted on
its essentially musical character: 'This sonnet shd. be almost sung:
it is most carefully timed in *tempo rubato*.' It also had its pictorial
aspect, beginning as a kind of sunset-landscape, symbolizing the

reduction of a varied, colourful world to black and white, of
human life's complexity to simple questions of right and wrong, all
that would matter in the next world. Readers, however, who doubt
if there will be one may find the poet's crowning achievement in
the series of sonnets, clear enough in meaning and almost
traditional in versification, which enacted his struggles with 'fits of
sadness' so acute, he told Bridges, as to 'resemble madness.' The
horror of these experiences was most unforgettably expressed in
such sonnets as 'No worst, there is none' and 'I wake and feel the
fell of dark, not day'; but the most endearing, and perhaps the
most valuable are those in which he tried, with wry touches of
humour, to cheer himself up. This for instance (once one has
puzzled out that 'betweenpie' means: 'give glorious glimpses of
dappled things between') demands admission to any depressive's
memory:

> My own heart let me more have pity on; let
> Me live to my sad self hereafter kind,
> Charitable; not live this tormented mind
> With this tormented mind tormenting yet.
>
> I cast for comfort I can no more get
> By groping round my comfortless, than blind
> Eyes in their dark can day, or thirst can find
> Thirst's all-in-all in all a world of wet.
>
> Soul, self; come, poor Jackself, I do advise
> You, jaded, let be; call off thoughts awhile
> Elsewhere; leave comfort root-room; let joy size
>
> At God knows when to God knows what; whose smile
> 's not wrung, see you; unforeseen times rather—as skies
> Betweenpie mountains—lights a lovely mile.

'I am so happy', Hopkins is said to have whispered three times
on his deathbed, at less than forty-five. He had not, it seems,
known very much happiness before. Yet the intense delight that he
found in physical life, epitomized in 'Spring', had never wholly
left him. In an unfinished 'Epithalamion', written the year before
he died, apparently while he was invigilating at one of those
endless examinations, he recaptured the exhilaration of swimming.
The fragment describes how 'a listless stranger' comes across some
boys bathing in a river. Fired with 'a sudden zest | Of summertime

joys', he 'hies to a pool neighbouring', hurriedly undresses, and plunges in himself:

Here he will then, here he will the fleet
Flinty kindcold element let break across his limbs
Long. Where we leave him, froliclavish, while he looks about him,
      laughs, swims.

It seems a good place to leave the last great Victorian poet.

9. Other Poets

As Byron reminded Southey, '*Non Di, non homines*—you know the rest', but Horace's ban on mediocre poets must be slightly relaxed in this period. Even when not very good, Victorian poets are often interesting, either because of their own eccentricity, or else because they were so popular with contemporary readers. Keble's motto, 'Don't be original' kept him well out of the former class, but he certainly comes into the latter. According to Bishop Westcott, a verse of Keble was worth volumes of Tennyson, and *The Christian Year* (1827) went into ninety-five editions during Keble's lifetime.[1] This was a kind of verse-commentary on the Prayer Book, designed to emphasize its 'soothing tendency', and was appropriately anodyne in form as well as content. Written mostly in hymn-book stanzas, the poems preached orthodox doctrine, without trace of doubt or inward struggle on the poet's part. His next volume, *Lyra Innocentium* (1846), had less success with the public, but now seems slightly more adventurous. His object-lessons, previously drawn from Nature, came here from various aspects of child-life, including such unexpected ones as 'Shyness' and 'Stammering'. But to anyone familiar with *Hymns Ancient and Modern* (of which Keble wrote eleven) the most obvious feature of his poetry is its predictability. What appeal it still has results chiefly from the impression it gives of his personality, of the 'simple earnestness and sweet gravity' that Newman observed in his preaching. His intellectual distinction showed itself not in poetry but in criticism.[2]

Unlike Keble, who had been an Oxford student before he became a don there, Sir Henry Taylor was largely self-educated.[3] While working in the Colonial Office, he made his name as a poet with a historical drama, *Philip van Artevelde* (1834). Though not meant for the stage, the plot is quite exciting when the hero storms

---

[1] John Keble, 1792–1866, was a fellow of Oriel College, Oxford, who became professor of poetry, 1831–41.

[2] See Chap. 15.

[3] Sir Henry Taylor, 1800–86. Besides verse-dramas, he wrote *The Statesman*, 1836, an account of how to succeed in the civil service. *Philip* was staged for six nights by Macready, 1847.

Bruges with an improvised army of starving people from Ghent. The characterization is thoughtful and the blank-verse dialogue, interspersed with lively songs, shows plenty of imagination but, happily, no straining after poetical effect.

Another self-educated poet was William Barnes, a Dorsetshire farmer's son who became a polymath, with special interests in languages and grammar.[4] Though not at all derivative, his *Poems of Rural Life in the Dorset Dialect* (1844) recalled Theocritus in their spirit, and had some of the earthy humour, though not the burlesque-element, of Gay's *Shepherd's Week*. Readers prepared to grapple with glossaries and phonetic notations have always found the poetry of Barnes rewarding, and he was much admired by Tennyson, Hopkins, and Hardy. His own tastes led him to study many languages, including Welsh, Hebrew, and Hindustani; but those whose appetite is less robust may have to accept relegation to the *profanum vulgus* who cannot fully enjoy his dialect poems.

A more accessible poet was Mrs Browning's correspondent, R. H. Horne.[5] Educated for the army, he fought in the Mexican navy, and twice narrowly escaped being eaten by a shark. His best-known poem, *Orion* (1843), was almost as bizarre as his adventures. An allegorical epic in blank verse, it included some graphic accounts of violence, as when Orion and two other giants demolished an enemy town. The allegory, as in Keats's *Endymion*, expressed psychological conflict in terms of competing love-affairs. The struggle, for instance, between the 'Intellectual' and the 'Sensuous' was sensationally dramatized in a scene where Orion tried to embrace the naked Artemis in her sleep. There was also conflict between Orion, as the spirit of progress, and other giants like the merely destructive Rhexergon, the cautious reactionary, Encolyon, and Akinetos 'the great Unmoved', representing fatalistic apathy. This part of the allegory gave scope for satirical humour, and for topical allusions to politics. *Orion* was designed as 'a novel experiment upon the mind of a nation', and it succeeded in making a great stir: it had gone into nine editions by

---

[4] William Barnes, 1801–86, was the son of a tenant farmer. He became first a schoolmaster, and finally the rector of Came, Dorset.

[5] Richard Henry or Hengist Horne, 1802–84, was born in London and went to Sandhurst. From 1839 he corresponded with Elizabeth Barrett. For his children's book see Chap. 20.

1872. It was originally sold at one farthing, 'to mark the public contempt into which epic poetry had fallen'; but, inflation apart, it is worth rather more than that, for some fine descriptive passages, for its Blake-like dramatization of the psyche, and for its interesting theory of history (III, 1).

None of the other poets born in the first decade of the century deserves much attention here. R. S. Hawker, the Vicar of Morwenstow, was a fascinating character who wrote rather dull poems.[6] Tennyson's friends Arthur Hallam and R. C. Trench the philologist were merely thinkers who had learned to versify.[7] Tennyson's brothers, Frederick and Charles, shared the family gift for verbal music and suggestive natural description, but showed no marked individuality.[8] R. M. Milnes, the editor of Keats, displayed a certain facility and lightness of touch in verse recalling the 'Ode to Fancy';[9] and the personal charm of Carlyle's friend, John Sterling, can be sensed through the delicate rhythms of a few short poems, as in the tenderly ironical 'Song of Eve to Cain'.[10] The decade ended with the portentous birth of a man once seriously recommended by a Professor of Poetry at Oxford for the post of Poet Laureate. This was Martin Tupper.[11] His *Proverbial Philosophy* (1838–42) was modelled on the Proverbs of Solomon, and written in rhythmical prose that reads like a prophetic parody of Whitman. It offered edifying advice on subjects ranging from 'Marriage' to 'Mystery': 'All things being are in mystery; we expound mysteries by mysteries'. But the greatest mystery of all is

[6] Robert Stephen Hawker, 1803–75. His publications included an Arthurian poem, *The Quest of the Sangraal*, 1864. For Baring-Gould's biography see Chap. 16.

[7] Arthur Henry Hallam, 1811–33, was the son of Henry Hallam, the historian, who edited his *Remains in Verse and Prose*, 1834, after his death from apoplexy in Vienna. Richard Chenevix Trench, 1807–86, was notable chiefly as a philologist. See Chap. 15. His collected poems were published, 1865.

[8] Both contributed with Tennyson to *Poems by Two Brothers*, 1827. Frederick, 1807–98, published *Days and Hours*, and several other volumes. Charles, later Tennyson Turner, 1808–79, specialized in sonnets, which were collected, 1880.

[9] Richard Monckton Milnes, later Baron Houghton, 1809–85. His literary friends included Tennyson, Thackeray, Swinburne, Burton, Patmore, and the Brownings. His *Poetical Works* were published, 1876.

[10] John Sterling, 1806–44. Before his *Poems*, 1839, he had published a novel set in the French Revolution, *Arthur Coningsby*, 1833. The literary group named after him had Tennyson, Milnes, and Mill among its members. For Carlyle's biography see Chap. 10.

[11] Martin Farquhar Tupper, 1810–89, went to Christ Church, Oxford, where he became a friend of Gladstone. The professor of poetry mentioned was Keble's anti-Tractarian successor, James Garbett.

why this book, platitudinous in thought, repetitive in style, and haphazard in structure, should have become a phenomenal best-seller and, like *In Memoriam*, included among its admirers Prince Albert and Queen Victoria.

In the second decade, which saw the birth of Browning, the crop of poets was equally variable. Alfred Domett wrote some pleasant verse, but none so interesting as the poem he inspired, Browning's 'Waring'.[12] W. B. Scott, the poet-painter friend of the Rossettis, made some effective poetry out of religious questioning, and also showed a gift for Burns-like grotesque comedy, and for handling life's little ironies almost in the manner of Hardy.[13] W. E. Aytoun celebrated romantic patriotism and courage in the manner of Scott and the old ballads, but his real gift was for parody.[14] Aubrey de Vere, Tennyson's Irish friend, wrote Wordsworthian nature-poetry, but cultivated 'tranquillity' to the point of insipidity.[15] And P. J. Bailey earned a popularity only slightly less mystifying than Tupper's, with a dramatic poem called *Festus* (1839).[16] Inspired by Goethe's *Faust*, and designed to give 'a sketch of world-life . . . on a theory of spiritual things', it consisted largely of conversations between Festus and Lucifer while wandering round the universe. Festus ends up in heaven, 'Saved'; but long before that, most modern readers will have acted on Lucifer's earlier suggestion: 'Let us away. We have had enough of this.' According to the Dedication, Bailey started writing the poem before 'twenty summers had imbrowned [his] brow', and it showed plenty of youthful exuberance, with a remarkable talent for versifying, and for spawning unlikely images ('Ye hate the truth as snails salt; it dissolves ye'). But the chief distinction of *Festus* was to pioneer a type of poetry that Aytoun would brilliantly parody in *Firmilian, or The Student of Badajoz: A Spasmodic Tragedy* (1854).

[12] Alfred Domett, 1811–87, became Prime Minister of New Zealand. Browning encouraged him to publish his long poem about Maoris, *Ranolf and Amohia*, 1872.

[13] William Bell Scott, 1811–90, contributed to *The Germ*, 1850, and then published *Poems*, 1854, and several other volumes.

[14] William Edmondstoune Aytoun, 1813–65. Born in Edinburgh, he worked as a barrister and became professor of rhetoric and *belles-lettres* at Edinburgh. He made his name as a serious poet by *Lays of the Scottish Cavaliers*, 1849. For his parodies see Chap. 21.

[15] Aubrey Thomas de Vere, 1814–1902, came from Limerick, became a friend of Newman, and followed him into the church of Rome, 1851. He made himself known as a poet by *The Search after Proserpine*, 1843.

[16] Philip James Bailey, 1816–1902, came from Nottingham. He was called to the bar, but practised only as a poet.

In this survey, *Festus* may also serve as a foil to Emily Brontë's poetry, which her sister Charlotte accurately described as 'condensed and terse, vigorous and genuine', with 'a peculiar music—wild, melancholy and elevating.[17] The effect of condensation was clearest in the twenty-one pieces by 'Ellis' in *Poems by Currer, Ellis, and Acton Bell* (1846), but has been somewhat obscured by the more recent publication from manuscripts of her whole poetical output which, read in chronological order, seems slightly repetitive and monotonous. Literary research may also be felt, like Keats's 'Philosophy', to have clipped an Angel's wings, by discovering the facts about 'Gondal'. This was an imaginary island in the North Pacific, about which the four Brontë children constructed a rather melodramatic saga. Many poems which seemed, as edited by Charlotte, to express Emily's personal feelings, have turned out to belong to this saga. Thus these lines from 'The Prisoner: A Fragment', which could once be quoted, out of their rather puzzling context, as evidence of Emily's mysticism, must now be seen as part of an absurdly Gothic love-affair between 'Julian M. and A. G. Rochelle':

> 'Then dawns the Invisible, the Unseen its truth reveals;
> My outward sense is gone, my inward essence feels—
> My wings are almost free, its home, its harbour found;
> Measuring the gulf it stoops and dares the final bound!
>
> Oh, dreadful is the check—intense the agony
> When the ear begins to hear and the eye begins to see;
> When the pulse begins to throb, the brain to think again,
> The soul to feel the flesh and the flesh to feel the chain!'

Presumably the Gondal saga did for Emily Brontë what some equally unimpressive librettos have done for great operatic composers: it served to activate her remarkable gift for lyric poetry. Its ubiquitous 'dungeon bars' doubtless symbolized her sense of restriction and frustration in the narrow world of Haworth parsonage. A longing for escape into a larger sphere came out in natural imagery inspired by her delight in the Yorkshire moors. And in this respect the whole Gondal fiction itself appears to have functioned as a kind of alternative world, in which she could

---

[17] Emily Jane Brontë, 1818–48, was born at Haworth, Yorkshire, where her Irish father was perpetual curate. She went to school for a short time with her sister Charlotte at Cowan Bridge, but was otherwise educated at home, and spent most of her short life there. Her novel, *Wuthering Heights*, will be discussed in another volume.

breathe more freely than in the real one. The connection between
Emily Brontë and her poems remains unusually indirect; but they
certainly create a vivid impression of a personality passionate,
intense, and stoical:

> Yes, as my swift days near their goal
> 'Tis all that I implore—
> Through life and death, a chainless soul
> With courage to endure!

Another poet better known as a novelist was Charles Kingsley,
the Christian Socialist who provoked Newman's *Apologia*.[18] His
social conscience and his anti-Catholicism (especially on the
question of celibacy) were prominent in *The Saint's Tragedy*
(1848), which dramatized the life of St Elizabeth of Hungary. He
presented her as the victim of a cruel religion that branded as
sinful her natural feelings towards her husband and children. Her
philanthropic work gave him scope for a blank-verse slum-
description almost as horrifying as the prose ones in *Alton Locke*,
and for implicit satire on Utilitarian arguments against 'indiscriminate charity', on the Corn Laws, and on *laissez-faire* economics. After a slow start the drama gathered speed and interest,
and ended with a sensational deathbed scene recalling the end of
The Duchess of Malfi, a canonization ceremony stressing the
hypocrisy of all concerned, and the murder of an ex-Inquisitor by
heretics. The versification, though varied and effective, was less
remarkable than in *Andromeda* (1858), where Kingsley managed to
make the English hexameter sound quite natural, achieving a
speed and lightness like Longfellow's in *Evangeline*, and happily
unlike Matthew Arnold's 'specimens' of 1861. When telling the
Andromeda story for children in *The Heroes* (1856), Kingsley had
of course minimized the erotic element. Here he seemed more
concerned with the sexual aspect of the myth than with heroic
achievement. Thus the poem repeated the anti-celibacy and anti-
priestcraft theme of the *Tragedy*, making Andromeda's ordeal
another black mark against the type of religion that he disliked.
The exciting narrative ended (more happily than his other fine

[18] Charles Kingsley, 1819–75, was born at Holme, Devonshire, where his father was
curate-in-charge. He went to Helston Grammar School, King's College, London, and
Magdalene College, Cambridge. Ordained 1842, he became rector of Eversley, Hampshire,
1844, and married Frances Grenfell the same year. For his clash with Newman and his
children's books see Chaps. 11 and 20.

poem, 'The Sands of Dee') with a wedding 'dear', not only to Aphrodite, but also to 'the wise unsullied Athené'.

Like 'The Sands of Dee', Jean Ingelow's 'High Tide on the Coast of Lincolnshire (1571)' was also about a girl drowned while calling the cattle home, but she took twenty-three stanzas to do what Kingsley did in four. In this respect the poem was symptomatic of the fatal fluency that tended to dilute the best features of her poetry, verbal melody and evocative description.[19] 'Divided' (1863) showed her special facility with anapaestic rhythms, and effectively pictured a landscape both literal and symbolic; but her most ambitious work, *A Story of Doom* (1867), a nine-book epic in pedestrian blank verse on the last days before the Flood, was all too aptly named. Still, *Poems* (1885) contained at least one example of her delicate imagination and prosodic gift. 'Echo and the Ferry' has haunting reverberations of its own:

'My Katie?' 'My Katie!' For gladness I break into laughter
And tears. Then it all comes again as from far-away years;
Again, some one else—oh, how softly! with laughter comes after,
Comes after—with laughter comes after.

Tears were more conspicuous than laughter in the poetry of W. J. Cory, whose famous version of Callimachus was more lachrymose than the original:

They told me, Heraclitus, they told me you were dead;
They brought me bitter news to hear and bitter tears to shed. . . .

But his own poems were much less repetitive, and recalled, in their lapidary style, the *Odes* of Horace.[20] The agnostic epicureanism of 'Mimnermus in Church' seems rather Horatian too, and his habit of literary allusion reminds us that Cory taught classics at Eton. The school was almost his whole life, and his deepest feelings were apparently those aroused by certain pupils. His few short poems were published anonymously in *Ionica* (1858), a title punning on his original surname, Johnson, while suggesting his Hellenism,

[19] Jean Ingelow, 1820–97, was born at Boston, Lincolnshire, but from 1863, when her *Poems* appeared, lived in London.

[20] William Johnson, 1823–92, was born at Torrington, Devonshire, and went to Eton and King's College, Cambridge, where he became a fellow, 1845. The same year he became a master at Eton, and taught there until 1872, when he changed his name to Cory. He then travelled for his health to Madeira, where he met and married the daughter of a Devonshire rector.

perhaps with the special connotation that the word had for Pater, when he wrote that Winckelmann's temperamental Hellenism was 'proved by his romantic, fervent friendships with young men'. Certainly the poetry itself was largely concerned with homosexual feelings and frustrations, delicately hinted at by allusions to Greek literature, such as Plato's *Phaedrus* or the *Idylls* of Theocritus. Though narrow in scope, Cory's poems show considerable artistry, and represent a type of epigrammatic lyricism most unusual in the period.

Nothing could be further from epigram than the work of Sydney Dobell, who qualified for inclusion in the 'Spasmodic School' of poetry by writing *Balder* (1854).[21] The plot of this dramatic poem is ludicrous. Balder is a poet who lives in a ruined tower with his unfortunate wife Amy. He spends his time writing an epic, reading extracts from it, and talking endlessly about himself, except when interrupted by songs of despair from Amy in the next room. Eventually she goes mad, not very surprisingly, and he feels it his duty to put her out of her misery, by murdering her. There is otherwise no real action, except when Balder threatens to throw the doctor off the rampart of the tower; but some suspense develops towards the end, as the hero, torn between love and a ruthless egotism masquerading as compassion, nerves himself to kill his wife. His speeches, though less boring than those in *Festus*, are an extraordinary mixture of imaginative eloquence and bathos. 'Have I trunk-hose of lead?' asks the reluctant murderer who, when the idea first came to him, expressed his horror by thirteen 'Ah!'s in succession. Only in Amy's lyrics can the poetry of *Balder* be taken at all seriously, and Dobell's lyrical gift was exploited with greater success in *England in Time of War* (1856). Here war was treated in a spirit, not of jingoism, as might have been feared, but of compassion for the separations, bereavements and disablements that it caused. Though much too long, like most of Dobell's poems, for its fairly simple theme, 'A Hero's Grave' contained at least one moving understatement by the hero's father: 'It was not glory I nursed on my knee.' The creation of atmosphere in 'Desolate' shows that Dobell was capable of thoughtful compression:

---

[21] Sydney Thompson Dobell, 1824–74, was born at Cranbrook, Kent, the son of a wine merchant. Precocious as a child, he never went to school or university. After an engagement contracted at fifteen, he married at twenty, and was said not to have been separated from his wife for thirty hours in the next thirty years.

From the sad eaves the drip-drop of the rain!
The water washing at the latchel door;
A slow step plashing by upon the moor;
A single beat far from the famished fold;
The clicking of an embered hearth and cold;
A rainy Robin tic-tac at the pane.

But the sick sensationalism that typified Spasmodic poetry was still prominent in 'Grass from the Battle-field', where a sparrow scavenging on the 'hacked and haggard head' of a dead horse was lovingly described.

To this sort of thing, the poetry of Tennyson's Irish friend William Allingham offers a refreshing contrast.[22] There seems no reason to doubt his claim, in *Poems* (1850), that his 'constant aim' was 'towards sincerity'. The volume contained not only his best-known poem, 'The Fairies', but also his first long one, 'The Music-Master', an idyll of young love set in an Irish village. Yeats called it 'tame and uninventive' and Patmore, perhaps rather more perceptively, 'the most touching poem I know'. Yeats also dismissed as 'dull' Allingham's *Laurence Bloomfield in Ireland: A Modern Poem* (1864); but this plea for land-reform, written in Crabbe-like couplets, contains some fine satirical portraits, some pleasant pictures of Irish country life, and a moving account, indignant but objective in tone, of the eviction, in pouring rain, of the whole population of a hamlet. Allingham was better, though, at short poems. 'The Dirty Old Man' told, with irony and pathos, a real-life story rather like Miss Havisham's in Dickens. 'George Levison, or, The School-fellows' acutely described the mixed feelings aroused by the visit of a down-and-out school-friend. Of several effective sonnets, one protested powerfully against the Afghan War, others immobilized the fleeting spirits of seasons, weather-conditions, or emotional experiences. In poems like 'The Wayside Well', 'The Lighthouse', or 'Wayconnell Tower' a vein of moralizing was made more acceptable by association with concrete symbols; but some of the best pieces do no more than record psychological fact:

> Four ducks on a pond,
> A grass bank beyond.

[22] William Allingham, 1824–89, came from Donegal, where he worked as a customs officer. He was transferred to Lymington in 1863, and frequently visited Tennyson at Farringford. His other friends included Carlyle, Patmore, and Rossetti. He edited *Fraser's Magazine*, 1874–9.

> A blue sky of spring,
> White clouds on the wing;
> What a little thing
> To remember for years—
> To remember with tears!

In his 'Familiar Epistle' to his son Allingham believed that the twentieth century would rather 'suit' him. His poems indeed seem to suit modern tastes rather better than those of his almost exact contemporary, George MacDonald, who has appealed to this century chiefly as a writer of fantasy in prose and of books for children.[23] His 'Faerie Romance for Men and Women', *Phantastes* (1858), begins invitingly with the emergence, from a secret compartment in a desk, of a tiny woman aged two hundred and thirty-seven; and those prepared to go on reading it for the story alone have usually enjoyed it. Its effect on C. S. Lewis was 'to convert, even to baptise' his imagination. It taught him, he wrote, to love 'goodness', and 'enchanted' him by what 'turned out to be the quality of the real universe, the divine, magical, terrifying and ecstatic reality in which we all live.' *Phantastes* has also been welcomed by psychoanalysts, as a kind of dream demanding interpretation, and it has been recently interpreted as a 'quest for love', especially in the relationship with 'the Mother'. But the poems were less adapted to modern interests. *Within and Without* (1855) was a dramatic poem compounded of insight and absurdity. It explored the matrimonial tensions between an ex-monk and his wife with some psychological realism, but did so in the context of a melodrama, where the wife appeared to have been seduced by a wicked Lord, while the husband and his small daughter re-enacted the pathetic wanderings of Little Nell. The narrative poem, 'A Hidden Life', was an equally odd mixture of autobiography and improbable romance. The hero's life on a farm, college education, and ill health through overwork were based on MacDonald's own experience; but the story centred on the lifelong inspiration that the farmer's son owed to a single smile from a lady on a horse. About to die of consumption, he told her all about it in a letter, giving his address, proleptically, as the churchyard, and the poem

[23] George MacDonald, 1824–1905, was born at Huntly, Aberdeenshire, the son of a farmer. He went to Aberdeen University and Highbury Theological College, and became a Congregational minister at Arundel, Sussex, 1850; but his congregation found him too unorthodox, and he resigned, 1853, though he continued to preach as a layman. His novels belong to another volume, but for his children's books see Chap. 20.

duly ended with her weeping on his grave. MacDonald's imagination had been stimulated by German romantics like Novalis and Fouqué, and he showed great fluency in conventional verse-forms. His religious poetry was most interesting when, as in *The Disciple* (1867), it showed the questioning spirit that had made him cease to be a Congregationalist minister. His poems for children had charm and inventiveness, but included the faintly nauseous 'Where did you come from, baby dear?'

A fourth product of 1824 was F. T. Palgrave, who as a child amused himself in church by turning the sermon into blank verse.[24] He grew up to compile *The Golden Treasury of Songs and Lyrics* (1861) and become Professor of Poetry at Oxford. His own *Visions of England* compared poorly with Macaulay's *Lays of Ancient Rome*, and his 'Lost Eurydice' with Hopkins's poem on the same subject; but he wrote a few well-turned lyrics like 'Eutopia' (1871), expressing nostalgia for childhood, and 'Margaret Wilson', inspired by his love of children. This celebrated, in the terse stanza of Tennyson's 'Two Voices', a remarkable case of child-heroism reported in the *Daily News* (1868).

Another of Tennyson's friends, who did two busts of him (with and without his beard) and provided him with the story of *Enoch Arden*, was Thomas Woolner.[25] 'Poetry', he rightly remarked, 'is not my proper work in this world; I must sculpture it, not write it.' But not all his poetry was negligible. As a member of the Pre-Raphaelite Brotherhood, he contributed to *The Germ*, and when it first appeared there, 'My Beautiful Lady' undoubtedly read like a parody of the 'rigid adherence to the simplicity of Nature' promised in the Preface. Expanded, however, into a semi-dramatic narrative poem which showed the influence of *Maud* and of *The Angel in the House*, My Beautiful Lady (1863) went into three editions. This can only be explained by the pleasant fluency of the versification, and the disarming effect of Woolner's naïve idealism—which had somehow survived his frustrating experiences as

[24] Francis Turner Palgrave, 1824–97, was born at Great Yarmouth, the son of a historian. He went to Charterhouse and Balliol College, Oxford, and worked in the education department, 1855–92. He became a close friend of Tennyson, who helped him make his selection for the *Golden Treasury*.

[25] Thomas Woolner, 1825–92, was born at Hadleigh, Suffolk, went to school at Ipswich, and studied sculpture from the age of twelve in London, where his father worked in the post office. In 1852 he went off to the Australian gold-fields, inspiring Brown's *The Last of England*. He found little gold, but earned some by making medallions and busts for local residents.

a gold-digger in Australia. After concentrating for eighteen years on his 'proper work' and becoming Professor of Sculpture at the Royal Academy, he returned to poetry with a series of blank-verse narrative poems based on Greek myths. Here, one feels, he was merely amusing himself, and the most amusing features for the reader were the incongruous adaptations of the myths to Woolner's personal concerns. The hero of *Pygmalion* (1881), for instance, is not merely absorbed with the technical problems of sculpture, but threatened by a conspiracy of critics to murder him. Like the Rhapsode in Plato's *Ion*, he then shows an unexpected talent for generalship, foils an invasion attempt by Egyptians, and is unanimously elected King of Cyprus. In *Silenus* (1884) Pan is held responsible for everything that Woolner disliked in the contemporary world: sexual licence, social anarchy, and even industrial capitalism. To the first charge Pan might well have replied that Syrinx had 'tossed | Aside her garment' almost as provocatively as Godiva had lowered hers in Woolner's marble statue of 1878.

The third Spasmodic, Alexander Smith, came to poetry from a humbler art than sculpture, that of lace-pattern designing.[26] Clough made it sound humbler still by calling him a 'Glasgow mechanic', when reviewing *A Life-Drama* (1853) and comparing it favourably with the poetry of Matthew Arnold. Clough's judgement and Smith's reputation were doubtless affected by inverted social snobbery; but both had a certain basis in fact. Though rightly accused of plagiarism (most obviously from Shakespeare, Shelley, Keats, and Tennyson), Smith had a genuine gift for poetry, which the absurdities of this poem did not wholly conceal. As a 'drama' it was ludicrous enough, consisting largely, like *Balder*, of long speeches by the poet-hero and recitations from his own works. The nearest approach to action is a love-affair with a girl called Violet. This appears to be ending happily when Walter proposes: 'Love's banquet spread, | Now let us feast our fills'. But remorse for thus yielding to passion causes a traumatic separation, during which he confides his sense of guilt to a startled prostitute on '*A Bridge in a City—Midnight*': 'I'll call thee "Sister"; do thou

call me "Brother".' The real happy ending comes when the lovers
are reunited, thanks to the phenomenal success of Walter's great
poem.

Apart from its emotional character (which Arnold rightly
assumed without reading it to be 'intensely immature') the most
striking feature of *A Life-Drama* may be summarized in Walter's
words about his dead poet-friend:

> But our chief joy
> Was to draw images from everything;
> And images lay thick upon our talk
> As shells on ocean sands.

Some of the images are rather silly ('The sun is dying like a cloven
king | In his own blood'), but many are both original and apt, and
at least one is mildly humorous: when the dead poet is described as
'A ginger-beer bottle burst'. A recurrent theme is that of Keats's
early sonnet,

> To one who has been long in city pent,
> 'Tis very sweet to look into the fair
> And open face of heaven ...

But Smith's most interesting contribution is not such praise of
natural beauty, but an attempt to find beauty in an industrial
landscape:

> As slow he journeyed home, the wanderer saw
> The labouring fires come out against the dark,
> For with the night the country seemed on flame:
> Innumerable furnaces and pits,
> And gloomy holds, in which that bright slave, Fire,
> Doth pant and toil all day and night for man,
> Threw large and angry lustres on the sky,
> And shifting lights across the long black roads.

The attempt was continued in *City Poems* (1857). In the fine
lyric, 'Glasgow', Smith tried to evoke 'the tragic hearts of towns',
to picture, like Turner's *Keelmen heaving in coals by night*,
'Another beauty, sad and stern', but in more than visual terms.
The river that had been a mere setting for melodrama in Walter's
talk with the prostitute was given deeper meaning as a 'black
disdainful stream'. As a 'long dark river of the dead', it anticipated
the symbolism of London Bridge in *The Waste Land*, while the

related image of 'the ebb and flow of streets' was made to imply the monotony of urban working life:

> Black Labour draws his weary waves,
> Into their secret-moaning caves;
>   But with the morning light,
> That sea again will overflow
> With a long weary sound of woe,
>   Again to faint in night.
> Wave am I in that sea of woes,
> Which, night and morning, ebbs and flows.

The volume also contained two efforts towards narrative realism, 'Horton' and 'Squire Maurice', and one rather touching story, 'A Boy's Poem', which must have been partly modelled on Smith's own experience. This personal element, which gave significance to *City Poems*, was absent from *Edwin of Deira* (1861). Based on Bede's account of the first Christian king of Northumbria, it offered little more than romanticized medievalism, with a proliferation of imagery all too reminiscent of Smith's earliest work. The best image in the book was Bede's own: the sparrow flying through a lighted hall. Expanded to almost a page, it lost one of its main points, brevity.

Edwin's story was told in somewhat Tennysonian blank verse, and he even suffered from something very like the 'weird seizures' of *The Princess*; but as a plagiarist, Smith could not compete with the Earl of Lytton, *alias* 'Owen Meredith', whose *Clytaemnestra* (1855) adopted famous phrases, not only from Aeschylus, but also from Marlowe and Shakespeare.[27] He did better imitating Browning's dramatic monologues in poems like 'The Portrait', 'Aux Italiens', and 'An Evening in Tuscany', and best of all in borrowing the plot of George Sand's *Lavinia* as the basis of his verse novel, *Lucile* (1860). His own conclusion to the story, in which George Sand's independent-minded heroine ends as a saintly nun nursing the wounded at Inkerman, was preposterous, but at least half the poem is still very readable, often recalling Byron's *Don Juan* in its witty and resourceful versification, and Oscar Wilde's *The Importance of Being Earnest* in its sophisticated

---

[27] Edward Robert Bulwer Lytton, first earl of Lytton, 1831–91, was the son of the novelist and playwright Bulwer-Lytton. Educated at Harrow and Bonn, he became a diplomat, and was Viceroy of India, 1876–80. His literary efforts were encouraged by his friend Forster.

flippancy. No one can fairly be asked to read *Glenaveril, or The
Metamorphoses* (1885), another verse-novel about two foster-
brothers who may or may not have got mixed up in childhood
('Think what thou wilt, then, Reader!'). The posthumous *King
Poppy*, however, which Lytton liked best of all his works, is quite
a strong argument against his classification by Swinburne as 'a
Seventh-rate Poet'. This allegorical fairy-tale in blank verse was at
least wholly original. Protesting, as the Preface explained, against
'the practical tendency of all the most popular formulas of social
and political improvement . . . to exclude the imaginative element
from the development of character and society, and to ignore its
influence', it made delightful fun of democratic government under
a constitutional monarchy. As Viceroy of India, Lytton had been
personally involved in such government, and he caricatured it in
the realm of Diadummiania, which was quite satisfactorily ruled,
without any help from the Queen, by her puppet double, a miracle
of technology controlled by the administration through 'a tele-
phonic apparatus'. This political satire of the 'real' world was
preceded by a 'Legend' in which, thanks to a god called Phantasos,
the Poppy becomes King of Dreamland, i.e. of the human
imagination. This part of the poem creates a world of romantic
fantasy in which the real Queen of Diadummiania ends up
dreaming for ever, with the Poppy on her breast. The fantasy has a
strangely haunting quality, especially in the love-story of the
Princess and the Shepherd Boy, who communicate at night by
musical telepathy, but never meet until he is dead and she
eternally asleep.

Like her, both Arnold and Morris had their nominal doubles,
who satisfied the public almost as well as the real thing. Sir Edwin
Arnold, editor of Matthew Arnold's butt, the *Daily Telegraph*, was
hailed as a major poet when he versified the life and teachings of
Siddartha or Gautama, the founder of Buddhism, in *The Light of
Asia* (1879).[28] Though the blank verse is only a good imitation of
Tennyson's, the poem is still worth reading for the inherent
interest of its subject, and for some grimly ironic moments in the
narrative that remind one of *Rasselas*, as when the young prince,

---

[28] Sir Edwin Arnold, 1832-1904, was born at Gravesend, went to King's School,
Rochester, King's College, London, and University College, Oxford, and became principal
of the government college at Poona, 1856. Returning to England, 1861, he joined the *Daily
Telegraph*, which he edited, 1873–88.

protected hitherto from harsh realities, sees an octogenarian beggar:

> Then spake the Prince—
> 'But shall this come to others, or to all,
> Or is it rare that one should be as he?'
> 'Most noble,' answered Channa, 'even as he,
> Will all these grow if they shall live so long.'
> 'But,' quoth the Prince, 'if I shall live as long
> Shall I be thus . . . ?'

To the challenge of *The Earthly Paradise* Sir Lewis Morris responded with his own collection of Greek myths, *The Epic of Hades* (1877), which one reviewer called 'certainly one of the most remarkable works of the latter half of the nineteenth century', while another confidently classed it 'among the poems in the English language which will live.'[29] Inspired, according to the lawyer-poet, by Tennyson's 'Tithonus' and mostly written 'amidst the not inappropriate sounds and gloom' of the London Underground, this 'epic' described a series of imagined interviews with mythological celebrities in Tartarus, in Hades, and on Mount Olympus. Tantalus confessed to having been a sex maniac driven by the law of diminishing returns to sadism. Phaedra, surprisingly, held feminist views. Sisyphus turned out to be a fraudulent financier, whose 'shameless' stone (Homer's adjective) re-enacted the failure of all his commercial schemes. Narcissus expressed the need for a worthy purpose in life, and Zeus, of all people, was finally praised for 'His Purity'. Such incongruous modernization was doubtless meant to mimic the 'modern touches' in Tennyson's 'The Epic'; but Morris's most impudent piece of imitation was *Gwen: A Drama in Monologue* (1879). This feeble tale of a secret marriage between 'a great peer's only son' and a 'peasant maiden' sometimes reads like a pirated text of *Maud*, reconstructed from vague memories of a single recitation. It also defied Horace by overrunning his five-act limit. Even so, its muffled echoes of Tennysonian music were enough to make it popular. 'Seldom', remarked the *Scotsman*, 'has literature been enriched by a more beautiful poem'.

[29] Sir Lewis Morris, 1833–1907, was the son of a Carmarthen solicitor. He took a first in classics at Jesus College, Oxford, where only his wealth prevented him from getting a fellowship, and practised as a barrister, 1861–80. He helped to establish the University of Wales, and had hopes of the Poet Laureateship, 1892.

Hopkins was surely guilty of almost equal exaggeration when he
wrote that one line in a poem by his friend R. W. Dixon ('Her eyes
like lilies shaken by the bees') had given him more delight than any
other single line in poetry.[30] But he certainly 'prized' Dixon's work
enough to copy out three long poems of his, 'St Paul', 'St John',
and 'Love's Consolation', to have by him when he ceased, as a
Jesuit, to possess any books of his own. Dixon had belonged to the
'Brotherhood' assembled by Morris and Burne-Jones at Oxford,
and the volume that so delighted Hopkins, *Christ's Company and
Other Poems* (1861), was typically Pre-Raphaelite in its tendency
towards aesthetic languor, static pictorialism, and quasi-medieval
religiosity. 'Love's Consolation' was a dramatic monologue by
'The Monk of Osneyford', on a theme drawn partly from Tennyson ('and if thy lady chide ... 'Tis better so, than never to have
been | An hour in love'), and partly from Emerson ('do thy thing').
The latter principle became Dixon's whole policy as a poet. Apart
from the early Pre-Raphaelite influence, his poetry seems intensely
private and personal: an honest attempt to tell himself in verse
what he really thought and felt. This often led to awkward or
obscure forms of expression, and a vocabulary odd enough to
require, as Hopkins put it, 'a Dixonery'. In *Mano* (1883), a
'Poetical History' written in *terza rima* by another medieval monk
about the confusing adventures of a Norman knight, Dixon set
forth his view of 'The mighty workers of this world's affairs, |
Fatality, infinity, these two'. Composed as an act of self-discipline,
it can be read only in the same spirit; but in shorter odes and
personal lyrics he wrote far more appealingly. Living a quiet life as
a country clergyman, he expressed through natural phenomena the
sadness of the human condition, as in 'Summer', 'The Fall of the
Leaf', and 'Fallen Rain' (for which Hopkins composed his best
musical setting). Dixon's extreme modesty came out pleasantly in
the quasi-Theocritan 'Polyphemus', where the monster feels
frustrated at being unable to make any social contacts, let alone
erotic ones. Thinking he has two eyes like everyone else, he cannot
make out why he is shunned in horror. 'Ode on Advancing Age'

---

[30] Richard Watson Dixon, 1833–1900, was born at Islington, the son of a Wesleyan
preacher. He went to King Edward's School, Birmingham, and Pembroke College, Oxford,
where he met Morris and Burne-Jones, and later lodged with them in Red Lion Square,
London. He became a minor canon of Carlisle Cathedral, and ended as vicar of Warkworth,
Northumberland.

described with majestic realism the sensation of becoming old, ending with a grimmer version of 'do thy thing': 'Be to the end what thou hast been before.' Happily, the progress towards 'silence' charted in that Ode brought Dixon, in 'Exeat', a Housman-like verbal economy:

> Thou hast neither laugh nor quip
> Longer on thy closed lip:
> All thy comrades say Depart
> For they love a merry heart.
> Weary too thy host become
> Bids thee quit his ruddy room.

Though best known for his *The City of Dreadful Night* (1874), it is clear from some entertaining letters, and from what his friends said about him, that James Thomson had 'a merry heart' too.[31] His life, however, could hardly be so described. His younger sister died when he was five, his father was paralysed a year later, his mother died when he was eight, and Matilda Weller, a pretty fourteen-year-old that he had grown fond of, died when he was nineteen. He also suffered from periodic fits of depression, which interacted with the alcoholism that killed him before he was forty-eight. In spite of all this, and of his initial poverty, he had enough *joie de vivre* to write 'Sunday at Hampstead: An Idle Idyll by a very humble Member of the great and noble London Mob'. This described with colloquial humour an outing of some young City workers to Hampstead Heath. Nor was he quite right to say, in an early sonnet, 'My mirth can laugh and talk, but cannot sing; | My grief finds harmonies in everything.' 'The Naked Goddess' celebrated natural life with a gaiety enhanced by ridicule of civilization, and by a rollicking, trochaic verse-form. Even on gloomy themes his poems were often humorous. 'A Real Vision of Sin' was a horrifying burlesque, less of Tennyson's 'Vision' than of his 'Two Voices'; for the theme was suicide, and the voices were those of an 'aged man and crone' in a setting even ghastlier than that of 'Childe Roland'. In the semi-supernatural fantasy, 'Vane's Story', Vane asked his dead girl-friend to use her influence in heaven to

---

[31] James Thomson, 1834–82, was born at Port Glasgow, the son of a merchant seaman. He went to a school for poor Scottish soldiers and sailors, trained as an army schoolmaster, and served in Ireland, where he met Matilda Weller and Charles Bradlaugh, then at Aldershot, in Jersey, and at Portsmouth, where he was discharged, probably for alcoholism, 1862. He then lived in London, initially with Bradlaugh, writing poetry and prose for periodicals. After 1881 he drank himself to death.

get him an early death. But the tone of their conversation is light-
hearted, even jocular, and the fun of taking her to a dance with his
friends on the last night of Vane's life is epitomized by his
suggestion that she should sing him one of Heine's love-poems to
the tune of a hymn by Bishop Heber. The best example of
Thomson's gift for the humorous treatment of suicide was 'In the
Room', which obliquely described, through a conversation
between pieces of furniture, how a hack writer came to kill himself.
Through all the hints of the dead man's misery the poet's love of
life made itself felt, especially in the references to the previous
tenant, Lucy, and even in the bed's final summary of human
experience, which included not only 'deaths' but also 'births and
bridal nights'.

Thomson's other notable poems include an all-too-lifelike
representation of 'Insomnia', and 'Weddah and Om-el-Bonain', a
grimly romantic narrative poem about a lover who is buried alive
by a jealous husband; but his greatest achievement was to do, in
The City of Dreadful Night, what Matthew Arnold had thought
impossible, to make enjoyable poetry out of 'a continuous state of
mental distress ... unrelieved by incident, hope, or resistance'.
The distress in question might be defined as acute endogenous
depression, exacerbated by atheism, and the poem succeeded
largely because of its central symbol, suggested by Dante's '*città
dolente*' and Shelley's 'Hell is a city much like London'. In a
rambling early poem, 'The Doom of a City', Thomson had
presented two such cities: a symbolic one, in which the inhabitants
were petrified for their sins, and the real city of London, through
which the insomniac poet paced alone by night. This aspect of
London, empty, lamplit, and made nightmarish by projected
misery and loneliness, now became the objective embodiment of a
subjective state. One advantage of the symbol was the scope it gave
for quasi-topographical exploration—for an illusion, at least, of
progress, as when a solitary walker followed by the poet keeps
turning right, and so keeps arriving at the same spot, the graveyard
where 'dead Faith, dead Love, dead Hope' are buried. Another
advantage was that London supplied a familiar spatial context for
some weird allegorical scenes, like that in the Cathedral, where an
atheist (doubtless modelled on Thomson's friend and publisher,
Charles Bradlaugh) preaches the sermon, or the encounter near 'a
suburb of the north', presumably Hampstead, with an old man

searching in the mud for the 'long-lost broken golden thread' to
reunite his present with his past.

Thus Thomson put variety into his picture of an essentially
monotonous mood. To structure his amorphous theme, he used
several compact forms of stanza, started with a Proem, and ended
with two descriptions of emblematic sculpture. The theme was
announced by two epigraphs, one from the notice over the gate of
Dante's *Inferno*, and the other from Leopardi, stressing cosmic
futility and inevitable human misery. The Proem then implied, by
a quotation from *Titus Andronicus*, that the poet was merely
'telling his sorrows to the stones', and appealing for mercy to gods
who, like the tribunes addressed by Titus, were not even there to
hear him. Section xx described two sculptured figures, an Angel
and a Sphinx, to image the replacement of a theocentric by a
materialistic view of the universe, and section xxi summed up the
whole feeling of the poem in 'a bronze colossus' of 'That City's
sombre Patroness and Queen', the 'Melencolia' of the engraving
by Dürer. Even the number of sections in the *City*, twenty-one,
was itself a kind of image. It must have referred to a conceit which
though, in Johnson's phrase, 'far-fetched' was surely 'worth the
carriage'. This was used about the man who kept turning right:

> He circled thus for ever tracing out
>   The series of the fraction left of Life;
> Perpetual recurrence in the scope
> Of but three terms, dead Faith, dead Love, dead Hope.

As a footnote explained, three score years and ten, divided by
$333 = 0.210$ recurring. The insertion, in such a context, of a
mathematical joke was as typical of Thomson's irrepressible
humour, as the story of the man who could not even get into Hell,
because he had no hope left to abandon. Paradoxically, it is this
undercurrent of gaiety that lends conviction to Thomson's masterpiece of gloom.

Alfred Austin wrote no masterpiece, and the funniest thing he
ever did was to get himself made Poet Laureate.[32] As a critic, in
The Poetry of the Period (1870) he had judged Tennyson a third-
rate poet, Browning 'not specifically a poet at all', Arnold and

[32] Alfred Austin, 1835–1913, was a lapsed Roman Catholic from Leeds, who was called
to the bar, but became a journalist. He edited the *National Review*, first with Courthope,
then alone, 1883–95. The Laureateship, 1896, was possibly a reward for supporting Lord
Salisbury's party.

Morris mere refugees from an age incapable of producing great poets. As a poet, he published twenty volumes; but in *English Lyrics* (1890) he inadvertently gave utterance to his best piece of criticism; 'Thou art dumb, my muse; thou art dumb, thou art dead, | As a waterless stream, as a leafless tree.' Austin Dobson's muse was far more attractive: elegant, witty, accomplished in versification, and above all concise.[33] In 'A Roman Round-Robin' he made affectionate fun of his most obvious model, Horace, for saying the same things so often, but his own range of subject-matter was hardly more extensive. Most of his best poems, from *Vignettes in Rhyme* (1873) onwards, were based on a single formula: the imaginative reconstruction of the life commemorated by some artefact—an old letter, an old picture, a Sèvres figurine, a manuscript. His melancholy, gently humorous antiquarianism shows no more variety than his delicate moralizing; yet subtle differences of approach and versification are enough to disguise the monotony of thought and feeling. Much of Dobson's output may fairly be called 'light verse', but there is something in his blend of humanity and artistry that seems worth taking more seriously, like the 'something vital' that he sensed in 'A Missal of the Thirteenth Century':

> Something that one still perceives
> Vaguely present in the leaves;
> Something from the worker lent;
> Something mute—but eloquent!

The special quality perceptible in the poetry of J. A. Symonds (best known for his *History of the Renaissance in Italy*) is rather less vague. It might be defined as intellectual and moral courage.[34] While living in the Swiss Alps and trying to recover from tuberculosis, he published three volumes of verse. *Many Moods* (1878) was a heterogeneous collection of poems, ranging from simple 'Pictures of Travel' to weird fantasies like 'Le Jeune Homme caressant sa Chimère', but unified, according to the

[33] Henry Austin Dobson, 1840–1921, was born at Plymouth, the son of a civil engineer. Educated partly in Strasbourg, he worked from the age of sixteen at the Board of Trade, 1856–1901, where Edmund Gosse was a colleague and friend. He wrote books on several eighteenth-century authors for the *English Men of Letters* series.

[34] John Addington Symonds, 1840–93, was born in Bristol, the son of a doctor. He went to Harrow and Balliol College, Oxford, and became a fellow of Magdalen. From 1878 until his death from tuberculosis, he lived chiefly at Davos. Lear, Swinburne, Stephen, and Stevenson were among his friends.

Preface, by the themes of 'Love, Friendship, Death, and Sleep'. Death figured prominently in two curious narrative poems centring on the immolation of a beautiful young man. This motif, which was doubtless connected with the poet's homosexuality, recurred in *New and Old* (1880); but the first volume also contained a more thoughtful and personal treatment of the death-theme in 'Sonnets on the Thought of Death'. These were followed, in the second, by two fine sonnet groups on the emotional implications of agnosticism, 'Intellectual Isolation' and 'An Old Gordian Knot'. In the third, *Animi Figura* (1882), some of these sonnets were integrated into a fairly coherent sequence. The title, from Tacitus's *Agricola*, implied that the book was meant to give a portrait of the poet's mind. Some of the sonnets express emotional frustration, or hint at feelings of guilt, but most are attempts to define an unorthodox position in morality, religion, or psychology. Conscious departure from convention was announced in the opening sonnets, 'The Innovators', and in 'Personality' the isolation of the individual consciousness, stressed by Pater in the 'Conclusion' to *The Renaissance*, was reasserted:

> Each self, from its own self concealed, is caught
> Thus in a cage of sense, sequestered far
> From comradeship, calling as calleth star
> To star across blank intermediate naught.

While seeing all creeds as merely human fictions, Symonds finally fell back on 'blind unwavering trust' that things were not quite so bad as they seemed. But he seems to have done it more in the spirit of J. S. Mill's 'Theism' than of *In Memoriam*;[35] and the concluding sonnet concentrated not on the ultimate solution of the 'Mystery of Mysteries' but on the present predicament of Man's 'staunch heart', imaged as Prometheus, alone upon a mountain, and without any prospect of release from torment. The work demands respect for its intellectual honesty, its precise and pointed diction, its flowing but disciplined verse, and its vivid presentation of an unusual personality.

Honesty was not the most obvious feature of the pseudonymous attack on Rossetti's poems, 'The Fleshly School of Poetry' (1871), but the man who wrote it, Robert Buchanan, had some other

[35] For Mill and Tennyson see Chaps. 14 and 2.

virtues as a poet.[36] His most interesting volume, *London Poems* (1866), had been dedicated to W. H. Dixon, the advocate of 'a great sexual insurrection of our Anglo-Teutonic race', whom Matthew Arnold would ridicule, and the *Pall Mall Gazette* would call 'a writer of indecent literature'. Buchanan's poems were not indecent, but certainly implied unconventional moral values. In a rather moving dramatic monologue, 'Nell', sympathy was demanded for the common-law wife of a man hanged for murder, and in a narrative poem, 'Jane Lewson', for an unmarried mother, ill-treated by her rigidly moral sisters. Buchanan also showed originality, however qualified by the prior appearance of Smith's *City Poems*, in trying

> to make
> The busy life of London musical,
> And phrase in modern song the troubled lives
> Of dwellers in the sunless lanes and streets.

His own life had been hard when he first came to London from Glasgow, and his picture of slum life, though tinged with melo-drama, was as realistic as his conventional verse-forms would allow. With Smith in mind, one can see additional point in the ironical story of 'Edward Crowhurst', a 'Labourer' who is turned by reviewers into a fashionable poet. He ends, like John Clare, in an asylum.

Where Buchanan tried to make music from the life of the man in the street, Arthur O'Shaughnessy made it from the inner life:

> We are the music makers,
>   And we are the dreamers of dreams,
> Wandering by lone sea-breakers,
>   And sitting by desolate streams;—
> World-losers and world-forsakers,
>   On whom the pale moon gleams . . .[37]

---

[36] Robert Williams Buchanan, 1841–1901, was born at Caverswall, Staffordshire. His father was a socialist and anti-religious tailor from Ayr, who later moved to Glasgow, where he owned and edited three socialist journals. After going to school and university there, Buchanan moved to London, 1860. Besides poetry and articles, he wrote novels and plays.

[37] Arthur William Edgar O'Shaughnessy, 1844–81, was born in London and privately educated. He worked in the British Museum from 1861. His promotion to assistant in the zoological department, 1863, was condemned by the Zoological Society, which thought him unqualified; but he made himself an expert in herpetology, and his death was deplored by his head of department as a loss to science.

His contempt for the outer world was explicit in his first volume,
An Epic of Women and Other Poems (1870):

> A common folk I walk among;
>   I speak dull things in their own tongue:
> But all the while within I hear
>   A song I do not sing for fear—
> How sweet, how different a thing!

Turning his back on such 'dull things' as herpetology, which he
had to study for his job at the British Museum, he yearned after a
romantic paradise where, among other assets, perfect love could be
enjoyed. The imperfection of earthly love was the theme of *An
Epic*, which roundly asserted that all *femmes* were *fatales*: 'so fair to
see, so false to love'. The thesis was proved by rhapsodic accounts
of how Aphrodite, Salome, and Helen behaved. The poem ended
with a dramatic monologue by a disillusioned lover (evidently a
disciple of Porphyria's), who goes to bed with a girl and then kills
her, explaining: 'It was the only way to keep her mine.' The sick
side of O'Shaughnessy's romanticism, though hinted at elsewhere,
was never flaunted so ludicrously, and his music-making, though
clearly stimulated by Swinburne, had its own originality and
charm. The intrinsic merits of his poetry were admittedly not
outstanding; but he seems admirably qualified to conclude a
survey of the period's minor poetry, since he heralded a shift of
interest, away from society and ethics, and towards Aesthetic
introversion, that would characterize much of the poetry of the
Nineties.

10. Carlyle

'INCESSANT scribbling', Carlyle warned his brother in 1831, 'is inevitable death to thought.'[1] He courted that disaster to the extent of thirty volumes, partly to earn a living, partly to practise his own gospel of Work, but chiefly, as he claimed in the same early letter, to communicate Truth: 'Nay, had I but two potatoes in the world, and one true idea, I should hold it my duty to part with one potato for paper and ink, and live upon the other till I got it written.' He did his duty so well that his ideas, whether true or false, sank deep into the public consciousness. Starting as the son of a barely literate Scottish stonemason, he ended as perhaps the most influential writer of his time. His audience at Edinburgh University had good reason to cheer their new Rector (1866) when he said: 'And now, after a long course, this is what we have come to.'

An important factor in this triumph of self-help was the invention of Carlylese. 'My style', he observed in his journal, 'is like no other man's'; but it must have been affected by his father's natural gift for talking: 'that bold glowing style of his, flowing free from the untutored Soul; full of metaphors (though he knew not what a metaphor was), with all manner of potent words (which he appropriated and applied with a *surprising* accuracy, you could not guess whence); brief, energetic . . .'. Other elements in Carlylese evidently came from Germany. The literary hack-work that was Carlyle's first defence against poverty included, besides reviewing for periodicals, translating and criticizing German literature. One author that specially appealed to him was 'Jean Paul' Richter, and

[1] Thomas Carlyle, 1795–1881, was born at Ecclefechan, Dumfriesshire, in a house that his father, a deeply religious stonemason, had built himself. He went to the village school, to Annan Academy, and to Edinburgh University, intending to become a minister; but he soon gave up that idea, and after some schoolteaching at Annan and Kirkcaldy, started to earn his living by writing. It was a hard struggle. From 1820 he supported himself by miscellaneous publications, including contributions to an encyclopaedia, articles and reviews in periodicals, and translations, chiefly from German. In 1826 he married Jane Baillie Welsh, a doctor's daughter from Haddington, East Lothian. From 1828 they lived in a remote farmhouse at Craigenputtoch, where he wrote *Sartor Resartus*, and in 1834 moved to Cheyne Walk, Chelsea. His fame began with *The French Revolution*, 1837, after which his home became a centre of London literary life. His wife died suddenly, 1866, while he was in Scotland, after giving his inaugural lecture as Rector of Edinburgh University.

this account of Richter's 'surface' is equally applicable to Carlyle's own future manner:

> He is a phenomenon from the very surface; he presents himself with a professed and determined singularity: his language itself is a stone of stumbling to the critic ... he ... deals with astonishing liberality in parentheses, dashes, and subsidiary clauses; invents hundreds of new words, alters old ones, or by hyphen chains and pairs and packs them together into most jarring combination; in short, produces sentences of the most heterogeneous, lumbering, interminable kind. Figures without limit; indeed the whole is one tissue of metaphors, and similes, and allusions to all the provinces of Earth, Sea and Air; interlaced with epigrammatic breaks, vehement bursts, or sardonic turns, interjections, quips, puns, and even oaths! A perfect Indian jungle it seems; a boundless, unparalleled imbroglio; nothing on all sides but darkness, dissonance, confusion worse confounded!

'As we approach more closely', Carlyle continued, 'many things grow clearer.' The same is true of reading him too, and patience with his superficial mannerisms is amply rewarded.

Before 1830, however, his surface was fairly conventional. Apart from a fragment of an autobiographical novel, *Wotton Reinfred*, his most interesting early work was 'Signs of the Times'. This anonymous article in the *Edinburgh Review* (1829) condemned all current trends of thought, especially Utilitarianism, as 'mechanical' rather than 'dynamic'. The metaphor (which Arnold would rework in *Culture and Anarchy*) served to link Utilitarianism with the triumphs of technology, via a tacit pun on James Mill's surname, and to unify a variety of complaints, all implying that the age had lost the sense of mystery, morality, and religion. The device inaugurated Carlyle's practice of making rather vague and general intuitions seem precise by an ingenious use of imagery.

Sartor Resartus (1833–4) was similarly built around the metaphor of clothes, which enabled Carlyle to say almost everything he most wanted to say at the time. In an allegorized autobiography by Professor Teufelsdröckh, an imaginary German philosopher specializing in Clothes, Carlyle sketched his own history: his humble origin, difficult choice of profession, unhappy love-affair, loss of religious faith, and discovery of a new one, free from specific theology, but otherwise closely resembling his parents' Calvinism. He also voiced his opinions on society and politics. He stressed the dangerous condition of England, divided into the

'Drudges' and the 'Dandies', the desperately poor and the irresponsible rich: 'the two nations', as Disraeli would call them. He satirized Malthusian acceptance of social misery, Utilitarian concentration on happiness, and Radical reliance on universal suffrage as the cure for all ills.

The complex form of the book developed from the Richteresque fiction that Carlyle was merely editing a massive monograph by a semi-comic professor, whose names suggested his function. 'Diogenes' implied not only a savage attack on convention by a half-naked philosopher who inhabits and thumps a tub, but also a kind of prophecy ('born of God'). 'Teufelsdröckh', meaning 'devil's dung' or asafoetida, implied not only a devil's advocate, but also a bitter stimulant to thought (on the theory that thought, like digestion, was a form of secretion). The point of the clothes-philosophy (clearly derived from Swift's *A Tale of a Tub*) was the distinction between eternal truth and passing fashion. Clothes changed with the fashion of the day, or wore out and had to be replaced, but the wearers remained the same. In that sense all human creeds and institutions were merely clothes. Thus the image expressed fundamental conservatism in religion, ethics, and politics, while urging superficial reform; and the title ('The Tailor Re-Tailored') epitomized the delicate balance between progress and reaction that characterized the whole period. The Tailor-Reformer, the creator of new forms, was presented in a new guise, as 'Hierophant and Hierarch' of mankind; but he was not encouraged to meddle with fundamental truths.

The fantasy of editing, criticizing, expounding, and selectively translating a German author was close to Carlyle's recent experience, but here it was functional rather than autobiographical. As propaganda for a type of mysticism then alien to English readers, it moved, by the same strategy as Tennyson would use to popularize feminism in *The Princess*, from ridicule to affirmation. It also gave scope for stylistic eccentricity, ostensibly based on German vocabulary and syntax. Finally it was an apt figure for the problems of literary creation. The green-spectacled 'Editor', struggling to decipher fragmentary, illegible, or unintelligible scribblings by a shadowy genius, vividly realized Carlyle's own situation, as he tried (in a phrase that he later applied to Tennyson) to manufacture the Chaos of his mind into Cosmos. *Sartor* was a turning-point in his writing. Unlike most of his earlier work, it was not deliberately contrived, but grew almost spontaneously from random jottings in his journal. By daring to trust the irrational side, he had found himself as an author.

Since his father thought poetry and fiction 'not only idle, but *false* and criminal', Carlyle grew up with a bias towards history. At twenty-one he read, with 'high esteem', the twelve volumes of Gibbon in as many days, and in two early articles (1830, 1833) he outlined his view of the historian's duty. This was to decipher the 'Letter of Instructions' from the past to the present. He also pointed out two great difficulties faced by the historian. First, the people involved in a historic crisis do not realize what is happening: 'no hammer in the Horologe of Time peals through the universe when there is a change from Era to Era.' Secondly, no plain narrative can express the three-dimensional movements of real life, the forces acting simultaneously in different places and at different levels of thought and feeling: 'Narrative is *linear*, Action is *solid*.' In *The French Revolution* (1837) he tried to perform this duty himself, and overcome these difficulties.

He presented the Revolution as a fearful exemplum of divine justice. A society without faith in God or Truth, where king and nobles were sham governors and priests sham teachers, was suddenly destroyed by the built-in 'Veracity' of the universe. Religious and social imposture was burnt up in a holocaust from which (as Teufelsdröckh had hoped) the Phoenix of a 'heaven-born young' society would eventually emerge. Thus even the worst horrors proved Providence, and the 'message' of the past to England, in the year that Chartism began, was that unless the upper classes behaved more responsibly, an English Revolution would soon follow.

The limited understanding of the people involved in a historical process was emphasized by various attempts to simulate how things seemed at the time. The story was told largely from contemporary sources, either quoted or paraphrased, and in the present tense. The style was dramatic and colloquial, full of questions and exclamations. Indeed the whole history might be described as a kind of dramatic monologue spoken by a series of separate voices, sometimes expressing the subjective reactions of an individual character, sometimes an undifferentiated consciousness representing some aspect of public opinion or feeling. Meanwhile the inevitable confusion in the contemporary mind was obliquely conveyed by a very allusive and elliptical form of expression. Readers without previous knowledge of the subject were left to guess at events through a fog of passing references, and thus experience something like the uncertainty that prevailed during the Revolution.

The 'solidity' of historic events was suggested by a cinematic technique of flashes back, forwards, and sideways, in both time and space; and also by special emphasis on the small human factors that might have momentous results. If, for instance, the post master at Varennes had not been in a bad temper that day, the King and Queen would never have been caught; but he 'was looking abroad, with that sharpness of faculty which stirred choler gives to man.'

Carlyle intended his history to be more than didactic. He also wanted 'to make an artistic picture of it', to create 'a work of art'. So he wrote it as a modern epic, factual and in prose, but otherwise comparable to the *Iliad*. He invited the comparison by often quoting from or alluding to Homer, and by giving his chief characters Homeric epithets. Mirabeau, like Agamemnon, was 'King of Men', and the 'atrabiliar' complexion of Robespierre earned him the formulaic adjective 'Sea-green', possibly to parallel the hint of jaundice in Homer's 'yellow Menelaus'. Of larger elements in the *Iliad*, Carlyle modelled his Procession of Deputies on the Catalogue of Ships, and on Helen's identification of Greek heroes from the walls of Troy. It gave him a neat method of introducing important figures, and glancing at the parts they would play in his story. More amusingly, the reconnaissance-balloon sent up by the French to spy on the Austrians was associated with the golden scales hung out in the sky by Zeus. It was not, however, by such deliberate connections with Homer that the work achieved epic status. It did so by the huge dimensions of the European crisis described, by the vigour and vividness of its narrative technique, and by the recurrence of certain powerful images (electricity, explosion, collapse into an abyss). These underlined Carlyle's concern, a concern that he had attributed to 'the Artist in History', with 'the Whole'. His treatment of that tragic whole was made more comprehensive, and so more epic, by the inclusion of its comic elements. The account of Marat's death, while 'stewing in slipper-bath', mocked life as well as Virgil: 'The helpful Washerwoman running in, there is no Friend of the

People, or Friend of the Washerwoman left; but his life with a groan gushes out, indignant, to the shades below.'

From the French, Carlyle now turned to the English sansculotte and the Irish 'Sanspotato'. In *Chartism* (1840) he attributed that movement to working-class poverty, the Corn Laws, the Poor Law Amendment Act of 1834, the *laissez-faire* policy recommended by economists and Malthusians and practised by Parliament, and the social disintegration caused by commercialism. For this last he coined a phrase that would find its way into the *Communist Manifesto*: 'Cash Payment has become the sole nexus of man to man!' He proposed two remedies: 'Emigration' and 'Universal Education'. So far his diagnosis was sound enough; but it was hardly realistic to interpret Chartist demands for Parliamentary representation as 'inarticulate prayers' for authoritarianism: 'Guide me, govern me! I am mad and miserable, and cannot guide myself!' What was wanted, he said, was a 'strong man', a 'leader', and a '*real* aristocracy' which would actually govern. Here the tendency to exaggerate, which he knew he inherited from his father, drove him beyond rational distrust of democracy into total rejection of it: 'Democracy is, by the nature of it, a self-cancelling business; and gives in the long run a net result of *zero*.' Quoting another fictitious German, Professor Sauerteig (Yeast), Carlyle went on to say that 'Might and Right' were in the long run 'identical', and that the 'strong thing is the just thing'. Like Teufelsdröckh, this persona added a fantastic quality to his rhetoric, thus increasing the impact of his ideas on the reader's mind; but he sweetened the pill more effectively by humour. The absurdity of total reliance on the laws of supply and demand was personified in the man who told his horses:

'Quadrupeds, I have no longer work for you; but work exists abundantly over the world: are you ignorant (or must I read you Political-Economy Lectures) that the Steam-engine always in the long run creates additional work? Railways are forming in one quarter of this earth, canals in another, much cartage is wanted; somewhere in Europe, Asia, Africa or America, doubt it not, ye will find cartage: go and seek cartage, and good go with you!'

The image of the 'strong man' was inflated to bursting-point in *Heroes, Hero-Worship and the Heroic in History* (1841). This was based on some public lectures by which Carlyle was then earning his living in London. In private life he enjoyed holding forth, but he hated these performances, and described them as a 'Detestable mixture of Prophecy and Play-actorism'. The book is certainly tedious, making at great length a few dubious statements: 'The History of the World is but the Biography of great men.' Hero-worship is a human instinct, 'the one fixed point' in the 'bottomless and shoreless' sea of 'modern revolutionary history'. Heroes are sincere, earnest, self-helping. They see through appearances to the reality, realize the 'infinite' difference between Right and Wrong, distinguish between the essential and 'surplusage', and usually start 'in a minority of one'. They are also very adaptable and may, according to circumstances, become pagan gods, prophets, poets, priests, men of letters, or kings. To judge by the examples given, the incidence of Heroism in Scotland, though lower than in England, is higher than anywhere else except in France.

While elaborating these ideas, Carlyle made some other assertions that proved more influential than they deserved. Like Browning's Bishop Blougram, he insisted that belief was what mattered in life. Doubt and scepticism were more than unhealthy. They were positively immoral, leading to 'a chronic atrophy and disease of the whole soul', and creating 'the whole tribe of social pestilences, French Revolutions, Chartisms, and what not'. Every writer should therefore preach some creed, and denounce folly and sin: 'on the whole, we are not altogether here to tolerate!' And the poet should preach in prose: 'I would advise all men who can speak their thought, not to sing it; to understand that, in a serious time, among serious men, there is no vocation in them for singing it.'

After all this wordy pontificating, *Past and Present* (1843) restores one's faith in Carlyle. From the start he was evidently trying to write more concisely, his preaching had a firmer basis in history, and the whole structure of the book showed an effort towards compression. The 'Letter of Instructions' was extracted from a short Latin document written in the twelfth century, and recently published by the Camden Society, *Chronica Jocelini de Brakelonda* (1840). This described everyday life in the monastery at Bury St Edmund's, recorded the procedure for electing a new Abbot, and told how the successful candidate, Samson, did his job. Here Carlyle found everything that he failed to find in his own period: universal belief, a society whose nexus was not cash but

community feeling, an election that actually chose the best man to
govern, and a benevolent dictatorship quite free from the corruption and inefficiency of Parliamentary democracy. In his style of
leadership, no less than in his name, Samson was every inch a
'strong man'. Thus *Chronica* epitomized the admirable *Past*. The
lamentable *Present* was similarly compressed, by some very
effective devices. One was to typify the whole 'condition of
England' by a sensational news item. Three children had been
murdered by their parents, 'to defraud a "burial-society" of some
£3 8s. due on the death of each child.' Carlyle enhanced the
symbolism by reference to Dante's *Inferno*, where Ugolino is
driven by hunger to eat his own children. Another device was to
summarize the current situation by a classical myth. Like Midas,
industrial England had a magical power of making money, but was
still an ass, and could only produce starvation. Like Oedipus
confronted by the Sphinx, the Victorians were set a riddle that
would be the death of them if they failed to solve it. A third device
was to translate *Present* into a kind of morality-play, with a cast of
representative characters, like Plugson of Undershot, the unscrupulous industrialist, Pandarus Dogdraught, the corrupt politician,
and the Hon. Alcides Dolittle, the Conservative MP. The allegory
developed an almost surrealist quality, when the Spinning Der-
vishes joined the cast, bizarre emblems of pointless activity in
Parliament, with a punning allusion to over-production in the
cotton industry. Commercial society finally became a nightmare,
'where the men go about as if by galvanism, with meaningless
glaring eyes, and have no soul, but only a beaver-faculty and a
stomach!'

We enjoy sermons less than the Victorians did, but even now
the tirades of *Past and Present* can stir up some vicarious
indignation, and its positive call to the achievement of the
'impossible' is still relevant, and effective as a booster of morale.
Its fragments of satirical fiction (which clearly inspired Arnold's
Friendship's Garland) are often very funny. The aristocrat who
wants to be paid even more through the Corn Laws for doing
nothing, is pictured as a lunatic, trying to jump through a plate-
glass window on to some iron railings, and so incur the fate of his
fellows in France:

Gracious Heaven, my brother, this that thou seest with those sick eyes is
no firm Eldorado, and Corn-Law Paradise of Donothings, but a dream of

thy own fevered brain. It is a glass-window, I tell thee, so many stories
from the street; where are iron spikes and the law of gravitation!

Carlyle's first big attempt to write history through the biography of a great man was an edition of *Oliver Cromwell's Letters
and Speeches, with Elucidations* (1845). The form suggested an
academic approach, but the work began with an attack on the
academic historian, in the character of 'Dryasdust'. *Cromwell* was
evidently meant as another epic poem, a 'Cromwelliad', distinguished from conventional history by its topical relevance. In
the forest of human life, the present grew from the past, most of
which had merely rotted down into mould, and

the grand difference between a Dryasdust and a sacred Poet, is very much
even this: To distinguish well what does still reach to the surface, and is
alive and frondent for us; and what reaches no longer to the surface, but
moulders safe underground, never to send forth leaves or fruit for
mankind any more . . .

Cromwell was still fruitful for mankind because he lived in a
'practical world based on Belief in God', because he was a 'strong
man', not a 'two-legged Rhetorical Phantasm', and because his
rigid morality was a salutary contrast to the modern 'indiscriminate mashing-up of Good and Evil into one universal patent-
treacle, and most unmedical electuary, of Rousseau Sentimentalism, universal Pardon and Benevolence, with dinner and drink and
one cheer more.' Cromwell was just what Victorian England
needed, in his severity with Levellers and 'a whole submarine
world of Calvinistic Sansculottism, Five-point Charter and the
Rights of Man', his contempt for 'rosewater surgery', his impatience with dilatory Parliaments, and his plan for a new House of
Lords, a 'Peerage of Fact' to replace the 'Peerage of Descent'. Best
of all, he never spoke 'distracted jargon' about abolishing capital
punishment.

Carlyle's sympathy with Cromwell was apparently increased by
the Protector's 'hypochondriac maladies', corresponding with his
own dyspepsia and insomnia: 'Samuel Johnson too had hypochon-
drias; all great souls are apt to have . . .'. So Carlyle worked hard to
vindicate every aspect of Cromwell's character and conduct, as
though raising a solitary protest against the 'stupidity' of historians
and the public. But he was not actually 'in a minority of one'.
Macaulay had written approvingly of Cromwell in 1828, calling

him 'emphatically a man', and stressing his unique talent for
sovereignty. Carlyle's line was unusual only in his anxiety to prove
Cromwell impeccable, not merely at some points, but at all. The
execution of Charles I, which Macaulay thought Cromwell's 'most
blameable act', was here a 'brave' experiment designed to free
humanity from fear of a 'Phantom-dynasty'. When he lost his
temper with the Rump Parliament, it was an 'inspiration'. When
he massacred the whole garrison of Tredah—'Here is a man whose
word represents a thing!' When he burnt a hundred men alive in a
church, and then called it 'a righteous judgment of God upon
these barbarous wretches', the historian clearly agreed with him.
And if the reader dared to disagree, he was simply excommunicated:

PROCUL PROFANI! The man is without a soul that looks into this Great
Soul of a man, radiant with the splendours of very Heaven, and sees
nothing there but the shadow of his own mean darkness. Ape of the Dead
Sea, peering asquint into the Holy of Holies, let us have done with *thy*
commentaries! Thou canst not fathom it.

Cromwell was an impressive piece of research, and its 'Elucidations' were far from dull; but the bad-tempered, hectoring tone,
which implies that the author stands alone in a world of knaves and
fools, makes the book hard to enjoy. What humour it contains is
sour, or silly, like the perorating pun:

The genius of England no longer soars Sunward, world-defiant, like an
Eagle through the storms . . . much liker an Ostrich intent on provender
and a whole skin mainly, [it] stands with its *Other* extremity Sunward . . .
No ostrich, intent on gross terren provender, and sticking its head into
Fallacies, but will be awakened one day,—in a terrible *à-posteriori* manner,
if not otherwise!

When Carlyle returned from history to more direct social
criticism, he did so in a character that finally alienated J. S. Mill
and all liberal friends, that of the 'moral desperado', as Arnold
aptly defined it.

His first performance in this role was 'An Occasional Discourse
on the Nigger Question' (1849). Campaigns by Evangelical philanthropists and missionary societies had led in 1833 to the abolition
of slavery in the British Empire. Among the results in the West
Indies was that freed negroes refused to work on the plantations
except for high wages. The planters' profits fell, the price of sugar

rose, and the English public faced the peril of having to drink its coffee unsweetened. Carlyle's answer to the problem was an imaginary speech by an anonymous intruder into a conference of philanthropists, urging them

to see well that our grand proposed Association of Associations, the UNIVERSAL ABOLITION-OF-PAIN ASSOCIATION, which is meant to be the consummate golden flower and summary of modern Philanthropisms all in one, do *not* issue as a universal 'Sluggard-and-Scoundrel Protection Society'.

The negro was presented as 'an idle Black gentleman, with his rum-bottle in his hand . . . no breeches on his body, pumpkin at discretion, and the fruitfulest region of the earth going back to jungle around him.' And the answer was that 'poor Quashee' should be forced back to work, 'with beneficent whip' if necessary, 'since other methods avail not'. For 'Niggers' like Chartists were really making a 'tacit prayer': 'Compel me!' Apart from some touches of humour, this attack on 'rose-pink Sentimentalism' was only redeemed from barbarity by two valid points in its argument: that English labourers who had no employer in charge of them might be worse off than slaves, and that the worst slavery of all was 'The slavery of Wisdom to Folly', as in a pure democracy.

Though equally unbalanced in their criticisms, *Latter-Day Pamphlets* (1850) were not even dramatic monologues. Here, in his own person, Carlyle did what his title implied: gave notice of an imminent Judgement on a foolish and sinful world. His list of sins and follies included Parliamentary government and democracy, in the light of the European revolutions and Chartist risings of 1848; the 'universal syllabub of philanthropic twaddle' about prison-reform; 'Stump-Oratory' and the 'vocal education' given by 'logic-shops' and 'nonsense-verse establishments' at Eton, Oxford, and Edinburgh; Jesuitism, emblematic of a 'Universe of Cant', happily suppressed by the French Revolution but resurgent in the re-establishment (1850) of the Catholic hierarchy in England; and finally 'Phallus-Worship, whose liturgy is in the Circulating Libraries'. In 'The Present Time' Carlyle proposed the conscription of paupers into an industrial army, where indolence would be punished, first by flogging, and ultimately by hanging. 'Model Prisons' deplored the abolition of the 'treadwheel', and ridiculed the idea of 'pity for the scoundrel-species'. It assumed

that the primitive instinct of revenge was the proper basis for a
penal code, and praised the old German system of plunging
criminals into 'the deepest convenient Peatbog', and driving an
oaken frame down over them. The drop of common sense in this
Pamphlet's ocean of savagery was to question the logic of making
convicts more comfortable in prison, while those struggling to be
useful members of society were left in horrible slums. To concentrate on being kind to the hopeless cases was 'a shockingly
unfruitful investment for your capital of Benevolence.' On the
whole, though, the views expressed in this book seem almost
insanely unenlightened, nor can it be defended as a Juvenalian
satire, to be read for its vivid expressions rather than for its
realism. True, there are some graphic images, like the picture of
post-revolutionary Europe as a house about to collapse, but still
kept up by 'rusty nails, wormeaten dovetailings, and secret
coherency of old carpentry.' Carlyle was not, however, composing
in a literary genre that invited vivid hyperbole, nor was there much
artistry in the rambling, repetitive style. A general decline in
creativity was most obvious in the peroration, which merely
modernized two famous passages in Lucretius and Horace:
'Mount into your railways; whirl from place to place, at the rate of
fifty, or if you like of five hundred miles an hour: you cannot
escape from that inexorable all-embracing ocean-moan of ennui.'

Certainly, *Latter-Day Pamphlets* offered no such escape; but
the *Life of John Sterling* (1851) was refreshingly different. Almost
genial in tone, it showed traces of impartiality, even of an inkling
that Carlyle might not always know best. Written as a tribute of
affection to his 'brilliant, beautiful and cheerful' friend, it was
meant to correct the impression given by J. C. Hare's memoir
(1848) that Sterling was no more than a lapsed clergyman. Sterling
had helped Carlyle in his struggle for recognition by an enthusiastic review of 1839, and in a novel, *Arthur Coningsby* (1833), had
set him a useful precedent for a sensational treatment of the
French Revolution. Carlyle must also have benefited from a clash
of views with Sterling over a long period. He now presented him as
a contemporary 'hero', a 'victorious *believer*' who, against formidable obstacles, especially chronic disease, was also a 'victorious
doer'. There was indeed something heroic about his persistent
attempts to write poetry, against every kind of discouragement,
particularly from Carlyle himself, who found him interesting less

as a poet than as 'an expressive emblem of his time'. He was emblematic chiefly in having succumbed to the fashion for democracy, and the religious influence of Coleridge. Instead of retreating into an obsolete orthodoxy, he should have worked his way forwards into a more valid, if less specific, faith. So the 'crowning error' of his life was to become (though only for eight months) a curate; but he redeemed it by resolutely shaking off the 'shadows of the surplice', until he had 'got the inky tints of that Coleridgean adventure completely bleached from his mind'.

Sterling seems to have brought out the best side of Carlyle, just as Cromwell brought out the worst. Sterling did not live to see *Cromwell* published, but shortly before his death the two friends had an argument about Cromwell in which, according to Carlyle, Sterling was 'trenchant, positive, and in some essential points wrong'. They also disagreed about slavery. When first trying to run a plantation in the West Indies, Sterling had thought the slaves 'cunning, deceitful and idle', and 'decidedly unfit for freedom'; but during a hurricane he found them behaving 'like so many Heroes of Antiquity', and he later formed 'extensive schemes' for 'Anti-Slavery Philanthropy'. When Carlyle suggested that it was 'really better' for a Negro to have a lifelong master than to be employed 'from day to day', Sterling laughed and said: 'I would have the Negroes themselves consulted as to that!' He would clearly have disapproved of 'The Nigger Question'. Perhaps Carlyle dimly recognized personality faults of his own, when he criticized Sterling for lack of genial humour, and of real feeling for music; but whatever the psychological explanation may be, the thought of his friend had a good effect on Carlyle, especially in mitigating his dogmatism. He now felt he had been rather too harsh in his judgements of Sterling's poems, and even admitted that Sterling might have been right, after all, to go on trying to be a poet. He also came near to admitting his own capacity for unconscious self-deception, when he observed that Sterling 'usually substituted for the primary determining motive and set of motives, some ultimate ostensible one', and added: 'as is the way, in a degree, with all men!'

The *Life* is full of interesting sidelights on the history of the period. It describes, for instance, the ill-fated Spanish expedition in which the young Tennyson and Arthur Hallam were peripherally involved, and contains a very funny account of Coleridge's conversation: 'I have heard Coleridge talk, with eager musical energy, two stricken hours, his face radiant and moist, and communicate no meaning whatsoever to any individual of his hearers . . .'. The wit of this passage, as of the whole work, results from an extremely precise use of words, quite unlike the indiscriminate verbiage of the *Pamphlets*. But the central achievement of the biography was to convey realistically the endearing but faintly ludicrous charm of Sterling's character. There is something touching as well as absurd in his deathbed promise to his unorthodox friend: 'Heaven bless you! If I can lend a hand when THERE, that will not be wanting.'

The History of Frederick the Great (1858–65) was hell to write and is not, except in patches, much fun to read. For pleasure, one might do better to try Macaulay's sardonic essay of 1842 on the same curious character, than struggle through Carlyle's six volumes. To him it seemed a kind of endurance test. 'It is a task', he told Emerson,

that generally seems to me not worth doing, and that yet must be done. No job approaching it in ugliness was ever cut out for me; nor had I any motive to go on except the sad negative one, 'Shall we be beaten in our old days?'

It took him twelve years to write, in an airless, windowless, allegedly sound-proof attic, and its constant cry of 'Courage, reader!' must have been really addressed to the author. Indeed, the whole work is like a soliloquy, or like Coleridge's conversation. Had he cared about his readers' reactions, he would hardly have kept reminding them what a 'weary' business it all was, and inviting them to skip. Nor would he have celebrated the end of the Seven Years' War with the exclamation: 'Oh, readers, do not at least you and I thank God to have done with it!'

Why, one may ask, did he ever choose a sitter at first sight even wartier than Cromwell? Though more ruthless and inhumane, Frederick had no religious or moral motives to justify his behaviour. His career of destruction began with a simple wish for self-aggrandisement. That he strangely combined the crudest militarism with a passion for music and literature, might well interest a psychologist; yet Carlyle was apparently attracted not by the contradictions in Frederick's character, but by the character itself. Was it doubt of his own virility that made him identify with Frederick, as this mention of *castrati* suggests?

He that will prefer Dilettantism in this world for his outfit, shall have it; but all the gods will depart from him; and manful veracity, earnestness of purpose, devout depth of soul, shall no more be his. He can if he like make himself a soprano, and sing for hire;—and probably that is the real goal for him.

Ostensibly, however, Frederick was Carlyle's hero because his style of government was what England needed, and because, in 'Universal History', he was the last real king before the liquidation of sham kings started. Frederick also had a close relationship with Voltaire, on whom Carlyle had written a sympathetic but censorious article in 1829; and here the earnest, positive, silent man of action could be neatly opposed to the frivolous negative master of 'Stump-Oratory'. Voltaire, the typical democrat, bowed to public opinion: Frederick, the archetypal king, was quite indifferent to it. Voltaire was 'feminine' in his spitefulness and morbid sensitivity, Frederick invariably 'manful' (hence the angry rejection of rumours that he was homosexual). Thus the two figures embodied the two great political trends of their period, leaving no room for doubt which was superior. The scheme made it necessary to idealize, not only Frederick himself but even his education. His almost insanely brutal and philistine father, Friedrich Wilhelm, became a 'veracious' hero, the indispensable 'drill-sergeant' of his country. His judicial murder of Frederick's friend Katte was 'like the doings of the gods, which are cruel, but not that alone'. By such outrageous treatment the father taught his son, not hypocrisy, but merely the 'the art of wearing ... a polite cloak-of-darkness.'

In everything he did, Frederick was tirelessly whitewashed. His initial aggression against Silesia was a case of 'crossing the Rubicon as it were in his sleep', like a railway-passenger; and from then on he was presented as more sinned against than sinning, a kindly, sensitive soul who somehow got into trouble and had to fight his way out of it. Carlyle did see the funny side of Whitefield's hailing Frederick as an 'authentic new Champion of Christendom', but quite ignored the irony of Frederick's *Anti-Macchiavell*, which Macaulay had called 'an edifying homily against rapacity, perfidy, arbitrary government, unjust war, in short, against almost everything for which the author is now remembered among men.' The breaking of Frederick's flute by his father might well have been used to symbolize the destruction of

the boy's most valuable potential. But Frederick's musical activities were usually treated as a joke: 'You can forget ... the
'Literature' of this young Majesty, as you would a staccato on the
flute by him!' Apparently his delightful flute concerto was a poorer
claim to fame than the devastation of Europe by twenty-three
years of war.

Emerson called *Frederick* 'the wittiest book in the world'. If
Polonius was right about the soul of wit, the praise seems
exaggerated. Sprawling and disproportionate in structure, the
work is no more than occasionally epigrammatic in style; but it
certainly sustains throughout its vast length great vitality of
expression. Its narrative, based on massive research, often produces an almost stereoscopic effect by the integration of evidence
from a variety of sources. For students of military history, there
are blow-by-blow accounts of all Frederick's campaigns. For non-
specialists, there are exciting stories of individual battles, as about
the 'mousetrap' strategy that led up to the battle of Hohenfried-
berg. Certain pictures stick in one's memory: the drunk Irish
deserter from the Austrian army, whose warning of a night-attack
cannot be understood till he is sobered up with tea; the three
hundred and sixty-four 'Pairs of Breeches' that Frederick finds
'hanging melancholy, in a widowed manner', in the Brühl Palace at
Dresden; the Prussians advancing under fire in perfect formation,
though sunk to the thighs in mud; the Russian Cossacks trapped at
the battle of Zorndorf who, though being 'sabred down like dead
oxen', break open brandy-flasks and meet death 'roaring drunk'.
Frederick himself emerges as a credible, if hardly likeable, person,
who gradually extorts admiration for his ability to turn defeat into
triumph. At the end he develops an almost tragic dimension,
arousing pity and fear by his 'great interior lake of sorrow', and his
'stern and lonely' death, after sitting for hours on a soldier's knee,
the only posture that allowed him to breathe. And even his
unspeakable father shows a flash of charm just before he dies.
Listening to his favourite hymn, he was struck by the words,
'Naked I came into the world, and naked shall I go.' 'No, not quite
naked,' he said. 'I shall have my uniform on.'

Carlyle was over seventy when he finished *Frederick*. As a
demonstration of will-power, it was a marvellous achievement.
And perhaps the most memorable part of the whole work is its
celebration of stoicism in the face of huge discouragements, old

age, and imminent death. If Carlyle's last great Hero is unacceptable as a person or a political ideal, he remains, like Satan, a splendid type of man's 'unconquerable will'.

There was little new or unpredictable in the other works published in Carlyle's lifetime, though some people who read his Inaugural Address at Edinburgh (1866) may have been surprised to learn, from such a source, that 'Silence withal is the eternal duty of a man.' 'Shooting Niagara: and After' (1867) predicted disastrous consequences from that year's Reform Act, and advised the aristocracy to withdraw from politics, turn their estates into miniature Utopias, and start drilling private armies to resist the forces of anarchy. *The Early Kings of Norway* (1875) returned nostalgically to the origins of 'real' government, i.e. to the primitive method of dealing with anarchy: '*conquest*, hard fighting, followed by wise guidance of the conquered'. Without 'something similar (little as men expect such now) no Cosmos of human society ever was got into existence, nor can ever again be.' Though his publications after 1865 merely repeated old ideas, Carlyle had already broken completely fresh ground in a work not originally meant for publication. His *Reminiscences*, edited and published after his death by his friend and future biographer, J. A. Froude (1881), revealed a new style, relaxed and unrhetorical, and a new personality, human, affectionate, depressive, and bitterly self-reproachful. Some of the material had been used before in conversation, when he entertained visitors with impromptu accounts of his experiences, and the first section, 'James Carlyle', had been written immediately after his father's death in 1832: 'I purpose now, while the impression is more pure and clear within me, to mark down the main things I can recollect of my Father ...'. The second, 'Jane Welsh Carlyle', was written while Carlyle was trying to cope with the shock of her sudden death in 1866, just before his return from Edinburgh. He then wrote about two important friends of his youth, Edward Irving, the Scottish minister who, by founding a fashionable sect in London, did something even worse than Sterling's 'clerical aberration', and Francis Jeffrey who, as editor of the *Edinburgh Review*, had given Carlyle his first real opening as an author. Among shorter sketches of other famous contemporaries, he portrayed Wordsworth as 'a rather dull, hard-tempered, unproductive and almost wearisome kind of man', and compared Southey to 'one of those huge sandstone grinding-cylinders ... turning with inconceivable velocity', until it finally disintegrated into 'a cartload of quiet sand'.

Like the letters and journals, the *Reminiscences* are indispensable for an understanding of Carlyle's background, character, and mind. They show the important influence of his 'brave, dear, and ever-honoured Peasant Father', whose stern and intimidating manner towards his children may partly explain Carlyle's willingness to think the best of Friedrich Wilhelm, and whose head was 'strikingly like that of the Poet Goethe', the man Carlyle regarded as his spiritual father, his 'evangelist'. But the most moving part of the book is 'Jane Welsh Carlyle'. It vividly describes her courage and gaiety, his agony at her loss, and his remorse at having sacrificed her, as well as himself, for all those years, to a self-imposed task that had 'now become *coprolite* to me, insignificant as the dung of a thousand centuries ago'. Though quite unstructured, the *Reminscences* might almost be said to recreate the past more powerfully than any of his histories. They also bring out a visual element in his imagination, which is concealed elsewhere by his concern with verbal rhetoric. Here he repeats a story told to his father about an 'Iron village':

On the platform of one of the furnaces, a solitary man ... was industriously minding his own business, now throwing-in new fuel and ore, now poking the white-hot molten mass that was already in; a poor old maniac woman silently joined him and looked, whom also he was used to, and did not mind; but, after a little, his back being turned towards the furnace mouth, he heard a strange thump or cracking puff; and turning suddenly the poor old maniac woman was not there; and, on advancing to the furnace-edge, he saw the figure of her, red-hot, semi-transparent, floating as ashes on the fearful element for some moments! This had printed itself on my Father's brain ... nor will it ever leave my brain either.

Any retrospect of Carlyle's literary career raises the question: what went wrong with his writing after *Past and Present*? Why, after such a brilliant start, did he deteriorate so rapidly into a bore, endlessly repeating the same prejudices, in a style that had gone stale? Had 'incessant scribbling' indeed brought 'death to thought'? Of many possible explanations, one may be found in his use of personae. *Past and Present* contains a fascinating passage about the problems of original composition:

For in fine, as Poet Dryden says, you do walk hand in hand with sheer Madness, all the way,—who is by no means pleasant company! You look fixedly into Madness, and *her* undiscovered, boundless, bottomless Night-empire; that you may extort new Wisdom out of it, as an Eurydice from Tartarus. The higher the Wisdom, the closer was its neighbourhood and kindred with mere Insanity; literally so;—and thou wilt, with a speechless feeling, observe how highest Wisdom, struggling up into this world, has oftentimes carried such tinctures and adhesions of Insanity still cleaving to it hither!

The originality of *Sartor*, written in the isolation of a farmhouse at Craigenputtoch, must have seemed to him all the more like madness, because Jeffrey had assured him that his eccentricity, his 'German mysticism', his exaggeration, and his 'earnestness' would preclude any success for him as an author. But he expressed these 'mad' qualities, and released his creativity, through the persona of Teufelsdröckh, whose ludicrous aspects were a calculated concession to Jeffrey's point of view. Here the 'Editor' kept his distance from the Professor, just as he had done with Professor Sauerteig in 'On Biography' (1832). Sauerteig performed the same function in 'Chartism', and even in 'The Nigger Question' the outrageous defence of slavery was voiced by an unknown speaker, and reported by Dr Phelim M'Quirk, whose name implied emotional eccentricity. But the Prime Minister in the *Pamphlets* who proposed to flog and shoot paupers was commended rather than disowned by the author, and the rest of the book, apart from the odd quotation from such characters as 'Crabbe' and Sauerteig, was written in Carlyle's own person. Of course he grew more opinionated with age, but he never actually went 'mad'. He did, however, start presenting his 'Wisdom' with more and more 'tinctures and adhesions of Insanity still cleaving to it'. Privately, he could still see two sides of a question, as when he wrote in his journal (1870), 'Anarchies, too, have their uses'. In public, it was more fun, and more exciting for the reader, to express only one side, in a wildly exaggerated form. So long as this was done through a sharply differentiated persona, all was well; but as the habit became addictive, the difference disappeared and eventually, like Stevenson's Mr Hyde, the persona took over.

11. Newman

FOR Newman, 'National Literature' was like a stinking 'horde of unconverted Germans' bathing in a stream.[1] It represented

the untutored movements of the reason, imagination, passions, and affections of the natural man, the leapings and the friskings, the plungings and the snortings, the sportings and the buffoonings, the clumsy play and the aimless toil, of the noble, lawless savage of God's intellectual creation.

Fortunately, though, he was not above having a bathe himself. He contributed largely to the period's literature, not only in sermons, tracts, and works of theology, but also in poems, novels, and autobiography. And though his work appeals most to the converted, it has much to offer the natural man, especially in polemical or satirical passages. Agnostics may often feel that he supports quite irrational beliefs by pseudo-rational arguments, and squanders a brilliant mind on theological details; but even they must find him interesting as a psychologist, for instance when he analyses mental processes and unconscious assumptions.

The first thing he published (jointly with an undergraduate friend) was a narrative poem, *St. Bartholomew's Eve* (1821), about a wicked monk whose 'gentler mind' had been corrupted by the 'zeal misguided' and 'mistaken worship' of Roman Catholicism. More characteristic of the future Cardinal was a passage associating the 'stillness' of night with the music of angels. He would always believe in angels, and love music and stillness: a footnote to the poem stated, contradicting Paley, that 'the happiness of oysters . . . consists in the silence they enjoy.' Music and stillness both figured in one of the first great moments of his life. Because of

---

[1] John Henry Newman, 1801–90, was born in London. His father was a banker, and his mother came from a Huguenot family. After a private school at Ealing he went to Trinity College, Oxford and became a fellow of Oriel, where he met Keble, Pusey, and R. H. Froude. From 1828 he was vicar of St Mary's, and in 1833 started *Tracts for the Times*. When *Tract* 90 was condemned, he retired to Littlemore, resigned his living, and set up the so-called 'Littlemore Monastery'. Converted to Roman Catholicism, 1845, he was ordained in Rome, and established the Birmingham Oratory, 1847, where, apart from four years in Ireland as Rector of the Catholic University in Dublin, 1854–8, he spent the rest of his life. He was made a cardinal, 1879.

overwork, he did badly in Schools at Oxford; but then he won a Fellowship to Oriel College. He was playing the violin when he heard the exciting news. 'Very well,' he said calmly, and went on playing.

As a young don, he published an article (1829) on Aristotle's *Poetics*. This foreshadowed his later view of education, in condemning the academic tendency to accumulate 'minute facts', and stressing 'the uses of knowledge in forming the intellectual and moral character'. He found Aristotle's conception of poetry too 'cold and formal' in its stress on the rational and 'artificial' elements in drama, and denied that Greek tragedy was, or should have been, remarkable for its plot-construction, which was merely 'a vehicle of more poetical matter'. Having put Aristotle right on this point, he then gave his own theory of poetry, as 'ultimately founded on correct moral perception', and inseparable from religion. Sceptics like Hume and Gibbon had 'radically unpoetical minds'. 'Revealed religion' and the 'virtues peculiarly Christian' were 'especially poetical'. 'With Christians', indeed, 'a poetical view of things is a duty—we are bid to colour all things with hues of faith, to see a divine meaning in every event, and a superhuman tendency.' But the 'poetical mind' had to look inwards as well as outwards, since 'poetry is the utterance of the inward emotions of a right moral feeling', and 'Nothing is more difficult than to analyse the feelings of our own minds.' In the sermons that Newman had already started preaching this difficulty was further emphasized.

The University Sermons, preached from 1826 onwards and published in 1843, were subtitled: *Chiefly on the Theory of Religious Belief*. While denying that Christians were irrational, Newman claimed that Christianity had been a pioneer of modern science, in first teaching the 'philosophical temper', that 'singleminded, modest, cautious, and generous spirit, which was, after a long time, found so necessary for success in the prosecution of philosophical researches.' But a far more convincing line of argument was summed up in 'Explicit and Implicit Reason' (1840). Faith was indeed satisfied with less evidence than 'Reason' would require, because Faith was itself a form of reasoning, though one so subtle, rapid, and personal as to be almost beyond analysis. The term 'Reason' had been monopolized by attempts to explain this mysterious process, i.e. by 'Explicit Reason'. 'Implicit Reason', however, came first, and bore the same relation to the 'Explicit' process as poetry to literary criticism. As a basic human instinct, it was generally reliable: 'Men do not mistake when their interest is concerned . . . They may argue badly, but they reason well.'

Here Newman marked a significant stage in the history of ideas, between Romantic epistemology, with its reliance on imagination, and modern theories of the unconscious. His literary achievement lay in the clarity with which he presented his rather subtle and novel argument, in the emotional appeal of his style, and in his suggestive imagery. Donne had glanced at the difficulty of climbing the hill of Truth ('and hee that will | Reach her, about must, and about must goe'). Newman, in a passage that may well have inspired Hopkins's 'O the mind, mind has mountains', brilliantly exploited the image to describe the actual thinking process:

The mind ranges to and fro, and spreads out, and advances forward with a quickness which has become a proverb, and a subtlety and versatility which baffle investigation. It passes on from point to point, gaining one by some indication; another on a probability; then availing itself of an association; then falling back on some received law; next seizing on testimony; then committing itself to some popular impression, or some inward instinct, or some obscure memory; and thus it makes progress not unlike a clamberer on a steep cliff, who, by quick eye, prompt hand, and firm foot, ascends how he knows not himself, by personal endowments and by practice, rather then by rule, leaving no track behind him, and unable to teach another.

In 1828 Newman became Vicar of St Mary's Church, and in that capacity preached the *Parochial Sermons* (1834–42). Their special impact was due partly to his unworldly character and presence, partly to his style of delivery, in which short passages of rapid speech were punctuated by long silences. To a future Professor of Poetry, J. C. Shairp, they sounded like 'high poems', like 'a fine strain of unearthly music', heard in 'the stillness of that high Gothic building'. This musical quality can be felt even in the printed text, but the modern reader may be more struck by the paradox that an intellectual of that period should be so literal-minded in his creed. Cremation was an 'irreverence' in view of 'the resurrection of the body'. Holiness was necessary, because 'a man of carnal and worldly mind' would never feel happy in Heaven — which would be much more like '*a church*' than anything else in this world. And in churchyards the Resurrection would be especially spectacular: 'Here the saints sleep, here they shall rise. A great sight will a Christian country then be, if earth remains what it is; when holy places pour out the worshippers who have for generations kept vigil therein, waiting through the long night for the bright coming of Christ!' But that would not be a happy day for everyone, and Newman protested against the current tendency to ignore 'the dark side of religion', i.e. 'eternal punishment':

it would be a gain to this country, were it vastly more superstitious, more bigoted, more gloomy, more fierce in its religion, than at present it shows itself to be ... better, far better is it, to torture the body all one's days, and to make this life a hell upon earth, than to remain in a brief tranquillity here, till the pit at length opens under us ...

If such doctrine seems archaic, there is still force in his demand for personal integrity, and his warnings against self-deception. 'Self-knowledge', he urged, 'is at the root of all real religious knowledge', and in 'Secret Faults' he wrote perceptively about unconscious motivation. Medieval in his creed, he was quite modern in his psychology.

The 'watchword' of these sermons was 'Deeds, not words and wishes', and since 1833 Newman, Keble, and R. H. Froude had been actively defending the Church, as a divine institution, against such encroachments of secular power as the recent plan to reorganize the Irish dioceses. In the penny pamphlet that launched *Tracts for the Times*, Newman urged his fellow-clergy to 'unlearn that idle habit, which has grown upon us, of owning the state of things to be bad, yet doing nothing to remedy it.' In *Tract* 2 he wrote: 'There is an unexceptionable sense in which a clergyman may, nay, must be *political*', and recommended the now familiar technique of the pressure group. As editor and chief author of the *Tracts*, he effectively publicized the Oxford Movement. In *The Prophetical Office of the Church* (1837) he outlined a 'Via Media' for the Anglican church to follow, between the 'errors' of Romanism (e.g. the claim to infallibility) and of Protestantism (e.g. total reliance on 'Private Judgement'). Finally he argued in *Tract* 90 (1841) that the Thirty-nine Articles, to which every Anglican clergyman had to subscribe, were quite compatible with traditional Catholicism. This caused a national outcry. The *Tract* was condemned by the University, and the Bishop of Oxford persuaded Newman to stop the series. The effect of Newman's propaganda for the Oxford Movement was certainly dramatic at the time; but his earnest attention to what now seem minor details of doctrine and church history make these works unrewarding for the general reader. Even the style, though fluent and lucid, tends to be monotonous. As a party spokesman, he doubtless felt he should avoid the kind of individuality that might have satisfied his own later definition of Literature: 'the personal use or exercise of language'.

The personal element was less subdued in Newman's contributions to *Lyra Apostolica* (1836), a collection of religious poems by anonymous Tractarians. The poem there entitled 'Deeds, not Words' not only expressed his 'watchword' but also suggested the principle of his poetic style:

> Prune thou thy words, the thoughts control
> That o'er thee swell and throng;
> They will condense within thy soul,
> And change to purpose strong.

The impression of strength given by Newman's poems was indeed produced by condensation, surprisingly combined with rhythmical fluency. His private tastes and intuitions, like his love of music and the Classics, and his belief in 'Guardian Angels', also came out clearly, and so did his reactions to the Mediterranean cruise (1832–3) on which many of the poems were written. Above all there was evidence of his mental struggles, as he felt himself gradually impelled towards decisive action. 'The Baptist' (later called 'Pusillanimity') showed his temperamental reluctance to 'dare some forward part', and his best-known poem, 'Lead, Kindly Light' (1833) showed reluctance giving way to blind faith in Implicit Reason, which would lead him to Roman Catholicism. He visited Rome on his cruise, and a poem that told how 'a foe' turned into 'The Good Samaritan', began with the wish: 'Oh that thy creed were sound! | For thou dost soothe the heart, Thou Church of Rome'. When in 1845 his head let him follow his heart, it felt, in the words of the *Apologia*, 'like coming into port after a rough sea'. He had had the same feeling at Gibraltar in 1832, when he wrote 'The Haven':

> Whence is this awe, by stillness spread
> O'er the world-fretted soul?
> Wave rear'd on wave its godless head,
> While my keen bark, by breezes sped,

Dashed fiercely through the ocean bed,
And chafed towards its goal.
But now there reigns so deep a rest,
That I could almost weep ...

In the month that *Tract* 90 was published (February 1841), Newman wrote something of far greater literary interest, *The Tamworth Reading Room*. These letters from 'Catholicus' to *The Times* challenged Sir Robert Peel's claim, when opening the reading room, that scientific education was conducive to morality and religion, and insisted that 'Christianity, and nothing short of it, must be made the element and principle of all education.' Quoting from the letters in *A Grammar of Assent*, nearly thirty years later, Newman observed that they were written 'with a freshness and force which I cannot now command'. Whatever may be thought of their thesis, its presentation was certainly delightful. Coupling the 'Conservative statesman' with the Whig Lord Brougham (who had founded the non-religious University of London) Newman mocked the flowery style of both 'eminent orators'. Peel's clumsy syntax was symbolic of his faulty logic: 'A long and complicated sentence, and no unfitting emblem of the demonstration it promises.' As for Brougham's prescription of 'intellectual occupation' as an anodyne:

He frankly offers us a philosophy of expedients: he shows us how to live by medicine. Digestive pills half an hour before dinner, and a posset at bedtime at the best; and at the worst, dram-drinking and opium,—the very remedy against broken hearts, or remorse of conscience, which is in request among the many, in gin-palaces not intellectual ... Such is this new art of living, offered to the labouring classes,—we will say, for instance, in a severe winter, snow on the ground, glass falling, bread rising, coal at 20d. the cwt., and no work.

But here the grim sarcasm is untypical. Newman's chief tool for demolishing 'the Knowledge School' was urbane humour, as when he ridiculed the idea that only '*virtuous* women' would be admitted to the reading room: 'To whom but to the vicious ought Sir Robert to discourse ... and who else would prove a fitter experiment, and a more glorious triumph, of scientific influences?' More seriously, he refuted the claim that science would stimulate religious faith, by a series of realistic epigrams:

The heart is commonly reached, not through the reason, but through the imagination ... Persons influence us, voices melt us, looks subdue us, deeds inflame us. Many a man will live and die upon a dogma: no man will be a martyr for a conclusion ... Life is not long enough for a religion of inferences; we shall never have done beginning, if we determine to begin with proof ... Life is for action. If we insist on proofs for everything, we shall never come to action: to act you must assume, and that assumption is faith.

That was how he decided to join the Church of Rome. Anxious 'to go by reason, not by feeling', he went through a long process of Explicit Reasoning about the relative claims of the Anglican and Roman churches to be the true successor of the Primitive Church; but in the end he acted on an assumption: 'I believed in a God on a ground of probability, ... I believed in Christianity on a probability, and, ... I believed in Catholicism on a probability ...'. Just after his conversion, feeling 'like one who, in the middle of his days, is beginning life again', he published *An Essay on the Development of Christian Doctrine* (1845). Here he retracted his criticisms of the Roman Church, and presented a theory by which the 'reputed corruptions of Rome' became true developments of primitive Christianity. This fascinating cross between Lamarckian evolution and the psychology of the two Reasons had been outlined in a University Sermon of 1843, and since then, with 'much thought and anxiety', worked out in detail. The sermon began with the hypothesis, no doubt suggested by Newman's own experience, that changes in a man's opinions were stages of organic growth. Such changes represented a continuous, unconscious process in the mind: 'the birth of an idea, the development, in explicit form, of what was already latent within it.' There was a parallel in literature: critics might find that a poet, throughout his writings, 'was possessed, ruled, guided by an unconscious idea.' Newman went on to argue that the Christian Revelation was a partly unconscious 'impression' of God, a piece of 'implicit knowledge' which had gradually grown more explicit as Catholic doctrines developed. On this principle 'corruptions' were merely temporary departures from the main line of development, inevitable in any great living idea, for 'here below to live is to change, and to be perfect is to have changed often.'

In the *Essay* this line of defence was made rather more convincing by being set in a much wider context. Newman's general theory of intellectual evolution was applied, not only to the

'Catholic idea', but to other seminal notions like the Rights of Man
and the Divine Right of Kings. It included an equivalent for
Lamarck's belief in the modifying effect of the environment: 'an
idea not only modifies, but . . . is modified or at least influenced by
the state of things in which it is carried out'. More interestingly, it
anticipated Darwin's 'struggle for existence':

And . . . it cannot develope at all, except by destroying, or modifying and
incorporating with itself, existing modes of thinking and acting . . . it is
the warfare of ideas, striving for the mastery, each of them enterprising,
engrossing, imperious, more or less incompatible with the rest, and
rallying followers or rousing foes according as it acts upon the faith, the
prejudices, or the interests of individuals.

Newman even implied that (as in Natural Selection) this warfare
was essential to the idea's evolution: 'It is elicited by trial, and
struggles into perfection.'

The argument of the sermon was enlivened, if hardly strengthened, by an outburst of enthusiasm for the sounds of music:
'they are echoes from our Home; they are the voice of Angels, or
the Magnificat of Saints, or the living laws of Divine Governance,
or the Divine Attributes.' As a writer 'beginning life again',
Newman evidently felt the impulse to explain his conversion in
more lively and personal terms. This he did in a novel, *Loss and
Gain* (1848). Provoked by a 'wantonly and preposterously fanciful'
story about Oxford converts to Roman Catholicism, he set out to
treat the subject realistically. Despite his denial that the novel was
'founded on fact', its undergraduate hero, Charles Reding, was a
recognizable self-portrait. He plays the violin, lives up to his
surname, and has a favourite sister called Mary. He is led by 'the
pillar of the cloud' to the 'harbour' of Rome, through a slow
mental process that is largely unconscious: 'he could not ultimately
escape his destiny of becoming a Catholic.' Newman's strange
combination of intellectual enterprise with willingness to submit
to authority is explained by Reding's conclusion that Private
Judgement is merely a homing-device to bring one into the
Church: something to be used 'in order ultimately to supersede it;
as a man out of doors uses a lamp in a dark night, and puts it out
when he gets home.' Reding reflects other aspects of Newman's
personality: his love of Oxford, his attraction to celibacy, his
capacity for male friendship. Exiled from Oxford (the *Loss* in the

title), Reding embraces the willows on the bank of the Cherwell. Seeing 'a young clergyman with a very pretty girl on his arm, whom her dress pronounced to be a bride', he feels faint, like 'a man on hearing a call for pork-chops when he was sea-sick.' A kiss on the cheek from his converted friend Willis inspires a mood of wild 'enthusiasm', in which he addresses the Roman Church as 'Mighty Mother', as if he were a self-castrating worshipper of the '*Magna Mater*', Cybele. This 'dark side' of Newman also appears in Reding's reaction to the sight of a man whipping himself beside a cross in the moonlight: '"O happy times," he cried, "when faith was one!"'

But a very different side of Newman was equally conspicuous in the novel. A friend who visited him in Rome while he was writing it often heard him laughing to himself over the manuscript, and the book was certainly full of humorous invention and satirical characterization. Bateman, 'a bore of at least the second magnitude', who like *Tract* 90 interprets the Thirty-nine Articles in a Catholic sense, has a passion for inessentials: 'I wear a scarf or stole, and have taken care that it should be two inches broader than usual.' Vincent, who has 'a great idea of the *via media* being the truth', is an amusing caricature of the non-committal academic. Dr Brownlow preaches a delightful parody of a Latitudinarian sermon. An Evangelical tea-party gravely discusses the sensational news that the late Pope 'died a believer'. And towards the end the comedy develops quite a flavour of Aristophanes. In *The Birds* the founder of Cloud-cuckoo-land is pestered by a series of impostors, anxious to exploit a new market. Reding, on the threshold of a new life, has the same experience. Since his doubts about Anglicanism have got into the newspapers, he finds himself 'in the market' for conversion, so is visited by a succession of religious cranks, in search of a proselyte. One offers him a 'Spiritual Elixir' in the form of a tract:

I have never known but one instance in which it seemed to fail, and that was the case of a wretched old man who held it in his hand a whole day in dead silence, without any apparent effect; but ... on further inquiry we found he could not read. So the tract was slowly administered to him by another person; and before it was finished, I protest to you, Mr. Reding, he fell into a deep and healthy slumber, perspired profusely, and woke up at the end of twelve hours a new creature, perfectly new, bran new, and fit for heaven—whither he went in the course of the week.

Reding finally scares this 'true Protestant' away by brandishing 'an idol' at him—that is, a small crucifix.

Humour and high spirits were no less evident in *Lectures on the Present Position of Catholics in England* (1851), a course of lectures which Newman thought the best-written of all his works. The printed text alone is quite enough to explain the peals of laughter that were heard from the room at Birmingham where Newman was addressing a lay audience of Roman Catholics; but he was making a serious effort to counter the anti-Catholic hysteria provoked by the 'Papal Aggression' of 1850, i.e. the establishment of a Roman Catholic hierarchy in England. Why is it, he asked, that

in this intelligent nation, and in this rational nineteenth century, we Catholics are so despised and hated by our own countrymen, with whom we have lived all our lives, that they are prompt to believe any story, however extravagant, that is told to our disadvantage?

Among many convincing answers, he mentioned the prejudices dating from the Elizabethan age and perpetuated in English literature, the fact that sensational fiction about Catholic wickedness sold better than factual accounts of them, and the unphilosophical assumptions made by Protestant intellectuals. He suggested two ways of improving the situation. The first was to try and dispel the general ignorance about Catholics:

Oblige men to know you; persuade them, importune them, shame them into knowing you. Make it so clear what you are, that they cannot affect not to see you, nor refuse to justify you . . . They will do all in their power not to see you; the nearer you come, they will close their eyelids all the tighter; they will be very angry and frightened, and give the alarm as if you were going to murder them. They will do anything but look at you.

The second was for Catholics to cultivate their minds, and so acquire 'those qualities and that character of mind which we denote by the word "gentleman". . . . Your opponents, my Brothers, are too often emphatically *not* gentlemen'. It was for Catholics to show gentlemanly generosity towards them, since it was 'far the most likely way, in the long run, to persuade and succeed'.

Readers who like Newman

firmly believe that saints in their life-time have before now raised the dead to life, crossed the sea without vessels, multiplied grain and bread, cured incurable diseases, and superseded the operation of the laws of the universe in a multitude of ways

will find the lectures' whole argument conclusive. Others will at least be impressed by his insight into the psychological mechanisms of propaganda and of unconscious assumptions, his identification of the pornographic element in much anti-Catholic fiction, his ridicule of narrow-mindedness, and his call for intellectual 'versatility'. The literary appeal of the work lies in its forceful epigrams and its humorous fantasies. Thus a Russian Count, while denouncing the English constitution, proves that 'Queen Victoria is distinctly pointed out in the Book of Revelations as having the number of the beast!' Still more entertaining is the account of a local myth, the 'Edgbaston Tradition', about the new Oratory building in Hagley Road, where an underground store-room was immediately assumed to be a dungeon. The idea failed to develop; but it might, said Newman, 'have been allotted ... a happier destiny',

and fifty years hence, if some sudden frenzy of the hour roused the anti-Catholic jealousy still lingering in the town, a mob might have swarmed about our innocent dwelling, to rescue certain legs of mutton and pats of butter from imprisonment, and to hold an inquest over a dozen packing-cases, some old hampers, a knife-board, and a range of empty blacking bottles.

Yet through all the fun one may sense what Newman's conversion cost him. There is, for instance, a speech by a father to his convert-son, which begins with the warmest affection and ends: 'I have duties to your brothers and sisters;—never see my face again'. Another passage seems as bitter and as moving as Shylock's famous protest against anti-Semitism:

We are regarded as something unclean, which a man would not touch, if he could help it: and our advances are met as would be those of some hideous baboon, or sloth, or rattlesnake, or toad, which strove to make itself agreeable.

Such attitudes were likely to be resented; but for 'lesser forms of moral obliquity' like resentment Newman had already prescribed a remedy: 'mental cultivation'. And he had just been given a chance of dispensing that prescription, not in England as he wished, but at least in Ireland. Asked to set up a Catholic university in Dublin, and become its Rector, Newman gladly took on the job; but he was frustrated by lack of co-operation from the Irish and from his clerical colleagues. He resigned the Rectorship in 1858, and his university survived only until 1882. Still, his failure to achieve what he later called 'an impossibility' had one great compensation. The attempt led him to write what he considered one of his 'two most perfect works, artistically'. This was *Discourses on the Scope and Nature of University Education* (1852), which formed the nucleus of *The Idea of a University Defined and Illustrated* (1873). In the *Discourses*, which included five lectures delivered in Dublin, Newman said that the function of a university was to impart 'culture' by teaching, 'at least implicitly', 'all branches of know-ledge'. 'Culture' was 'a good in itself', and also 'of great secular utility, as constituting the best and highest formation of the intellect for social and political life'. The 'instrument and result' of such culture was 'Liberal Knowledge', and in some ways culture resembled Christianity; but because of that very resemblance, culture was sometimes Christianity's 'insidious and dangerous foe'. It was therefore essential for a university to teach Catholic theology, as a branch of 'Universal Knowledge', and to come under the 'direct and active jurisdiction of the Church'. Theology, as 'the Science of God, or the truths we know about God put into system', was not only a segment of the 'circle of universal science': it was virtually the centre of that circle, since all other sciences were affected by it. 'In a word, Religious Truth is not only a portion, but a condition of general knowledge.'

The assumption that theology is a science may be felt to invalidate Newman's whole idea of a university—especially when it appears that 'Religious Truth' may include a statement like this: 'in the science of history, the preservation of our race in Noah's ark is an historical fact, which history never could arrive at without Revelation.' But the soundness of his general argument against over-specialization is quite unaffected by his religious bias. He defines most persuasively the 'philosophical habit' of mind that should be the end of university teaching, and the connection between 'culture' and the intellectual character of a 'gentleman'. And if he sometimes slightly exaggerates the personal and social utility of non-vocational education, he is most realistic in his comments on the learning-process, his warning against 'undigested knowledge', and his satire on those 'who have over-stimulated the Memory'.

The style of the *Discourses* has been rather over-praised. It may have achieved his avowed aim in all his writings, 'to express clearly and exactly my meaning', but much of it was disappointingly formal, perhaps in deference to the academic context. Even the more colourful passages were ponderous in their dignity: 'The most insignificant or unsightly insect is from Him ... the restless ever-spreading vegetation which creeps like a garment over the whole earth, the lofty cedar, the umbrageous banana ...'. The theory, however, of style was well handled in 'Literature' (1858), the best of the pieces added to the *Discourses* to make up *The Idea*:

> ... style is a thinking out into language ... A great author ... is one who has something to say and knows how to say it ... He is master of the two-fold Logos, the thought and the word, distinct, but inseparable from each other. He may, if so be, elaborate his compositions, or he may pour out his improvisations, but in either case he has but one aim ... That aim is to give forth what he has within him ... Whatever be his subject, high or low, he treats it suitably and for its own sake.

This lecture also contributes to literary history an account of how 'a great classic' exerts 'a tyranny' over later writers, until he produces 'a re-action; and thus other authors and other schools arise'. As for English literature, though Protestant, and like all literature 'prone to disorder and excess, to error and to sin', it has 'very considerable alleviations': 'it is neither atheistical nor immoral'.

A striking example of human error and sin had been the state of the army in the Crimea. In a series of letters to the *Catholic Herald* entitled 'Who's to Blame?' (1855) Newman had gently ridiculed the 'independent, self-governing, self-reliant Englishman':

> wherever we go all over the earth, it is the solitary Briton, the London agent, or the *Milordos*, who is walking restlessly about, abusing the natives, and raising a colossus, or setting the Thames on fire, in the East or the West. He is on the top of the Andes, or in a diving-bell in the Pacific, or taking notes at Timbuctoo, or grubbing at the Pyramids, or scouring over the Pampas, or acting as prime minister to the king of Dahomey, or smoking the pipe of friendship with the Red Indians, or hutting at the Pole.

But in politics this admirable character had drawbacks. He had

created a democracy incapable of decisive action: 'You canot eat
your cake and have it; you cannot be at once a self-governing
nation and have a strong government.' So, Who's to Blame?—'the
ignorant, intemperate public, who clamour for an unwise war' and
then 'proceed to beat their zealous servants in the midst of the
fight for not doing impossibilities.'

Thus polemic journalism brought back life to Newman's style,
and it was probably a wish to controvert Kingsley's *Hypatia* (1853)
that made him return to imaginative fiction and complete *Callista*
(1856). Kingsley's novel about a Greek philosopher in fifth-
century Alexandria had been a veiled attack on Tractarians and
Roman Catholics. In a sermon published in 1843, Newman had
called monks and nuns 'Christians after the very pattern given us
in Scripture'. By way of comment, Kingsley's noble heroine was
torn to pieces by a mob of monks. Newman's novel contained
scenes of equal horror, in which first a Tertullianist and then a
Christian cook are torn to pieces by a mob of pagans. As if to
confirm that the early Christians had no monopoly of atrocities, it
ended with a detailed account of the torture by which Callista
became a Christian martyr and saint. As her name (most beautiful)
implied, Callista represented, like Hypatia, the finest aspect of
Greek culture, and the novel traced, with psychological realism,
the slow process of her conversion, and that of her unsuccessful
suitor, Agellius. But it had a wider historical aim, to 'imagine and
express the feelings and mutual relations of Christians and
heathens' in the third century. In attempting this reconstruction,
Newman was conscientious enough to point out one minor
anachronism, and especially convincing in his account of the
administrative difficulties that Christians created for the Roman
authorities. But the novel suffered from an excessive concern with
cruelty and mob-violence, not adequately explained either by
Kingsley's example or by a curious reference to the *Bacchae* of
Euripides, and was generally much inferior to *Loss and Gain*.

For the next few years Newman's life seemed to be all losses.
Returning to Birmingham after his Dublin frustration, he found
tension between his Oratory and its London offshoot. A welcome
invitation to prepare a new translation of the Bible led to nothing.
From 1859 he became doctrinally suspect in the Vatican. His
books had stopped selling well, and he felt generally unpopular
and ineffective. 'I am *passé*, in decay; I am untrustworthy', he

wrote in 1863. Just then the cold war between *Hypatia* and
Callista flared up into open hostilities, from which Newman
emerged more popular than ever before. Kingsley started it, with a
remark in a review of Froude's *History* (*Macmillan's Magazine*,
January 1864): 'Truth for its own sake, had never been a virtue
with the Roman clergy. Father Newman informs us that it need
not, and on the whole ought not to be ...'. This charge, from a
happily married Anglican clergyman with great faith in the saving
power of nuptial love, was based purely on *odium theologicum* and a
careless reading of a sermon published twenty years before, on
'Wisdom and Innocence'. But despite Newman's private protests,
it was never withdrawn or substantiated. The dispute was made
public in two pamphlets, Newman's *Mr. Kingsley and Dr. Newman: A Correspondence on the Question 'Whether Dr. Newman
teaches that Truth is No Virtue?'* and Kingsley's *'What then does
Dr. Newman mean?'* Both pamphlets were cleverly and amusingly
written; but they make it quite clear that Newman was the
honester disputant. Kingsley's last pages implied that, however
conclusively Newman might prove his innocence, the proof would
be one more instance of 'sleight-of-hand logic' or 'cunning
equivocation'. This left Newman in the position of Socrates:
forced to defend himself, not against any specific charge, but
against a general prejudice. Socrates had begun his *apologia* with a
piece of autobiography, explaining how, out of respect for a god,
he had made himself unpopular. Finding himself, in Kingsley's
own words, 'on his trial', Newman followed Socrates' example,
and also his own advice to Catholics in Birmingham: 'Oblige men
to know you'. As he put it in his *Apologia pro Vita sua* (1864):

I must, I said, give the true key to my whole life; I must show what I am
that it may be seen what I am not, and that the phantom may be
extinguished which gibbers instead of me. I wish to be known as a living
man, and not as a scarecrow which is dressed up in my clothes ... I will
draw out, as far as may be, the history of my mind ...

He found it 'a cruel operation, the ripping up of old griefs', and
his task was made still harder by having to work against time, since
he had decided to publish in weekly instalments. One day he
worked on the book for sixteen hours without a break, another day,
for twenty-two. 'I have been constantly in tears', he told a friend in
May, 'and constantly crying out with distress.' But it was worth it.

The work proved an instant success, and he was felt to have established his integrity. From then on he was able to influence a much larger section of the public, and greatly reduce anti-Catholic feeling. The 1864 edition was described on the title-page as a reply to Kingsley's pamphlet. It began with complaints about his unfair methods of argument, and went on to answer his charges in detail. But by 1865 Newman had ceased to feel 'on trial', so the second edition cut out all references to Kingsley, with most of the polemical matter, and was simply entitled: *History of My Religious Opinions*. In the version prepared about four years before his death, these words became the subtitle, and the main one was again *Apologia pro vita sua*—though the 'Defence' was then probably intended for a higher court.

Though perhaps his most famous work, the *Apologia* is less interesting as literature than as part of a success story which readers can enjoy only vicariously. It was the happy ending to a tale like *Cinderella* of unjust persecution, but for non-theologians it is rather disappointing reading. It does indeed give a strong impression of sincerity, dignity, and charm. It issues a challenge that everyone should try to meet: 'Be large-minded enough to believe, that men may reason and feel very differently from yourselves'. It expands our view of things by its picture of a most unusual mind; but it conveys no more than the outline of a human personality, and thus fails to qualify as a great autobiography. The only hints that Newman was ever a child are that he once wished 'the Arabian Tales were true', suspected that 'life might be a dream, or I an Angel', and used to cross himself 'on going into the dark'. The sole light thrown on his extraordinary magnetism comes from indications that it was involuntary and almost unconscious: 'it was not I who sought friends, but friends who sought me.' 'I was not the person to take the lead of a party.' 'I never recognized the hold I had over young men.' Glimpses of human frailty are the more welcome for their rarity. He had, for instance, enough malice to enjoy Socratizing: 'I was not unwilling to draw an opponent on step by step, by virtue of his own opinions, to the brink of some intellectual absurdity, and to leave him to get back as he could.' His happiness at Oxford is barely mentioned, though his pain at leaving it is powerfully suggested:

Trinity had never been unkind to me. There used to be much snapdragon growing on the walls opposite my freshman's rooms there, and I had for years taken it as the emblem of my own perpetual residence even unto death in my University.

On the morning of the 23rd I left the Observatory. I have never seen Oxford since, excepting its spires, as they are seen from the railway.

The *Apologia* was Newman's *Odyssey*. It described an epic journey through strange seas of thought, ending in a home-haven. But the temptations and perils now seem equally unreal. Calypso was merely the *Via Media*, and as for the Polyphemus that made the hero 'seriously alarmed':

My stronghold was Antiquity; now here, in the middle of the fifth century, I found, as it seemed to me, Christendom of the sixteenth and the nineteenth centuries reflected. I saw my face in that mirror, and I was a Monophysite.

Yet the book often shows mastery of 'the two-fold Logos'. Intellectual and verbal virtuosity is most evident in the defence of the paradox that the Church's Infallibility actually promotes Private Judgement; but many readers may find the *Apologia* more convincing in its analysis of long-term mental development:

For myself, it was not logic that carried me on; as well might one say that the quicksilver in the barometer changes the weather. It is the concrete being that reasons; pass a number of years, and I find my mind in a new place; how? the whole man moves; paper logic is but the record of it.

'Woe unto you, when all men shall speak well of you!' quoted Newman uneasily in 1868. His new popularity with Protestants as well as Catholics had been increased by *The Dream of Gerontius* (1865). This dramatic poem, in which a dying Catholic dreams he is already in the next world, was spontaneously produced at a time when Newman thought his own death was imminent: 'it came into my head to write it, I really can't tell how. And I wrote on till it was finished on small bits of paper, and I could no more write anything else by willing it than I could fly.' The return to poetry synchronized with a return to music. He had not played the violin for years, but now two friends gave him 'a very beautiful fiddle', and he played Beethoven until he was 'obliged to lay down the instrument and literally cry out with delight'. It no longer seemed a self-indulgent distraction from his work: 'I really think it will add to my power of working, and the length of my life. I never wrote more than when I played the fiddle . . . Perhaps thought is music.' During most of *The Dream* Gerontius is blind, and all his experience comes to him through music: songs, choruses, hymns (including the famous 'Praise to the Holiest in the height'), and a final psalm. Even the Demons make their presence felt by 'sour' and 'uncouth . . . dissonance'. In fact, the work was an oratorio long before Elgar composed his setting for it (1900).

Newman's original music made good use, as in *Lyra Apostolica*, of traditional metres and stanzas; but it also showed great resourcefulness in dramatizing thoughts and feelings by subtle variations of rhythm and language. Thus the dying man's sense of physical disintegration was marked by an increasingly unpredictable line-length and rhyme-scheme:

> I can no more; for now it comes again,
> That sense of ruin, which is worse than pain,
> That masterful negation and collapse
> Of all that makes me man; as though I bent
> Over the dizzy brink
> Of some sheer infinite descent;
> Or worse, as though
> Down, down for ever I was falling through
> The solid framework of created things,
> And needs must sink and sink
> Into the vast abyss.

The Demons' resentment was voiced in short explosive lines, brusque syntax, near-colloquial diction, and almost 'sprung' rhythm.

The poem had a wide appeal in its day. A stocking-weaver made his wife keep reading it to him as he died, and General Gordon's copy was heavily underlined. It still seems a work of great imaginative power, which sums up the most sympathetic aspect of Newman's literary character:

> There will I sing my sad perpetual strain,
>   Until the morn.
> There will I sing, and soothe my stricken breast,
>   Which ne'er can cease
> To throb, and pine, and languish, till possest
>   Of its Sole Peace.

Despite its forbidding title, *A Grammar of Assent* (1870) has its

sympathetic side too. Though written as 'a sort of duty' which had
become an 'incubus' on Newman's mind, it can be read with
pleasure even by non-philosophers. Here he tried to answer the
question: how could Christians justify their certainty about things
for which there could be no scientific evidence? His answer was
roughly this: science, being founded on 'Inference', could lead
only to 'Notional', never to 'Real Assent', since it dealt not with
'things' but with 'notions', i.e. 'abstractions and generalizations,
which have no existence, no counterpart' outside the mind. For
'genuine proof in concrete matter', and so for 'Real Assent', 'we
require an *organon* more delicate, versatile, and elastic than verbal
argumentation.' This was the 'Illative Sense', a wordless, largely
unconscious action of the mind, evidently related to 'Implicit
Reason': 'It determines what science cannot determine, the limit
of converging probabilities and the reasons sufficient for a proof.'
On this theory Newman built a superstructure of dogma, which
some readers may think not merely unproved but also highly
improbable. But such people were 'mentally crooked': 'I have not
the power to change [their principles or their conclusions] any
more than I can make a crooked man straight.' In other words,
'*quot homines tot sententiae*, but my *sententia* happens to be right.'
The book's last pages oddly illustrate the kind of 'reasons' that he
himself found 'sufficient for a proof'. To prove that the early
history of Christianity manifested 'the Hand of God', he gave a
long catalogue of tortures endured by martyrs: 'Whence came this
tremendous spirit, scaring, nay, offending the fastidious criticism
of our delicate days?'

   The central argument is not so rigidly pursued as to exclude all
concern with literature. An interesting digression discusses the
text of *Henry V*. Lucretius is charged with writing 'dishonourably'
in complaining of the 'yoke of religion' after rejoicing in 'Alma
Venus'. A distinction is drawn between the scientific and the
poetic use of language. As a piece of literature in itself, *A Grammar*
is chiefly remarkable for investing an abstract argument with so
much human charm. In this it is the supreme example of
Newman's ability (to borrow a phrase from his early piece on
Aristotle) 'to make friends with the reader's imagination'.

12. Ruskin

WHEN Ruskin was about four, he entertained his mother's friends by preaching to them 'over the red sofa cushions'.[1] The sermon was eleven words long, and began: 'People, be good'. He soon outgrew such exemplary brevity, and his idea of goodness became humanistic rather than religious; but though he wrote and lectured on many subjects, including art, literature, science, economics, and mythology, it was always in the spirit and manner of this early performance. His style was at first orotund and over-explicit, with a strictly logical system of sections and subsections. In middle age he tried hard to be less showy, more lucid, and more concise. His later style was delightfully informal and spontaneous, but almost unstructured. As it came closer to a pure stream of consciousness, it made more and more puzzling connections between apparently unrelated topics.

His parents had much to answer for when they paid their small son a shilling for every page he wrote. Thus encouraged, he produced nearly forty fat volumes, not easily envisaged as a single whole; but a kind of conspectus may be based on his own comparison of a picture to a window. In most of his works he was either looking at pictures and other artefacts, or looking through them at the world outside. As an art critic he thought pictures useful in drawing attention to natural facts and beauties that would otherwise go unnoticed; in communicating the vision of a superior mind; and in stimulating that of the viewer. At his most naïvely religious, he was almost a natural theologian: the function of art was to demonstrate God's creation, and draw the morals that it was designed to teach. As he moved towards humanism, he made

---

[1] John Ruskin, 1819–1900, was born in London, the only child of a wine merchant and his strictly evangelical cousin. Educated at home, he had already started publishing before he went to Christ Church, Oxford, 1836. His marriage, 1848, to Euphemia (Effie) Chalmers Gray was annulled on grounds of non-consummation, 1854, and she then married Millais, whose Pre-Raphaelite paintings Ruskin had defended in 1851. At Turin, 1858 (so he claimed in 1877), he was 'conclusively *un*converted' from Evangelical Christianity. He became Slade professor of fine art at Oxford, 1870, and settled at Coniston in the Lake District, 1871. In 1875 Rose La Touche, to whom he had proposed in 1866 when she was eighteen, died insane. Three years later he had the first of a series of mental breakdowns, and after 1889 wrote nothing and seldom spoke.

art reveal social as well as natural facts. Meanwhile his 'picture' came to include, besides art, all forms of symbol and myth; and the view from that 'window' took in, not merely objective reality, but the sum of subjective reactions to it. Thus flowers and birds became, not just what botanists and ornithologists classified, but also what poets and myth-makers had made of them. Crystals physically enacted moral truths. 'The Storm-Cloud of the Nineteenth Century', a form of industrial smog that Ruskin observed and recorded quite scientifically, was seen as an embodiment of spiritual darkness.

This confusion of 'picture' with 'window' in his later work was doubtless connected with the series of mental breakdowns that started in 1878; but even in his early writings he had often blurred the distinction between fact and symbol. In a delightful fairy-tale, *The King of the Golden River*, written when he was twenty for the twelve-year-old girl that he later, disastrously, married, the gold of an optical illusion became real wealth. And in *Modern Painters* (1843) Turner's picture of a slave-ship was presented as simultaneously realistic and symbolic. Its sea accurately transcribed natural fact, its slavers were a horrible image of commercial exploitation, and its sunset, which 'burns like gold and bathes like blood', expressed a sort of cosmic morality:

Purple and blue, the lurid shadows of the hollow breakers are cast upon the mist of night, which gathers cold and low, advancing like the shadow of death upon the guilty ship as it labours amidst the lightning of the sea, its thin masts written upon the sky in lines of blood, girded with condemnation in that fearful hue which signs the sky with horror, and mixes its flaming flood with the sunlight, and, cast far along the desolate heave of the sepulchral waves, incarnadines the multitudinous sea.

This seems rather like the 'pathetic fallacy' that Ruskin was to condemn (1856) in Kingsley's 'cruel, crawling foam', and attribute generally to second-rate poets. He wanted at first to be a poet himself, and by the age of eight had written enough poems to require classification, under headings like 'Poetry Discriptive'; but they gave no indication that he would ever rise even to 'the second order of poets'.

The prose juvenilia were more promising. The early diaries recorded in notes and sketches what Ruskin had seen on tours through Europe with his parents, and showed, especially in the geological and meteorological observations, the scientific approach and first-hand knowledge that would support the argument of *Modern Painters* i. So did the contributions to the *Magazine of Natural History* (1834, 1836), attempting to explain such things as the colour of the Rhine, and the hardening of soft sandstone in ancient buildings. A paper published by the recently founded Meteorological Society (1839) exemplified his special concern with the subject, and also stressed a concept central to his later social criticism, 'co-operation'. A footnote (1840) to a book on landscape-gardening anticipated his use in art criticism of optical data: 'only one *point* can be clearly and distinctly seen by the fixed eye, at a given moment'.

The Poetry of Architecture (1837–8), published when he was eighteen, related the features of cottages and villas in England and Europe to national character and to natural scenery. Despite the Englishman's lack of taste, Ruskin found the chimney-styles of 'sweet carbonaceous England' the only ones worth imitating, since 'what is most adapted to its purpose is most beautiful'. The subject and method prefigured *The Stones of Venice*, and his pseudonym, 'Kata Phusin', i.e. 'According to Nature', epitomized a basic principle of *Modern Painters*. But the real germ of that work was an angry defence of Turner's current style, written in 1836. A facetious critic in *Blackwood's Magazine* had complained that *Juliet and her Nurse* was not true to nature. Ruskin replied with evidence of its topographical accuracy, praise of its colour and treatment of sunlight, and a claim that Turner ranked with Shakespeare in his poetic imagination. When Turner saw this piece, he discouraged publication: 'I never move in these matters.' But it developed over the next seven years into Ruskin's first great book.

Modern Painters was designed to prove that Turner was 'the greatest painter of *all* time'. Volume i defined 'the greatest picture' as 'that which conveys to the mind of the spectator the greatest number of the greatest ideas.' Such ideas might be of 'Power', 'Imitation', 'Truth', 'Beauty', or 'Relation', the last perceptible only by active thought. 'Imitation', the type of 'jugglery' by which a picture might actually be mistaken for a window, was vastly inferior to 'Truth', the accurate statement of objective fact. But 'Truth' was not attainable by photography, for calotypes and daguerrotypes lacked the vital element of 'Love'; and though 'the first end of art' was the 'representation of facts', its 'real and only important end' was to represent 'thoughts'. So Ruskin began by insisting on Turner's 'Truth', not as his most important quality, but as the one denied by his critics, and yet most easily proved.

Ruskin's form of proof, which he compared to a theorem in Euclid, was simply to describe from his own observations what such things as sunsets, shadows, clouds, rocks, mountains, water surfaces, and trees really looked like; then to show how they were misrepresented by the 'old masters' (one of Claude's trees, for instance, was 'a very faithful portrait of a large boa-constrictor, with a handsome tail'); and lastly to demonstrate how the chief of Modern Painters had depicted them. Here Turner's mountain-drawings were recommended as visual aids to the study of geology. The approach was scientific: 'my business is not to talk sentiment'. But existing sciences were subordinated to a new 'science of appearances', based on the data of 'the disciplined eye', which were, Ruskin claimed, worth more to the artist than any knowledge of botany or optics. The Preface, written at twenty-four, explained that the anonymous 'Graduate of Oxford' had himself 'been devoted from his youth to the laborious study of practical art'. To the reader who has not, the volume can still come as a revelation, offering a new awareness of the natural environment, and of the seeing process itself.

As literature the book is enjoyable not for its style of argument, which is rather wordy and pompous, but for the brilliant word-paintings of which Ruskin would later feel ashamed. These were not just rhetorical exercises in the ancient genre of the *ekphrasis*. In the days before colour photography they were the only effective way to suggest the visual character of pictures and natural spectacles referred to; and it was not until the third volume that the text was illustrated even by black-and-white engravings from his own drawings. In the first, too, the purple patches were essential to the argument. This peroration, for instance, about a sunset seen near Albano led up to a QED:

... and over all, the multitudinous bars of amber and rose, the sacred clouds that have no darkness, and only exist to illumine, were seen in fathomless intervals between the solemn and orbed repose of the stone pines, passing to lose themselves in the last, white, blinding lustre of the measureless line where the Campagna melted into the blaze of the sea.

Tell me who is likest this, Poussin or Turner?

Modern Painters ii (1846) proceeded, as originally planned, from ideas of 'Truth' to ideas of 'Beauty', but then went off at a tangent. Tintoretto's *Crucifixion* had opened 'a new world' to Ruskin, and he had become as pious as his Evangelical mother could have wished. According to his ironic retrospect of 1883, he was well on his way to becoming 'the Catholic Archbishop of York'. So Turner was replaced by Angelico, the manner of Euclid by that of Hooker, the 'disciplined eye' by the 'moral retina', and all traces of humour by an insistence that art was serious. In expounding a theory that beauty typified the attributes of God, Ruskin even rejected the term 'Aesthetic' in favour of 'Theoretic', since the former, by derivation, implied 'mere sensual perception': 'I wholly deny that the impressions of beauty are in any way sensual; they are neither sensual nor intellectual, but moral.' The *Ethics* of Aristotle had defined perfect happiness as a contemplative (*theoretike*) activity, beyond the scope of animals and fully enjoyable only by the gods. Ruskin Christianized the concept. 'Theoria' was unselfish and other-worldly: 'her home is in heaven', where the angels practised it, kindly contemplating the happiness of all living things.

One notable feature of the argument was the notion of co-operation, which would form the chief link between Ruskin's ideas about art and society. The strength of human spirits, as of all 'earthly creatures' was 'in their co-working and army fellowship, and their delight . . . in the giving and receiving of alternate and perpetual good.' So, too, in pictorial composition, the 'Associative imagination' made everything work together to a single end:

nothing comes amiss to it; but whatever rude matter it receives, it instantly so arranges that it comes right; all things fall into their place, and appear in that place perfect, useful, and evidently not to be spared; so that . . . wherever it passes, among the dead bones and dust of things, behold! a shaking, and the bones come together bone to his bone.

The art with the most social implications was clearly architecture, which had fascinated Ruskin since the age of five or six, when he played with wooden bricks and amused himself by counting the bricks in the houses across the street. In *The Seven Lamps of Architecture* (1849) he called it a 'distinctively political art', and urged architects not to sacrifice morality to expediency, as politicians did. The 'Lamps', by a metaphor taken from the Psalms, were aspects of divine law. According to one of them, Beauty could only be based on the forms of nature. Thus the pointed arch reflected 'the termination of every leaf that shakes in summer wind'. Equally characteristic of Ruskin's approach to art was the lamp of 'Truth', which forbade the surreptitious use of iron to support a stone structure, or of machine-made ornament to increase the 'apparent labour'. In the light of 'Truth' several famous buildings stood condemned: King's College Chapel at Cambridge for 'architectural juggling', St Sophia at Istanbul (which Ruskin had never seen) for 'affectedly inadequate supports', and presumably the Crystal Palace, two years before its erection, for its 'metallic framework'.

Contemporary society was equally condemned, from the 'domestic vanities' of the middle classes, 'living between a Turkey carpet and a gilded ceiling, beside a steel grate and polished fender', to the 'popular discontent' expressed by surburban housing, those 'gloomy rows of formalised minuteness, alike without difference and without fellowship, as solitary as similar'. Worst of all was the 'railroad': 'It transmutes a man from a traveller into a living parcel. For the time he has parted with the nobler characteristics of his humanity for the sake of a planetary power of locomotion.' The railways were also responsible for destroying the 'quietness of nature' and creating, in navvies, a 'reckless, unmanageable, and dangerous' class of men. The effect of wrong employment on the workman was the main social point of the book. The important question to ask about any ornament was, whether the carver had been happy in his work. If you turned a man into a machine by giving him a dull job, you made him a malcontent. All the political turmoil of 1848 had stemmed from 'idle energy' which ought to have gone into handicrafts. And *The Seven Lamps* ended with a hint that Ruskin would soon tackle social problems more directly: 'I have some strange notions . . . which it is perhaps wiser not loosely to set down.' He elaborated them in what he called 'the more considered and careful statements' of *The Stones of Venice* (1851–3), and by 1879 had come to think most of the earlier book 'utterly useless twaddle . . . shallow piety and sonorous talk'.

The purpose of *The Stones of Venice* was variously defined by its author. According to its first page, it was an attempt to 'trace the . . . image' of Venice, before the city disappeared beneath the waves, and also to record its history, as a 'warning' to the commercial pride of England. By 1866 its sole aim had become:

to show that the Gothic architecture of Venice had arisen out of, and indicated in all its features, a state of pure national faith, and of domestic virtue; and that its Renaissance architecture had arisen out of, and in all its features indicated, a state of concealed national infidelity, and of domestic corruption.

Its 'chief purpose' (1877) was to show that the 'beauty' of Venetian architecture depended on 'the happiness and fancy of the workman', and that 'no architect could claim the title to authority of *magister* unless he himself wrought at the head of his men, captain of manual skill.'

Several less explicit objectives may be inferred from the work itself: to give the first reliable account, from personal observation, measurements, and drawings, of early Venetian architecture; to combine the functions of an architectural primer, a tourist's guide, and an entertaining travelogue; to denigrate all Renaissance art, and popularize the Gothic style of architecture, for general building purposes; and to denounce, as a product of the Renaissance spirit, everything that Ruskin deplored in Victorian society. This included indifference to religion, faith in science and technology, commercialism, classical education, disdain for manual as opposed to intellectual work, and the soul-destroying labour imposed on factory employees.

To find a structure that would serve so many purposes, and reduce to order over six hundred pages of closely-written notes, with hundreds of sketches and diagrams, was a difficult problem, and Ruskin cannot be said to have solved it completely. But he gave an air of coherence to his massive book, by the titles of its three volumes. 'The Foundations' set out the basic principles of architecture, and justified the Gothic style on grounds of practical efficiency, and Gothic ornamentation on grounds of religion, since by imitating natural form it expressed 'man's delight in God's work'. 'The Sea-Stories' dealt with the Byzantine and Gothic stages of Venice's architectural history, and 'The Fall' (implying sin as well as artistic decline) denounced all aspects of the Renaissance spirit.

The first volume still offers a most inviting introduction to the theory of building, though even the most innocent reader may suspect some rashness of dogmatism: 'there never can be any new system of architectural forms invented ... all vertical support must be, to the end of time, best obtained by shafts and capitals.' The most important chapter in the second volume (and, as Ruskin thought, in the whole book) was 'The Nature of Gothic'. Here, besides such external features as the pointed arch, Ruskin listed six 'mental characters which make up the soul of Gothic'. Two of these, 'Savageness' and 'Changefulness', stemmed from the Gothic workman's freedom to choose his own type of ornament, instead of being compelled, as by Renaissance architects, to do only what he could do perfectly, i.e. execute a series of geometrical or symmetrical patterns. At this point Ruskin charged the English public with equal inhumanity, in demanding a perfect finish on all consumer goods. This degraded the workman into 'an animated tool', and so created social unrest. Consumers should therefore discourage 'the manufacture of any article, not absolutely necessary, in the production of which *Invention* has no share', and realize the human meaning of that 'division of labour' which Adam Smith had called 'the greatest improvement' in political economy:

It is not, truly speaking, the labour that is divided; but the men:— Divided into mere segments of men—broken into small fragments and crumbs of life; so that all the little piece of intelligence that is left in a man is not enough to make a pin, or a nail, but exhausts itself in making the point of a pin, or the head of a nail.

The third volume ranged even more widely in its criticisms. It condemned Renaissance architecture from the Casa Grimani in Venice to Whitehall and St Paul's in London, and listed the 'moral, or immoral elements' of the Renaissance mentality: 'Infidelity', 'Pride', 'Science', 'State', and 'System'. The coldness and ostentation of Renaissance buildings was 'full of insult to the poor'. The scientific spirit was mere gluttony: 'We no more live to know than we live to eat.' It was better to be an artist, 'a seeing and feeling creature'. The systematic approach, which turned architecture into a 'fetter-dance', was also responsible for 'this age of perfect machinery'. Ruskin had evidently had enough of his own systematic research in Venice. Six years later he wrote:

I went through so much hard, dry, mechanical toil there, that I quite lost, before I left it, the charm of the place. Analysis is an abominable business. I am quite sure that people who work out subjects thoroughly are disagreeable wretches. One only feels as one should when one doesn't know much about the matter.

This revulsion against 'System' resulted in a confessedly 'rambling' Conclusion, which summed up the book's central principle like this: 'art is valuable or otherwise, only as it expresses the personality, activity, and living perception of a good and great human soul.' The soul was more important than either knowledge or technique, and once this was recognized, there would be a new understanding of the 'great symbolic language of past ages, which has now so long been unspoken.'

In *The Stones of Venice* Ruskin's own instinct for symbolism was still kept under control. He derided the idea that Gothic spires expressed religious 'aspiration': 'the chances of damp in the cellar, or of loose tiles in the roof, have, unhappily, much more to do with the fashions of a man's house building than his ideas of celestial happiness or angelic virtue.' When he wrote that 'the arch line is the moral character of the arch, and the adverse forces are its temptations', he was hardly more serious than when he suggested that the small doors of English cathedrals were designed 'for the surreptitious drainage of a stagnant congregation'. Indeed, one great merit of the book is its straightforward presentation of facts, in a style 'aimed chiefly', he said, 'at clear intelligibility; that any one, however little versed in the subject, might be able to take up the book, and understand what it meant forthwith'. Such lucid exposition is given extra charm by imaginative interludes, like the simulated flight from the Mediterranean to the Arctic Circle, relating architecture to climate (II. vi), and the remembered journey, by stage-coach and gondola, from Padua to Venice (I. xxx). This served as 'Vestibule' to the central theme, and ended with a view of Venice which subtly suggested much of what Ruskin meant by its 'Fall':

Now we can see nothing but what seems a low and monotonous dockyard wall, with flat arches to let the tide through it;—this is the railroad bridge, conspicuous above all things. But at the end of those dismal arches there rises, out of the wide water, a straggling line of low and confused brick buildings, which, but for the many towers which are mingled among them, might be the suburbs of an English manufacturing town. Four or five domes, pale, and apparently at a greater distance, rise over the centre of the line; but the object which first catches the eye is a sullen cloud of black smoke brooding over the northern half of it, and which issues from the belfry of a church.

It is Venice.

When the Working Men's College was founded in 1854, 'The Nature of Gothic' was used as its manifesto, and Ruskin began to teach art there, while studying political economy. He soon decided that 'Nobody knows anything about that', and set about showing that he did. *Modern Painters*, iii–iv (1856), though ostensibly an 'epitaph' for Turner, was quite un-Turnerian in its signs of social concern. The third volume lived up to its title, 'Of Many Things', and to Ruskin's initial warning that he did not mean to be 'laboriously systematic', but would pursue 'the different questions ... just as they occur to us, without too great scrupulousness in marking connections, or insisting on sequence.' The questions ranged from the 'Grand Style' to the 'Pathetic Fallacy' and a survey of Greek, medieval, and modern attitudes to landscape. The only common denominator was an uneasy blend of realism and humanitarianism. The 'central and highest branch of ideal art' was that which 'concerns itself simply with things as they ARE, and accepts, in all of them, alike the evil and the good.' This type of 'naturalism' was represented by Turner and the Pre-Raphaelites. But such acceptance of evil conflicted with the feeling for human welfare. Yet if, while enjoying the sight of an Alp, one let one's thoughts run off on to 'the causes of the prosperity or misfortune of the Alpine villagers', or 'the political economy of the mountaineers', one ceased to *see* the mountain. In 'The Moral Landscape' Ruskin explored this dilemma, and questioned the relation between art and human happiness. The nearest he came to a conclusion was to imply that landscape-painting might help to restore a sense of true values:

To watch the corn grow, and the blossoms set; to draw hard breath over ploughshare or spade; to read, to think, to love, to hope, to pray,—these are the things that make men happy ... The world's prosperity or adversity depends upon our knowing and teaching these few things: but upon iron, or glass, or electricity, or steam, in no wise.

Volume iv, 'Of Mountain Beauty', was primarily designed to demonstrate Turner's 'truthfulness' in depicting mountain scenery. It began, however, with a piece of social satire, suggested by a notice about 'a Genteel House' to let, on the English middle classes: 'our serenity of perfection, our peace of conceit, the spirit of well-principled housemaids everywhere . . .'. Before long Ruskin was satirizing the 'heartless' lover of the picturesque:

Poverty, and darkness, and guilt, bring in their several contributions to his treasury of pleasant thoughts. The shattered window, opening into black and ghastly rents of wall, the foul rag or straw wisp stopping them, the dangerous roof, decrepit floor and stair, ragged misery, or wasting age of the inhabitants,—all these conduce, each in due measure, to the fulness of his satisfaction. What is it to him that the old man has passed his seventy years in helpless darkness and untaught waste of soul? The old man has at last accomplished his destiny, and filled the corner of a sketch, where something of an unshapely nature was wanting.

'The Mountain Gloom' even threw doubt on the natural theologian's view of mountains. Their beauty might manifest 'the beauty of God's working', but what about the wretchedness of Alpine peasants' lives? 'Black bread, rude roof, dark night, laborious day, weary arm at sunset; and life ebbs away.' The problem suggested an economic solution. If opera-goers in London and Paris stopped paying to see 'simulacra' of happy Swiss peasants, and used the money to improve the living-conditions of the real ones, it might turn out better, not only for the peasants, but even for the audiences.

Two years later, Ruskin was finding mountains 'stupid'. Two years more, and he was doubting 'the real use to mankind' either of Turner's or 'any other transcendent art'. After another eight, he would preach, if not practise, the doctrine that 'art must not be talked about'. Thus his interest gradually shifted from art to society, and by 1860 he was even prepared to say that the 'digressions respecting social questions', which had 'warped and broken' much of his art criticism, had interested him ten times more than the work that he had been 'forced into undertaking'. Social questions had now become his central theme, and for purposes of propaganda he chose the medium of public lectures 'in all the manufacturing towns'.

Invited to lecture at Manchester, the home of industrial wealth and *laissez-faire* economics, during an exhibition of 'Art Treasures', he used that phrase as an excuse to talk about *The Political Economy of Art* (1857). Here he stressed the social responsibilities of wealth, and also the need for 'Discipline and Interference' by government, to produce 'its soldiers of the ploughshare as well as its soldiers of the sword'. For the 'wise management of labour' in art, he proposed the establishment of special art schools, and the employment of artists on work that was 'easy', 'lasting', and 'various', including the supply of visual aids for ordinary schools. So long as there was 'no glut of it, nor contempt', art should be distributed as widely as possible. The 1880 title, *A Joy for Ever*, was made to reinforce this point: 'the beauty which is indeed a joy for ever, must be a joy for all.' Claiming to have read no political economists but Adam Smith 'twenty years ago', Ruskin laid down his own 'general principles' for running a country as one would manage a household. Simple models like a farm, and a group of castaways on a desert island were used to ridicule the idea of unemployment and competition. The purchase of luxury goods was melodramatically denounced: 'the angels do see—on those gay white dresses of yours . . . spots of the inextinguishable red that all the seas cannot wash away.' But most of the style was admirably plain, rising to this final denial that only the sensible poor deserved consideration:

What do you suppose fools were made for? That you might tread upon them, and get the better of them in every possible way? By no means. They were made that wise men might take care of them.

The Two Paths (1859) again used art as an opening for general social criticism. Based on lectures given partly extempore, in London, Bradford, Manchester, and Tunbridge Wells, the book began by urging students of art and industrial design not to study conventional styles of abstract decoration (which the Indian Mutiny had shown to be morally corrupting), but to imitate 'Organic Form', on which 'all noble design, in any kind' was based. Opposing the current theory that industrial design could be taught like industrial technology, Ruskin insisted that art and manufacture 'must be followed separately', and that drawing was 'the basis of all manual arts whatever' (hence his own textbook, *The Elements of Drawing*). In a totally industrialized country, however, there would be no organic form left to imitate, so he went on to protest against the obliteration of natural scenery by coal-pits, brick-fields, quarries, and machinery. Finally, in 'The Work of Iron, in Nature, Art, and Policy', he used iron as Browne used the quincunx, to unify quite heterogeneous observations. Iron railings, the mark of 'respectability', always meant 'thieves out-side, or Bedlam inside'. In the ploughshare and the needle, iron served to confirm Carlyle's gospel of Work, and Patmore's view of Woman: 'a happy nation may be defined as one in which the husband's hand is on the plough, and the housewife's on the needle'. In 'Fetters' iron typified the 'restraint or subjection necessary in a nation', thus contradicting Mill's *On Liberty*, published the same year: 'No human being, however great, or powerful, was ever so free as a fish'. As a symbol of hard-heartedness, iron meant the exploitation of the poor by buying goods below their real value, and so using the worker's 'hunger, or domestic affliction' as 'a thumbscrew to extort property' from him. One aspect of this iron rule over the 'labouring man' was 'the oppression of expecting too much' of him:

'Be assured, my good man,'—you say to him,—'that if you work steadily for ten hours a day all your life long, and if you drink nothing but water, or the very mildest beer, and live on very plain food, and never lose your temper, and go to church every Sunday, and always remain content in the position in which Providence has placed you, and never grumble, nor swear; and always keep your clothes decent, and rise early, and use every opportunity of improving yourself, you will get on very well, and never come to the parish.'

At this point Ruskin's father told him: 'John, if you don't finish that book now I shall never see it.' So, working 'in a careless, listless way', Ruskin finished *Modern Painters*. The work had raised, he said, too many questions for him to 'conclude' it adequately, and volume v (1860) was certainly inconclusive. It treated, according to the title, 'Leaf Beauty', 'Cloud Beauty', and 'Ideas of Relation'. The last included disjointed comments on Turner's life, work, and character, and an interesting account of pictorial composition, in terms equally applicable to an animal or vegetable organism, or to social organization:

Composition may be best defined as the help of everything in the picture by everything else . . . Government and co-operation are in all things and eternally the laws of life. Anarchy and competition, eternally, and in all things, the laws of death.

The study of clouds had made Ruskin re-read the *Clouds* of Aristophanes, whom he had earlier praised for his accurate cloud-description. He then read the *Plutus*, a comic allegory in which good men finally become rich. This led to a new interest in the interpretation of Greek myths, which Max Müller's *Comparative Mythology* (1856) had pioneered in England. The results in this volume were the enigmatic chapters, 'The Nereid's Guard' and 'The Hesperid Aeglé'. Here Ruskin analysed, by reference to Hesiod and other primary sources, Turner's *Goddess of Discord Choosing the Apple of Contention in the Garden of the Hesperides.* The results of this 'complete analysis' were surprising. One of the Hesperides, named Aeglé (sunlight), signified 'especially the spirit of brightness or cheerfulness; including even the subordinate idea of household neatness or cleanliness'. Turner's Dragon represented, physically, 'the Simoom' and morally, 'the evil spirit of wealth, as possessed in households'. Thus Turner's 'first great religious picture' depicted 'the Assumption', not of St George, but of 'our British Madonna', the Dragon. The myth was then turned to express Turner's own sadness, as 'the painter of the loveliness of nature, with the worm at its root'. The 'sorrow of night' in Turner was made more specific in the last chapter, 'Peace'. Taking his title, and his black-white contrast from Turner's pictorial epitaph for Wilkie, Ruskin set Turner's 'brightest qualities of mind' against 'the absolute darkness' of the age's 'infidelity'. Of this, the supreme example was the political economists' assumption that the Christian ethic 'would not work'.

The title of *Unto This Last* (1862) implied the opposite: that labour-problems like the builders' strike of 1859 could best be solved by the fixed-wage system of the Gospel parable (Matthew 20: 1–15). Here, in four short essays, which caused such an outcry that the *Cornhill Magazine* stopped publishing them, Ruskin outlined an alternative to conventional political economy. For 'economic man', an abstraction 'actuated by no other moral influences than those which affect rats or swine', and prepared to work only 'for pay, or under pressure', he substituted a 'curious engine' 'whose motive power is a Soul', which ran best on 'its own proper fuel', i.e. such emotions as loyalty and affection. For the 'merchant ... presumed to act always selfishly', Ruskin substituted a public-spirited person, who distributed the best possible goods 'at the cheapest price' to the places where they were 'most needed', and treated his employees like sons or daughters. He distinguished between 'mercantile' and 'political' economy. The first was 'the science of getting rich', or rather 'the art of keeping your neighbour poor'. The second was concerned with the 'production, preservation, and distribution, at fittest time and place, of useful or pleasurable things', since 'the final outcome and consummation of all wealth is the producing as many as possible full-breathed, bright-eyed, and happy-hearted human creatures.' As for the supposedly unalterable 'laws of demand and supply', they were just like the law that a stream flows downwards: 'Whether the stream shall be a curse or a blessing, depends upon man's labour, and administering intelligence.'

Ruskin thought *Unto This Last* the best thing he had written, and it was certainly the most readable and convincing. The general soundness of its argument was marred only by a rash contradiction of Malthus: 'There is not yet, nor will yet for ages be, any real over-population in the world.' The expression, concise but colourful, was unfailingly lucid, except for one outbreak of mythology, when Ixion's wheel got entangled with the wheels of Ezekiel. A sequel to this work, *Munera Pulveris* (1862–3), was much less satisfactory. Dedicated to Carlyle, it showed the bad influence of *Latter-Day Pamphlets* in its acceptance of slavery, and of 'the whip', as methods of making people 'do right'. Claimed by Ruskin to be 'the first accurate analysis of the laws of Political Economy', it was rambling and unsystematic, full of dubious etymology, literary allusions, and eccentric interpretation of myth.

Like *Munera Pulveris*, *Sesame and Lilies* (1865) concealed its themes under a cryptic title. *Sesame*, the first of two lectures given in Manchester, used the story of Ali Baba and a dialogue by Lucian to imply the value of reading, the right approach to it, and the wrongness of political economists. Books would not open their treasures to 'robbers', but only to those with a sense of social justice; Adam Smith and Ricardo were like Lucian's bogus philosophers. *Lilies*, by way of the 'Queen lily' in *Maud*, and the Gospel 'lilies of the field', discussed the position and education of women; it was written while Ruskin was a guest at a progressive girls' school. Professing to steer a course between the 'wilder words' of feminism, and the 'perhaps even more foolishly wrong' idea that women were naturally inferior, Ruskin produced a prose specification for Patmore's *Angel*: a house-bound, home-creating, moral guide and supporter of Man. His view of female education was hardly more advanced than Rousseau's: it should be 'nearly the same as a boy's'; 'but quite differently directed', for 'a man

ought to know any language or science he learns, thoroughly—
while a woman ought to know the same language, or science, only
so far as may enable her to sympathize in her husband's pleasures,
and in those of his best friends.'

Sesame and Lilies immediately became Ruskin's most popular
work; but the male chauvinism of the second lecture, and the
blend of Jeremiah and Dutch uncle in its rhetoric make it now
barely readable. A third lecture, added in 1871, 'The Mystery of
Life and its Arts', has lasted much better. Ruskin wrote it under a
sense of failure and disappointment: nobody came to his exhibition
of Turner's drawings, Gothic architecture would not go with 'the
squalid misery of modern cities', and poetry, painting, and
sculpture, 'though only great when they strove to teach us
something about the gods', have never 'taught us anything
trustworthy' about them. The great problem was to find the
'motive' of life itself. Even those who professed to believe in
Heaven and Hell did not act on that belief. 'Wise practical men'
such as 'capitalists and men of business' were like children fighting
for 'brass-headed nails'. Only the manual workers who did
'something useful' had anything important to teach—but to
understand it, one had to join them. Their lesson was that
although a 'continued sense of failure' was inevitable the best way
of being as happy as human nature allowed was to do one's work as
well as one possibly could. The practical message of the lecture
was that one should stop wasting 'vital power' on 'religious
sentiment', and use it 'first in feeding people, then in dressing
people, then in lodging people, and lastly in rightly pleasing
people, with arts, or sciences, or any other subject of thought.' One
might start by repairing slum houses, or even just tidying up: 'I
myself have washed a flight of stone stairs all down, with bucket
and broom, in a Savoy inn, where they hadn't washed their stairs
since they first went up them; and I never made a better sketch
than that afternoon.'

So, when the working classes got the vote in 1867, Ruskin
turned to them, as the only people who might still resist 'the
deadly influence of moneyed power'. The result was *Time and
Tide: Twenty-five Letters to a Working Man of Sunderland on the
Laws of Work* (1867). The medium encouraged simple language,
but was death to coherent structure, since it gave 'sufficient reason
for saying, in or out of order, everything that the chances of the

day bring into one's head, in connection with the matter in hand.' This one-sided correspondence between the son of a sherry-merchant and a reluctant supplier of corks to public houses told the workers that their representation in Parliament would not be 'worth a rat's squeak' until they thought seriously what they wanted, advised them to elect a parliament of their own, and outlined a non-socialist, paternalistic Utopia, in which there were no idle *rentiers*, everyone did some manual work, marriage required a permit but gave the right to a state allowance, and Bishops (i.e. *episkopoi*, overseers) acted as social workers and probation officers. They also kept moral dossiers on all members of the population—though here Ruskin prudently registered a *nolo episcopari*. Finding his subject 'now branched, and worse than branched, reticulated, in so many directions, that I hardly know which shoot of it to trace, or which knot to lay hold of first', he protested against the prostitution of Mozart's genius, the misuse of Cruikshank's, the all-girl cast of a pantomime, the 'vicious' character of the cancan, and the blasphemous choice of Gustave Doré to illustrate, not merely the Bible, but even Tennyson's 'Elaine'. He warned his 'working friend' that the Devil was the real 'person to be "voted" against', told him that the soundest attitude to the Bible gave it no more authority than the sacred books of Egypt, Greece, Persia, and India, and claimed that 'all Christ's main teachings' were about 'the use and misuse of *money*'. As a spendthrift who gave up his birthright, the Prodigal Son had both an economic and a political meaning.

So had the Sirens, and here Ruskin drifted into the field of his next book, *The Queen of the Air: A Study of the Greek Myths of Cloud and Storm* (1869). Max Müller had called mythology 'an ancient form of language', 'applicable to all things'. Ruskin now tried to translate some of that language, and explain its grammar. He saw each mythical figure as a term for three types of idea: a 'physical existence, sun, or sky, or cloud, or sea', a 'personal incarnation of that', and a 'moral significance', which 'is in all the great myths eternally and beneficently true'. Concentrating on Athena, he found her, physically, 'queen of the air', and spiritually, queen of man's breathing in every sense, including his 'inspiration', his 'moral health and habitual wisdom; wisdom of conduct and of the heart'. Under the heading of 'Athena Ergane' (i.e. the worker) he not only elaborated his theory of political

economy, but discussed a subject that would become crucial in the
late twentieth century, the choice between sources of energy.
Human muscles should be used first, then 'inexpensive natural
forces' like wind and water, and only as a last resort, 'artificially
produced mechanical power', as of steam-engines. 'Instead of
dragging petroleum with a steam-engine, put it on a canal, and
drag it with human arms and shoulders. Petroleum cannot possibly be in a hurry to arrive anywhere.'

The translation of mythical language, like his favourite publicity
media, the informal letter and the semi-impromptu lecture,
encouraged Ruskin to pursue quite private trains of thought,
unchecked by common sense, and guided chiefly by free association. The results, though often silly, were usually interesting.
Science, for instance, was condemned as inadequately anthropo-
centric. So the vegetation fostered by Athena was described, as in
Proserpina (1875–86), primarily from a human angle. Potatoes
were 'innocent', garlic was a 'powerful means of degrading peasant
life', and tobacco was 'the worst natural curse of modern civilization'. Since people liked the look of flowers, the flower was 'the
end and proper object of the seed, not the seed of the flower'. *The
Queen of the Air* contains many good points and good passages.
These include a revealing account of Ruskin's 'three different ways
of writing', and a provocative answer to the doctrines of artistic
and political liberty. But the total effect of the book is to make one
transfer to its author this description of Turner's decline:

... helpless and guideless, he indulges his idiosyncrasies till they change
into insanities; ... all the purpose of life degenerating into instinct; and
the web of his work wrought, at last, of beauties too subtle to be
understood, his liberty, with vices too singular to be forgiven—all
useless, because magnificent idiosyncrasy had become solitude, or contention, in the midst of a reckless populace ...

The impression of 'solitude' and 'contention' was too amply
confirmed by *Fors Clavigera: Letters to the Workmen and Labourers
of Great Britain* (1871–84). 'I live', he wrote, 'in the midst of a
nation of thieves and murderers ... this festering mass of scum of
the earth, and miserable coagulation of frog-spawn soaked in
ditch-water.' In his savage isolation, he made no real effort to
communicate with his nominal addressees. The British workman
could hardly have understood even the title of this 650,000-word

soliloquy. Among Ruskin's conflicting translations of the Latin words, the most apt was 'Fortune ... Nail-bearing', since the sequence of ideas was governed throughout by pure chance, and much of the work was written in the spirit of Jael, when she hammered a nail into her sleeping guest's head:

> Here is the first economical fact I have been trying to teach, these fifteen years; and can't get it, yet, into the desperate, leathern-skinned, death-helmeted skull of this wretched England—till Jael-Atropos drive it down, through skull and all, into the ground ...

The 'fact' in question was the high cost of living 'in a saucepan full of steam, with no potatoes in it!' But in every respect England was a 'Kakotopia', to be replaced by a Utopia of Ruskin's own devising. This he tried to realize by founding the 'Guild of St George', a charitable project to cultivate barren land and educate farm workers. By 1884 it had only fifty-seven contributors, with Ruskin (who had contributed £7,000) as its 'Master'. From what was said of its basic principles in Fors, the Guild seems scarcely to have deserved any greater success. Utopia turned out to be a place where Ruskin had despotic power, where nobody ate sugar without sugar-tongs, and where there was no credit or interest. The Master had some difficulty in explaining why he continued to draw dividends from consols. Eventually he confessed that he 'entirely hated' running the Guild, and had started writing Fors Clavigera merely 'as a byework to quiet my conscience, that I might be happy in what I supposed to be my own proper life of Art-teaching, at Oxford and elsewhere.' Thus art and society had once more changed places in his esteem.

If the thought of Fors Clavigera was notably incoherent, the writing was nearly always lively, and admirably direct. 'Sir, your house is on fire', was now the norm, rather than the ornate style of his early works, here contemptuously parodied: 'Sir, the abode in which you probably passed the delightful days of youth is in a state of inflammation.' Exasperating when read continuously, the letters are most rewarding to skip through. They show great agility of mind and freshness of approach; and one of their most absurd features was justified by its sequel. The assumption that his readers needed to know the most intimate or most trivial details of his private life made him broadcast the information that 'the woman I hoped would have been my wife [i.e. Rose La Touche] is dying' and that 'My hostess's white cat, Lily, woke me at half-past five by piteous mewing at my window', but it also made him include, at the slightest excuse, whole passages of autobiography in his letters. By 1875 he was facing Tristram Shandy's problem: 'I must steadily do a little bit more autobiography in every Fors, now, or I shall never bring myself to be of age before I die ...'. And the little bits finally developed into the most delightful of all his books, *Praeterita* (1885–9).

In this unfinished autobiography, written between attacks of mental illness, Ruskin tried to avoid being 'disagreeable or querulous', to 'set the facts down continuously' in a 'plain' rather than 'piquant' style, and to 'unpeel the authorial skin' from 'the "natural" me'. He achieved a genial tone by including only what it gave him 'joy to remember', which meant saying nothing about his marriage to Effie Gray, or his traumatic love for Rose la Touche. Predictably, the narrative soon ceased to be 'continuous', on the reasonable ground that, for 'clearness of exposition', the growth of certain 'forces' could not be traced chronologically. But the inevitable relapse into rambling was happily delayed until the third volume. The 'plain' style turned out to have a piquancy of its own, in a quiet irony suggesting suppressed laughter. This was quite new in Ruskin's writings.

By 'unpeeling' his infallibility, he became quite an endearing character. 'If I get tiresome', he remarked, 'the reader must skip'. Instead of elaborating his 'strong insights into the faults of others', he concentrated on his own: his selfishness, arrogance, conceit, lack of affection, and social ineptitude; his bigoted Protestantism, inadequate classical scholarship, and curious methods of courtship (e.g. by writing the lady a nine-page essay to refute her opinions); in short, the aptness of the crest that his father had chosen for him: 'a pig'. The 'great pain, and shame' that he felt on 'meeting' himself, 'face to face' produced a crop of self-satirizing images: 'a little black silkworm in the middle of its first mulberry leaf', 'a skate in an aquarium trying to get up the glass', 'a just open-eyed puppy, disconsolate at the existence of the moon', 'a little floppy and soppy tadpole,—little more than a stomach with a tail to it'. But even the power of development implied by the last two pictures of his former self was sadly negated:

... looking back from 1886 to ... 1837 ... I find myself in nothing whatsoever *changed*. Some of me is dead, more of me stronger. I have learned a few things, forgotten many; in the total of me, I am but the same youth, disappointed and rheumatic.

The egotism of childhood was beautifully defined: 'My parents were—in a sort—visible powers of nature to me, no more loved than the sun and the moon; only I should have been annoyed and puzzled if either of them had gone out.' So was the child's bewilderment at adult taboos, as when Ruskin suggested Byron's 'Juan and Haidée' for after-dinner reading aloud. There was gentle ridicule of his parents' blend of piety and snobbishness, of their stifling protectiveness and baffled ambitions for him: 'he would have been a Bishop'. However, the pleasantest passages of description are about his travels with them. It was they who first introduced him to the joys of 'windows' like the 'large moving oriel' of the 'chariot' in which they toured Europe, and of 'pictures' like the ones he saw when his father took him to visit his customers' country houses.

Praeterita is indispensable for filling in the background of Ruskin's other works. It shows, for instance, his attitude to writing ('My own literary work ... was always done as quietly and methodically as a piece of tapestry'); his delight in drawing, and his habit of 'staring', i.e. 'looking exclusively at the thing before my eyes till I could see it'. It also records certain key experiences in his aesthetic and religious development, like the 'bit of ivy' that he drew on the road to Norwood, or his 'unconversion' at Turin in 1858, when Veronese's *Queen of Sheba* convinced him that 'the gorgeousness of life' could not really be as sinful as he had been brought up to believe. Such accounts should not, of course, be taken too literally, since they doubtless expressed the results of conscious reflection and hindsight. Despite its claim to unpeel a 'natural' personality, *Praeterita* was itself a literary creation. For hints of what he felt at a deeper level, one must turn to his diaries. What the unpeeling process really cost him may be dimly guessed from a dream he recorded in 1875, after some months of writing autobiography. He dreamt he was examining a picture of 'an old surgeon dying by dissecting himself! It was worse than dissecting—*tearing*: and with circumstances of horror about the treatment of the head into which I will not enter.'

13. Pater

'WHAT is this song or picture, this engaging personality presented in life or in a book, to *me*?' That, said Pater, was the first question the 'aesthetic critic' should ask.[1] If one asks it about Pater himself one must, for a start, confess that his personality, whether in life or in his books, was not very engaging. A withdrawn, fastidious, unmarried don, who loved travelling but hated being with strangers, he lived almost wholly in the world of art, literature, and philosophy, and spent most of his time as a writer laboriously searching for the perfect phrase. The resulting style can certainly be beautiful, but is apt to be soporific. Its lack of spontaneity deadens the reader's responses, its steady tempo puts all narrative into slow motion, and its conscientious precision sometimes leads to sentences so long, and syntax so complicated, as to obscure the meaning. Beneath this highly-wrought surface one occasionally glimpses a morbid taste for violence and cruelty. More generally, Pater's work suffers from the very fault that he found in Coleridge's prose: 'excess of seriousness'. Though he admired the 'levity' of Matthew Arnold, Carroll, and Wilde, he seldom achieved anything like it himself. For all this, he was an original and stimulating thinker, a perceptive critic of art and literature, and the pioneer of a new type of English fiction, particularly effective in conveying spiritual atmosphere, slow changes of mental attitude, and subtle reactions to physical environment.

Pater's thoughts seem to have revolved round a small group of images—crystal or precious stone, flame, focus, web, and rebirth or *renaissance*. The 'clear crystal nature' was the theme of his earliest surviving essay, 'Diaphaneitè (i.e. *diaphanéité*, trans-

---

[1] Walter Horatio Pater, 1839–94, was born at Shadwell, east London. His father was a doctor of Dutch descent, who died soon afterwards. His mother also died before he was fifteen, and an aunt became his guardian. He went to a school at Enfield, King's School, Canterbury, and Queen's College, Oxford, where he won a fellowship at Brasenose, 1864. From 1869 he lived with his unmarried sisters. That year he got to know some of the Pre-Raphaelites, especially Rossetti and Swinburne. Another of his friends was Pattison. He usually spent his vacations travelling in Europe, and 1882 worked in Rome on the background to *Marius*; but 1885–93 he lived with his sisters in London during vacations. They then moved back to Oxford, where he died suddenly, when thought to be convalescent after rheumatic fever.

parency), written soon after he became a Fellow of Brasenose
College, Oxford in 1864. Here he defined, in some rather opaque
epigrams, a 'type of character ... rare, precious above all to the
artist', that might bring about 'the regeneration of the world'. It
was 'transparent' in that nothing clouded its view of external
reality, or concealed its inner self from observation. It might
indeed seem 'colourless' since, like the colours in white light, its
many gifts were blended in a 'just equipoise': 'no single gift, or
virtue, or idea, has an unmusical predominance'. Like Matthew
Arnold's Criticism, Pater's 'crystal nature' saw the world and itself
'as they are', with the disinterested 'repose of perfect intellectual
culture'. It was 'revolutionist', not in practice but in spirit, 'from
the direct sense of personal worth, that χλιδή, that pride of life,
which to the Greek was a heavenly grace.' Thus Pater's Hellenism
was more egocentric than Arnold's, and its 'criticism of life' more
aesthetic than intellectual or moral. The crystal character 'treated
life in the spirit of art'.

The character was also compared to 'that fine edge of light,
where the elements of our moral nature refine themselves to the
burning point.' Here the image of flame merged into that of focus
(in Latin a literal 'burning point', a hearth). Pater associated flame
with the 'perpetual flux' of Heraclitus, for whom, according to
Plato and Platonism, the 'incoherency of fire' was a 'lively
instance' of the general 'principle of disintegration'. The web
image, too, was hinted at in the early essay, where 'transparency'
was 'a thread of pure white light that one might disentwine from
the tumultuary richness of Goethe's nature'; it would be made
more explicit in a famous passage about 'the passage and dissolu-
tion of impressions, images, sensations ... that continual vanish-
ing away, that strange, perpetual weaving and unweaving of
ourselves.' As for the images of *renaissance*, it would develop from
its first appearance as 'the regeneration of the world' into the title
and theme of Pater's best-known book. In his work as a whole it
took many different forms, including such figures of Spring as
waking from sleep and the emergence of life from underground,
resurrection myths like those of Dionysus and Persephone, and
fantasies of reincarnation inspired by Heine's *'Die Götter im Exil'*.
This was a satirical account of how the Greek gods managed to
survive in the medieval world, Apollo disguised as an Austrian
shepherd, Bacchus as a Tyrolean monk, and Zeus as a poor old

man dressed in rabbit-skins, on an island in the far north. In Pater's mind, however, such metempsychosis was not exclusively reserved for gods. Greek culture might similarly be reborn in a later age, and Winckelmann, who pioneered the study of Greek art in the eighteenth century, owed his special 'understanding of the Greek spirit' to 'his own nature—itself like a relic of classical antiquity laid open by accident to our alien modern atmosphere.'

Most of the thought expressed or generated by these central images may be subsumed under an equally small group of concepts: the supreme value of sensuous beauty; the imminence of death; the transience and subjectivity of human experience, with its corollary, relativism; the need for a 'sense of freedom' in 'modern life', and for 'simplicity' in an increasingly complex world. These ideas persisted through Pater's writing career, but with some changes of emphasis. His early paganism and amorality, for instance, gave way to greater sympathy, if mainly for aesthetic reasons, with Christian ethics.

Having read 'Diaphaneitè' to a University literary society, Pater published articles on Coleridge, Winckelmann, and Morris in the *Westminster Review* (1866–8). Coleridge, he claimed, had destroyed himself as a poet, by resisting the 'relative spirit', of 'modern thought' and clinging to 'the absolute'. The 'germ' of relativism, first produced by an 'ancient philosopher', presumably Heraclitus, had been 'fecundated' by modern science, presumably Darwinian, which showed 'types of life evanescing into each other by inexpressible refinements of change'. From biology, intent on 'distinguishing and fixing delicate and fugitive details', relativism had 'invaded moral philosophy': 'Hard and abstract moralities are yielding to a more exact estimate of the subtlety and complexity of our life.' The true relationship between the individual and his environment was not a matter of 'eternal outlines effected once for all', but of 'fine gradations and subtly linked conditions, shifting intricately as we ourselves change'. The idea of 'ontology' was just a mistake: 'Who would change the colour or curve of a roseleaf' for the 'colourless, formless, intangible' reality postulated in Plato's *Phaedrus*? But Coleridge had done so. He had let the 'sentiment or instinct' that he shared with Wordsworth of a 'mind in nature' freeze into a 'scientific or pseudo-scientific theory', and tried to 'found a religious philosophy'. Thus he declined from a poet into a writer of 'bundles of notes', and even as a literary critic, he 'withdraws us too far from what we can see, hear, and feel.' His 'first buoyant, irresistible self-assertion' had been 'a temporary escape of the spirit from routine', but his theology had been 'humdrum, insipid', and his whole 'pathetic history' proved the need for 'a more elastic moral philosophy than his', the inadequacy of 'every formula less living and flexible than life itself'.

In happy contrast to Coleridge, Winckelmann was a pagan, saved from 'bloodless routine' by his passion for art. A 'transparent' character in all but his politic conversion to Roman Catholicism, he was inclined by temperament to escape from 'abstract theory to intuition, to the exercise of sight and touch', and form 'romantic, fervid friendships with young men', which showed his natural affinity with the Greeks, and their special feeling for bodily beauty. Thus naturally qualified, he gave the human spirit, in Hegel's phrase, 'a new organ' by rediscovering Hellenism. Here again Pater subordinated religion to art. Greek religion had been based on the 'universal pagan sentiment' of sadness at the prospect of death and of being at the mercy of 'irresistible natural powers'. Like all primitive religions, it had started with prophylactic 'charms and talismans' and ritual, to which an 'aesthetic element', i.e. 'the myth, the religious conception', had been 'accidentally' attached. And the whole value of Greek religion had been its ability 'to transform itself into an artistic ideal'.

The essence of this ideal had been the acceptance of the sensuous element in life. Gifted with a 'perfect animal nature', the Greeks did not at first aspire, like Christians, to 'independence of the flesh'. In their art 'the idea does not outstrip or lie beyond its sensible embodiment'. There was none of the quality found in the work of Angelico, for instance, the 'crushing of the sensuous, the shutting of the door upon it, the flesh-outstripping interest.' The defence of flesh was continued in the article on the poetry of Morris. There medieval religion was 'but a beautiful disease or disorder of the senses'. By denying the flesh it caused a chronic neurosis, of which Courtly Love was the most obvious symptom: 'a love defined by the absence of the beloved, choosing to be without hope, protesting against all lower uses of love, barren, extravagant, antinomian.' In poetry this morbid condition appeared as 'a wild, convulsed sensuousness', a 'tension of nerve, in which the sensible world comes to one with a reinforced brilliance and relief—all redness is turned into blood, all water

into tears.' In Morris's *Defence of Guenevere* Pater found this
'electric atmosphere' powerfully conveyed. *Jason* was then praised
for its return to the sensuous simplicity of Hellenism, and thus re-
enacting 'a transition which, under many forms, is one law of the
life of the human spirit, and of which what we call the Renaissance
is only a supreme instance.' Finally *The Earthly Paradise* set off,
with 'exquisite dexterity', the 'grace of Hellenism . . . against the
sorrow of the middle age'.

After admitting that this last poem lacked 'concentration', and
justifying its 'mere mass' as 'itself the first condition of an art
which deals with broad atmospheric effects', Pater concluded his
review with three pages of admirably concentrated prose. Here he
answered the charge that Morris's poetry was behind the times,
because it ignored modern 'truths' and, 'assuming artistic beauty
of form to be an end in itself', wasted time and effort in retelling
'pagan fables'. His reply was roughly this: since 'modern philosophy' reduces human life, both physical and mental, to 'a drift of
momentary acts of sight and passion and thought', the most
practical way of spending the little time at one's disposal is to make
each of those momentary acts as intense as one possibly can. And
the 'wisest' method of doing it is to devote one's life to 'art and
song':

For our one chance is in expanding that interval, in getting as many
pulsations as possible into the given time. High passions give one this
quickened sense of life, ecstasy and sorrow of love, political or religious
enthusiasm, or 'the enthusiasm of humanity.' Only, be sure it is passion,
that it does yield you this fruit of a quickened, multiplied consciousness.
Of this wisdom, the poetic passion, the desire of beauty, the love of art for
art's sake, has most; for art comes to you professing frankly to give
nothing but the highest quality to your moments as they pass, and simply
for those moments' sake.

Thus the doctrine of *l'art pour l'art*, preached by Théophile
Gautier in 1835, was made to follow logically from the view of life
presented by such philosophers and scientists as Hume, J. S. Mill,
and T. H. Huxley. In a lecture 'On the Physical Basis of Life',
delivered about the time that Pater's article came out, Huxley
explained to his audience that his own 'living protoplasm' was
'always dying': 'Every word uttered by a speaker costs him some
physical loss . . . he burns that others may have light.' Pater used
the same image in a less altruistic sense:

A counted number of pulses only is given to us of a variegated dramatic life. How may we see in them all that is to be seen in them by the finest senses? How can we pass most swiftly from point to point, and be present always at the focus where the greatest number of vital forces unite in their purest energy?

To burn always with this hard gem-like flame, to maintain this ecstasy, is success in life.

If the type of hedonism recommended was egocentric, that too followed from the solipsistic element in modern thought:

Experience, already reduced to a swarm of impressions, is ringed round for each one of us by that thick wall of personality through which no real voice has ever pierced on its way to us, or from us to that, which we can only conjecture to be without. Every one of these impressions is the impression of an individual in his isolation, each mind keeping as a solitary prisoner its own dream of a world.

Oscar Wilde's *Dorian Gray* would show up the ugly side of Aesthetic Epicureanism, but though Pater's version of it rejected 'abstract morality', it was hardly calculated to make an exponent end up 'loathsome of visage': 'While all melts under our feet, we may well catch at any exquisite passion, or any contribution to knowledge that seems by a lifted horizon to set the spirit free for a moment, or any stirring of the senses, strange dyes, strange flowers and curious odours, or work of the artist's hands, or the face of one's friend.' Whatever may be thought of such a life-style, these pages certainly expressed the bleakness of the human situation, and the argument for *carpe diem*, with a specially poignant blend of poetry and logic.

When the end of this anonymous article was republished under Pater's name as the 'Conclusion' to *Studies in the History of the Renaissance* (1873), it was much criticized by the orthodox, officially condemned by the Bishop of Oxford, parodied in W. H. Mallock's *The New Republic*, and diplomatically excluded from the 1877 edition. The rest of the work was less provocative. It consisted of a 'Preface' explaining the principles of 'aesthetic criticism', and chapters, including four articles republished from the *Fortnightly Review*, on individual aspects of the Renaissance. The first chapter found in the 'sweetness' of two thirteenth-century French prose-romances the 'seed of the classical revival'. In the second, the attempt of the fifteenth-century humanist, Pico

della Mirandola, to reconcile Greek religion with Christianity was
related to the fusion of pagan and Christian imagery in the Italian
art of his period. Four great Florentine artists of the *Quattrocento*
were then discussed separately, to be joined in the 1888 edition by
the Venetian Giorgione. The story ended with the sixteenth-
century poet and critic, Joachim du Bellay, representing what was
'called the Renaissance in France' but was really 'the finest and
subtlest phase of the Middle Ages itself'. By way of epilogue,
before the 'Conclusion', the article on Winckelmann was used
again, since he was 'the last fruit of the Renaissance' and explained
'in a striking way its motives and tendencies'.

The Preface politely corrected Matthew Arnold's critical position. Despite his preference for 'specimens' and 'touchstones',
Arnold was prepared to generalize about literary value. For Pater,
all abstract definitions of beauty were 'metaphysical questions, as
unprofitable as metaphysical questions elsewhere' (a remark glibly
echoed by Oscar Wilde's Gwendolen). Beauty could only be
defined in the 'concrete', since it, 'like all other qualities presented
to human experience', was relative. Yet a statement by Arnold,
which seems to imply the existence of an absolute reality, was then
quoted with approval:

'To see the object as in itself it really is,' has been justly said to be the aim
of all true criticism whatever; and in aesthetic criticism the first step
towards seeing one's object as it really is, is to know one's own impression
as it really is, to discriminate it, to realize it distinctly.

The next step was to account for it, and here again Pater showed
traces of absolutism:

... the function of the aesthetic critic is to distinguish, to analyse, and
separate from its adjuncts, the virtue by which a picture, a landscape, a
fair personality in life or in a book, produces this special impression of
beauty or pleasure, to indicate what the source of the impression is, and
under what conditions it is experienced. His end is reached when he has
disengaged that virtue, and noted it, as a chemist notes some natural
element, for himself and others ...

But however self-contradictory, Pater's insistence that personal
impressions are the 'primary data' for criticism seems less unreasonable than Arnold's later implication that a 'real estimate' can
be reached through simply dismissing the 'personal estimate'.

By this quite unhistorical method Pater pursued his studies in what the book's first title called 'the History of the Renaissance'. He looked for the special 'virtue' not only of individual artists, but also of periods: 'In whom did the stir, the genius, the sentiment of the period find itself?' The 'virtue' of the whole Renaissance he identified as 'the care for physical beauty, the worship of the body, the breaking down of those limits which the religious system of the Middle Ages imposed on the heart and the imagination.' An early plea for this 'liberty of the heart' Pater found in the Tannhäuser legend, which justified sexual enjoyment through its image of rebirth, the blossoming of the dry staff. A more explicit attempt to reconcile pagan with Christian values was made by Pico della Mirandola who, though gently mocked for trying (like Gladstone in 1858) to find a Christian meaning in Homer, was hailed as 'a true *humanist*' for believing that 'nothing which has ever interested living men and women can wholly lose its vitality'. Thus, too, Botticelli's *Birth of Venus* reinforced the Tannhäuser figure of 'mediaeval Renaissance': 'the return of that ancient Venus, not dead, but only hidden for a time in the caves of Venusberg'. Botticelli's own 'virtue' was a blend of 'sympathy for humanity in its uncertain condition' with 'consciousness of the shadow upon it of the great things from which it shrinks.' So his Venuses were 'never without some shadow of death in the gray flesh and wan flowers', and his 'peevish-looking Madonnas', too human to enjoy the 'intolerable honour' done to them, show on their faces a preference for a 'middle world' between heaven and hell.

Turning to sculpture, Pater discussed the problem of getting 'individualized expression', the 'equivalent of colour', into hard, white stone. Luca della Robbia had solved it by bas-relief, Michelangelo by a 'studied incompleteness', suggesting but not realizing 'solid form'. The formula for Michelangelo's art was 'sweetness and strength, pleasure with surprise', qualities found also in his life and in his poems, which had been republished in 1863. But the chapter-title, 'The Poetry of Michelangelo', referred to more than these. It meant that all his works were poetic in their suggestiveness, in the 'vague fancies, misgivings, presentiments', for instance, that Pater found in the symbolic figures on the Medici tomb, and translated into his own type of prose-poetry. Here, like 'the promptings of a piece of music', were hints of ideas about 'the disembodied soul':

at last, far off, thin and vague . . . the new body . . . a dream that lingers a moment, retreating in the dawn, incomplete, aimless, helpless; a thing with faint hearing, faint memory, faint power of touch; a breath, a flame in the doorway, a feather in the wind.

In the work of Leonardo da Vinci, too, Pater sensed meanings 'subtle and vague as a piece of music', and defined those of the *Mona Lisa* in a much-quoted passage, which figures as *vers libre* in Yeats's *Oxford Book of Modern Verse* (1936). Vasari called the sitter's smile 'pleasant', and explained that Leonardo employed musicians, singers, and jesters to 'keep her merry' while he painted the portrait. For Pater it was an 'unfathomable smile . . . with a touch of something sinister in it'; and the picture represented, not merely an embodiment of the artist's thought (as in Rossetti's 'Hand and Soul'), but even 'the modern idea' of 'humanity as wrought upon by, and summing up in itself, all modes of thought and life.' Compounded of 'curiosity and the desire of beauty', Leonardo's genius came especially close to the 'modern spirit' in that the curiosity was scientific. Leonardo also came close to Pater's own ideals, in having a soul like 'clear glass', and showing 'carelessness in the work of art of all but art itself'.

The analogy between art and music, already touched on twice, was elaborated in 'The School of Giorgione', a painter who invited such an approach by the subject of his *Concert Champêtre*, on which Rossetti had written a sonnet, and also by his skill as a lutanist. Here, without naming Ruskin, Pater contradicted his view that 'pictures' and 'poems' were 'synonymous', and his denial that 'impressions of beauty are in any way sensual'. Borrowing a term from Matthew Arnold, Pater claimed that all art 'addresses . . . the "imaginative reason" through the senses', but that each art had 'its own peculiar and untranslatable sensuous charm'. So what mattered most in a picture was its 'essential pictorial quality', the effect of its 'pure line and colour':

In its primary aspect, a great picture has no more definite message for us than an accidental play of sunlight and shadow for a few moments on the wall or floor: is itself, in truth, a space of such fallen light, caught as the colours are in an Eastern carpet, but refined upon, and dealt with more subtly and exquisitely than by nature itself.

Still, every art tended to 'pass into the condition of some other art', and '*All art constantly aspires toward the condition of music*'. Here

Pater referred to 'German critics', but some of his wording, including the term 'aspire', was clearly taken from Baudelaire. Music, not poetry, he explained, was 'the true type or measure of perfected art', because of its 'perfect identification of matter and form'. The '*vraie vérité*' about Giorgione was then defined in musical terms, including one phrase that might well puzzle a musicologist: 'that modulated unison of landscape and persons'.

From music as an artistic ideal Pater turned to music in poetry. An 'insatiable' appetite for music was 'almost the only serious thing in the poetry of the Pléiade', and Du Bellay's one important poem was 'a thing in which matter is almost nothing, the form almost everything'. Like the work of Giorgione, which 'presents us with a kind of profoundly significant and animated instant . . . an intense consciousness of the present', this poem concentrated, in the spirit of the Conclusion, on the experience of a moment: 'A sudden light transfigures a trivial thing, a weathervane, a windmill, a winnowing flail, the dust in the barn door; a moment—and the thing has vanished . . .'.

The academic characer of *The Renaissance* was pleasantly relieved by traces of interest in the subjective experience of children; by this comment, for instance, on a Botticelli Madonna's face: 'The white light on it is cast up hard and cheerless from below, as when snow lies upon the ground, and the children look up with surprise at the strange whiteness of the ceiling.' In 'Winckelmann', pagan 'sadness' at the thought of death was like 'a rush of homesickness' for the earth. Du Bellay's *Les Regrets*, written in Rome, expressed 'nostalgia, homesickness—that pre-eminently childish, but so suggestive sorrow', that of 'the schoolboy far from home'.

Homesickness became a central theme in Pater's first short story, 'The Child in the House' (*Macmillan's Magazine*, August 1878). He called it 'a portrait', a literary genre as old as the *Eikones* of Lucian (who also wrote art criticism), and it was largely a self-portrait. The idea of portraying his own soul may have come from Rossetti's 'Hand and Soul', and that of identifying a house with a personality, from the same poet's *The House of Life*. In an essay on Wordsworth (1874) Pater had referred to 'the airy building of the brain', and here he began his own *Prelude*, describing 'that process of brain-building by which we are, each one of us, what we are.' Even Simon Lee may be glimpsed in the first sentence, where Florian Deleal does a kind deed to 'a poor aged man'. The name

Florian, for a person whose memories of home formed 'parts of the great chain wherewith we are bound' to the earth, was perhaps meant to recall the 'flowery band' by which Keats's things of beauty 'bind us to the earth'. As for Deleal, it sounds almost like a punning allusion to the leader of the Parnassians, Leconte de Lisle, and to one meaning of his name: 'The Story of the Island' would be an apt title for this study of the impressions of an 'individual in his isolation'.

Here Pater conveyed a vivid sense of how a child may react to his physical environment, and how that environment may grow inseparable from his mental and emotional life. Thus all forms of experience

belong to this or the other well-remembered place in the material habitation—that little white room with the window across which the heavy blossoms could beat so peevishly in the wind, with just that particular catch or throb, such a sense of teasing in it, on gusty mornings; and the early habitation thus gradually becomes a sort of material shrine or sanctuary of sentiment; a system of visible symbolism interweaves itself through all our thoughts and passions ...

Florian was fostered not quite by beauty and fear, like Wordsworth in *Prelude*, but by 'beauty', 'pain', and 'a strange biblical awe'. One visitation of beauty was the sudden sight of 'a great red hawthorn in full flower ... crimson fire out of the heart of the dry wood', as if by the Tannhäuser miracle. Pain came to him most 'poignantly' in the cry of an 'aged woman' announcing his father's death, the sufferings of a dying cat, and those of a caged starling that he felt obliged (like the young Leonardo da Vinci) to set free. As for the biblical awe, it tended to counteract his melancholy at the thought of death. So he became devoted to the externals of religion, but regarded its 'sacred history' as more 'ideal' than historical: 'a complementary strain or burden, applied to our every-day existence, whereby the stray snatches of music in it re-set themselves, and fall into the scheme of some higher and more consistent harmony.'

The story was framed by the image of a road, suggesting the journey from youth to age, and unified by allusions to a caged bird, which qualify the comforting connotations of the House, by implying that the 'thick wall of personality' encloses, as in the Conclusion, a 'solitary prisoner'. The style, slow, dreamy, and unruffled, was perfectly adapted to describing the experience of a child for whom, as he sat with his mother in the garden, 'time seemed to move ever more slowly to the murmur of the bees in it, till it almost stood still on June afternoons.'

Pater had less excuse for letting time, and the narrative, move quite so slowly in *Marius the Epicurean* (1885), a novel-length 'portrait' of an earnest young Roman of the second century AD. Here, like Newman in both his novels, Pater traced the progress of a mind from one religion to another. The hero's spiritual journey, associated with certain literal ones, was in four stages. Initially a devotee of traditional Roman religions, Marius is attracted first to Epicureanism, then to Stoicism, and finally to Christianity. He dies rather like Sydney Carton, in the place of a Christian friend, and is given the last rites and buried as a Christian, but he remains to the end an Epicurean. Instinctively altruistic, he has always tried not to hurt other people: '*Tristem neminem fecit*—he repeated to himself; his old prayer shaping itself now almost as his epitaph.' Yet he never believes in Christianity: he just gets aesthetic pleasure from its 'vision' of 'a perfect humanity, in a perfect world', from its way of life, and 'above all' from 'the touching image of Jesus'. Having enjoyed this 'vision', he can say, with Horace, '*Vixi!*'

The first stage, dominated by conscience, ritual, and family feeling, results from the environment of White-nights, the dreamy old country house in Etruria, where Marius passes his childhood with his widowed mother. The second stage is connected with a school-friend at Pisa called Flavian. The name suggests 'golden', with hints of the '"golden" book of that day', Apuleius' *Golden Ass*, which the two boys study in the sunshine, and of the 'golden lads and lasses' who celebrate springtime and love in the *Pervigilium Veneris*, a poem of unknown authorship that Pater attributes to Flavian. The third stage centres on the Emperor Marcus Aurelius, whose secretary Marius becomes in Rome; and the fourth on Cornelius, a young aristocrat who befriends Marius, and turns out to be a Christian.

Marius and Pater had much in common. They were both interested in poetry, prose-style, and visual art, the atmosphere of White-nights was almost indistinguishable from that of 'the House', and Marius, like Pater, used as a child to play at being a priest. And when Marius defined his 'New Cyrenaicism', he was virtually defending Pater's Conclusion against a hostile review entitled 'Modern Cyrenaicism'. But, though tinged with autobiography, the novel was firmly based on the history of the period, and ingeniously documented by extracts from its literature. Thus the story in Apuleius of Cupid and Psyche was translated with some expurgation and idealization: 'So the famous story composed itself in the memory of Marius, with an expression changed in some ways from the original and on the whole graver.' In this form it gave Marius the idea of 'a perfect imaginative love, centred upon a type of beauty entirely flawless and clean', and so led him to improve on the mainly sensual hedonism of Aristippus. The *Pervigilium*, too, which served to illustrate Flavian's character and philosophy by its 'pagan' delight in sex, gave Pater a plausible pretext for the fiction that its author died while composing it, since the poem concludes: 'I have lost the Muse in silence . . .'. Marius's flirtation with Stoicism was similarly authenticated by free translation from the *Meditations*, and his rejection of Stoicism in favour of Christianity, by a version of Lucian's *Hermotimus*, containing this suggestive comment on the godlike creatures who attained the heights of Stoic philosophy: 'Strange! And do they never come down again from the heights to help those whom they left below?'

Though cleverly devised, this scholarly infrastructure threatens to turn the novel into a mere compilation; but some sense of unity is given by the style, which maintains the same tone and tempo whatever the context, and by the repetition of certain ideas and images, those of children, of home, of animals, and of the eye. The miraculous birth of 'the child Romulus' on page one points forward to that of Psyche's semi-divine daughter Voluptas, and finally to that of Jesus. Throughout the narrative children stimulate or represent that human sympathy which Marius finds so appealing in Christianity. Pater's old image of rebirth took on a Christian meaning, first when St Peter brought a dead child to life (instead of the adult Tabitha as in Acts 9) and then, with a touch of the macabre, when a 'baby' hand protruding from a tiny, broken coffin hinted at the notion of being born again. It was 'the crying of the children' (with or without any thought of Euripides or Mrs Browning) that made the dying Marius dimly aware of the 'touching image of Jesus'; and he tried to 'fix his mind . . . on all the persons he had loved in life', 'like a child thinking over the toys it loves', before it falls asleep.

The theme of home was prominent from the start, with references to the Lares and Penates, and to Domiduca, the goddess of home-coming. For Marius, home, family, and religion are inseparable, and his death in the bosom of a Christian family is even more of a home-coming than his final visit to White-nights. His disillusionment with Marcus Aurelius and Stoicism is completed when the Emperor displays for ridicule in his triumphal procession 'our own ancestor, representative of subject Germany', complete with 'the very house he had lived in ... a wattled cottage'. As for the animal-theme, Marius first glimpses the great philosopher's feet of clay, when he presides over 'a show, in which mere cruelty to animals, their useless suffering and death, formed the main point of interest'; and in other passages Marius' concern for animals helped him to develop a general ideal of humanity towards all suffering creatures.

Most pervasive of all was the theme of the eye, connected with pictures, dreams, and visions. In a dreamlike interview, the priest of Aesculapius recommended to Marius 'a diligent promotion of the capacity of the eye, inasmuch as in the eye would lie for him the determining influence of life.' Through a special aperture in the wall of the shrine he was shown a picture-like 'vision of a new world', prefiguring his 'vision of the church in Cecilia's house', and his lifelong tendency to get all his spiritual enlightenment from visual experience. Pater, it seems, was the same: he saw the unworthy side of Aurelius' triumph most clearly in a picture by Mantegna. And perhaps the revolting account of flaying in the Circus, which suggests a sadistic streak in the author himself, was really a humanitarian response to Titian's *Flaying of Marsyas*.

In the novel itself, however, the visual element was less conspicuous than the intellectual. Despite some pleasant passages of description, Pater's treatment was hardly pictorial, except in its static quality. Its style, long-winded and far from crystal-clear, was not well adapted to fiction, though based on a theory which seemed convincing enough, when applied to the 'Euphuism' of Apuleius and Flavian. The theory was that even the most 'assiduous cultivation of manner' was all right, so long as it presented 'matter':

That preoccupation of the *dilettante* with what might seem mere details of form, after all, did but serve the purpose of bringing to the surface, sincerely and in their integrity, certain strong personal intuitions, a certain vision or apprehension of things as really being, with important results, thus rather than thus,—intuitions which the artistic or literary faculty was called upon to follow, with the exactness of wax or clay, clothing the model within.

This notion that perfect style meant perfect fidelity to 'the true nature of one's own impression' would be more neatly expressed in *Appreciations*. Here it was just one ingredient in a work less interesting for its literary criticism, or indeed as a novel, than as evidence of Pater's personal development. *Marius* marked his emergence from what he now saw as the 'isolating narrowness', the 'subjective and partial ideals' of the *Renaissance* Conclusion. Failure in life was no longer 'to form habits': 'Surely evil was a real thing, and the wise man wanting in the sense of it, where, not to have been, by instinctive election, on the right side, was to have failed in life.'

This subordination of the intellectual to the moral was con-tinued in 'Sebastian van Storck', one of the four short stories that made up *Imaginary Portraits* (1887). Sebastian, a character sug-gested by the winter landscapes of the Dutch painter Hendrick Avercamp, is a skater both literally and symbolically. For him, the 'lively purpose of life' has been 'frozen out of it' by an intellectual theory of the 'Infinite', which makes him skate over everything human as wholly unimportant. On this principle he cruelly rejects the girl who loves him, and is punished by a fit of 'black melancholy'. He finally redeems himself by dying in the act of rescuing a child from a flood. The moral of 'Denys l'Auxerrois' was less straightforward. Here Dionysus was reincarnated in thirteenth-century Auxerre, where he inaugurated a kind of Hellenic 'golden age'; but his 'dark or antipathetic side' proved unacceptable in a world that had outgrown 'childish conscious-ness, or rather unconsciousness', and his innocent savagery outraged more advanced moral values. He was finally torn to pieces by a mob whose 'evil passions' he had himself stimulated.

Imaginary Portraits showed great ingenuity in adapting myths, pictures, and historical facts to form new vehicles for Pater's old ideas. Thus in 'A Prince of Court Painters' Watteau was made to prefigure something very like that 'regeneration of the world' envisaged in the essay of 1864: 'a new era now dawning upon the world, of fraternity, liberty, humanity, of a novel sort of social freedom in which men's natural goodness of heart will blossom at a thousand points ...'. 'Duke Carl of Rosenmold', the 'northern Apollo' whose passion for the products of the Renaissance in the south led to the German *Aufklärung*, did more than represent two mythical light-bringers, Apollo and Balder: his return to life after a sham funeral, true to the *Resurgam* on his empty coffin, was itself a kind of *renaissance*. As fiction, however, the *Portraits* are unsatisfactory. The characters seldom speak, but only think or write. The narrative technique is undramatic. Even the death of Denys is described in a laconic retrospect:

The soul of Denys was already at rest, as his body, now borne along in front of the crowd, was tossed hither and thither, torn at last limb from limb. The men stuck little shreds of his flesh, or, failing that, of his torn raiment, into their caps; the women lending their long hairpins for the purpose.

Only some psychological insight, as in the characterization of Sebastian, and some hints of humour, as in the account of the ball-game in Auxerre cathedral, make the pieces a little more acceptable, if read simply as short stories.

Since 1866 Pater had been publishing literary criticism in various periodicals, and since 1880 in T. H. Ward's *English Poets*. Such articles were collected in *Appreciations* (1889), which included studies of Wordsworth, Coleridge, Shakespeare's *Measure for Measure*, and the poems of D. G. Rossetti. Wordsworth was praised for 'that sincerity, that perfect fidelity to one's own inward presentations, to the precise features of the picture within, without which any profound poetry is impossible', but also, less predictably, for his wisdom in protesting against a modern mistake that F. M. Alexander has called 'end-gaining': 'Justify rather the end by the means [his poetry] seems to say: whatever may become of the fruit, make sure of the flowers and the leaves.' 'Coleridge', while repeating some of the early attack on the prose, found one 'secret' of the poetry in the 'identification of the poet's thought, of himself, with the image or figure which serves him'. '"Measure for Measure"' stressed the 'ethical interest' of the play in showing 'the intricacy and subtlety of the moral world itself ... the difficulty of just judgment'. Rossetti was commended both for such Arnoldian virtues as 'serious beauty' and 'a great style', and also for Paterian ones like 'sincerity' and 'transparency', and for 'the adding to poetry of fresh poetic material . . . a new order of phenomena'.

The 'appreciations' were framed by two essays in literary theory, one on 'Style' and one on the distinction between classicism and romanticism. In this 'Postscript' Pater linked classicism with 'the absolute beauty of . . . artistic form', and 'the charm of familiarity', romanticism with 'strangeness': 'It is the addition of strangeness to beauty, that constitutes the romantic character in art; and the desire of beauty being a fixed element in every artistic organization, it is the addition of curiosity to this desire of beauty, that constitutes the romantic temper.' These two impulses (which had been called in *The Renaissance* 'the two elementary forces in Leonardo's genius') appeared in varying proportions in every artist and in every period of art. So like 'all critical terms' the words 'classical' and 'romantic' were 'relative', and the critic should not be 'overmuch occupied concerning them':

For, in truth, the legitimate contention is, not of one age or school of literary art against another, but of all successive schools alike, against the stupidity which is dead to the substance, and the vulgarity which is dead to form.

The disdainful note in this last sentence of the book, as of 'a fugitive and cloister'd vertue', had been struck before in the first essay, on 'style':

Different classes of persons, at different times, make, of course, very various demands upon literature. Still, scholars, I suppose, and not only scholars, but all distinterested lovers of books, will always look to it, as to all other fine art, for a refuge, a sort of cloistral refuge, from a certain vulgarity in the actual world.

But the rest of the essay was less donnish, and was sound in its main thesis:

Say what you have to say, what you have a will to say, in the simplest, the most direct and exact manner possible, with no surplusage:—there, is the justification of the sentence so fortunately born, 'entire, smooth, and round,' that it needs no punctuation, and also (that is the point) of the most elaborate period, if it be right in its elaboration. Here is the office of ornament: here also the purpose of restraint in ornament.

Pater's own style in *Appreciations* was seldom 'so fortunately born'. Heavily punctuated, and sometimes rather clumsy, it hardly lived up to his own theoretical standards. He charged Dryden with an 'imperfect mastery of the relative pronoun', and prescribed 'minute and constant' attention to the 'physiognomy' of words; but this was how he concluded his account of the 'finer justice' in *Measure for Measure*: 'for this true justice is dependent on just those finer appreciations which poetry cultivates in us the power of making, those peculiar valuations of action and its effect which poetry actually requires.'

Apart from six chapters of a novel, *Gaston de Latour*, which threatened to be a dull imitation of *Marius*, and two works of scholarship, *Plato and Platonism* and *Greek Studies*, Pater wrote little else of interest before his early death in 1894. But his last two stories, 'Emerald Uthwart' (1892) and 'Apollo in Picardy' (1893), formed an apt conclusion to his career, both because of their own merits, and because their common theme, the pointless destruction of a promising young man, makes one conscious of something disappointing about Pater's own life and work.

Inspired by a visit to his old school at Canterbury, the first story reads like a protest against his early education. Instead of burning, true to his name, with a hard, gem-like flame, and enjoying 'the sweets of the sensible world', Emerald is turned by school discipline into a 'submissive', 'repressible', 'self-restrained' stoic. As a soldier in action, he commits 'almost the sole irregular or undisciplined act' of his life, while 'still following his senior', by helping a friend do a deed of 'thoughtless bravery'. The friend is executed, and Emerald dishonourably discharged from the army, to die later of an 'old gun-shot wound'. The writing was occasionally banal: at the execution 'there was hardly a dry eye, and several young soldiers fainted'. The climax was deliberately macabre: a post-mortem operation to remove the rusty ball, after which the corpse was replaced in its coffin, with so many flowers that nothing remained visible but 'the hands and the peak of the handsome nose'. But this ironically completed an effective pattern of imagery, by which Emerald was a '*Flos Parietis*! thus carelessly plucked forth.' Thus an unconvincing plot was redeemed by its symbolic structure; and there was no lack of realism in one part of the story, at least—the account of a sensitive boy's reactions to a public-school education in a beautiful cathedral city.

'Apollo in Picardy' transferred the myth of Hyacinthus from ancient Greece to medieval France. It came nearer to Heine's fantasy than 'Denys l'Auxerrois', in its touches of sly humour at the expense of Prior Saint-Jean. This 'strenuous, self-possessed, much-honoured monastic student' is sent mad by a god of 'light' disguised as a handsome young farm-hand called, not Apollo, but Apollyon (the destroyer). Here, in his last and most haunting image of the Renaissance, Pater stressed the inconsistency of Apollo's character. Like Morris an 'idle singer', he was both a culture-god and a cause of demonic possession; an animal-lover who slaughters pigeons like 'a wild-cat, or other savage beast'; a god of health and of plague. In him the pagan ethic of 'untutored natural impulse, of natural inspiration' was shown to revivify culture but prove morally unacceptable either to the medieval or to the modern consciousness. Pater presented the problem without offering any solution, in an attractive story with a sensational climax:

Under the overcast sky it is in darkness they are playing, by guess and touch chiefly; and suddenly an icy blast of wind has lifted the roof from the old chapel, the trees are moaning in wild circular motion, and their devil's penny-piece, when Apollyon throws it for the last time, is itself but a twirling leaf in the wind, till it sinks edgewise, sawing through the boy's face, uplifted in the dark to trace it, crushing in the tender skull upon the brain.

The wilfully gruesome language, while indicating something not quite healthy in Pater's mind, was functional in its context. It served to sharpen the ambivalence of the tacit allusion to Myron's famous statue, the *Discobolus*, here made to typify not only the beauty of Hellenism, but also its moral inadequacy. As Matthew Arnold had said, 'the world could not live by it', and Pater's poor Prior could not do so either. He is last seen, mentally confused and 'under suspicion of murder', but still gazing nostalgically into the 'blue distance', towards the pagan world in which he has spent a brief holiday.

14. Four Notable Authors

'Every schoolboy knows who imprisoned Montezuma, and who strangled Atahualpa.' So thought Macaulay, rashly extrapolating from his own experience.[1] Since the age of three he had been absorbing the contents of books, apparently 'through the skin', as one observer put it, and remembering everything he read. He knew *Paradise Lost* by heart, and found it just as easy to memorize unrelated facts. 'Any fool,' he once remarked, 'could say his Archbishops of Canterbury backwards'. His computer-like mind gave his writings a tone of slightly insensitive dogmatism, and encouraged a method of argument that relied too much on apt quotations and examples; but his immense knowledge and incisive style make him hard to disagree with, at least at the moment of reading him.

He was thus ideally qualified for a legal or political career. Called to the Bar in 1826, he was never a practising lawyer, but distinguished himself in that field by drafting a new penal code for India in 1837. An MP from 1830, he soon reached Cabinet rank, and was active in politics until his heart-attack in 1852. But his chief interest was in literature and scholarship. He never married, and the people who meant most to him seem to have been his sisters. To one of them he confided: 'Books are becoming everything to me. If I had at this moment my choice of life, I would bury myself in one of those immense libraries . . . and never pass a waking hour without a book before me.' When that sister died, and the other got married, he told a friend: 'Literature has saved my life and my reason. Even now, I dare not, in the intervals of business, remain alone for a minute without a book in my hand.' Books enabled him to live 'with the past, the future, the distant,

---

[1] Thomas Babington Macaulay, 1800–59, was born in Leicestershire, the son of a philanthropic but soon prosperous merchant, and brought up at Clapham. He went to Trinity College, Cambridge, where he won a fellowship, 1824. By then his father was no longer prosperous, and became partly dependent on his son, who started writing for the *Edinburgh Review*, 1825. His parliamentary career began 1830, and he was a member of the supreme council in India, 1834–8. After his sister Hannah married Charles Trevelyan, he lived with them, and their son G. O. Trevelyan became his biographer. From 1852 he was a semi-invalid.

and the unreal.' Of these he preferred the past, and his own books were primarily historical.

From 1825 to 1844 he wrote articles in the Whig *Edinburgh Review*, most of which were collected in *Critical and Historical Essays* (1843). The first, written to please his father Zachary Macaulay, an ardent abolitionist, associated 'Tories and Radicals' with the defence of slavery in the West Indies, and subsequent articles had the same political slant. 'Milton' began as literary criticism, but ended by vindicating the poet as a propagandist for revolution and regicide. 'Southey's Colloquies' ridiculed the Tory *Quarterly Review* in the person of one of its contributors, and denounced 'Mr. Southey's idol, the omniscient and omnipotent State'. The article decided the Whig politician Lord Lansdowne to offer Macaulay a pocket borough, and in 1831 he made his first great speech in support of the Reform Bill. Oratory tightened and strengthened his written style, and three months later he produced his witty essay on Byron, as a poet whose 'political opinions . . . leaned strongly towards the side of liberty.' It ended with a delightful satire on Byronism, as practised by 'hopeful undergraduates and medical students': 'From the poetry of Lord Byron they drew a system of ethics, compounded of misanthropy and voluptuousness, a system in which the two great commandments were, to hate your neighbour, and to love your neighbour's wife.'

Though loosely linked to recent publications, the subjects of the essays show the movement of Macaulay's interests, from contemporary politics to history. 'Samuel Johnson' exposed the editorial incompetence of the Tory, J. W. Croker, but also praised Boswell's *Life* for its method of historical portraiture. Between 1831 and 1838, when he outlined the plan of his *History*, Macaulay wrote essays on several figures in the seventeenth and eighteenth centuries. Of these, Horace Walpole was dismissed as an entertaining writer, too frivolous to be more than a nominal Whig. Bacon was an unscrupulous politician but, as a scientist, represented the kind of progress that the *History* would celebrate. Swift's patron, Sir William Temple, censured for being a 'mere holiday-politician', was possibly a scapegoat for Macaulay's own impulse to escape from active politics into literature. Among these studies of historical figures appeared one of a historian, 'Sir James Mackintosh'. This touched on the theme of the *History*, the 'beneficial' effects of the 1688 Revolution, and listed some qualifications for writing history: one must be a 'judge', not an 'advocate'; have 'imagination' and a gift for 'lively' narrative; and possess 'that eminent qualification' (which Macaulay certainly had himself) of having 'spoken history, acted history, lived history'. Two later essays, 'Clive' and 'Warren Hastings', were products of his four years in India, as Law Member in the Governor's Supreme Council. Both showed a growing talent for 'lively' story-telling, perfected in 'Frederick the Great'; and 'Madame d'Arblay', in lamenting the stylistic decline in Fanny Burney's novels, reflected Macaulay's ambition (confessed in a letter of 1841) to write a history that would 'for a few supersede the last fashionable novel on the tables of young ladies'.

In themselves, the *Essays* are interesting chiefly for their style, their characterization, and their literary criticism. Though much longer than the average modern article, they consist of short, forcible sentences, rich in epigram: 'Voltaire could not build: he could only pull down: he was the very Vitruvius of ruin.' 'See', he once wrote in a letter, 'how antitheses drop from my pen in its most rapid and unstudied movements.' He liked them in character as well as in prose: he was fascinated by contradictions. Machiavelli was both 'the martyr of freedom' and 'the apostle of tyranny', Bacon, 'the checkered spectacle of so much glory and so much shame.' Clive, the brilliant general and administrator, forged a signature on a treaty. Frederick, the military genius, had a 'passion for writing indifferent poetry'. In moral issues, Macaulay stressed such discrepancies for the sake of historical truth. Always at war with hagiographers, he emphasized the discreditable facts about his heroes, as when Bacon 'went to the Tower to listen to the yells of Peacham' under torture. Here, true to his principle of not judging one period by the standards of another, Macaulay pointed out that Bacon was 'distinctly behind his age'. And in literary criticism, though it was never his main concern, Macaulay showed considerable acuteness, as in recognizing Restoration Comedy as an over-reaction to Puritanism, defining the Byronic hero and heroine, and distinguishing between Johnson's spoken and written language: '"*The Rehearsal*," he said, very unjustly, "has not wit enough to keep it sweet"; then, after a pause, "it has not vitality enough to preserve it from putrefaction."'

Matthew Arnold was equally unjust when he called Macaulay's *Lays of Ancient Rome* (1842) 'pinchbeck *Roman Ballads*'. The author of *Merope* should have been more charitable. Begun when Macaulay was reading Livy in India, the *Lays* were based on a theory revived by Niebuhr, that Livy's sources for the early history of Rome were 'lost ballads'. Macaulay reconstructed four such ballads, all somewhat Whiggish in sentiment. 'Horatius', composed by a discontented Plebeian, and 'The Battle of the Lake Regillus' sang of victories over supporters of the Tarquin monarchy. 'Virginia' was a piece of anti-Patrician propaganda designed to back the Tribunes of the Plebs in their efforts for political reform. 'The Prophecy of Capys' marked the triumph of the Roman Republic over a Greek king. Macaulay took pains to adjust each Lay to its historical context, and pointed out one anachronism, only to put the blame for it on the minstrel: 'he troubles himself little about dates'. Even the versification, based mainly on that of Scott and 'our own old ballads', was occasionally just rough enough to suggest the irregularity of early Latin verse. As a work of historical rather than poetic imagination, the *Lays* cannot fairly be compared with the type of poem that Tennyson published the same year; but they tell their stories well, and their boyish enthusiasm for a rather unappealing ethic is strangely infectious. When Horatius finally gets his head above water, even the most critical reader can 'scarce forbear to cheer'.

Still, the *Lays*, like the *Essays*, were merely preludes to Macaulay's greatest work, the *History of England from the Accession of James II* (1849–61). As he told his sister Margaret, his imagination had always been fired by history: 'The Past is in my mind soon constructed into a romance ... I am no sooner in the streets than I am in Greece, in Rome, in the midst of the French Revolution.' In an essay of 1828 he had outlined his theory of 'what a history ought to be', stressing the need for factual accuracy, impartiality, philosophical generalization, lifelike characterization, and 'the art of narration, the art of interesting the affections, and presenting pictures to the imagination.' This meant that no significant detail should be excluded as 'beneath the dignity' of history. The historian's job was to show the whole 'character and spirit of an age ... in miniature'. One who confined his attention to 'battles, treaties', and grand political events was like 'a gnat mounted on an elephant, and laying down theories as to the whole internal structure of the vast animal, from the phenomena of the hide.' A 'truly great historian' would display an 'intimate knowledge of the domestic history of nations', and 'reclaim those materials which the novelist has appropriated'. While confessing that such a paragon 'would indeed be an intellectual prodigy', Macaulay resolved to write a history of his own, starting with the 1688 Revolution, and possibly ending just before the 1832 Reform Act. In the event, his Parliamentary duties and subsequent ill health prevented the completion of the plan. The posthumous fifth volume went no further than William's death in 1702.

Though still respected by historians, Macaulay's *History* has been charged with misrepresentation due to political prejudice. Of that only specialists can judge; but no one has questioned the quality that made it a bestseller, its immense readability. For the rest, it seems fairest to assess it by his own standards. To achieve factual accuracy, he went to unprecedented lengths in consulting not only official documents but newspapers, manuscript newsletters, pamphlets, lampoons, satires, and every kind of literature. He also travelled extensively to inspect historical sites. Where Thucydides, despite his policy of excluding the 'fabulous', invented speeches for his characters, Macaulay studded his narrative with authentic sayings, like Charles II's characteristic apology for being 'a most unconscionable time dying', or James II's question when his tyranny was finally overthrown: '"What have I done?" he demanded of the Kentish squires who attended him. "Tell me the truth. What error have I committed?"' This was one of the methods by which Macaulay emulated the vivid characterization that he had praised in Tacitus. Another was the use of undignified detail. Thus the ungracious side of his hero, William, was epitomized in his gobbling up a whole dish of green peas, without offering a single spoonful to Princess Anne. Such willingness to see conflicting aspects of a character went far to realize Macaulay's ideal of impartiality. He clearly hated Judge Jeffreys, and confessed that, when one of his victims spotted him, disguised as a sailor and black with coal dust, the incident could 'hardly be related without a feeling of vindictive pleasure'. And yet Macaulay had allowed him traces of humanity, as when, drunk and practically naked, he was 'with difficulty prevented from climbing up a signpost to drink his Majesty's health.' In the Tower he became a 'pitiable spectacle'; and the record closed with his astonishing refusal to admit that 'he had done anything that deserved reproach'.

The 1828 essay had required the historian to identify 'principles'. The first principle of the *History* was that the 1688 Revolution, 'of all revolutions the least violent, [had] been of all revolutions the most beneficent.' The peroration of volume ii, written and published just after the European revolutions of 1848, implicitly repeated what Macaulay had said in Parliament in 1831: 'Reform, that you may preserve': 'It is because we had a preserving revolution in the seventeenth century that we have not had a destroying revolution in the nineteenth.' The second 'principle' was that 'the history of our country during the last hundred and sixty years is eminently the history of physical, of moral, and of intellectual improvement.' This thesis was powerfully supported by a fascinating, if not wholly reliable, chapter of social history (iii, 'The State of England in 1685'), and by frequent reference to penal atrocities and other signs of barbarism, in the periods covered. Macaulay's assumption of progress has been ridiculed as an example of Victorian complacency; but he was right in claiming that the Victorians did not invent the social evils for which they are now notorious: they were the first to recognize, and try to eliminate them. Nor did his sense of progress imply that he was satisfied with contemporary society. There was pointed sarcasm in his fantasy that it might be fashionable in the twentieth century 'to talk of the reign of Queen Victoria as the time when England was truly merry England, when all classes were bound together by brotherly sympathy, when the rich did not grind the faces of the poor, and when the poor did not envy the splendour of the rich.'

But the real charm of the *History* was its 'narrative art'. It is most exciting to read, either as a kind of novel, or as a collection of short stories. Its large-scale structure can be enjoyed by tracing the growth of resistance to James II, through the dispute with Magdalen College, Oxford, and the trial of the bishops, to the climactic proclamation of William and Mary. Shorter units, relatively self-contained and varying widely in their type of appeal, include the death of Charles II, an appalling record of iatrogenic suffering; the gruesome but inspiring siege of Londonderry; the grimly comic episodes of the Darien Scheme and of Captain Kidd, the official pirate-hunter who became a pirate himself; the death of James II, making sure that his forgiveness of the Emperor ('the hardest of all exercises of Christian charity') should not pass unnoticed; and William's final heroism:

His end was worthy of his life. His intellect was not for a moment clouded. His fortitude was the more admirable because he was not willing to die. He had very lately said to one of those whom he most loved: 'You know that I never feared death; there have been times when I should have wished it; but, now that this great new prospect is opening before me, I do wish to stay here a little longer.' Yet no weakness, no querulousness, disgraced the noble close of that noble career. To the physicians the King returned his thanks graciously and gently. 'I know that you have done all that skill and learning could do for me: but the case is beyond your art; and I submit.'

To Harriet Martineau, Macaulay's *History* was just 'a brilliant fancypiece'.[2] Her own brilliance was less obvious but equally real. She worked against obstacles of poverty and chronic ill health that make Macaulay's life seem relatively easy, and her famous ear-trumpet epitomized her triumph over circumstances. Deaf from the age of fourteen, and left penniless at twenty-seven, she made herself one of the best-known authors in her period. Once mistaken, on a steamer near Malta, for a megaphone, the ear-trumpet may also serve to symbolize her type of authorship. Heterogeneous information, from both oral and written sources, was funnelled into her brain, where it was rapidly processed and broadcast to her readers in more simple and vivid terms. Supremely successful as a researcher and educator, she did herself less than justice in an obituary written twenty years too soon:

With small imaginative and suggestive powers, and therefore nothing approaching to genius, she could see clearly what she did see, and give a clear expression to what she had to say. In short, she could popularize, while she could neither discover nor invent.

All her work was didactic. She made her name with short stories designed to teach economic theory. She then undertook to tell the public the facts about America, and about domestic service. Her novels and children's books were meant to teach history or morality or both. Next, from her own experience, she gave instruction about illness and its cure. The account of her Middle

[2] Harriet Martineau, 1802-76, sister of James Martineau the theologian, was the daughter of a Unitarian manufacturer, who died when she was twenty-four. In 1829 the family lost what little money he had left them, by a failed investment, and she had to earn her own living. On the success of the *Illustrations* she moved to London, 1832, then to Tynemouth, 1840, after her health broke down. When she recovered, 1845, she had a house built at Ambleside, Lake District, which became her final home.

Eastern travels became a treatise on comparative religion. Her *History* was intended to impart 'sound political knowledge and views'; and even the *Autobiography* was written as a 'duty': she had 'derived profit' from other people's autobiographies, and rightly assumed that her own would be equally profitable.

The *Illustrations of Political Economy*, of *Poor Laws and Paupers*, and of *Taxation* (1832–4) were produced at phenomenal speed, 'thirty-four little volumes', she recorded, 'in two years and a half,—the greater part of the time being one unceasing whirl of business and social excitement.' Here, improving on the method of Mrs Jane Marcet's *Conversations on Political Economy* (1816), Harriet Martineau tried to show how the principles of Adam Smith, Malthus, and Ricardo operated in real life, appending to each story a brief 'Summary of Principles illustrated'. Sometimes these abstract principles monopolized the narrative, in dreary arguments between interested parties, or lectures by economic experts, but in the best stories they were fully dramatized. Thus the Luddite workers in 'The Hill and the Valley', failing to understand that 'Machinery, by assisting the growth of Capital, therefore increases the demand for labour', set fire to a factory, and so destroy their only chance of employment in the area. Malthusian theory was similarly enforced by 'Weal and Woe in Garveloch', a grim tale of famine on a remote Scottish island.

Despite their repellent title, the *Illustrations* were rich in fictional variety. The settings, all carefully researched, included not only industrial Manchester and a Tyneside mining village, but also such places as a plantation in Demerara, a labour-camp in Siberia, seventeenth-century Amsterdam, and a pearl-fishery in Ceylon. The characters were equally varied. The most unexpected was Archie in 'Ella of Garveloch', an endearing version of Wordsworth's Idiot Boy, who, 'as if suddenly inspired by reason', saves his brother from drowning at the cost of his own life. The most convincing one was William Allen in 'A Manchester Strike', a reluctant strikeleader who tries to obey his conscience and common sense, against great pressure from his union, his employers, and his own wife and family.

The series was so popular that the struggling young author from Norwich became instantly a London 'lion'. It is still very far from 'unreadable', as the *Dictionary of National Biography* called it in 1909. At times the approach seems coldly doctrinaire, as when 'indiscriminate charity' is condemned in 'Cousin Marshall', or child-labour is condoned in 'A Manchester Strike'; but there is plenty of human feeling in the treatment of press-gangs and of slavery. The thesis of 'Demerara' is that slavery 'inflicts an incalculable amount of human suffering, for the sake of making a wholesale waste of labour and capital', and the suffering is powerfully conveyed. When a runaway slave is torn to pieces by bloodhounds and his sister is caught, the horror is enhanced by irony: 'She was asleep or in a stupor when brought back to her hut, a circumstance which was pointed out by a white as conclusive of the fact that negroes have no feeling.' The *Illustrations* opened up new material for Victorian fiction, anticipating the novels of industrial conflict, of politics, and of social issues. 'For Each and for All', an attack on Owenite theory, was Trollopian in exploiting the relation between a politician's public and private life, and also pioneered the feminist heroine in the lively character of Letitia, the ex-actress wife of a government minister. More generally, later novelists seem to have taken her husband's advice when he said: 'The true romance of life lies among the poorer classes ... yet these things are almost untouched by our artists; ... be they dramatists, painters, or novelists ... let humble life be shown.'

Society in America (1837) was based on a tour lasting almost two years. It was a sociological survey, closer to Alexis de Tocqueville's *La démocratie en Amérique* (1835) than Frances Trollope's *Domestic Manners of the Americans* (1832), which Harriet Martineau thought too personal and prejudiced. Like Tocqueville she found an undue fear of nonconformity, and like Arnold fifty years later, much vulgarity; but her chief complaints were more philosophical: the contradiction between democratic egalitarianism and the facts of slavery and the subordination of women. She praised American manners ('the best I ever saw') and the freedom allowed to children, and was sympathetic to the idea of socialism, as a butterfly-state at which the American caterpillar would eventually arrive, however much it now disliked the prospect. Meanwhile she satirized certain aspects of the American character, as in the man who told her that

there had been a time when he believed, like other people, that he might be mistaken; but that experience had convinced him that he never was; and he had in consequence cast behind him the fear of error. I told him I was afraid the place he lived in must be terribly dull,—having an oracle in it to settle everything. He replied that the worst of it was, other people were not so convinced of his being always in the right as he was himself. There was no joke here. He is a literal and serious-minded man.

A Retrospect of Western Travel (1838) was written to meet a demand for a more 'personal narrative' of her American experience, and of 'the lighter characteristics of men, and incidents of travel'. The 'lighter' material included much damning evidence against slavery in the South, with descriptions of a prison, a lunatic asylum, two homes for deaf mutes, and a mechanized slaughterhouse for pigs in Cincinnati, the only unpleasant thing that she refused to see for herself. In the 'personal' category came some delightful glimpses of the author, braving, for instance, the messy process of eating corn on the cob: 'Surrendering such a vegetable from considerations of grace is not to be thought of.' Humour, moral courage, and common sense had brought her through what sounds like a gruelling ordeal. Among the 'annoyances' of sea-travel she noted: 'hard beds ... Remedy, patience. Perhaps air-cushions may be better still.' As for America itself, she painted a vivid panorama, with a few great landmarks. One was Emerson, 'without knowing whom it is not too much to say that the United States cannot be fully known.' Another was New Orleans, 'the last place in which men are gathered together where one who prizes his Humanity would wish to live.'

Her own humanity was less obvious in *The Housemaid* (1839), a pamphlet published for the Poor Law Commissioners to recruit and train domestic servants, than in her two novels. With American slavery in mind, she thought first of writing one on the Negro revolutionary, Toussaint l'Ouverture (1743–1803); but a friend discouraged the idea, so she began with *Deerbrook* (1839). The setting was a contemporary English village, the manner influenced by admiration for Jane Austen, and the plot suggested by the author's mistaken belief that a family friend had married one of two sisters, while really in love with the other. That is what her apothecary-hero, Edward Hope, does, and the strain on the marriage is increased when the unmarried sister joins the household. Hope's problems are professional as well as domestic. His medical practice is almost destroyed by the enmity of the local squire, outraged that Hope has not voted for him in an election, and the machinations of a neighbour called Mrs Rowland, who resents his marrying a relation of her social rival. By a resolute exercise of faith, hope, and charity, the hero makes his marriage a success, and regains his professional reputation, having proved in a cholera epidemic the villagers' only hope.

The novel resembles a morality play in more than this use of a name. Apart from a general ethic compounded of Christianity, Stoicism, and Homeric self-respect, it inculcated some of its author's characteristic beliefs: that a voter should obey his conscience, regardless of consequences; that poverty was unimportant, a mere 'deficiency of the comforts of life', to be met by stern retrenchment; and that in medicine, as in all things, a rational approach was essential. But, despite its didacticism, *Deerbrook* can be enjoyed as a novel. Except for the stage-villainess Mrs Rowland, the characters are interesting and realistic. Hester, the wife, is a hypersensitive neurotic, as tiresome in her remorse and self-abasement as in her ruthless egotism, but responding well to a crisis that calls for 'magnanimity'. Miss Young, the crippled governess, who philosophically accepts sexual privation, may well reflect an aspect of Harriet Martineau's own adjustment to life.

Wordsworth made Toussaint l'Ouverture a symbol of 'man's unconquerable mind', and *The Hour and the Man* (1841), a historical novel about him, was itself a triumph of mind over matter, being written when its author was seriously ill and practically bedridden. Her initial source had been an article in the *Quarterly Review* (April 1819), and after extensive research she had actually visited the 'cold, damp, gloomy dungeon' in the fortress of Joux, where Napoleon had imprisoned Toussaint until he died. He was certainly a remarkable man, who read Epictetus, Caesar, and Plutarch while still a slave, and when in power, maintained a policy of 'No Retaliation' in spite of atrocities committed by the whites. In the novel he appears as not only a saint and martyr, but also a military, diplomatic, and political genius. True to his name, he is 'the portal of freedom to his race', 'the way which God had opened' to Negro emancipation. Though the total effect is more like hagiography than history, the concluding chapters are genuinely moving, even inspiring; but the stiffness of the narrative style, and the absurd elegance of the dialogue, where the speakers are supposed to be illiterate, make the work very hard to read as a novel.

The five children's stories in *The Playfellow* (1841), though equally edifying, were much more readable, but their outlook seems faintly morbid, possibly because they were written when Harriet Martineau still thought of herself as an invalid. 'The Crofton Boys', for instance, preached the virtues of endurance, self-reliance, and forgiveness, but made no protest against the barbarous conditions in which they were exhibited. In Crofton School a 'passionate' boy might be buried up to his neck in the ground by a mob of his 'playfellows', or have his foot crushed by a coping-stone so that it had to be amputated. Hugh was praised for his courage in undergoing this operation, but nothing was said against the headmaster for allowing such a thing to happen. 'Feats on the Fiord' was an exciting adventure story with a villain who had thrown three children to the wolves, to save his own life. 'The Peasant', set shortly before the French Revolution, ended happily for one family, but with a gloomy reference to 'many hundred thousand miserable' ones. 'The Prince' was a harrowing biography of Louis XVII, which attributed the sorrows of his family to the ignorance of Marie Antoinette, 'especially her ignorance of men and common life'. 'The Settlers at Home' taught self-reliance by a grim tale of how some children coped with total isolation by a flood. The one casualty was their baby brother, but they resourcefully improvised a funeral service, constructed a stone coffin, and buried him under a tree—unearthing in the process a mummified corpse of great antiquity.

A healthier product of Harriet Martineau's illness was *Life in the Sick-room: Essays by an invalid* (1844). This was not, as Carlyle thought, an appeal for sympathy, 'as if she were a female Christ, saying, "Look at me: see how I am suffering!"' It was a 'conversation' with other invalids, warning them against the moral dangers of their situation, such as irritability, and suggesting compensations for illness, which included having time to read *all* the newspapers, not just the angled reports of one or two. The book also urged friends and nurses to be honest with patients ('When the time approaches that I am to die, let me be told that I am to die, and when'); and urged tolerance of empirical forms of treatment like homoeopathy and mesmerism. It was mesmerism, or her faith in it, that then restored her to health, and her *Letters on Mesmerism* (1845), published and later ridiculed in the *Athenaeum*, told the fascinating story of how this happened. Modern believers in alternative medicine will take her account more seriously than her contemporaries did, and it is beyond dispute that a year later the invalid was sufficiently recovered to start an arduous tour of Egypt, Palestine, Syria, and the Lebanon.

Eastern Life, Present and Past (1848) is the most entertaining of all her books. A lively blend of travelogue and guide-book, it gave a personal impression of many famous sights. Petra, for all its 'distressingly gaudy' rock-colours and the 'colonial vulgarity' of its Roman ornaments, was 'the most romantic vision of the travels of my life'. She presented a bizarre picture of the intrepid Victorian tourist, coping with huge discomforts and difficulties, and handling the natives with confident paternalism: 'We treated them as children: and this answered perfectly well.' As for the invalid herself, she narrowly avoided falling from her horse down a precipice; ironed collars and gowns for her fellow-travellers while being rowed up the Nile; amused members of a harem by saying 'Bo!' into her ear-trumpet; bathed in the Red Sea, though warned against sharks; and enjoyed every minute of it—except when riding a camel. But she scorned so 'undutiful a levity' as travelling 'for nothing but picturesque and amusing impressions'. Slavery, polygamy, and ignorance of political economy were castigated wherever she found them, and the whole book was designed as a study in religious development, from the beliefs of ancient Egypt to Judaism, Christianity, and Islam. It concluded that all 'Faiths' should be respected, but none considered definitive: 'all genuine faith is—other circumstances being the same,—of about equal value. The value is in the act of faith, more than in the object'.

Her own faith by this time had developed from the Unitarianism of her youth to a humanistic faith in 'great ideas'. Reviewing the period she had lived through in her *History of England during the Thirty Years' Peace* (1849–50), she identified the 'great idea' of the age as Reform in every sphere. Having registered the progress made in that direction, she predicted that the 'central fact' of the following period would be the solution of the 'tremendous Labour Question . . . the question whether the toil of a life is not to provide a sufficiency of bread.' The *History* itself was more like a chronicle, being largely based on Hansard and the *Annual Register*. Researched and written at speed, it was generally pedestrian in style, but rose to eloquence or satirical wit on subjects close to the author's heart, such as popular education, Parliamentary Reform, and women's rights. Of an article arguing against the Infants'

Custody Bill of 1839 she wrote: 'This ... proceeded on the supposition that all women are bent on mischief; and that the only way to manage them is to place them under the absolute despotism of their husbands.'

'The retrospect of one's own life, from the stillness of the sick-room', she had observed in 1844, 'is unendurable to any considerate person, except in the light of the deepest religious humility.' Told by two doctors in 1855 that she might die at any moment, she faced the ordeal and started writing her *Autobiography* (1877). She need not have hurried, but it is fortunate that she wrote it in her intellectual prime. Using a relaxed and conversational but always pithy style, she vividly described her world and her own experience. The most interesting passages were on her early childhood, the *Illustrations*, her gradual transformation from a 'remarkably religious child' into a Comtean free thinker, her methods of composition, and her final attitude to death. Her childhood was marked by many irrational terrors, as of a magic-lantern show, for instance; but she had at least one happy moment before she was five, when she 'wickedly' opened her bedroom window before anyone else was awake, and stood her baby brother James on a chair to admire a 'gorgeous' dawn sky. The dramatic success story of the *Illustrations* involved a notable display of courage and determination: 'The people wanted the book; and they should have it.' A momentous stage of her religious development was her conversion to Necessarianism, when she felt 'it was better to take the chance of being damned than be always quacking one's self in the fear of it.' Her account of how she wrote contained a sentence that every would-be writer should memorize:

I have suffered, like other writers, from indolence, irresolution, distaste to my work, absence of 'inspiration', and all that: but I have also found that sitting down, however reluctantly, with the pen in my hand, I have never worked for one quarter of an hour without finding myself in full train ...

As for death, she faced it with a delightful mixture of insouciance and open-mindedness: 'If I am mistaken in supposing that I am now vacating my place in the universe, which is to be filled by another,—if I find myself conscious after the lapse of life,—it will be all right, of course; but, as I said, the supposition appears to me absurd.'

For John Stuart Mill open-mindedness was a basic principle.[3] He claimed no greater distinction than a 'willingness and ability to learn from everybody', and he always tried to recognize the 'substratum of truth' in views that he thought generally wrong. Thus his textbook of capitalist economics included arguments for socialism, his last sceptical essay on religion tolerated 'simple Hope' of an afterlife, and his feminist manifesto admitted the existence of domineering wives who were 'a proper subject for the law of divorce'. One of his arguments against censorship was that 'the silenced opinion' might 'contain a portion of the truth'; and he valued the clash of opinions enough to found a debating society before he was twenty, and play an active part in another, where the speakers included not only Benthamites but Liberals, Coleridgeans, and 'two excellent Tory speakers'—though Tories had proved rather hard to recruit. He seems to have viewed marriage as a kind of debating society, in which husband and wife could 'have alternatively the pleasure of leading and of being led in the path of development'. He developed such a marriage of minds with Harriet Taylor, which became after twenty years, when her husband died, a more conventional one; and Harriet did her share of leading. But in every sphere Mill believed in a marriage of opposites. A strict Benthamite complained in 1840: 'he was most emphatically a philosopher, but then he read Wordsworth, and that muddled him, and he has been in a strange confusion ever since, endeavouring to unite poetry and philosophy.' Though most of his works were on non-literary subjects—logic, economics, political theory, or what 'by a convenient barbarism', as he said, had 'been termed Sociology'—his interest in poetry and feeling, his tendency to treat every subject in a broad human context, and the lucid precision of his style entitle him to a place in literary history.

There were four obvious stages in his development. Until 1826, when he fell into a state of deep depression, his mind was dominated by his father James Mill, and by Benthamite theory.

[3] John Stuart Mill, 1806–73, was born in Pentonville, London, the son of Bentham's friend James Mill, who systematically educated him, and got him a job in his own department of India House. There he worked for the next thirty-five years, 1823–58. In 1831 he met and formed a close relationship with Mrs Harriet Taylor, whom he married, 1851, after her husband died. In 1858 she died at Avignon, where he continued to live for half of each year, spending the other half at Blackheath.

Until about 1843 he was working out a synthetic philosophy of his own, which included elements drawn, not only from the Utilitarians, but also from Coleridge and Carlyle. Until Harriet's death in 1858 his books were, according to him, written in close collaboration with her, though he possibly exaggerated her contribution when he prefaced *On Liberty* (1859) with the statement that they belonged 'as much to her as to me'. For the rest of his life he was apparently carrying out, with whatever fresh thoughts of his own, a programme of book-production on which they had previously agreed.

'I never was a boy,' said Mill in 1833, 'never played at cricket; it is better to let Nature have her own way.' His father had thought otherwise. He put his baby son through a crash course in general culture, which enabled him to write, at six and a half, a ten-page 'History of Rome'. At less than eighteen he published an article (*Westminster Review*, April 1824), condemning the *Edinburgh Review* for two vices that he would soon consider virtues: an interest in 'mere feelings', and a 'spirit of compromise', in which it 'preached alternately, first on the one side and then on the other' of every question. But on one point he had already ceased to be a mouthpiece for his father. James Mill had argued that women did not need a vote, since their interests were usually 'involved' in those of their fathers or husbands. His son ridiculed the *Edinburgh's* similar attitudes:

In a woman, it is esteemed amiable to be a coward. To be entirely dependant upon her husband for every pleasure, and for exemption from every pain; to feel secure, only when under his protection; to be incapable of forming any opinion, or of taking any resolution without his advice and aid; this is amiable, this is delicate, this is feminine: while all who infringe on any of the prerogatives which man thinks proper to reserve for himself; all who can or will be of any use, either to themselves or to the world, otherwise than as the slaves and drudges of their husbands, are called masculine, and other names intended to convey disapprobation.

The first important product of Mill's second period was 'The Spirit of the Age', published in the Radical *Examiner* (1831). This presented the age as at a 'crisis of transition' from government by rich men and nobles to government by 'fitter' persons. While welcoming such a change, Mill warned against rushing from one extreme to another. When 'men break loose from an error', he observed, they usually resolve that the new light which has broken in on them shall be the sole light; and they wilfully and passionately blow out the ancient lamp, which, though it did not show them what they now see, served very well to enlighten the objects in the immediate neighbourhood.

Thus the new light of democracy was apt to obscure the facts of history, and the need for expert knowledge and scientific method. Common sense was not enough. Experience showed that 'the men who place implicit faith in their own common sense are, without exception, the most wrong-headed and impracticable persons.' Here, with a pleasant touch of humour, Mill formulated one of his central ideas:

men ... have in general an invincible propensity to split the truth, and take half, or less than half of it; and a habit of erecting their quills and bristling up like a porcupine against anyone who brings them the other half, as if he were attempting to deprive them of the portion which they have.

These quite rational articles made Carlyle exclaim, 'here is a new Mystic', and led to a friendship between the two men. For what he called 'a long period' Mill greatly admired Carlyle, but found his works helpful 'not as philosophy to instruct, but as poetry to animate'. His own article 'On Genius' (1831), which interpreted genius chiefly as thinking for oneself, and deplored the replacement of education by 'cram', used Carlyle's emphasis on 'spirit' to introduce an implicit criticism of Bentham: even 'the most absolute utilitarianism must come to the same conclusion', i.e. that without such 'higher endowments' as 'wisdom and virtue', 'happiness' was impossible. 'Prose', said Bentham, 'is when all the lines except the last go on to the end. Poetry is when some of them fall short of it.' In 'What is Poetry?' and 'The Two Kinds of Poetry' (1833) Mill improved on the later definition: 'poetry is overheard ... is feeling, confessing itself to itself in moments of solitude.' If this seems a mere paraphrase of Shelley, there was originality in Mill's distinction between poets 'of nature' and 'of culture', and in the suggestion that a 'mere poet' and the 'philosophical poet' represented two different ways of arriving at 'truth', which would ideally be combined in the same person. Hoping that Tennyson might become such a person, Mill urged him, in a perceptive review of his poems (1835), to 'cultivate, and with no half devotion, philosophy as well as poetry'. He implied something similar in a review of Carlyle's *French Revolution* (1837). Having praised the work highly as 'an epic poem', he complained that its author, using the artist's method of 'figuring things to himself as wholes', went 'as much too far in his distrust of analysis and generalization, as others ... went too far in their reliance upon it'.

The principle of finding truth in contrasting forms of thought was finally elaborated in 'Bentham' and 'Coleridge' (*Westminster Review*, 1838, 1840). Here the two thinkers were presented as 'contraries', 'not hostile, but supplementary to one another'. Bentham was praised for his 'questioning spirit', his 'warfare against absurdity', his 'sifting and anatomizing method', but criticized for lack of human experience, sympathy, and poetic feeling; above all for his one-sidedness, his contempt for previous thinkers, and his inability to learn from others. Coleridge was praised as an 'unsectarian' poet who, instead of despising ancient institutions, tried to find out their meaning, and the reasons for their survival; who realized that most errors were 'truths misunderstood', or 'half-truths taken as a whole'. The articles marked Mill's emancipation from crude Utilitarianism, and posed the political question: 'Is it, at all times and places, good for mankind to be under the absolute authority of the majority of themselves?' Answering Bentham's charge that 'All Poetry is misrepresentation', he justified hyperbole as a means to emotional effect: 'All writing addressed to the feelings has a natural tendency to exaggeration; but Bentham should have remembered that in this, as in many things, we must aim at too much, to be assured of doing enough.' Bentham was also blamed for 'perpetually aiming at impracticable precision', and so making his prose unreadable:

He could not bear, for the sake of clearness and the reader's ease, to say, as ordinary men are content to do, a little more than the truth in one sentence, and correct it in the next. The whole of the qualifying remarks which he intended to make, he insisted on imbedding as parentheses in the very middle of the sentence itself.

The *System of Logic* (1843) was the last work of Mill's on which Harriet Taylor had no direct influence. Its chief interest for the non-logician lies in its concluding call for a new science of psychology, its scepticism about the 'long list of mental and moral differences ... observed, or supposed to exist, between men and women', and its demand that political economy should take more account of human nature. This demand Mill himself tried to meet in his *Principles of Political Economy* (1848). The human aspect of his approach was most conspicuous in three chapters, on the 'Stationary State', the 'Probable Future of the Labouring Classes', and 'Property'. The first protested against the effects of industrial progress on the quality of life and the environment. The second, on which Harriet apparently insisted, rejected paternalistic reforms in favour of greater self-government by the working classes themselves. The third set out the pros and cons of socialism. Mill's gravest objection to it was that it would probably result in monotony, uniformity, and loss of personal freedom: 'no one's way of life, occupations, or movements, would depend on choice, but each would be the slave of all'.

The *Principles* ended with a protest against such 'government interference' as the censorship of opinions; for instance, the recent imprisonment of 'several individuals . . . for the public profession, sometimes in a very temperate manner, of infidel opinions'. Soon afterwards Mill wrote, but did not publish, two infidel essays of his own. 'Nature', with a dry humour meant to recall 'the Socratic Elenchus, as exhibited and improved by Plato', systematically refuted the argument of Paley's *Natural Theology*. The world was too cruel and unjust to have been created by a God both benevolent and omnipotent: 'If the maker of the world *can* all that he will, he wills misery, and there is no escape from the conclusion.' 'The Utility of Religion' similarly refuted the idea that religious belief was essential to morality and social welfare. In fact, the fear of Hell (that 'dreadful idealization of wickedness') had proved quite ineffective as 'a more cunning sort of police', and morality would be better served by a quasi-religious devotion to the good of one's species. Here Mill anticipated Matthew Arnold in seeing theology as poetry taken too literally.

The thesis of *On Liberty* had already been stated in the *Principles*: 'there is a circle round every individual human being which no government . . . ought to be permitted to overstep . . . within which the individuality of the person ought to reign uncontrolled either by any other individual or by the public collectively . . . '. The later work defined this area more precisely, added supporting arguments, and discussed practical applications. Censorship was condemned because it might, in various ways, 'put down' truth. Personal freedom was desirable, not only for the individual, but also for society, since individuals were the growing-points of humanity, the sources of all energy, originality, and progress: 'it is useful . . . that there should be different experiments of living'. The arguments were compelling; but the literary value of the book lay in its persuasive power, as a work designed (to use a phrase from 'Bentham') 'to make men feel truths as well as see them'. This was achieved, partly by infectious enthusiasm for the idea of individuality, partly by satire directed against 'the despotism of Public Opinion', and partly by a pervasive image of organic growth:

Human nature is not a machine to be built after a model, and set to do exactly the work prescribed for it, but a tree, which requires to grow and develop itself on all sides, according to the tendency of the inward forces which make it a living thing.

But 'narrow' theorists preferred people 'cramped and dwarfed . . . just as many have thought that trees are a much finer thing when clipped into pollards, or cut into figures of animals, than as nature made them.'

Utilitarianism (1861) was an attempt to 'make men feel' that Utilitarians were not narrow theorists, but admirable human beings. This meant first discarding Bentham's simple faith in arithmetic. To his theory that, 'quantity of pleasure being equal, push-pin is as good as poetry', Mill added the notion of quality: 'It is better to be a human being dissatisfied than a pig satisfied.' The humanizing process went on, until Utilitarians had become, not merely altruists, but even good Christians: 'In the golden rule of Jesus of Nazareth we read the complete spirit of the ethics of utility.' The questionable logic of Mill's improvements on the 'Greatest Happiness Principle' was concealed by the charm of the style, brisk, almost conversational, and occasionally humorous; while the ethic itself was given a highly respectable pedigree reaching back into the past that Bentham had despised, to Epicurus and ultimately Socrates.

The book ended with a vision of a future, in which the 'aristocracies of colour, race, and sex' would all have been abolished. Mill struck his first effective blow against the third type of 'aristocrat' when, as MP for Westminster, he proposed that the word 'man' in the 1867 Reform Bill should be replaced by

'person'. Though Harriet had written an article on 'The Enfranchisement of Women' in 1851, this was not a subject on which she
had done the 'leading'. He had been a feminist since long before he
met her, and woman suffrage must have seemed to him a corollary
of Bentham's dictum, 'everybody to count for one, nobody for
more than one'. In 1869, observing the rapid growth of the society
that he had helped to found, for the Representation of Women,
Mill felt that the time was ripe to publish a book written eight
years before, *On the Subjection of Women*. This carefully reasoned
protest against all forms of injustice to women now seems at times
to be labouring the obvious, but the converted may still enjoy
Mill's preaching, for the cogency of its logic, its imaginative
rhetoric, and the empathy with which it presents the frustrations
of the 'subjected'. Here Mill must have learnt something, not only
from Harriet but also from Florence Nightingale, whose 'Cassan-
dra' he quoted to explain why women had not yet distinguished
themselves in philosophy, science, or art: 'A celebrated woman, in
a work which I hope will some day be published, remarks truly
that everything a woman does is done at odd times.' But the real
brilliance of *On the Subjection* lay less in its arguments than in its
literary strategy. Confronted, as he knew, by prejudices so ancient
as to be almost instinctive, he exploited the fashionable belief in
evolutionary progress, by presenting the current position of
women as a relic of barbarism,

a single relic of an old world of thought and practice exploded in
everything else, but retained in the one thing of most universal interest;
as if a gigantic dolmen, or a vast temple of Jupiter Olympius, occupied
the site of St. Paul's and received daily worship, while the surrounding
Christian churches were only resorted to on fasts and festivals.

The implied association of progress with Christianity was not
merely diplomatic. 'Theism', written around the time when *On the
Subjection* was published, was more tolerant of religion than the
two previous essays on the subject. He was also more tolerant of
socialism in 'Chapters on Socialism' (1879) than he had been in the
Principles. That his views were always changing was one of his
reasons for writing his *Autobiography* (1873):

in an age of transition in opinions, there may be somewhat both of
interest and of benefit in noting the successive phases of any mind which

was always pressing forward, equally ready to learn and to unlearn from its own thoughts or from those of others.

Another motive was to record his 'unusual and remarkable' education, which included being taught Greek at the age of three, and finally gave him 'an advantage of a quarter of a century over [his] cotemporaries'. It also precipitated a psychological 'crisis' at twenty, in which he lost all interest in life:

I was thus ... left stranded at the commencement of my voyage, with a well equipped ship and a rudder, but no sail; without any real desire for the ends which I had been so carefully fitted out to work for: no delight in virtue or the general good, but also just as little in anything else.

He was cured by reading Wordsworth, in whose poetry he found 'the very culture of the feelings' that he lacked, and from then on the 'cultivation of the feelings became one of the cardinal points in [his] ethical and philosophical creed.' The whole story is enthralling, especially in the early draft of 1853–4 which, alone among Mill's works, revealed the human being behind the philosopher. The rest of the *Autobiography*, besides throwing much light on the intellectual life of the period, showed how his non-literary experience affected his writing. Bureaucrats are not generally admired for their prose, but Mill's work at the India Office contributed to his technique of persuasion:

I could not issue an order or express an opinion, without satisfying various persons very unlike myself, that the thing was fit to be done. I was thus in a good position for finding out by practice the mode of putting a thought which gives it easiest admission into minds not prepared for it by habit ...

Such tactful writing was not Samuel Butler's way.[4] 'O God! O Montreal!' he exclaimed in a poem about a museum that kept the Discobolus in an attic because 'He has neither vest nor pants with

---

[4] Samuel Butler, 1835–1902, was born at Langar, Nottinghamshire, the son of the rector. He went to Shrewsbury, where his grandfather Bishop Butler had been headmaster, and St John's College, Cambridge. His father tried to make him a clergyman too, and he was already a lay reader at St James's, Piccadilly, when doubts about the efficacy of baptism made him prefer to become an artist. When his father refused to finance art-training, he made some money as a sheep-farmer in New Zealand, then settled at Clifford's Inn, studied painting, and exhibited eleven pictures at the Royal Academy. His closest relationships were with Charles Paine Pauli, Eliza Mary Ann Savage, and Henry Festing Jones, who wrote his biography. Nearly all his books were published at his own expense, and none but *Erewhon* was ever popular in his lifetime.

which to cover his limbs'; and he loved making fun of people who were so easily shocked. But he was more than a satirist of Victorian conventions. He was also a kind of Democritus, a laughing philosopher, whose best ideas came from jocular reversals of the orthodox. Thus in *Erewhon* (a literal reversal of Nowhere or Utopia) crime was treated as an illness, and illness as a crime. 'When I have turned a proposition inside out,' he wrote, 'put it to stand on its head, and shaken it, I have often been surprised to find how much came out of it.' That was his formula, not only for epigrams like 'An honest God's the noblest work of man', but also for theses. The proposition that Jesus rose from the dead was turned into a theory that he never died. The 'Origin of Species' was not to be found in the survival and reproduction of chance variations, but in the 'Origin of Variations', i.e. in the 'needs and experience of the creatures varying'. The *Odyssey* was not, as Longinus said, the work of an old man, but of a young woman. How seriously Butler believed in his own theories was never quite clear. 'The one serious conviction that a man should have', he once wrote, 'is that nothing is to be taken too seriously.' But his arguments were always plausible as well as entertaining, and however outrageous they might seem, never failed to bring out some neglected aspects of reality.

His first book was the exception, since it was edited and published by his strictly conventional father, from letters that Butler had sent home while sheep-farming in New Zealand. So *A First Year in Canterbury Settlement* (1863) is interesting chiefly because the experience there described suggested the setting of *Erewhon*, just as the anonymous pamphlet on the *Evidence for the Resurrection* (1865) merely formulated a theory that would be handled more inventively in *The Fair Haven*. Butler's first, and only, great success with the contemporary public was *Erewhon or Over the Range* (1872). This, like the pamphlet, was published anonymously, but the author's name was added when a second edition was needed within a few weeks.

As a Utopian novel, *Erewhon* had all the attractions of Lytton's *The Coming Race*, which had popularized the genre the previous year. It was an imaginative satire on contemporary society, which could be enjoyed for the story alone. From the moment when the narrator (later called Higgs) set off into unknown territory until he finally got back to England, having escaped from Erewhon by balloon, his adventures were genuinely exciting, for all the ironic humour of the style. As for the satiric content, it was both more thoughtful and more ambiguous than Lytton's. Conventional religion was caricatured in the Musical Banks of Erewhon, which were housed in fine old buildings, and patronized by all respectable people, but dealt in a currency that was never used in practical life. What everyone really believed in, and acted on, was the worship of Ydgrun, i.e. Mrs Grundy. Here Butler was not condemning respect for public opinion as such, but low standards of public opinion; for what he called 'high Ydgrunites' were 'gentlemen in the full sense of the word', and he fully shared their 'Only religion . . . that of self-respect and consideration for other people'. It is harder to define the precise implications of the Erewhonian ban on machinery. On the face of it this was a *reductio ad absurdum* of a reactionary attitude with which Butler sympathized. He had handled the subject before, in two contributions to a New Zealand paper. 'Darwin among the Machines' (1863) had warned that machines were a new species destined to supersede *Homo sapiens*. 'Lucubratio Ebria' (i.e. Drunk Dissertation, 1865) suggested that they were merely supplementary limbs, developed in the process of human evolution. Both theories were ingeniously and amusingly worked out, and the computer has now made the warning of 1863 seem increasingly relevant; but perhaps, like these two pieces, the whole discussion of machinery in *Erewhon* is best classed under a heading that Butler once jotted down in a list of possible titles and subjects for future works: 'Fooling Around'.

How far the same applies to the discussion of crime and illness is again debatable. The treatment of criminals as psychological cases may nowadays look progressive, and the trial of the man 'accused of pulmonary consumption' certainly seems to imply that the English penal system was equally heartless. Yet Butler showed few signs elsewhere of an active social conscience, and his meaning here may not have been profound. In one Erewhonian institution, however, Butler made his real feelings quite plain. The Birth Formula, by which babies absolved their parents from all responsibility for their children's welfare, immortalized a conviction summed up in 1883: 'My most implacable enemy from childhood onward has certainly been my father.'

The upbringing that had prompted this belief was pleasantly burlesqued in the 'Memoir of the late John Pickard Owen', the alleged author of *The Fair Haven* (1873). The work itself was an elaborate hoax, which took some of its readers in. Ostensibly a 'Defence of the Miraculous Element' in Christianity against such rationalist criticism as Butler's own early pamphlet, it parodied the weaknesses of Christian apologists, by the confusion, inconsistency, and sophistry of its arguments. Thus he explained 'the partial obscurity—I might have almost written, the incomparable *chiaroscuro*' of the Gospel-record as God's way of enhancing the aesthetic appeal of the 'Christ-Ideal', yet concluded that the 'pilot' that had brought him safely into the Fair Haven of Christian brotherhood was 'Candour'. The solemn practical joke was played at far too great length, but the story in the Memoir of how J. P. Owen originally lost his faith had several delightful episodes, as when the small son of fundamentalist parents has to share a bedroom with a lady guest, and finds that, if he pretends to be asleep, she does not bother to say her prayers.

It was typical of Butler that, when Natural Selection was a revolutionary doctrine, he had defended it in a 'Dialogue' (1862), but once it was widely accepted, he passionately opposed Darwin's version of evolution. His own version, first announced in *Life and Habit* (1878), stood Paley's Natural Theology on its head. For Paley the ingenious 'contrivances' of organic structure proved a designing Creator; for Butler, they proved infinite numbers of designing creatures. He thus gave the credit for evolution to the evolvers themselves, rather than to chance variations which enabled certain individual organisms to survive and reproduce. As for Darwin's account of how an orchid chanced to be fertilized by a bee:

I can no more believe that all this has come about without design on the part of the orchid, and a gradual perception of the advantages it is able to take over the bee, and a righteous determination to enjoy them, than . . . that a mouse-trap or a steam-engine is the result of the accumulation of blind minute fortuitous variations in a creature called man, which creature has never wanted either mouse-traps or steam-engines, but has had a sort of promiscuous tendency to make them, and was benefited by making them, so that those of the race who had a tendency to make them survived and left issue, which issue would thus naturally tend to make more mouse-traps and more steam-engines.

The flippant tone resembled that of Lucian's satire on dogmatic scientists, the *Icaromenippus*, from which the book's epigraphs were taken, and Butler's professed aim was 'simply to entertain and interest the numerous class of people who, like myself, know nothing of science, but who enjoy speculating and reflecting (not too deeply) upon the phenomena around them.' He finally confessed, however, that though he had not at first seriously believed in his theory, he now thought it a 'talisman of inestimable value'. By veiled allusions to *Natural Theology* and *In Memoriam* he even implied that it was a 'pebble' at least as significant as the 'stone' that introduced Paley's famous watch, and a 'dream' as well worth 'holding true' as Tennyson's.

'I know nothing about science', Butler announced and, though he had clearly read a great deal about it, scientists are no more likely to accept his conclusions now than they were then; but his arguments are full of human interest and incidental insights. Having observed that habitual actions became unconscious, and that special skills, like playing music from a score, were the result of conscious practice unconsciously remembered, Butler argued that all animal instincts, embryological processes, and developments of new organs were of similar origin. Thus a chick developed a beak with which to break out of its egg, because it unconsciously remembered that long practice had shown this to be the best procedure. In the human sphere it followed that each individual drew on the experience of its parents, and was ultimately inseparable from them; and that personality was 'a nebulous and indefinable aggregation of many component parts which war not a little among themselves'. The argument also involved an approach to pantheism: 'we are only component atoms of a single compound creature, *LIFE*, which has probably a distinct conception of its own personality though none whatever of ours, more than we of our own units.'

Having thus treated the subject of evolution 'artistically', as he put it, and continued his argument against Darwin in two more books, Butler turned to art criticism in *Alps and Sanctuaries* (1881) and *Ex Voto* (1888). He had once meant to be a professional artist himself, and had painted two oddly satirical pictures, *Family Prayers* (1864) and *Mr. Heatherley's Holiday* (1874). Now, in these books, he described, with drawings of his own, various art objects that he had seen while on holiday in Italy and Ticino. Chatty and rambling in style, both works are more interesting for their comments on life than on art. Universities, for instance, were condemned 'because they push young men too fast through doorways that the universities have provided, and so discourage the habit of being on the look-out for others.' There was also a reasoned attack on Earnestness, 'the last enemy that shall be subdued'.

Meanwhile Butler had started composing Handelian music with his friend and biographer, H. F. Jones: first short piano pieces, then a satirical cantata about the Stock Exchange, and finally an oratorio, *Ulysses* (published 1904). While checking his Greekless collaborator's plan for this piece, he reread and was fascinated by the *Odyssey*. It opened a new 'doorway' for him, which led to three most entertaining works: a lecture on 'The Humour of Homer', given at the Working Men's College in 1892; a version of the *Odyssey* in fairly modern prose (1900), pioneering the type of Homeric translation popularized by E. V. Rieu in 1946; and *The Authoress of the Odyssey* (1897). Though Butler's thesis that the *Odyssey* was written by Nausicaa has made no more impression on classicists than his theory of evolution has on scientists, this book is not only very readable in itself, but makes a valuable contribution to the perceptive reading of the original poem. For all his mockery of the 'hypothetical language' taught in *Erewhon*, Butler's classical education made him react with great sensitivity to the text, and notice many features of the narrative that more 'earnest' students had overlooked. The same sort of close reading was less convincing in *Shakespeare's Sonnets Reconsidered* (1899), where one suspects that the characterization of 'Mr. W. H.' reflected Butler's own disillusionment about his friend Pauli.

'Mr. W. H.' took on a different character in *Erewhon Revisited* (1901), when John, Higgs's son by Arowhena, found George, Higgs's illegitimate son by Yram, the equal of anyone in 'the blazon of beauty's best'. The great beauty of George was his resemblance to 'all who love truth and hate lies'. His 'fearless frankness' made him wish his father to repudiate his divine status in Erewhon, and so demolish the whole fictitious religion that had developed from his 'ascension' by balloon twenty years before. This Higgs eventually did, in a temple built for his own worship, only to be treated as 'a dangerous lunatic'. The satirical force of the book was concentrated on religious hypocrisy, chiefly personified in Professors Hanky and Panky, who had a vested interest in the state religion, and were quite prepared to defend it, even when

its mythology had been disproved. As a novel, the work was far
more coherent than *Erewhon*, while equally exciting and amusing
in its narrative. In Yram Butler had produced for the first time a
character not merely satirical, but rounded and realistic. And even
his last word on the fictitious religion showed a new breadth of
outlook: 'if you cannot abolish me altogether', Higgs advises an
Erewhonian academic, 'make me a peg on which to hang all your
own best ethical and spiritual conceptions'.

The truth-loving George was succeeded in *The Way of All Flesh*
(1903) by Ernest Pontifex's Aunt Alethea, whose name means
truth. Her function was to help the young Ernest (brought up in
the spirit of 'the last enemy') to disentangle his 'true self' from the
'lies' by which he has been 'surrounded on every side'. Alethea was
based on Butler's close friend, Miss E. M. A. Savage, who had
encouraged him to start writing the novel in 1873. He continued
work on it until her death in 1885, and then abandoned it, leaving
the second part unrevised. In making Alethea rich and good-
looking Butler improved on his original, but Theobald, Christina,
and Dr Skinner were unkind, though not wholly unjust, portraits
of his father, mother, and headmaster at Shrewsbury. Besides
being partly autobiographical, the novel dramatized the theory of
Life and Habit. Thus Ernest's evolution was traced through four
generations. He himself was an 'organ' developed by Theobald, in
order to vent his spleen 'with least risk and greatest satisfaction'.
Fortunately, Ernest had access to the instinctive wisdom of his
great-grandfather, a carpenter who built a church-organ, and he
was encouraged by Alethea to learn carpentry and start building an
organ too. But even without her help, ancestral wisdom came to
him through his unconscious self, whose influence was translated
into a long lecture on the theme: 'This conscious self of yours,
Ernest, is a prig begotten of prigs and trained in priggishness; I
will not allow it to shape your actions, though it will doubtless
shape your words for many a year to come.' The story of Ernest's
slow development is immensely entertaining and, apart from one
or two incidents, psychologically convincing. Though most
remembered as a witty and sometimes horrifying indictment of a
repressive Victorian upbringing, the book still has a positive value
for any adolescent trying to sort out his own ideas from among
those of his parents. In this it justifies Butler's claim in his
notebooks not merely to have been 'unorthodox and militant in

every book' he wrote, to have been 'the *enfant terrible* of literature and science', but also to have tried to make his 'own work belong to the youth of a public opinion'. During his lifetime he was never a popular author; but this novel, published the year after his death, has certainly brought him the 'posthumous fame' that he professed to have always 'gone in for'.

15. Other Prose Writers

As Horace explained, writing verse means more than turning out 'two hundred lines an hour, while standing on one leg', and the same applies to prose. So the term 'prose-writer' here excludes any who worked, however interestingly or voluminously, in the spirit of M. Jourdain. All the authors mentioned were conscious of their medium and concerned to use it effectively. Some were directly engaged in forms of literary or linguistic criticism. And a third type of qualification for inclusion in this chapter has been subject-matter broad enough in scope to be called, in Arnold's vague but useful phrase, 'criticism of life'.

Historically, John Keble's most important piece of prose was his sermon on 'National Apostasy' (1833), since it started the Oxford Movement; but the literary interest of his *Praelectiones Academicae* (1844) was far greater.[1] These lectures, which he had given as Professor of Poetry at Oxford, were written in Latin (a tradition first broken by his godson Matthew Arnold). While questioning his own ability to express in a foreign language what he 'thought he thought' about poetry ('*quae mente animoque videre mihi videor*'), he contrived to present very gracefully some quite subtle ideas, in a tone that was admirably tentative. A critic, he realized, was like a doctor taking a pulse: he had to be sure that the heartbeats he felt were not merely his own. The medical image was central to the whole work, which was entitled '*De Poeticae Vi Medica*' (on the healing power of poetry). Here Wordsworth's 'spontaneous overflow of powerful feelings' was seen as a psychological safety-valve. Powerful feelings were painful if unexpressed, and might cause mental breakdown; but civilized people instinctively kept such feelings to themselves, either from shame (*verecundia*), or because their feelings were too sublime for expression in everyday speech. Poetry was a Heaven-sent solution of the problem, and poets could thus be sorted into two classes: 'Primary' ones, who composed purely to relieve their own feelings, and 'Secondary' ones, who merely imitated 'Primary' poetry. Keble then examined some

---

[1] John Keble, 1792–1866. For his poetry see Chap. 9.

famous candidates, allotting Firsts and Seconds. The procedure anticipated that of Arnold's inaugural lecture, but the results were different. Here Sophocles' 'cheerfulness' counted against him, since it implied a lack of deep feeling; but Lucretius was classed as Primary, on the strength of his feeling for Nature, and was even thought to have prepared the way for true religion. In Keble's view, religion and poetry were almost inseparable, but so, more surprisingly, were poetry and politics. When Odysseus preferred Penelope to Calypso, he showed himself a true conservative, while the Suitors were revolutionary demagogues. Indeed, real poets like Homer were naturally anti-democratic, anti-utilitarian, and traditionalist in morals, law, and religion.

By the last criterion (as by most others) Francis Newman was no poet.[2] *The Soul* (1849) was a protest against traditional theology, in which he depreciated the 'historical and miraculous side' of Christianity, rejected Sabbatarianism ('More sins of every kind . . . are committed on Sunday than on any other day of the week'), and denied that the Bible had any special authority over 'man's understanding, conscience or soul'. The 'True Basis of Theology' was individual experience of a personal God. Biblical criticism had merely turned Christianity into 'a LITERATURE', and its teachers into 'a literary profession'. To reverse this trend, Newman offered a 'scientific' account of the 'organ' by which Man experienced God. *Phases of Faith* (1850) was much livelier. Avowedly 'egotistical' in form, it traced Newman's development from fundamentalism to an undogmatic creed based on the 'inward instincts of the soul', 'pruned and chastened by the sceptical understanding'. Though often ridiculed by writers on Matthew Arnold, the author of this book deserves respect for his devotion to 'truth, as such, and truthfulness, more than any creed', and for his refusal to defend orthodox doctrine by 'any shiftings and shufflings of language'. There is drama, too, in the story of how his mind grew, 'expanding slowly under pressure' from a society that equated

---

[2] Francis William Newman, 1805–97, was born in London, the brother of J. H. Newman. He went to Worcester College, Oxford, and decided to resist his brother's influence when he found a picture of the Virgin on the wall of his college room, and learned that John had had it put there. He resigned his fellowship at Balliol, 1830, rather than sign the Articles. He then made a three-year trip to Baghdad, and in 1848 became professor of Latin at University College, London. He published verse translations of Horace's *Odes* and the *Iliad* (for Arnold's reactions see Chap. 5), and Latin versions of *Hiawatha* and *Robinson Crusoe*.

scepticism with immorality. 'Oh Dogma! Dogma!' he once
exclaimed, 'how dost thou trample under foot love, truth, conscience, justice!' The style, however, was not usually so histrionic,
but objective, pithy, and at times jocose. Even if the word *aionios*
meant 'secular' not 'eternal',

how was I to think that a good-humoured voluptuary deserved to be
raised from the dead in order to be tormented in fire for 100 years? and
what shorter time could be called secular? Or if he was to be destroyed
instantaneously, and 'secular' meant only 'in a future age,' was he worth
the effort of a divine miracle to bring him back to life and again annihilate
him?

For similar doubts about Eternal Punishment, more hesitantly
expressed in *Theological Essays* (1853), F. D. Maurice lost his
Chair of English literature and history at King's College London.[3]
Dedicated to his friend Tennyson, the book attempted to 'Ring in
the Christ that is to be', on the principle that 'a Theology which
does not correspond to the deepest thoughts and feelings of human
beings cannot be a true Theology.' What exactly Maurice believed
had not been made very clear in his first major work (after a novel
about the French Revolution), *The Kingdom of Christ* (1838).
Wordy and vague in style, this stated his faith in the Church of
England as a God-created and socially indispensable institution,
but makes little impression, except of a pleasant personality and an
admirably humble approach to controversy. As Tennyson put it in
a poem, Maurice was one 'of that honest few, | Who give the Fiend
himself his due', and here he treated the views of every sect in 'a
tender and reverent spirit', intent on reconciling discordant
beliefs. Having suffered as a child from religious disputes in his
family, he had developed a talent for mediation, which made him a
key figure in the Broad Church movement; but on religious topics,
topics, his unfailing fairness to the Fiend tended to make him a
rather dull writer.

On adult education he was much better. A year after founding

---

[3] John Frederick Denison Maurice, 1805–72, was born near Lowestoft, the son of a
Unitarian minister, and went to Trinity College and Trinity Hall, Cambridge. In 1834 he
became an Anglican priest, and published a novel, *Eustace Conway*. He became chaplain to
Guy's Hospital, 1838, and professor of English literature and history at King's College,
London, 1840. In 1848 he founded Queen's College for Women, and promoted Christian
Socialism. He founded the Working Men's College, 1854, and became professor of moral
philosophy at Cambridge, 1866.

the Working Men's College, he explained and publicized the new venture in *Learning and Working* (1855). Here he glanced at historical precedents, refuted the idea that manual work was incompatible with learning, and then outlined the principles on which the College would be run: 'What we want is not to put things into our pupils' minds, so much as to set in order what we find there, to untie knots, to disentangle complicated threads.' Thus his natural humility suggested an appropriate type of instruction, and his policy of collecting elements of truth from contradictory creeds suggested a hopeful method of teaching such subjects as politics. More happily still, the lecture-form in which the book was written, and the practical need for effective communication transformed Maurice's style. Short emphatic sentences replaced the shapeless, rambling periods of *The Kingdom*.

The same was true of the lectures on literature collected in *The Friendship of Books* (1873), but here the content was less interesting. Chatty and anecdotal, the lectures were critically unadventurous, merely suggesting that one should treat books like people, and learn from them rather than find fault with them. The most enterprising piece in the collection was a lecture 'On Words', delivered to medical students at Guy's Hospital in 1838, when Maurice was chaplain there. In deference to his audience, his method was pseudo-scientific, but his conclusions were almost mystical. Contradicting the materialism implicit in J. H. Tooke's philology, Maurice made words 'testify, and that not weakly or obscurely, of man as a spiritual being.' With much emotive imagery, which he denied to be 'metaphysical', he insisted that there was 'as much a vital principle in a word as in a tree or a flower'; and by 'a few experiments on words' demonstrated that language embodied spiritual truths. Thus the etymology of *conscience* proved the presence of God in the human soul.

This type of moralizing philology was popularized in *The Study of Words* (1851) by R. C. Trench, the clerical poet who originated (1858) the scheme of the *New English Dictionary* (*OED*).[4] Elaborating Emerson's description of language as 'fossil poetry', Trench claimed that it was also 'fossil ethics' and 'fossil history'—even a kind of sacred history, for it recorded the Fall of Man:

---

[4] Richard Chenevix Trench, 1807–86, was born in Dublin, the son of a barrister. He went to Trinity College, Cambridge, where he was an Apostle with Tennyson. He became dean of Westminster, 1856, and archbishop of Dublin, 1863. See Chap. 9.

I open the first letter of the alphabet; what means this 'Ah,' this 'Alas,' these deep and long-drawn sighs of humanity, which at once encounter us there? And then presently follow words such as these, Affliction, Agony, Anguish, Assassin, Atheist, Avarice, and twenty more ... it is a melancholy thing to observe how much richer is every vocabulary in words that set forth sins, than in those that set forth graces.

Social questions too could be decided by etymology. Four years after his friend Tennyson had tried, in *The Princess*, to improve on the primitive view, 'Man for the field and woman for the hearth', Trench found it confirmed by language. The word *wife* had 'its lesson', since it hinted at 'earnest in-door stay-at-home occupations, as being the fittest for her who bears this name'. As for the husband, 'the very name may put him in mind of his authority'. In its main thesis, however, that language was 'the amber in which a thousand subtle and precious thoughts have been safely embedded and preserved', *The Study* was both convincing and fascinating. And such quasi-poetic imagery gave it an extra-philological eloquence, as in this protest against any scheme of phonetic spelling:

Words are now a nation, grouped into tribes and families ... this change would go far to reduce them to a promiscuous and barbarous horde. Now they are often translucent with their idea, as an alabaster vase is lighted up by a lamp placed within it; in how many cases would this inner light be then quenched.

There was no such tincture of poetry in the prose of W. E. Gladstone.[5] Even his *Studies on Homer* (1858) proposed that Homer should be examined 'under other aspects than such as are merely poetical'; and though the third volume was ostensibly on Homer's poetry, it did little more than discuss Homer's feeling for the picturesque, his sense of colour, and his relation to later writers of epic like Virgil, Tasso, and Milton. Gladstone's real concern was with the 'inner Homeric world of which his verse is the tabernacle and his poetic genius the exponent', the 'world of religion and ethics, of civil polity, of history and ethnology, of manners and arts, so widely separated from all following ex-

---

[5] William Ewart Gladstone, 1809–98, was born in Liverpool, the son of a merchant who owned plantations and slaves in Demerara. He went to Eton, where he became a friend of Arthur Hallam, and Christ Church, Oxford. His friendship with Tennyson dated from 1837. Primarily a Liberal politician who was four times Prime Minister, he wrote *Studies on Homer* when out of office from 1855. In 1858 he was sent to the Ionian Islands, then a British Protectorate, where he tried in vain to discourage agitation for union with Greece.

perience, that we may properly call them palaeozoic.' Along with the poetry, Gladstone brushed aside the then very lively Homeric Question as 'all but dead', and assumed that both *Iliad* and *Odyssey* were produced by 'a designing mind' in 'the heroic age itself'. He saw Homer as 'a paramount historical authority', and also as a theologian, whose poems complemented the early sections of the Bible. Thus Jupiter, Neptune, and Pluto (so Latinized) were a debased version of the Trinity, Latona, of the Virgin Mary, and the Titans and Giants, of Satan.

The sermonizing instinct seen in Trench and Gladstone took a secular form in Samuel Smiles.[6] Though he disparaged 'literary culture', one can hardly exclude from literary history an author whose best-known book, *Self-help* (1859) sold a quarter of a million copies during his life-time, and was translated into many languages, both European and oriental. Here, in a chatty, anecdotal style, he used the careers of famous men in every walk of life to illustrate the theme that individual effort, even with 'mediocre abilities', can lead to great achievements. His argument, which depreciated 'legislation as an agent in human advancement', was open to political objections, and his glorification of the self-made man in trade and industry invited the kind of ridicule that Matthew Arnold poured on 'Mrs Gooch's Golden Rule': 'Ever remember, my dear Dan, that you should look forward to being some day manager of that concern!' But the book itself, which developed from talks given to a 'mutual improvement' group of young workmen in Leeds, still retains its human value. Like Emerson's 'Self-Reliance', though at a much humbler level, *Self-help* is a useful piece of equipment for practical life.

Educated chiefly by his father, on a principle of 'self-help carried out in all directions', Herbert Spencer accumulated great quantities of miscellaneous information in his youth, and went on to write on a huge variety of subjects.[7] At twenty he developed 'a

[6] Samuel Smiles, 1812–1904, was born at Haddington, one of the eleven children of a paper-maker. He went to the local grammar school and Edinburgh University. He practised briefly as a doctor, edited the *Leeds Times*, 1838–42, became secretary of the South-Eastern Railway, and published a life of George Stephenson, 1857. After *Self-Help* he wrote *Character*, 1871, *Thrift*, 1875, *Duty*, 1880, and *Life and Labour*, 1887.

[7] Herbert Spencer, 1820–1903, was born in Derby, the son of a schoolmaster married to the daughter of a local plumber. He worked as a civil engineer on the railway, 1837–41, and as sub-editor of the *Economist*, 1848–53. Internationally famous in his day, he now seems to be remembered less for his evolutionary philosophy than for his pioneering work in sociology, and his friendship with George Eliot.

decided leaning' towards the idea of evolution, and in *Social Statics* (1851) he assumed a general progress towards 'perfection' which, in human terms, meant a 'condition in which the individuality of each may be unfolded without limit, save the like individualities of others.' This ideal condition required equal rights not only for women but also for children; and the current method of dealing with children who misbehaved was amusingly satirized:

Paternity with knit brows, and in a severe tone, commands desistance— visits anything like reluctant submission with a sharp 'Do as I bid you'— if need be, hints at a whipping or the black hole—in short carries coercion, or the threat of coercion, far enough to produce obedience. After sundry exhibitions of perverse feeling, the child gives in; showing, however, by its sullenness the animosity it entertains. Meanwhile paternity pokes the fire and complacently resumes the newspaper under the impression that all is as it should be ...

Less humanely, Spencer condemned 'sigh-wise and groan-foolish' people who tried, by Poor-Laws or other forms of state-philanthropy, to change the 'natural order of things'. This was that the 'unhealthy, imbecile, slow, vacillating, faithless members' of society, whether animal or human, were 'excreted' from the system. He came even nearer to anticipating Darwin's Natural Selection in 'the Theory of Population' (1852), and later coined a phrase which Darwin adopted, 'the survival of the fittest'. In his ten-volume *System of Synthetic Philosophy* (1860–96) Spencer elaborated the 'hypothesis of a fundamental unity, extending from the simplest inorganic actions up to the most complex associations of thought and the most involved social processes.' This massive attempt to integrate biology, psychology, sociology, ethics, and politics into a single theory was a triumph of research and creative thinking, but his style became less witty and more diffuse, partly, as he realized, because in 1859 he started dictating his books. But he was always very readable, and in a perceptive essay on the 'Philosophy of Style' (1852) he stressed the 'importance of economizing the reader's or hearer's attention', by presenting ideas in such a way that they could be 'apprehended with the least possible mental effort'. Though he used 'Mariana' to illustrate this principle, and had once been 'enthusiastic' about *Prometheus Unbound*, his general preference was for 'little poetry and of the best'. In *Education* (1861) he rejected literature and the classics in favour of science, as the subject 'most worth knowing', and emphasized the importance of enjoyable physical training. But he was no Philistine. A not uncritical admirer of Turner's paintings, he drew and modelled himself, wrote interestingly about music, and at one time found his 'chief gratification' in part-singing. Though fiction had been excluded from his early reading, by 1852 he was urging George Eliot to start writing novels. His own nearest approach to that form was a fascinating *Autobiography* (1904). Among many pieces of vivid narrative, it recorded a 'rebellious' walk at the age of thirteen from Bath to Cheltenham, which bears comparison with David Copperfield's epic journey from London to Canterbury.

Like Spencer, Walter Bagehot applied Natural Selection to politics, was impatient of long poems ('Poetry should be memorable and emphatic, intense, and *soon over*'), and believed in enjoying life: 'The essence of Toryism is enjoyment.'[8] But in most respects the two authors were antithetical. Bagehot regarded science not as the thing 'most worth knowing' but as a regrettable distraction from the 'proper study of mankind': 'Some people are unfortunately born scientific. They take much interest in the objects of nature. They feel a curiosity about snails, horses, butterflies. They are delighted at an ichthyosaurus, and excited at a polyp ... '. He attributed the aberration to 'the absence of an intense and vivid nature ... a want of sympathy'. Instead of spending a long life on a work in ten volumes, Bagehot spent a short one writing miscellaneous articles. His criterion of style was not ease in transmitting ideas, but entertainment value. When, in 'the First Edinburgh Reviewers' (1855) he compared 'modern writing' to 'the talk of a man of the world', he precisely defined his own literary manner:

the talk of the manifold talker, glancing lightly from topic to topic, suggesting deep things in a jest, unfolding unanswerable arguments in an absurd illustration, expounding nothing, completing nothing, exhausting nothing, yet really suggesting the lessons of a wider experience ... and what is more to the purpose, pleasing all that hear him, charming high

---

[8] Walter Bagehot, 1826–77, was born at Langport, Somerset, the son of a banker and shipowner whose business he joined in 1852. He went to school in Bristol and University College, London, then studied law and was called to the bar, but never practised. He had spent some months in Paris during Louis Napoleon's *coup d'état*, 1851, which he then strongly defended. He edited the *Economist* from 1860 until his death in Langport.

and low, in season and out of season, with a word of illustration for each, and a touch of humour intelligible to all . . .

Bagehot's 'talk' occasionally lapses into chatter, and his habit of 'glancing lightly from topic to topic' becomes tedious after a while; but in small doses his prose is delightful to read, full of witty epigrams and surprising images. His comments on literature were always interesting but sometimes rather superficial. 'Shakespeare—The Individual' (1853) was a resourceful attempt to reconstruct the poet's personality from his works. In contrast to Shakespeare's 'experiencing nature', 'Macaulay' (1856, 1859) had an '*in*experiencing' one, a quasi-scientific 'insensibility' to ordinary human emotions, which precluded any development. 'Shelley' (1856) was more fairly defined as a 'pure impulsive character' whose form of self-expression was paradoxically 'intellectual'. 'Wordsworth, Tennyson, and Browning; or Pure, Ornate, and Grotesque Art in English Poetry' (1864), though Bagehot's best-known piece of literary criticism, was quite unworthy of him. Its defence of Tenyson's 'ornateness' in *Enoch Arden* was rather silly: 'A dirty sailor who did *not* go home to his wife is not an agreeable being: a varnish must be put on him to make him shine.' So was the 'error' attributed to 'Caliban upon Setebos', that Caliban was 'a nasty creature—a gross animal, uncontrolled and unelevated by any feeling of religion or duty', who spoke 'very difficult' and 'unpleasant' lines. On Clough, who had been a close friend, Bagehot wrote far more perceptively (1862), describing the '*flavour* of his mind' as 'a sort of truthful scepticism', and demonstrating the brilliance of *Amours de Voyage*, while admitting the 'awkwardness' that disqualified him for wide popularity.

Still, the best things in Bagehot are not his critical judgements but his *obiter dicta*. In 'Edward Gibbon', for instance, he made fun of the 'literary man':

He sits beside a library-fire, with nice white paper, a good pen, a capital style, every means of saying everything, but nothing to say . . . What a gain if something would happen! then one could describe it. Something has happened, and that something is history . . . Perhaps when a Visigoth broke a head, he thought that was all. Not so; he was making history; Gibbon has written it down.

The best subject that Bagehot himself found to write about was *The English Constitution* (1867). This too was something that simply 'happened': 'We have made, or rather stumbled on, a constitution which—though full of every species of incidental defect, though of the worst *workmanship* in out-of-the-way matters of any constitution in the world—yet has two capital merits.' It consisted of 'a simple efficient part' which could, when necessary, work better than 'any instrument of government that has yet been tried', and various 'historical, complex, august, theatrical parts, which it has inherited from a long past—which *take* the multitude—which guide by an insensible but an omnipotent influence the associations of its subjects.' In describing the 'efficient' part, as in his article on 'Parliamentary Reform' (1859), Bagehot expressed a moderate reaction against the democratic trend that produced the 1867 Reform Act; but he showed most individuality in explaining, with ironic wit and psychological insight, the practical use of the chief 'theatrical' part, the monarchy. On one point, however, recent experience seems to have proved him wrong: 'secrecy is . . . essential to the utility of English royalty as it now is. Above all things our royalty is to be reverenced, and if you begin to poke about it you cannot reverence it.'

In *Physics and Politics* (1872) Bagehot translated Natural Selection into political terms, arguing that human society could only survive by evolving from primitive forms of despotism to 'government by discussion'. The main thesis was obscured by rambling presentation, but, while trying to explain how national character developed, he suggested a very interesting analogy in literary history: an original author was like one of Darwin's chance variations. If he happened to satisfy the demands of his environment, his style would be 'propagated' by imitation. If not, he would be 'eliminated': 'What writers are expected to write, they write; or else they do not write at all; but . . . stop discouraged, live disheartened, and die leaving fragments which their friends treasure, but which the rushing world never heeds.'

Here Bagehot was probably thinking of Clough; but another example of such 'elimination' might have been found in E. S. Dallas, whose attempt to make literary criticism scientific had to wait for 'propagation' by Northrop Frye in a more congenial climate of opinion.[9] In Dallas's *Poetics* (1852), poetry was the

---

[9] Eneas Sweetland Dallas, 1828–79, was born in Jamaica, where his Scottish father was a planter. He went to Edinburgh University, and became a journalist on the staff of *The Times*, to which he sent letters from Paris during the siege, 1870. He also wrote a *Manual of Cookery*, 1877.

record of a pleasure felt by the poet, and was meant to give pleasure to the reader. The poet's pleasure was termed *poetry* and the record, *poesy*. Pleasure was the 'harmonious and unconscious activity of the soul', and *poetry*, the 'imaginative, harmonious and unconscious activity of the soul'. These definitions embodied three 'Laws', of Activity, Harmony, and Unconsciousness. The third was the most important, since 'Pleasure says to every one of us what we say to children. Open your mouth and shut your eyes.' So no form of self-consciousness, 'didactic', 'artistic', or 'satiric', could be 'admitted into a poem without doing much harm.' The 'kinds' of *poesy* were then elaborately classified, with references to ethnology, chronology, and grammar. Thus romantic art was dramatic, classical art was epic, divine or primitive art was lyrical. The Greek 'dwelt in the past', the Hebrew in the future, the modern in the present. A diagram showed Drama linked with the Present, Plurality, and You; Epic with the Past, Totality, and He; Lyric with the future, Unity, and I. To complete the symmetry of the scheme, Time, heard by the ear as metre, balanced Space 'chiefly marked by the eye' as imagery. Only 'a dreamy Aristotle', wrote Dallas, could fully explain poetry; but he was Platonic enough himself to give it a religious title: 'that which it receives by charter of inspiration—Joy of the Holy Ghost'.

The Gay Science (1866) was a more ambitious effort to 'settle the first principles of Criticism, and to show how alone it can be raised to the dignity of a science.' While punning on a Troubadour term for Poetry, the title implied that scientific criticism must start with the psychology of pleasure, rather than with philosophical 'ideas', as Matthew Arnold had just claimed in 'The Function of Criticism'. Indeed Dallas dismissed Arnold, his junior by only six years, as a 'delightful writer' whose style showed 'intense juvenility, a boy-power to the *nth*'. But the most interesting chapter in the book, on 'The Hidden Soul', was a prose-equivalent of Arnold's poem, 'The Buried Life', describing

a mental existence within us . . . a secret flow of thought which is not less energetic than the conscious flow, an absent mind which haunts us like a ghost or a dream, and is an essential part of our lives.

Attributing the concept of unconscious thought to Leibniz, Mill, Spencer, and Hamilton, Dallas was original in bringing out the exciting side of the theory, and in linking it firmly with poetry. For him Imagination was merely a name for the Unconscious, 'this lubber-fiend who toils for us when we are asleep or when we are not looking.' Hence all art was magical and mysterious: 'the most wonderful, the most vital, of all the elements of art' was 'the element of mystery, that sense of the unseen, that passion of the far-away, that glimmer of infinity, that incommunicable secret, that know-not-what . . . '. Thus the 'dignity of science' ended in an '*O altitudo!*' and the promise of 'systematic' criticism in a rambling last chapter on 'The Ethical Current', i.e. general trends in contemporary literature and society. However disappointing as a scientist, Dallas was an attractive writer with a fertile mind and a style that proved juvenile enough to make him a very successful journalist.

Dallas's aspiration towards scientific criticism was partly shared by a much more important critic, Leslie Stephen: 'After all, though criticism cannot boast of being a science, it ought to aim at something like a scientific basis, or at least to proceed in a scientific spirit.'[10] But in practice he tended to regard books as people, and judge them on moral grounds; while he stressed the subjective element in criticism almost as much as Pater: 'Every critic is in effect criticising himself as well as his author; and I confess that to my mind an obviously sincere record of impressions, however onesided they may be, is infinitely refreshing.' That was why he admired Johnson as a critic, for all his limitations, and his 'blunder' about 'Lycidas'. 'The first point', Stephen wrote, 'is to have the rare courage of admitting your own feelings,' and in 1887 he warned students of English literature at St Andrews: 'Never persuade yourselves that you like what you don't like.' His own largest gesture towards objective criticism was to pioneer the theory that literature was 'a kind of by-product' of social conditions. Stephen's literary criticism, however, first collected in *Hours in a Library* (1847–9), was only a part of his output. Writing in a concise and witty style that resembled but surpassed Bagehot's, he also produced two major works on the history of

[10] Sir Leslie Stephen, 1832–1904, was born in London, the son of an under-secretary of state for the colonies who became professor of modern history at Cambridge. His mother was the daughter of John Venn, the Evangelical rector of Clapham. He went to Eton and Trinity Hall, Cambridge, where he became tutor, 1856. This required him to take orders, which he did, 1859, but he soon found Christian doctrine incredible, and in 1864 left Cambridge for literary journalism in London. He edited the *Cornhill*, 1871–82, when he became editor of the *DNB*. He had climbed his first Swiss mountain, 1857.

philosophy, and edited the Dictionary of National Biography (1882–91), contributing three hundred and seventy-eight of the articles himself.

He began as a social satirist, with *Sketches from Cambridge, by a Don* (1865). Here he made fun of the academic life that he had just abandoned to become a periodical journalist in London. Posing as a complacent classicist, ostensibly busy editing an ancient text ('it is not necessary that your performance should ever get beyond a publisher's list'), he described his university as a place where nobody came 'with a view to learning chiefly', and where education was 'not the main object, but the incidental result' of the system. The agnosticism that had made him resign his tutorship appeared in gentle mockery of Maurice, 'muscular Christianity', Tractarianism, and the 'limited thinking power' of country parsons. He also touched on values that he would later assert less flippantly ('sincerity', 'manly qualities', 'free speech and honest ... inquiry'), and showed the 'hard-headed, energetic' common sense that would mark all his thinking.

While discussing the prominence of rowing in 'our intellectual machinery', Stephen observed that it was 'fortunately not a chronic complaint', like the 'infection of mountaineering'. He had this himself at twenty-five, and in *The Playground of Europe* (1871) he vividly described some of the symptoms. After pointing out how the Alps had developed from 'hideous excrescences' in the eighteenth century to objects of worship in the nineteenth, he argued that most worshippers were 'insincere', since they merely followed the fashion. The real beauty of the Alps could not be felt unless one risked one's life trying to climb them. The thesis was supported by exciting stories of actual climbs, with accounts of the climber's emotional 'rewards'. One of these was supplied by the Wetterhorn:

The awful gulf which intervened between me and the green meadows struck the imagination by its invisibility. It was like the view which may be seen from the ridge of a cathedral-roof, where the eaves have for their immediate background the pavement of the streets below; only this cathedral was 9,000 feet high. Now, any one standing at the foot of the Wetterhorn may admire [its] stupendous massiveness and steepness; but to feel [its] influence enter in the very marrow of one's bones, it is necessary to stand on the summit, and to fancy the one little slide down the short ice-slope, to be followed apparently by a bound into clear air and a fall down to the houses ...

For Stephen, the Alps offered refuge from himself and his neighbours, an escape from 'the commonplace' to 'vigorous originality'. Like his agnosticism, they presented a challenge to his courage and sincerity. The two challenges were explicitly linked in *Essays on Freethinking and Plainspeaking* (1873). Here the initial over-reaction of 'sound divines' to Darwinism was compared to the terror of a man clinging 'through the dark hours of the night' to the edge of a supposed precipice, only to discover, when he finally fell, that 'his feet had been all the time within a couple of inches' of the ground. In a later chapter, 'A Bad Five Minutes in the Alps', the simile was developed into a gripping short story. Clinging to a narrow ledge two hundred feet above a mountain torrent, the narrator searched his mind for ideas or beliefs that might help him face imminent death. His hopes of a future life proved 'too shadowy to be grasped with much satisfaction', but 'another difficulty was really more invincible. The instinctive feeling remained that I would not die with a lie on my lips.' The concluding moral of the book, 'Take courage and speak the truth' was the principle of all his writing, and the literary character that he projected was infinitely more attractive than his daughter's portrait of him as Mr Ramsay in *To the Lighthouse*. His lecture, for instance, on Matthew Arnold (1893) had an ironic charm quite equal to his victim's:

I must confess that, as a good Philistine, I often felt, and hope I profited by the feeling, that he had pierced me to the quick, and I submitted to his castigations as I have had to submit to the probings of a dentist—I knew they were for my good. And I often wished, I must also confess, that I too had a little sweetness and light that I might be able to say such nasty things of my enemies.

He had enough of both to be described as 'kind, serene, genial, penetrating, ripe' by another uncompromising rationalist, John Morley.[11] Like Stephen, Morley made his name as a freelance journalist. He wrote chiefly for the *Fortnightly Review*, which he edited for fifteen years, distinguished himself as a critic and

---

[11] John Morley, first viscount Morley of Blackburn, 1838–1923, was born at Blackburn, the son of a surgeon who had been a Wesleyan but became an Anglican. He went to Cheltenham College and Lincoln College, Oxford, which he left with a pass degree. He then struggled as a freelance journalist, 1860–3, when he joined the staff of the *Saturday Review*. That year he became a friend of Meredith, and later of J. S. Mill. After two unsuccessful attempts to enter Parliament, he became MP for Newcastle upon Tyne, 1883. A close supporter of Gladstone, he was chief secretary for Ireland, 1886 and 1892.

biographer, edited the English Men of Letters series, and finally
became a Liberal politician and cabinet minister. In articles
published from 1870 onwards, he approached literature as part of
the history of ideas, describing major poets as 'great historic
forces':

For these we need synthetic criticism, which, after analysis has done its
work, and disclosed to us the peculiar qualities of form, conception, and
treatment, shall collect the products of this first process, construct for us
the poet's mental figure in its integrity and just coherence, and then
finally, as the sum of its work, shall trace the relations of the poet's ideas,
either direct or indirect, through the central currents of thought, to the
visible tendencies of an existing age.

Thus Byron was seen, not as a writer of poems, but as a
propagandist of 'revolutionary emotion'. *Don Juan* was mentioned
only to regret its 'antisocial and licentious sentiment': 'Let us
condemn and pass on, homily undelivered.' Carlyle had the merit
of pointing out 'the profoundly important crisis in the midst of
which we are living', but the fault of being 'a sentimentalist, not a
reasoner'. Rationalist authors, of course, were most sympathetically analysed. Harriet Martineau was valued for her intellectual
'manliness', and J. S. Mill for 'the radiance of a clear vision and a
beneficent purpose', though later reproached for his backsliding in
'Theism' towards Christianity. George Eliot was 'a great moral
force at that epoch', and Pater was encouraged for his 'intellectual
firmness', while being warned against further stylistic 'excess'. In
style, as in thought, Morley hated anything vague: 'firmness is
certainly one of the first qualities that good writing must have.' Yet
he found Macaulay's prose too stiff; 'not like a flowing vestment to
his thought, but like a suit of armour.' His own early style was
rather ponderous, though enlivened by the occasional epigram
('Labels are devices for saving talkative persons the trouble of
thinking'), and by the directness of his derogatory terms, of which
'fatuous' was his favourite. Gradually he started aiming at 'the
excision of superfluous words, of connecting particles, introductory phrases, and the like things, that seem more trivial for a
reader's comfort than they are.' This resulted in the staccato
lucidity of *On Compromise* (1874):

If I have found my way to the light, there must be others groping after it
very close in my neighbourhood. My discovery is their goal. They are

prepared to receive the new truth, which they were not prepared to find for themselves. The fact that the mass are not yet ready to receive, any more than to find, is no reason why the possessor of the new truth should run to hide under a bushel the candle which has been lighted for him.

Though the image came from a Gospel, the chief 'truth' about which the whole book discouraged compromise was the untruth of orthodox Christianity. From J. S. Mill's doctrine that social progress demanded freedom for the individual, Morley went on to urge individuals to have the courage of their convictions. Since progress was 'not automatic', it was the duty of 'every intelligent man' to have 'some clear ideas' about important issues, and to pass those ideas on to others. To conceal them was to betray humanity. 'A considerable proportion of people, men no less than women, are born invertebrate', Morley complained. His sermon against pusillanimity included some scathing satire, on clergymen, for instance, who went 'through life masked and gagged' in order to earn a living, and on infidel husbands who kept their thoughts from their wives, and presided at family prayers. Not even Matthew Arnold's Oxford was quite what it seemed: ' ... "the sweet city with her dreaming spires," where there has ever been so much detachment from the world, alongside of the coarsest and fiercest hunt after the grosser prizes of the world.'

Oxford's MP, however, was immune to any such charge. The *Life of Gladstone* (1903) showed Morley's 'whole-hearted and candid attachment' to his friend and political colleague, despite Gladstone's attachment to religion. Completed in only four years, while Morley was still busy in Parliament, the work was a triumph of research, not only into Parliamentary reports, but also into 'a huge mountain of material at Hawarden', including sixty thousand letters addressed to Gladstone:

To overmaster and compress the raw material, and to produce from it the lineaments of a singularly subtle and elastic mind, and the qualities of one of the most powerful and long-lived athletes that ever threw himself into the parliamentary arena—*hic labor, hoc opus!*

Morley had no great gift for narrative, and without a special interest in the details of political history the three fat volumes may be found slow reading. But the 'lineaments' that emerge of a powerful, if strangely humourless, personality are indeed remarkable; and it was typical of the period's 'free-thinking' that Morley should both censure Mill for failing 'to keep the agnostic lamps well trimmed', and yet praise Gladstone for carrying, in his religiously-based morality, 'a golden lamp':

Events from season to season are taken to teach sinister lessons, that the Real is the only Rational, force is the test of right or wrong, the state has nothing to do with the restraints of morals, the ruler is emancipated. Speculations in physical science were distorted for alien purposes, and survival of the fittest was taken to give brutality a more decent name . . . This gospel it was Mr. Gladstone's felicity to hold at bay.

He was equally resistant to old age, and so was his biographer. In his *Recollections* (1917), published when he was seventy-nine, Morley called Arnold's 'Growing Old' 'terribly true, unless we resist . . . '. To judge from this lively work, he was still very far from being 'the phanton of himself'. It contained many acute comments on contemporary authors, a chapter inspired by Clough's 'Easter Day', and some final thoughts, in the context of an evening walk with his dog, on the intellectual life of his period. Questioning whether the influence of rationalism over the last two generations had really proved 'so much more potent than the gospel of the various churches', Morley ended in a mood of indulgence rather than respect for the pretensions of philosophy: 'My little humble friend squat on her haunches, looking wistfully up, eager to resume her endless hunt after she knows not what, just like the chartered metaphysician.'

Though a founder-member of the Metaphysical Society, Henry Sidgwick did know what he was hunting for, only he failed to find it.[12] He was after some method of reconciling his 'religious instinct' with his 'growing conviction that both individual and social morality ought to be placed on an inductive basis'. That was how he described his dilemma in 1861, and two subsequent articles suggest that he was arguing, first against one horn and then the other. Reviewing *Ecce Homo* in 1866, he systematically refuted the idea that this edifying work had 'contrived somehow to set Christianity upon a basis impregnable to the assaults of modern criticism and science.' In 'The Prophet of Culture' (1867) he found fault equally with Matthew Arnold's claim that culture,

---

[12] Henry Sidgwick, 1838–1900, was born at Skipton, Yorkshire, where his father was headmaster of the grammar school. He went to Rugby and Trinity College, Cambridge, of which he became a fellow, 1859. He was largely responsible for the founding of Newnham College, 1876, and that year married Eleanor Mildred Balfour, who became its principal, 1892–1910. From 1883 he was professor of moral philosophy at Cambridge.

consisting of 'the scientific passion for pure knowledge' plus 'the moral and social passion for doing good', was destined to 'transform and govern' the idea of religion. Here he even called Arnold a Philistine, for being so superficial in his approach to religion:

He seems to me (if so humble a simile may be pardoned) to judge of religious organisations as a dog judges of human beings, chiefly by the scent . . . he will not stoop down and look into them; he is not sufficiently interested in their dynamical importance.

Clough, however, he found a wholly congenial poet, and followed his example in 1869 by resigning his fellowship at Trinity College Cambridge, rather than subscribe to a religious test. The same year Sidgwick reviewed Clough's *Poems and Prose Remains* for the *Westminster Review*, showing a remarkable degree of insight, not only into Clough's thought, but also into his poetical technique:

All English hexameters written quite *au sérieux* seem to us to fail; the line ought to be unconscious of being a hexameter, and yet never is. But Clough's line is, and is meant to be, conscious of being a hexameter: it is always suggestive of and allusive to the ancient serious hexameters, with a faint but deliberate air of burlesque, a wink implying that the bard is singing academically to an academical audience, and catering for their artificial tastes in versification. This academic flavour suits each poem in a different way . . . In *Amours de Voyage*, it suits the over-cultured, artificial refinement of the hero's mind: he is, we may say, in his abnormal difficulties of action and emotion, a scholastic or academic personage.

In *The Methods of Ethics* (1874) Sidgwick made his most serious attempt to rationalize morality. Here he considered, impartially, three possible methods of doing so, Egoism, Intuitionism, and Utilitarianism. Egoism was rejected, as offering only 'dubious guidance to an ignoble end—dubious, because one never knew what would really make one happy, so the deliberate pursuit of one's own happiness was often self-defeating. Intuitionism would not do either, since it relied on the 'Morality of Common Sense', which was shown in many cases to be uncertain and contradictory. Utilitarianism came out best, though J. S. Mill's version of it was found defective in certain points, especially in its 'qualitative comparison of pleasures'. But the general soundness of common-sense morality was attributed to its 'unconscious Utilitarianism', and some of its anomalies were thought defensible on Utilitarian principles. In sexual ethics, for instance, it was not so irrational as it seemed to condemn, 'with special vehemence and severity, acts of which the immediate effect is pleasure not obviously outweighed by subsequent pain.' Victorian prudery was ultimately 'felicific', a 'thoroughly justified' means to an important social end: 'the maintenance, namely, of the permanent unions which are held to be necessary for the proper rearing and training of children.' Yet even Utilitarianism was not wholly rational. Why should one try to promote the general happiness at the possible expense of one's own? That was clearly unreasonable, unless there was a God who rewarded virtuous behaviour. But Sidgwick firmly refused to create a God simply to prop up an ethical theory. He did not even feel morally bound to regard all his 'duties *as if they were* commandments of God'. He found such a state of mind inconceivable, 'except as a momentary half-wilful irrationality, committed in a violent access of philosophical despair.'

It is for such intellectual integrity that most readers will admire *The Methods*. Though its argument is clear and engrossing, the style is too neutral to give much pleasure, and there are few traces of the humour that apparently made Sidgwick's conversation delightful. In this respect F. H. Bradley's *Ethical Studies* (1876) were much more appealing.[13] In a style that T. S. Eliot compared to Matthew Arnold's, Bradley dismissed Arnold's claim that religion was 'morality touched by emotion': '*All* morality is, in one sense or another, "touched by emotion".' He burlesqued Arnold's definition of God: 'the habit of washing ourselves might be termed "the Eternal not ourselves that makes for cleanliness" . . . "the Eternal", in short, is nothing in the world but a piece of literary clap-trap.' He was scathing about Sidgwick: 'on the subject of Hedonism I can not honestly say more than that he seems to me to have left the question exactly where he found it.' He also ridiculed J. S. Mill's *Utilitarianism*, using the author's own 'pig satisfied' to demolish the alleged 'proof' that 'each person's happiness is a good to that person, and the general happiness, therefore, a good to the aggregate of all persons.'

[13] Francis Herbert Bradley, 1846–1924, brother of the Shakespearian scholar, A. C. Bradley, was born at Clapham, where his father was incumbent of St James's Chapel. He went to Cheltenham College, Marlborough, while his half-brother was headmaster, and University College, Oxford. From 1870 he was a fellow of Merton College, Oxford, where he lived until his death.

Whether our 'great modern logician' thought that by this he had proved that the happiness of all was desirable for each, I will not undertake to say. He either meant to prove this, or has proved what he started with, viz. that each desires his own pleasure. And yet there is a certain plausibility about it. If many pigs are fed at one trough, each desires his own food, and somehow as a consequence does seem to desire the food of all; and by parity of reasoning it should follow that each pig, desiring his own pleasure, desires also the pleasure of all. But as this scarcely seems conformable to experience, I suppose there must be something wrong with the argument, and so likewise with the argument of our philosopher.

Logic and humour, however, were not Bradley's only weapons against Utilitarian Hedonism. He also appealed to human experience, using an effective type of rhetoric to contend that pleasure did not bring happiness:

Pleasures, we saw, were a perishing series. This one comes, and the intense self-feeling proclaims satisfaction. It is gone, and *we* are not satisfied. It was not that one, then, but this one now; and this one now is gone. It was not that one, then, but another and another; but another and another do not give us what we want; we are still left eager and confident, till the flush of feeling dies down, and when that is gone there is nothing left. We are where we began, so far as the getting happiness goes; and we have not found ourselves, and we are not satisfied.

Finding oneself, or '*self-realization*' was for Bradley the 'end in itself' of morality, but not in an egoistic or individualistic sense. It meant: 'Realize yourself as the self-conscious member of an infinite whole, by realizing that whole in yourself.' As for 'the whole', it meant first 'the state', which was 'the moral organism, the real identity of might and right', and later 'an organic human-divine totality', alias God. The positive conclusion of the *Studies*, which incorporates a phrase from *In Memoriam*, seems hardly more precise that that of the poem:

Here our morality is consummated in oneness with God, and everywhere we find that 'immortal Love', which builds itself for ever on contradiction, but in which the contradiction is eternally resolved.

Bradley's merits as a prose writer appear chiefly in the negative parts of the book, where he demolished opposing theories with witty paradoxes and epigrams; but he was clearly concerned throughout to entertain 'the plain man', whose ethical views were treated with greater respect than those of professional philosophers.

The plain man was not catered for in *Appearance and Reality* (1893). By a long series of subtle arguments, Bradley proved that all the first principles on which metaphysicians had relied to explain the nature of reality were self-contradictory. From this he drew inferences strangely reminiscent of Swinburne's parody, 'The Higher Pantheism in a Nutshell':

All is appearance, and no appearance, nor any combination of these, is the same as Reality. This is half the truth, and by itself is a dangerous error. We must turn at once to correct it by adding its counterpart and supplement. The Absolute *is* its appearances, it really is all and every one of them ... Every attitude of experience, every sphere or level of the world, is a necessary factor in the Absolute. Each in its own way satisfies, until compared with that which is more than itself. Hence appearance is error, if you will, but not every error is illusion.

'That metaphysics should approve itself to common sense', Bradley realized, 'is indeed out of the question. For neither in its processes nor in its results can it expect, or even hope, to be generally intelligible.' But even the plain man's interest may be caught by the chapters on the 'Self' and 'Solipsism'. He may also find some evidence to support T. S. Eliot's view that 'of wisdom Bradley had a large share'. Having accepted that a future life was 'decidedly improbable', he made a comment worthy at least of Tennyson's 'Ancient Sage': 'There is in life always, I admit, a note of sadness; but it ought not to prevail, nor can we truly assert that it does so.'

16. History, Biography, Autobiography

THE course of historiography during the period might be described in Carlylese as a gradual degradation of the Sacred Poet into Dryasdust. As the inspired amateur gave way to the objective professional, the writing tended to become duller; but the decline was by no means continuous, and the divorce between literature and science was never made absolute. Even Niebuhr, who pioneered the scientific approach to Roman history (1827-8), relied heavily on his own intuition, and Connop Thirlwall, who with J. C. Hare translated Niebuhr's *History* into English (1828-42), and followed its principles in his own *History of Greece* (1835-44), wrote in a style less colourless than some critics have suggested.[1] Deliberately unrhetorical, it was clear and fluent in narrative as well as in argument. J. S. Mill thought Thirlwall the best speaker he had ever heard, and his written prose, syntactically simple and economically worded, was well adapted for reading aloud. He brought out the full comedy of the occasion when Nicias called Cleon's bluff in the Assembly, and the slowly mounting tragedy of the Sicilian expedition, especially where disaster was finally assured by the superstitious scruples of Nicias about a lunar eclipse.

After Carlyle's first specimen of 'poetical' history, *The French Revolution* (1837), Thomas Arnold tried to cultivate Niebuhr's 'master art of doubting rightly and believing rightly', in his own *History of Rome* (1838-43).[2] Yet Arnold's judgements of fact were

[1] Connop Thirlwall, 1797-1875, was born at Stepney, the son of a clergyman. He started Latin at three, read Greek at four, and had his first book published at eleven. He went to Charterhouse and Trinity College, Cambridge, where he became a fellow. Not wishing then to be a clergyman, he trained as a barrister, but was ordained and returned to Cambridge, 1827, and held several college offices. He was forced to resign his fellowship, 1834, because he opposed compulsory chapel for dissenters. From 1840 he was Bishop of St David's, and in the House of Lords was progressive on most issues, though he voted to condemn *Essays and Reviews*, 1860. A cat-loving bachelor, he shared a grave with Grote.

[2] For *The French Revolution* see Chap. 10. Thomas Arnold, 1795-1842, the father of Matthew Arnold, was born at East Cowes, Isle of Wight, the son of a customs-collector. He went to Winchester and Corpus Christi College, Oxford. Ordained deacon, he settled at

clearly influenced by his faith that history showed Providence at work, and illustrated certain 'truths in moral and political science', such as the bad results of 'legalized oppression'. Thus the outcome of the Punic Wars was providential, since 'it was clearly for the good of mankind that Hannibal should be conquered: his triumph would have stopped the progress of the world.' While aiming to be 'impartial in his judgements of men and parties', Arnold never pretended to be 'indifferent to those principles which were involved more or less purely in their defeat or triumph.' So he told his story with the earnestness of a preacher and the personal involvement of an eye-witness, always quick to applaud a fine action, and to sympathize with suffering, even that of Hannibal's 'poor' elephants. For the early history of Rome, which Niebuhr thought to have survived in legends and ballads, Arnold used a 'more antiquated' style, faintly poetic and biblical. For the rest, his prose was admirably lucid and emphatic, if rather stiff and orotund. The best of his narrative described Hannibal's campaigns in Italy, which Niebuhr had not lived to handle. Here Arnold's treatment went far to support his claim that these wars, unlike most others, had 'the interest of a romance', and thus kept 'their hold on the imaginations and feelings of all ages and countries.'

There was not much romance in George Finlay's *Greece under the Romans* (1844)—except for one bizarre anecdote about the Empress Eudocia, which Gibbon had dismissed in a footnote as 'fit only for the Arabian Nights'.[3] Finlay, a law student who had been with Byron at Missolonghi, was chiefly interested in 'the effects of the ancient [Greek] institutions on the fortunes of the people under the Roman government', and how 'these institutions were modified or supported by other circumstances.' His interest was not purely academic. After Independence he had bought an estate in Attica, and had been disillusioned by his experience of Greek society. The book became the first instalment of a *History of*

Laleham on the Thames, took private pupils, and married a clergyman's daughter, who died in 1829. He was headmaster of Rugby from 1828, published an edition of Thucydides, 1830–5, and became professor of modern history at Oxford, 1841. He was a Broad-Churchman, advocating church reform and Catholic emancipation, and attacking the Oxford Movement. For Stanley's biography see below.

[3] George Finlay, 1799–1875, was born at Faversham, Kent, the son of an army officer, and studied law at Glasgow and Göttingen, but spent most of his life in Greece. It was, he wrote, only his failure to 'improve the land' that led him to 'the sterile task of recording its misfortunes'.

Greece from its Conquest by the Romans (1877), which put a new emphasis on social and economic conditions in the Byzantine Empire, and was hailed by a contemporary as the greatest work of English historical literature since Gibbon. Its literary appeal, however, was small. He mentioned 'vivid pictures' in Strabo and Pausanias, but painted none himself. Only rare flashes of humour enlivened the dry precision of his prose; and though he shared Arnold's view of 'legalized oppression', he lacked Arnold's vigour in denouncing it.

In George Grote's *History of Greece* (1846–56) profound scholarship was a vehicle for political propaganda.[4] Though the son of a Tory banker, Grote had become a disciple of James Mill, campaigned for Parliamentary Reform, and been active in Parliament as a Philosophical Radical. So Athenian democracy, which in William Mitford's *History* (1785–1810) had been condemned as the direct cause of despotism, was in Grote's 'the active transforming cause' which had made Athens 'the most progressive and most intellectual city in the ancient world'. This

grand and new idea of the sovereign People, composed of free and equal citizens—or liberty and equality, to use words which so profoundly moved the French nation half a century ago . . . acted with electric effect upon the Athenians, creating within them a host of sentiments, motives, sympathies, and capacities, to which they had before been strangers.

In formulating the idea, Pericles had foreseen the danger against which J. S. Mill would warn in *On Liberty*; for Pericles had stressed 'the liberty of thought and action at Athens, not merely from excessive restraint of law, but also from practical intolerance between man and man, and tyranny of the majority over individual dissenters in taste and pursuit.' Even the demagogue Cleon showed traces of a halo: qualified by his 'violent temper' to become 'what is called a great opposition speaker', he probably made enemies 'by helping poor persons, who had been wronged, to obtain justice before the dikastery'. Grote's political fervour made his *History* carry conviction, but the work is not easy or pleasant reading. His polysyllabic diction, ponderous syntax, and abstract

---

[4] George Grote, 1794–1871, was born near Beckenham, Kent, the eldest of a banker's eleven children. He went to Charterhouse, where he met Thirlwall, then worked, 1810–43, in the bank founded by his grandfather, an immigrant from Bremen. He was MP for the City of London, 1832–41.

forms of expression were ill-adapted for narrative. As Grote told the story, even the battle of Salamis became undramatic.

Harriet Martineau's *History of England during the Thirty Years' Peace* (1849–50) and Macaulay's *History of England from the Accession of James II* (1849–61), both discussed elsewhere in this volume, were in different ways innovative; but Charles Merivale's *History of the Romans under the Empire* (1850–62) was old-fashioned in method as well as outlook.[5] While Mommsen was showing the historical importance of inscriptions, Merivale continued to rely on literary sources; while Macaulay was preaching liberalism and Grote democracy, Merivale saw the Empire as a providential phase in the growth of monarchy:

The sublime vaticinations of the Virgilian Sibyl, bringing the predictions of the Hebrew prophets home to the breasts of the Italians, foreshadowed a reign of peace, equality, and unity, whether under a political or a moral law. At last, with the birth of the monarchy, there sprang up the germ of the greatest of social revolutions, the religion of Christ.

Thus Julius Caesar, of whom Arnold had written, 'Never did any man occasion so large an amount of human misery with so little provocation', became a kind of John the Baptist. He started a 'humane experiment' in creating 'popular monarchy', on the 'general principle' of the 'elevation of a middle class of citizens, to constitute the ultimate source of all political authority'. Only the Ides of March frustrated his 'liberal schemes'. For 'inscrutable reasons' the 'Great Disposer' left Augustus and his successors to carry them out—including, presumably, Nero and Domitian. Though fluent and dignified, Merivale's prose lacked tension and variety. He realized that the battle of Actium 'must have presented' an 'exciting spectacle', yet added, more characteristically: 'But the moral setting of the picture endues it with a still higher charm.' A moralist rather than a story-teller, he was best at relating incidents with a moral aspect, like the death of Cicero, or of Pliny the elder.

Excitement and moral earnestness were splendidly combined in

---

[5] For Harriet Martineau and Macaulay see Chap. 14. Charles Merivale, 1808–93, was born in London, the son of a barrister who wrote poems and translations. He went to Harrow, Haileybury, and St John's College, Cambridge, where he became a fellow. He had earlier recited *Timbuctoo* in the Senate House, when Tennyson was too shy to do so, and also distinguished himself by walking from Cambridge to London in a day. He became dean of Ely, 1869.

J. A. Froude's *History of England, from the Fall of Wolsey to the Defeat of the Spanish Armada* (1856–70).[6] A superb story-teller, a colourful writer, and a passionate sceptic, Froude was Merivale's antithesis. The scepticism had first surfaced when, caught up like his brother R. H. Froude in the Tractarian movement, he wrote for Newman's series a life of St Neot, which concluded: 'This is all, or perhaps rather more than all, that is known of his life.' When Newman became a Roman Catholic, Froude expressed his own loss of faith in a novel, *The Nemesis of Faith* (1849), which was publicly burnt by the Sub-Rector of Exeter College, Oxford. Froude resigned his fellowship there, and started work on his history, in a mood of indignation against Romanism and religious intolerance. His subject was 'the great religious drama of the sixteenth century', 'the great duel with Rome', and his plan was to trace 'the transition from the Catholic England with which the century opened, the England of a dominant Church and monasteries and pilgrimages, into the England of progressive intelligence.' For him the English Reformation, like Athenian democracy for Grote, began 'a vast intellectual revolution':

The recognition that false dogmas had for many centuries been violently intruded upon mankind—and the consequent revolt against the authority which imposed them, were in reality a protest against the dogmatic system, and an admission of the rights of conscience.

The Reformation led to the 'reciprocal toleration' of 'a multitude of opinions', and the experience 'that men of different persuasions can live together with mutual advantage and mutual respect, has untwisted slowly the grasp of the theological fingers from the human throat.' The 'duel with Rome' was also 'the struggle which transferred from Spain to England the sovereignty of the seas', and laid the foundations of the British Empire. The thesis involved the glorification, not only of Protestant heroes and martyrs, but also of Henry VIII. Despite his 'many faults' he was not a tyrant, but a man who, 'with the strength of irresistible will', swept England

---

[6] James Anthony Froude, 1818–94, brother of the Tractarian R. H. Froude, was born at Dartington, Devonshire, the son of the rector. He went to Westminster and Oriel College, Oxford, where his rooms were just above Newman's. He took deacon's orders, 1844, but renounced them as soon as the law allowed it, 1872. His friends included Clough, Emerson, Kingsley, whose sister-in-law he married, and Carlyle, whose life he wrote (see below). He edited *Fraser's Magazine*, 1860–74, and from 1892 was professor of modern history at Oxford (living at Cherwell Edge, now Linacre College). He died at Kingsbridge, Devonshire.

forward into a new age. His religious persecutions, including the execution of More, were understandable, if not forgivable, on grounds of national security; though Froude stopped short of condoning 'deliberate cruelty'.

Froude wrote with strong feeling, but scrupulously balanced evidence, arguments, and probabilities, as when discussing the charges against Anne Boleyn; and though charged by contemporary liberals with reckless inaccuracy, he had done an unusual amount of research into manuscript sources. His reputation as a historian now stands higher than it did, but his literary merits have always been recognized. His vivid characterization and compelling narrative may best be sampled in the accounts of Darnley's murder and of Mary Stuart's execution. A disciple of Carlyle, Froude helped to delay the dispossession of the Sacred Poet by a witty lecture of 1864, rejecting H. T. Buckle's proposal that history should become a science. Science, he argued, implied ability to predict future phenomena, but human beings were essentially unpredictable: 'you will make nothing of [them] except from the old-fashioned moral—or, if you please, imaginative—point of view.' The best models for history were *Macbeth*, the *Iliad*, and the *Odyssey*.

The argument seems less conclusive when one reads Buckle's *History of Civilization in England* (1857–61).[7] Buckle based his case on the data of statistics, which suggested that, though individual human beings were unpredictable, human behaviour 'at large' was to some extent regular and uniform. For instance, the number of murders and suicides was much the same every year, and one could roughly predict how many people would forget to address their letters before posting them. In an attempt to formulate 'the laws of European history' and of English civilization, Buckle produced four hypotheses: that human progress depended on scientific progress; that this depended on the diffusion of 'a spirit of scepticism'; that scientific discoveries made intellectual truths more influential than moral ones; and that this movement towards civilization was chiefly retarded by 'the protec-

[7] Henry Thomas Buckle, 1821–62, was born at Lee, Kent, the son of a London shipowner, who died in 1840. Delicate from childhood, he was at first taught by his mother, then briefly at a private school in Kentish Town, but for the most part educated himself, by extensive reading and travelling. He had a remarkable memory, distinguished himself in international chess-contests, and grudged no expenditure on books or cigars. He died of typhoid at Damascus.

tive spirit ... the notion that society cannot prosper, unless the affairs of life are watched over and protected at nearly every turn by the state and the church.' The hypotheses were to be checked against the facts of history in Germany, America, Scotland, and Spain, after which the main treatment of civilization in England would have begun, but for Buckle's sudden death after publishing the first two volumes. He had time, however, to attribute the melancholy backwardness of Spain to the crushing of all scepticism and individual initiative by the Church, and to expose the paradox that 'brilliant, inquisitive, and sceptical writers like Hume and Adam Smith did nothing to reduce the general superstition and religious intolerance in Scotland.' Unfinished as it was, Buckle's *History* incorporated a remarkable range of historical knowledge, raised interesting questions about the effect of climate and physical environment on national character, and was most persuasively worded: to ensure continuity, he had composed each paragraph in his head before writing it down. His enthusiasm about 'the glorious principle of universal and undeviating regularity' in human life is surprisingly infectious. One feels, behind the description of his ideal historian in the second volume, the intense frustration that he voiced when he was dying: 'Oh, my book, my book! I shall never finish my book.'

The history of civilization was approached from another angle in Henry Maine's *Ancient Law: its Connection with the Early History of Society and its Relation to Modern Ideas* (1861).[8] Tracing the evolution of modern from ancient law, Maine found superstitious adherence to the customs of 'a barbarous society' an 'absolutely fatal' obstacle to 'progress in civilization'. One such relic of barbarism was the legal position of married women. To the general reader the book is chiefly interesting for its passing comments on contemporary issues like feminism, political economy, the rights of property, and revolution. Otherwise it belongs to scholarship rather than literature. A. W. Kinglake's *The Invasion of the Crimea* (1863–87) had a much wider appeal.[9] Kinglake

[8] Sir Henry James Sumner Maine, 1822–88, was nearly killed as a baby by an overdose of opium, but survived to go to Christ's Hospital, London, and Trinity Hall, Cambridge, of which he became master, 1877. Called to the bar, 1850, he went to India, 1862, as legal member of the supreme council, and held the chair of jurisprudence at Oxford, 1869–78. Always delicate, he died of apoplexy at Cannes.

[9] Alexander William Kinglake, 1809–91, was born at Taunton, Somerset, the son of a banker and solicitor. He went to Eton and Trinity College, Cambridge, where he met

had witnessed the battle of Alma himself, and then done prolonged research into written sources, including the complete papers of Lord Raglan. Believing Napoleon III to have been mainly responsible for the war, Kinglake began with an indignant account of the 1851 *coup d'état*, culminating in a massacre of civilians on a Paris boulevard. The whole work was enormously diffuse, but, as might be expected from the author of *Eothen*, was full of graphic realism and ironic wit. Describing the hand-to-hand fighting at Inkerman, Kinglake pointed the paradox of 'an Englishman's love of "fair play"':

Bancroft—fighting for his life with one upstanding antagonist, and clutched at the same time round his legs by the one who had fallen— could only repress the fierce energy of the man on the ground by stunning him with kicks in the head . . . Serjeant Alger called out to him, from a spot some way off, and forbade him to 'kick the man that was down.'

S. R. Gardiner's *History of England from the Accession of James I*, which also began to come out in 1863, was a more austere work.[10] Himself a descendant of Cromwell, he set out to write the history of the Puritan revolution. His Puritan sympathies appeared even in his style. He warned his readers not to expect any 'striking dramatic interest', or any 'well-known anecdote', 'however amusing', as the 'anecdote-mongers' were 'thoroughly untrustworthy'. Sure enough, he wrote almost impersonally, without any trace of excitement or humour. So, though his work has been called by a historian, 'the most solid and enduring achievement of British historiography in the latter half of the nineteenth century', other readers may find it dull, as in its conscientious refusal to exploit the dramatic element even in the Gunpowder Plot. But here, and throughout the history, one must admire Gardiner's efforts to 'judge the actors fairly'. Thus Bacon's mixed motives and 'moral

---

Tennyson and Thackeray. After the travels described in *Eothen* (see Chap. 18), he was called to the bar, 1837. He went to the Crimea, 1854, fell off his pony at Alma near Lord Raglan, became his friend, and was thus given access to his papers after his death. He was Liberal MP for Bridgwater, 1857–68.

[10] Samuel Rawson Gardiner, 1829–1902, was born at Alresford, Hampshire, grandson of a descendant of Cromwell's eldest daughter. He went to Winchester and Christ Church, Oxford. After his marriage, 1856, he lived in London, researching at the British Museum. He became professor of modern history at King's College, London, and a popular extension lecturer, 1877–94. Having refused an invitation to succeed Froude at Oxford, he was Ford Lecturer there, 1896.

failings' are patiently analysed, until 'his conduct becomes at least intelligible.' Understanding the past, rather than bringing it to life, was Gardiner's main object.

W. E. H. Lecky was a more attractive writer.[11] An admirer of Buckle, he made his name, in a *History of the Rise and Influence of the Spirit of Rationalism in Europe* (1865), as a historian of ideas, who studied them in a broad, human context: 'It is impossible to lay down a railway without creating an intellectual influence.' Here he traced not only the social effects of the 'Declining Sense of the Miraculous' but also its manifestations in science, art, ethics, politics, and industry. Though rationalist in temper as well as subject, the book conveyed strong feeling, chiefly indignation at the cruelty caused by superstitious beliefs and doctrines of 'exclusive salvation'. But that feeling was expressed, not in passionate rhetoric, but in a dry form of wit. Describing the massacres of Jews and trials for witchcraft precipitated by the Black Death in Switzerland, Lecky mentioned one 'explanation' of the plague: 'Boots with pointed toes had been lately introduced, and were supposed by many to have been peculiarly offensive to the Almighty.' Stressing 'the idea of absurdity' in religious persecution, the *History* resembled a Swiftian satire, full of *saeva indignatio* but often very funny. In his *History of European Morals from Augustus to Charlemagne* (1869) Lecky blamed Christianity for obstructing intellectual progress, and ridiculed its attitude to sex. In the twelfth century, for instance, 'a lake of mingled lead, pitch, and resin' was supposed to be reserved in hell 'for the punishment of married people who had lain together on Church festivals or fast days.' Recording the 'Natural History of Morals' with clinical detachment, Lecky was mildly revolutionary in his approach to all sexual questions, including divorce and the status of women. Though loosely constructed, the whole work was very readable, rich in ironic epigram and neatly exploited quotation. His *History of England in the Eighteenth Century* (1878–90) covered all 'the permanent forces of the nation' and 'the more enduring

---

[11] William Edward Hartpole Lecky, 1838–1903, was born near Dublin, the son of a landowner who had been called to the bar, but was too rich to need to practise. After graduating, 1859, at Trinity College, Dublin, he published a book of poems, thought of becoming a clergyman, but soon decided to be an author. His *History of Rationalism* was an instant success. In 1871 he married and settled in London, where his literary friends included Tennyson, Browning, Stephen, Huxley, and Spencer. He was MP for Dublin University, 1895–1902.

features of national life' in every sphere, but ideas were again central, and one of the best chapters described 'The Religious Revival', and the rise of Methodism. It contained a vivid, if satirical, portrait of Wesley, and some entertaining comments on Whitefield's preaching, and 'intolerably tedious' writings: 'Of the even profane imagery to which he could descend it is sufficient to say that he once spoke of Christ as "roasted, as it were, in the Father's wrath, and therefore fitly styled the Lamb of God".'

In 1866, the year after the *History of Rationalism*, the appointment of William Stubbs to the Chair of History at Oxford had marked the advent of the professional historian.[12] Having distinguished himself as an editor of medieval source-material, Stubbs went on to produce what has been called 'one of the most astonishing achievements of the Victorian mind', his *Constitutional History of England* (1874–8). He warned his readers that the subject afforded 'little of the romantic incident or of the picturesque grouping which constitutes the charm of History in general', and held out 'small temptations to the mind that requires to be tempted to the study of Truth'. Such minds were certainly not catered for. The subject of *Murder in the Cathedral* was covered by one censorious sentence, and Henry V, far from being thought worthy of a 'Muse of fire', was curtly reduced to a kind of epitaph: 'a laborious man of business, a self-denying and hardy warrior, a cultivated scholar, and a most devout and charitable Christian.' The style was ponderous and abstract, except when, possibly recalling a passage in Browning's *Paracelsus*, Stubbs envisaged the 'good' in the Dark Ages as 'lying deep down and having yet to wait long before it reaches the surface, [but] already striving towards the sunlight that is to come.'

Another member of the Oxford School, E. A. Freeman, offered more in the way of 'temptation'.[13] His *History of the Norman*

---

[12] William Stubbs, 1825–1901, was the son of a Knaresborough solicitor. He went to Ripon Grammar School and Christ Church, Oxford, where he became a fellow of Trinity, then vicar of Navestock, Essex. There he 'knew every toe on every baby in the parish', married an ex-schoolmistress, and fathered six more babies, while researching on medieval sources. In 1859 he privately coached Swinburne. As Regius professor of history at Oxford, 1866–84, he lived in Broad Street and gave scrupulously prepared lectures to small audiences. He was made Bishop of Chester, 1884, and of Oxford, 1888.

[13] Edward Augustus Freeman, 1823–92, was born at Harborne, Staffordshire. Orphaned as a baby, he was brought up by a grandmother. He became a fellow of Trinity College, Oxford, 1845, married his former tutor's daughter, and lived first in Gloucestershire and then in Somerset. After publishing a history of architecture, and a book of poems, he wrote

Conquest (1867–79), which helped to inspire Tennyson's *Harold*, was meant to 'throw some life' into a period 'commonly presented to ordinary readers in the guise either of fantastic legends or else of summaries of the most repulsive dryness.' Freeman saw the Conquest as 'a turning-point' at which an essentially Teutonic nation was temporarily subjected to an alien power, and the whole work glowed with patriotism and hero-worship. The Greek epigraph from Ecclesiasticus, 'Let us now praise famous men,' introduced a series of 'great' kings, from Alfred, 'the most perfect character in history', to Edward I, 'the first king of the new stock who deserved to be called an Englishman.' Traces of the Sacred Poet survived in allusions to classical literature. The last line of the *Iliad* was quoted to link Harold with Hector and, with several similar references, to suggest the feeling of a national epic. In the same way Xerxes was invoked to associate Freeman's 'great drama' with Aeschylus' patriotic tragedy, the *Persae*. While scrupulously collecting and assessing 'every scrap of evidence', Freeman clearly enjoyed legends for their own sake. His own gift for story-telling was conspicuous in Chapter 15, on 'The Norman Invasion and the campaign of Hastings'. Despite some lapses into ham rhetoric and Wardour Street English ('The King turned him to depart'), and a general tendency to long-windedness, Freeman's style was quite lively and readable.

By literary standards, however, the best of the Oxford School was J. R. Green.[14] His *Short History of the English People* (1874), which was enlarged from one volume to four, as the *History of the English People* (1877–80), was a brilliantly concise account of the period from 607 to 1815, with an Epilogue sketching further developments up to 1873. With a patriotic enthusiasm like Freeman's, but in a much more epigrammatic style, Green told the story of English progress. He found room for a surprising number

---

constantly for the *Saturday Review*, starting an argument with Trollope, 1869, on 'The Morality of Field Sports'. He succeeded Stubbs at Oxford, 1884. Passionate about history and politics, he was a violent controversialist, as when attacking Kingsley and Froude. He travelled extensively, and died of smallpox at Alicante.

[14] John Richard Green, 1837–83, was born in Oxford, where he went to Magdalen College School and Jesus College. Ordained, 1860, he worked as a clergyman in Hoxton and Stepney, spending his free time at the British Museum. Encouraged by Stubbs and Freeman, he started writing for the *Saturday Review*, and became librarian at Lambeth, 1868. Next year he began to suffer from tuberculosis, which eventually killed him. His *Short History* sold 150,000 copies in fifteen years.

of striking details, quotations, and anecdotes. He also managed to cover not merely political but also 'intellectual and social advance'. Resolving not to write a 'drum and trumpet history ... a mere record of the butchery of men by their fellow-men', he celebrated 'the triumphs of peace', including literature and science, with some 'figures little heeded in common history ... the missionary, the poet, the printer, the merchant ... the philosopher.' His feeling for poetry and left-wing sympathies came out well in a passage on *Piers Plowman* and the Peasants' Revolt, while his view of drums and trumpets did not prevent him from making an excellent story of the Napoleonic Wars, with its climax at Waterloo. Though he called his own period 'the greatest indeed of all in real importance and interest', he vividly pictured the spirit of the Elizabethan age, in a mosaic of seemingly unrelated historical facts. With the 'prodigal use of glass ... in domestic architecture' Green associated a 'prodigal enjoyment of light and sunshine', a 'lavishness of new wealth [which] united with a lavishness of life, a love of beauty, of colour, of display, to revolutionize English dress':

Men 'wore a manor on their backs.' The old sober notions of thrift melted before the strange revolutions of fortune wrought by the New World. Gallants gambled away a fortune at a sitting, and sailed off to make a fresh one in the Indies. Visions of galleons loaded to the brim with pearls and diamonds and ingots of silver ... threw a haze of prodigality and profusion over the imagination of the meanest seaman ... It was to this turmoil of men's minds, this wayward luxuriance and prodigality of fancy, that we owe the revival of English letters under Elizabeth.

Encouraged by the popularity of this 'wee book' (as Freeman called it), Green started a series of shilling primers, and asked another Oxford friend, Mandell Creighton, to do one on Roman History.[15] Completed in three weeks, this too sold well (1875), for which Creighton had a modest explanation: it was just the right size, he said, for schoolboys to throw at one another's heads, so it constantly needed replacing. He took longer to finish his *History of*

---

[15] Mandell Creighton, 1843–1901, was born in Carlisle. He went to Durham Grammar School and Merton College, Oxford, where he became a fellow, 1866. Ordained, 1870, he married the daughter of a London merchant, and took a college living at Embleton, Northumberland. He was first professor of ecclesiastical history at Cambridge, 1884, and first editor of the *English Historical Review*, 1886. He was made bishop of Peterborough, 1891, and of London, 1897.

the Papacy during the period of the Reformation (1882–94), but this clearly gained from the early exercise in writing shortly and simply. Regarding the decline of papal authority from the Great Schism to the Sack of Rome as one cause of the Reformation, and the Reformation as a turning-point in both political and intellectual history, Creighton set out 'to trace, within a limited sphere, the working of the causes which brought about the change from medieval to modern times.' He did it 'from a strictly historical point of view', by simply 'watching events and noting the gradual development of affairs'. He cultivated such detachment in moral as well as religious questions. Though he showed some indignation at the horrors of the Sack of Rome, his usual tone, even when relating the conduct of the Borgias, was humorous and tolerant. Thus Pope Alexander VI was a 'handsome, joyous, and genial' character, who liked 'to do unpleasant things in a pleasant manner', who played the 'game' of politics according to the rules of his period, and whose only mistake was frankness: 'The exceptional infamy that attaches to [him] is largely due to the fact that he did not add hypocrisy to his other vices.'

Much of Creighton's material was sensational or bizarre, like Lorenzo Strozzi's macabre dinner-party; but he excelled in realistic portraiture, as of Luther, and also had Lecky's knack of enlivening serious discussions with entertaining details. Examining the complex relation between the Reformation and the Renaissance, he exploited all the humour of the *Epistolae Obscurorum Virorum*; and while stressing the paradox that the 'cultivated tolerance of Leo X's court' should have resolved to crush Luther, drew an interesting comparison between the spirits of Luther and of Raphael. 'When events are tedious,' wrote Creighton, 'you must be tedious', and he warned his readers: 'Much that is interesting has been omitted, much that is dull has been told at length.' But, thanks to his laconic wit, his writing was seldom dull. Having told how, after 'a comedy of exalted patriotism', the Roman people meekly accepted occupation by an invading army, Creighton remarked: 'Patriotism and enthusiasm were too precious in word to be rudely expressed in deed.'

Less tolerant than Creighton, J. R. Seeley called the Papacy 'the burning heart of all human discord'.[16] In his anonymous *Ecce*

---

[16] Sir John Robert Seeley, 1834–95, was born in London, the son of a publisher. He went to the City of London School, where he read *Paradise Lost* four or five times, and Christ's

Homo: A Survey of the Life and Work of Jesus Christ (1866), he had
treated his subject as a historian, and presented Jesus primarily as
'the Legislator of a world-wide society', a 'new and unique
Commonwealth' ruled by 'the enthusiasm of humanity' and 'the
law of philanthropy'. A rather similar 'world-state' was the theme
of *The Expansion of England* (1883). Based on lectures that he had
given as Professor of Modern History at Cambridge, the book
argued the importance of an unconscious movement in English
history, the growth of 'Greater Britain': 'We seem, as it were, to
have conquered and peopled half the world in a fit of absence of
mind.' The best reason for studying the past was to get guidance
for political action in the present, and since 'the God who is
revealed in history' evidently meant England to become a federal
empire, the unconscious process should now be consciously
continued. Though *The Expansion* proved very popular, its version of imperialism was not merely an appeal to emotion. Seeley
dissociated himself from the 'bombastic' school of thought, which
believed in maintaining the Empire 'as a point of honour or
sentiment'. He admitted that 'crime [had] gone to the making of
it', and could only 'hope' and 'trust' that India, on balance, had
gained from British rule: 'Our Western civilisation is perhaps not
absolutely the glorious thing we like to imagine it.'

He was equally sceptical about the literary element in historiography. He ridiculed Thackeray's suggestion that history should
be modelled on the novel, called Carlyle and Macaulay 'charla-
tans', and disdained 'a foppish kind of history which aims only at
literary display, which produces delightful books hovering
between poetry and prose.' He even depreciated the story element
in history. 'Break the drowsy spell of narrative,' he urged his
students, 'ask yourself questions; set yourself problems; your mind
will at once take up a new attitude; you will become an investiga-
tor; you will cease to be solemn and begin to be serious.' Happily
his medium contradicted his message. With such views he should
have written like Dryasdust, but his prose was dramatic, epigrammatic, and imaginative. Incorrigibly concerned with literary effect,

---

College, Cambridge, where he met Calverley, and became a fellow and classical lecturer. In
1859 he published a book of poems, and left Cambridge to teach classics at his old school.
From 1863 he was professor of Latin at University College, London, and in 1869 succeeded
Kingsley as professor of modern history at Cambridge, where his lectures attracted large
audiences.

he even offered his theory of Greater Britain as a method of avoiding anticlimax:

Does not Aristotle say that a drama ends, but an epic poem only leaves off? English history, as it is popularly related, not only has no distinct end, but leaves off in . . . a gradual manner, growing feebler and feebler, duller and duller, towards the close . . . our historians . . . lead their readers to think of English history as leading up to nothing . . . like the Heart of Midlothian, of which the whole last volume is dull and superfluous.

'Many of the greatest men that ever lived have written biography. Boswell was one of the smallest men that ever lived, and he has beaten them all.' Macaulay's remark of 1831 must have encouraged modest authors, for by 1876 biography writing had become, as G. O. Trevelyan put it, 'the custom of the age'. Modesty led to a high proportion of extracts from letters and journals, a trend which culminated in J. W. Cross's attempt to 'form an *autobiography* (if the term may be permitted)' of his dead wife, George Eliot. Thus a 'Life' was apt to degenerate into a shapeless compilation; but modern critics of the period's biographies have paid less attention to their structure than to their habit of expurgation, against which Carlyle was the first to protest: 'How delicate, decent, is English biography, bless its mealy mouth! . . . The English biographer has long felt that if . . . he wrote down anything that could by possibility offend any man, he had written wrong.' Using this criterion one might assume a simple line of development from Stanley's *Arnold* (1844) to Froude's *Carlyle* (1882–4), i.e. from hagiography to warts and all. But no such line can be easily traced, and the criterion seems inappropriate. A biographer is not a sensational journalist, or even a psychoanalyst. More relevant questions may be asked about a biography. Does it convey the impression of a real person in a real environment? Does it present its material effectively, or in an artistic form? Is it well written, and interesting to read? Judged from these angles, the period's contributions to the genre make Harold Nicolson's reference (1927) to 'the catastrophic failure of Victorian biography' seem absurd.

In the *Life and Correspondence of Thomas Arnold* the expurgation was explicit. A. P. Stanley omitted any allusions 'which would have been painful to living individuals', and any 'domestic details, which, however characteristic, could not yet have been published without a greater infringement on privacy than is yet possible.'[17] He presented his old headmaster chiefly as a public figure, feeling unable to give 'more than a faint shadow' of his 'inner life . . . what he was.' Arnold's work as an educationist and his professional persona were interestingly described, including 'that awful frown . . . almost always the expression, not of personal resentment, but of deep, ineffable scorn and indignation at the sight of vice and sin.' The natural man was glimpsed beneath the headmaster, when Arnold was said to find early rising difficult, and later discovered at dawn, marking school exercises at Rugby, on the day of his inaugural lecture at Oxford. 'Faint shadows' of his inner life appeared in quotations from the diary that he kept for a few weeks before he died; but for the most part he was viewed from a respectful distance. He emerged as an impressively original, yet wholly mysterious figure, since the reader was given no idea what it was like to *be* Arnold. And even the outward signs of his dynamic personality were obscured by a certain stuffiness in Stanley's manner of writing.

John Forster's *Life and Adventures of Oliver Goldsmith* (1848) was free from such defects.[18] Writing in a conversational, semi-dramatic style, developed in journalism and theatrical criticism, he showed affectionate sympathy with Goldsmith's odd personality. Far from putting him on a pedestal, he stressed his human weaknesses, and saw 'the true beginning of Goldsmith's literary career' in the 'Discipline of Sorrow' which transformed the feckless youth into a mature adult. At this point, destitute and insulted by the bookseller for whom he had been slaving, Goldsmith defended his character with dignity and courage, and graduated from 'Authorship by Compulsion' to 'Authorship by

[17] Arthur Penrhyn Stanley, 1815–81, was born at Alderley, Cheshire, the son of the rector. He went to Rugby under Dr Arnold, whose influence he described as 'the lodestar of my life', and to Balliol College, Oxford. A leading Broad-Churchman and a church historian, he was professor of ecclesiastical history at Oxford from 1856, and dean of Westminster, 1864–81.

[18] John Forster, 1812–76, was the son of a Newcastle cattle-dealer. He went to Newcastle Grammar School and University College, London, then studied law and was called to the bar, 1843. He had had a play performed, 1828, become a dramatic critic, 1832, and went on to edit the *Daily News*, 1846, and the *Examiner*, 1847–55. He had started writing biographies in Lardner's *Cyclopaedia*, 1836–9. His friends included Leigh Hunt, Lamb, Lytton, and Landor, whose life he wrote, 1859. He left a library of eighteen thousand books, now in the Victoria and Albert Museum.

Choice'. This moral interpretation of Goldsmith's career supplied the biography with a firm structure, which compensated for the chatty and rambling character of Forster's prose. His gift for drama came out in scenes like the one where Goldsmith's brother arrived in 'that garret near Salisbury-Square', hoping to share in Oliver's supposed success: '"All in good time, my dear boy," cried Oliver joyfully, to check the bitterness of despair; "all in good time: I shall be richer bye and bye . . .".' His frustrated scheme to make a living as a doctor 'on the coast of Coromandel' was described with a mixture of pathos and humour not unlike that in the poem for which Edward Lear adopted that haunting phrase.

In its tone of critical affection, Carlyle's *John Sterling* (1851) resembled Forster's *Goldsmith*;[19] but Mrs Gaskell's *Life of Charlotte Brontë* (1857) was too affectionate to criticize: 'I cannot measure or judge such a character as hers. I cannot map out vices, and virtues, and debateable land.'[20] Setting out to 'show what a noble, true, and tender woman Charlotte Brontë really was', despite false accounts of her as a writer of 'coarse' love-stories, Mrs Gaskell tried to do so, not by idealizing her friend's character, but by using the rest of her family as foils. Thus her father's violence, her brother's depravity, and her sister Emily's ruthlessness (as when she punched her dog's 'red fierce eyes' until it was half-blind) served to make Charlotte relatively appealing. Some of the best stories about these foils turn out to have been apocryphal; but they added to the pleasure of reading the book, and the resultant portrait of Charlotte seemed entirely realistic, especially against the almost surrealist savagery of her background. As gripping as a novel, the *Life* was also remarkable for its imaginative structure. The special significance of Charlotte's environment was initially introduced by an account, as in a guide-book, of a journey from Keighley to Haworth, and this perspective was reinforced in the penultimate chapter, when the biographer first made the same journey. The opening view of the Parsonage, surrounded by a graveyard 'terribly full of upright tombstones', and the epitaphs of the seven Brontës inside the church, announced the theme of

---

[19] For the *Life of Sterling* see Chap. 10.
[20] Mrs Elizabeth Cleghorn Gaskell, 1810–65, was born in Chelsea, the daughter of William Stevenson, then a treasury official, and was brought up by her aunt at Knutsford, Cheshire. She married a Unitarian minister in Manchester, 1832. Her novels will be discussed in another volume.

death, which was repeated with variations throughout the work, culminating in Charlotte's own funeral—at which one of those who mourned the alleged author of 'naughty books' was 'a village girl who had been seduced some little time before, but who had found a holy sister in Charlotte.' While professing to have 'openly laid bare' the facts of her friend's life, Mrs Gaskell concealed Charlotte's real feelings towards M. Héger; but here she sinned more against history than literature.

The converse might be said of David Masson's *Life of John Milton: Narrated in Connexion with the Political, Ecclesiastical, and Literary History of his Time* (1859–80).[21] Here he promised to write Milton's life 'fully, deliberately, and minutely', and congratulated himself, twenty years later, on having persevered 'to the very end in the original plan, omitting nothing, slurring nothing, that the plan required.' For all his industry and scholarship, the work would have been more readable if he had omitted and slurred more freely, and expressed himself less verbosely. But beneath his ponderous prose lurked a certain dry humour, which surfaced when Milton's doctrine of divorce was said to envisage a man 'living in the centre of a perfect solar system of discarded wives, moving in nearer or farther orbits round him, according to the times when they were thrown off, and each with her one or two satellites of little darlings!' Masson supported the higher education of women, and the subject of Milton's relations with them made him quite lively and imaginative; but the 'Literary History' mentioned in the title indicated no comparable feeling for literature. Posterity, he claimed, had become 'utterly impatient of Donne's poetry', which was best represented by 'The Progresse of the Soule'. And even of Milton's poems his judgement seems questionable: 'he never wrote anything more beautiful, more perfect than *Comus*.'

A more attractive 'bit of literary navvy work' (as Carlyle called it) was James Spedding's *The Letters and the Life of Francis Bacon*

---

[21] David Masson, 1822–1907, was the son of an Aberdeen stone-cutter. He went to the grammar school and university there, then to Edinburgh University. He wrote textbooks for W. & R. Chambers, then moved to London, 1847, where he already knew the Carlyles, and contributed to periodicals. From 1853 he was professor of English literature at University College, London, and he founded and edited *Macmillan's Magazine*, 1859–67. In 1865 he succeeded Aytoun as professor of rhetoric at Edinburgh, and produced numerous biographies and editions.

(1861–72).[22] This professed to be just an edition of Bacon's occasional writings, with a 'Commentary Biographical and Historical', and Spedding assumed that his readers wished 'not to be amused or delighted, but to be informed'. He tried, however, and managed to make his explanations 'not only accurate but readable'. Though wary of 'trespassing upon the province of the novelist', he was quite prepared to use imagination and empathy to describe not only Bacon's expressed thoughts but also 'the condition of his mind', as in a most convincing 'Review of his position', after Bacon had been convicted and imprisoned:

Had the loss of fortune only and reputation in the world's eyes been added . . . still he would have had Job's consolation: he would have boldly stood upon his integrity and challenged censure. But to see all go, and to feel that he had only himself and his own fault to blame, even though the blame were not much in itself, was a terrible catastrophe . . .

Criticized for the alleged 'absence' of the man, Francis Bacon, from the scene, Spedding replied that everything in large print was of that man's composition. Yet it is true that, though Bacon's thoughts and actions were made clear enough, he rarely emerged as a living personality. One sympathizes with critics who demanded 'Less of the raw material of biography and more of the manufactured article.' But Spedding could always silence such complaints: 'the work is constructed on the supposition that both the comment and the text will be read; nor do I regard any one who skips either the one or the other as having read the book or qualified himself to criticize it.'

There is no temptation to skip the 'text' (written or spoken by Blake himself) in Gilchrist's *Life* of him (1863).[23] This belonged to

[22] James Spedding, 1808–81, was born at Mirehouse, near Bassenthwaite, the son of a rich landowner. He went to Trinity College, Cambridge, where he was an Apostle with Tennyson, who called him the wisest man he knew. His first work on Bacon, 1845, was a privately printed reply to Macaulay's 1842 essay. He worked briefly in the colonial office, and refused an invitation to be under-secretary of state. He died after being run over by a cab, and taking special pains to exculpate the driver.

[23] Alexander Gilchrist, 1828–61, was born at Newington Green, the son of a Unitarian minister. He went to University College School and trained as a barrister, but started writing art criticism in periodicals. In 1851 he married Anne Burrows, a solicitor's daughter, 1828-85, who published her own first article in *Household Words*, 1857. His life of Etty had come out, 1855, and he started work on Blake; but he died of scarlet fever before the book was finished, and Anne Gilchrist completed it. She later wrote two articles on Whitman, a life of Mary Lamb, 1883, and was writing a study of Carlyle when that too was interrupted by death.

what Gilchrist called 'that modern school of biography wherein authentic letters form the basis and the hero draws his own portrait.' The portrait was fascinating, thanks to the biographer's gift for identifying facts and details that were 'mentally physiognomic'. He described Blake's life as 'romantic, though incident be slight'; but it contained several bizarre episodes, like the enactment of Adam and Eve in the summer-house, the exit of Robert Blake's spirit through the ceiling, William's trial for sedition, and Hayley's 'eccentric habit of using an umbrella on horseback'. The uneasy relations between that patron and his protégé were presented with considerable understanding and humour. So too was the then central question, 'Mad or not Mad?', to which Gilchrist's final answer was: 'So far as I am concerned, I would infinitely rather be mad with William Blake than sane with nine-tenths of the world.' Though his work has been very important in the history of literary criticism, pioneering the view that Blake's poetry was to be taken seriously, and thus laying the foundations for the twentieth-century industry of Blake-explication, Gilchrist did not himself throw much light upon the poems: 'criticism is idle. How analyse a violet's perfume, or dissect the bloom on a butterfly's wing?' So he contented himself with this sort of comment on 'Spring': 'Can we not see the little three-year-old prattler stroking the white lamb, her feelings made articulate for her?' As for the Prophetic Books, he did little more than register their 'delicate mystic beauty', and amusingly express the average reader's bewilderment: 'dim surmises hurtle in the mind'.

When writing the *Life* of his friend Dickens (1872–4), Forster faced problems not of interpretation but of tact. Since Mrs Dickens was still alive, he played down her husband's 'domestic discontents' and concealed his affair with Ellen Ternan; but he otherwise drew a frank and realistic portrait of the novelist, admitting the 'grave defects' in his character, such as his incapacity for 'renunciation and self-sacrifice' in marriage, and stressing the restless, impatient, and obsessional aspect of his personality. Otherwise the 'Life' was mainly a book-by-book account of a literary career, on the pretext that, with Dickens, the written work 'formed the whole of that inner life which essentially constituted the man.' Though this sounds like an overstatement, Forster made out a good case for assuming that the novels served Dickens as an alternative world to live in, which he found less frustrating than the real one:

It was the world he could bend to his will, and make subserve to all his desires . . . He had his own creations always by his side. They were living, speaking companions. With them only he was thoroughly identified.

The biography was so crowded with superficial detail that its underlying structure was not always clear; but the work was implicitly shaped into a memorable tragic myth: a genius works his way, by superhuman efforts, from shameful poverty to unprecedented fame—but not to happiness. He finally works himself to death, not just to make money, but to escape from his own 'spectres', on the grim principle: 'It is much better to go on and fret, than to stop and fret.' Yet the tragedy was relieved by unfailing 'animal spirits', which could always turn deep depression into wild comedy, as in this picture of a man suffering from the climate at Bonchurch:

He has no purpose, power, or object in existence whatever. When he brushes his hair in the morning, he is so weak that he is obliged to sit upon a chair to do it . . . And his bilious system is so utterly overthrown, that a ball of boiling fat appears to be always behind the top of the bridge of his nose, simmering between his haggard eyes.

Another man who worked himself to death was Mark Pattison's *Isaac Casaubon* (1875), but he was otherwise quite unlike Dickens.[24] He had no 'animal spirits', but a 'depressed nervous organism'. Far from being stimulated by crowds, he hated being interrupted in his work by 'the plague of friends'. He was 'destitute of imagination . . . the inventive imagination of the poet, that dangerous faculty which enlivens fact, but too often also supersedes it.' When talking or writing, he 'drew from his memory, and not from his mother-wit.' He was a genius only in the sense that 'Industry was Casaubon's genius. Not the industry of the pen, but the industry of the brain.' This unpromising subject for biography had no obvious human appeal, except for his relations with his wife, whom he loved dearly despite her tendency to interrupt his work, and who, but for being 'too prolific—they had eighteen children— . . . proved an excellent scholar's wife.' Yet the book was extremely engaging, both for its wit, and also for

[24] Mark Pattison, 1813–84, was born at Hornby, Yorkshire, the eldest of the twelve children of the curate-in-charge. He went to Oriel College, Oxford, became a fellow of Lincoln, 1839, and its rector, 1861. His marriage that year has been thought to have inspired Casaubon's in *Middlemarch*. He had contributed to *Essays and Reviews*, 1860.

Pattison's sympathy with his hero's aims and frustrations. Himself a refugee from Tractarian theology to scholarship, Pattison clearly felt for Casaubon in his 'disease of double-mindedness', torn between the Classics and the Fathers. A victim of college intrigue at Oxford, he felt for one deprived by Court intrigue of a professorship in Paris. Above all he felt for a scholar working against time, constantly interrupted, thwarted by the difficulty of getting the books he needed, and perpetually thinking: 'Research is infinite; it can never be finished.' Almost like Browning in 'A Grammarian's Funeral', Pattison stressed the heroic absurdity of such a life:

The result of this sustained mental endeavour is not a book, but a man. It cannot be embodied in print, it consists in the living word ... There came the death summons, and at fifty-six all those stores which had been painfully gathered by the toil of forty years were swept away, and nothing left but some lifeless books, which can do little more than a gravestone can do, perpetuate the name...

Even so, Casaubon's 'example' had its lesson for a generation whose literature 'bore the stamp of half knowledge ... the dogmatism of the smatterer.'

As if to confirm this view of the period's literature, Sabine Baring-Gould's *The Vicar of Morwenstow* (1876) was chatty, disorganized, and inaccurate.[25] Confessedly 'a gossiping book', it was full of amusing anecdotes. R. S. Hawker was an exuberant eccentric who, as a curate, visited parishioners with a tame pig in tow, and, as a vicar, 'would pat his cats or scratch them under their chins' while saying prayers in church: 'Originally ten cats accompanied him to church, but one having caught, killed, and eaten a mouse on a Sunday, was excommunicated, and from that day was not allowed again within the sanctuary.' The biography gave a vivid impression of his personality, but made no attempt to explain it. Baring-Gould, who had written a book on werewolves and started publishing *The Lives of the Saints* in seventeen volumes, was content to call Hawker 'an anachronism' that really belonged 'to the Middle Ages and to the East'.

[25] Sabine Baring-Gould, 1834–1924, was born at Exeter, the eldest son of a landowner. Privately educated, he went to Clare College, Cambridge. He was ordained priest, 1865, succeeded to his father's estate, 1872, and in 1881 presented himself to the family living of Lew Trenchard. His extensive travels included a trip to Iceland, 1861, and among his numerous publications were novels, works on folklore and religion, and the hymn, 'Onward, Christian Soldiers'.

No doubt Hawker would have found Macaulay equally inexplicable when he said of dog-owners: 'How odd that people of sense should find any pleasure in being accompanied by a beast who is always spoiling conversation!' The remark, quoted in G. O. Trevelyan's *Life and Letters of Lord Macaulay* (1876) indicated one of those gaps in his uncle's sensibility which Trevelyan conscientiously recorded.[26] Others were his indifference to music, the tactlessness which allowed him to address a letter to his constituents as from Windsor Castle, and his naïve partisanship: 'There is something almost pathetic in this unbounded, and unshaken, faith in the virtues of a political party.' Yet another was 'the intensity and, in some cases (it must be confessed), the wilfulness of his literary conservatism', which made him 'prefer a third-rate author' of a traditional type to authors like Carlyle or Ruskin. While taking such precautions against charges of 'partiality', Trevelyan made no attempt to conceal his own affection and admiration for his uncle, or his pleasure in writing about 'one of the happiest lives that it has ever fallen to the lot of a biographer to record.' The result was a fascinating account of an intellectual prodigy, presented as a credible, if not wholly comprehensible, human being. His unusual devotion to his sisters was neither ignored nor made an excuse for psychological speculation. On the evidence shown his moral character was not unduly idealized, though the claim that 'unselfishness was the key' to it certainly invites scepticism. His courage and resilience were confirmed by his diary. Advised of his disabling heart-condition, and convinced that the rest of the *History* was therefore 'certain to be a failure', he struggled to make the best of the situation: 'my reason tells me that hardly any man living has so much to be thankful for. And I will be thankful.' Though Trevelyan went on to become a historian himself, he had started as a humorous writer, and the charm of this biography owed much to his delicate wit. There was artistry, too, in the overall structure. Since Macaulay's rise to fame was too easy to offer any drama, Trevelyan supplied the missing element by his opening account of Macaulay's father Zachary. The prelude served two other purposes. Zachary's campaign against slavery

[26] Sir George Otto Trevelyan, 1838–1928, Macaulay's nephew, was born at Rothley Temple, Leicestershire, the son of an Indian Civil Servant who had just returned to England. He went to Harrow and Trinity College, Cambridge. His distinguished political career began in 1865, when he became Liberal MP for Tynemouth. He also published humorous verse, a comedy, and descriptions of Anglo-Indian life.

announced the theme on which his son performed political variations, and Zachary's personal misfortunes accentuated his son's good luck. For 'fate seemed determined that Zachary Macaulay should not be indulged in any great share of personal happiness.' He celebrated his son's birth by falling off his horse and breaking both arms. So 'he spent in a sick-room the remainder of the only holiday worth the name which . . . he ever took during his married life'; and when he at last stopped work, it was only to live in 'trouble', 'sorrow', and 'gloom'. It was an effective background for Macaulay's sunny existence.

'Cherish . . . manly feelings,' Carlyle urged one of his brothers. 'They lead to . . . sunshine within which nothing can destroy or eclipse.' That was not to be his own experience, to judge from J. A. Froude's biography (1882–4).[27] His manliness was admittedly patchy: 'if his little finger ached he imagined that no mortal had ever suffered so before.' But 'when in real trouble', like the loss of his *French Revolution* manuscript, he 'faced his difficulties like a man', and he showed immense courage in slowly working his way from obscure poverty to fame. Yet even when he was famous he still found life intolerable. Far from having sunshine within, he was a choleric, depressive egotist who, perhaps for that reason, suffered from chronic dyspepsia. Since Froude's 'master' had said he wanted 'to be known as he was', Froude never tried to conceal the negative side of Carlyle's character, which was confirmed by extracts from his own journals and letters. Thinking it a biographer's business to 'throw in some moral remarks' as well as record the facts, Froude even underlined the selfishness, self-deception, and insensitivity that marked Carlyle's dealings with his wife. But he also pointed out that 'Mrs. Carlyle, like her husband, was not easy to live with', and made constant efforts throughout to paint a balanced picture. If Carlyle made his wife miserable, he was never 'intentionally unkind'. If he sometimes behaved 'like a child, and like a very naughty one', he was still above criticism by ordinary standards: 'Such faults as these were but as the vapours which hang about a mountain, inseparable from the nature of the man.' Froude's *Carlyle* has been charged, first with wanton iconoclasm and then with careless or unscrupulous editing. It was, however, so delicate in its ironic realism that it contrived to humanize

[27] See Chap. 10.

without seriously reducing its subject. It conveyed the impression of a living personality, but left the aura of genius intact. This was largely due to the quality of its humour:

Carlyle came home with the fixed determination to be amiable and good and make his wife happy ... but he came home to drive her immediately distracted, not by unkindness ... but through inability to endure with ordinary patience the smallest inconveniences of life ... on the fourth morning the young lady next door began upon her fatal piano, and then the tempest burst out...

He would have been equally irritated by J. W. Cross's *George Eliot's Life as Related in her Letters and Journals* (1885).[28] 'Each letter', he explained, 'has been pruned of everything that seemed to me irrelevant to my purpose—of everything that I thought my wife would have wished to be omitted.' To dignify her character, he cut out all signs of humour, frivolity, or spontaneity, and apparently destroyed the first forty-six pages of a journal written in her early thirties. He thus made a conventional sage out of a woman who had defied sexual convention, and made a brilliant author sound rather dull. This was perhaps the nadir of the period's biography. But the survey need not end quite so bathetically. Edward Dowden's *Life of Percy Bysshe Shelley* (1886) was a scholarly attempt to present the facts without forfeiting all sympathy for the poet.[29] Though charged with occasionally manipulating the evidence for Shelley's benefit, Dowden was prepared to reprove Shelley's 'judicial decree' of separation from Harriet, '—issued, as I believe, rashly—by himself as judge in his own cause'. The fantastic element in Shelley's life-story was enough to make any such book entertaining, and the circumstances of his death, exhumation, and cremation offered a ready-made peroration. Dowden's narrative made the most of such material, and his comments showed humour and humanity. The worst feature of the book was its style, which was sometimes mawkish and pseudo-poetical, as when describing Shelley's beauty 'in the halcyon nest of babyhood'. Yet Dowden was also capable of economical wit. When Harriet begged to be rescued from her school:

[28] John Walter Cross, 1840–1924, was a banker from New York. He first met George Eliot in Rome, 1869, and married her, 1880.
[29] Edward Dowden, 1843–1913, was born at Cork, the son of a merchant and landowner. He went to Queen's College there, and Trinity College, Dublin, where he became professor of English literature in 1867. He was best known as a Shakespearian scholar.

It was the cry of Andromeda chained to the rock, while the obscene monster of brute tyranny opened its jaws, to Perseus riding high in air, and Perseus was pledged to abolish all brute tyrannies from the face of the earth.

'Perseus riding high in air' defined Shelley far more accurately than Arnold's 'ineffectual angel'.

Authors' lives are apt to be dull, and those who turn author only to tell the story of their lives are unlikely to write well. Against such odds, the period produced a surprising amount of good work in autobiography. That of Newman, J. S. Mill, Harriet Martineau, Carlyle, and Ruskin has already been discussed,[30] but there were several other notable productions in the genre. Dundonald's *Autobiography of a Seaman* (1860) was an apologia for a life more eventful than Newman's.[31] Dundonald was defending himself against a charge of complicity in a Stock Exchange swindle of 1814, for which he had been fined, imprisoned, dishonourably discharged from the Navy, deprived of his seat in Parliament, and even sentenced to stand in the pillory. Given a 'free pardon' in 1832, he had become an admiral in 1854; but he wanted to clear his name before he died, and prove that he had been a victim of 'persecution' by the Admiralty and the government, largely because of his efforts for naval and parliamentary reform. Born thirteen years before Byron, he had been a kind of naval Corsair, whose whole career was fabulous and sensational: 'Without a particle of romance in my composition, my life has been one of the most romantic on record.' His naval exploits included an attempt to destroy the French fleet by 'explosive vessels' of his own invention; the capture of a cargo of Papal Bulls and dispensations bound for 'the Mexican sin-market'; and the theft of a document from the water-closet of an Admiralty Court official. His parliamentary activity began with a refusal to bribe the electors at the going rate of £5 per head. After his defeat he gave each of his supporters £10, as a reward for resisting bribery—and was returned unopposed at the next election. His adventures were both

---

[30] For Newman, Mill, Harriet Martineau, Carlyle, and Ruskin see Chaps. 11, 14, 14, 10, and 12 respectively.

[31] Thomas Cochrane, tenth earl of Dundonald, 1775–1860, joined the navy, 1793, spent a half-year at Edinburgh University, 1802, became MP for Honiton, 1806, and for Westminster, 1807. He died in his eighty-fifth year and was buried in Westminster Abbey.

exciting and amusing, and his style, though mostly that of official correspondence, was often forceful and vivid. In its lack of structure, as well as its sensational content, the work resembled a picaresque novel; but it had at least a neat peroration, quoted from the back of the £1,000 banknote with which he had bought his release from prison:

My health having suffered by long and close confinement, and my oppressors being resolved to deprive me of property or life, I submit to robbery to protect myself from murder, in the hope that I shall live to bring the delinquents to justice.

Dundonald wrote much better than might be expected of a 'Seaman', and Anthony Trollope's life was far more interesting than those of most professional authors.[32] The basic story of his *Autobiography* (1883) was a spectacular rise to greatness, recalling the transformation of Odysseus in Ithaca from a beggar into a king. As a day-boarder at Harrow, who had to walk twelve miles to school, from a 'wretched tumble-down farmhouse', through 'those miserably dirty lanes', Trollope felt humiliated: 'What right had a wretched farmer's boy, reeking from a dunghill, to sit next to the sons of peers,—or worse still, next to the sons of big tradesmen who had made their ten thousand a year!' He ended as a member of the Athenaeum, frankly enjoying 'the society of distinguished people'. And it was all done by Odyssean enterprise and endurance. The heroic note was first struck in the picture of Frances Trollope, the family bread-winner, sitting up

night after night nursing the dying ones and writing novels the while,— so that there might be a decent roof for them to die under. Had she failed to write the novels, I do not know where the roof would have been found.

Her son followed her example, writing novels at a predetermined speed of '250 words every quarter of an hour', even on 'a terribly rough voyage to Alexandria . . . more than once I left my paper on the cabin table, rushing away to be sick in the privacy of my stateroom . . . but still I did my work.' In the context of such moral achievements the details of Trollope's commercial success developed as much human interest as the account of his school-days

[32] Anthony Trollope, 1815–82, was born in London, the son of an old Wykehamist barrister who had lost a fortune trying to be a farmer, and Frances Trollope, the novelist and critic of America. He went to Harrow and Winchester, then worked in the Post Office, 1834–67. His novels will be discussed in another volume.

and early difficulties in the Post Office. He claimed to have written only a 'so-called autobiography', since it made no attempt to record his 'inner life. No man ever did so truly,—and no man ever will.' But it vividly presented a delightful and admirable character. The book's humour and narrative skill were predictable from the novels. More unexpected, considering that he had absorbed Latin 'through the skin', by having it thrashed into him, were the signs that Roman literature had now become one of his 'chief delights'. Having proudly listed his publications, he finally reduced them to the status of fallen autumn-leaves, by a graceful allusion to the *Aeneid*: 'Now I stretch out my hand, and from the further shore I bid adieu to all who have cared to read any among the many words that I have written.'

Published in the year that *Praeterita* was giving glimpses of Ruskin's early childhood, Mark Pattison's *Memoirs* (1885) said nothing about his own, except that he loved his sisters and disliked his father. Fearing that he might not live long enough to complete his recollections, he began with his arrival at Oxford in 1832, and died before he could put his first nineteen, or last twenty-three, years on record. So the book was chiefly concerned with his self-education.

I really have no history but a mental history ... All my energy was directed upon one end—to improve myself, to form my own mind, to sound things thoroughly, to free myself from the bondage of unreason, and the traditional prejudices which, when I began first to think, constituted the whole of my intellectual fabric.

He recognized in *The Prelude* something like his own experience; but his equivalent for Wordsworth's lapse into Godwinism was when he was 'drawn into the whirlpool of Tractarianism', and found himself 'trying to suppress that which was, all the time, my real self, and to put on the new man—the type by which I was surrounded.' Happily his real self, of which 'the master-idea' was rationalism, reasserted itself, and he escaped from that 'degrading superstition' to his 'old original ideal', the 'pure and unselfish conception of the life of a true student'. His life was temporarily shattered by his failure to become Rector of his college in 1851; and though the violence of his reaction to this disappointment was not very admirable, it had the good effect of sharpening his satire against those who had obstructed his efforts towards reform.

Complaining that his college was dominated by 'fossil specimens of the genus Fellow', he went on:

They besides could fetch up from no great distance—Northampton—another wretched *crétin* of the name of Gibbs, who was always glad to come and booze at the college port a week or two when his vote was wanted in support of old abuses.

Thus anger tended to vitalize Pattison's style, and the whole work marked a new departure in English autobiography, as an essay in rather unsympathetic self-analysis, which recognized the part of 'the Unconscious—*das Unbewusste*' in the evolution of ideas.

Pattison clearly felt he had improved over the years; but the evolution of Charles Darwin, as traced in his *Autobiography* (1887), seemed to confirm the 'possibility', first admitted in 1866, 'of some forms having retrograded in organization'.[33] No doubt the scientist who shocked his contemporaries by his theory of Natural Selection was more scrupulous than the little boy who claimed to have produced 'variously coloured Polyanthuses and Primroses by watering them with certain coloured fluids', and who was 'much given to inventing deliberate falsehoods . . . for the sake of causing excitement.' Emotionally and aesthetically, however, he felt he had deteriorated. Having been 'very affectionate' at school, he had now 'lost the power of being deeply attached to anyone'. When he wrote the *Origin*, his religious scepticism had been tempered by a sense of awe at 'this immense and wonderful universe', but all that had faded away. Music, at Cambridge, had given him such 'intense pleasure' that his 'backbone would sometimes shiver', and he had once greatly enjoyed many kinds of poetry: 'But now for many years I cannot endure to read a line of poetry: I have tried lately to read Shakespeare and found it so intolerably dull that it nauseated me.' Altogether, his feelings had atrophied, and his mind become 'a kind of machine for grinding general laws out of

[33] Charles Robert Darwin, 1809–82, was born at Shrewsbury, the son of a doctor and grandson of the poet and evolutionist, Erasmus Darwin. He went to Shrewsbury School, Edinburgh University, and Christ's College, Cambridge. He joined HMS *Beagle* as a naturalist for a scientific expedition to South America, 1831–6. He married Emma Wedgwood, 1837, lived in London until 1842, then settled at Down, a small village near Beckenham, Kent. In 1858 he received from A. R. Wallace a sketch of an evolutionary theory essentially the same as the one he had been working out since his return to England, and they presented a joint paper to the Linnean Society. For his scientific writing and travel-writing see Chaps. 17 and 18.

large collections of facts.' Thus the argument of Arnold's recent 'Literature and Science' was strikingly confirmed, and in another life Darwin himself would have 'made it a rule to read some poetry and listen to some music at least once every week.'

Written to 'amuse' himself, and 'possibly interest' his children and grandchildren, Darwin's *Autobiography* was full of entertaining anecdotes, and admirably objective in its approach, but its form was undistinguished. 'I have taken no pains', he confessed, 'about my style of writing', which was indeed careless and unstructured. It was enlivened, however, by ironical humour, and by malicious comments on his contemporaries, most of which were excised by his first editor. For Thomas Huxley, though, he had nothing but praise: 'He never says and never writes anything flat.' Since this was hardly an exaggeration, it is fortunate that chronology allows the survey to end with him.[34]

Huxley had a 'profound objection' to writing about himself but, fearing that a volume of 'biographical sketches' might otherwise say something 'all wrong' about him, he wrote a thirteen-page 'Autobiography' for it (1890), warning the compiler that 'autobiographies are essentially works of fiction, whatever biographies may be.' His own was fictional to the extent of suppressing two important facts, the difficulty he had in marrying a girl he met in Australia, and the death of their first child at four. But he certainly made a very good story of his life. It opened with his failure to emulate Pindar, when his nurse excluded some bees from his nursery:

If that well-meaning woman had only abstained from her ill-timed interference, the swarm might have settled on my lips, and I should have been endowed with that mellifluous eloquence which, in this country, leads far more surely than worth, capacity, or honest work, to the highest places in Church and State. But the opportunity was lost, and I have been obliged to content myself through life with saying what I mean in the plainest of plain language; than which, I suppose, there is no habit more ruinous to a man's prospects of advancement.

---

[34] Thomas Henry Huxley, 1825–95, was born at Ealing, the son of a schoolmaster. He studied medicine at Charing Cross Hospital, joined the Navy as a surgeon, and went to sea in HMS *Rattlesnake*, 1846–50. In Sydney he met and fell in love with Henrietta Anne Heathorn, and in 1855, having been offered a lectureship, initially part-time, at the School of Mines, London, he married her. He had become an FRS, 1851. For his scientific writing see Chap. 17.

Though thus prevented from becoming a bishop like his future adversary Samuel Wilberforce, he showed, like the young Ruskin, 'strong clerical affinities', turning his 'pinafore wrong side forwards, and preaching to [his] mother's maids in the kitchen ... one Sunday morning when the rest of the family were at church.' But his final gospel could not well have been preached in a surplice:

there is no alleviation for the sufferings of mankind except veracity of thought and of action, and the resolute facing of the world as it is, when the garment of makebelieve, by which pious hands have hidden its uglier features, is stripped off.

The type of non-mellifluous eloquence that he achieved in many sermons on this theme may be sampled in this realistic comment on his own life:

Men are said to be partial judges of themselves—young men may be, I doubt if old men are. Life seems terribly foreshortened as they look back; and the mountain they set themselves to climb in youth turns out to be a mere spur of immeasurably higher ranges, when, with failing breath, they reach the top.

17. Science

'Have not many sciences such as Astronomy or Geology a side of feeling which is poetry?' So asked Benjamin Jowett in 1858, and in 1889 Tennyson reported that those two 'terrible Muses' had taken over Parnassus. Victorian scientists have several claims to a place in literary history, quite apart from their influence on literary authors. Some were poets in Jowett's sense, reacting with awe and wonder to natural phenomena. Some were romantic individualists, whose delight in their own discoveries made them effective propagandists, or satirists of all theories that contradicted theirs. Some were lucid exponents of unfamiliar concepts, or popularizers of work done by more original researchers. And some brought science into general literature, by discussing the wider implications, religious, social, or simply human, of scientific progress.

Charles Lyell's *Principles of Geology* (1830–3) was 'an attempt to explain the former changes of the earth's surface by reference to causes now in operation', so the work consisted chiefly of factual description designed to illustrate such causes.[1] Earlier geologists were charged with having 'felt themselves at liberty to indulge their imaginations, in guessing at what *might be*, rather than in inquiring *what is*.' Yet Lyell's own imagination was much in evidence. 'Let us imagine' was one of his favourite phrases, and his argument included some pleasant fantasies. To show how geologists had been misled by underestimating the age of the earth, he asked what would have become of Egyptology, if it had been assumed that the banks of the Nile had never been inhabited before the nineteenth century. Mummies would have been attributed to 'some *plastic* virtue residing in the interior of the earth', or regarded as 'abortions of nature produced by her incipient efforts in the work of creation'. But such humour was exceptional. The general tone was sad and solemn, as Lyell catalogued floods, earthquakes, volcanic eruptions, exterminations of species, and

[1] Sir Charles Lyell, 1797–1875, was born at Kinnordy, Forfarshire, the son of a botanist who translated Dante. He went to school at Ringwood, Salisbury, and Midhurst, then to Exeter College, Oxford, where he read classics but went to Buckland's lectures on geology. After making two geological tours of Europe, he became professor of geology at King's College, London, 1831–3, and president of the Geological Society, 1835–6 and 1849–50.

other 'vicissitudes' of the earth's crust and of its inhabitants. Though the style was often pedestrian, the sheer accumulation of disasters had a strong emotional effect, not wholly unlike that of Ecclesiastes, or 'The Vanity of Human Wishes'. Darwin said that the work 'altered the whole tone of one's mind', and its effect on Tennyson's is clear from *In Memoriam*. Nor was its presentation untouched by traditional culture. Lyell found occasion to describe, almost in Ruskin's manner, a picture by Bewick, and the scenery round Mount Etna; and he often quoted from English and classical poetry. Pressing his case for Uniformitarianism, he listed 'the convulsions even of the last thirty years', and neatly turned a Horatian tag against the type of geologist who still maintained that the earth had at last settled into a state of 'repose'. If he ignored such recent evidence, no 'proofs of similar convulsions' in the past would ever 'shake his tenacity of purpose. "Si fractus illabatur orbis / Impavidum ferient ruinae"'. [If the universe shattered and fell on him, its ruins would strike him undismayed.]

Mary Somerville's survey of scientific research, *On the Connexion of the Physical Sciences* (1834), began and ended with the other 'terrible Muse', Astronomy.[2] She also dealt with meteorology, the theory of tides, botanical geography, sound, light, heat, electricity, and magnetism. The last four seemed to her 'so connected' that they would probably turn out to be derived from a single 'power ... in conformity with the general economy of the system of the world, where the most varied and complicated effects are produced by a small number of universal laws.' Such economy was typical of the Creator's methods. Thus the law of gravitation 'must have been selected by Divine Wisdom out of an infinity of others, as being the most simple.' Mary Somerville was a pioneer, not in science, but in popularizing science. Her explanatory version (1831) of Laplace's *Mécanique Céleste* was doubtless the model for Lady Psyche's lecture in *The Princess*, and *On the Connexion* was designed to be a primer in scientific education. Though its readers were not spared technical details or precise figures, the style was reassuringly lucid and direct, and occasional efforts were made to

[2] Mary Somerville, née Fairfax, 1780–1872, was born at Jedburgh, the daughter of an admiral. At her Musselburgh boarding-school she concentrated on Euclid, and also on Latin, so as to read Newton's *Principia*. With her second husband, William Somerville, an army surgeon, she moved from Edinburgh to London, 1816, where she made many intellectual friends, and was asked by Brougham to write on Laplace for the Society for the Diffusion of Useful Knowledge. Somerville College, Oxford was named after her.

stimulate feeling and imagination. The student was encouraged to picture how 'splendid an object' the earth must appear from the moon, how strange it would feel to be relatively weightless on a smaller planet, or to live on one without an atmosphere, and so in 'a death-like silence'. An account of underwater vegetation echoed the wonder, and almost the wording, of Gray's allusion to the flora of 'dark unfathomed caves of ocean'; and Browning's fine simile in *Paracelsus* about 'plants in mines which never saw the sun,/But dream of him', may well have been inspired by Mary Somerville's description, published the year before, of 'green plants growing in complete darkness at the bottom of one of the mines at Freuburg'. Above all, the book conveyed a great sense of excitement about the latest science, electricity.

Michael Faraday's *Experimental Researches in Electricity* (1839–55) was a 'plain unvarnished tale' of marvels greater than any reported by Othello, but less effectively told.[3] Here he wrote only for scientists, in a style that was mostly impersonal, though from time to time he confessed feelings of 'interest', 'anxiety', and 'disappointment', or of delight at a positive finding: 'How beautifully does the curvature of the ramifications illustrate the curved form of the lines of inductive force previous to the discharge!' Such rare exclamations reflected an awe like Mary Somerville's at the craftsmanship shown by the 'Author of all things', the 'universal correlation of the physical forces of matter, and their mutual conversion one into another.' But Faraday's own artistry was most impressive in the little books printed from verbatim reports of his 'Christmas Courses of Lectures Adapted to a Juvenile Auditory'. Here, in an easy, colloquial, and often humorous style, he exploited the theatrical possibilities of his subject. While talking, for instance, about *The Various Forces of Matter* (1860), he demonstrated the conduction of electricity 'along wires and other bodies' by sitting on an insulated stool, electrifying himself, and then lighting a gaslight with a spark from his finger. The best of these courses, in which he tried, like Shelley's poet, to strip away 'the veil of familiarity from the beauty of the

---

[3] Michael Faraday, 1791–1867, was born at Newington Butts, London, the son of a blacksmith. Apprenticed at thirteen to a bookbinder, he made electrical experiments in his spare time. When one of the customers gave him tickets for some lectures by Humphry Davy, he sent Davy his notes of them, bound in a quarto volume, and asked for his help. He became Davy's assistant, and succeeded, 1827, to his chair of chemistry at the Royal Institution.

world ... the film of familiarity which obscures from us the wonder of our being' was *On the Chemical History of a Candle* (1861). One need not be 'juvenile' to enjoy this imaginatively structured work, which uses an apparently commonplace object to introduce a whole range of sciences, from chemistry to biology, with passing references to the need for better ventilation in slum houses, and the type of ink used by scribes in Herculaneum. For his conclusion, the seventy-year-old scientist gracefully adapted famous images from *Macbeth* and *The Merchant of Venice* to point 'the analogy between respiration and combustion':

Indeed, all I can say to you at the end of these lectures (for we must come to an end at one time or another) is to express a wish that you may, in your generation, be fit to compare to a candle; that you may, like it, shine as lights to those about you; that, in all your actions, you may justify the beauty of the taper by making your deeds honourable and effectual in the discharge of your duty to your fellow-men.

In the year that Faraday had started to enlighten his generation about electricity (1839), Darwin had begun to teach them 'geology and natural history'; but as the scientific significance of his researches from the *Beagle* was not made clear until twenty years later, his *Journal* of that voyage will not be discussed here, but in the chapter on travel literature.[4] Meanwhile Lamarck's theory of evolution, already dismissed by Lyell, was pleasantly ridiculed in Hugh Miller's *The Old Red Sandstone* (1841).[5] The 'ingenious foreigner ... bearing home in triumph ... the skeleton of some huge salamander or crocodile' might doubtless like to think he had 'possessed himself of the bones of his grandfather,—a grandfather removed, of course, to a remote degree of consanguinity by the intervention of a few hundred thousand *great-greats*', but the Scottish palaeontologist ascribed successive 'orders of being' to a series of divine creations. To him these represented 'a progress Godwards', destined to culminate in a 'dominant race' of which Enoch, Elias, and Jesus were 'fit representatives'. Miller's chief

---

[4] See Chap. 18.
[5] Hugh Miller, 1802–56, was born at Cromarty, the son of a sailor who was lost at sea five years later. He left the local school after a violent clash with the dominie, and was apprenticed at seventeen to a stone-mason. He published a book of poems, 1829, and from 1841 edited a sectarian newspaper, the *Witness*. In 1847 he published a reply to *Vestiges of Creation*. His lungs had been damaged by his work as a stone-mason, and he committed suicide.

contribution to science was the discovery and description of fossil fish, notably the *Pterichthys Milleri*: 'Had Lamarck been the discoverer, he would unquestionably have held that he had caught a fish almost in the act of wishing itself into a bird'. But his literary achievement was to make geology appealing to non-scientists. Like Faraday almost self-educated, he became passionately interested in geology while working as an apprentice stonemason in a quarry. 'Geology,' he wrote, 'of all the sciences, addresses itself most powerfully to the imagination', and he specialized in imaginative descriptions of landscapes and other geological data. Thus from fossils in the Orkneys he created a vivid impression of 'some terrible catastrophe' which had left 'all the ichthyolites' in 'attitudes of fear, anger, and pain'. He had first published as a poet, and his prose-style was highly dramatic, full of unexpected images from literature, mythology, or contemporary life. He also showed a feeling for visual art, both in his own drawings and in his tendency to treat palaeontological specimens as *objets d'art*. He discussed 'the microscopic beauty of these ancient fishes' in terms of architectural 'style', and even found a hint of divine aestheticism in their having been 'consigned to the twilight depths of a primeval ocean': 'Art comes to be pursued for its own sake . . . It would be perhaps over-bold to attribute any such o'ermastering feeling to the Creator, yet . . . '.

In a series of popular lectures, published posthumously as *The Testimony of the Rocks* (1857), Miller tried to reconcile geology with the Bible. Each 'day' of creation was a period 'mayhap millenniums of centuries' long. The Flood was a 'providential' rather than 'miraculous' effect, not of rain, but of the depression of 'an area about two thousand miles each way' which let in the sea to drown the 'human family, still amounting to several millions, though greatly reduced by exterminating wars and exhausting vices.' But that deluge could not have been universal, for how could all the thousands of known species have got into an Ark containing, at most, about one seventh of the floor-space in the Crystal Palace? And how, without 'an enormous expense of miracle', could they have been returned to their natural habitat? 'The sloths and armadilloes,—little fitted by nature for long journeys,—would have required to be ferried across the Atlantic.' Though his own position now seems untenable, Miller made excellent fun of other believers in a final chapter on 'The Geology

of the Anti-Geologists'. One of the book's charms was this curious
blend of humorous satire and humourless fantasy. In the second
class came his account, 'as the successive scenes of a great
air-drawn panorama', of the visions that served Moses as
source-material for Genesis. Here Miller's model was not merely
Paradise Lost but also the Victorian equivalent of the cinema, the
diorama.

The 'ingenious foreigner' mocked by Miller was treated almost
as rudely by Robert Chambers in his anonymous *Vestiges of the
Natural History of Creation* (1844), where Lamarck's suggestion
that new organs were developed in response to new environments
and needs was classed 'with pity among the follies of the wise'.[6]
This was ungracious, since the book propounded an evolutionary
theory clearly influenced by Lamarck's: 'It has pleased Providence
to arrange that one species should give birth to another, until the
second highest gave birth to man, who is the very highest.' In
support of this theory Chambers stated, as a recent finding in
embryology, 'that every individual among us passes through the
characters of the insect, the fish, the reptile (to speak nothing of
others) before he is permitted to breathe the breath of life!' But
Chambers was not himself an embryologist, nor a scientist at all,
but a publisher with a gift for popular writing on a wide range of
subjects. In Darwin's view (1859) the book showed 'little accurate
knowledge', and 'a great want of scientific caution', but he praised
its 'powerful and brilliant style', and thought it had been useful in
'preparing the ground for the reception of analogous views'.
Though ridiculed by Disraeli in *Tancred*, and bitterly attacked by
the orthodox, *Vestiges* had gone into twelve editions by 1887. Its
success was due partly to its tactful presentation, partly to its
attractiveness as a general introduction to modern science, and
partly to its colourful writing. 'My sincere desire', Chambers
explained, 'was to give the true view of the history of nature, with
as little disturbance as possible to existing beliefs, whether philosophical or religious.' While undermining the arguments of Paley's
Natural Theology and of the *Bridgewater Treatises*, he maintained
their pious and reassuring message. Though a world that worked
exclusively by general laws might cause suffering and apparent

---

[6] Robert Chambers, 1802–71, was born at Peebles, the son of a cotton-merchant. He
went to the local school and at ten started 'roaming like a bee' through his father's
Encyclopaedia Britannica. With his brother William he founded the Edinburgh publishing
firm that produced *Chambers's Encyclopaedia* and many other educational books.

injustice to individuals, perhaps 'the present system is but a part of
a whole, a stage in a Great Progress, and ... the Redress is in
reserve.' Despite the 'apparent ruthlessness', there might be 'a
system of Mercy and Grace behind the screen of nature.' As a
miniature *Chambers's Encyclopaedia* of modern science, the book
was full of fascinating information, ranging from Astronomy to
Zoology, and including the alleged creation of a living insect in a
laboratory. As for stylistic colour, this is how Chambers warned
his short-lived readers not to question the truth of his theory:

Suppose that an ephemeron, hovering over a pool for its one April day of
life, were capable of observing the fry of the frog in the water below. In
its aged afternoon, having seen no change upon them for such a long
time, it would be little qualified to conceive that the external branchiae of
these creatures were to decay, and be replaced by internal lungs, that feet
were to be developed, the tail erased, and the animal then to become a
denizen of the land.

A similar effort to overcome natural scepticism was made by Sir
John Herschel in his *Outlines of Astronomy* (1849).[7] To show 'that
central thread of common sense on which the pearls of analytical
research are invariably strung', he explained why the earth did not
seem to be moving, by appealing to common experiences of
unperceived motion, 'in a carriage with the blinds down', in a train
'especially by night or in a tunnel', on 'aeronautic voyages ... with
closed eyes', and in the cabin of a big ship. He even confirmed the
antiquity of the illusion by an apt quotation from the *Aeneid*.
Having thus initiated the non-scientist into the mysteries of
astronomy, he seemed to lose interest in imaginative presentation,
and ended his densely fact-filled book with a bald table of figures.
He had, however, sometimes glanced beyond technicalities, as
when he wondered why the 'Creator' should have made the fixed
stars: 'Surely not to illuminate *our* nights, which an additional
moon of the thousandth part of the size of our own would do much
better, nor to sparkle as a pageant void of meaning and reality.'
Besides scientific works Herschel published original poems and
verse translations, including a quite readable version of the *Iliad* in
hexameters. Traces of poetic feelings about the 'realms of

[7] Sir John Frederick William Herschel, 1792–1871, was born at Slough, the son of the
astronomer, Sir William Herschel. He went to Eton and St John's College, Cambridge,
where he was senior wrangler, and became a fellow. He was President of the Astronomical
Society, 1827–32.

unspeakable glory' (as he called the night sky when translating the famous simile at the end of Book VIII) may be found in *Outlines*, but his emotional reactions to his subject were more eloquently expressed in his less technical *Essays* (1857). Here, while congratulating the compilers of a new star catalogue, he celebrated both the practical value of astronomy to humanity, and the function of stars in the divine economy:

The stars are the landmarks of the universe; and amidst the endless and complicated fluctuations of our system, seem placed by its Creator as guides and records, not merely to elevate our minds by the contemplation of what is vast, but to teach us to direct our actions by reference to what is immutable in his works ...

Not the immutability of stars, but the mutability of species on this planet was now to become the main question for science. To the zoologist Philip Gosse, the theory of *Vestiges* was self-evidently absurd: 'Coolly bowing aside His authority, this writer has hatched a scheme, by which the immediate ancestor of Adam was a Chimpanzee, and his remote ancestor a Maggot!'[8] Gosse's own *Aquarium: An Unveiling of the Wonders of the Deep Sea* (1854) had a fundamentalist epigraph, 'The sea is HIS and He made it'; and while detailing the structure and behaviour of marine organisms, he pointed out every clue to 'HIS' intentions. Thus 'the Prawn washing himself after dinner' exemplified the curse under which the whole creation has groaned since the Fall, 'the perpetual round of strife with dirt'. Still, the curse was not 'unmitigated': 'What crimes have been prevented, what proficiency in iniquity cut short by the necessity of labour for the support of life!' It was a poem 'Link'd with one virtue and a thousand crimes', *Lara*, that had first inspired Gosse to become an author, and like Byron he was fond of writing about himself. So the *Aquarium* had

somewhat of the form of a personal narrative; sufficient, at least, to constitute a link of connexion between myself and my reader, not only in the *things* described, but also in the feelings they excite in my own mind.

His main feelings were of religious awe and aesthetic delight, both

[8] Philip Henry Gosse, 1810–88, was the father described in Edmund Gosse's *Father and Son*, 1907. Born at Worcester, the son of a miniature-painter, he went to school at Poole and at Blandford, then worked as a clerk in Newfoundland, a farmer in Canada, a schoolmaster in Alabama, and a naturalist in Jamaica, before returning to England, where he finally settled, 1852, at St Marychurch, Devonshire. He was made an FRS, 1856.

in scenery and weather conditions, and also in the miniature beauties of individual organisms, as when he saw candle-light reflected in the eyes of a prawn, 'like two little globes of fire'. His writing was lively and dramatic, but as full of irrelevance as *Don Juan*. Edmund Gosse was to recall his father's 'extraordinary way of saying anything that came up into his mind'. One thing that came up in the *Aquarium* was the local pronunciation of the 'unpoetical name' of a steamer sighted off Weymouth.

Omphalos (1857) was much less discursive. It argued closely, if not quite convincingly, that the testimony of Adam's navel (*omphalos*) and of the whole earth's crust was false. Adam had no mother, and the earth had no history, before the moment of creation. This was no deception on the Creator's part, but an inevitable corollary of 'the fact of creation'. At whatever point in its life-cycle one chose to create a cow, its physiology would show traces of 'another parent cow', and these could be traced back 'through a vista of receding cows', indefinitely. But no such antecedent cows would have existed. If the world had been created in 1857, it would have been precisely as it was that year:

whatever is now existent would appear, precisely as it does appear. There would be cities filled with swarms of men; there would be houses half-built; castles fallen into ruins; pictures on artists' easels just sketched in; wardrobes filled with half-worn garments; ships sailing over the sea; marks of bird's footsteps on the mud; skeletons whitening the desert sands; human bodies in every stage of decay in the burial-grounds.

In its imaginative logic and dramatic presentation this refutation of the geologists was, if nothing else, a literary *tour de force*, comparable to Browning's defences of indefensible characters.

For Charles Darwin Gosse had 'a profound esteem', but the feeling was not reciprocated.[9] *The Origin of Species* (1859) asked wonderingly if certain 'authors' could 'really believe' that mammals were 'created bearing the false marks of nourishment from the mother's womb?' *The Origin* broke the tradition of natural theology which had previously dominated popular works on science. Yet, when he wrote it, Darwin confessed later, he still felt 'compelled to look to a First Cause having an intelligent mind in some degree analogous to that of a man', and his residual theism

---

[9] Charles Robert Darwin, 1809–82. For his autobiography and his travel-writing see Chaps. 16 and 18.

was perceptible in his wording. Even while arguing against Paley's claim that the structure of the eye was conclusive evidence of a Creative Design, he virtually deified Natural Selection as 'a power always intently watching each slight accidental alteration' in layers of transparent tissue, 'and carefully selecting each alteration' which might tend to produce a distincter image'. Thus, over 'millions on millions of years',

natural selection will pick out with unerring skill each improvement . . . and may we not believe that a living optical instrument might thus be formed as superior to one of glass, as the works of the Creator are to those of man?

The inconsistency of the last few words was compounded by allusions to Genesis, either explicit, like the reference to Jacob's methods of cattle-breeding, or implicit, like the extended simile of 'the great Tree of Life, which fills with its dead and broken branches the crust of the earth, and covers the surface with its ever branching and beautiful ramifications.'

No doubt such relics of orthodoxy contributed to the book's success in overcoming contemporary resistance to a revolutionary theory, and perhaps they were partly designed for that purpose. Certainly *The Origin*'s literary value lay more in its strategy than its style, which tended to confirm Darwin's complaint at sixty-seven:

I have as much difficulty as ever in expressing myself clearly and concisely . . . There seems to be a sort of fatality in my mind leading me to put at first my statement and proposition in a wrong or awkward form.

By constant revision he achieved a dignified clarity, but seldom any ease or grace. The work was, however, highly persuasive. In preaching his new doctrine, he adopted the personal tone of a recent convert to the faith, recalling, as stages in his own conversion, the special things that 'struck' him, and stressing the 'difficulties' that had worried him, like the complexity of the eye, and the shortage of 'links' between species in the geological record. His favourite phrase, 'I suspect', suggested a diffidence more convincing than dogmatism. It was only in the last few pages that he took a firm stand against 'the blindness of preconceived opinion'. One of his subtlest manœuvres was to recommend ideas that his readers might think wildly conjectural, by saying it would

be rash to assume the contrary. Thus, of the eye: 'We should be
extremely cautious in concluding that an organ could not have
been formed by transitional gradations of some kind.' The whole
book was, as he put it, 'one long argument', supported by long lists
of facts; but he tried occasionally to appeal to the reader's sense of
humour, visual imagination, or humane feelings. The application
of Malthus to the 'whole animal and vegetable kingdom' was
introduced by a mild joke ('in this case there can be ... no
prudential restraint from marriage') and enforced by droll fantasies. Without 'checks' on Man's reproduction,

in a few thousand years, there would literally not be standing room for his
progeny ... The elephant is reckoned to be the slowest breeder of all
known animals ... at the end of the fifth century there would be alive
fifteen million elephants, descended from the first pair.

To illustrate 'the great battle of life', and again as an epilogue to
the whole work, Darwin painted an outwardly idyllic picture of 'an
entangled bank'. While refuting Paley's claim that 'it is a happy
world after all', he did his best to sweeten the pill of realism:

When we reflect on this struggle, we may console ourselves with the full
belief, that the war of nature is not incessant, that no fear is felt, that
death is generally prompt, and that the vigorous, the healthy, and the
happy survive and multiply.

Of the human species *The Origin* said little, except to find fault
with its structure ('every particle of food and drink which we
swallow has to pass over the orifice of the trachea, with some risk
of falling into the lungs'), to point out the resemblance between
'the hand of a man, wing of a bat, fin of the porpoise, and leg of a
horse', and to predict that 'in the distant future' light would be
thrown on 'the origin of man and his history'. This more sensitive
subject was tackled first by Thomas Huxley, and then by Darwin
himself in *The Descent of Man* (1871). By that time he no longer
needed to defend his theory, and was free to speculate on its wider
implications for ethics and society. Rejecting Utilitarian ethics, he
derived the 'moral sense' from Man's instincts as 'a social animal'.
In a fire, for instance,

when a man endeavours to save a fellow-creature without a moment's
hesitation, he can hardly feel pleasure; and still less has he time to reflect
on the dissatisfaction which he might subsequently experience if he did
not make the attempt.

In retrospect, the man 'would feel that there lies within him an impulsive power widely different from a search after pleasure or happiness; and this seems to be the deeply planted social instinct.' Darwin also disagreed with J. S. Mill's view that the sexes were intellectually equal. Man, he argued, had 'ultimately become superior to woman', since woman's greater powers of 'intuition, of rapid perception, and perhaps of imitation' were faculties characteristic 'of the lower races, and therefore of a past and lower state of civilization'. But for the law among mammals 'of the equal transmission of characters to both sexes', man would probably have become 'as superior in mental endowment to woman, as the peacock is in ornamental plumage to the peahen.' Apart from such applications of evolutionary theory to social and moral issues, and from many bizarre references (e.g. the man 'who could pitch several heavy books from his head by the movement of the scalp alone', the parrot 'which was the sole living creature that could speak a word of the language of a lost tribe'), the chief interest of *The Descent* for the general reader lies in glimpses of Darwin's personal feelings:

For my own part I would as soon be descended from that heroic little monkey, who braved his dreaded enemy in order to save the life of his keeper, or from that old baboon, who descending from the mountains, carried away in triumph his young comrade from a crowd of astonished dogs—as from a savage who delights to torture his enemies, offers up bloody sacrifices, practises infanticide without remorse, treats his wives like slaves, knows no decency, and is haunted by the grossest superstitions.

The personal element was stronger in *The Expression of the Emotions in Man and Animals* (1872), and the style was less formal. He suggested three principles as governing instinctive expression. Movements 'serviceable in gratifying some desire, or in relieving some sensation' were habitually repeated 'whenever the same desire or sensation [was] felt'. Movements associated with one feeling were reversed to express an opposite one, as in dogs the wagging tail of friendliness was the 'antithesis' of the 'erect and quite rigid' tail of aggression. The third principle was 'the direct action of the excited nervous system on the body, independently of the will, and independently, in large part, of habit.' This covered a range of physiological reactions, from sweating with fear, to turning down the corners of the mouth from grief. With unexpected sensitivity

Darwin described expressions that he had observed in individuals. These included animals, psychiatric patients, and 'one of my own infants'. One story of a successful diagnosis showed a delicate balance between scientific satisfaction and human sympathy:

An old lady with a comfortable but absorbed expression sat nearly opposite to me in a railway carriage. Whilst I was looking at her, I saw that her *depressores anguli oris* became very slightly, yet decidedly contracted; but as her countenance remained as placid as ever, I reflected how meaningless was this contraction, and how easily one might be deceived. The thought had hardly occurred to me when I saw that her eyes suddenly became suffused with tears almost to overflowing, and her whole countenance fell. There could now be no doubt that some painful recollection, perhaps that of a long-lost child, was passing through her mind.

Twelve years earlier, at an Oxford meeting of the British Association for the Advancement of Science, Bishop Samuel Wilberforce had tried (as he put it privately) to 'smash Darwin'. In the event it was Darwin's champion, Thomas Huxley, that smashed Wilberforce.[10] He completed the process with a 'crushing rejoinder' so legendary that its precise wording remains in doubt, but its gist is clear enough. Asked whether he claimed descent from an ape on his grandfather's or grandmother's side, he replied that he would rather have an ape for his ancestor than a man with as little intellectual integrity as the bishop. This set the tone for a series of books, articles, and lectures defending Darwinism, confuting clergymen, and supporting on moral as well as scientific grounds a position for which he coined the term 'agnostic'. He also became a powerful advocate of scientific education, a brilliant teacher of science to the general public, and a philosopher of the relation between science and human life.

Man's Place in Nature (1863) presented conclusive evidence of Man's animal origin. It also placed the discovery in a historical context, starting with half-mythical sightings of anthropoid apes as in the *Periplous* of Hanno (*c*.490 BC), and describing the recognition of Man's real status as a momentous point in the history of thought, 'a new ecdysis' in the development of 'the human larva'. To reconcile that status with human dignity, Huxley compared Man to a peak in the Alps or the Andes, 'of one substance with the dullest clay, but raised by inward forces to that place of proud

---

[10] Thomas Henry Huxley, 1825–95. For his autobiography see Chap. 16.

and seemingly inaccessible glory.' That Man was consubstantial, not only with apes, but with nettles, with a fungus on rotting vegetation, and with 'those broad disks of glassy jelly which may be seen pulsating through the waters of a calm sea', was the theme of a lecture 'On the Physical Basis of Life' (1868). Here he rejected 'the materialistic position that there is nothing in the world but matter, force, and necessity' as being 'as utterly devoid of justification as the most baseless of theological dogmas'. But he vigorously attacked such dogmas, as upheld by the Archbiship of York, borrowing the language of religion to express his anti-religious views. By eating mutton for supper after the lecture, he hoped to 'transubstantiate sheep into man'; and he warned his audience that his arguments might lure them on to 'the first rung of a ladder which, in most people's estimation, is the reverse of Jacob's'. An almost lyrical account of the varied forms assumed by protoplasm recalled Job's leviathan:

... picture to yourselves the great Finner whale, hugest of beasts that live, or have lived, disporting his eighty or ninety feet of bone, muscle, and blubber, with easy roll, among waves in which the stoutest ship that ever left dockyard would flounder hopelessly; and contrast him with the invisible animalcules—mere gelatinous specks, multitudes of which could, in fact, dance upon the point of a needle with the same ease as the angels of the Schoolmen could, in imagination.

Unlike Darwin, Huxley was a born writer, who remembered being, as a boy, 'a voracious and omnivorous reader; a dreamer and speculator of the first water, well endowed with that splendid courage in attacking any and every subject, which is the blessed compensation of youth and inexperience.' The subject of proto-plasm inspired a brief meditation on mortality, with allusions to Dante and Horace; and an imaginative picture of scientific progress in its apparently threatening aspect, as being sure to extend the 'realm of matter and law until it is co-extensive with knowledge, with feeling, and with action.'

The consciousness of this great truth weighs like a nightmare, I believe, upon many of the best minds of these days. They watch what they conceive to be the progress of materialism, in such fear and powerless anger as a savage feels, when, during an eclipse, the great shadow creeps over the face of the sun. The advancing tide of matter threatens to drown their souls; the tightening grasp of law impedes their freedom; they are alarmed lest man's moral nature be debased by the increase of his wisdom.

Such fears, however, Huxley thought gratuitous. Matter and spirit were merely names for the unknown, 'for the imaginary substrata of groups of natural phenomena ... Why trouble ourselves about matters of which ... we do know nothing, and can know nothing? We live in a world which is full of misery and ignorance, and the plain duty of each and all of us is to try to make the little corner he can influence somewhat less miserable and somewhat less ignorant than it was before he entered it.'

This duty led to a dispute with Gladstone about the Gadarene Swine, in which Huxley argued with great inventiveness and urbanity. Complaining (1890) about Gladstone's 'controversial method', he gave a fair account of his own. He said he had come to regard polemics as 'a branch of the fine arts, and to take an impartial and aesthetic interest in the way in which it is conducted.' Since 1854 he had been practising the art on the subject of education. While doubting if 'the dead soul of Peter Bell ... would have been a whit roused from its apathy by the information that the primrose is a Dicotyledonous Exogen, with a monopetalous corolla and central placentation', he claimed that scientific training tended 'to increase our sense of the beautiful in natural objects'. In 'A Liberal Education and Where to Find it' (1868) he amusingly satirized the exclusively classical syllabus of public schools and those 'educational cities of the plain', the older universities, but admitted: 'if my opportunities had lain in that direction, there is no investigation into which I could have thrown myself with greater delight than that of antiquity.' His 'Science and Culture' (1880) was the challenge that called forth Arnold's 'Literature and Science':[11]

I should say that an army, without weapons of precision and with no particular base of operations, might more hopefully enter upon a campaign on the Rhine, than a man, devoid of a knowledge of what physical science has done in the last century, upon a criticism of life.

Carrying the war into the enemy's camp, Huxley also found fault with the Hellenism of the 'Levites in charge of the ark of culture':

We cannot know all the best thoughts and sayings of the Greeks unless

[11] See Chap. 5.

we know what they thought about natural phenomena ... We falsely pretend to be the inheritors of their culture, unless we are penetrated, as the best minds among them were, with an unhesitating faith that the free employment of reason, in accordance with scientific method, is the sole method of reaching truth.

Yet here too Huxley saw both sides of the issue:

I am the last person to question the importance of genuine literary education, or to suppose that intellectual culture can be complete without it. An exclusively scientific training will bring about a mental twist as surely as an exclusively literary training.

According to his own definition of culture (A 'scientific "criticism of life"') an 'assertion which outstrips evidence is not only a blunder but a crime', and his arguments against religion were full of moral fervour. 'Agnosticism and Christianity' (1889) denounced the idea of encouraging religious belief as a prop for public morality: 'Surely, the attempt to cast out Beelzebub by the aid of Beelzebub is a hopeful procedure as compared with that of preserving morality by the aid of immorality.' And the principle of Agnosticism was 'as much ethical as intellectual': 'it is wrong for a man to say that he is certain of the objective truth of any proposition unless he can produce evidence which logically justifies that certainty.'

The finest, if most depressing, product of Huxley's intellectual conscience was *Evolution and Ethics* (1893–4). This was a protest against 'the fanatical individualism of our time [which] attempts to apply the analogy of cosmic nature to society', i.e. against ethical theories based on Natural Selection. The analogy was false in two respects. The 'survival of the fittest' did not, in 'cosmic nature' mean 'of the best'. If 'our hemisphere were to cool again', the survivors 'in the vegetable kingdom ... might be nothing but lichens, diatoms, and such microscopic organisms as those which give red snow its colour.' And secondly the qualifications for success in the natural 'struggle for existence' were essentially antisocial. Primitive man succeeded largely because of 'those qualities which he shares with the ape and the tiger'. Civilized man 'would be only too pleased to see "the ape and tiger die"':

But they decline to suit his convenience; and the unwelcome intrusion of these boon companions of his hot youth into the ranged existence of civil life adds pains and griefs, innumerable and immeasurably great, to those which the cosmic process necessarily brings on the mere animal. In fact, civilized man brands all these ape and tiger promptings with the name of sins; he punishes many of the acts which flow from them as crimes; and in extreme cases, he does his best to put an end to the survival of the fittest of former days by axe and rope.

Despite the charm of Huxley's rhetoric, with its witty allusions to *Henry IV* and *In Memoriam*, the final effect of the paradox, and of the whole book, was uncharacteristically sombre. The cosmic and ethical processes proved irreconcilably opposed, and the cosmic would ultimately win. All one could do was to fight a losing battle against it, in the spirit of Tennyson's 'Ulysses', knowing that the 'garden' of human civilization would one day revert to a wilderness:

That which lies before the human race is a constant struggle to maintain and improve, in opposition to the State of Nature, the State of Art of an organized polity; in which, and by which, man may develop a worthy civilization, capable of maintaining and constantly improving itself, until the evolution of our globe shall have entered so far upon its downward course that the cosmic process resumes its sway; and, once more, the State of Nature prevails over the surface of our planet.

Another believer in Natural Selection who preferred the State of Art was Darwin's cousin, Francis Galton.[12] His *Hereditary Genius: An Enquiry into its Laws and Consequences* (1869) developed from his observation, to be signally confirmed by the Huxleys, that intellectual distinction tended to run in families. *The Origin* had begun with an account of the artificial selection practised by breeders of 'domesticated animals and plants', all 'trying to possess and breed from the best individual' specimens, and Galton proposed to apply the same procedure, for which he coined the term 'eugenics', to human beings:

as it is easy . . . to obtain by careful selection a permanent breed of dogs or horses gifted with peculiar powers of running, or of doing anything else, so it would be quite practicable to produce a highly-gifted race of men by judicious marriages during several consecutive generations.

---

[12] Sir Francis Galton, 1822–1901, was born in Birmingham, the son of a banker and grandson of Erasmus Darwin. He went to King Edward's School, Birmingham, and was apprenticed to two local doctors, before studying medicine at King's College, London. After a brief trip to Turkey, he went to Trinity College, Cambridge, 1840. Finding himself well off after his father's death, 1844, he travelled widely, and explored new territory in South Africa. He became an authority on meteorology, and pioneered the collection of anthropometric statistics, and the use of fingerprints. He was made an FRS, 1856, and received an honorary DCL from Oxford, 1892.

The proposal was supported by tables showing 'Records of Families' of eminent men in a number of different fields. The categories ranged from judges to 'Senior Classics of Cambridge', including scientists, poets, musicians, and artists, and supplemented by 'two short chapters on muscle', in the persons of 'Oarsmen' and 'Wrestlers of the North Country'. Galton was not exaggerating when he called these tables 'capricious'. In a sample of fifty-six 'Poets' from various periods and nations, Milton rubbed shoulders with Milman and Praed. But the tables were full of fascinating biographical details, and the whole book was highly entertaining. By a kind of lateral thinking Galton assembled his facts in novel combinations, and reached some surprising conclusions; as when he gravely pointed out that success as a military commander involved not getting shot too soon. This was best achieved by presenting a relatively small target: 'Had Nelson been a large man, instead of a mere feather-weight, the probability is that he would not have survived so long.' Such passages had an air of humorous fantasy; but those of most general interest were the ones where, in the course of psychological typing, Galton obliquely satirized his contemporaries. The difference between a scientist and a classicist might be traced back to their mothers. The scientist's mother did not, like most women, keep saying things like, 'do not ask questions about this or that, for it is wrong to doubt', but made it clear that 'indifference or insincerity in the search after truth is one of the most degrading of sins'.

Of two men with equal abilities, the one who had a truth-loving mother would be the more likely to follow the career of science; while the other, if bred up under extremely narrowing circumstances, would become as the gifted children in China, nothing better than a student and professor of some dead literature.

Trying to explain 'the apparent anomaly that the children of extremely pious parents occasionally turn out very badly', Galton found the answer in the parents' unstable characters.

Very devout people are apt to style themselves the most miserable of sinners, and I think they may be taken to a considerable extent at their word ... their disposition is to sin more frequently and to repent more fervently then those whose constitutions are stoical, and therefore of a more symmetrical and orderly character.

If the child 'inherits great instability without morality, he will be very likely to disgrace his name'. For there was no reason why morality and instability should necessarily go together, and indeed Galton, like Huxley, found the stoical sceptic morally superior to the devout believer. Since the general effect of the period's scientific literature was to increase scepticism, the survey may fitly end with Galton's portrait of 'a contented sceptic':

he must have confidence in himself, that he is qualified to stand absolutely alone in the presence of the severest trials of life, and of the terrors of impending death. His nature must have sufficient self-assertion and stoicism to make him believe that he can act the whole of his part upon earth without assistance ... The man of religious constitution considers the contented sceptic to be foolhardy and sure to fail miserably; the sceptic considers the man of an extremely pious disposition to be slavish and inclined to superstition.

18. Travel

'To *see* the cities, and *know* the minds of men', said Ford's bulky but entertaining *Hand-Book for Travellers in Spain* (1845), 'has been, since the days of the Odyssey, the object of travel.'[1] Like Odysseus, Victorian travel-writers were keen anthropologists. Faced by difficulties almost as great as Polyphemus or Scylla and Charybdis, some earned the status of epic heroes. Some were mere 'wanderers', even tourists, trying to escape the pressures of urbanization, but most of those mentioned here were in some sense explorers, or else pursued some interest like biology, geology, archaeology, or missionary work, which added an extra dimension to the story of their adventures. Travellers also tended to be individualists, intent on projecting and justifying their own personalities. So the travel-book of the period was often a rich mixture of elements from other genres, from epic, the picaresque novel, the scientific or religious treatise, and from autobiography.

Darwin's *Journal of Researches* on the voyage of the *Beagle* (1839) recorded the initial field-work that led to his theory of evolution.[2] He had joined the surveying ship as a naturalist (his passport read 'El Naturalista Don Carlos'), and in the Galapagos Islands he felt 'brought somewhat near to that great fact—that mystery of mysteries—the first appearance of new beings on this earth'. His 'astonishment' at the savages of Tierra del Fuego foreshadowed *The Descent of Man*: 'One's mind hurries back over past centuries, and then asks, could our progenitors have been men like these?—men, whose very signs and expressions are less intelligible to us than those of the domesticated animals . . . '. But the book was much more than a scientific report. It was a fascinating narrative of a five-year expedition, in the course of

[1] Richard Ford, 1796–1858, came from an old Sussex family. His father became MP for East Grinstead, and finally chief police magistrate in London. He went to Winchester and Trinity College, Cambridge, and was called to the bar but never practised. He travelled all over Spain on horseback, making sketches, 1830–4, wrote articles on Spanish art for the *Quarterly*, and introduced Velazquez to the English public. A friend of Borrow, he advised Murray to publish *The Bible in Spain*.

[2] Charles Robert Darwin, 1809–82. For his autobiography and his scientific writing see Chaps. 16 and 17.

which Darwin rode about four hundred miles on horseback through uninhabited country, with only one Gaucho for company. The style was plain but often humorous, with occasional flashes of caustic wit. Of a runaway slave who killed herself to avoid recapture he observed: 'In a Roman matron this would have been called the noble love of freedom: in a poor negress it is mere brutal obstinacy.' His aesthetic tastes were unconventional: 'what are the boasted glories of the illimitable ocean? A tedious waste . . . '. He preferred bizarre sights like a frozen horse pedestalled on a column of ice. 'with its hind legs straight up in the air', or a real-life centaur: 'A naked man on a naked horse is a fine spectacle; I had no idea how well the two animals suited each other.' He found beauty in the flight of the condor, and above all in the 'wild luxuriance' of a tropical forest: 'Epithet after epithet was found too weak to convey to those who have not visited the intertropical regions, the sensation of delight which the mind experiences.' He delighted even in the 'arid wastes' of Patagonia: 'I can scarcely analyze these feelings; but it must be partly owing to the free scope given to the imagination.' Freedom, it seems, was what he enjoyed most:

This was the first night which I passed under the open sky . . . There is high enjoyment in the independence of the Gaucho life—to be able at any moment to pull up your horse, and say, 'Here we will pass the night.' The death-like stillness of the plain, the dogs keeping watch, the gipsy-group of Gauchos making their beds round the fire, have left in my mind a strongly marked picture . . . which will never be forgotten . . . It has been said that the love of the chase is an inherent delight in man—a relic of an instinctive passion. If so, I am sure the pleasure of living in the open air, with the sky for a roof and the ground for a table, is part of the same feeling; it is the savage returning to his wild and native habits.

The feeling was strong in George Borrow, who claimed to have 'lived in habits of intimacy' with gypsies in 'various and distant countries', and had added Romany to his large repertoire of languages.[3] *The Bible in Spain* (1843) described his adventures there, while trying to distribute translations of the Bible for the

---

[3] George Henry Borrow, 1803–81, was born at East Dereham, Norfolk, the son of a recruiting officer, then constantly on the move. He went to school in Edinburgh and Norwich, where he was articled to a solicitor before opting for authorship. He travelled through France, Russia, Spain, and the East, becoming a remarkable linguist. As a novelist he belongs to another volume.

British and Foreign Bible Society. The persona of a missionary who found it 'a pleasant thing to be persecuted for the Gospel's sake' conflicted with the brash personality of the philological adventurer: threatened with imprisonment in Madrid, Borrow welcomed the chance to complete his 'vocabulary of the language of the Madrilenian thieves'. In other respects, the book gave no great impression of veracity. Though often very dramatic and entertaining, the passages of dialogue had a fictional flavour, and the general effect was of a picaresque novel, based only roughly on personal experience. The structure was rambling and episodic, but the episodes were frequently sensational, like the storm in the Bay of Biscay, the robbing of the mail-coach, or the public execution. Some were oddly humorous, like the saga of the half-witted guide. The style was always lively and ironical, and Borrow amply justified his remark that 'Spain is the land of extraordinary characters.' In one of many bizarre scenes, he conversed in Latin with 'a frightful ragged object' in a market-place—a blind girl who corrected his unclassical use of *Anglia* rather than *Britannia*. But perhaps the best example of his narrative was the passage where he was arrested on Cape Finisterre, in mistake for the pretender Don Carlos, and finally released because the local magistrate admired 'the grand Baintham', i.e. Jeremy Bentham, and thought 'he could be ranked as a poet with Lope de Vega'.

The Bible in Spain ended with a trip to Tangier, on which Borrow came across a *haji*, and the following year Kinglake's *Eothen* (1844) went much further into the world of the Koran.[4] His title, which he hoped was 'the only hard word to be found in the book', was Homeric Greek for 'from the East', and referred to a journey made nine years before, from Belgrade to the south coast of Turkey, via Constantinople, the Troad, Cyprus, Beirut, Palestine, and Egypt. This delightful work fully vindicated Horace's advice not to publish for nine years by the calculated charm of its style. Kinglake was determined not to write an ordinary travel-book:

... the book is quite superficial in its character. I have endeavoured to discard from it all valuable matter derived from the works of others, and it appears to me that my efforts in this direction have been attended with great success; I believe I may truly acknowledge, that from all details of

---

[4] Alexander William Kinglake, 1809–91. For his writing of history see Chap. 16.

geographical discovery, of antiquarian research—from all display of
'sound learning, and religious knowledge'—from all historical and
scientific illustrations—from all useful statistics—from all political dis-
quisitions—and from all good moral reflections, the volume is thoroughly
free.

Professing to write solely for his 'own genial friend', i.e. Eliot
Warburton, he concentrated 'precisely upon those matters which
happened to interest [him], and upon none other'; and no reader
could fail to find them interesting too. A 'headstrong and not very
amiable traveller', as he fairly described himself, he miraculously
survived the plague in Cairo, and then landed at Satalieh in
defiance of the quarantine regulations, on the strength of his
'unbounded faith in the feebleness of Asiatic potentates'. But he
also showed great courage and resourcefulness. Finding himself
alone in the desert, he welcomed the challenge: 'now, at last . . . *I
myself, and no other, had charge of my life.*' Navigating by the sun,
as he had no compass, he 'pushed on alone' towards the Red Sea,
and finally greeted it in the words of Xenophon: 'Thalatta!
Thalatta!' Outside Suez he fell off his camel and lost it in the dark.
Though he knew 'hardly one word of Arabic', he commandeered a
donkey from some bandits: 'somehow or other I contrived to
announce it as my absolute will and pleasure that these fellows
should find me the means of gaining Suez.' In a rather self-
conscious piece of fine writing he described the rough burial of an
old pilgrim in the Holy Land; but the whole book was in a more
acceptable sense finely written, and in less serious contexts the
literary self-consciousness was one of *Eothen's* most attractive
features, as in the delicately turned phrases used to describe 'one
of those coffin-shaped bundles of white linen that implies an
Ottoman lady.'

In *The Crescent and the Cross* (1845) Eliot Warburton denied
having 'intentionally followed in the footsteps . . . of any author',
but his book reads like a cheap imitation of his friend's.[5] Apart
from visiting Greece instead of Turkey, Warburton had travelled

[5] Eliot (Bartholomew Elliott George) Warburton, 1810–52, was born at Tullamore,
Offaly, Ireland, the son of a former inspector-general of constabulary in Ireland. Privately
educated at Wakefield, Yorkshire, he went to Queens' College, then Trinity College,
Cambridge, where he acted in *Much Ado about Nothing* with Milnes, Kemble, and Arthur
Hallam. Called to the Irish bar, 1837, he gave up that profession to travel and write. He
published two historical novels, and had collected material for a 'History of the Poor', when
he lost his life on a ship that caught fire off Land's End.

on a route similar to Kinglake's, bathing like him in the Dead Sea, and inspecting the Pyramids; but he travelled more in the spirit of a modern tourist, and his style, though often lively and amusing, sometimes lapsed into that of a novelette or a holiday-brochure. He wrote, and apparently thought, in clichés. Thus a member of a harem was 'one of Eve's brightest daughters, in Eve's own loving land ... that perfection in living woman which Praxiteles scarcely realized.' The view from the Mount of Olives 'laid bare every fibre of the great heart of Palestine'. Kinglake had smiled at the 'many geographical surprises' in the church of the Holy Sepulchre: 'mount Calvary, Signor? eccolo! it is *upstairs—on the first floor.*' Warburton was unsurprised: 'I see no reason to doubt that Calvary (never mentioned as a *hill* in the sacred writings) occupied the neighbouring locality.' But he was happiest shooting crocodiles:

I took aim at the throat of the supercilious brute ... Bang went the gun; whizz flew the bullet, and my excited ear could catch the *thud* with which it plunged into the scaly leather of his neck ... There was blood on the water ...

Perhaps it gave him confidence when confronted by a 'very picturesque' encampment of pirates. Warned of his danger, and asked, 'On what protection do you rely?' he answered: 'On the name of Englishman.' He then strolled past, warning the pirates: 'the first man that puts out a hand dies as surely as I live.' While he spoke, 'The moonlight glimmered on the barrel of my pistol.' No doubt such touches of melodrama partly explain why the book went into seventeen editions.

The subject-matter of *Eothen* was further popularized in Thackeray's *Notes of a Journey from Cornhill to Grand Cairo by way of Lisbon, Athens, Constantinople, and Jerusalem* (1846).[6] If Warburton resembled a tourist, Thackeray was one. Given a free ticket for an 'excursion in the Mediterranean by the Peninsular and Oriental Steam Navigation Company', he repaid the debt with a Preface that was almost an advertisement. In two months of 'incessant sight-seeing' he found Athens 'a disappointment', the

---

[6] William Makepeace Thackeray, 1811–63, was born in Calcutta, the son of an East India Company official. He went to Charterhouse and Trinity College, Cambridge, 1829, where his friends included Fitzgerald, Kinglake, Milnes, Spedding, and Tennyson. He studied art in London and Paris, then earned his living by miscellaneous journalism in London. His novels will be discussed in another volume, but for his work as a children's writer and a parodist see Chaps. 20 and 21.

'real camels' of Smyrna like 'the fairy dreams of boyhood', Constantinople like a 'Stanfield diorama', Cairo 'magnificently picturesque', but the Pyramids 'an exaggeration of bricks'. The Summer Palace suggested first a wish 'just to have *one* peep ... at all those wondrous beauties' in the harem, and then the inevitable reference to sacks in the Bosphorus. Having complained of fleas, bugs, and mosquitoes, Roman Catholic 'credulity' and the Rhodian Jews' 'genius for filth', he concluded that 'The Life of the East is a life of brutes', full of 'horrible sensuality'. But his first-hand knowledge of that life was rather sketchy. In Turkey, where he 'knew not a syllable of the language', he offered some wine to 'a good old Turk':

his eyes twinkled with every fresh glass, and he wiped his old beard delighted, and talked and chirped a good deal, and, I dare say, told us the whole state of the empire. He was the only Mussulman with whom I attained any degree of intimacy ... and you will see that, for obvious reasons, I cannot divulge the particulars of our conversation. 'You have nothing to say, and you own it.' says somebody: 'then why write?'

His best answer would have been that he sometimes wrote rather amusingly, as when describing a Turkish bath: 'the choking sensation went off, and I felt a sort of pleasure presently in a soft boiling simmer, which, no doubt, potatoes feel when they are steaming.'

In *Nineveh and its Remains* (1849) Layard had more interesting things to say, and his approach to the natives was more serious-minded:

When I first employed the Arabs, the women were sorely ill-treated, and subjected to great hardships. I endeavoured to introduce some reform in their domestic arrangements, and punished severely those who inflicted corporal punishment on their wives.[7]

The contrast between the conventional language and the Quixotic enterprise was typical of the man. Though he had no special gift for writing, his story was one to fire the imagination. It inspired, for instance, a poem by Rossetti, and a fine image in Tennyson's

---

[7] Sir Austen Henry Layard, 1817–94, was born in Paris, the son of a Ceylon Civil Servant. After some years in Italy, he studied law with a solicitor uncle in London, then started travelling overland to Ceylon, 1839, becoming interested in Nimrud on the way. He was MP for Aylesbury, 1852–7, under-secretary for foreign affairs, 1861–6, and then held diplomatic appointments in Madrid and Constantinople.

Maud. Before becoming an archaeologist, Layard had started 'wandering through Asia Minor and Syria', 'without guide or servants', and with only one friend for company, relying solely on his gift for making friends with Turks and Arabs. To excavate the supposed site of Nineveh, he had to overcome severe financial problems, obstructive local authorities, and a very difficult climate. The hot summers made life in a tent unbearable, so he made himself a study in a river-bank, only to be joined there by 'scorpions and other reptiles, which issued from the earth forming the walls of my apartment'. Once his whole encampment of huts and tents was blown hundreds of yards apart by a whirlwind, and he had to crouch for shelter under one of his winged lions. But the most exciting passage in the book described the first stage of the Assyrian Bull's journey to the British Museum. While four groups of men retarded the descent with unreliable ropes, its huge weight was slowly lowered from the mound:

It was a moment of great anxiety. The drums, and shrill pipes of the Kurdish musicians, increased the din and confusion caused by the war-cry of the Arabs, who were half-frantic with excitement . . . The bull once in motion, it was no longer possible to obtain a hearing. The loudest cries I could produce were buried in the heap of discordant sounds . . . The cables and ropes stretched more and more. Dry from the climate, as they felt the strain, they creaked and threw out dust. Water was thrown over them, but in vain, for they all broke together when the sculpture was within four or five feet of the rollers . . . A sudden silence succeeded to the clamour. I rushed into the trenches, prepared to find the bull in many pieces . . .

The story behind some of the medieval manuscripts in the British Museum was even more exciting, as told by Robert Curzon in his *Visits to Monasteries in the Levant* (1849).[8] His quest for manuscripts as material for a never-completed history of handwriting took him to some of the most inaccessible places in Egypt, Palestine, Albania, and Greece, including the monasteries perched on perpendicular rocks at Meteora. The book gave detailed accounts of the art, architecture, and scenery that he saw, with its

[8] Robert Curzon, fourteenth Baron Zouche, 1810–72, was born in London, the son of Baroness Zouche and the Hon. Robert Curzon. He went to Charterhouse and Christ Church, Oxford, which he left without a degree, 1831, to become for one year an MP. He was made an attaché at the Constantinople embassy, 1841, and sent to Erzerum, 1843–4, on a commission to define the Turco-Persian border. He later travelled in Italy, again collecting manuscripts.

historical background; but the most enjoyable passages were about the people that he met, and about his own adventures. On Mount Athos he was entertained in a kiosk 'like a large bird-cage' by the Turkish aga, 'who is in fact a sort of sheep-dog to the flock of helpless monks who pasture among the trees and rocks of the peninsula.' It turned out that his host had broken the rules of the Holy Mountain, by bringing with him from Stamboul 'a *she*-cat! a cat feminine!', to remind him of his home and family far away.

I promised to make no scandal about the cat, and took my leave; and as I rode off I saw him looking at me out of his cage with the cat sitting by his side. I was sorry I could not take aga and cat and all with me to Stamboul, the poor gentleman looked so solitary and melancholy.

Such humour and humanity formed part of the book's appeal; but Curzon was also good at relating sensational incidents, like the battle in the church of the Holy Sepulchre, his own capture by bandits on the way to St Sabba, his climb up a series of ladders to St Barlaam, or that most literal of cliff-hangers when the horse he was riding struggled to hold up the weight of a baggage-mule that was roped to it, and had practically fallen over a precipice, but still 'endeavoured to retain his hold with his chin and his fore-legs. There we were—the mule's eyeballs almost starting out of his head, and all his muscles quivering with the exertion.'

Curzon was a natural story-teller, but Alfred Wallace often contrived, in *Travels on the Amazon and Rio Negro* (1853), to make equally sensational experiences seem rather dull.[9] In his four-year quest for zoological specimens, he negotiated waterfalls and rapids in a twenty-foot-long canoe, was attacked by a swarm of wasps, came face to face with a black jaguar, and finally spent nine days in an open boat, when his ship caught fire about seven hundred miles from land. He found the burning ship a 'magnificent spectacle', was struck by the beauty of an orchid growing out of a rotting tree, and had enough interest in language and literature to translate an improvised native epic into what he called 'very dreary blank

---

[9] Alfred Russel Wallace, 1823–1913, was born at Usk, Gwent, one of the eight children of a man who had tried various trades, and lost most of his money in a literary venture. He went to Hertford Grammar School at fourteen, and in 1844 started teaching at a Leicester school. There he met the naturalist, H. W. Bates, with whom he went off to the Amazon, 1848. The idea of natural selection occurred to him independently, 1858, and when he wrote to Darwin about it, the two agreed to give a joint paper on the subject to the Linnean Society.

verse'. His own prose had flashes of imagination and irony, as when ants gave an 'apparition of scraps of paper, dead leaves, and feathers, endued with locomotive powers', or when Indian parents, finding the Padre too ill to baptize their baby, had to 'bring back the poor little unsanctified creature, liable, according to their ideas, should it die, to eternal perdition.' But in general his narrative style suffered from a surfeit of litotes. Embarking on the Amazon in his first canoe, and observing that passengers and cargo 'sank the little boat to within two inches of the water's edge', Wallace 'felt rather nervous'. He then found that it leaked, and needed continuous bailing: 'but after a few miles we got used to it, and looked to the safe termination of our voyage as not altogether improbable.' On the return journey, 'fifty-two live animals (monkeys, parrots, etc.) . . . in a small canoe, were no little trouble and annoyance.' Though humanly admirable, Wallace's determination to minimize his own difficulties had the literary effect of eliminating drama and tension. The reader feels cheated of the subjective element in travel-writing.

No such complaint can be made against Richard Burton's *Personal Narrative of a Pilgrimage to El-Medinah and Meccah* (1855-6).[10] A flamboyant poseur, Burton had good reason to think that his book might seem 'egotistical', 'mere outpourings of a mind full of self'. His 'pilgrimage' to a city banned to non-Muslims was an act of bravado, designed to wipe out 'that opprobrium to modern adventure, the huge white blot which in our maps still notes the Eastern and the Central regions of Arabia', and the sight of the shrine at Mecca filled him, not with 'religious enthusiasm', but with 'the ecstasy of gratified pride'. He travelled in real danger, disguised first as a Persian prince, then as a wandering Dervish, then as an Afghan doctor, relying solely on his presence of mind, his gift for acting, his knowledge of languages and of the Muslim religion, and 'a single bottle of Cognac, coloured and scented to resemble medicine.' But he was no ordinary adventurer. Kissing the Black Stone at Mecca, he identified it as an aerolite. Satirizing the use of hackneyed quotations in Persian conversation,

[10] Sir Richard Francis Burton, 1821-90, was born in Hertfordshire, the son of a colonel. Irregularly educated in France and Germany, he spent five terms at Trinity College, Oxford, where he started learning Arabic. He joined the Indian army, 1842. In the course of his travels he is said to have learnt thirty-five languages. Besides more than forty travel-books, he published poetry and translation, notably an unexpurgated version of the *Arabian Nights*, 1885-8.

he concluded with a pun on Horace: 'I took my leave, delighted with the truly Persian "apparatus" of the scene.' The polygamy of mosque servants made him think of Juvenal's sixth *Satire*, and the sound of water-wheels on the way to Kuba set off a train of associations, ending with the emotional impact of 'Lochaber no more', among a regiment of Highlanders in the West Indies. While distinguishing between 'the effect of Arab poetry' and that of European, he threw out a criticism of contemporary painting: 'we Europeans and moderns, by stippling and minute touches, produce a miniature on a large scale so objective as to exhaust rather than to arouse reflection.' The variety of his interests was matched by that of his style. This was usually full of energy, and ruthlessly direct, as in describing how he dealt with an 'offensively republican' donkey-boy: 'A pinch of the windpipe, and a spin over the ground, altered his plans at the outset of execution. He gnawed his hand with impotent rage, and went away ... '. Yet for a night-journey across rough ground such aggressive staccato was replaced by an eerie legato:

Darkness fell upon us like a pall. The camels tripped and stumbled, tossing their litters like cockboats in a short sea ... It was a strange, wild scene. The black basaltic field was dotted with the huge and doubtful forms of spongy-footed camels with silent tread, looming like phantoms in the midnight air; the hot wind moaned, and whirled from the torches flakes and sheets of flame and fiery smoke, whilst ever and anon a swift-travelling Takht-rawan, drawn by mules, and surrounded by runners bearing gigantic mashals or cressets, threw a passing glow of red light upon the dark road and the dusky multitude.

First Footsteps in East Africa (1856) began with another piece of bravado. Since 'no white man had ever succeeded in entering' Harar, Burton felt it 'a point of honour' to do so himself. He arrived there in disguise, then boldly announced his identity to the Amir, and was lucky enough to be treated as a guest. He went to bed 'profoundly impressed by the poésie' of his situation:

I was under the roof of a bigoted prince whose least word was death, amongst a people who detest foreigners, the only European that had ever passed over their inhospitable threshold, and the fated instrument of their future downfall.

He then crossed a desert on a mule, supplied with 'five biscuits, a few limes, and sundry lumps of sugar', to join three other officers

from India, including J. H. Speke, and their camp was attacked
one night by three hundred and fifty Somalis. One of their party
was killed, Speke escaped with eleven wounds, and Burton himself
survived being speared through both his cheeks and his palate. In
this book, too, exciting narrative was laced with literary culture.
While describing social life at Zayla, Burton mentioned 'that
power of quotation which in the East makes a polite man', proved
his own politeness by quoting from Pope and Tennyson, and
translated two Arabic poems into verse. He also noted the paradox
that the *Arabian Nights* (which he would later translate himself)
was, though the

most familiar of books in England, next to the Bible ... one of the least
known, the reason being that about one-fifth is utterly unfit for
translation; and the most sanguine Orientalist would not dare to render
literally more than three-quarters of the remainder.

Still, Burton wrote much more interestingly about life than
literature, and the most memorable passages in the book are about
the night-attack, and the earlier ordeal in the desert:

For twenty-four hours we did not taste water, the sun parched our
brains, the mirage mocked us at every turn, and the effect was a species of
monomania. As I jogged on with eyes closed against the fiery air, no
image unconnected with water suggested itself ... I opened my eyes to a
heat-reeking plain, and a sky of that metallic blue so lovely to painter and
poet, so blank and deathlike to us, whose καλόν was tempest, rain-storm,
and the huge purple nimbus.

Burton clearly enjoyed writing, and produced over forty travel-
books. In this and most other respects David Livingstone was very
different.[11] 'I think', he confessed in *Missionary Travels and
Researches in South Africa* (1857), 'I would rather cross the African
continent again than undertake to write another book. It is far
easier to travel than to write about it.' Burton was chiefly impelled
by egotism: Livingstone was intent on 'the alleviation of human
misery' and the propagation of Christianity. Burton seemed to

[11] David Livingstone, 1813-73, was born at Blantyre, Lanarkshire, the son of a tailor
who became a tea-dealer. From the age of ten he worked in a cotton factory, and educated
himself. Ordained in 1840, he left for Africa under the auspices of the London Missionary
Society. He discovered Lake Ngami, Lake Nyasa, and the Victoria Falls. An expedition to
investigate the sources of the Nile, 1865, ended in his being found by Stanley at Ujiji, 1871.
But he went on exploring, and died at Ilala.

dislike Africans: Livingstone often found them rather endearing ('They are a merry set of mortals—a feeble joke sends them off into fits of laughter') and knew how to get the best out of them. 'The invariably kind and respectful treatment that I have received from these and many other heathen tribes in this central country have led me to the belief that, if one exerts himself for their good, he will never be ill-treated.' It was a belief that sometimes required considerable courage. When a Chiboque chief demanded tribute from him, and surrounded his camp with armed men, Livingstone sat calmly on his camp-stool with a gun across his knees:

I then said that, as one thing after another had failed to satisfy them, it was evident that *they* wanted to fight while *we* wanted only to pass peaceably through their country; that they must begin first to bear the guilt before God. We would not fight till they struck the first blow. I then sat silent for some time. It was rather trying for me because I knew that the Chiboque would aim at the white man first, but I was careful not to appear flurried, and having four barrels ready for instant action, looked quietly at the savage scene around. The Chiboque countenance, by no means handsome, is not improved by their practice of filing their teeth to a point.

Apart from such touches of humour, Livingstone's prose was no livelier than Wallace's, but it described some thrilling experiences, as when he was attacked by a lion ('Growling horribly close to my ear, he shook me as a terrier dog does a rat'), and gave a strong impression of a genuinely heroic personality. His humane tolerance of heathen frailties wavered only at impropriety, as in the 'frightful nudity' of the 'Balonda ladies', or a 'quite singular' form of greeting which involved rolling stark naked on one's back, slapping one's thighs 'as expressions of thankfulness', and 'uttering the words '*Kina bomba*'. For the country itself he showed an almost Wordsworthian passion, especially when describing the Victoria Falls: 'No one can imagine the beauty from anything witnessed in England. It had never been seen before by European eyes; but scenes so lovely must have been gazed upon by angels in their flight.'

For Burton, Africa was now 'the coal-hole of the East'. *The Lake Regions of Central Africa* (1860) professed to give 'a Dutch picture' of 'African adventure' from 'the more popular and picturesque points of view', but was actually one long grumble about his 'African sufferings'. It told how he had tried, with Speke as his assistant, to find the source of the Nile. Everything had gone wrong, but Burton's main complaint was against Speke himself who, after a bitter disagreement, had independently discovered Victoria Nyanza, and correctly identified it as one of the Nile's sources. He had then gone home, while Burton was still convalescing in Zanzibar, and taken the credit for an expedition '*cujus pars minima fuit*', as Burton put it, reversing a Virgilian tag to imply that he, not Speke, was the real hero of that epic journey. Though the book was written with characteristic vitality, contained many amusing character-sketches, and a fascinating account of East African life and culture, it was spoiled by its sour tone, and petty satire on 'my invalid sub'. Not content with sneering at 'the Anglo-Indian's complete ignorance of Eastern manners and customs, and of any Oriental language beyond, at least, a few words of the debased Anglo-Indian jargon', Burton was even catty about Speke's sufferings: 'My companion ... suffered from a painful ophthalmia, and from a curious distortion of face, which made him chew sideways, like a ruminant.'

Speke's reply to all this was his *Journal of the Discovery of the Source of the Nile* (1863).[12] This described, without mention of Burton, Speke's third expedition. In a blunt and forcible but mostly pedestrian style, with a certain amount of broad humour, it described some astonishing adventures, and revealed a personality that explained much of Burton's antagonism. Speke had all the qualifications for success in the Army, courage, resource, personal authority, and a rare gift for coping with awkward situations and customers, but also a degree of simple-mindedness and insensitivity. In a tribe where 'fattening [was] the first duty of fashionable female life', he carefully took the measurements of 'A Fattened Princess':

All of these are exact except the height, and I believe I could have obtained this more accurately if I could have had her laid on the floor. Not knowing what difficulties I should have to contend with in such a piece of engineering, I tried to get her height by raising her up. This, after infinite exertions on the part of us both, was accomplished, when she sank down again, fainting, for her blood had rushed into her head.

[12] John Hanning Speke, 1827–64, was born near Ilminster, Somerset, the son of an army officer. He joined the Indian army at seventeen, and before taking part in Burton's Somaliland expedition of 1864, had fought in the Punjab, and gone shooting in the Himalayas. He discovered Lake Victoria Nyanza and Lake Tanganyika. He died near Bath by accidentally shooting himself instead of a partridge.

This parallel with the problem that faced the Lilliputian tailors was not the only point at which Speke's travels resembled Gulliver's. Like Gulliver at the court of the Emperor Golbasto, Speke had the farcical but deeply frustrating experience of being kept hanging about for months in Uganda, as the guest, prisoner, and court-entertainer of King Mtesa, where court etiquette was very like that of Luggnagg:

> ... both Wakungú, as is the custom in Uganda, thanked their lord in a very enthusiastic manner, kneeling on the ground ... in an attitude of prayer ... when, thinking they had done enough of this, and heated with the exertion, they threw themselves flat upon their stomachs, and, floundering about like fish on land, repeated the same words over and over again, and rose ... with their faces covered with earth; for majesty in Uganda is never satisfied till subjects have grovelled before it like the most abject worms.

Mtesa was a 'capricious barbarian', very fond of Speke, and with a certain childlike charm, but capable of the utmost cruelty. When he ordered one of his wives to be executed for daring to give him some fruit, Speke abandoned his non-intervention policy: 'This last act of barbarism was too much for my English blood to stand.' He demanded a reprieve, and the 'novelty of interference' made the king smile and change his mind.

Like Speke, Winwood Reade had been made a 'prisoner of hospitality' by an African king, but there the resemblance ended.[13] His *Savage Africa* (1863) gave an account of the Negro designed to ridicule the idea of the 'Noble Savage', and was often absurdly racist: 'negroes can only tell lies by exaggeration, or by turning truth inside out; they cannot create falsehood.' Arguing that the slave-trade would never be stopped until Africa was 'walled with civilization', he then flippantly defined that millennium as a time when 'hotels and guide-books are established at the Sources of the Nile', when 'young ladies on camp-stools under palm-trees will read with tears "*The Last of the Negroes*"; and the Niger will

---

[13] William Winwood Reade, 1838–75, nephew of the novelist Charles Reade, was born in Oxfordshire, and went to Magdalen Hall, Oxford, 1856, but left the university without a degree. After his first African travels of 1861, he studied medicine at St Mary's Hospital, London, and worked at the Southampton cholera hospital. He started exploring the sources of the Niger, 1869, and returned to Africa, 1873, as correspondent for *The Times* on the Ashantee war, joining the 42nd Highlanders. Besides novels and travel-books, he published an anti-religious work, *The Martyrdom of Man*, 1872.

become as romantic a river as the Rhine.' The tone of the book was accurately described in the Preface:

I make, of course, no pretensions to the title of Explorer. If I have any merit, it is that of having been the first young man about town to make a *bonâ fide* tour in Western Africa; to travel in this agreeable and salubrious country with no special object and at his own expense; to *flâner* in the virgin forest; to flirt with pretty savages; and to smoke a cigar among cannibals.

After trying to become a novelist like his uncle Charles, Reade had gone to Gabon to satisfy his curiosity about gorillas, and travelled up the Casemanche, Gambia, and Senegal rivers. His book, written at twenty-five, showed great efforts to be smart and witty, and contained some quite funny epigrams like: 'When one travels in the company of cannibals it is bad policy to let them become too hungry'; but the effect was made less enjoyable by the author's obvious immaturity, and lack of humane feeling. After shooting a gazelle, and sentimentalizing over 'those tender eyes' and 'her poor little body', he concluded: 'We had her cutlets dressed *à la papillote*. Exquisite as her beauty, I ate them to indigestion.' Just before ascribing 'the cruelty of the negro' to 'ignorance', he told how a negro had carried him across some mud:

a tall man stooped down like a camel and I sat astride on the back of his neck, his head making an excellent pommel and atoning for the shortness of the wool bridle. Presently he began to flounder, I instinctively pressed his head between my knees, and his struggles increasing, my shooting boots began to play the devil's own tattoo on his belly. But now I found that from a camel my man had become a horse. He was sinking in the mud . . .

The only 'great discovery' which Reade claimed to have made in Africa was his 'own ignorance', but that was not the kind of ignorance he meant. His final message to his 'dear reader' was merely this: 'I go to study with humble industry, the elements of science, the grammar of Nature'.

One returns with relief to Livingstone, who in *The Zambesi and its Tributaries* (1865) reaffirmed his faith in 'the magic power of kindness—a charm which may be said to be one of the discoveries of modern days.' Describing an expedition to explore new territory, investigate natural resources for commerce, and find further evidence of 'the misery entailed by the slave-trade in its inland phases', he also protested against the 'indiscriminate slaughter of wild animals' encouraged by some travel-books, and estimated that 30,000 elephants were being killed each year. Based on journals written by Livingstone and his brother Charles, the book included two striking anecdotes. One was about a man who sold himself into slavery, and on the proceeds started a profitable business as a slave-owner. The other told how two English sailors rescued and bandaged up a slave-girl whose leg had been bitten off by a crocodile. They took her back to her village, but next morning found her, with her bandages ripped off, thrown out to die. 'I believe', remarked one sailor, 'her master was angry with us for saving her life, seeing as how she had lost her leg.'

Also in 1865, W. G. Palgrave's *Personal Narrative of a Year's Journey through Central and Eastern Arabia* reported (and possibly improved on) a Burtonesque feat of audacity.[14] Having learned Arabic and mixed freely with Arabs while a Jesuit missionary in Syria, Palgrave posed as a Syrian doctor and travelled in constant danger through an area then closed to Europeans. His story was extremely exciting, especially when a Prince at Riyadh denounced him publicly as a Christian spy and revolutionary, and when, finally shipwrecked, he drifted through a stormy sea in an overcrowded, open boat. In the best passages, however, danger was merely the background to a strange type of ordinary life, as in the account of his work as a general practitioner in Ḥā'yel. Happily, the sensational character of his adventures was not wholly obscured by his narrative style, which was verbose, painfully whimsical ('Wilt thou go on with me, gentle reader, for an Arab trip?'), and ponderously facetious: 'it is a great blessing in Arabia that neither gnats nor mosquitoes, nor a certain saltatory insect very common in Southern Europe and in Syria ("letters four do form its name") are here known.'

In *The Malay Archipelago* (1869) Wallace's own personality came out more clearly than in his earlier book. Though his main interest, as before, was in collecting 'specimens of natural history', he now showed some aesthetic feelings. He was 'delighted with the

[14] William Gifford Palgrave, 1826–88, brother of the *Golden Treasury's* editor, was born in London, went to Charterhouse and Trinity College, Cambridge, and then became an officer in the Bombay Native Infantry. He was later a Jesuit priest and missionary in Syria. The journey described in his book was financed by Napoleon III. He then left the Jesuits, went on a diplomatic mission to Abyssinia, and was consul in various places, including Montevideo, where he died of bronchitis.

beauty of the human form . . . the unrestrained grace of the naked savage.' It made him 'melancholy' to think there was nobody to enjoy the beauty of the tropical forest, and that if 'civilized man' did ever live there, he would rapidly destroy it by disturbing the delicate balance of nature. The colourful fish and vegetation in the harbour of Amboyna were 'a sight to gaze at for hours, and no description can do justice to its surpassing beauty and interest.' Yet he ridiculed the conventional raptures of travel-writers. The tropics were not full, as they implied, with 'bright flowers and gorgeous masses of blossom', nor were all Rajah's daughters glamorous:

And here I might (if I followed the example of most travellers) launch out into a glowing description of the charms of these damsels . . . But, alas!, regard for truth will not allow me to expatiate too admiringly on such topics, determined as I am to give as far as I can a true picture of the people and places I visit.

In collecting his 125,660 'specimens' Wallace had to do a great deal of slaughtering, even if his scientific purpose took it out of Livingstone's 'indiscriminate' category; but he did feel some compunction. Having shot an '*orangutan*' in a tree, and then found that her young had 'fallen face downwards in the bog', he tried to feed it like a baby, with 'rice-water from a bottle with a quill in the cork, which after a few trials it learned to suck very well', and even made it 'an artificial mother, by wrapping up a piece of buffalo-skin into a bundle, and suspending it about a foot above the floor.' But it died three months later: 'I much regretted the loss of my little pet. It had given me daily amusement by its curious ways and the inimitably ludicrous expression of its little countenance.' He also had many more upsetting experiences, like spending a night during an earthquake in a village on the edge of a ravine, or going to bed one night, blowing out his candle, reaching for his handkerchief, and putting his hand on a snake: 'there he was, sure enough, nicely coiled up, with his head just raised to inquire who had disturbed him.'

One of the first travel-books to exploit, not unknown territory, but an unusual form of transport, was John MacGregor's *A Thousand Miles in the Rob Roy Canoe on Rivers and Lakes of Europe* (1870).[15] Here a London barrister, who had already travelled

[15] John MacGregor, 1825–92, was the son of a general. He went to Trinity College,

widely in the Middle East, Russia, South Africa, and America, described a holiday-tour of France, Germany, and Switzerland in a boat of his own design. The tone of the book was set by a pun: 'On this new world of waters, then, we are to launch the boat, the man, and his baggage, for we must describe all three. "Arma, virumque canoe".' The story ended in Paris, with a tacit tribute to 'The Yarn of the Nancy Bell': 'I could not believe that any person there had enjoyed his summer months with such delight as the captain, the purser, the ship's cook, and cabin-boy of the Rob Roy Canoe.' The sense of enjoyment was effectively conveyed by a style that hovered between facetiousness and wit; but it was not to parody *The Bible in Spain* that MacGregor carried 'Scripture anecdotes and other papers in French and German' in his 'very limited baggage' for use on 'appropriate occasions'. A deeply religious man, he had in his youth wanted to be a missionary. He was serious too, though he expressed it humorously, in the feeling that he shared with Borrow, Darwin, and many other travel writers:

So now, let the wind blow as it liked. I could run before it, and breakfast at this village; or cross to that point to bathe; or row round that bay, and lunch on the other side of the lake, or anywhere else on the shore, or in the boat itself, as it pleased me. I felt as a dog must feel on its travels who has no luggage and no collar, and has only one coat, which always fits him, and is always getting new.

When Livingstone had set off again to explore the Central African rivers, he too had felt 'quite exhilarated ... The mere emotional pleasure of travelling in a wild unexplored country is very great.' But unreliable porters, obstructive natives, inter-tribal wars, his own illness, and the theft of his medicine box by deserters had made the expedition a disaster. His journal showed amazing stoicism; but when he finally reached Ujiji in 1871 he was 'reduced to a skeleton' and, finding that his stores there had been stolen, felt 'at his wits' end'. At that point H. M. Stanley, sent out by the *New York Herald* to find him, acted the *deus ex machina*.[16]

Dublin, and Trinity College, Cambridge, and became a barrister, 1851. He travelled in Europe, America, and the Middle East. A philanthropist, he became vice-president of the Ragged School Union, and gave all his literary earnings to charity.

[16] Sir Henry Morton Stanley (originally John Rowlands) was born at Denbigh, Wales. He assumed the name of a cotton-broker who befriended and adopted him in New Orleans,

Born of poor parents in Denbigh, this enterprising journalist had first emulated Nicholas Nickleby by thrashing his workhouse schoolmaster, then crossed the Atlantic as a cabin-boy, fought in the Civil War, and finally become a special correspondent. His *How I found Livingstone* (1872) was understandably a bestseller. It told the whole story of his gruelling assignment in a sensationally graphic style which, if often carelessly worded, gave a lively impression of the obstacles overcome, both external and internal — as when he described the psychological effects of malaria. His famous first words to Livingstone had a more complex mental background than they themselves might suggest. He was thinking less of the tragic hero than of the chorus of natives surrounding him:

My heart beats fast, but I must not let my face betray my emotions, lest it shall detract from the dignity of the white man appearing under such extraordinary circumstances.

So I did what I thought was most dignified ... I would have run to him, only I was a coward in the face of such a mob — would have embraced him, but that I did not know how he would receive me; so I did what moral cowardice and false pride suggested was the best thing — walked deliberately to him, took off my hat, and said:

'DR. LIVINGSTONE, I PRESUME?'

'And now, dear reader,' Stanley concluded, 'the time has come for you and I to part.'

Though more elegant in grammar and phrasing, Winwood Reade's *African Sketch-Book* (1873) was otherwise far less impressive than Stanley's historic work. Reade meant it to be 'not only a narrative of travel ... but a sketch-book of African life', and to make it 'comprehensive and complete' he included much heterogeneous material. Besides recapitulating his 'previously published travels', and describing a second expedition (1869), he added essays on various subjects, and even fictitious 'tales' suggested by his travels or his reading. Designed to be 'popular' and interest 'many lady-readers', it was tiresomely dilettante in manner, and certainly gave a very sketchy idea of life or travel in Africa.

1859. Before his search for Livingstone he had been to Abyssinia and Spain, and travelled through Palestine, Turkey, Southern Russia, and Persia to India. After Livingstone's death, he went on exploring Africa, and published *Through the Dark Continent*, 1878, and *In Darkest Africa*, 1890.

Fred Burnaby's *Ride to Khiva: Travels and Adventures in Central Asia* (1876) was a better story by a tougher traveller.[17] The Russians had just occupied Khiva, and forbidden foreigners to enter the area. In the 'contradictorious' spirit that his nurse had found in him as a child, Burnaby defied the ban. He also wished to confirm his suspicion that Russia was preparing bases from which to attack India. He travelled from St Petersburg partly by train, partly by sleigh (once drawn by three camels), and partly on horseback, riding three hundred miles across a steppe when the temperature was twenty degrees below zero. He wrote sometimes like a novelist, with plenty of dialogue, but mostly like a fluent, observant, and entertaining raconteur. His 'Adventures' included having to jump, in heavy clothing, across a large hole in ice; being driven in a sleigh down a steep, winding road on the edge of a precipice; nearly losing his hands from frost-bite; and being shaved in front of a huge crowd at Khiva, after being warned that if he went there without an escort, the Khan would probably put his eyes out or throw him into a dungeon: 'the idea occurred to me that, if the barber were fanatically disposed, he might think that it would be doing a good deed in the eyes of Allah and of his countrymen, if he were forthwith to cut the throat of the unbeliever.' One of his lesser ordeals was to find himself riding 'a camel in love':

He was a very long and a very tall camel, and in an instant he commenced to rear . . . I found that I was, as it were, slipping down the steep roof of a house, with nothing to hold on by but a peg about four inches long, which projected from the front part of the saddle. It was an awful moment, but he did not keep me long in suspense. Performing an extraordinary movement, he suddenly swung himself round on his hind legs, and ran as fast as he could in the direction of the fair enticer . . . At this moment my steed was seized with a strange and convulsive twitching which threatened to capsize the saddle. My position became each moment more ridiculous and more appalling. I was a shuttlecock, Romeo's back was the battledore . . .

On Horseback through Asia Minor (1877) described a journey

[17] Frederick Gustavus Burnaby, 1842–85, was born at Bedford, the son of a clergyman, and educated at Bedford Grammar School, Harrow, and privately in Germany. He joined a cavalry regiment, 1859, and became colonel, 1881. His *Ride Across the Channel*, 1882, described a balloon-flight from Dover to Envermeu, Normandy. He was killed on the Khartoum relief expedition by a spear-wound in the throat.

from Scutari to Erzerum fitted, like the other *Ride*, into a few month's leave from the Royal Horse Guards. This time Burnaby's object was to find out if the Turks were really 'such awful scoundrels' as Gladstone said they were, and to assess the threat of further Russian encroachment over the Turkish frontier. He concluded that the Turks were much maligned, and that 'We should accept the challenge, and draw our swords for Turkey.' Promising 'a sort of verbal photograph . . . of what [he] saw and heard during [his] journey', he duly recorded his conversations with Turks and his visits to Turkish prisons. Apart from nearly dropping down a chasm while crossing a snow-covered mountain, and having his photograph posted at all the frontier-stations as '*un ennemi acharné*' of Russia, who was to be expelled if he crossed the border, he had few startling adventures. But many of his experiences were pleasantly bizarre. Falling ill in a small village, he was put to bed in a stable, where a Hungarian doctor diagnosed rheumatic fever, and prescribed a herbal 'febrifuge'. 'The day wore on. In the evening the cows inside my bedroom were joined by three buffaloes.' At last he managed to sleep. 'I was awakened late the following afternoon by something cold and clammy against my hand.' It was a cow, meditatively licking his fingers.

The cattle that figured in Robert Louis Stevenson's *An Inland Voyage* (1878) included 'one beast, with a white head and the rest of the body glossy black', like a 'preposterous clergyman . . . A moment after I heard a loud plunge, and, turning my head, saw the clergyman struggling to shore. The bank had given way under his feet.'[18] The reader was left to catch the ironic allusion to Tennyson's 'ever-breaking shore | That tumbled in the Godless deep', and the subtlety of the effect showed how little Stevenson was playing 'the sedulous ape' to MacGregor. His account of a canoe-trip with his friend Walter Simpson on the rivers and canals of Belgium and France was in some ways a traditional travel-book. It made an amusing story out of the problems of travel, as when the voyagers, looking like 'a pair of damp rag-and-bone men' were refused beds at 'a capital inn'. It contained some striking

[18] Robert Louis (originally Lewis) Balfour Stevenson, 1850–94, was born in Edinburgh, the son of a lighthouse engineer. He studied engineering, then law, at Edinburgh University, and was called to the Scottish bar, 1875, but never practised. He had a chronic bronchial ailment, probably tubercular, and in 1876 started travelling for his health. After his early travel-books, he published novels and poems, which will be discussed in other volumes.

word-pictures, like that of Noyon Cathedral, and some interesting
character-sketches, like the old woman in 'Church Interiors':

To each shrine she dedicated an equal number of beads and an equal
length of time. Like a prudent capitalist with a somewhat cynical view of
the commercial prospect, she desired to place her supplications in a great
variety of heavenly securities.

But the work was unusual in its genre for the breadth and
intelligence of its moralizing, its introspective quality, and its
verbal artistry. Travelling to overcome chronic ill health, Stevenson envisaged one experience on a river as part of his struggle with
death. When the current drove him into a fallen tree, swept away
his canoe, and left him desperately trying to pull himself out of the
water:

Death himself had me by the heels, for this was his last ambuscado, and
he must now join personally in the fray. And still I held to my paddle . . .
On my tomb, if ever I have one, I mean to get these words inscribed: "He
clung to his paddle."

The hypnotic effect of using that paddle on the return journey was
wittily described:

The central bureau of nerves, what in some moods we call Ourselves,
enjoyed its holiday without disturbance, like a Government Office. The
great wheels of intelligence turned idly in the head, like fly-wheels,
grinding no grist . . . There is nothing captious about a man who has
attained to this, the one possible apotheosis in life, the Apotheosis of
Stupidity; and he begins to feel dignified and longaevous like a tree . . .
This frame of mind was the great exploit of our voyage, take it all in all. It
was the farthest piece of travel accomplished.

Stevenson's *Travels with a Donkey* (1879) did not cover much
ground either—Modestine saw to that—but he travelled further
through the mountains of the mind than through those of the
Cévennes. 'For my part, I travel not to go anywhere, but to go. I
travel for travel's sake. The great affair is to move . . . '. He needed
to take his thoughts off his separation from Mrs Fanny Osbourne,
whom he married after her divorce the following year; and he told
his friend Sidney Colvin that the book was full of 'mere protesta-
tions to F.'. Far more obvious in the text was his love-hate
relationship with his 'diminutive she-ass', Modestine. This part of
his story, though humorously told, now seems the least enjoyable.

When he finally sold her, he professed to feel the 'bereavement' as deeply as Wordsworth felt the death of 'Lucy'; but he had previously mentioned her chiefly as a frustrating form of transport for his luggage, and when, after much thrashing and goading, he found her load had made 'her two forelegs no better than raw beef on the inside', his only reaction was annoyance: 'What the devil was the good of a she-ass if she could not carry a sleeping-bag and a few necessaries?' The sleeping-bag figured, however, in the two most delightful chapters of the book, 'A Camp in the Dark' and 'A Night among the Pines'. In the first, after going to sleep on a supper of chocolate and Bologna sausage washed down with brandy, he woke to find himself in a brave new world:

Ulysses, left on Ithaca, and with a mind unsettled by the goddess, was not more pleasantly astray. I have been after an adventure all my life, a pure dispassionate adventure, such as fell early and heroic voyagers; and thus to be found by morning in a random woodside nook in Gévaudan—not knowing north from south, as strange to my surroundings as the first man upon the earth, an island castaway—was to find a fraction of my day-dreams realised.

In the other chapter, his 'night's lodging' in his 'green caravan-serai' was so exquisite that 'in a half-laughing way' he left 'pieces of money on the turf' to pay for it. On 'The Last Day', beneath some chestnuts overlooking 'an amphitheatre of hill, sunlit and green with leaves', he 'moved in an atmosphere of pleasure'. That is the reader's feeling throughout the book; but the pleasure is that of reflection as well as 'Stupidity'. Stevenson's agnosticism had caused a painful rift with his parents, and the question of religious belief kept recurring in various contexts: in his visit to a Trappist monastery, and the attempts made there to convert him, in his conversation with a Plymouth Brother, and in the story of the Camisards, ironically confirming the Lucretian view: '*Tantum religio potuit suadere malorum*'. Stevenson concluded that one's religious creed was an integral part of one's personality,

the poetry of the man's experience, the philosophy of the history of his life . . . And I think I should not leave my old creed for another, changing only words for other words; but by some brave reading, embrace it in spirit and truth, and find wrong as wrong for me as for the best of other communions.

Under pressure far greater than Stevenson had to resist in the monastery, Charles Doughty also refused to change 'words for other words'.[19] Before an ugly mob of fanatical Muslims at Hâyil, a Moorish 'brute-man' called for a knife to circumcise the 'cursed Nasrâny' (Christian), and virtually demanded his apostasy or his life: 'for one thing ... we will be friends with thee; say, there is none God but the Lord and His apostle is Mohammed: and art thou poor we will also enrich thee.' 'I count your silver as the dust,' replied Doughty. 'Though you gave me this castle, and ... the sacks of hoarded silver which ye say to lie therein, I would not change my faith.' His *Travels in Arabia Deserta* (1888) were much more dangerous than Burton's or Palgrave's because he refused to conceal his identity. Nor was his project simply an act of bravado. He wished to investigate some 'rock cities' like Petra of which he had heard on a previous geological expedition; but when the Royal Geographical Society failed to get the necessary firman from the Sultan, in time for him to join the next caravan of pilgrims to Mecca, he felt obliged to go without official backing. And when the British Consul in Damascus refused to accept any responsibility for him ('he had as much regard for me, would I take such dangerous ways, as of his old hat'), Doughty felt he had no option but to rely on his own resources, and to a large extent on Bedouin hospitality. So off he went, with a revolver, an aneroid barometer, two small notebooks, and a black-letter *Canterbury Tales* among the few contents of his camel-bags.

His two-year pilgrimage from Damascus to Jidda on the Red Sea proved a gruelling ordeal, in which he 'many times [came] nigh to be foully murdered!' On one such occasion he was threatened with a knife by a 'mad sherif', and hemmed in by 'more than a dozen cameleers', while bystanders were shouting: 'Let us hack him in morsels, the cursed one! what hinders?—fellows, let us hack him in morsels!' That was the only time he drew his revolver—but, having no chance of escaping if he used it, handed it over to his attackers and still managed to survive. The whole

[19] Charles Montagu Doughty, 1843–1926, was born at Theberton Hall, Suffolk, the son of a clerical landowner. Rejected on medical grounds by the navy, he read geology at Cambridge, first at Caius, then at Downing. Before taking the natural sciences tripos, he studied glaciers in Norway, and read a paper on them to the British Association, 1864. Planning to write poetry which would revive the diction of Chaucer and Spenser, he did linguistic and antiquarian research, then started travelling, 1870, through Europe to Greece, Syria, Palestine, and Egypt, watching *en route* an eruption of Vesuvius. The journey described in his book began from Damascus, 1876. His poetry will be dealt with in another volume.

enterprise was a wonderful human achievement. Doughty had an immensely interesting and exciting story to tell; but he also had a literary theory to illustrate. He wanted 'to continue the older tradition of Chaucer and Spenser, resisting ... the decadence of the English language'; or, as he put it in 1913:

The Arabia Deserta volumes had necessarily a personal tone. A principal cause of writing them was besides the interest of the Semitic life in tents, my dislike of the Victorian English; and I wished to show, and thought I might be able to show, that there was something else.

The alternative offered was a dialect of his own invention, highly Arabicized and full of English archaisms. It has been much admired, notably by William Morris, Robert Bridges, and W. S. Blunt, who claimed to have been 'one of the first to recognize the position of the book as the best prose work of the XIXth century.' It is easier to sympathize with the publisher's reader who found 'the style of the book so peculiar as to be at times unintelligible', and thought 'most readers and all reviewers would ... say that parts of it are not English at all'. But the content of the work was unquestionably fascinating. It gave a realistic picture of life in Arabia, which was endorsed by T. E. Lawrence: 'It is the true Arabia, the land with its smells and dirt, as well as its nobility and freedom ... There is no sentiment, nothing merely picturesque ... There is nothing we would take away, little we could add.' If *Arabia Deserta* was not quite the 'contribution ... to literature' that Doughty intended, it at least lived up to its epigraph: 'PROSIT VERITATI'.

That was the only claim that Jerome K. Jerome made for *Three Men in a Boat* (1889):

The chief beauty of this book lies not so much in its literary style, or in the extent and usefulness of the information it conveys, as in its simple truthfulness ... Other works may excel this in depth of thought and knowledge of human nature: other books may rival it in originality and size; but for hopeless and incurable veracity, nothing yet discovered can surpass it.[20]

---

[20] Jerome Klapka Jerome, 1859–1927, was born at Walsall, the son of a Nonconformist colliery-owner who became a London ironmonger. He left Marylebone Grammar School at fourteen, and after working as a railway clerk, an actor, and a schoolmaster, became a journalist. He later wrote plays, notably *The Passing of the Third Floor Back*, produced 1908. *Three Men in a Boat* was translated into many languages, and had a huge circulation in Russia.

This account of a trip up the Thames in a rowing-boat to Oxford, and back to Pangbourne, had a historical basis, and was originally designed, as *The Story of the Thames*, to describe the history and scenery of that river. But all that came easily was the 'humorous relief', and when by 'grim determination' Jerome succeeded in writing 'a dozen or so slabs of history and working them in', they were promptly excised by his editor. The result was perhaps the funniest book of the period. As such, it was not a travel-book in the normal sense, especially as its author confessed to having 'coloured', i.e. fictionalized, his 'record of events that really happened'. But it belongs here, as the climax of the tendency, from MacGregor onwards, for travel-writers to parody the genre. When all the equipment for the expedition, including a frying-pan, and recalling the cargo of Wallace's canoe, first appeared on the pavement outside No 42, it caused much speculation:

'They ain't a-going to starve, are they?' said the gentleman from the boot-shop.

'Ah! you'd want to take a thing or two with *you*,' retorted the Blue Posts, 'if you was a-going to cross the Atlantic in a small boat.'

'They ain't a-going to cross the Atlantic', struck in Biggs's boy, 'they're a-going to find Stanley.'

19. Drama

'A Slough of Despond in the wide well-tilled field of English Literature'. That was how one of the period's best playwrights, Henry Arthur Jones, described Victorian drama up to 1891. For him plays were primarily pieces of literature, and 'the worst and deadliest enemy of the English drama [was]—the English theatre.' He explained himself further in 1894:

It is often said in the theatre that the test of a play is, will it act? This is merely a theatrical test, and can be refuted by all the heaps of forgotten theatrical rubbish that have been popular successes during the past two hundred years. Believe me, the true test of a play is, will it act and read?

For a history of literature this seems an appropriate criterion. All the plays mentioned in this chapter acted well enough to succeed in the theatre: the only question asked will be how well they read.

To start with 'theatrical rubbish', a popular melodrama in the 1830s was *Maria Marten; or, the Murder in the Red Barn*. This anonymous dramatization of a real-life murder illustrates two of the most pernicious influences on early Victorian drama: those of Shakespeare and of an illiterate, working-class audience. The first, which infected serious plays also, from Sheridan Knowles's *Virginius* (1820) to Tennyson's *Queen Mary* (1875), showed itself here in prose dialogue that threatened to become blank verse, and in rephrasings of famous Shakespearian lines.[1] 'Come, shroud me, demons!' cries the villain before the murder. 'Hide, hide my thoughts within your black abyss!' The second influence appeared in the crude sensationalism of the plot. Until Queen Victoria started trying, in 1848, to make the theatre respectable, most plays continued to reflect the tastes and intellects of what Jones called 'the mob'. For many other reasons, including Evangelical prejudice against the theatre, and the fact that Drury Lane and Covent garden were too large for any subtlety of effect, the period's drama certainly began in a Slough of Despond, but it ended in a kind of Celestial City, where melodrama was partially transfigured by

---

[1] For Tennyson see Chap. 2. He had five plays performed in his lifetime, but his only theatrical success came after his death, when Henry Irving produced *Becket*, in 1893.

'ideas', as in Jones's *Saints and Sinners* (1884), and farce, free from
the slapstick of Jerrold's *Mr Paul Pry* (1826), was etherealized by
fantastic wit, as in Gilbert's *Engaged* (1877) and the Savoy Operas.
In general, there was a Playwright's Progress from physical to
intellectual, from spectacular to literary, from stagy to realistic.
Though clearly linked with rising standards of education, this was
also connected with the development of theatrical resources and
techniques, as technical improvements in scenery, costume, and
lighting were combined with better stage-management and direct-
ing, and actors set off along the road from Ham to Method.

The movement towards realism was only faintly perceptible in
Douglas Jerrold's 'nautical drama', *Black-Eyed Susan* (1829).[2]
Inspired by his own experience as a midshipman, it was based, not
on Gothic fantasy, like such earlier melodramas as Isaac Pocock's
The Miller and his Men (1813), but on contemporary social
conflict. Thus it expressed working-class distrust of officers and
landlords, and had a lower-deck hero, William. Yet William's
character, diction, and history were remote from real life. About to
be executed for resisting a lecherous attack on his wife by the
Captain, he tells the Lieutenant: 'I bear no malice, your honour, I
loved the Captain.' Elsewhere he supplies comic relief by his
addiction to nautical metaphor, as when he sees some girls
approaching:

There's my Susan! now pipe all hands for a royal salute; there she is,
schooner-rigged—I'd swear to her canvas from a whole fleet. Now she
makes more sail—outs with her studding booms—mounts her royals,
moon-rakers and sky-scrapers; now she lies to—now—now—eh? May I
be put on six-water grub for a lubber ... 'Tisn't she—'tisn't my craft.

The happy ending was delayed until the last drop of pathos had
been extracted from his farewell to Susan, and was brought about
by the news that William had been officially discharged from the
Navy before he struck the Captain.

John Walker's *The Factory Lad* (1832) ended less happily but
more sensationally, with a shot fired by an indignant poacher
across the court of a magistrate called Bias, at a callous industrial-

---

[2] Douglas William Jerrold, 1803–57, was the son of an actor–manager. Born in London,
he was taught to read and write by a member of the cast, and then taught himself Latin,
French, and Italian. Before writing plays for the Surrey Theatre, he had served in the navy,
been apprenticed to a printer, and acted in other London theatres. He later became a
journalist, writing especially for *Punch*.

ist, who had sacked his whole labour-force because 'Steam supersedes manual labour!'[3] Staged at the same working-class theatre as *Black-Eyed Susan*, this play handled industrial realities in the language of melodrama, but in a spirit almost as serious as that of Harriet Martineau's 'A Manchester Strike', published the same year.[4] Walker's thoughtful and conscientious hero, Allen, shared a name and a character with hers, and the curtain went down on an appeal for social justice: 'Spurn a helpless and imploring woman, whose heart is broken—whose mind is crazed? If her *voice* is weak, my *arm* is not. Justice shall have its due. Die, tyrant! Quick, to where water quencheth not!'

The contrast between Allen's character and his social predica-ment was more tragic in its effect than Browning's *Strafford: A Tragedy* (1837), which was also less effective as a historical drama than Edward Bulwer-Lytton's *Richelieu* (1839).[5] Though written in the blank verse then thought necessary for serious drama, this had the vitality and some of the features of a melodrama. Its ingenious plot culminated in a kind of resurrection-scene where Richelieu, previously reported to be dead and now apparently dying, was instantaneously restored to health and political power by the arrival of a page, 'whose pourpoint is streaked with blood', carrying vital documents. *Richelieu* gave Macready a far better acting part than *Strafford* had done, and it is still quite entertain-ing even to read.

Macready not only produced and acted in Lytton's best play, *Money* (1840), but had also helped him to write it. The comedy moved further towards realism in the colloquial wit of its prose dialogue, and its satire on fashionable attitudes to wealth and class, though its plot was wildly improbable. When a scholarly poor relation called Evelyn is suddenly left a fortune, he finds himself able, at last, to marry the girl he loves, but for being engaged to another girl, who loves him only for his money. He solves the problem by pretending to squander his whole fortune on gambling

---

[3] Nothing seems to be known about John Walker, but that he wrote several other plays.

[4] See Chap. 14.

[5] For Browning see Chap. 3. Edward George Earle Lytton Bulwer-Lytton, first Baron Lytton, 1803–73, was born in London, the son of General Bulwer. He went to Trinity College, Cambridge, thought himself insulted by a tutor, so moved to Trinity Hall. In 1827 he started publishing novels, which will be discussed in another volume, and in 1831 began a political career. The first of his plays was performed in 1838.

and extravagance. In certain ways the play was traditional. Evelyn's view of society was like Juvenal's in his third *Satire*. The scene where he appeared surrounded by hopeful tradesmen was evidently modelled on the second plate of Hogarth's *A Rake's Progress*. The mixture of humour and romantic sentiment was in the manner of Sheridan. But the more recent influence of melodrama was seen in the denouement, where Evelyn's reprieve from marriage to the mercenary Georgina and his reunion with Clara were contrived at the last possible moment by the identification of an anonymous letter-writer. The device was used, however, with an air of parody; and the whole piece was marked by the flippant cynicism that Oscar Wilde would cultivate. This was most conspicuous in the will-reading scene, and in the closing lines, where Evelyn's tribute to 'the everlasting holiness of truth and love' was followed by a list of requisites for happiness, concluding with: 'plenty of Money'.

Boucicault's *London Assurance* (1841) was in much the same spirit.[6] Having started his career not like Lytton as a novelist, but as an actor, Boucicault feared that his first attempt at 'a modern comedy' would 'not bear analysis as a literary production', but it reads extremely well, as a kind of inspired farce. Like Jack in *The Importance of Being Earnest* (1895) its hero, Young Courtly, was a 'Bunburyist'. Under his country name of Augustus Hamilton, he made love to his father's fiancée, Grace; but when he had to kill Augustus off 'in a frightful accident on the London road', he found the dead man had supplanted him in her affections: 'Since you press me into a confession,—which nothing but this could bring me to speak—know I did love poor Augustus Hamilton, but he—he is no more! Pray, spare me, sir.' The play's title was personified in the irresponsible dandy, Richard Dazzle, who reflected the Irish ebullience of Boucicault's own character, and also anticipated Jack, in having 'not the remotest idea' who he actually was by birth. Written for Covent Garden, which with Drury Lane had a legal monopoly of serious drama until 1843, the piece was not wholly frivolous. Grace's mockery of love, besides echoing Rosa-

---

[6] Dionysius Lardner Boucicault (Bourcicault, Boursiquot), 1820–90, was born in Dublin, of Huguenot extraction. He went to University College School in London, and first appeared on the stage as an actor in 1838. After the success of *London Assurance* he wrote or adapted about 250 plays. He helped to get the American dramatic copyright law passed in 1856, and was the first English playwright to receive royalties, 1861.

lind's, touched on the realities of the 'marriage mart' in a coolly feminist tone: 'Why should I lay out my life in love's bonds upon the bare security of a man's word?' And even Lady Gay Spanker, otherwise merely a stage-caricature, complained of married life in terms not simply paradoxical: 'I am never contradicted, so there are none of those enlivening ... little differences which so pleasantly diversify the monotony of conjugal life, like spots of verdure; no quarrels, like oases in the desert of matrimony; no rows.'

A humbler type of farce was performed at the Adelphi Theatre, where the audiences were lower-class, with a high proportion of Irish. J. S. Coyne's *How to Settle Accounts with your Laundress* (1847) was exactly what they liked.[7] Coyne came from Ireland himself, and the one-act piece was introduced by an Irish servant called Barney Toole, whose master insisted on calling him Twill, 'because Twill, he says, is genteeler'. The master, a tailor named Widgetts, was similarly ridiculed for his pretensions to 'gentility' when he told his laundress, Mary: 'Walking's vulgar, my dear'. The whole play was about her manœuvres to make him honour a promise of marriage written on twenty-nine unpaid laundry-bills. She did this chiefly by pretending to have committed suicide— dressing a tailor's dummy in a woman's clothes, and sticking it head down in a water-butt, the legs encased in a pair of green boots. While still dazed by the discovery of the supposed corpse, Widgetts delivered a soliloquy full of puns and allusions to *Hamlet*: 'Oh! I haven't strength to open the door with them green boots kicking at my conscience ... There's poor Mary White gone on a weeping and *wailing* voyage to that bourne from whence no traveller gets a return ticket.'

Not Shakespeare, but romantic drama was burlesqued, with far greater art, in J. M. Morton's *Box and Cox* (also 1847).[8] This 'Romance of Real Life', which combined the plots of two French

---

[7] John Stirling Coyne, 1803–68, was born at Birr, King's County, Ireland, the son of a port surveyor, and went to Dungannon School. His first farce was produced in Dublin, 1835, and he moved to London, 1836. He wrote about seventy plays, half of them farces, and was also a journalist, writing especially for *Punch*, and drama critic of the *Sunday Times*.

[8] John Maddison Morton, 1811–91, was born at Pangbourne, the son of a playwright, and was educated in France. He wrote over 125 plays, 100 of them farces, mostly taken from the French. *Box and Cox*, a rewriting of *The Double-Bedded Room*, 1843, was said to have made him £7,000.

farces, was about two young men, a night-shift printer and a
salesman in a hat-shop, who found they were both tenants of the
same bed-sitting-room. The dialogue was unfailingly facetious,
but the funniest effects arose from the gradual process of discovery, and from the play's formal symmetry. Box and Cox were
like mirror-images of one another. As though to confirm Bergson's
later theory that laughter was a reaction to a '*mécanisation de la
vie*', Box had only to start cooking bacon, for Cox automatically to
start cooking a chop. The series of chance resemblances continued
until both young men turned out to be engaged to the same widow
of a 'proprietor of bathing-machines', and culminated in a delightful parody of romantic melodrama:

BOX. You'll excuse the apparent insanity of the remark, but the more I
   gaze on your features, the more I'm convinced that you're my long-
   lost brother.
COX. The very observation I was going to make to you!
BOX. Ah, tell me—in mercy tell me—have you such a thing as a
   strawberry mark on your left arm?
COX. No!
BOX. Then it is he!

                              [*They rush into each other's arms.*

   Such parody did nothing to reduce the popularity of plays like
Boucicault's *The Corsican Brothers* (1852), which Queen Victoria
went four times to see. Cox had called duelling 'a barbarous
practice', except with unloaded pistols; but this piece, adapted
from a French dramatization of a novel by Dumas *père*, ended
every act with a sensational duel. The twin-heroes were telepathi-
cally linked, so that Fabien, in Corsica, was instantly aware that his
brother was being killed at Fontainebleau. When Louis had finally
been avenged, his ghost appeared, 'rising gradually through the
earth, and placing his hand on [Fabien's] shoulder': 'Mourn not,
my brother,' he said, as the curtain slowly fell, 'we shall meet
again.' Though the vision of Louis's death at Fontainebleau recalls
the dream of the murder in *Maria Marten*, Boucicault's melodrama was of a new type. Written for the Princess's Theatre,
where Charles Kean had been producing Shakespeare, it gave
scope for Kean's relatively subdued acting-style, while presenting an aristocratic world as unrealistic as Shakespeare's Bohemia.
It also exploited recent improvements in scenery and stage-
technology, especially in the appearance of the ghost.

A similar taste for improbable stage-effects was shown by Tom Taylor and Charles Reade in *Masks and Faces* (1852).[9] Here they adapted the statue-scene in *The Winter's Tale* to satirical purposes, making an art-critic complain that a portrait of Peg Woffington was 'not a bit like' her, though the face was in fact her own, showing through a hole in the canvas. Such satire was mixed with contrived sentiment: the eighteenth-century actress was presented as more like a Cheeryble than a Corsican Brother, in her efforts to relieve the misery of a Grub Street author and artist, and his starving family. She also set an example for Wilde's Cecily and Gwendolen to parody, in her generosity towards her lover's wife, Mabel:

WOFFINGTON. And you will let me call you friend?
MABEL. Friend! no—not friend!
WOFFINGTON. Alas!
MABEL [*timidly and pleadingly*]. Let me call you sister? I have no sister!
WOFFINGTON. Sister! oh yes! call me sister!

[*They embrace.*

Apart from this kind of thing, the play was quite witty and entertaining, and the playwrights (who had been Fellows of colleges, at Cambridge and Oxford respectively) gave a lively and convincing reconstruction of theatrical society in the eighteenth century.

With *The Colleen Bawn* (1860) Boucicault inaugurated a new form of romantic melodrama, no less fantastic in plot than *The Corsican Brothers*, but realistic in so far as the diction and character-types were based on his own experience of country life in Ireland. The aristocratic twins were replaced by an odd pair of foster-brothers: Hardress, a gentleman threatened by foreclosure of the mortgage on his family estate, and his hunchbacked servant Danny Mann, whose devotion had been increased rather than reduced by the fact that his disability had been accidentally caused

---

[9] Tom Taylor was born in Sunderland, the son of a self-educated farm-labourer who had become a brewer. He went to Glasgow University and Trinity College, Cambridge, of which he became a fellow. He was professor of English literature at University College, London, 1845–7, practised briefly as a barrister, and for twenty years worked as a civil servant in the health department. He edited *Punch*, 1874–80. An amateur actor, he wrote or adapted some hundred pieces for the stage. Charles Reade, 1814–84, was born at Ipsden, Oxfordshire, the son of a squire. He went to Magdalen College, Oxford, where he became a fellow. He began his theatrical career with *Masks and Faces*, and then turned it into a novel, *Peg Woffington*, 1853. His novels will be discussed in another volume.

by his foster-brother. The Colleen Bawn was a beautiful peasant-girl whom Hardress had rashly married, and when she seemed likely to obstruct her husband's social and financial progress, the devoted Danny tried to murder her, by pushing her off a flat rock, centre-stage, into a lake of 'gauze waters'. Like many characters in melodrama, she came back to life in the last scene, having been fished out just in time by a poacher-smuggler called Myles (acted by Boucicault himself), who supplied comic relief like Autolycus, and also personified the Irish quality of the whole play. The Irish brogue and idiom served two purposes. They appealed to the Irish element in lower-class audiences, especially when the snobbish Hardress finally accepted that, in his wife's mouth at least, 'Spake is the right sound' for *speak*; and, now that stage-dialogue was normally in prose, they restored some poetry to drama in the way of rhythmical speech, fantastic hyperbole, and picturesque imagery. When Myles, having settled the heroine for the night in his hillside shanty, went off to sleep elsewhere, he could, without sounding too literary, speak like this: 'There ye are like a pearl in an oyster; now I'll go to my bed as usual on the mountain above—the bolster is stuffed with rocks, and I'll have a cloud round me for a blanket.'

There was no trace of poetry in *Lady Audley's Secret* (1863), C. H. Hazlewood's dramatization of a novel by M. E. Braddon, though the original had at one point compared Lady Audley's smiles to 'sunbeams on a river, which make us forget the dark depths which lie hidden beneath the surface.'[10] The contrast between the novel and the play fully justified Jones's distrust of the theatre. Despite an improbable plot, the novel was quite a thoughtful work. The 'Secret' was very gradually revealed by a young barrister's investigations, and a serious effort was made to explain Lady Audley's state of mind. The realistic style, plausible characterization, and humane approach to the issues raised made the book well worth reading; but the play, designed for the rowdy audiences of the Royal Victoria Theatre, was entirely crude in its effects. The nearest approach to psychological analysis was a

[10] Colin Henry Hazlewood, 1823–75, was a comedian on the Lincoln, York, and western circuits, who started his career as a playwright with a successful farce, 1850. Mary Elizabeth Braddon, 1837–1915, was born in London, the daughter of a solicitor from an old Cornish family. Privately educated, she worked as an actress for three years, and in 1861 published a book of poems, and the first of more than seventy novels. In 1874 she married John Maxwell, a publisher, whose first wife had died insane.

statement just before the final curtain that Lady Audley was mad. 'Aye—aye!' she agreed, laughing wildly. 'Mad, mad, that is the word.' Her attempt to murder her first husband, only dimly suspected for most of the novel, was enacted early in the play, *coram populo*. Having pushed him down a well in the middle of the stage, she told the audience: 'He is gone—gone! and no one was a witness to the deed!' 'Except me!' added Luke, her blackmailer, in a thunderous aside. In the novel, her victim's unlikely escape with a broken arm was progressively disclosed in the course of a rambling death-bed confession by the drunken Luke; in the play, it became an abrupt resurrection:

ROBERT. Friends, hear me:—I accuse that woman of the murder of my friend, George Talboys.

LADY AUDLEY. How and where?

LUKE [*revives*]. I—I will tell that. She pushed him down that well, [*Points to well, all start*] but it will be useless to search there now, for George Talboys is—

Enter GEORGE TALBOYS.

GEORGE. Here!

OMNES. Alive!

LADY AUDLEY [*petrified*]. Alive! alive! you alive!

There was a more convincing return to life at the end of Tom Taylor's *The Ticket-of-Leave Man* (1863), when Brierly, found bleeding and unconscious after a desperate struggle with a criminal, opened his eyes and reassured his wife: 'It's only a clip on the head. I'm none the worse. It was all my game to snare those villains.' As the kindly detective Hawkshaw (the first member of his profession to appear on the English stage) realistically remarked, 'Men don't die so easily.' Taylor's efforts to add some realism to melodrama showed themselves in the setting of the opening scene, a South-London tea-garden, and in the colloquial dialogue, coloured with criminals' slang. The plot, adapted from a recent French play, drew attention to a current social problem, the rehabilitation of ex-convicts. Sent to prison for having been an unconscious accessory to the passing of forged currency, Brierly was sacked by every employer who learned of his record—until he managed to snare the real villains. Apart from its exciting story, and the comedy supplied by the garrulous Cockney landlady, Mrs Willoughby, the play was notable for its faithful representation of lower-middle-class culture.

The farces of William Brough and Andrew Halliday were set still further down the social scale.[11] The scene of *The Area Belle* (1864), for instance, was a basement-kitchen, where a pretty cook-general called Penelope received her three suitors, when not frustrated by the unpredictable movements of her employer: 'What a nuisance missuses are—they're really more trouble than they're worth.' *Hamlet*, however, was more in evidence than the *Odyssey*. When the policeman had been hidden in the copper, and there apparently 'boiled alive . . . like a raw lobster', he returned to life only to be mistaken for a ghost, and commanded: 'Rest, perturbed spirit!'

'Leave sentiment to servant wenches who sweetheart the police-men; it's unworthy of a lady.' So said Lady Ptarmigant in T. W. Robertson's *Society* (1865).[12] This brilliant comedy was the first of a series produced at the Prince of Wales's, a theatre small enough to encourage an intimate style of acting, and stage sets realistic in every detail. Robertson had worked since childhood in every department of theatrical production, and he pioneered new tech-niques of stage-direction, giving detailed instructions in his plays how the stage was to be furnished, and certain passages were to be acted. Catering for a fashionable, middle-class audience, he wrote amusing domestic dramas about contemporary social issues. Lady Ptarmigant foreshadowed Lady Bracknell in her mercenary snob-bishness. At first she urged her penniless niece Maud to marry a very rich but intensely vulgar young man called Chodd, rather than the 'shabby writer' whom she loved, Sidney Daryl; but when Sidney inherited a title and a fortune and became an MP, she instantly changed her mind: 'Why, you wicked girl, you wouldn't marry a man you didn't love, would you? Where are your

[11] William Brough, 1826–70, was born in London, the son of an unsuccessful brewer. Apprenticed to a printer, he became a journalist, and wrote many burlesques, farces, and extravaganzas for the stage. Andrew Halliday Duff, 1830–77, was born at Marnoch, Banffshire, the son of a minister. Educated at Marischal College and the University, Aberdeen, he moved to London, 1849, and became a journalist, contributing the article on 'Beggars' to Henry Mayhew's *London Labour and the London Poor*, 1851. With Brough he wrote thirteen farces and one drama, 1861–5.

[12] Thomas William Robertson, 1829–71, was born at Newark-on-Trent, the eldest of an actor's twenty-two children, who included the actress Madge Kendal. He grew up in the theatre, acting both as a child and when grown up. He moved to London, 1848, where his first play had been produced in 1845, with only moderate success. He then published *David Garrick*, a novel based on a French comedy, and turned it into a play under the same name. Produced at the Haymarket, 1864, this made him known to the public, and the series of his best plays began the following year.

principles? ... My niece marry a Chodd!' But Lady Ptarmigant
was more than a satirical caricature. Her heartless opportunism
was explained in human terms:

Men are a set of brutes. I was jilted myself when I was twenty-three—
and oh, how I loved the fellow! But I asserted my dignity, and married
Lord Ptarmigant, and *he*, and *he* only, can tell you how I have avenged
my sex! Cheer up, my darling! love, sentiment, and romance are
humbug!—but wealth, position, jewels, balls, presentations, a country
house, town mansion, society, power—that's true, solid happiness, and if
it isn't, I don't know what is?

Apart from its witty dialogue and its delicate blend of satire,
realism, and romance, the play contained some ironic stage-effects,
as when Chodd attempted to woo Maud on stage, while Sidney
was heard off stage, more effectively wooing the voters. It also
showed a capacity for the use of symbolic detail, as when the
jealous Sidney, getting more and more drunk in the ball-scene,
and fiddling with a cuff-link that Maud had given him, grumbled:
'This link will *not* hold', and finally gave it to Chodd.

Ours (1866) was about the private life of some officers in 'Our'
regiment just before and during the Crimean War. It exploited the
pathos of wartime separations, and their visual effect: the parting
of the lovers Angus and Blanche, for instance, was meant to
imitate *The Black Brunswicker* of Millais. It also exploited the
ironies of that particular war: Blanche's unsuccessful lover was a
magnanimous Russian Prince. The real theme, however, was not
war but marriage. As in *Society*, separate passages of dialogue were
ingeniously interwoven, when the billing and cooing of Angus and
Blanche alternated with the bickering of Sir Alexander and Lady
Shendryn to form a continuous conversation. The device enforced
one message of the play, the contrast between the relationship of
lovers and of married couples. An observer of the older pair shook
his head and wondered: 'How people with these before their eyes
can fall in love?' When Blanche asked, 'Why do girls get married?'
Lady Shendryn replied: 'Marriage is one of those— ... blessings,
which cannot be avoided.' But the final moral of the play was more
positive. Hinted at in the opening jokes about 'this here joyful
double-barrelled event', the birth of the sergeant's twins, it was
that marriage was equally double-barrelled—at once a state of
'mutual conflict' and the essence of human solidarity. 'And what

are we?' asked Blanche, just before the curtain fell. 'Ours!' said Angus.

After these two plays, Robertson's more famous *Caste* (1867) seems rather disappointing. A play with such a title, produced in the same year as a new working-class electorate, might be expected to treat the problems of inter-class marriage more seriously than they had been treated in *The Colleen Bawn*; but the ostensible theme was partly obscured by farce and melodrama. Yet the piece began well enough. The social incompatibility of Esther Eccles and the Hon. George D'Alroy was accurately objectified in the set descriptions for 'The Little House at Stangate' and 'The Lodgings in Mayfair', and all the Stangate characters except Esther were perfectly designed to disgust the D'Alroys. Class-prejudice was explicitly discussed, and justified by tacit allusion to Darwin's chapter on 'Hybridism' in *The Origin*, and by reference to the railways. Captain Hawtree warned his friend George about 'the inexorable law of caste . . . that commands like to mate with like, and forbids a giraffe to fall in love with a squirrel.' 'People', said Sam Gerridge, a gas-fitter engaged to Polly Eccles,

should stick to their own class. Life's a railway journey, and Mankind's a passenger—first class, second class, third class. Any person found riding in a superior class to that for which he has taken his ticket will be removed at the first station stopped at, according to the bye-laws of the company.

Esther's drunken father, a remote ancestor of Shaw's Mr Doolittle, amusingly oscillated between obsequiousness and self-pitying tirades against 'the wrongs . . . of the workin' classes'; but George's mother, the Marquise de St Maur, was a purely farcical figure, devoid of humanity or even common courtesy, and apt to quote lengthily from Froissart, as if to imply that snobbishness was a relic of the Middle Ages. Thematically the piece culminated in a reconciliation-scene, where Sam and Hawtree, as class-representatives, apologized to one another, shook hands, and then instantly reverted to type: Sam taking advantage of the situation to advertise his new business, and Hawtree recovering from his lapse into camaraderie and resuming 'his Pall Mall manner as he goes out'. The theatrical climax, however, was a mixture of farce and melodrama. George, who was thought to have died in India, outdid his namesake in *Lady Audley's Secret* by suddenly appearing on stage carrying a milk-can, like one of the *Area Belle's* admirers. Like another of them, he was promptly taken for his own ghost, and Polly Eccles, true to the spirit of that play, sank in terror beneath the table.

The resurrection theme was repeated at the end of *Progress* (1869), where Eva, instantaneously cured of a fatal illness by being told that she can marry Ferne after all, looked forward to tottering 'down the avenue' next summer, supported by her fiancé on one side and her great-uncle Lord Mompesson on the other: 'My path must lead to happiness when love and hope conduct me, and affection and experience guide me—[*smiling*] That's Progress!' Thus progress would depend on the reconciliation of an aristocratic past and a technological future—for Ferne was an engineer. But this real-life issue was associated with a novelettish love-story. Eva was a character much too like Tennyson's May Queen, whose example she tried at one point to follow by standing on a balcony in a snow-storm, wearing only a petticoat and coughing frequently. Apart from such romantic absurdities, the contemporary conflict between new and old values was well handled, most explicitly in a debate between Ferne and Arthur Mompesson, a passionate *laudator temporis acti*. For him, Progress was 'the modern slang for the destruction of everything high and noble, and the substitution of everything base and degrading.' For Ferne, who planned to build a railway-station on the site of Mompesson Abbey, it was the railway:

I spread civilisation wherever I sit a-straddle of my steed of vapour, whom I guide with reins of iron and feed with flames. As for the tumbledown old ruins I knock down in passing, what matter? Where I halt towns rise, and cities spring up into being. 'Tis the train that is the master of the hour. As it moves it shrieks out to the dull ear of prejudice, 'Make room for me! I must pass and I will! and those who dare oppose my progress shall be crushed!'

As things turned out, Arthur was as quickly converted to trains as Kenneth Grahame's Toad would be to motor-cars; but the play had most to say about the least attractive aspects of modernity, personified in Bob Bunnythorne, a would-be poet whose favourite quotation from his own unpublished works was: 'Patience, my heart, oh rest, my brain, oh wait, my weary soul!' The soul would take flesh, as Bunthorne, in Gilbert's *Patience*, but Bob's best

moment in *Progress* was when he and his father, both equally
drunk, were trying to convince each other that they were sober.
The mirror-image effect, which had been used in *Box and Cox*,
and would be used more literally in the Marx Brothers' film, *Duck
Soup*, was here the subject of a stage-direction:

Both assume an air of excessive sobriety and dignity ... their resemblance to each other must be carried out by the actors' gestures and
manners being arranged so as to be identical. Whatever action is used by
Bunnythorne is also used inadvertently and unconsciously by Bob.

In another play of 1869, *New Men and Old Acres*, Tom Taylor
and Augustus William Dubourg handled the same issue rather
more subtly.[13] The Mompessons were paralleled by the Vavasours,
and Ferne by a Liverpool merchant called Brown; but Eva's
gushing poeticism was almost parodied in Fanny Bunter, when she
exclaimed, 'Give me art and intellect, sweetness and light, you
know—a cottage and a crust—a lovely landscape and the "Stones
of Venice." Oh, I could live upon Ruskin!' This suited Fanny's
character as the daughter of 'a self-made man', and as a scion of
the nobility Lilian Vavasour was more convincing than Eva,
especially when she pretended not to mind being turned out of her
family home, keeping back her tears until she was left alone.
Brown was an equal improvement upon Ferne, whose chief
distinguishing features had been faith in technology and a gift for
falling in love when the plot required it. Brown was a much more
sensitive and intelligent person, who responded to Lady Matilda's
snobbishness with tolerant irony:

Yes—I've her full consent. In fact, she's been kind enough to plan our
married life for us. My trade mark is to be got rid of, as burglars punch
the cypher out of plate. I'm to be recast into a fine gentleman, with a seat
in Parliament and a post under Government.

The love-story was quite realistically treated, and set in an exciting
plot, plausibly related to commerce and finance. This ended with
the foiling of Bunter's scheme to buy and foreclose the mortgage
on the Abbey, because he knew the park contained valuable
deposits of iron. Bunter's defeat was made even more enjoyable by

---

[13] Augustus William Dubourg, 1830–1910, was the great-grandson of the violinist who
led the orchestra for the first performance of Handel's *Messiah*. He worked as a clerk in the
House of Lords, published one novel, 1877, and wrote or collaborated in fourteen stage-
plays, 1866–92.

touches of satire. He had reason to call Lady Matilda 'a disgustin' hippercrit'; but he himself was a sanctimonious Dissenter, who had shown his 'Cheristian principles' by donating a consignment of sub-standard bricks towards the building of a chapel. The upper classes, too, were satirized. Lilian's slang-phrases were condemned by the middle-class Brown as 'rather strong expressions for a lady', and her cousin Bertie Fitz-Urse, who might have become Lord Bearholm, was quite uneducated. Still, he hoped that family influence would get him into the Foreign Office: 'None but swells at the F.O.—come at one and go at seven. Asked everywhere—up to everything. There's only one thing: F.O. is so deucedly expensive. Salary won't keep a fellow in cigars and eau de cologne.'

The more intellectual character of this comedy showed up the weak side of Robertson's theatrical successes. The weakest and most successful of these was *School* (also 1869). Based on a German dramatization of the Cinderella myth, it described the amorous results of a visit to a girls' school by two young men. Its chief interest now is that the unpleasant teacher, Krux, was modelled on a former colleague of Robertson's in a school at Utrecht. Its best piece of comic invention was making a stock character, that of the elderly dandy Beau Farintosh, extremely short-sighted.

In *Birth* (1870) Robertson reworked his old themes, class-prejudice and the conflict between industrialists and the landed aristocracy. The conflict was symbolized, as in Harriet Martineau's 'The Hill and the Valley', by the setting. Paul Hewitt and his sister ran a factory in the valley, while the Earl of Eagleclyffe and his sister lived in a castle on the hill. The class-war was intensified by an ancient feud between the families, but eventually ended by intermarriage. Robertson had nothing new to say about the contemporary issue, but produced a theatrical novelty in the character of Jack Randall. This friend of both families, who had lost all his money and now planned to earn a living by 'literature', was apparently meant to stress the literary aspect of the play. He compared the family feud to the one in *Romeo and Juliet*, and the castle ghost to Wilkie Collins's *The Woman in White*. He even quoted at length from Byron's *Don Juan*, while pretending to describe the Earl's 'splendid conduct' in the Crimean War. Pirandello's 'six characters' would be in search of an author, but

Jack was an author in search of a plot. Having decided to 'write a comedy ... *au naturel* ... I mean, to write raw! from the life', he went about with a notebook taking down each 'capital incident' in the Hewitt-Eagleclyffe saga, and commenting on its dramatic possibilities. Thus Robertson's play and Jack's projected play became practically the same thing, and the chief question raised was: what kind of a play was it? In the course of the denouement, factory-workers invaded the castle, threatening to lynch the Earl for the supposed murder of Paul Hewitt, who then appeared 'with his arm in a sling', to be formally asked by the Earl for his 'sister's hand in marriage'. 'Capital!' said Jack, taking notes and wiping his eyes. 'Very effective comedy—no, melodrama—no, bother!' The status of *Birth* remains questionable. As a piece of experimental theatre it anticipated anti-illusionist trends in modern drama; but it also suggested a decline in Robertson's creativity, by its return to old plot-material, and a narrowing of his interests, by its abandonment of social criticism for criticism of the theatre. As a kind of self-parody, however, it still reads amusingly.

In 1866 Robertson had encouraged William Schwenck Gilbert to start writing plays.[14] Gilbert said he had learned a great deal from his friend, especially 'how to give life and variety and nature to the scene by breaking it up with all sorts of little incidents and delicate by-play', but his first great success, *The Palace of Truth* (1870), was hardly in Robertson's line. It was a 'fairy comedy' in blank verse, with the fantastic wit and cynicism of the *Bab Ballads* (1869). All who entered the Palace were unconsciously impelled to speak the truth (unless they carried a special crystal box, of which an ineffective replica also existed). The results were sometimes quite funny, as when a courtier heard the Princess singing:

> Oh, I protest, my ears have never heard
> A goodly song more miserably sung.
> [*Clapping hands*] Oh, very poor indeed—oh, very weak;
> No voice—no execution—out of tune—
> Pretentious too—oh, very, very poor!
> [*Applauding as if in ecstasies*]

[14] Sir William Schwenck Gilbert, 1836–1911, was born in London, the son of a retired naval surgeon, who had written poetry and later published novels. A much-travelled baby, he was kidnapped by brigands at Naples, and ransomed for £25. His pet-name, 'Bab', became his pseudonym. He went to King's College, London, worked as a barrister, then started publishing comic verse with his own illustrations, chiefly in *Fun*. The *Bab Ballads* started appearing in 1866, and were collected in 1869. His first theatrical piece was a burlesque, 1866. His collaboration with Arthur Sullivan began with *Thespis*, 1871.

It transpired that only two of the characters were sincere. Even the King, who owned both the Palace and the crystal box, had no scruples about deceiving his wife.

Sweethearts: An Original Dramatic Contrast (1874) was more clearly influenced by Robertson. It juxtaposed two conversations separated by an interval of thirty years. In the first the young 'sweethearts' planted a sycamore in the garden where they had played together as children. Harry, about to leave for India, tried to get some response to his love for Jenny; but she, partly to tease him and partly from pique at not being told of his departure sooner, concealed her own feeling by flippant small-talk. In the second act Jenny had to put on her spectacles, and Harry a double eye-glass, before they could recognize each other. Harry, when reminded of it, claimed to have an 'absolutely photographic' memory of their farewell-scene, but insisted that he had given her a camellia, not a rose:

Nonsense, Jane—come, come, you hardly looked at it, miserable little flirt that you were; and you pretend, after thirty years, to stake your recollection of the circumstance against mine? No, no, Jane, take my word for it, it was a camellia.

In a beautifully contrived climax to the argument, Jenny produced 'a withered rose from a pocket-book'. Thus, with an irony subtler than Robertson's, Gilbert echoed the sad realism of *Ours*.

He then parodied, in a 'Farcical Comedy', *Tom Cobb* (1875), Robertson's pictorial allusion. The 'romantic' Effinghams were posed to resemble not a painting by Millais but a family photograph, with Caroline 'seated in a picturesque attitude ... and Bulstrode standing gloomily behind'. Caroline, 'a romantic-looking young lady, with long curls and gushing, poetical demeanour', was like a caricature of Eva. She fell in love with 'the soul', as expressed in his poems, of a Major-General in India, became engaged to him by correspondence, and later decided to sue him for breach of promise. Parody, however, was only one element in the creation of pure nonsense. This took the form of zany dialogue, and an ingeniously incredible plot, about a young surgeon who, having pretended to be dead, was discouraged by everyone from coming back to life. When he tried to kiss his own fiancée, he was sternly reprimanded by another surgeon:

Sir, misled by a resemblance which I admit to be striking, you have come

here under the impression that you are my departed friend. I can excuse
the error; but now that it's been pointed out to you, if ever you attempt to
embrace this young lady, I'll break your leg and set it myself.

The farce ended on the same note as Lytton's *Money*. Asked if
she could still love Tom 'as a wealthy but unromantic apothecary',
Caroline replied, 'I can love you as a wealthy anything!' The note
was repeated in Gilbert's best play, *Engaged* (1877). 'What a
terrible thing is this incessant craving after money!' said Symperson, shocked at his daughter's refusal to earn him two thousand
pounds by marrying a man that she thought had lost all his money.
The comic effect was to be achieved by making such blatant
hypocrisy sound unconscious. A Note by Gilbert directed that 'the
characters, one and all, should appear to believe, throughout, in
the perfect sincerity of their words and actions.' The universal
hypocrisy applied to sentiments as well as moral principles.
Having told Belvawney that she loved him 'with an imperishable
ardour which mocks the power of words', Miss Treherne went on:

But ... business is business, and unless I can see some distinct
probability that your income will be permanent, I shall have no
alternative but to weep my heart out in all the anguish of maiden
solitude—uncared for, unloved, and alone!

As this hint of Gwendolen suggests, *Engaged* was a milestone on
the road from Robertson to Wilde. Its 'peasant lad' Angus
Macalister, named after the hero of *Ours*, was a wrecker of trains in
pursuit of 'sic chance custom as the poor delayed passengers'
might bring to his cottage. His pastoral love for Maggie did not
prevent him from selling her to one such passenger for the sum of
two pounds. Like Jack after killing off 'poor' Ernest, Belinda
Treherne appeared in deep mourning, and then showed an
appetite for tarts as keen as Algernon's for muffins. The mercenary
philanderer Belvawney developed, like Bunbury, into a disrepu-
table verb. And Symperson's advice to his daughter on marriage
stood midway between the Shendryns' bickering and Lady Bracknell's boast never to have undeceived her husband on any
question:

If you would be truly happy in the married state, be sure you have your
own way in everything. Brook no contradictions. Never yield to outside
pressure. Give in to no argument. Admit no appeal. However wrong you

may be, maintain a firm, resolute, and determined front. These were your angel mother's principles through life, and she was a happy woman indeed. I neglected these principles, and while she lived I was a miserable wretch.

For all its brilliance, *Engaged* was disliked in its day for its heartless cynicism; and satire so purely destructive needed something like the verse-form of the *Bab Ballads* to make it sympathetic. This was supplied by Sullivan's music in the Savoy Operas (1875–96), where the spiteful and almost sadistic character of Gilbert's wit was obscured by the warmth and gaiety of the musical settings. So the libretti tend to fail Jones's test of reading well. Of course, there is pleasure to be got from the prosodic virtuosity of some lyrics, from the plots' exuberant defiance of probability, and from passages of prose dialogue where even unpleasant jokes may flower into a sort of nonsense poetry. Thus Gilbert's love of jeering at plain or elderly women does not wholly spoil the beauty of Katisha's speech in *The Mikado*:

You hold that I am not beautiful because my face is plain. But you know nothing; you are still unenlightened. Learn, then, that it is not in the face alone that beauty is to be sought. But I have a left shoulder-blade that is a miracle of loveliness. People come miles to see it. My right elbow has a fascination that few can resist. It is on view Tuesdays and Fridays, on presentation of visiting-card. As for my circulation, it is the largest in the world.

In themselves, the libretti are chiefly interesting for their satire on everything established, conventional, or fashionable: on marriage, the Church, commercial advertising, democracy, egalitarianism, humanitarianism, Evangelicalism, respectability, the armed forces, the Civil Service, Aesthetic poetry, melodrama, and the whole system of law and government, including the monarchy. When *The Pirates of Penzance* had the police at their mercy, they were instantly reduced to tears and submission by 'Queen Victoria's name.' In 1885, while the Poet Laureate celebrated the wedding of Princess Beatrice, 'True daughter, whose all-faithful, filial eyes | Have seen the loneliness of earthly thrones', this was Gilbert's contribution to the occasion:

MIKADO. From every kind of man
        Obedience I expect;
        I'm the Emperor of Japan.

KATISHA. And I'm his daughter-in-law elect!
        He'll marry his son
        (He has only got one)
        To his daughter-in-law elect.
MIKADO. My morals have been declared
        Particularly correct;
KATISHA. But they're nothing at all, compared
        With those of his daughter-in-law elect!
        Bow! Bow!
        To his daughter-in-law elect!

While Gilbert had been raising farce to a new level, H. A. Jones had been doing the same thing for melodrama. *The Silver King* (1882), in which Henry Herman collaborated, used the basic formula of *The Ticket-of-Leave Man*, by which an innocent man got involved with criminals, but finally struggled free with the help of a kindly detective.[15] Here, however, the exciting plot was complicated by Denver's unawareness of his own innocence. Since he had been drunk at the time, and remembered later that he had gone off to the murdered man's house in a fit of jealous rage, he assumed that he was indeed the murderer. The arrest of the real murderer, Skinner, was reserved for a traditionally melodramatic denouement:

SKINNER. Mr Baxter, do your duty and arrest the murderer of Geoffrey Ware.
BAXTER. Very well . . .

                                       [puts handcuffs on Skinner

There was plenty of pity as well as terror in Denver's previous adventures, especially when, still wanted by the police, he talked to his small daughter Cissy, without saying who he was. The feeling in such passages may now seem somewhat contrived, but Matthew Arnold did not greatly exaggerate when he wrote that 'in general throughout the piece the diction and sentiments are natural, they have sobriety and propriety, they are literature.' The lack of 'lubricity' that he found in the play may have made him over-

[15] Henry Arthur Jones, 1851–1929, was born at Grandborough, Buckinghamshire, the son of a farmer of Welsh descent. He left school at Winslow at the age of twelve, to work as a draper's assistant and warehouseman, then as a commercial traveller, until his first play was produced at Exeter, 1878. *The Silver King* was his first London success. Henry Herman, 1832–94, was educated in Alsace, then went to America, and lost an eye fighting in the Civil War. He produced his first play in London in 1875, and went on to write many other plays and also novels.

enthusiastic; but at least it was, as he said, a 'hopeful sign to find playwrights capable of writing in this style, actors capable of rendering it, and a public capable of enjoying it.'

Jones's *Saints and Sinners* (1884) must have appealed to Arnold even more, since its villains, Prabble and Hoggard, were Dissenting Philistines, who tried to use their influence over a chapel congregation to further their commercial ends. Prabble, a small grocer who was being undersold by the local Stores, was outraged when his Minister, Jacob Fletcher, refused to preach against them: 'If I support your chapel, I expect you to get the congregation to support my shop. That's only fair.' Hoggard threatened to sack the Minister, unless he connived at a financial fraud. Fletcher, an admirable yet quite believable character, defied this threat, but then had to resist blackmail when his daughter Letty was tricked into living with the unscrupulous Captain Fanshawe. The seduction theme was a relic of early melodrama, and the diction corresponded: 'Worse than death?' asks Letty's true lover. 'There is but one thing worse than death. Is it that?' Fanshawe, however, was a fairly lifelike character, and the message implied by the title, that sexual sinners might be better people than self-righteous puritans, was effectively dramatized in the scene where the Minister, before resigning, made a final appeal to his congregation. Letty proved her sainthood by working herself to death as a nurse in an epidemic. The news that she and her father had finally been 'forgiven' by the congregation came too late either to save her life, or to make her feel less guilty. As she 'shrieked' in her delirium: 'Yes—I have sinned, but can you never forgive me? I have tried so hard to live it down. Oh you Christians, will you never learn to forgive?'

From such beginnings in melodrama, Jones went on to represent the 'theatre of ideas' in the period covered by the next volume. Another playwright who straddled the two periods was Arthur Wing Pinero.[16] He began as a writer of farce. *The*

---

[6] Arthur Wing Pinero, 1855–1934, was born at Islington, London, the son of a solicitor of Portuguese-Jewish descent. Spasmodically educated in private schools and at evening classes in the Birkbeck Institute (now Birkbeck College), he studied law from the age of ten in his father's office, but wanted to be an actor. His first stage appearance was in Edinburgh, 1874. Happily mistaken for another actor, he was given a part in a London production, 1876, then toured playing the King to Henry Irving's Hamlet, and was described by a Birmingham critic as 'the worst Claudius the city has ever seen.' His first play was produced at the Globe in 1877, and *The Magistrate* made him popular.

Magistrate (1885) incorporated elements of slapstick from such pieces as *The Area Belle*, which had exploited the humour of unsuitable hiding-places like cupboards, coppers, or under tables. Here one character had to stand on an unsafe balcony in pouring rain, while a dinner-party went on indoors; and the hilarious scene ended with six guests in evening dress crouching in the dark under a table, while a policemen with a lantern listened to find out how many people were breathing. But the main source of comic effect was subtler: All those hiding were intent on maintaining their dignity or keeping up appearances. The paradox was underlined when the Magistrate turned up in court next morning, in muddy evening dress, tieless, and with 'a small strip of black plaster' across his nose, to pass judgement on his wife and the others who had shared his hiding-place. Though the plot was farcical, the play touched on the serious theme of *Measure for Measure*, that judges are only human; and as a human being, middle-class, professional, and relatively conscientious, Mr Posket was perfectly credible. He thus illustrated Pinero's theory of farce, expounded in a note to *The Cabinet Minister* (1890):

Thus Mr. Pinero holds that farce should treat of probable people placed in possible circumstances, but regarded from a point of view which exaggerates their sentiments and magnifies their foibles. In this light it is permitted to this type of play, not only to deal with ridiculous incongruities of incident and character, but to satirize society, and to wring laughter from those possible distresses of life which might trace their origin to fallacies of feeling and extravagances of motive.

Having thus made farce serious, Pinero proceeded to turn melodrama into the 'problem play'. Like *Lady Audley's Secret*, *The Second Mrs. Tanqueray* (1893) was about a woman with an inconvenient past: her previous lovers included the young man that her husband's daughter by his first marriage wanted to marry. But this melodramatic situation was used to question the prevailing sexual ethic, and Paula Tanqueray's character was brilliantly conceived and horribly lifelike. To Hedda Gabler's neurotic aggressiveness and discontent she added a kind of tragic philosophy: 'I believe the future is only the past again, entered through another gate.'

20. Children's Books

This large section of the period's output has of late been much researched; but two broad statements made by experts in the field need taking with a pinch of salt. One is that most of these books are not 'literature', only interesting social documents. The average standard of writing was in fact quite high, perhaps because the authors felt obliged to express themselves briefly and simply. They showed, as a class, no less imagination than contemporary poets or novelists, and were often more skilled at manipulating their readers' emotions. Their observation of adult as well as juvenile behaviour was generally acute, and their criticism of life was not necessarily superficial or immature. If their works be not literature, a Dr Johnson might well ask, where is literature to be found?

The other statement is that children's literature developed during the nineteenth century from books intended, in Mrs Trimmer's words, 'to improve the heart' and 'cultivate the understanding', to books meant simply to entertain the young. Certainly the development began with a reaction against the didacticism of Maria Edgeworth's *Early Lessons* (1801), against the moral tales recommended by Mrs Trimmer's *Guardian of Education* (1802–5), and against her condemnation of fairy-tales, especially after the Grimms' *Kinder- und Hausmärchen* and Andersen's *Eventyr fortalte for Børn* had started appearing in English (1823, 1846). But, except in the Nonsense of Lear and Carroll, didacticism remained a constant element in children's books. What changed and became more sophisticated was the didactic technique. A critic observed in the *Quarterly Review* (1860):

At present so many ingenious devices have been discovered for insinuating moral or scientific truths into story-books, that children are never safe. The pleasant picture of a fireside, and the most promising anecdote or conversation of some children with their papa, are too often only the prelude to a conversation on chemistry ... Children are so often entrapped in this way that they learn to suspect that the inevitable schoolmaster is lying *perdu* under every variety of innocent disguise.

The schoolmaster and the parson were still there when the period ended. Henty claimed that *The Young Buglers* (1880) would enable

a boy 'to pass an examination as to the leading events of the
Peninsular War'. Mrs Ewing's 'Daddy Darwin's Dovecote' (1881)
was a moral tale about the conversion of a misanthropic miser into
a good Christian. George MacDonald's *The Princess and Curdie*
(1877) began with a moral awakening: 'I was doing the wrong of
never wanting or trying to be better.' And Carroll's *Sylvie and
Bruno* (1889) featured 'one of the Fairies that teach children to be
good'.

The first children's book of the period that was fun to read was
Catherine Sinclair's *Holiday House* (1839).[1] Here she tried to
portray not prize pupils or little saints but

that species of noisy, frolicsome, mischievous children, now almost
extinct, wishing to preserve a sort of fabulous remembrance of days long
past, when young people were like wild horses on the prairies, rather than
like well-broken hacks on the road.

Miss Edgeworth's Harry and Lucy liked nothing better than being
told by Papa how a thermometer worked. Miss Sinclair's Harry
preferred playing with a lighted candle, setting fire to a bedroom,
and then shutting the door so that the flames should not be seen.
Her Laura, equally full of scientific curiosity, experimented with a
pair of scissors that she had been 'positively forbid to touch', until
she had cut off all her hair. Their greatest friend was their nice
Uncle David, who treated such tiresome behaviour as a joke, and
generally undermined their strict nurse's authority. His faith,
shared by the author, was that however naughty the children were,
they were good at heart, and needed only gentle guidance to
develop into admirable adults. The theory was confirmed by their
elder brother Frank who, thanks to the influence of 'his kind, good
mamma' before she died, became a saintly midshipman, whose
premature but edifying death turned Harry and Laura from
'merry, thoughtless young creatures' into sadder and wiser ones,
alerted to 'the frailty of all earthly joy' and 'the importance of
religion'. Frank was modelled on the author's 'deeply loved and

---

[1] Catherine Sinclair, 1800–64, was the daughter of a landowner and politician who
became first president of the board of agriculture, and published thirty-nine books,
including one tragedy, and 367 pamphlets. Until his death, 1835, she worked as his
secretary, and published only a conventional children's book about a good aunt and a bad
aunt. After *Holiday House* she wrote adult novels, until her very successful *Picture Letters*
for children, 1861–4.

deeply lamented' brother, and her grief may be felt to excuse the lachrymose sermonizing with which the book ended.

The element of play, which had dominated the rest of *Holiday House*, was minimal in Harriet Martineau's *The Playfellow* (1841).[2] This contained early specimens of the *Coral Island* situation, and of the school story, in neither of which was the 'schoolmaster' *perdu*. Felix Summerly's (i.e. Henry Cole's) *The Home Treasury*, a series started in 1843, was designed to be equally educational, but in a different way.[3] Protesting against the purely intellectual syllabus of the Peter Parley books by the American S. G. Goodrich and his English imitators, Cole set out to cultivate 'the other and certainly not less important elements of a little child's mind, its fancy, imagination, sympathies, affections', by publishing well-illustrated editions of traditional fairy-tales and nursery-rhymes. The rehabilitation of fancy and imagination went much further in 1846 with the appearance of Lear's *Book of Nonsense*, Mary Howitt's *Wonderful Stories for Children* (translated from Hans Andersen), and her friend R. H. Horne's *Memoirs of a London Doll, Written by Herself. Edited by Mrs Fairstar* (an apt pseudonym for the author of *Orion*).[4] This delightful work traced the progress of a wooden doll from a workshop in High Holborn, through a series of homes with various child-'mammas', to a country house where, with every luxury and a most attentive mamma, she felt comfortably 'settled for life'. Her progress gave her experience of several social classes, and Horne, who had helped to prepare the report on conditions of child employment that inspired 'The Cry of the Children', described in one harrowing chapter how badly 'The Little Milliners' were treated. Mrs Browning praised the book, but complained of 'one great omission': that it failed to cater for the child's 'sense of God'. For this he might surely have blamed his persona. Certainly his social criticism gained force from the wooden objectivity of the narrator. So far as the perspective was human at all, it was convincingly

---

[2] See Chap. 14.

[3] Sir Henry Cole, 1808–82, was born at Bath, the son of a captain in the Dragoons. He worked in the Public Record Office, sat on the committee of the Great Exhibition, 1851, and founded the museum that became the Victoria and Albert.

[4] Edward Lear, 1812–88. For Lear's Nonsense see Chap. 21. Mary Howitt, née Botham, 1799–1888, became popular as a children's poet. Her 'Will you walk into my parlour?' inspired the Mock Turtle's song in Lewis Carroll's *Alice's Adventures in Wonderland*. Richard Henry or Hengist Horne, 1802–84. For his poetry see Chap. 9.

childlike. 'Look there, dear!' said one mamma, pointing to a statue in Hyde Park, '. . . that is the strongest and largest doll ever seen in London. His name is "Achilles,"—and the ladies of London had him made of iron and brass, because the Duke of Wellington was so lucky in playing at ball on the fields of Waterloo!'

In other mid-century books for, or much read by, English children, the sense of God was pervasive. The heroine of *The Wide, Wide World* (1850) spent much of her time reading the Bible, learning hymns, and struggling against great obstacles 'to be a Christian'. *Uncle Tom's Cabin* (1851–2) was almost as much a religious as an abolitionist tract. Ruskin's *The King of the Golden River* (1851) took advantage of the new interest in fairy-tales to preach the old Christian ethic of unselfishness. Charlotte Yonge's *The Heir of Redclyffe* (1853), written under Keble's influence, had an equally exemplary plot. It ended with the Heir forgiving his cousin's malice, nursing him through a fever, catching it himself, and thus dying a martyr to his faith.[5]

That novel was meant for adults but became popular with children. Thackeray's 'Fireside Pantomime', *The Rose and the Ring* (1855) was meant for both classes of reader or, as on the title-page, 'for Great and Small Children'.[6] The adults were offered incidental satire on monarchy, politics, the Crimean War, the novels of G. P. R. James, and conventional morality: 'Then came an empty cart, returning from market; and the driver being a kind man, and seeing such a very pretty girl trudging along the road with bare feet, most good-naturedly gave her a seat.' The children were offered an exciting story, amusingly told in a quasi-impromptu style, full of nonsensical hyperbole, as when an owl and a cat, the only creatures that could see Rosalba in the darkness of her dungeon, immediately fell in love with her, and 'the toads . . . came and kissed her feet, and the vipers wound round her neck and arms, and never hurt her, so charming was this poor Princess in

---

[5] *The Wide, Wide World* was by 'Elizabeth Wetherell', i.e. Susan Bogert Warner, 1819–85. *Uncle Tom's Cabin* was by Mrs Harriet Elizabeth Beecher Stowe, 1811–96. For *The King of the Golden River* see Chap. 12. Charlotte Mary Yonge, 1823–1901, the daughter of an ex-army officer, was born and spent all her life at Otterbourne, Hampshire. She was much influenced by the Tractarian John Keble, who became vicar of Hursley, then the same parish as Otterbourne, when she was twelve. As a novelist, she belongs to another volume. For Keble see Chaps. 9 and 15.

[6] William Makepeace Thackeray, 1811–63. For his travel-writing and his parodies see Chaps. 18 and 21.

the midst of her misfortunes.' But the last word underlined the moral of the piece, pronounced over Rosalba's cradle by the Fairy Blackstick: 'as for this little lady, the best thing I can wish her is a *little misfortune.*' Thus the whole piece could be read as a Trimmeresque moral tale, a warning for spoilt children against laziness and conceit. It could also be read as a parody of a moral tale. To make up for his idleness as a child, Prince Giglio worked so hard at the University of Bosforo, i.e. Oxford, that his rhetoric was enough to subdue an army of thirty thousand men:

... stepping well forward on to the balcony, the royal youth, *without preparation*, delivered a speech so magnificent, that no report can do justice to it. It was all in blank verse (in which, from this time, he invariably spoke, as more becoming his majestic station). It lasted for three days and three nights, during which not a single person who heard him was tired, or remarked the difference between daylight and dark ... Such were the consequences of having employed his time well at College!

Despite such ridicule, didactic stories for children remained popular. Mrs Gatty's *Parables from Nature* (1855–71) showed how gracefully and charmingly this sort of thing could still be done.[7] In prose that precisely captured the tone of an affectionate mother telling a small child a bedtime story, she gave elementary instruction in religion, morality, and science. Faith in a future life was encouraged by a fable of a caterpillar who refused to believe that it would ever become a butterfly. The need for obedience was shown by the chaos created in a hive by some egalitarian bees. Cheerfulness and hope were embodied in a robin who, against the advice of a tortoise, stayed awake and kept singing through a hard winter. Meteorology was anthropomorphized, as by Shelley in 'The Cloud', in a speech by 'the Vapours':

Behold, we pour into the earth as rain, or slide into it as moisture; and lo, the soil gives its gases into our care, and the roots of the plants draw us and them up together, and feeding on them, expand and flourish, and grow; and when the useful deed is done, and the sun shines down on our labour, up we ascend to its absorbing rays, to be carried forward again and again, to other gracious deeds.

[7] Margaret Gatty, née Scott, 1809–73, was born at Burnham, Essex, the daughter of a bibliophile clergyman who had been Nelson's chaplain in the *Victory*, and who brought her up when her mother died, two years later. In 1839 she married the vicar of Ecclesfield, Yorkshire, where she spent the rest of her life. Her first children's book, *The Fairy Godmothers*, came out in 1851.

Later *Parables*, if less suitable for children, had a more interesting message. In 'Imperfect Instruments', a short story reminiscent of Herbert's poetry, a young curate's intolerance of human weakness was associated with his assumption that an organ could be tuned in perfect fifths and fourths.

The parabolic method was applied more loosely to Greek myths in Kingsley's *The Heroes* (1856).[8] Nathaniel Hawthorne had described these myths as 'brimming over with everything that is most abhorrent to our Christianised moral sense', but Kingsley gave them a meaning which 'is true, and true for ever, and that is—"Do right, and God will help you."' This generalized interpretation relieved him of the duty to expurgate, when retelling the stories of Perseus, Jason, and Theseus as if to his own three children, though he mentioned Medea's revenge only as 'too terrible to speak of here'. Denying that the Argonauts had gone off merely in search of gold, he credited them with the instinct for selfless service that had motivated Jesus, the Apostles, English explorers, and the soldiers and nurses in the Crimean War: 'No, children, there is a better thing on earth than wealth, a better thing than life itself; and that is, to have done something before you die, for which good men may honour you, and God your Father smile upon your work.'

The pursuit of wealth was similarly disparaged in Frances Browne's *Granny's Wonderful Chair and its tales of Fairy Times* (1856).[9] This ended with King Winwealth's unpleasant wife and daughter, Wantall and Greedalind, grubbing for gold at the bottom of a deep pit, while Prince Wisewit, released from a spell that had turned him into a white pigeon, set to work to 'make all things right again' in the kingdom. As a pigeon, he had been shut up under the cushion of the wonderful chair, and had expressed his anti-plutocratic wisdom through a series of stories, each of which had made a moral point. Though the proper names suggest a crude form of didacticism, the stories were compellingly written, and their symbolism was highly imaginative. Among the book's memorable images was that of the old man in 'The Story of Merrymind', who kept marching round a valley where nobody did

---

[8] Charles Kingsley, 1819–75. For his poetry and his clash with Newman see Chaps. 9 and 11.

[9] Frances Browne, 1816–79, was born in Donegal. Blinded by smallpox when a baby, she managed to earn her living in London by writing, especially for the *Leisure Hour* magazine. She published fifteen other books, including poems and novels.

anything but work, carrying a huge pannier of dust. It is easy to understand how Frances Hodgson Burnett, having read the work as a child, and found no trace of its survival, was able to rewrite part of it from memory, for publication in an American magazine (1887).[10]

Few children would remember with such pleasure either Thomas Hughes's *Tom Brown's Schooldays* or Mrs Gatty's *Proverbs Illustrated* (both 1857).[11] The first, based on personal experience of life at Rugby, is interesting historically; but the passages that stick in the memory are examples of bullying, of 'fighting with fists' as 'the natural and English way for English boys to settle their quarrels', and of thrashing, as the best way to turn a bully into 'a very good fellow' and 'a credit to his School'. The same faith in flogging infected even Mrs Gatty's *Proverbs*. As the 'delicate, wayward, and spoilt' narrator of 'The Footstep on the Stairs' put it: 'My uncle flogged me that night, with no pity for my weakness and no respect for my mother's tears. He told me he stood in my father's place, and he would not have the sin of Eli on his head. And he was right.' The boy's subsequent history suggested otherwise, for he became a drunkard, and nearly killed a man in a panic explicitly linked with that early traumatic experience. But Mrs Gatty seemed blind to the logic of her own story, perhaps because she was more concerned with its ingenious structure. This was based on the recurrence of the 'footstep' in different contexts. The last time the narrator heard it, he thought it was 'the Doctor come to tell me—me, the reckless, intemperate fool—that I must die!' In fact, the doctor judged his case 'not hopeless—quite', a verdict applicable to the tale itself.

Corporal punishment was even more prominent in Farrar's *Eric, or Little by Little: A Tale of Rosslyn School* (1858).[12] After several canings, the first 'excruciating' and quite undeserved, Eric took to drink, and started on a downward slope which finally led to

---

[10] For her own *Little Lord Fauntleroy* see below.

[11] Thomas Hughes, 1822–96, was born at Uffington, Berkshire, the son of a travel-writer and poet. He went to Rugby under Dr Arnold, and Oriel College, Oxford. With F. D. Maurice he supported working-men's education and Christian Socialism. His view of life was nicknamed 'muscular Christianity'.

[12] Frederick William Farrar, 1831–1903, was born in India, the son of a missionary. He went to King William's College, Isle of Man, and Trinity College, Cambridge, where he got a fellowship. After teaching at Marlborough, he was ordained and became a housemaster at Harrow. From 1871 he was headmaster of Marlborough, and from 1895 dean of Canterbury. Besides sermons and theology he published two historical novels.

his death, after a brutal lashing with a rope-end on board a ship. Yet his moral decline was attributed not to the way he was treated but to his love of popularity, which made him 'follow the multitude to do evil'. Based on the author's experience both as a schoolboy in the Isle of Man and as a master at Marlborough and Harrow, the book showed some efforts towards realism. Farrar recognized, for instance, 'that there must be in boyhood a pseudo-instinctive cruelty', touched darkly on the problem of sex, and even hinted, in Eric's friendship with 'little Wildney', at the threat of homosexuality. He also told his story rather well, especially in 'The Adventure of the Stack'. Still, *Eric* was a very sick book. Farrar later explained its excessive 'lacrimosity' as arising from 'the state of mind in which [he] wrote it'; but it suffered much more from an unpleasant blend of religiosity with a near-sadistic tolerance of physical cruelty.

The morality of another moral tale published that year, A.L.O.E.'s *The Story of a Needle*, was less dubious.[13] This fanciful autobiography preached service and consideration for others, along with some scientific information, chiefly about metals. Having explained the process of her manufacture, the Needle recorded conversations with a conceited pair of Scissors, and a sweet-tempered silver Thimble. She also told the story of a spoilt and tiresome brother and sister, their thoughtful and industrious elder brother, their overworked mother, and their gloomy and rather insensitive father. The mother was portrayed quite realistically: coping with the constant demands of her two small children, while listening for sounds of trouble from the baby upstairs, and trying to deal with household bills. The older brother was a little too good to be true, but creative enough to invent an edifying fairy tale for the benefit of his juniors about a Prince and Princess who learned 'how great is the value of time, and opportunity to do some good to others', by being turned for seven years into a compass and a needle.

Even seen through the eye of a needle, the picture of the older boy telling stories, while his small brother and sister helped him

[13] A.L.O.E. (= 'A Lady of England') was Charlotte Maria Tucker, 1821–93. She was born at Barnet, the daughter of an ex-Indian Civil Servant who had become an East India Company director despite having spent six months in prison for attempted rape, and refusing to support missionary work in India. Educated at home, she became a workhouse visitor, but published nothing until her father died. She then produced 142 separate works. In 1875 she went as a missionary to India, where she worked until her death at Amritsar.

wind a skein of wool, was a pleasant one; and a similar picture in real life had inspired Mrs Gatty's *Aunt Judy's Tales* (1858): 'There is not a more charming sight in the domestic world, than that of the elder girl in a large family, amusing what are called *the little ones*.' Mrs Gatty was thinking of her own daughter Juliana Horatia, whose family nickname was Aunt Judy, and whose married name would be Ewing. The stories here attributed to her, like the accounts of their contexts and of audience reactions, were entertainingly educational. They made fun of children who grumbled at being made to wash their hands or go to bed; encouraged consideration for servants by a dramatic monologue expressing the cook's point of view; discouraged No. 8's tendency to get under people's feet when they were busy by a tale of a conceited young German who was 'always thrusting himself forward, and always getting pushed back in consequence'; and answered the complaint that there was 'nothing to do' with an Eastern fable posing the social problem of real unemployment. The book made ample amends for *Proverbs Illustrated*, and achieved the liveliness of *Holiday House*, but with subtler humour and more convincing dialogue.

The middle-class nursery was replaced in R. M. Ballantyne's *The Coral Island* (1858) by a world of cannibals and pirates, but here again the purpose was educational.[14] The Preface promised 'valuable information, much pleasure, great profit, and unbounded amusement'. The information was mostly about natural history, geology, and anthropology in the Pacific islands; the profit was both moral and religious. When shipwrecked on a desert island, the three boys instantly resolved to make the best of it. 'I have made up my mind', said Peterkin, 'that it's capital—first rate—the best thing that ever happened to us, and the most splendid prospect that ever lay before three jolly young tars.' Coping resourcefully with the practical problems of survival, they also devised a method of calculating which day was the Sabbath, and observing it as a day of rest. Though Ralph's Bible had gone down

[14] Robert Michael Ballantyne, 1825–94, was born in Edinburgh, the son of a newspaper proprietor whose brother printed Scott's novels. When the Ballantynes were involved in Scott's financial problems, Robert was taken away from school at sixteen and sent off to Canada, as an apprentice in the Hudson Bay Company. In 1848 he published a diary of his life there, and in 1856 an adventure story based on his experiences, *The Young Fur-Traders*. Encouraged by its success, he wrote a series of similar books, for which he deliberately acquired the relevant experience. *Coral Island* was his most popular and influential work.

with the ship, he always said his prayers, and was later able to quote two biblical texts from memory to comfort the pirate, Bloody Bill, when he was dying, penitent but doubtful of his salvation. The scenery often turned Ralph's 'thoughts to the great and kind Creator of this beautiful world', and the book ended with a splendid advertisement for the London Missionary Society: when about to be slaughtered by cannibals, the boys were saved in the nick of time by an English missionary, who promptly converted the whole tribe to Christianity. Having supervised a bonfire of native idols, the three returned to England on the pirate ship— which Ralph had earlier sailed single-handed, although with 'a most imperfect knowledge of navigation, and in a schooner requiring at least eight men for her proper crew'. Their adventures, which were sometimes plausibly melodramatic, included such horrific incidents as the launching of a native canoe over living human bodies: 'Oh, reader, this is no fiction. I could not, for the sake of thrilling you with horror, invent so terrible a scene.'

Whether fiction or fact, it seems hardly suitable in a children's book, and the same may be said of the sexual undertones in Christina Rossetti's fairy-story, *Goblin Market* (1862), and of the powerful image of mortality in Mrs Ewing's *Melchior's Dream*, published the same year.[15] Here a family was pictured as riding in a coach at high speed along a crowded road. Every so often, a brother or sister would get out, and disappear in the crowd, or be suddenly led off by 'a figure wrapped in a cloak, gliding in and out among the people, unnoticed, if not unseen.' But this disturbing 'Allegory' was delicately adapted to its context and its purpose, which was to educate a self-centred elder brother, who had just exclaimed, 'I wish there were no such things as brothers and sisters!' He was already cynical about improving literature:

I don't like stories like tracts ... There was an usher at a school I was at, and he used to read tracts about good boys and bad boys to the fellows on Sunday afternoon. He always took out the real names, and put in the names of the fellows instead ... He didn't like me, and I was always put in as a bad boy, and I came to so many untimely ends I got sick of it. I

[15] For *Goblin Market* see Chap. 7. Juliana Horatia Ewing, 1841–85, was born at Ecclesfield, Yorkshire, the daughter of Mrs Gatty, her second name referring to her grandfather's connection with Nelson. She showed an early interest not only in story-telling but in modern languages and classical literature. In 1867 she married a major in the army pay department, who published translations from Turkish and German. After two years in Canada, she lived at Aldershot and elsewhere in England. She died at Bath.

was hanged twice, and transported once for sheep-stealing; I committed suicide one week, and broke into the bank the next; I ruined three families, became a hopeless drunkard, and broke the hearts of twelve distinct parents.

He yielded, however, to Mrs Ewing's more oblique type ot didacticism, and most adult readers, too, will find her stories irresistible. Their 'whole tone and aim', according to her mother, was 'so unmistakably high, that even those who criticize the style will be apt to respect the writer.' But the style was extremely attractive, gently humorous, and always on the verge of blossoming into epigram. The tone of her thought was civilized and humane, if somewhat class-conscious, as when, elsewhere in the same collection of tales, a small girl's ungracious behaviour was attributed by her aristocratic godmother to spending too much time below stairs:

'That is where you learned your little *toss* and your trick of grumbling, my dear,' my godmother said, planting her gold eye-glasses on her high nose; 'and that is why your mouth is growing out of shape, and your forehead getting puckered, and your chin poked, and—and your boots bulged crooked ... No boots will keep in shape if you shake your hips and kick with your heels like a servant out Sunday walking.'

That bad behaviour ruined faces as well as boots or, as Charles Kingsley put it, 'that your soul makes your body', was said to be 'the one, true ... doctrine' of his 'wonderful fairy tale', *The Water-Babies* (1863). Sure enough, Tom's body as well as his soul 'grew all prickly with naughty tempers', and the rest of the book's moral message was personified in the motherly Mrs Doasyouwouldbedoneby and the stern disciplinarian, Mrs Bedonebyasyoudid. So far, the book was just one more moral fable which, while satirizing the Peter Parley books under the name of Cousin Cramchild, was equally instructive on the subject of marine and freshwater natural history. But much of the work was really directed at adults. Tom's treatment by Grimes, the chimney-sweep, was a protest against current conditions of child-employment; and children were surely not meant to enjoy the allusions to the controversy between Huxley and Richard Owen about the hippocampus major—even when called the 'hippopotamus major'. Written at speed, the book had the charm of an improvisation by an agile and well-stocked mind; yet its structure seems rather clumsy after Mrs Ewing's precise artistry, and its sarcasm ponderous after her delicate irony. For all its fame as a children's classic, the best of *The Water-Babies* was over when Tom became one, half-way through the second chapter. The work is otherwise memorable chiefly for the rich suggestiveness of its central image, an escape from a dirty world of cruelty and injustice into a clean one ruled by fairness and kindness. One may also remember the 'History of the . . . Doasyoulikes', less for their exemplary decline from human beings into gorillas than for the Lear-like Nonsense describing their original way of life:

They were very fond of music, but it was too much trouble to learn the piano or the violin; and as for dancing, that would have been too great an exertion. So they sat on ant-hills all day long, and played on the Jew's harp; and, if the ants bit them they just got up and went to the next ant-hill, till they were bitten there likewise.

And they sat under the flapdoodle-trees, and let the flap-doodle drop into their mouths . . .

The Nonsense in Lewis Carroll's *Alice's Adventures in Wonderland* (1865) began with a burlesque of didactic literature for children.[16] Thus the 'busy bee' of Isaac Watts's poem was replaced as a moral exemplum by the hypocritical crocodile, while the altruism preached by moral fables was converted (as if by Callicles in Plato's *Gorgias*) into egotistical pleonexia: 'there's a large mustard-mine near here. And the moral of that is—"The more there is of mine, the less there is of yours."'' Yet even *Alice* had its educational side, if chiefly in the field of logic and semantics:

'Take some more tea,' the March Hare said to Alice, very earnestly.
'I've had nothing yet,' Alice replied in an offended tone: 'so I ca'n't take more.'
'You mean you ca'n't take *less*,' said the Hatter: 'it's very easy to take *more* than nothing.'

Still, teaching was not the purpose of the book, and Mrs Gatty's *Aunt Judy's Magazine for Young People* (founded 1866) was right to warn parents that in this 'exquisitely wild, fantastic, impossible,

[16] Lewis Carroll was Charles Lutwidge Dodgson, 1832–98. He was born at Daresbury, near Warrington, one of the eleven children of a clergyman who had taken a double first (classics and mathematics) at Christ Church, Oxford. He went to Rugby, then to his father's college, where he did better at mathematics than classics, became a mathematical lecturer, 1855–81, was ordained deacon, 1861, and spent most of his life. That he was never ordained priest has been attributed to his shyness and his stammer. He was a gifted photographer, especially of children, whose company he particularly enjoyed. He died at Guildford, where he had lived in vacations since his father's death. See Chap. 21.

yet most natural history' they would not find much 'knowledge in disguise'.

In the *Magazine* itself they had been assured, 'they need not fear an overflowing of mere amusement'. So, though the first story began with a misunderstanding caused by quoting one of Lear's limericks without acknowledgement, most of the contents were improving or informative. They included 'emblems' of 'moral truths' by Mrs Gatty herself, 'facts and anecdotes, historical, biographical, or otherwise', and a regular dose of natural history. The first number started serializing her daughter J.H.G.'s *Mrs Overtheway's Remembrances*, in which a 'little old lady' told stories about her own childhood to a small orphan girl. She started with one so introspective in tone that it sent the audience to sleep, and showed the narrator her mistake:

it is a child's story, but the moral is more for me than for her . . . Alas! my grown-up friend, are there now no passionate, foolish longings, for which we blind ourselves to obvious truth, and of which the vanity does not lessen the disappointment?

The moral of Mrs Gatty's 'The Little Sick Child' was more outward-looking and practical. Written to support a fund-raising campaign for the Great Ormond Street Children's Hospital, it realistically described the position of a nine-year-old boy who had been bedridden since he was three with a tubercular hip.

The sufferings of poor children became a favourite theme of the Evangelical authors published by the Religious Tract Society. Among the most popular of these was 'Hesba Stretton', i.e. Sarah Smith, a founder of the London Society for the Prevention of Cruelty to Children.[17] Her *Jessica's First Prayer* (1867) was about a fatherless child who lived with her drunken mother in a slum attic. Her first prayer was : 'O God! I want to know about you. And please pay Mr Dan'el for all the warm coffee he's given me.' It was duly answered. She found out all about God by surreptitious attendance at the chapel where Mr Daniel worked as pew-opener; and she herself paid him back by changing him from a selfish miser into a good Christian. In return he saved her life when she was dying of fever, and finally adopted her. The saintly

[17] Sarah Smith, 1832–1911, was born at Wellington, Shropshire, the daughter of a bookseller-publisher and his evangelical wife, and went to a local school. Her first story was published by Dickens in *Household Words*, 1859. *Jessica's First Prayer* sold over a million and a half copies, and was translated into most European languages, and many Asiatic and African ones.

child, the hard-hearted money-grubber, and the philanthropic clergyman were stereotypes, and the religious message was extraordinarily naïve; but there was realism in the account of Jessica's living-conditions, and a touch of satire on chapel-goers. Daniel kept his coffee-stall a secret, for fear that the 'very grand' congregation might sack him for pursuing such a 'low and mean' trade. He also tried at first to keep Jessica out of the chapel, lest the 'ladies and gentlemen' should be shocked by the presence of 'a ragged little heathen'. The style was simple and unemotional, and the total effect more moving than this summary suggests.

In *Little Meg's Children* (1868) Hesba Stretton laid even greater stress on the efficacy of prayer. Here the ten-year-old daughter of a seaman, who had left his wife and children living in a slum attic, accessible only by ladder, became at her mother's death both mater- and paterfamilias:

'Pray God,' said Little Meg, 'you've let mother die, and father be took bad at the other side of the world, and there's nobody to take care of us 'cept you: and Jesus says, if we ask you, you'll give us bread, and everything we want, just like father and mother. Pray God, do! I'm not a grown-up person yet, and Robin's a very little boy, and baby can't talk or walk at all; but there's nobody else to do anything for us, and we'll try as hard as we can to be good.'

With an adequate suspension of disbelief, the book might well make a powerful impression. As a form of applied literature with a specific missionary purpose, it was a miniature masterpiece.

'It's so dreadful to be poor!' sighed another Meg that year, in Louisa May Alcott's *Little Women*.[18] She only wanted a new dress for Christmas, but the poverty pictured in George MacDonald's *At the Back of the North Wind* (1868–9) was more like the English Meg's.[19] The story involved a girl crossing-sweeper, who lived with a drunken old woman in a cellar, until she fell ill, and was put in the Children's Hospital by 'one of the kindest men in London'. The boy-hero, Diamond, had to become the family bread-winner while his father was ill, by driving his cab for him. He was also even better than Little Meg at looking after babies. Besides his external problems, Diamond had an exciting and puzzling inner life. Instead of firmly believing in a kind God, Diamond exper-

[18] Louisa May Alcott, 1832–88, was born in Pennsylvania, and experienced real poverty as a child.
[19] George MacDonald, 1824–1905. For his poetry see Chap. 9.

ienced supernatural power in the ambiguous character of the North Wind, a protean female combining the qualities of a loving mother and a ruthless destroyer. Being 'a true child in this, that he was given to metaphysics', Diamond wrestled with the theological difficulty: 'Here you are taking care of a poor little boy with one arm, and there you are sinking a ship with the other. It can't be like you.' 'Ah! but which is me? I can't be two mes, you know.'

If metaphysics bulked larger than might have been expected in a children's book, so did literary allusion. The 'back of the North Wind' was first connected with the Hyperboreans mentioned by Herodotus, then with Dante's *Purgatorio*. Diamond's dream about angels digging for stars, and his subsequent appearance as a cabman, or charioteer, driving a good horse, clearly alluded to a famous passage in Plato's *Phaedrus*. In its general outline, the story corresponded with that of Shelley's 'Alastor', where a poet was finally led to his death by a beautiful, visionary female; and the Shelleyan poet dominated the whole landscape of the book. After the North Wind had shown Diamond 'a poet' in a boat, defining the term as 'a man who is glad of something, and tries to make other people glad of it too', the boy started to become one himself: singing songs to the tune of a river at the back of the North Wind, improvising songs for the baby, and finally comforting a lady who could not sleep for pain, with an unheard song that went straight into her heart.

As a semi-realistic fairy-tale with an admixture of theology and poetic symbolism, the book was something new in children's literature, but the old didacticism remained. Like Little Meg, Diamond was an exemplary character:

The whole ways and look of the child, so full of quiet wisdom, yet so ready to accept the judgment of others in his own dispraise, took hold of my heart ... It seemed to me, somehow, as if little Diamond possessed the secret of life, and was himself what he was so willing to think the lowest living thing—an angel of God with something special to say or do.

Humphrey, the seven-year-old hero of Florence Montgomery's *Misunderstood* (1869) was no such paragon.[20] Hyperactive and generally tiresome, he caused his own death by his disobedience, in climbing with his younger brother on to a branch overhanging a

[20] Florence Sophia Montgomery, 1843–1923, was born in County Donegal, the daughter of a baronet. *Misunderstood* was aimed at adults, but she also wrote *Moral Tales for Children*, 1886, and other children's books.

pond. His fate was meant to be a warning, not to children, but to adults—for he was not really naughty, only playful, and suffering from inward grief for the death of his mother. Thus, misunderstood by his father, who thought he had 'not much heart', he finally figured in a deathbed scene that made Paul Dombey's seem relatively unemotional: bequeathing his total capital of twopence to a little cripple that he knew, and trying to remember a consoling text from Revelation. Yet there was more in the book than false sentiment. The author's attempts 'to view life as it appears to a child' were sometimes both convincing and amusing, as when Humphrey, dressing his small brother for an unauthorized mushroom-hunt before their nurse woke up, was baffled by the complexity of underwear. In its tolerance for the naughty child *Misunderstood* was a decendant of *Holiday House* and a remote ancestor of Richmal Crompton's *William* (1922).

With *The Brownies and Other Tales* (1870) Mrs Ewing continued her efforts to make naughty children better, before they reached the point of having to make their wills. The title-story (from which Lord Baden-Powell would take the name for junior Girl Guides) told how two thoughtless and untidy brothers were converted into 'domesticated Brownies', who secretly did the housework before their father was awake. The moral was obliquely conveyed to them by a wise old owl, part mother-figure, part cryptically sardonic oracle.

The Brownies reappeared in MacDonald's *The Princess and the Goblin* (1870–1) to conclude another process of moral improvement, when the hideously ugly and malicious Goblins 'grew milder in character, and indeed became very much like the Scotch Brownies.' The first chapter seems to invite an almost Freudian interpretation of the Goblins, as natural impulses repressed by 'too severe taxes' and ever 'stricter laws', and thus driven underground, to grow 'misshapen' and delight 'in every way they could think of to annoy the people who lived in the open-air storey above them.' But whatever they were meant to symbolize, their moral improvement was paralleled by the gentler moral education of the eight-year-old Princess. This was chiefly effected by visits to her great-great-grandmother, a wise and beautiful old lady of miraculous powers who lived at the top of a tower, and acted as a kind of guardian angel. The mysterious communion between these two, which took place mainly in a world of imagination, was linked to a thrilling adventure-story in the 'real' world, of which a young miner called Curdie was the hero. He foiled the Goblins' attempt to invade the house through the wine-cellar, and drowned most of them in the 'subterranean waters' by which they had planned to destroy the human population. Thus the book strangely combined didacticism with obscurely symbolic fantasy, real narrative excitement, and also grotesque humour, as in the sensitivity of the Goblins' feet, and their horror at 'verse of every kind'. The result was immensely readable and suggestive, though its suggestions were seldom made so explicit as this: 'Here I should like to remark, for the sake of princes and princesses in general, that it is a low and contemptible thing to refuse to confess a fault, or even an error.'

The fault that led to Humphrey's fall in *Misunderstood* had been disobedience; yet for purposes of pathos he was associated not with Adam but with Humpty Dumpty. In Carroll's *Through the Looking-Glass* (1872) a pre-lapsarian Humpty Dumpty gave Alice a tutorial on language and logic.[21] Other children's writers, however, continued to teach morality and religion. The hero of Mrs Ewing's *Lob Lie-by-the-fire* (1874) was a foundling adopted by two elderly spinsters, who obeyed Matthew 6:3 so literally that each sister kept her charities a secret from the other. He was ungrateful enough to run away from them, but later adopted their policy of doing good by stealth, by pretending to be a Brownie, 'the rough, hairy, Good-fellow who worked at night that others might be idle by day.' The moral was given piquancy by the author's ironic wit and psychological insight, especially in describing the conflict between the small boy's gypsy instincts, and the *Cranford*-like atmosphere of his adoptive home.

The only trace of irony in the Evangelical preaching of Mrs O. F. Walton's *Christie's Old Organ* (1874) appeared in the opening scene, where an aged organ-grinder, living alone in a dismal attic, was found playing his favourite tune, 'Home, Sweet Home'.[22] The rest of the story was relentlessly direct in its message. The 'poor, forlorn old man, without a friend in the world', was befriended by 'a little ragged boy' called Christie, and had his sins washed away in the blood of Jesus, just in time for his

---

[21] See Chap. 21.

[22] Amy Catherine Walton, 1849–1939, had several other stories published by the Religious Tract Society, including *Christie the King's Servant: A Sequel to Christie's Old Organ*, 1898.

transfer to our best, our brightest "HOME, SWEET HOME!"'". Christie, who had done the necessary research in the local mission-room, finally became a clergyman, got married, and, while waiting for the real thing, set up a 'dear little earthly home' of his own. Though the style was more commonplace, and the sentiment more shamelessly contrived, the narrative had the same type of appeal as *Jessica's First Prayer*.

Mrs Molesworth's *Tell me a Story* (1875) belonged to a different class, both socially and intellectually.[23] Told by an aunt in a middle-class family to children ranging in age from a toddler to a twelve-year-old, these stories showed less concern with religion than with child-psychology. In one of them a small girl, told that her dead sister had been taken to Heaven by Jesus, asked anxiously: 'Had she only her little pink dressing-gown on? Wouldn't she be cold?' Every story had an obvious moral, but the plots were imaginative, as when a boy who loved fairy tales and hated lessons was imprisoned by fairies inside a mountain; and the children were convincingly characterized. The same was true of *Carrots: Just a Little Boy* (1876), which went far to justify its claim to be 'the history of a *real* little boy and girl, not fancy children'. Here, as in *Misunderstood*, the moral was chiefly for adults: not to judge small children hastily or harshly. Through an unsuspected uncertainty about the meaning of 'a half-sovereign', the six-year-old hero was wrongly assumed to have stolen one from his nurse's drawer, hidden it, and added lying to theft when it was discovered in his paint-box. His absentee father, a naval officer possibly modelled on the author's military husband, saw only the circumstantial evidence, and was not easily dissuaded by his wiser wife from whipping the young criminal.

In trying to represent the small child's mental world, Mrs Molesworth was too apt to imitate its language. 'Where are that cuckoo? Does *you* know?' asked Master Phil in *The Cuckoo Clock* (1877). But the rest of the book was delightful. Griselda (apparently named on the *lucus a non lucendo* principle) was a little girl

---

[23] Mary Louisa Molesworth, née Stewart, 1839–1921, was born in Rotterdam, the daughter of a Scottish business man. Brought up in Manchester, Scotland, and Switzerland, she was educated by her mother, and also by Mrs Gaskell's husband. In 1861 she married an army major with a very violent temper, attributed to a head-wound in the Crimean war. She started publishing pseudonymous and unsuccessful novels about incompatible couples; but from 1875 she wrote children's books, many of which were illustrated by Walter Crane.

sent to stay with two spinster great-aunts in a very old house, where she received the best part of her moral and academic schooling from a cuckoo in a clock. His method was a kind of affectionate teasing, as in this comment on her besetting sin of impatience:

'Why will you jump at conclusions so? It's a very bad habit, for very often you jump *over* them, you see, and go too far. One should always *walk* up to conclusions, very slowly and evenly, right foot first, then left, one with another—that's the way to get where you want to go, and feel sure of your ground. Do you see?'

He also taught her astronomy, while carrying her on his back to the other side of the moon, and history, by taking her to fantastic places suggested by the old-fashioned furniture. Such adventures were fun for children, while adult readers could enjoy the realistic interaction between old age and extreme youth, and the loving satire on the two ladies. Their first reaction to the news that Griselda had been playing with Master Phil was horror: 'A *boy*, a rude, common, impertinent *boy*' — until they heard that he was 'quite a little boy' and 'quite a little gentleman'. '"A little gentleman," repeated Miss Grizzel, "and not six years old! That is less objectionable than I expected."'

Rosalie, the twelve-year-old heroine of Mrs Walton's *A Peep behind the Scenes* (1877), had far more objectionable people to deal with, most notably her father, who forced her to go through a song-and-dance routine in his travelling theatre, while her mother was dying in the family caravan. The harrowing account of her life 'behind the scenes' was functional, because theatres, fairs, and circuses were used to epitomize 'the world's glitter and glare and vain show'. Such 'lessons' of the story were constantly spelt out, and the book was full of preaching, Bible-reading, hymn-singing, and praying. Images of the Good Shepherd were ubiquitous, and the characters were frequently described as sheep or lambs, lost or otherwise. Threatened with the workhouse by her cruel step-mother, Rosalie set off from London, with a kitten, twopence in her pocket, and 'a piece of bread . . . saved from breakfast', to find her way to her aunt's home in the country. When she opened 'her little Testament', she promptly found a text about a sheep, and the memory of another one guided her to the house of a kindly couple, who called her a 'poor lamb'—and started family prayers with a

reading of Psalm 23. The aunt duly gave her a good home, or, as
Rosalie preferred to put it, 'a very green pasture'. In spite of all
this, her previous environment was quite realistically described,
the story was vividly told and occasionally rather touching, and
there were even traces of humour, as when the giant explained his
reluctance to be seen outside the fair ('we mustn't make ourselves
too cheap, you know'), or the midget, happily 'found', asked: 'Oh,
Good Shepherd, have you got any work for a woman that's only
three feet high?'

One sign that Rosalie's father was 'lost' was the way he treated
his horse, and Anna Sewell's *Black Beauty: The Autobiography of
a Horse* (also 1877) was another protest against such treatment.[24]
Lucian's *Lucius or The Ass* had complained of similar cruelty, and
so had the Comtesse de Ségur's *Mémoires d'un Âne* (1860), but the
'translator' of this sad autobiography 'from the original equine'
was not interested in literary precedents. A crippled Quaker who
could only get about in a pony-cart, she used neither whip nor
reins, relying solely on appeals to the animal's better nature, like:
'Now thee must go a little faster. Thee would be sorry for us to be
late at the station.' Her instinctive feeling for horses enabled her to
speak for them without sounding fanciful, and dictated a habit of
stoical understatement, which made her criticisms of human
behaviour all the more telling. Thus an old mare commented on a
hunting accident, with all the wisdom, but without the dogmatism,
of a Houyhnhnm:

I never yet could make out why men are so fond of this sport; they often
hurt themselves, often spoil good horses, and tear up the fields, and all for
a hare or a fox, or a stag, that they could get more easily some other way;
but we are only horses, and don't know.

'I have heard people talk about war as if it was a very fine thing',
said Black Beauty to a cab-horse who had been in the charge of the
Light Brigade. 'Ah!' said the veteran, 'I should think they never
saw it . . . but the enemy must have been awfully wicked people, if
it was right to go all that way over the sea on purpose to kill them.'
Fashion, 'the drink devil', religious 'shams and humbugs', and
party politics were as summarily dismissed; but the humanitarian

[24] Anna Sewell, 1820–78, was born at Great Yarmouth, Norfolk, the daughter of a
banker and his Quaker wife Mary, who published moral tales, mostly in verse. Told in 1871
that she had only eighteen months to live, she started writing *Black Beauty*, and died shortly
after it came out, unaware of its great success. By 1894 nearly 100,000 copies had been sold.

message remained central, compellingly conveyed in a painfully realistic life-history.

The same theme was found, with strange variations, in Mac-Donald's *The Princess and Curdie* (1877). Here Curdie's moral progress began with remorse at having wantonly injured a white pigeon, and was confirmed by his friendship with a dog-like monster called Lina. With forty-nine other monsters called the 'Uglies' she helped him complete his 'mission' to foil a murderous plot against the King, and punish the wicked courtiers and servants involved. Lina was an endearing character, who had once been a 'naughty' woman, but was now 'growing good.' Thus, like Kingsley in *The Water Babies*, MacDonald moralized the notion of retrograde evolution. Once a woman 'travelling beastward', Lina was now a beast becoming human. The image of beasts being turned into men and then 'reeling back into the beast' must have come from *Idylls of the King*, and MacDonald's King failed, like Arthur, to effect any permanent improvement in human beings. In its satire on Victorian values, as dominated more by profit and self-interest than Christianity, this children's book was curiously sour. At one point Curdie seemed a kind of John the Baptist, warning the wicked servants to repent and flee from the wrath to come; but there was a most unchristian delight in the punishments inflicted, as when Lina was told to take the wicked doctor by the leg: 'Curdie heard the one scrunch with which she crushed the bone like a stick of celery.' 'Vengeance', indeed, was the subject of two whole chapters; yet however dubious its moral teaching, the book was full of thrilling adventures, grotesque humour, and an element of mystery, as when Curdie opened the door of the old Princess's room, and saw 'neither walls nor floor, only darkness and the great sky'.

After this work's sour misanthropy, Mrs Ewing's *Jackanapes* (1879) came near to seeming saccharine; but this story of altruistic heroism on the battlefield, set against the peaceful life of a small village, was redeemed by its subtle humour, its epigrammatic style, and its symbolic structure, which hinted at parallels between the human and animal life on Goose Green. Thus the speckled hen's surprise, when her foster-chick developed a passion for the pond, reflected the feelings of the elderly lady who was bringing Jackanapes up, when he showed an inherited instinct for riding and daring escapades. And the Grey Goose served amusingly as a

Chorus, who could not understand the disinterested values represented by the hero:

The Grey Goose always ran away at the first approach of the caravans,
and never came back to the Green till there was nothing left of the Fair
but foot-marks and oyster-shells. Running away was her pet principle;
the only system, she maintained, by which you can live long and easily,
and lose nothing. If you run away when you see danger, you can come
back when all is safe. Run quickly, return slowly, hold your head high,
and gabble as loud as you can, and you'll preserve the respect of the
Goose Green to a peaceful old age.

Such artistry must have appealed chiefly to parents reading
aloud, whereas children probably preferred another book published that year, Mrs Molesworth's *The Tapestry Room*. This,
though loosely constructed and written in a style without any
distinction but clarity, was well designed to stimulate a youthful
imagination. In its story, mysterious atmosphere, and bizarre
fantasies it resembled *The Cuckoo Clock*, but Dudu the raven was a
less amusing guide and instructor than the Cuckoo; and its 'white
lady' seemed like a poor imitation of MacDonald's 'great-great-
grandmother'. After waiting three hundred years for Hugh and
Jeanne to visit her, all she could tell them was a version of a
traditional folk-tale recommending patience. 'I'm a boy, you
know', said Hugh at one point to Jeanne, 'so it's right I should go
first in case of meeting anything that might frighten you.' In other
ways the book hardly catered for boys, who were then beginning to
read Penny Dreadfuls about *Spring-heeled Jack* or *The Wild Boys
of London* (1866). To counteract these sensational and sometimes
pornographic publications, the Religious Tract Society produced a
more edifying pennyworth, *The Boy's Own Paper* (1879). This
promised educational adventure-stories which, without 'direct
doctrinal teaching', would encourage 'true religion' as a spirit
pervading all life, in work, in play'. The formula had already been
used in *Coral Island*, and now became the basis of G. A. Henty's
vast output of works like *The Young Buglers* (1880).[25] Here two
'regular young pickles' from Eton joined the army as buglers

[25] George Alfred Henty, 1832–1902, was born at Trumpington, near Cambridge, the son
of a stockbroker and mine-owner. He went to Westminster and Caius College, Cambridge,
but joined the army when war broke out and left without a degree for the Crimea, 1855.
There he became a war correspondent, which continued to be his job in Italy, Abyssinia,
Ashanti, Spain, Paris, and elsewhere. He published about a dozen novels for adults, but
from 1871 produced a long series of boys' adventure stories, written at the rate of four a
year.

(having rapidly taught themselves Spanish as well as bugle-playing), acted as spies for Wellesley, fought at Albuera, and outwitted a villainous guerilla-leader called Nunez, who had kidnapped one of them, and hung him upside down over a slow fire. Throughout their breath-taking adventures they were unfailingly brave and resourceful, and always maintained a high moral tone, resisting every kind of foreign wickedness in the spirit of English gentlemen—though this included impaling Nunez on a pitchfork, and throwing him on to the fire. Wildly unrealistic, and stereotyped in characterization and moral outlook, Henty's books were yet brilliantly adapted to juvenile taste in their day, and for at least two generations after it.

The young buglers' love of practical jokes (like putting peas in other people's bugles) was a throw-back to the 'species of noisy, frolicsome, mischievous children' that Catherine Sinclair had called 'almost extinct' in 1839. Had she lived to read Frances Hodgson Burnett's *Little Lord Fauntleroy* (1886), she might have deleted the 'almost'.[26] Though his mother described him as 'a very boyish little boy, sometimes', Cedric showed no trace of mischief. He was, in fact, a moral paragon, who was always thinking of others, and always thinking the best of them. His love and trust had the same effect on the disagreeable old Earl as Jessica's had on Mr Daniel. 'You're a very good man, aren't you, Mr Dan'el?' said Jessica. 'You are always doing good, aren't you?' Cedric told his grandfather, and again the treatment worked. Thus the children's literature of the period ended as it had begun, with an attempt to 'improve the heart' and 'cultivate the understanding'. But there was 'entertainment' too, if chiefly for adult readers, in the form of ironic humour. Suspecting certain inaccuracies in an old sailor's account of his 'asperiences', Cedric suggested a possible excuse: 'Being scalped a great many times might make a person forgetful.' Nor was the Earl's character wholly implausible. When he finally brought himself to apologize to Cedric's mother for years of inhuman treatment, he remained true to himself in his choice of words: 'I suppose I have treated you badly.'

[26] Frances Eliza Hodgson, 1849–1924, was born in the north of England, the daughter of an ironmonger, who died when she was three. In 1865 her mother took her to live at Knoxville, Tennessee, where she met and later married Swan Burnett, the son of a local doctor. When her mother died, 1870, Frances supported the family by writing magazine stories, and from 1877 published novels, which later showed the influence of Henry James. Towards the end of her life, after two unhappy marriages, she lived partly in America, partly in Kent, writing children's books again, notably *The Secret Garden*, 1911.

21. Comic Verse, Parody, Nonsense

OSCAR WILDE was not the first Victorian to question the importance of being earnest. Just as the age's prudery finally led to the eleven volumes of *My Secret Life* (*c*.1890), so the proscription of 'levity' by Carlyle, the Evangelicals, and the Agnostics stimulated the mass-production of light literature. But there was nothing secret about it. With the birth of *Punch* in 1841 the making of jokes became a national industry. Though *Punch* was originally serious in its Radical politics, it claimed in its first number to be simply a 'Guffawgraph'. Its motto, taken from Byron's *Don Juan*, was: 'laugh at all things'. Its philosophy, far from Hamlet's notion of 'looking before and after', was to make 'the most of the present, regardless of the past or future', and countless humorists wrote in the same spirit. Their quest for 'the loud laugh that spoke the vacant mind' now seems faintly frenetic, and much of the period's guffawgraphy was as strained as its pornography. *Punch*'s 'Facetiae' make very tedious reading, and Walter Hamilton's six large volumes of *Parodies of the Works of English and American Writers* (1884–9) seldom rise much above this level:

> Break, break, break,
> O slavey, my crock–e–ry!
> And I would that my tongue dared utter
> The wrath that's astir in me.

Yet the Victorian urge to be funny had three happy results for literature. It produced some excellent comic verse, some wonderfully accurate parodies, and a whole new subgenre, Nonsense.

The humour of Barham's *Ingoldsby Legends* (1840–7) was usually as black as Thomas Hood's.[1] One told of a husband

---

[1] Richard Harris Barham, 1788–1845, was born at Canterbury, the son of a landowner, who died seven years later. In 1802 he had an arm partly crippled for life in a coach-accident on the way to St Paul's School. He went to Brasenose College, Oxford, 1807, where he made friends with Theodore Hook (the humorist who volunteered to sign Forty Articles if the authorities required it). Ordained in 1813, he became a minor canon at St Paul's Cathedral.

carefully dismembered by his wife and her lover, only to be miraculously reassembled on a dinner-table. Then the murderess sat on a cushion stuffed with her late husband's beard, 'shriek'd with pain', and 'From that hour to her last | She could never get rid of that comfortless "Bustle!"' Such mixtures of farce, horror, and the supernatural were presented in resourcefully improvised verse, with a wealth of polysyllabic rhymes. The stories were mildly amusing, but much too long: only 'The Jackdaw of Rheims' showed any tightness of structure. While ridiculing medieval legends, the Anglican poet doubtless satirized Catholicism; and 'The Execution', about an all-night party planned to culminate in a public hanging, must have been meant as social criticism. Otherwise the fun was pointless, and when a 'Moral' was appended, it was merely flippant.

There was some point, however, in *The Book of Ballads: Edited by Bon Gaultier* (1845). This was a collection of parodies by W. E. Aytoun and Theodore Martin.[2] Their pseudonym, meaning '*bon vivant*', was taken from the Prologue to *Gargantua*, and implied that their work, like Rabelais's, made serious points under cover of boisterous humour. Certainly the parodies of Tennyson suggested valid criticisms. The exaggerated protests of the lover in 'Locksley Hall' were mocked by further exaggeration: 'I will wed some savage woman—nay, I'll wed at least a dozen.' And the inflated sentiments of the 'May Queen' were deservedly punctured:

> You may lay me in my bed, mother,—my head is throbbing sore;
> And, mother, prithee, let the sheets be duly aired before;
> And, if you'd do a kindness to your poor desponding child,
> Draw me a pot of beer, mother—and, mother, draw it mild!

There was no nonsense about this May Queen, who had been hoping to attract a 'nobler suitor' than her rustic admirer; but making a poet talk nonsense was a form of parody as old as the *Frogs* of Aristophanes, and Lewis Carroll would soon apply it to

---

The *Legends* first appeared from 1837 in *Bentley's Miscellany* and *The New Monthly Magazine*.

[2] For Aytoun's poetry see Chap. 9. Sir Theodore Martin, 1816–1909, was born at Edinburgh, the son of a solicitor. He went to Edinburgh University, practised as a solicitor, and moved to London, 1846, having already started writing for *Tait's* and *Fraser's*. He published translations from Latin, German, and Italian, including a lively verse-rendering of Horace's *Odes*, 1860, a life of Prince Albert, 1875–80, and reminiscences of Queen Victoria, 1902.

Tennyson. Meanwhile it was Edward Lear who first specialized in nonsense for its own sake, taking his favourite verse-form, the limerick, from an anonymous collection of them called *Anecdotes and Adventures of Fifteen Gentlemen* (*c*.1821).[3]

A Book of Nonsense (1846) was ascribed on the title-page to 'Derry Down Derry', who, according to the limerick on the cover, 'loved to see little folks merry'. Lear undoubtedly did so, and had started improvising these limericks to amuse the children at Knowsley Hall, where he was working as a zoological draughtsman for Lord Stanley. One of his many 'Old Men' epitomized the nature of his own rapport with the young:

> There was an Old Person of Chili,
> Whose conduct was painful and silly,
> He sat on the stairs, eating apples and pears,
> That imprudent Old Person of Chili.

The comparative youth who appeared in Lear's illustration, with spectacles, dark hair, and moustache, resembled Lear himself, in a portrait of 1840, except that the expression was changed from faint melancholy to joyous insouciance. The book was full of such Persons, who thoroughly enjoyed doing things that children were taught to think silly or naughty. The general defiance of convention, common sense, and morality must have been a great comfort to repressed Victorian children. And nonconformist adults must have warmed to the limericks too, especially if they agreed with J. S. Mill that 'Precisely because the tyranny of opinion is such as to make eccentricity a reproach, it is desirable, in order to break through that tyranny, that people should be eccentric.' *A Book of Nonsense* was a *Golden Legend* of eccentrics, and many of them were martyred by a tyrannous majority, which constantly figured as 'they':

[3] Edward Lear, 1812–88, was born at Holloway, London (then a quiet village), the twentieth child of a stockbroker who was ruined in 1816. From the age of fifteen he had to earn his own living, first by medical drawings, then by drawing birds and animals for the Zoological Society, and for Lord Stanley at Knowsley Hall, near Liverpool, 1832–6. In 1837, having trouble with his eyesight, he was sent for his health to Rome, where he started landscape-painting. He then lived mostly abroad, but on various visits to England he gave drawing lessons to Queen Victoria, became a friend of Tennyson and Holman Hunt, and formed a deep attachment to Franklin Lushington. After travelling in Greece and Palestine and visiting India, he died at San Remo.

> There was an Old Man of Whitehaven,
> Who danced a quadrille with a Raven;
> But they said—'It's absurd, to encourage this bird!'
> So they smashed that Old Man of Whitehaven.

This Old Man, and the Young Lady who said, 'all the birds in the air | Are welcome to sit on my bonnet' reflected Lear's interest in ornithology, and several other limericks were faintly autobiographical. As the twentieth child of a man who went bankrupt when Lear was four, he had reason to censure as 'very peculiar' the conduct of a father who 'fed twenty sons upon nothing but buns'. Asthmatic, mildly epileptic, and often deeply depressed, he must have felt for the Old Man of Cape Horn, 'Who wished he had never been born'. And at least two limericks may help to explain why he never married: the 'unfortunate Man of Peru' whose wife baked him 'by mistake' in a stove, and this equally grim metaphor for monogamy:

> There was an Old Man on some rocks,
> Who shut his wife up in a box,
> When she said, 'Let me out,' he exclaimed, 'Without doubt,
> You will pass all your life in that box.'

Parody works best when the subject is similarly confined: novels are harder to parody than short poems. In *Mr Punch's Prize Novelists* (1847) Thackeray solved the problem by encapsulating the weaknesses of Disraeli, Lever, Lytton, Mrs Gore, G. P. R. James, and Fenimore Cooper in a series of short stories.[4] The best of them, 'Codlingsby', reduced Disraeli's high-minded hero to 'a pretty fighter' who, in a battle between Town and Gown, unsuccessfully challenged 'the most famous bruiser of Cambridge'. 'I likes whopping a Lord!' said the bruiser as he did so. Thackeray's cheapest joke was to suggest the Jewish novelist's exclusion from University education by making him confuse the topography of Oxford and Cambridge: 'From the Addenbrooke's hospital to the Blenheim turnpike, all Cambridge was in an uproar . . .'. A more legitimate target was the incredible character in *Coningsby* of the Jewish superman, Sidonia. This fabulous plutocrat, who 'had exhausted all the sources of human knowledge' and

---

[4] W. M. Thackeray. For his travel-writing and his *Rose and the Ring* see Chaps. 18 and 20.

whose advice was 'courted' by 'monarchs and ministers of all countries', was absurd enough in the original, but not at all funny. Thackeray made him so by simply increasing the hyperbole. His Mendoza kept a bundle of thousand-pound notes on the piano, for relighting cigars. Where Sidonia had merely won a four-mile steeplechase with thirty-nine jumps in less than fifteen minutes, Mendoza, 'with a few rapid strokes of his flashing paddles', kept his canoe well ahead of a Cambridge boat-race, pausing now and then to send up 'volumes of odour' from his oriental pipe.

Amusing as these pieces were, their literary criticism was less acute than that of Aytoun's *Firmilian, or The Student of Badajoz: A Spasmodic Tragedy. By T. Percy Jones.*[5] This parody of Alexander Smith's *A Life-Drama* and Sydney Dobell's *Balder* began as a review of the imaginary author's work (*Blackwood's Magazine*, May, 1854), where Jones was hailed as 'the coming Poet', far superior to the other members of his school:

You can always tell what Percy Jones is after, even when he is dealing with 'shuddering stars', 'gibbous moons', 'imposthumes of hell', and the like; whereas you may read through twenty pages of the more ordinary stuff without being able to discern what the writers mean—and no wonder, for they really mean nothing. They are simply writing nonsense-verses; but they contrive, by blazing away whole rounds of metaphor, to mask their absolute poverty of thought, and to convey the impression that there must be something stupendous under so heavy a canopy of smoke.

Besides mimicking Smith and Dobell's extravagant imagery, *Firmilian* burlesqued their plots. To write his *magnum opus*, a tragedy about Cain, Firmilian needed first-hand experience of remorse. So he poisoned three friends, blew up a cathedral with its whole congregation of 'Uninspired dullards, unpoetic knaves', and flung a Poet off the top of St Simeon Stylites' pillar, crushing a Critic who had just prayed to Apollo: 'I do beseech thee, send a poet down!' Still unable to feel remorse, Firmilian abandoned tragedy for love-poetry, and began by inviting a rose, a lily, and a 'dark full-scented night-stock', i.e. two white girls and a negress, to join him in a *ménage à quatre*. He was finally led into a quarry by a chorus of Ignes Fatui, whose music sounded at first like 'the echo of an inward voice'.

[5] William Edmoundstoune Aytoun, 1813–65. See Chap. 9.

The echoes of other poets in C. S. Calverley's *Verses and Translations* (1862) led to nothing much better:[6]

> Now unto mine inn must I,
> Your 'poor moralist,' betake me,
> In my 'solitary fly.'

The punning allusion to Gray was as fatuous as the application of 'Break, break, break', to crockery; and no critical point was made by turning Longfellow's 'I was a Viking old!' into 'I have a liking old', or his 'Skeleton in Armour' into an 'Ode to Tobacco'. There was relevance, though, in the opening reference to Horace, and the whole Ode was Horatian in the *curiosa felicitas* of its versification, and the delicacy of its humour:

> Thou who, when fears attack,
> Bidst them avaunt, and Black
> Care, at the horseman's back
>   Perching, unseatest;
> Sweet when the morn is gray;
> Sweet, when they've cleared away
> Lunch; and at close of day
>   Possibly sweetest . . .

Calverley would become one of the period's finest parodists, but as yet he was only an accomplished verse-humorist, and a translator and imitator of classical poetry. The volume included versions of 'Lycidas' in Virgilian hexameters, of a passage from *In Memoriam* in Horatian alcaics, of Lucretius and Homer in English hexameters, and of Theocritus in sub-Tennysonian blank verse. There was also an original poem in quasi-Juvenalian hexameters, satirizing student life at Cambridge, with pseudo-scholarly notes, also in Latin, where quotations from Virgil's *Eclogues* were glossed as references to smoking. The best attempt at direct parody was aimed at too easy a target: Tupper's *Proverbial Philosophy*.

Another by-product of the academic life was *Alice's Adventures in Wonderland* (1865), by 'Lewis Carroll', i.e. Charles Lutwidge

---

[6] Charles Stuart Blayds, 1831–84, was born at Martley, Worcestershire, the son of a clergyman. The family reverted to its old name, Calverley, 1852. He went to Marlborough, Harrow, and Balliol College, Oxford, from which he was removed for a disciplinary offence, then to Christ's College, Cambridge, where he became a fellow. He was called to the bar, 1865, but brain-damage caused by a skating accident in the winter of 1866 gradually incapacitated him for serious work. He also suffered from Bright's disease and consequent depression, and died before he was fifty-three.

Dodgson.[7] His previous publications had been chiefly on mathematics, but included two contributions to a magazine called *The Train* (1856). One was a serious but sentimental tribute to Florence Nightingale, written partly in blank verse and partly in a pastiche of Tennyson's 'The Two Voices'. The other parodied that poem as 'The Three Voices'. This brilliantly reproduced Tennyson's style, but implied no criticism of his poetry, except that it was pretentious nonsense. His doctrine seemed to be personified in a grotesque, governess-like character 'With huge umbrella, lank and brown', on whom the victim of the argumentative 'voices' commented:

> 'Her style was anything but clear,
> And most unpleasantly severe;
> Her epithets were very queer.

> 'And yet, so grand were her replies,
> I could not choose but deem her wise,
> I did not dare to criticise...

The parodies in *Alice* showed the same spirit: that of a child rebelling against its teachers by turning their wise words into nonsense, or playfully reversing their morality. Thus Southey's didactic poem, 'The Old Man's Comforts and How He Gained Them', taught that a happy old age was the reward of prudence in youth. Carroll's 'You are old, Father William' taught a more juvenile ethic: that the best way to stay young was to do exactly what one liked.

So Carroll's Nonsense may be said to have started as childishly subversive parody. Like Lear, he 'loved to see little folks merry', and identified strongly with them; but unlike Lear, he seems to have preferred their company to any other. He had many 'child-friends', as he called them, and enjoyed nothing more than making up stories to amuse them. He improvised one for Alice Liddell, the lexicographer's ten-year-old daughter, while he and his friend Duckworth (the Dodo and the Duck) took her with her sisters Lorina and Edith (the Lory and the Eaglet) on a boat-trip up the Isis in the summer of 1862. The story was full of allusions to people, places, and events within the children's experience, and Carroll first recorded it in a four-chapter version called *Alice's*

---

[7] See Chap. 20.

Adventures Under Ground. This, beautifully written and illustrated, was his Christmas present to Alice in 1864. It suggests, rather touchingly, how a young don whose stammer made relations with adults uneasy, sympathized with the problems of a growing child; for beneath all the jokes, puns, parodies, and nonsensical fantasies appeared a continuous theme: the problem of growing up. By making Alice a Gulliver who never knows for long whether he is in Brobdingnag or Lilliput, Carroll seems to have hinted at her shifting relations with the adult world. At one moment she felt small enough to be 'ordered about' by her elders (as she was by every character she met in the book): at the next, she felt big enough to criticize adult behaviour as absurdly irrational.

The theme was obscured, and the structure made less coherent in the twelve-chapter *Alice's Adventures in Wonderland*, which, as a children's book, was less obviously attractive than its predecessor. But few children would regret the addition of Nonsense so quintessential as that of the Mad Tea-Party, nor would most adults complain of the increase in intellectually provocative humour; as when Alice is made to distinguish between 'say what you mean' and 'mean what you say', or told that the right way to go from here 'depends a good deal on where you want to get to'.

Like Carroll's, Gilbert's Nonsense began as parody.[8] 'The Yarn of the Nancy Bell' (1866), republished in the *Bab Ballads* (1869), was a skit on 'The Ancient Mariner'. In Gilbert's version the compulsive story-teller, having survived by eating the rest of the ship's company, reduced the whole experience to 'a single joke', endlessly repeated in a 'singular minor key':

> 'Oh, I am a cook and a captain bold,
>   And the mate of the *Nancy* brig,
> And a bo'sun tight, and a midshipmite,
>   And the crew of the captain's gig.'

The savage humour, which made *Punch* reject the poem as 'too cannibalistic', was in the tradition of Barham and Hood, but the 'singular minor key' was peculiar to Gilbert. The subtitle of the *Bab Ballads* (so called after his pet name as a child) was: 'much sound and little sense'; and the primacy of sound appeared in verbal music that was delightful in itself. This resulted not just from exquisite versification but often from melodious

[8] W. S. Gilbert, 1836–1911. For his plays see Chap. 19.

malapropisms. Burlesquing the fashion started by Moore and
Byron for oriental tales, he deliberately misused foreign words:

> Each morning he went to his garden, to cull
> A bunch of zenana or sprig of bul-bul,
> And offered the bouquet, in exquisite bloom,
> To BACKSHEESH, the daughter of RAHAT LAKOUM.

He did the same thing with unfamiliar words in English:

> Of AGIB, who could readily, at sight,
> Strum a march upon the loud Theodolite.
> He would diligently play
> On the Zoetrope all day,
> And blow the gay Pantechnicon all night.

Then there were proper names, perfectly embodying character
and also determining their poems' rhythmical structure:

> KING BORRIA BUNGALEE BOO
> Was a man-eating African swell;
> His sigh was a hullaballo,
> His whisper a horrible yell—
> A horrible, horrible yell!

But the *Ballads* were more than musical nonsense. Like the
Savoy Operas, which used some of the same plot-material, they
were full of social satire. Gilbert had much in common with the
'disagreeable man' in his *Princess Ida*: 'Each little fault of temper
and each social defect | In my erring fellow-creatures I endeavour
to correct.' His view of them gave a special meaning to his jokes
about cannibalism. 'For, oh', as he would put it in 'The Thief's
Apology' (1884), 'we live in a wicked world where dog eats dog,
and likes it.' His favourite butts were clergymen and democratic or
humanitarian idealists. Captain Reece RN was so anxious to
'Promote the comfort of his crew' that he finally allowed them to
marry all his female relations. To 'humour' a congregation who
'lived on scalps served up in rum', the Bishop of Rum-ti-Foo
adopted the same diet. Yet slaves to convention were equally
ridiculed. In 'Etiquette' two castaways on a small desert island
could not speak to one another, because they had never been
introduced—until it turned out that they both knew a man called
Robinson.

There were no such problems to frustrate the idyllic love of

'The Owl and the Pussy-Cat' in Lear's *Nonsense Songs* (1871). Though conventional enough to want to get married, they just 'sailed away for a year and a day, | To the land where the Bong-tree grows', bought a ring from a 'Piggy-wig' (who agreed to the sale in the words of the Marriage Service), got a Turkey to conduct the ceremony, and lived happily ever after:

> And hand in hand, on the edge of the sand,
>   They danced by the light of the moon,
>   The moon,
>   The moon,
>   They danced by the light of the moon.

Here nonsense was made to convey the essence of romantic feeling, with a touch of melancholy—as if such happiness was inconceivable except in a nonsense-world. Other expressions of Lear's own wanderlust were similarly tinged with realism. Those intrepid travellers, 'The Jumblies', lived happily for twenty years in a 'Western Sea' utopia, and were congratulated on having 'been to the Lakes, and the Torrible Zone, | And the hills of the Chankly Bore'; yet the refrain stressed that they were a privileged minority, remote from ordinary human experience:

> Far and few, far and few,
>   Are the lands where the Jumblies live;
> Their heads are green, and their hands are blue,
>   And they went to sea in a sieve.

As for 'The Nutcrackers and the Sugar-tongs', who 'galloped away to the beautiful shore' to escape from 'this stupid existence', their grand gesture ended in their simply ceasing to exist: 'They faded away—And they never came back!' The last phrase became a refrain in 'Calico Pie', where it seemed like an echo of Tennyson's lament: 'But the tender grace of a day that is dead | Will never come back to me.'

While Lear's Nonsense was developing into romantic poetry, Carroll's had become more cerebral. *Through the Looking-Glass* (1872) originated from stories told to the Liddell girls when they were learning chess; and, as Carroll explained in 1896, Alice's movements in the book represented 'a chess-problem ... correctly worked out ... strictly in accordance with the laws of the game.' The mirror-image theme, suggested by a remark of his young cousin, Alice Raikes, was worked out with equal ingenuity. In the mirror-world even time was reversed. One 'effect of living backwards', as the White Queen put it, was that her finger started to bleed before she pricked it. Within this carefully contrived framework were several wild parodies of the *Alice's Adventures in Wonderland* type. Thus the remarks attributed in *Maud* to the roses, the lily, and the larkspur were exaggerated into a whole conversation with talking flowers. Wordsworth's fine poem, 'Resolution and Independence', was burlesqued in 'The Aged Aged Man', and the schoolmaster-murderer's kindly attitude towards his pupils in Hood's *Dream of Eugene Aram* was mocked, rather more thoughtfully, in 'The Walrus and the Carpenter':

> 'I weep for you,' the Walrus said:
>   'I deeply sympathize.'
> With sobs and tears he sorted out
>   Those of the largest size,
> Holding his pocket-handkerchief
>   Before his streaming eyes.

After the splendid nonsense-ballad, 'Jabberwocky', which had begun as a parody of Anglo-Saxon poetry in 1855, Humpty Dumpty's scholarly footnotes came as an anticlimax; and, like his discussion of semantics, many passages in the book showed nonsense shading off into linguistic or philosophical speculation, as when the White King wished he had good enough eyes to 'see nobody on the road', or when Tweedledum and Tweedledee argued on Berkeleyan lines that Alice was 'only a sort of thing' in the Red King's dream. But this type of intellectualism has delighted modern critics, who have found in Carroll's nonsense every possible kind of sense. In 1966 the primly conventional, clerical author of the *Alice* books was said to have created 'a comic myth of man's insoluble problem of meaning in a meaningless world'.

The problem of meaning in Pre-Raphaelite poetry was easily solved by Calverley in *Fly Leaves* (1872):

> Her sheep follow'd her, as their tails did them.
>   (*Butter and eggs and a pound of cheese*)
> And this song is consider'd a perfect gem,
>   And as to the meaning, it's what you please.

One wonders if Calverley realized what subtle effects could be achieved by a not obviously relevant refrain, like Morris's '*Two red roses across the moon*'. He was, in the words of a reviewer, a 'remarkably good mocking-bird', as this volume showed; but he was better at parroting poets' styles than understanding them. 'The Wanderers', for instance, precisely caught Tennyson's manner in blank verse, but pointlessly turned 'The Brook' into a travelling tinker. Nor did Calverley's comic masterpiece, 'The Cock and the Bull' suggest awareness of anything below the surface of *The Ring and the Book*:

> *Ut*,
> Instance: *Sol ruit*, down flops sun, *et*, and
> *Montes umbrantur*, out flounce mountains, Pah!
> Excuse me, sir, I think I'm going mad.
> You see the trick on't though, and can yourself
> Continue the discourse *ad libitum*.
> It takes up about eighty thousand lines,
> A thing imagination boggles at:
> And might, odds-bobs, sir! in judicious hands,
> Extend from here to Mesopotamy.

Though less extensive, Carroll's *The Hunting of the Snark* (1876) has always made imaginations boggle, and almost every reader has his own interpretation. One critic has called it (1962) 'a poem about being and non-being, an existential poem, a poem of existential agony'. As a quest-poem with an unhappy ending, it was, perhaps, partly a parody of three recent publications, Morris's *Jason* and *The Earthly Paradise*, and Tennyson's 'Holy Grail'. Where Arthur's knights had followed 'wandering fires', the Bellman's crew hunted something 'With a flavour of Will-o'the-Wisp'. Henry Holiday's first illustration made the Bellman look very like Tennyson, and Carroll's text described him in terms that recalled 'The Three Voices': 'Such solemnity too! One could see he was wise, | The moment one looked in his face!' But the Bellman was probably Liddell as well as Tennyson. Four years earlier, in *The New Belfry of Christ Church, Oxford*, Carroll had ridiculed the 'head of the House' for having the bells removed from the Cathedral and temporarily housed in a kind of wooden box above the Hall staircase. This eyesore was compared to a meatsafe, a Greek Lexicon, and finally to the containers used for packaging ersatz China tea: 'Was there not something prophetic in the choice? What traveler is there, to whose lips, when first he enters the great educational establishment and gazes on its newest decoration, the words do not rise unbidden—"Thou tea-chest"?'

Apart, however, from such parody and satire, the poem seems to have a more general meaning. Carroll claimed not to know what it was, and to have intended nothing but nonsense; but he explained that the whole poem 'pieced itself together' from a single line that suddenly came into his head: 'For the Snark *was* a Boojum, you see.' He wrote later that he was glad to accept whatever 'good' meanings' could be found in the piece, and that, of interpretations suggested to him, the one he liked best took the poem as 'an allegory for the pursuit of happiness'. In that case, everything would presumably turn on pursuing the right *kind* of happiness. As the Baker's uncle put it: 'If your Snark be a Snark, that is right: | Fetch it home by all means . . . But . . . If your Snark be a Boojum! . . . You will softly and suddenly vanish away, | And never be met with again!' Carroll himself would doubtless have taken this in a Christian sense; but Plato's Socrates, too, would have thought it a 'good' meaning, and as a tragicomic modernization of 'The Vanity of Human Wishes' *The Hunting* is still an impressive as well as amusing poem:

> They sought it with thimbles, they sought it with care;
>   They pursued it with forks and hope;
> They threatened its life with a railway-share;
>   They charmed it with smiles and soap . . .
> In the midst of the word he was trying to say,
>   In the midst of his laughter and glee,
> He had softly and silently vanished away—
>   For the Snark *was* a Boojum, you see.

The nonsense-poetry in Lear's *Laughable Lyrics* (1877) was less grim but almost more melancholy. 'The Dong with a Luminous Nose' was a casualty of the Jumblies' happy visit to the Hills of the Chankly Bore. He had fallen in love with a Jumbly Girl, only to be left on 'the cruel shore', like Ariadne on Naxos, when the travellers sailed home. His disconsolate wanderings were made no less pathetic by their parody of the Scholar-Gipsy's 'fugitive and gracious light . . . shy to illumine':

> Lonely and wild—all night he goes—
> The Dong with a luminous Nose!
> And all who watch at the midnight hour,
> From Hall or Terrace, or lofty Tower,

> Cry, as they trace the Meteor bright,
> Moving along through the dreary night,—
>   'This is the hour when forth he goes,
>   'The Dong with a luminous Nose!'

'The Courtship of the Yonghy-Bonghy-Bò was another sad story of frustrated love, and 'The Pobble Who Has No Toes' offered no consolation for irreparable loss but one that sounds deeply ironical: 'It's a fact the whole world knows, | That Pobbles are happier without their toes.' The melancholy, however, was expressed through an oddly attractive blend of humour and verbal music. The former came mostly from the habit, conspicuous in Lear's letters, of playing about with words, spellings, ideas, and visual images, so as to create an almost surrealist world; the latter must have stemmed from the instinct which enabled him, without any musical training, to compose effective settings for poems (including some lyrics of Tennyson).

Carroll's *Dreamland* (1882) was a work of the opposite kind—a poem written to fit a melody composed in a dream by a friend. Though melody, even verbal, was not Carroll's strong point, the best, if not the only good things in *Sylvie and Bruno* (1889) were the Gardener's eight songs, each on this pattern:

> He thought he saw a Rattlesnake,
>   That questioned him in Greek:
> He looked again, and found it was
>   The Middle of Next Week.
> 'The one thing I regret', he said,
>   'Is that it cannot speak!'

The book had developed from a short story called 'Bruno's Revenge' (*Aunty Judy's Magazine*, 1867), in which a cross boy fairy was persuaded to improve his sister's garden instead of spoiling it. While expanding this moral tale, Carroll incorporated 'a huge unwieldy mass of litterature—if the reader will kindly excuse the spelling', accumulated from 'all sorts of odd ideas, and fragments of dialogue' that had occurred to him over the years. Along with 'nonsense for children' he claimed to have introduced 'some of the graver thoughts of human life'. The result was not happy. The baby-talk was more painful than the worst in Mrs Molesworth, and the adult world was treated in the spirit of a moralizing, sentimental novel.

Rather than end a chapter, and a volume, with a work so disappointing, we must, like the White Queen, live backwards for nine years. A worthier conclusion to the period's humorous efforts may be found in Swinburne's *Seven against Sense* (1880).[9] There, 'in a Nutshell', is not only Tennyson's 'Higher Pantheism', but the whole age's talent for self-ridicule:

One, who is not, we see: but one, whom we see not, is;
Surely this is not that: but that is assuredly this . . .
Doubt is faith in the main: but faith, on the whole, is doubt;
We cannot believe by proof: but could we believe without? . . .
God, whom we see not, is: and God, who is not, we see;
Fiddle, we know, is diddle: and diddle, we take it, is dee.

[9] A. C. Swinburne, 1837–1909. See Chap. 7.

Chronological Table

Date	General History	Literary History
1832	Grey PM. First Reform Act. Durham University founded. Constable, *Grove, Hampstead*. Turner, *Staffa, Fingal's Cave*. Mendelssohn, *Fingal's Cave*. Chopin's first Paris concert. Wilkins, National Gallery (to 1838).	Bentham d. Crabbe d. Scott d. Goethe d. E. Arnold b. 'Lewis Carroll' b. Henty b. Stephen b. *Penny Magazine. Chambers's Journal.* Goethe, *Faust*, ii.
1833	Slavery abolished in British colonies (as from Aug. 1834). Factory Act forbids employment of children under nine. First government grant for schools. Oxford Movement starts. Landseer, *Hunted Stag*. Mendelssohn, 'Italian' Symphony.	Hannah More d. A. H. Hallam d. Dixon b. *Penny Cyclopaedia* (to 1844). *Bridgewater Treatises* (to 1836). A. de Musset, *André del Sarto*. Béranger, *Chansons nouvelles et dernières*.
1834	Owen's Grand National Trades Union. 'Tolpuddle Martyrs'. Melbourne PM, then Peel. His Tamworth Manifesto commits Tories to reform. Houses of Parliament burnt down. Poor Law Amendment Act starts workhouses. Turner, *Venice*. Berlioz, *Harold en Italie*.	Coleridge d. Lamb d. Malthus d. Seeley b. Thomson b. A. de Musset, *On ne badine pas avec l'amour*.
1835	Melbourne PM. Municipal Corporations Act reforms local government. Turner, *Burning of the Houses of Lords and Commons, Keelmen Heaving in Coals by Night*. Donizetti, *Lucia di Lammermoor*.	Cobbett d. Mrs Hemans d. J. Hogg d. Austin b. Butler b. 'Mark Twain' b. Hans Andersen, *Eventyr fortalte for Børn*. Gautier, *Mademoiselle de Maupin*, with preface expounding doctrine of *l'art pour l'art*. Strauss, *Das Leben Jesu* (to 1836). Tocqueville, *La démocratie en Amérique*

Verse	Prose	Drama (date of acting)
Tennyson, *Poems* ('1833').	Lyell, *Principles of Geology*, ii. Martineau, *Illustrations of Political Economy* (to 1834).	Walker, *The Factory Lad*.
E. Barrett, *Prometheus Bound, translated from Aeschylus and Miscellaneous Poems*. Browning, *Pauline*. Newman writes 'Lead, Kindly Light'.	Carlyle, *Sartor Resartus* (to 1834), 'On History Again'. Keble, 'National Apostasy'. Lyell, *Principles of Geology*, iii. Macaulay, 'Horace Walpole'. Mill, 'What is Poetry?', 'Two Kinds of Poetry'. Newman *et al.*, *Tracts for the Times* (to 1841). Sterling, *Arthur Coningsby*.	
Taylor, *Philip van Artevelde*.	Hallam, *Essays and Remains*. Martineau, *Illustrations of Taxation*. Newman, *Parochial Sermons* (to 1842). Somerville, *On the Connexion of the Physical Sciences*.	
Browning, *Paracelsus*.	Macaulay, 'Sir James Mackintosh'. Mill, review of Tennyson's poems. Thirlwall, *History of Greece* (to 1844).	

Date	General History	Literary History
1836	Newspaper tax reduced. London University given royal charter as examining body. London Working Men's Association leads towards Chartism. First train in London (to Greenwich). Forms of telegraph being devised in America and England. Pugin's *Contrasts* advocates Gothic architecture. Turner, *Juliet and her Nurse*.	Godwin d. James Mill d. Gilbert b. *Dublin Review*. Eckermann, *Gespräche mit Goethe*. Gogol, *Inspector-General*. Heine, *Die Romantische Schule*.
1837	William IV d. Accession of Queen Victoria. Paper duty halved. Isaac Pitman, *Stenographic Sound-Hand*. Landseer, *Old Shepherd's Chief Mourner*. Turner, *Interior at Petworth*. Basnevi, Fitzwilliam Museum, Cambridge (to 1847)	Green b. Swinburne b. Leopardi b. Pushkin d. *Bentley's Miscellany*.
1838	Afghan War. Irish Poor Law. Cobden's Anti-Corn Law League. Working Men's Association drafts People's Charter. Chartist *Northern Star*: circulation 50,000. Public Record Office. Regular steamship service between England and USA. London–Birmingham railway completed. Royal Orthopaedic Hospital. Barry, Reform Club (to 1840). Donizetti's *Lucia* produced in London.	Landon d. Lecky b. Morley b. Sidgwick b. Newman, Keble, Pusey (edd.), *Library of the Fathers of the Holy Catholic Church* (to 1885).
1839	War with China: Hong Kong taken. Chartist riots. Photography invented (Daguerre, Fox Talbot). Maclise, *Charles Dickens*. Turner, *Fighting Téméraire*. Berlioz, *Roméo et Juliette*.	Galt d. Praed d. Pater b.
1840	Queen Victoria marries Prince Albert. Afghans surrender. Maoris yield sovereignty of New Zealand. Rowland Hill starts penny post. Barry and Pugin, Houses of Parliament (to 1865). Etty, *Mars, Venus and Attendant*. Turner, *Slavers*, Schumann, *Dichterliebe*.	Fanny Burney d. Blunt b. Hardy b. Symonds b. *Chronica Jocelini de Brakelonda* published by Camden Society. Sainte-Beuve, *Port-Royal* (to 1859).

Verse	*Prose*	*Drama (date of acting)*
Browning, 'Porphyria's Lover', 'Johannes Agricola in Meditation'. Newman, Keble *et al.*, *Lyra Apostolica*.	Ruskin writes defence of Turner against criticisms in *Blackwood's Magazine*; contributes to *Magazine of Natural History*.	
	Carlyle, *French Revolution*. Macaulay, 'Francis Bacon'. Martineau, *Society in America*. Mill, review of Carlyle's *French Revolution*. Newman, *The Prophetical Office of the Church*. Ruskin, *The Poetry of Architecture* (to 1838).	Browning, *Strafford*.
Barrett, *Seraphim*. Tupper, *Proverbial Philosophy* (to 1842).	T. Arnold, *History of Rome* (to 1843). Macaulay, 'Sir William Temple'. Martineau, *A Retrospect of Western Travel*. Maurice, *The Kingdom of Christ*, lecture on 'Words'. Mill, 'Bentham'.	
Bailey, *Festus* (to 1889). Sterling, *Poems*.	Carlyle, *Chartism*. Darwin, *Journal of Researches into the Geology and Natural History of the various countries visited by H.M.S. Beagle*. Martineau, *Deerbrook, The Housemaid*. Sinclair, *Holiday House*.	Lytton, *Richelieu*.
Barham, *Ingoldsby Legends* (to 1847). Browning, *Sordello*.	Macaulay, 'Lord Clive'. Mill, 'Coleridge'. Newman, sermon on 'Explicit and Implicit Reason'.	Lytton, *Money*.

Date	General History	Literary History
1841	Hong Kong, New Zealand proclaimed British. Peel PM. Second Afghan War. Arc-lamp street-lighting demonstrated in Paris. Scott, Martyrs' Memorial, Oxford.	Newman's *Tract* 90 condemned by Oxford University. *Punch*. Emerson, *Essays*. Feuerbach, *Das Wesen des Christentums*. London Library.
1842	End of wars with China and Afghanistan. Mines Act. Chadwick report on 'sanitary condition' of working classes. Chartist riots. Turner, *Snow Storm, Peace*. Wagner, *Rienzi*.	T. Arnold d. Copyright Act. Mallarmé b.
1843	Sind, Natal annexed. Brunel, Thames Tunnel. Landseer, *Queen Victoria, Prince Consort and Princess*. Watts, *Lady Holland*. Wagner, *Fliegende Holländer*.	Southey d. Wordsworth Poet Laureate. Doughty b. Dowden b. 'Felix Summerly' *The Home Treasury* series. *Economist*. Liddell and Scott, *Greek-English Lexicon*.
1844	Factory Act limits working hours for women and children. 'Rochdale Pioneers': first co-operative society. Ragged School Union. Washington-Baltimore telegraph. First public baths (Liverpool). London YMCA. Turner, *Rain, Steam, and Speed*. Joachim plays Beethoven in London, Mendelssohn conducting. Berlioz, *Carnaval Romain*.	Campbell d. Bridges b. Hopkins b. Lang b. *North British Review*. R. Chambers, *Cyclopaedia of English Literature*. W. Smith, *Dictionary of Greek and Roman Biography and Mythology* (to 1849). Heine, *Neue Gedichte*. Nietzsche b. Verlaine b.
1845	Expedition against Madagascar. War with Sikhs. Potato famine in Ireland. Maynooth grant for Irish education. Stephenson and Thompson, Britannia Bridge, Menai Strait. Franklin, North-West Passage expedition. Wagner, *Tannhäuser*.	Barham d. Hood d. Sydney Smith d. Colvin b. Saintsbury b. Browning meets Elizabeth Barrett. Layard starts excavating Nimrud. Engels, *Die Lage der arbeitenden Klassen in England*. Hoffmann, *Struwwelpeter*.

Verse	Prose	Drama (date of acting)
Browning, *Pippa Passes.*	Carlyle, *On Heroes, Hero-Worship, and the, Heroic in History.* Macaulay, 'Warren Hastings'. Martineau, *The Playfellow, The Hour and the Man.* Miller, *The Old Red Sandstone.* Newman, *Tract* 90, *The Tamworth Reading Room.*	Boucicault, *London Assurance.*
Browning, *King Victor and King Charles, Dramatic Lyrics.* Macaulay, *Lays of Ancient Rome.* Tennyson, *Poems.*	Macaulay, 'Frederic the Great'.	
Browning, *Return of the Druses.* Horne, *Orion.*	Borrow, *The Bible in Spain.* Carlyle, *Past and Present.* Macaulay, *Essays, Critical and Historical.* Mill, *System of Logic.* Newman, *Sermons Preached Before the University of Oxford.* Ruskin, *Modern Painters,* i.	Browning, *A Blot in the 'Scutcheon.*
Barnes, *Poems of Rural Life in the Dorset Dialect.* Barrett, *Poems.* Browning, *Colombe's Birthday.* Patmore, *Poems.*	(R. Chambers), *Vestiges of the Natural History of Creation.* Finlay, *Greece under the Romans.* Keble, *Praelectiones Academicae.* Kinglake, *Eothen.* Martineau, *Life in the Sick-room.* Newman (ed.), *Lives of the English Saints* (to 1845). Stanley, *Life and Correspondence of Thomas Arnold.*	
(Aytoun & Martin), *The Book of Ballads: Edited by Bon Gaultier.* Browning, *Dramatic Romances and Lyrics.*	Carlyle, *Oliver Cromwell's Letters and Speeches, with Elucidations.* Ford, *Handbook for Travellers in Spain.* Martineau, *Letters on Mesmerism.* Newman, *An Essay on the Development of Christian Doctrine.* Warburton, *The Crescent and the Cross.*	

Date	General History	Literary History
1846	Sikhs defeated. Louis Napoleon escapes from prison to England. Corn Laws repealed. Russell PM. Planet Neptune, protoplasm discovered. Rawlinson deciphers cuneiform. Ether used as anaesthetic in operation. Evangelical Alliance to stop 'encroachments of Popery and Puseyism'. Turner, *Angel Standing in the Sun*. Mendelssohn conducts *Elijah* in Birmingham.	Frere d. F. H. Bradley b. Brownings' secret marriage and journey to Pisa. Hakluyt Society (to publish travel-books). Bohn's *Standard Library*. *Daily News*. George Eliot's translation of *Das Leben Jesu*. Mary Howitt, *Wonderful Stories for Children* (from Hans Andersen). Senancour d.
1847	Factory Act: ten-hour day for women and young persons. Simpson uses chloroform as anaesthetic. Jenny Lind sings in England. Smirke, British Museum south front completed. Cruikshank, *The Bottle*. Verdi, *Macbeth*.	Alice Meynell b. Emerson, *Poems*. Longfellow, *Evangeline*.
1848	Revolutions in Europe. Louis Napoleon President of France. Second Sikh War. Cholera in England. Public Health Act. Marx–Engels *Communist Manifesto* (first printed in London). Chartist demonstration ends in fiasco. Rossetti, Millais, and Hunt form Pre-Raphaelite Brotherhood. Queen's College for women founded.	E. Brontë d. I. D'Israeli d. Bohn's *Classical Library*. Milnes (ed.), *Life, Letters and Literary Remains of John Keats*. Chateaubriand d.
1849	Sikhs surrender, Punjab annexed. Rome proclaimed republic under Mazzini, then taken by French. Communist riots suppressed in Paris. Revolt against British in Montreal. Disraeli becomes Conservative leader. Bedford College for women. Maurice, Kingsley, Hughes preach Christian Socialism. Millais, *Isabella*. Rossetti, *Girlhood of Mary Virgin, Dante drawing an Angel*. Hunt, *Rienzi*. Liszt, *Tasso*.	Barton d. Beddoes d. A. Brontë d. H. Coleridge d. Elliott d. E. Gosse b. Henley b. *Notes and Queries*. Poe d. Strindberg b.

Verse	Prose	Drama (date of acting)
(Charlotte, Emily, Anne Brontë), *Poems by Currer, Ellis and Acton Bell.* Browning, *Luria, A Soul's Tragedy.* Keble, *Lyra Innocentium.* Lear, *Book of Nonsense.*	Clough, Letters to *The Balance* on political economy. Grote, *History of Greece* (to 1856). (Horne), *Memoirs of a London Doll, Written by Herself.* Ruskin, *Modern Painters,* ii. Thackeray, *Notes of a Journey from Cornhill to Grand Cairo.*	
Tennyson, *The Princess.*	Clough, *Consideration of Objections Against the Retrenchment Association.* Thackeray, *Mr Punch's Prize Novelists.*	Coyne, *How to Settle Accounts with your Laundress.* Morton, *Box and Cox.*
Aytoun, *Lays of the Scottish Cavaliers.* Clough, *The Bothie of Toper-na-fuosich;* starts writing *Adam and Eve.* Kingsley, *The Saint's Tragedy.*	Forster, *Life and Adventures of Oliver Goldsmith.* Martineau, *Eastern Life, Present and Past.* Mill, *Principles of Political Economy.* Newman, *Loss and Gain.*	
(Arnold), *The Strayed Reveller and Other Poems by A.* Clough (with Burbidge), *Ambarvalia.* Clough starts writing *Amours de Voyage.*	Carlyle, 'Occasional Discourse on the Nigger Question'. Curzon, *Visits to Monasteries in the Levant.* Herschel, *Outlines of Astronomy.* Layard, *Nineveh and its Remains.* Macaulay, *History of England,* i–ii. Martineau, *History of England during the Thirty Years' Peace* (to 1850). F. W. Newman, *The Soul.* Ruskin, *The Seven Lamps of Architecture.*	

Date	General History	Literary History
1850	Navy blockades Piraeus for Gibraltarian Don Pacifico. Anglo-Kaffir War. Forts on Gold Coast bought from Denmark. Public Libraries Act. Factory Act: sixty-hour week for women and young persons. Miss Buss starts North London Collegiate School. Re-establishment of RC hierarchy: 'Papal Aggression'. First Dover-Calais telegraph-cable. Butterfield, All Saints', Margaret Street (to 1859). Millais, *Christ in the House of his Parents*. Rossetti, *Ecce Ancilla Domini*. Hunt, *Claudio and Isabella*. Collins, *Convent Thoughts*. Wagner, *Lohengrin*.	Bowles d. Jeffrey d. Wordsworth d. Tennyson Poet Laureate. Stevenson b. *Harper's Magazine* (to republish English authors in America). *Household Words*. *The Germ*. *Christian Socialist*. Warner, *The Wide, Wide World*. Turgenev, *A Month in the Country*.
1851	Louis Napoleon's *coup d'état*. Great Exhibition in Paxton's Crystal Palace (Hyde Park). Mayhew, *London Labour and the London Poor*. Tenniel starts cartoons in *Punch*. Cubitt, King's Cross Station (to 1852). Millais, *Mariana*. Hunt, *Hireling Shepherd*.	Lingard d. A. C. Bradley b. H. A. Jones b. *New York Times*. Hawthorne, *Wonder-Book for Boys and Girls*. H. B. Stowe, *Uncle Tom's Cabin* (to 1852).
1852	Louis Napoleon proclaimed Emperor Napoleon III. Derby PM, then Aberdeen. Burmese War. Duke of Wellington d. Brunel and Wyatt, Paddington Station (to 1854). Millais, *Ophelia*. Hunt, *Awakening Conscience*. Brown, *Work* (to 1865). Schumann, *Manfred*.	Moore d. Lady Gregory b. Roget, *Thesaurus*. Gautier, *Émaux et Camées*. Leconte de Lisle, *Poèmes antiques*.
1853	Turkey rejects Russian ultimatum, declares war on Russia. Turkish fleet destroyed, Anglo-French fleet off Dardanelles. Hunt, *Light of the World*. Verdi's *Rigoletto* produced in London.	*Encyclopaedia Britannica*, 8th edn. (to 1860). Hawthorne, *Tanglewood Tales for Girls and Boys*. Heine, *Die Götter im Exil*.

Verse	*Prose*	*Drama (date of acting)*
Allingham, *Poems*. E. B. Browning, *Sonnets from the Portuguese* (in *Poems*). Browning, *Christmas-Eve and Easter-Day*. Clough starts writing *Dipsychus*. C. Rossetti (in *Germ*), 'Dreamland'. Rossetti (ibid.) 'Blessed Damozel', 'My Sister's Sleep'. Tennyson, *In Memoriam A.H.H.* Wordsworth, *The Prelude*.	Carlyle, *Latter-Day Pamphlets*. Clough writing letter on socialism. Merivale, *History of the Romans under the Empire*. F. W. Newman, *Phases of Faith*. Rossetti (in *Germ*), 'Hand and Soul'.	
E. B. Browning, *Casa Guidi Windows*. Meredith, *Poems*.	Carlyle, *Life of John Sterling*. Fitzgerald, *Euphranor: A Dialogue on Youth*. Newman, *Lectures on the Present Position of Catholics in England*. Ruskin, *King of the Golden River*, *The Stones of Venice*, i. Spencer, *Social Statics*. Trench, *The Study of Words*.	
Arnold, *Empedocles on Etna and Other Poems*. Tennyson, *Ode on the Death of the Duke of Wellington*.	Browning, 'Shelley'. Dallas, *Poetics*. Newman, *Discourses on the Scope and Nature of University Education*. Florence Nightingale starts writing 'Cassandra' (to 1859). Spencer, 'Philosophy of Style', 'Theory of Population'.	Boucicault, *The Corsican Brothers*. Taylor and Reade, *Masks and Faces*.
Arnold, *Poems*. Fitzgerald, *Six Dramas of Calderon freely translated*. Patmore, *Tamerton Church-Tower and Other Poems*. Smith, *A Life-Drama* (in *Poems*)	Bagehot, 'Shakespeare—The Individual'. Maurice, *Theological Essays*. Ruskin, *The Stones of Venice*, ii–iii. Wallace, *Travels on the Amazon and Rio Negro*. Yonge, *The Heir of Redclyffe*.	Browning, *Colombe's Birthday*.

Date	General History	Literary History
1854	Crimean War: Alma, siege of Sebastopol, Balaclava (Charge of Light Brigade), Inkerman. Maurice founds Working Men's College. University College, Dublin. Pius IX makes Immaculate Conception article of faith. Florence Nightingale at Scutari. Frith, *Ramsgate Sands*. Millais, *John Ruskin*. Hunt, *Scapegoat*. Brown, *English Autumn Afternoon*. Rossetti begins *Found*.	S. Ferrier d. Lockhart d. Wilson d. Wilde b. 'George Eliot', translation of Feuerbach. Thoreau, *Walden*. Rimbaud b. G. de Nerval, *Les Chimères*.
1855	Palmerston PM. Fall of Sebastopol. London–Balaclava telegraph. Deane and Woodward, Oxford University Museum (to 1859). Brown, *Last of England*. Hughes, *April Love* (to 1856). Rossetti, *Paolo and Francesca*. London production of Verdi's *Il Trovatore*. Wagner conducts Philharmonic Society concerts.	Mary Mitford d. Rogers d. Pinero b. Smith, *Latin-English Dictionary*. Newspaper tax abolished. First Hoe rotary press in England. *Daily Telegraph* (first London daily for a penny). *Saturday Review*. Longfellow, *Song of Hiawatha*. Whitman, *Leaves of Grass*. Nerval d.
1856	Crimean War ends. Queen institutes VC. Second Chinese War. War with Persia. Bessemer patents steel-making process. Oudh annexed. First stage appearance of Henry Irving. Millais, *Blind Girl, Autumn Leaves*. Wallis, *Death of Chatterton*. London production of Verdi's *La Traviata*.	Miller d. Shaw b. *Oxford and Cambridge Magazine*. *The Train*. Emerson, *English Traits*. Hugo, *Les Contemplations*. Heine d.
1857	Persian War ends. Chinese fleet destroyed. Indian Mutiny. Transatlantic cable laid (to 1865). Divorce Courts established. Queen opens Museum of Ornamental Art (Victoria and Albert Museum, 1899). Millais, *Sir Isumbras at the Ford*. Rossetti, *Tune of Seven Towers, The Wedding of St George*. Wallis, *The Stonebreaker*.	Jerrold d. Davidson b. Arnold Professor of Poetry at Oxford. Oxford Union frescos: Rossetti, Morris, Burne-Jones, Swinburne, 'Jovial Campaign'. Baudelaire, *Les Fleurs du Mal*. Musset d.

Verse	*Prose*	*Drama (date of acting)*
Allingham, *Day and Night Songs*. Arnold, 'Balder Dead'. Aytoun, *Firmilian, or The Student of Badajoz: A Spasmodic Tragedy*. Dobell, *Balder*. Patmore, *The Angel in the House: Betrothal*. Tennyson, 'The Charge of the Light Brigade'.	P. Gosse, *Aquarium: An Unveiling of the Wonders of the Deep Sea*. Huxley, 'On the Educational Value of the Natural History Sciences'.	
Arnold, 'Stanzas from the Grande Chartreuse'. Browning, *Men and Women*. Clough, 'Say not the Struggle nought availeth'. MacDonald, *Within and Without*. 'Owen Meredith', *Clytemnestra*. Tennyson, *Maud and Other Poems*.	Bagehot, 'First Edinburgh Reviewers'. Burton, *Personal Narrative of a Pilgrimage to El-Medinah and Meccah*. Gatty, *Parables from Nature* (to 1871). Macaulay, *History of England*, iii–iv. Maurice, *Learning and Working*. Newman, 'Who's to Blame?' Thackeray, *The Rose and the Ring*.	
Dobell, *England in Time of War*. Fitzgerald, *Salámán and Absál: An Allegory translated from the Persian of Jámí*. Patmore, *Angel in the House: Espousals*.	Browne, *Granny's Wonderful Chair and its Tales of Fairy Times*. Burton, *First Footsteps in East Africa*. Froude, *History of England* (to 1870). Kingsley, *The Heroes*. Morris, 'Story of the Unknown Church', 'Lindenborg Pool' (in *Oxford and Cambridge Magazine*). Newman, *Callista*. Ruskin, *Modern Painters*, iii–iv.	
E. B. Browning, *Aurora Leigh*. MacDonald, *Poems*. Smith, *City Poems*.	Arnold, lecture on 'Modern Element in Literature'. Buckle, *History of Civilization in England* (to 1861). Gaskell, *Life of Charlotte Brontë*. Gatty, *Proverbs Illustrated*. P. Gosse, *Omphalos*. Hughes, *Tom Brown's Schooldays*. Livingstone, *Missionary Travels and Researches in South Africa*. Miller, *The Testimony of the Rocks*. Ruskin, *The Political Economy of Art*.	

Date	General History	Literary History
1858	Derby PM. Chinese War ends. Indian Mutiny suppressed. Powers of East India Company transferred to Crown. Jewish Disabilities Act. Property qualification for MPs abolished. Fenian Brotherhood in Ireland. I. K. Brunel's *Great Eastern* (biggest ship ever built). Darwin and Wallace give joint paper on evolution. Frith, *Derby Day*. Millais, *William Gladstone*. Morris, *Queen Guinevere*. E. M. Barry, Covent Garden Opera House. Offenbach, *Orphée aux enfers*.	R. Owen d. Watson b. Ruskin's 'unconversion' in Turin.
1859	Palmerston PM, Gladstone Chancellor of Exchequer. Franco–Austrian War. Austrian defeat at Solferino. Peace of Villafranca. Napoleon III negotiates to form Italian Confederation. Nightingale, *Notes on Hospitals, Notes on Nursing*. Webb, Red House for Morris (to 1860). Millet, *L'Angélus*. Gounod, *Faust*.	De Quincey d. H. Hallam d. Leigh Hunt d. Macaulay d. K. Grahame b. Housman b. F. Thompson b. *Chambers's Encyclopaedia* (to 1868), *Macmillan's Magazine*. Hugo, *La Légende des siècles* (to 1883).
1860	Maori War. First Italian Parliament. Lincoln President of USA. Huxley–Wilberforce debate at Oxford. Scott, St Pancras Station. Hunt, *Finding of the Saviour in the Temple*. Millais, *Black Brunswicker*. W. B. Scott, *A. C. Swinburne*.	Barrie b. Inge b. *Cornhill Magazine*, ed. Thackeray: 120,000 copies sold. Bradlaugh's *National Reformer*. Burckhard, *Die Kultur der Renaissance in Italien*. Schopenhauer d.
1861	Prince Consort d. Victor Emmanuel King of Italy. Maori War ends. American Civil War starts. Lowe's Revised Code: payment by results in grants to schools. Post Office Savings Bank. HMS *Warrior* (all-iron warship). Mrs Beeton, *Household Management*. Hughes, *Home from Work*. Brahms, first piano concerto.	E. B. Browning d. Clough d. Hewlett b. Raleigh b. Palgrave's *The Golden Treasury of Songs and Lyrics*. Baker's *Hymns Ancient and Modern*. Morris and Company founded. Max Müller, *Science of Languages* (to 1864). Paper tax abolished.

Verse	*Prose*	*Drama (date of acting)*
Arnold, *Merope*. Clough, *Amours de Voyage*. Cory, *Ionica*. Kingsley, *Andromeda and Other Poems*. Morris, *The Defence of Guenevere and Other Poems*.	A.L.O.E., *The Story of a Needle*. Ballantyne, *The Coral Island*. Carlyle, *History of Friedrich II of Prussia, called Frederick the Great*, i–ii. Farrar, *Eric, or Little by Little*. Gatty, *Aunt Judy's Tales*. Gladstone, *Studies on Homer*. MacDonald, *Phantastes*.	
Fitzgerald, *Rubáiyát of Omar Khayyám*. Tennyson, *Idylls of the King* ('Enid', 'Vivien', 'Elaine', 'Guinevere').	Arnold, *England and the Italian Question*. Bagehot, 'Parliamentary Reform'. Darwin, *The Origin of Species by means of Natural Selection*. Masson, *Life of John Milton*. Mill, *On Liberty*. Nightingale, 'Cassandra' (priv. ptd.). Ruskin, *The Two Paths, Elements of Drawing*. Smiles, *Self-Help*.	
'Owen Meredith', *Lucile*. Patmore, *The Angel in the House: Faithful for Ever*.	Burton, *Lake Regions of Central Africa*. Dundonald, *Autobiography of a Seaman*. Faraday, *Various Forces of Matter*. Ruskin, *Modern Painters*, v. Spencer, *System of Synthetic Philosophy* (to 1896). Swinburne writes 'La Fille du Policeman'. Wilson, Temple, Williams, Powell, Pattison, Jowett, Goodwin, *Essays and Reviews*.	Boucicault, *The Colleen Bawn*.
Dixon, *Christ's Company and Other Poems*. Rossetti (tr.), *Early Italian Poets together with Dante's Vita Nuova*. Smith, *Edwin of Deira*.	Arnold, *On Translating Homer*, 'Democracy' (in *Popular Education of France*). Faraday, *On the Chemical History of a Candle*. Macaulay, *History of England*, v. Maine, *Ancient Law*. Mill, *Utilitarianism*. F. W. Newman, *Homeric*	

Date	General History	Literary History
1862	*Alabama*, built at Birkenhead for Confederates, allowed to sail. Bismarck Prussian premier. Lancashire cotton famine. Companies Act: Limited Liability. H. Dunant, *Souvenir de Solferino* leads to international Red Cross. Frith, *Railway Station*. Verdi, *Forza del Destino*.	Buckle d. Knowles d. Elizabeth (Siddal) Rossetti d. Newbolt b. 'Lewis Carroll' takes Liddell girls up the Isis. Thoreau d. Maeterlinck b.
1863	Palmerston cedes Ionian Islands to Greece. Metropolitan line opened. Scott, Albert Memorial (to 1872). Hughes, *Home from Sea*. Gounod's *Faust* produced in London. Bizet, *Pêcheurs de perles*. Stanislavsky b.	Thackeray d. Quiller-Couch b. Rossetti (ed.), 'Selections' of Blake (in Gilchrist's *Life*). Renan, *Vie de Jésus*. Sainte-Beuve, *Nouveaux Lundis* (to 1870). Taine, *Histoire de la littérature anglaise*. Vigny d.
1864	Sherman marches through Georgia. Lincoln re-elected President. Geneva Convention. International Working Men's Association founded in London. Octavia Hill starts work on slums. Pius IX condemns liberalism, socialism, rationalism. Clerk-Maxwell predicts electromagnetic radiation. Butler, *Family Prayers*. Landseer, *Man Proposes, God Disposes*. Rossetti, *Beata Beatrix* (to 1870). Whistler, *Symphony in White No 2*.	Clare d. Landor d. Phillips b. *The Month*.

Verse	Prose	Drama (date of acting)
	Translation in Theory and Practice. Spencer, Education. Spedding, The Letters and the Life of Francis Bacon.	
Calverley, Verses and Translations. Clough, Mari Magno (in Poems). Hopkins writes 'Vision of Mermaids'. Meredith, Modern Love and Poems of the English Roadside. Patmore, The Angel in the House: Victories of Love. C. Rossetti, Goblin Market and Other Poems.	Arnold, On Translating Homer: Last Words. Braddon, Lady Audley's Secret. Butler, 'Darwin on the Origin of Species: A Dialogue'. Carlyle, Friedrich, iii. 'Carroll' starts writing Alice's Adventures Under Ground. Ewing, Melchior's Dream. Ruskin, Unto this Last; Munera Pulveris (to 1863). Swinburne writing Lesbia Brandon.	
Hopkins, 'Winter with the Gulf Stream'. Ingelow, Poems. Woolner, My Beautiful Lady.	Butler, A First Year in Canterbury Settlement, 'Darwin among the Machines'. Gardiner, History of England from the Accession of James I (to 1882). Gilchrist, Life of William Blake. Huxley, Man's Place in Nature. Kinglake, The Invasion of the Crimea (to 1887). Kingsley, The Water-Babies. Speke, Journal of the Discovery of the Source of the Nile. Winwood Reade, Savage Africa.	Hazlewood, Lady Audley's Secret. Taylor, The Ticket-of-Leave Man.
Allingham, Laurence Bloomfield in Ireland: A Modern Poem. Browning, Dramatis Personae, Hawker, Quest of the Sangraal. Hopkins writes 'Heaven-Haven'. Tennyson, Enoch Arden and Other Poems.	Bagehot, 'Wordsworth, Tennyson, and Browning or Pure, Ornate, and Grotesque Art in English Poetry.' Carlyle, Friedrich, iv. Kingsley, What then does Dr Newman Mean? Newman, Mr Kingsley and Dr Newman's Correspondence, Apologia pro Vita sua. Pater writes 'Diaphaneitè'.	Brough and Halliday, The Area Belle.

Date	General History	Literary History
1865	Lincoln assassinated. Civil War ends. Slavery abolished in USA Palmerston d. Russell PM. Transatlantic cable completed. Eyre suppresses Negro revolt in Jamaica. Booth founds Salvation Army. Wagner, *Tristan und Isolde*.	Aytoun d. Kipling b. Yeats b. *Argosy. Fortnightly Review. Pall Mall Gazette*. Whitman, *Drum-Taps*.
1866	Fenians active in Ireland. Habeas Corpus suspended. Derby PM. Elizabeth Garrett opens dispensary for women. Dr Barnardo starts children's homes. Pasteur, *Études sur le vin* (pasteurization). Work starts on London underground railway. Rossetti, *Monna Vanna*. Smetana, *Bartered Bride*. Thomas, *Mignon*.	Jane Welsh Carlyle d. Keble d. Peacock d. Gilbert Murray b. Hopkins received by Newman into RC Church. Stubbs Professor of History at Oxford. *Aunt Judy's Magazine. Contemporary Review*. Ibsen, *Brand. Le Parnasse contemporain*. Verlaine, *Poèmes saturniens*.
1867	Fenian outrages in England. Canada becomes Dominion. Second Reform Act. Factory Act. Lister describes antiseptic surgery in *Lancet*. Albert Hall (to 1871). Marx, *Das Kapital*, i. Bizet, *Jolie Fille de Perth*. Strauss, 'Blue Danube' waltz. Verdi's *Forza* produced in London.	Faraday d. Smith d. Dowson b. Galsworthy b. Johnson b. Ibsen, *Peer Gynt*. Baudelaire d. Pirandello b.

Verse	Prose	Drama (date of acting)
Allingham, *Fifty Modern Poems*. Clough, *Dipsychus* (in *Letters and Remains*, priv. ptd.). Fitzgerald, *Agamemnon: A Tragedy, taken from Aeschylus* (priv. ptd.). Hopkins, 'Barnfloor and Winepress'. Newman, *The Dream of Gerontius*. Swinburne, *Atalanta in Calydon*. Thomson, 'Naked Goddess'.	Arnold, *Essays in Criticism*. Butler, *Evidence for the Resurrection*, 'Lucubratio ebria'. Carlyle, *Friedrich*, v–vi. 'Carroll', *Alice's Adventures in Wonderland*. Hopkins writes 'On the Origin of Beauty: A Platonic Dialogue'. Lecky, *History of the Rise and Influence of the Spirit of Rationalism in Europe*. Livingstone, *The Zambesi and its Tributaries*. W. G. Palgrave, *Personal Narrative of the Year's Journey through Central and Eastern Arabia*. Ruskin, *Sesame and Lilies*. (Seeley), *Ecce Homo* ('1866'), reviewed by Sidgwick.	Robertson, *Society*.
Arnold, 'Thyrsis'. Buchanan, *London Poems*. Gilbert, 'Yarn of the Nancy Bell'. Hopkins writes 'Habit of Perfection'. C. Rossetti, *Prince's Progress and Other Poems*. Swinburne, *Poems and Ballads*. Thomson, 'Sunday at Hampstead'.	Carlyle, *Inaugural Address at Edinburgh: On the Choice of Books*. Dallas, *The Gay Science*. Ewing, *Mrs Overtheway's Remembrances* (to 1868). Hopkins starts writing *Journal*. Pater, 'Coleridge'.	Robertson, *Ours*.
Arnold, 'Dover Beach', 'Rugby Chapel' (in *New Poems*). Ingelow, *A Story of Doom*. MacDonald, *The Disciple and Other Poems*. Morris, *The Life and Death of Jason*. Swinburne, *Song of Italy*.	Bagehot, *The English Constitution*. Carlyle, 'Shooting Niagara'. Freeman, *History of the Norman Conquest* (to 1879). Pater, 'Winckelmann'. Ruskin, *Time and Tide*. Sidgwick, 'Prophet of Culture'. 'Hesba Stretton', *Jessica's First Prayer*.	Robertson, *Caste*.

Date	General History	Literary History
1868	Disraeli PM. Basutoland annexed. Gladstone PM. Keble College, Oxford founded. Expedition against Abyssinia. Maori War. Hodgson, *European Curiosities*. Watts, *Thomas Carlyle*. Wagner, *Die Meistersinger von Nürnberg*.	Brougham d. Milman d. Gertrude Bell b. Hopkins becomes Jesuit. Alcott, *Little Women*.
1869	Irish Church disestablished. Suez Canal opened. Emily Davies starts Girton College at Hitchin (moved to Cambridge 1873). Sophia Jex-Blake begins medical training at Edinburgh. Wagner, *Rheingold*.	Binyon b. *Graphic*. Alcott, *Good Wives*. 'Mark Twain', *Innocents Abroad*. Lamartine d. Sainte-Beuve d.
1870	Franco-Prussian War. Irish Land Act: loans to peasants. Married Women's Property Act gives wives rights over own earnings. Forster's Education Act: board schools funded by local rates. Siege of Paris. Vatican asserts Papal Infallibility. Civil Service opened to competitive examination. Butterfield, Keble College, Oxford. Pearson, St Augustine's, Kilburn (to 1880). Burne-Jones, *The Mill*. Delibes, *Coppélia*.	Dickens d. Belloc b. Sturge Moore b. *Brewer's Dictionary of Phrase and Fable*. W. M. Rossetti's edn. of Shelley. English Literature made a subject in elementary schools.
1871	Fall of Paris ends war. Paris Commune set up and suppressed. Bismarck's *Kulturkampf* against Catholics. Kimberley diamond fields annexed. Stanley finds Livingstone. Purchase of army commissions stopped. Religious tests abolished at Oxford, Cambridge, and Durham universities. Anne Clough starts house of residence at Cambridge (Newnham College in 1876). Starley's 'penny-farthing' bicycle. Rossetti, *Dante's Dream*. Leighton, *Hercules Wrestling with Death for the Body of Alcestis*.	Grote d. Robertson d. W. H. Davies b. Synge b. Valéry b.

Verse	*Prose*	*Drama (date of acting)*
Browning, *The Ring and the Book* (to 1869). Morris, *The Earthly Paradise* (to 1870). Newman, *Verses on Various Occasions*.	Huxley, 'Liberal Education and Where to Find It'. Lecture 'On the Physical Basis of Life'. MacDonald, *At the Back of the North Wind* (to 1869). Pater, 'Poems of William Morris'. 'Stretton', *Little Meg's Children*. Swinburne, *William Blake: A Critical Essay*.	
Clough, *Poems and Prose Remains*. Gilbert, *Bab Ballads*. Rossetti, sonnets 'Of Life, Love, and Death'. Tennyson, *Holy Grail and Other Poems*.	Arnold, *Culture and Anarchy*. Galton, *Hereditary Genius*. Lecky, *History of European Morals*. Mill, *On the Subjection of Women*. Montgomery, *Misunderstood*. Ruskin, *The Queen of the Air*. Sidgwick reviews Clough's *Poems*. Wallace, *The Malay Archipelago*.	Robertson, *School, Progress*. Taylor and Dubourg, *New Men and Old Acres*.
O'Shaughnessy, *An Epic of Women and Other Poems*. Rossetti, *Poems* (including fifty sonnets for *The House of Life*).	Arnold, *St. Paul and Protestantism*. Austin, *The Poetry of the Period*. Ewing, *The Brownies*. MacDonald, *The Princess and the Goblin* (to 1871). MacGregor, *A Thousand Miles in the Rob Roy Canoe*. Newman, *A Grammar of Assent*.	Gilbert, *The Palace of Truth*. Robertson, *Birth*.
Browning, *Balaustion's Adventure, Prince Hohenstiel-Schwangau*. Lear, *Nonsense Songs*. Swinburne, *Songs before Sunrise*.	Arnold, *Friendship's Garland*. Buchanan, 'The Fleshly School of Poetry'. Darwin, *The Descent of Man*. Lytton, *Coming Race*. Rossetti, 'Stealthy School of Criticism'. Ruskin, *Fors Clavigera*. 'Mystery of Life and its Arts'. Stephen, *The Playground of Europe*.	

Date	General History	Literary History
1872	Trading posts on Gold Coast bought from Holland. Viceroy of India murdered. Jesuits expelled from Germany. Conscription in France. Ballot Act in England. Rossetti, *Bower Meadow*. Bizet, *L'Arlésienne*.	Maurice d. Beerbohm b. Russell b. Gautier d. Nietzsche, *Geburt der Tragödie*.
1873	Napoleon III d. at Chislehurst. Ashanti War. Falk Laws in Germany. Russians annexe Khiva. Remington typewriter. Moody and Sankey evangelize England. Cambridge University starts extension lectures. Butterfield, Keble College Chapel (to 1876). Rossetti, *La Ghirlandata*. Brahms, *German Requiem* performed in London.	Mill d. Lytton d. Walter de la Mare b. Rimbaud, *Une Saison en enfer*.
1874	Duke of Edinburgh marries Grand Duchess Marie Alexandrovna. Disraeli PM. LSE opened to women. Strike of agricultural workers. Fiji Islands annexed. Tichborne claimant convicted of perjury. Impressionist exhibition in Paris. Butler, *Mr. Heatherley's Holiday*. Burne-Jones, *Beguiling of Merlin*. Strauss, *Fledermaus*. Smetana, *Má Vlast* (to 1879)	Dobell d. Baring b. Chesterton b. Winston Churchill b. W. M. Rossetti (ed.) Blake.
1875	France becomes Republic. Wreck of *Deutschland*. Disraeli buys Suez Canal shares. Public Health Act. Prince of Wales visits India. Madame Blavatsky founds Theosophical Society. Mary Baker Eddy, *Science and Health*. Rossetti, *Blessed Damozel* (to 1878). Bizet, *Carmen*. Verdi conducts his *Requiem* in London.	Finlay d. Lyell d. Thirlwall d. *Encyclopaedia Britannica*, 9th edn. (to 1889).

Verse	Prose	Drama (date of acting)
Browning, *Fifine at the Fair*. Calverley, *Fly Leaves*. Lear, *More Nonsense*. Morris, *Love is Enough*. Tennyson, *Gareth and Lynette*. Thomson, 'In the Room'.	Bagehot, *Physics and Politics*. Butler, *Erewhon or Over the Range*. 'Carroll', *Through the Looking-Glass* (issued 1871), *The New Belfry of Christ Church, Oxford*. Darwin, *The Expression of the Emotions of Man and Animals*. Forster, *Life of Charles Dickens* (to 1874). Stanley, *How I found Livingstone*.	
Browning, *Red Cotton Night-Cap Country: or Turf and Towers*. Dobson, *Vignettes in Rhyme*.	Arnold, *Literature and Dogma*. Butler, *The Fair Haven*; starts writing *The Way of All Flesh* (to 1885). Hopkins writing lecture-notes on Rhetoric (to 1874). Maurice, *The Friendship of Books*. Mill, *Autobiography*. Newman, *The Idea of a University Defined and Illustrated*. Pater, *Studies in the Renaissance*. Winwood Reade, *African Sketch-Book*. Stephen, *Freethinking and Plainspeaking*.	
O'Shaughnessy, 'We are the music-makers' (in *Music and Moonlight*). Thomson, *The City of Dreadful Night*.	Ewing, *Lob Lie-by-the-Fire*. Green, *Short History of the English People*. Mill, *Three Essays on Religion*. Morley, *On Compromise*. Sidgwick, *The Methods of Ethics*. Stephen, *Hours in a Library* (to 1879). Stubbs, *Constitutional History of England* (to 1878). Walton, *Christie's Old Organ*.	Gilbert, *Sweethearts: An Original Dramatic Contrast*.
Browning, *Inn Album*. Hopkins writes 'The Wreck of the Deutschland' (Dec.–Jan.). 'Owen Meredith', *King Poppy* (priv. ptd.).	Carlyle, *The Early Kings of Norway*. Creighton, *History of Rome*. Molesworth, *Tell me a Story*. Pattison, *Isaac Casaubon*. Ruskin, *Proserpina* (to 1886).	Gilbert, *Tom Cobb*. With Sullivan, *Trial by Jury*.

Date	General History	Literary History
1876	Turks massacre Bulgarians. Disraeli becomes Earl of Beaconsfield. Bell patents telephone. Otto's four-stroke internal-combustion engine. Rossetti, *Spirit of the rainbow*. Brahms, first symphony. Wagner, *Ring des Nibelungen*. Tchaikovsky, *Swan Lake*.	Forster d. Harriet Martineau d. G. M. Trevelyan b.
1877	Queen proclaimed Empress of India. Transvaal annexed. Praxiteles' *Hermes* found at Olympia. Edison invents phonograph. Pasteur starts work on causes of infectious diseases. Burne-Jones, *Perseus Slaying the Sea-Serpent* (*c.*1875–7). Rossetti, *Astarte Syriaca*. Whistler, *Nocturne in Black and Gold*. Brahms, second symphony.	Bagehot d. Granville-Barker b. *Nineteenth Century*. Morris, Webb, Faulkner found Society for Protection of Ancient Buildings. Ibsen, *Pillars of Society*.
1878	'Jingoism' against Russia. Beaconsfield gets Cyprus from Turkey in return for promise of protection. Afghan War. First electric street-lighting in London. Booth founds Salvation Army. 'Cleopatra's Needle' brought to London. London University opens all degrees to women. Woolner, *Lady Godiva Unrobing*.	G. H. Lewes d. Masefield b. Thomas b. Whistler gets farthing damages against Ruskin for libel. *English Men of Letters* series.
1879	Zulu War. British legation massacred at Kabul: Afghanistan invaded. Electric light bulb invented. Ayrton addresses British Association on 'Electricity as a Motive Power'. Somerville Hall (later College) founded at Oxford. Pearson, Truro Cathedral (to 1910). Tchaikovsky, *Eugen Onegin*. Joachim plays Brahms violin concerto.	E. M. Forster b. Monro b. Hopkins parish-priest at St Aloysius', Oxford. *Cambridge Review*. *The Boys' Own Paper*. Skeat's *Etymological Dictionary of the English Language*. Lewis and Short's *Latin Dictionary*. Grove's *Dictionary of Music and Musicians* (to 1889). Henry George, *Progress and Poverty*. Ibsen, *A Doll's House*.

Verse	Prose	Drama (date of acting)
Browning, *Pacchiarotto*. 'Carroll', *The Hunting of the Snark*. Fitzgerald, *Agamemnon* (published). Hopkins, 'Silver Jubilee'. Morris, *Sigurd the Volsung* ('1877'). Milnes, *Collected Works*. Tennyson, *Harold*.	Baring-Gould, *The Vicar of Morwenstow*. Bradley, *Ethical Studies*. Burnaby, *Ride to Khiva*. Molesworth, *Carrots: Just a Little Boy*. Stephen, *History of English Thought in the Eighteenth Century*. G. O. Trevelyan, *Life and Letters of Lord Macaulay*.	Tennyson, *Queen Mary*.
Browning (tr.), Aeschylus' *Agamemnon*. Dobson, *Proverbs in Porcelain*. Hopkins writes 'God's Grandeur', 'Starlight Night', 'Spring', 'In the Valley of the Elwy', 'Sea and the Skylark', 'Windhover', 'Pied Beauty', 'Hurrahing in Harvest', 'Caged Skylark', 'Lantern out of Doors'. Lear, *Laughable Lyrics*. L. Morris, *The Epic of Hades*. Patmore, *The Unknown Eros*.	Burnaby, *On Horseback through Asia Minor*. Finlay, *History of Greece from its Conquest by the Romans*. Green, *History of the English People*. MacDonald, *The Princess and Curdie*. Martineau, *Autobiography*. Meredith, *Idea of Comedy*. Sewell, *Black Beauty*. (Swinburne) *A Year's Letters* 'by Mrs Horace Manners'. Walton, *A Peep behind the Scenes*.	Gilbert, *Engaged*. With Sullivan, *The Sorcerer*.
Browning, *La Saisiaz*. Butler, 'Psalm of Montreal'. Hopkins writes 'Loss of the Eurydice', 'May Magnificat'. Patmore, *Amelia, etc. with prefatory study on English Metrical Law*. Symonds, *Many Moods*.	Butler, *Life and Habit*. Lecky, *History of England in the Eighteenth Century*. Pater, 'Child in the House'. Stevenson, *An Inland Voyage*.	Gilbert and Sullivan, *HMS Pinafore*.
E. Arnold, *The Light of Asia*. Browning, *Dramatic Idyls* (to 1880). Hopkins writes 'Binsey Poplars', 'Duns Scotus's Oxford', 'Henry Purcell', 'Candle Indoors', 'Handsome Heart', 'Bugler's First Communion', 'Morning, Midday, and Evening Sacrifice', 'Andromeda', 'Peace', 'At the Wedding March'. L. Morris, *Gwen: A Drama in Monologue*. Tennyson, *Lover's Tale* (started 1827–8, parts i–ii printed 1832).	Arnold, *Mixed Essays*. Butler, *Evolution, Old and New*. Ewing, *Jackanapes*. Mill, 'Chapters on Socialism'. Morris, 'Art of the People'. Stevenson, *Travels with a Donkey*.	Tennyson, *The Falcon*.

Date	General History	Literary History
1880	Gladstone PM. Bradlaugh, MP, refuses to swear on Bible. Attendance at elementary schools made compulsory. Manchester University founded. Burne-Jones, *Golden Stairs.* Dvorak, symphony in D.	'George Eliot' d. Taylor d. Noyes d. Lytton Strachey b. Ward's *English Poets* (to 1881). Ibsen's *Pillars of Society* (tr. Archer, as *Quicksands*) staged in London. Apollinaire b.
1881	Defeat by Boers at Majuba Hill. Habeas Corpus suspended in Ireland. Gladstone's Irish Land Act. South Kensington Natural History Museum. Flogging abolished in army. Hyndman forms Marxist Democratic Federation. Savoy Theatre lit by electricity. Rossetti, *Pia de' Tolomei.* Brahms, *Academic Festival Overture.* Offenbach, *Tales of Hoffmann.*	Beaconsfield d. Borrow d. Carlyle d. O'Shaughnessy d. Stanley d. Abercrombie b. P. G. Wodehouse b. Browning Society founded. Hopkins composes melody for Dixon's 'Fallen Rain'. Revised Version of New Testament. Westcott and Hort (ed.), *New Testament in Greek.* Ibsen, *Ghosts.* Verlaine, *Sagesse.*
1882	Phoenix Park murders. Europeans massacred in Egypt. Navy bombards Alexandria. Cairo occupied. Agrarian outrages in Ireland. Primrose League. Married Women's Property Act: rights of separate ownership. Street, Law Courts completed. Burne-Jones, *Hours, Tree of Forgiveness.* Watts, *Cardinal Manning.* Brahms, second piano concerto.	Darwin d. Rossetti d. Thomson d. Drinkwater b. Stephens b. Giraudoux b. Ibsen, *Enemy of the People.*
1883	Irish terrorism in London. Baring British Agent in Egypt. Frith, *Private View at the Royal Academy, 1881.* Tissot, *Frederick Gustavus Burnaby.* Royal College of Music (Grove Director). Brahms, third symphony.	Fitzgerald d. Green d. Jebb (ed.), Sophocles (to 1896). Nietzsche, *Also sprach Zarathustra.*

Verse	*Prose*	*Drama (date of acting)*
Hopkins writes 'Felix Randal', 'Brothers', 'Spring and Fall'. Swinburne, *Specimens of Modern Poets: Heptalogia, or The Seven against Sense*. Symonds, *New and Old*.	Arnold, 'Study of Poetry'. Henty, *The Young Buglers*. Hopkins writes notes on *Spiritual Exercises*. Huxley, 'Science and Culture'.	Gilbert and Sullivan, *The Pirates of Penzance*.
Hopkins writes 'Inversnaid'. C. Rossetti, 'Monna Innominata' (in *Pageant and Other Poems*). Rossetti, Ballads and Sonnets (with *The House of Life* expanded to 101 sonnets). Palgrave, *Visions of England*. Thomson, *Vane's Story and Other Poems*.	Butler, *Alps and Sanctuaries*. Carlyle, *Reminiscences*. Ewing, *Daddy Darwin's Dovecote*. Morris, 'Pattern-designing'.	Gilbert and Sullivan, *Patience*. Tennyson, *The Cup*.
'Carroll', 'Dreamland'. Hopkins writes 'Ribblesdale', 'Leaden Echo and Golden Echo'. Swinburne, *Tristram of Lyonesse*. Symonds, *Animi Figura*.	Arnold, 'A Word about America'. Creighton, *History of the Papacy* (1894). Froude, *History of the First Forty Years of Carlyle's Life*.	Gilbert and Sullivan, *Iolanthe*. Jones and Herman, *The Silver King*. Tennyson, *The Promise of the May*.
Browning, *Jocoseria*. Dixon, *Mano*. Hopkins, '"The Child is Father to the Man" (Wordsworth)'. Writes 'Blessed Virgin compared to the Air we Breathe'. Meredith, *Poems and Lyrics of the Joy of Earth*.	Jane Welsh Carlyle, *Letters and Memorials*, prepared by Carlyle, ed. Froude. Morris, 'Art, Wealth and Riches'. Seeley, *The Expansion of England*. Trollope, *Autobiography*.	

Date	General History	Literary History
1884	Third Reform Act. Fabian Society. Burne-Jones, *King Cophetua and the Beggar Maid.* Moore, *Reading Aloud.* Massenet, *Manon.*	Calverley d. Horne d. Pattison d. Flecker b. O'Casey b. Hamilton (ed.), *Parodies of the Works of English and American Writers* (to 1889). *New English Dictionary on Historical Principles* (i.e. *OED* to 1928). Ibsen, *The Wild Duck.* Leconte de Lisle, *Poèmes tragiques.*
1885	Gordon killed at Khartoum. Salisbury PM. Burmese War. Starley's 'Rover' safety bicycle. Benz's first motor car (three wheels, one cylinder). Pasteur's successful rabies inoculation. Marx, *Das Kapital,* ii. Sargent, *Robert Louis Stevenson and his Wife.* Brahms, fourth symphony.	Milnes d. *Dictionary of National Biography* (to 1900). *Commonweal.* Revised Version of Old Testament. Merton Professorship of English Language and Literature at Oxford. Hugo d. Ezra Pound b.
1886	Upper Burma annexed. Gladstone PM but defeated on Irish Home Rule. Salisbury PM. St Hugh's Hall (later College) Oxford. Severn Tunnel. Daimler's first motor car (four wheels). Millais, *Bubbles* bought for £2,200 to advertise Pears' soap. Watts, *Hope.* Bartholdi, *Liberty enlightening the World* (New York).	Taylor d. Trench d. Shelley Society. Ibsen, *Rosmersholm.*
1887	Queen's Golden Jubilee. Zululand annexed. 'Bloody Sunday' in Trafalgar Square. Zamenhof, textbook of Esperanto. Burne-Jones, *Depths of the Sea.* Brahms, double concerto. Stainer, *Crucifixion.* Verdi, *Otello.*	Rupert Brooke b. Edwin Muir b. Edith Sitwell b. Chekhov, *Ivanov.* Strindberg, *The Father.*

Verse	*Prose*	*Drama (date of acting)*
Hopkins writes 'Spelt from Sibyl's Leaves' (?1884-5). Tennyson, *Becket*. Thomson, 'Real Vision of Sin', 'Insomnia'.	Froude, *Carlyle's Life in London*. Morris, 'Art and Socialism'. Ruskin, *The Storm-Cloud of the Nineteenth Century*. Spencer, *The Man versus the State*.	Gilbert and Sullivan, *Princess Ida*. Jones, *Saints and Sinners*.
Hopkins writes 'To what serves Mortal Beauty', 'Soldier', 'Carrion Comfort', 'No worst, there is none', 'To seem the stranger', 'I wake and feel', 'Patience, hard thing!', 'My own heart'. Ingelow, *Poems*. 'Owen Meredith', *Glenaveril, or The Metamorphoses*. Morris, *Pilgrims of Hope*. Tennyson, *Tiresias and Other Poems* (adding 'Balin and Balan' to *Idylls of the King*).	Arnold, 'A Word More about America'. Cross, *George Eliot's Life as Related in her Letters and Journals*. Pater, *Marius the Epicurean*. Pattison, *Memoirs*. Ruskin, *Praeterita* (to 1889).	Gilbert and Sullivan, *The Mikado*. Pinero, *The Magistrate*.
Tennyson, *Locksley Hall Sixty Years After*.	Burnett, *Little Lord Fauntleroy*. Dowden, *Life of Percy Bysshe Shelley*. Morris, *A Dream of John Ball* (to 1887).	
Browning, *Parleyings with Certain People of Importance in their Day*. Hopkins writes 'Tom's Garland', 'Harry Ploughman'. Meredith, *Ballads and Poems of Tragic Life*.	Butler, *Luck or Cunning?* Darwin, *Autobiography*. Pater, *Imaginary Portraits*.	Gilbert and Sullivan, *Ruddigore*.

Date	General History	Literary History
1888	Local Government Act. Rhodes gets mining rights in Matabeleland. Eastman's 'Kodak' box-camera. Dunlop's pneumatic tyre. Hertz verifies Clerk-Maxwell's prediction of 1864 by demonstrating 'wireless' transmission of electromagnetic energy. Alma–Tadema, *Favourite Poet*. Rimsky-Korsakov, *Scheherazade*. R. Strauss, *Don Juan*. Butler and Festing Jones, *Narcissus* (oratorio).	Arnold d. Lear d. Maine d. T. S. Eliot b. T. E. Lawrence b. Eugene O'Neill b. Bellamy, *Looking Backward: 2000–1887*. Strindberg, *Miss Julie*.
1889	London Dock Strike ('Red Flag' written). Rhodes given Royal Charter for British South Africa Company. Eastman's celluloid roll-film. Sargent, *Paul Helleu Sketching with his Wife*. César Franck, symphony. Elgar, *Salut d' Amour*.	Allingham d. Browning d. (12 Dec.), having recorded recitation of 'How they Brought the Good News' on wax cylinder (7 Apr.). Hopkins d. Tupper d. Middleton Murry b. W. J. R. Turner b. *Granta*. Ibsen's *Doll's House* (tr. Archer) produced in London.
1890	International anti-slavery conference in Brussels. Rhodes PM of Cape Colony. Bechuanaland and Uganda under British control. Housing of the Working Classes Act. Deptford power-station. First electric underground railway starts operating in London (fare 2*d.*). Forth Bridge opened by Prince of Wales. Moore, *Summer Night*. Elgar, *Froissart*. Mascagni, *Cavalleria Rusticana*.	Newman d. W. B. Scott d. Morris founds Kelmscott Press. Tennyson records 'Blow, bugle, blow', 'The Charge of the Light Brigade', 'Come into the garden, Maud' on wax cylinders. Frazer, *Golden Bough*, i. William James, *Principles of Psychology*. Ibsen, *Hedda Gabler*.

Verse	*Prose*	*Drama (date of acting)*
Hopkins writes 'That Nature is a Heraclitean Fire', 'St Alphonsus Rodriguez'; starts 'Epithalamion'.	Arnold, *Essays in Criticism*, ii., 'Civilization in the United States'. Butler, *Ex Voto*. Doughty, *Travels in Arabia Deserta*.	Gilbert and Sullivan, *The Yeomen of the Guard*.
E. B. Browning, *Poetical Works* (with prefatory note by Browning). Browning (12 Dec.) *Asolando*. Fitzgerald (tr.), Attár's *Mantik-ut-tair* (in *Literary Remains*). Hopkins writes 'Thou art indeed just', 'The shepherd's brow', 'To R.B.' (i.e. Bridges). Swinburne, *Poems and Ballads*, iii. Tennyson, 'Crossing the Bar' (in *Demeter and Other Poems*.)	'Carroll', *Sylvie and Bruno*. Huxley, 'Agnosticism and Christianity'. Jerome, *Three Men in a Boat*. Morris, *House of the Wolfings*. Pater, *Appreciations*.	Gilbert and Sullivan, *The Gondoliers*.
Austin, *English Lyrics*. Gilbert, *Songs of a Savoyard, Illustrated by the Author*.	Anon., *My Secret Life* (printed *c.* 1890). Huxley, 'Keepers of the Herd of Swine'. Morris, *News from Nowhere*.	Pinero, *The Cabinet Minister*.

Select Bibliography

A. Bibliographical Guides

The New Cambridge Bibliography of English Literature, ed. G. Watson, vol. iii (Cambridge, 1969; abbrev.: *NCBEL*).
A Guide to English and American Literature, 3rd edn., ed. F. W. Bateson and H. T. Meserole (London, 1976).
The Victorian Poets: A Guide to Research, ed. F. E. Faverty, 2nd edn. (Cambridge, Mass., 1968; abbrev.: *Fav*).
Victorian Prose: A Guide to Research, ed. D. J. DeLaura (New York, 1973; abbrev.: *DeL*).
The Wellesley Index to Victorian Periodicals, ed. W. E. Houghton (Toronto, 1966–).

Annual Bibliographies
The Year's Work in English Studies (The English Association, 1919–).
Annual Bibliography of English Language and Literature (The Modern Humanities Research Association, 1920–).
International Bibliography of Books and Articles on the Modern Languages and Literatures (The Modern Language Association of America, 1969–).
Abstracts of English Studies (Boulder, Colo., 1958–).
'Victorian Bibliography', in *Victorian Studies* (Bloomington, Ind., 1958–).
'Guide to the Year's Work in Victorian Poetry', in *Victorian Poetry* (Morgantown, W. V., 1974–).
'Recent Studies in the Nineteenth Century', in *Studies in English Literature 1500–1900* (Houston, Tex., 1961–).

B. Books on Chapter-subjects

1. THE SPIRIT OF THE AGE

[See *Bibliography of British History 1789–1851*, ed. L. M. Brown and I. R. Christie (Oxford, 1977); *Bibliography of British History 1851–1914*, ed. H. J. Hanham (Oxford, 1976); *Victorian England 1837–1901*, ed. J. L. Altholz (Cambridge, 1970); *How to Find Out About the Victorian Period: A Guide to Sources of Information*, ed. L. Madden (Oxford, 1970)]

A. POLITICAL AND SOCIAL HISTORY

Best, G., *Mid-Victorian Britain 1851–1875* (London, 1971).

Dyos, H. J. and M. Wolff, *The Victorian City* (London, 1973).

Ensor, R. C. K., *England 1870–1914* (Oxford, 1936).

Harrison, J. F. C., *The Early Victorians 1832–1851* (London, 1971).

Hellerstein, E. O., L. P. Hume and K. M. Offen (eds.), *Victorian Women* (Brighton, 1981).

Humpherys, A., *Travels into the Poor Man's Country: The Work of Henry Mayhew* (Athens, Ga., 1977).

Jones, G. S., *Outcast London: A Study in the Relationship between Classes in Victorian Society* (Oxford, 1971).

Marcus, S., *Engels, Manchester, and the Working Class* (London, 1974).

Mitchell, S., *The Fallen Angel: Chastity, Class and Women's Reading 1835–1880* (Bowling Green, Ohio, 1981).

Trudgill, E., *Madonnas and Magdalens: The Origins and Development of Victorian Sexual Attitudes* (London, 1976).

Vicinus, M (ed.), *Suffer and be Still: Women in the Victorian Age* (Bloomington, Ind. 1972).

—— (ed.), *A Widening Sphere: Changing Roles of Victorian Women* (London, 1980).

Woodward, E. L., *The Age of Reform 1815–1870*, 2nd edn. (Oxford, 1962).

B. LITERARY AND CULTURAL HISTORY

General Studies

Altholz, J. L. (ed.), *The Mind and Art of Victorian England* (Minneapolis, Minn., 1976).

Altick, R. D., *The English Common Reader: A Social History of the Mass Reading Public 1800–1900* (Chicago, 1957).

—— *Victorian People and Ideas* (London, 1973).

Auerbach, N., *Woman and the Demon: The Life of a Victorian Myth* (Cambridge, Mass., 1982).

Batho, E. C. and B. Dobrée (edd.), *The Victorians and After 1830–1914* (London, 1938).

Buckler, W. E., *The Victorian Imagination: Essays in Aesthetic Exploration* (Brighton, 1980).

Conrad, P., *The Victorian Treasure-House* (London, 1973).

Elton, O., *A Survey of English Literature 1830–1880* (London, 1920).

Ford, B. (ed.), *The Pelican Guide to English Literature*, vol. vi, *From Dickens to Hardy*, rev. edn. (Harmondsworth, 1982).

Houghton, W. E., *The Victorian Frame of Mind* (New Haven, Conn., 1957).

Jenkyns, R., *The Victorians and Ancient Greece* (Oxford, 1980).

Kincaid, J. R. and A. J. Kuhn (edd.), *Victorian Literature and Society: Essays Presented to R. D. Altick* (Columbus, Ohio, 1983).

Knoepflmacher, U. C. and G. B. Tennyson (edd.), *Nature and the Victorian Imagination* (Berkeley, 1977).

Pollard, A., *The Victorians* (London, 1970).

Ricks, C. (ed.), *The New Oxford Book of Victorian Verse* (Oxford, 1987).

Sussman, H. L., *Victorians and the Machine: The Literary Response to Technology* (Cambridge, Mass., 1968).

Tillotson, G., *A View of Victorian Literature* (Oxford, 1978).

Turner, F. M., *The Greek Heritage in Victorian Britain* (New Haven, Conn., 1981).

Vicinus, M., *The Industrial Muse: A Study of Nineteenth-Century Working-Class Literature* (London, 1974).

Ward, A. W. and A. R. Waller (edd.), *The Cambridge History of English Literature*, vols. xii–xiv (Cambridge, 1915–16).

Wellek, R., *A History of Modern Criticism 1750–1950*, vol. iii, *The Age of Transition* (New Haven, Conn., 1964).

Williams, R., *Culture and Society 1780–1950* (London, 1967).

Religion

Bradley, I., *The Call to Seriousness: The Evangelical Impact on the Victorians* (London, 1976).

Briggs, J. and I. Sellers (edd.), *Victorian Nonconformity* (London, 1973).

Chadwick, O., *The Victorian Church* (London, 1966–70).

Clark, G. K., *Churchmen and the Condition of England 1832–1885* (London, 1973).

Jay, E. (ed.), *The Evangelical and Oxford Movements* (Cambridge, 1983).

Prickett, S., *Romanticism and Religion: The Tradition of Coleridge and Wordsworth in the Victorian Church* (Cambridge, 1976).

Reardon, B. M. G., *From Coleridge to Gore: A Century of Religious Thought in Britain* (London, 1971).

Rowell, G., *Hell and the Victorians: A Study of the Nineteenth-Century Theological Controversies Concerning Eternal Punishment and the Future Life* (Oxford, 1974).

Turner, F. M., *Between Science and Religion: The Reaction to Scientific Naturalism in Late Nineteenth-Century England* (New Haven, Conn., 1974).

Science

Bowler, P. J., *Evolution: The History of an Idea* (Berkeley, 1984).

Hall, M. B., *All Scientists Now: The Royal Society in the Nineteenth Century* (Cambridge, 1984).

Harré, R. (ed.), *Some Nineteenth-Century Scientists* (Oxford, 1969).

Singer, C. J., *A Short History of Scientific Ideas to 1900* (Oxford, 1959).

Education

Allen, P., *The Cambridge Apostles: The Early Years* (Cambridge, 1978).

Armytage, W. H. G., *Four Hundred Years of English Education*, 2nd edn. (Cambridge, 1970).

Kelly, T., *A History of Adult Education in England*, 2nd edn. (Liverpool, 1970).

Palmer, D. J., *The Rise of English Studies: An Account of the Study of English*

Language and Literature from the Origins to the Making of the Oxford English School (London, 1965).

Rothblatt, S., *The Revolution of the Dons: Cambridge and Society in Victorian England* (London, 1978).

Journalism

[See L. Madden and D. Dixon, *The Nineteenth-Century Periodical Press in Britain: A Bibliography of Modern Studies 1901–1971* (New York, 1976) and J. D. Vann and R. T. Van Arsdel (edd.), *Victorian Periodicals: A Guide to Research* (New York, 1978)]

Armstrong, I., *Victorian Scrutinies: Reviews of Poetry 1830–1870* (London, 1972).

Wolff, M. (ed.), *The Victorian Periodical Press: Samplings and Soundings* (Leicester, 1982).

Music

Abraham, G., *New Oxford History of Music*, vol. ix, *Romanticism 1830–1890* (Oxford, 1889).

Colles, H. C., *Oxford History of Music*, vol. vii, *Symphony and Drama 1850–1900* (Oxford, 1934).

Russell, D., *Popular Music in England 1840–1914: A Social Survey* (Manchester 1987).

The Visual Arts

[See E. Arntzen and B. Rainwater (edd.), *Guide to the Literature of Art History* (Chicago, 1980)]

Bendiner, K., *An Introduction to Victorian Painting* (New Haven, Conn., 1985).

Boase, T. S. R., *English Art 1800–1870* (Oxford, 1959).

Farr, D., *English Art 1870–1940* (Oxford, 1978).

Girouard, M., *The Victorian Country House* (Oxford, 1971).

Harrison, M., *Victorian Stained Glass* (London, 1980).

Hitchcock, H.-R., *Architecture: Nineteenth and Twentieth Centuries* (Harmondsworth, 1958).

Jordan, R. F., *Victorian Architecture* (Harmondsworth, 1966).

Maas, J., *Victorian Painters* (London, 1969).

Ormond, R., *Early Victorian Portraits* (London, 1973).

—— and M. Rogers (edd.), *Dictionary of British Portraiture*, vol. iii, *The Victorians* (New York, 1981).

Ovenden, G. (ed.), *A Victorian Album: Julia Margaret Cameron and her Circle* (London, 1975).

Read, B., *Victorian Sculpture* (New Haven, Conn., 1982).

Reynolds, A. G., *Victorian Painting* (London, 1966).

Thompson, P., *Victorian and Modern Architecture* (Harmondsworth, 1965).

White, J. F., *The Cambridge Movement: The Ecclesiologists and the Gothic Revival* (Cambridge, 1962).

Wood, C., *Victorian Panorama: Paintings of Victorian Life* (London, 1976).

2. TENNYSON

[See K. H. Beetz, *Tennyson: A Bibliography 1827–1982* (Metuchen, NJ, 1984)]

Albright, D., *Tennyson: The Muses' Tug-of-War* (Charlottesville, 1986).

Assad, T. J., *Tennysonian Lyric: 'Songs of the Deeper Kind' and 'In Memoriam'* (New Orleans, 1984).

Colley, A. C., *Tennyson and Madness* (Athens, Ga., 1983).

Gray, J. M. (ed.), *Idylls of the King* (Harmondsworth, 1983).

Lang, C. Y. and E. F. Shannon (edd.), *The Letters of Alfred Lord Tennyson*, vol. i, 1821–1850, vol. ii, 1851–1870 (Oxford, 1982, 1987).

Peltason, T., *Reading 'In Memoriam'* (Princeton, NJ, 1985).

Ricks, C. (ed.), *The Poems of Tennyson, Second Edition, incorporating the Trinity College Manuscripts* (Harlow, 1987).

—— and A. Day (edd.), *The Tennyson Archive* (New York, 1987–   ).

Shatto, S. (ed.), *Tennyson's 'Maud': A Definitive Edition* (London, 1986).

—— and M. Shaw (edd.), *In Memoriam* (Oxford, 1982).

Tillotson, K. M. and S. Race, *Tennyson: Two Talks* (Lincoln, 1985).

3. BROWNING

[See L. N. Broughton, C. S. Northup and R. Pearsall, *Robert Browning: A Bibliography 1830–1950* (Ithaca, 1953); W. S. Peterson, *Robert Browning and Elizabeth Barrett Browning: An Annotated Bibliography 1951–1970* (New York, 1974); P. Kelley and R. Hudson, *The Brownings' Correspondence: A Checklist* (New York, 1978); V. P. Anderson, *Robert Browning as a Religious Poet: An Annotated Bibliography of the Criticism* (Troy, NY, 1983)]

Altick, R. D. (ed.), *The Ring and the Book* (Harmondsworth, 1971).

Armstrong, I. (ed.), *Robert Browning* (London, 1974).

Bloom, H. and I. Munich (edd.), *Robert Browning: A Collection of Critical Essays* (Englewood Cliffs, 1979).

Brugière, B., *L'univers imaginaire de Robert Browning* (Paris, 1979).

Chell, S. L., *The Dynamic Self: Browning's Poetry of Duration* (Victoria, BC, 1984).

Crowell, N. B., *A Reader's Guide to Robert Browning* (Albuquerque, N. Mex., 1972).

Erickson, L., *Robert Browning: His Poetry and His Audiences* (Ithaca, 1984).

Gridley, R., *Browning* (London, 1972).

Hair, D. S., *Browning's Experiments with Genre* (Edinburgh, 1972).

Hassett, C. W., *The Elusive Self in the Poetry of Robert Browning* (Athens, Ohio, 1982).

Irvine, W. and P. Honan, *The Book, the Ring, and the Poet: A Biography of Robert Browning* (New York, 1975).

Jack, I., *Browning's Major Poetry* (Oxford, 1973).

—— and M. Smith (edd.), *The Poetical Works of Robert Browning* (Oxford, 1983–).

Karlin, D., *The Courtship of Robert Browning and Elizabeth Barrett* (Oxford, 1985).

Kelley, P. and R. Hudson (edd.), *The Brownings' Correspondence* (Winfield, Kan., 1984–).

Khatab, E. A., *The Critical Reception of 'The Ring and the Book' 1868–1889 and 1951–1968* (Salzburg, 1977).

King, R. A. (gen. ed.), *The Complete Works of Robert Browning, with Variant Readings and Annotations* (Athens, Ohio, 1969–).

Korg, J., *Browning and Italy* (Athens, Ohio, 1983).

Lawson, E. Le R., *Very Sure of God: Religious Language in the Poetry of Robert Browning* (Nashville, 1974).

Maynard, J., *Browning's Youth* (Cambridge, Mass., 1977).

Montaut, M., *Robert Browning: Men and Women* (Harlow, 1984).

Peterson, W. S. (ed.), *Browning's Trumpeter: The Correspondence of Robert Browning and Frederick J. Furnivall 1872–1889* (Washington, DC, 1979).

Pettigrew, J. and T. J. Collins (edd.), *Robert Browning: The Poems* (Harmondsworth, 1981).

Phipps, C. T., *Browning's Clerical Characters* (Salzburg, 1976).

Rivers, C. L., *Robert Browning's Theory of the Poet 1833–1841* (Salzburg, 1976).

Ryals, C. de L., *Browning's Later Poetry 1871–1889* (Ithaca, 1975).

—— *Becoming Browning: The Poems and Plays of Robert Browning 1833–1846* (Columbus, Ohio, 1983).

Slinn, E. W., *Browning and the Fictions of Identity* (London, 1982).

Thomas, D. S., *Robert Browning: A Life Within Life* (London, 1982).

Trickett, R., *Browning's Lyricism* (London, 1971).

Tucker, H. F., *Browning's Beginnings: The Art of Disclosure* (Minneapolis, 1980).

Turner, P. (ed.), *Men and Women* (London, 1972).

Watson, J. R. (ed.), *Men and Women and Other Poems: A Casebook* (London, 1974).

4. CLOUGH

[See R. M. Gollin, W. E. Houghton and M. Timko, *Arthur Hugh Clough: A Descriptive Catalogue: Poetry, Prose, Biography and Criticism* (New York, 1967); M. Timko, 'Arthur Hugh Clough' in *Fav*; P. G. Scott, *The Early Editions of Arthur Hugh Clough* (New York, 1977)]

Biswas, R. K., *Arthur Hugh Clough: Towards a Reconsideration* (Oxford, 1972).

Greenberger, E. B., *Arthur Hugh Clough: The Growth of a Poet's Mind* (Cambridge, Mass., 1970).

Harris, W. V., *Arthur Hugh Clough* (New York, 1970).

Mulhauser, F. L. (ed.), *The Poems of Arthur Hugh Clough*, 2nd edn., with translations ed. J. Turner (Oxford, 1974).

Scott, P. G. (ed.), *Amours de Voyage* (St Lucia, 1974).

—— (ed.), *The Bothie: The Text of 1848* (St Lucia, 1976).

Thorpe, M. (ed.), *Clough: The Critical Heritage* (London, 1972).

Williams, D., *Too Quick Depairer: A Life of Arthur Hugh Clough* (London, 1969).

5. MATTHEW ARNOLD

[See F. E. Faverty, 'Matthew Arnold' in *Fav*; J. Bertram, 'Arnold' in A. E. Dyson (ed.), *English Poetry: Select Bibliographical Guides* (London, 1971); V. L. Tollers, *A Bibliography of Matthew Arnold 1932–1970* (University Park, 1974); A. K. Davis, *Matthew Arnold's Letters: A Descriptive Checklist* (Charlottesville, 1968)]

Allott, K. (ed.), *Matthew Arnold* (London, 1975).

—— (ed.), *The Poems of Matthew Arnold* (2nd edn., ed. M. Allott; London, 1979).

Allott, M. and R. H. Super (edd.), *Matthew Arnold* (Oxford, 1986).

ApRoberts, R., *Arnold and God* (Berkeley, 1983).

Buckler, W. E., *On the Poetry of Matthew Arnold: Essays in Critical Reconstruction* (New York, 1982).

—— *Matthew Arnold's Prose: Three Essays in Literary Enlargement* (New York, 1983).

Bush, D., *Matthew Arnold: A Survey of His Poetry and Prose* (London, 1971).

Carroll, J., *The Cultural Theory of Matthew Arnold* (Berkeley, 1982).

Coulling, S., *Matthew Arnold and his Critics: A Study of Arnold's Controversies* (Ohio, 1974).

Dawson, C. (ed.), *Matthew Arnold: The Poetry: The Critical Heritage* (London, 1973).

—— and J. Pfordresher (edd.), *Matthew Arnold: Prose Writings: The Critical Heritage* (London, 1979).

Honan, P., *Matthew Arnold: A Life* (London, 1981).

Robbins, W., *The Arnoldian Principle of Flexibility* (Victoria, BC, 1979).

Rowse, A. L., *Matthew Arnold: Poet and Prophet* (London, 1976).

Simpson, J., *Matthew Arnold and Goethe* (London, 1979).

Super, R. H. (ed.), *The Complete Prose Works of Matthew Arnold* (Ann Arbor, 1960–77).

Tesdorpf, I.-M., *Die Auseinandersetzung Matthew Arnolds mit Heinrich Heine* (Frankfurt am Main, 1971).

6. FOUR LESSER POETS

Mrs Browning

[See M. Timko, 'Elizabeth Barrett Browning' in *Fav*, and W. S. Peterson, *Robert and Elizabeth Barrett Browning: An Annotated Bibliography 1951–1970* (New York, 1974). See also Bibliography to Chap. 3 above)]

Berridge, E. (ed.), *The Barretts at Hope End: The Early Diary of Elizabeth Barrett Browning* (London, 1974).

Heydon, P. N. and P. Kelley (edd.), *Elizabeth Barrett's Letters to Mrs. David Ogilvy 1849–1861* (New York, 1973).

Leighton, A., *Elizabeth Barrett Browning* (Brighton, 1986).

Mander, R., *Mrs Browning: The Story of Elizabeth Barrett* (London, 1980).

Peterson, W. S. (ed.), *Sonnets from the Portuguese: A Facsimile Edition of the British Library Manuscript* (New York, 1977).

Pope, W. B. (ed.), *Invisible Friends: The Correspondence of Elizabeth Barrett and Benjamin Robert Haydon 1842–1845* (Cambridge, Mass., 1972).

Fitzgerald

[See M. Timko, 'Edward Fitzgerald' in *Fav*]

Graves, R. and O. Ali-Shah (tr.), *The Rubaiyyat of Omar Khayaam: A New Translation with Critical Commentaries* (London, 1968).

Hayter, A. (ed.), *Fitzgerald to His Friends: Selected Letters of Edward Fitzgerald* (London, 1979).

Kasra, P. (tr.), *The Ruba'iyat of 'Umar Khayyam: Translated with an Introduction* (New York, 1975).

Martin, R. B., *With Friends Possessed: A Life of Edward Fitzgerald* (London, 1985).

Terhune, A. M. and A. B. (edd.), *The Letters of Edward Fitzgerald* (Princeton, NJ, 1980).

Patmore

[See L. Stevenson, 'Coventry Patmore' in *Fav*]

Weinig, M. A., *Coventry Patmore* (Boston, Mass., 1981).

Meredith

[See L. Stevenson, 'George Meredith' in *Fav*; and M. Collie, *George Meredith: A Bibliography* (no secondary material; Folkestone, 1974)]

Bartlett, P. B. (ed.), *The Poems of George Meredith* (New Haven, Conn., 1978).

Beer, G. and M. Harris (edd.), *The Notebooks of George Meredith* (Salzburg, 1983).

Bernstein, C. L., *Precarious Enchantment: A Reading of Meredith's Poetry* (Washington, DC, 1979).
Cline, C. L. (ed.), *The Letters of George Meredith* (Oxford, 1970).
Hanley, K. (ed.), *George Meredith: Selected Poems* (Manchester, 1983).
Johnson, D., *The True Story of the First Mrs. Meredith and Other Lesser Lives* (London, 1972).
Singh, P., *George Meredith: The Poet* (New Delhi, 1973).
Williams, J. (ed.), *Meredith: The Critical Heritage* (London, 1971).

7. THE PRE-RAPHAELITES

[See W. E. Fredeman, *Pre-Raphaelitism: A Bibliocritical Study* (Cambridge, Mass., 1965) and 'The Pre-Raphaelites' in *Fav*]

Fredeman, W. E. (ed.), *The P.R.B. Journal: William Michael Rossetti's Diary of the Pre-Raphaelite Brotherhood 1849–1853, together with Other Pre-Raphaelite Fragments* (Oxford, 1975).
Hilton, T., *The Pre-Raphaelites, with 157 Illustrations, 21 in Colour* (London, 1970).
Hunt, J. D., *The Pre-Raphaelite Imagination 1848–1900* (London, 1968).
Lang, C. Y. (ed.), *The Pre-Raphaelites and Their Circle: with the Rubáiyat of Omar Khayyám* (Boston, Mass., 1968).
Nicoll, J., *The Pre-Raphaelites* (London, 1970).
Rose, A. (ed.), *The Germ: The Literary Magazine of the Pre-Raphaelites* (Oxford, 1979).
Stanford, D. (ed.), *Pre-Raphaelite Writing: An Anthology* (London, 1973).
Stevenson, L., *The Pre-Raphaelite Poets* (Chapel Hill, 1972).
Watkinson, R., *Pre-Raphaelite Art and Design* (London, 1970).

D. G. Rossetti

[See F. L. Fennell, *Dante Gabriel Rossetti: An Annotated Bibliography* (New York, 1982)]

Fredeman, W. E. (ed.), *Victorian Poetry: An Issue Devoted to the Works of Dante Gabriel Rossetti* (Morgantown, 1982).
Rees, J., *The Poetry of Dante Gabriel Rossetti: Modes of Self-Expression* (Cambridge, 1981).

C. G. Rossetti

[See R. W. Crump, *Christina Rossetti: A Reference Guide* (Boston, Mass., 1976)]

Battiscombe, G., *Christina Rossetti: A Divided Life* (London, 1981).
Bellas, R. A., *Christina Rossetti* (Boston, Mass., 1977).
Charles, E. K., *Christina Rossetti: Critical Perspectives 1862–1892* (London, 1985).
Crump, R. W. (ed.), *The Complete Poems of Christina Rossetti: A Variorum Edition* (Baton Rouge, La., 1979–   ).

Weintraub, S., *Four Rossettis: A Victorian Biography* (London, 1978).

Morris

[See W. E. Fredeman, 'William Morris' in *Fav*]

Bradley, I., *William Morris and His World: with 145 Illustrations* (London, 1978).
Clark, F., *William Morris: Wallpapers and Chintzes* (London, 1973).
Fairclough, O. and E. Leary, *Textiles by William Morris and Morris & Co 1861–1940* (London, 1981).
Faulkner, P. (ed.), *Early Romances in Prose and Verse* (London, 1973).
—— (ed.), *William Morris: The Critical Heritage* (London, 1973).
—— *Against the Age: An Introduction to William Morris* (London, 1980).
Fitzgerald, P. (ed.), *The Novel on Blue Paper by William Morris* (London, 1982).
Gardner, D. R., *An 'Idle Singer' and His Audience: A Study of William Morris's Reputation in England 1858–1900* (The Hague, 1975).
Johnson, F. (ed.), *Ornamentation and Illustrations from the Kelmscott Chaucer, with an Introduction* (New York, 1973).
Kelvin, N. (ed.), *William Morris: The Collected Letters* (Princeton, NJ, 1984–).
LeMire, E. D. (ed.), *The Unpublished Lectures of William Morris* (Detroit, 1969).
Lindsay, J., *William Morris: His Life and Work* (London, 1975).
Meier, P., *La Pensée utopique de William Morris*, tr. W. Gubb as *William Morris, the Marxist Dreamer* (Hassocks, Sussex, 1978).
Oberg, C. H., *A Pagan Prophet: William Morris* (Charlottesville, 1978).
Peterson, W. S. (ed.), *The Ideal Book: Essays and Lectures on the Arts of the Book by William Morris* (Berkeley, 1982).
Robinson, D. and S. Wildman *Morris and Company in Cambridge* (Cambridge, 1980).
Stansky, P., *William Morris* (Oxford, 1983).
—— *Redesigning the World: William Morris, the 1880s, and the Arts and Crafts* (Princeton, NJ, 1985).

Swinburne

[See C. L. Hyder, 'Algernon Charles Swinburne' in *Fav*]

Findlay, L. M. (ed.), *Algernon Charles Swinburne: Selected Poems* (Manchester, 1982).
Fuller, J. O., *Swinburne: A Critical Biography* (London, 1968).
Henderson, P., *Swinburne: The Portrait of a Poet* (London, 1974).
Hyder, C. L. (ed.), *Swinburne: The Critical Heritage* (London, 1970).
McGann, J. J., *Swinburne: An Experiment in Criticism* (Chicago, 1972).
Panter-Downes, M., *At The Pines: Swinburne and Watts-Dunton in Putney* (London, 1971).
Peckham, M. (ed.), *Poems and Ballads, Atalanta in Calydon* (Indianapolis, 1970).

Sypher, F. J. (ed.), *A Year's Letters* (New York, 1974).

—— (ed.), *Undergraduate Papers: An Oxford Journal Conducted by A. C. Swinburne . . . and Others* (Delmar, NY, 1974).

Walder, A., *Swinburne's Flowers of Evil: Baudelaire's Influence on 'Poems and Ballads', First Series* (Uppsala, 1976).

8. HOPKINS

(See T. Dunne, *Gerard Manley Hopkins: A Comprehensive Bibliography* (to 1970; Oxford, 1976)]

Bergonzi, B., *Gerard Manley Hopkins* (London, 1977).

Bottrall, M. (ed.), *Gerard Manley Hopkins: A Casebook* (London, 1975).

Bump, J., *Gerard Manley Hopkins* (Boston, Mass., 1982).

Davies, W. (ed.), *Gerard Manley Hopkins: The Major Poems* (London, 1979).

Downes, D. A., *The Great Sacrifice: Studies in Hopkins* (New York, 1983).

Harris, D. A., *Inspirations Unbidden: The 'Terrible Sonnets' of Gerard Manley Hopkins* (Berkeley, 1982).

Kitchen, P., *Gerard Manley Hopkins* (London, 1978).

MacKenzie, N. H., *A Reader's Guide to Gerard Manley Hopkins* (London, 1981).

Milroy, J., *The Language of Gerard Manley Hopkins* (London, 1977).

Milward, P., *Landscape and Inscape* (London, 1975).

—— (ed.), *Readings of 'The Wreck'* (Chicago, 1976).

Motto, M., *Mined with a Motion: The Poetry of Gerard Manley Hopkins* (New Brunswick, NJ, 1984).

North, J. S. and M. D. Moore (edd.), *Vital Candle: Victorian and Modern Bearings in Gerard Manley Hopkins* (Waterloo, 1984).

Peters, W. A. M., *Gerard Manley Hopkins: A Tribute* (Chicago, 1984).

Phillips, C. (ed.), *Gerard Manley Hopkins* (Oxford, 1986).

Roberts, G. (ed.), *Gerard Manley Hopkins: Selected Prose* (Oxford, 1980).

—— (ed.), *Gerard Manley Hopkins: The Critical Heritage* (London, 1987).

Robinson, J., *In Extremity: A Study of Gerard Manley Hopkins* (Cambridge, 1978).

Russell, J. F. J., *A Critical Commentary on Gerard Manley Hopkins's 'Poems'* (London, 1971).

Storey, G., *Gerard Manley Hopkins* (London, 1984).

Sulloway, A. G., *Gerard Manley Hopkins and the Victorian Temper* (London, 1972).

Thornton, R. K. R., *Gerard Manley Hopkins: The Poems* (London, 1973).

—— (ed.), *All My Eyes See: The Visual World of Gerard Manley Hopkins* (Sunderland, 1975).

Walhout, D., *Send My Roots Rain: A Study of Religious Experience in the Poetry of Gerard Manley Hopkins* (Ohio, 1981).

9. OTHER POETS

[See 'Minor Poetry' in *NCBEL*]

Keble

Battiscombe, G., *John Keble: A Study in Limitations* (London, 1963).
Martin, B. W., *John Keble: Priest, Professor and Poet* (London, 1976).
Tennyson, G. B., *Victorian Devotional Poetry: The Tractarian Mode* (Cambridge, Mass., 1981).

Barnes

Forster, E. M., 'William Barnes' in *One Hundred Poems* (Blandford Forum, 1971).
Jones, B. (ed.), *The Poems of William Barnes* (London, 1962).
Keen, L. and C. Lindgren, *William Barnes: The Dorset Engravings* (Dorchester, 1986).
Wrigley, C. (ed.), *William Barnes, the Dorset Poet: Introduced and Selected* (Stanbridge, 1984).

Horne

Blainey, A., *The Farthing Poet: A Biography of Richard Hengist Horne 1802–84, A Lesser Literary Lion* (London, 1968).

Hawker

Brendon, P., *Hawker of Morwenstow: Portrait of a Victorian Eccentric* (London, 1975).
Tregellas, A., *The Vicar in Sea Boots: Rev. R. S. Hawker* (Padstow, 1975).

Hallam

Kolb, J., *The Hero and His Worshippers: The History of A. H. Hallam's Letters* (Manchester, 1973).
—— (ed.), *The Letters of Arthur Henry Hallam* (Columbus, Ohio, 1981).

Aytoun

Weinstein, M. A., *William Edmonstoune Aytoun and the Spasmodic Controversy* (New Haven, Conn., 1968).

E. Brontë

[See J. M. Barclay, *Emily Brontë Criticism 1900–1968: An Annotated Checklist* (New York, 1974) and G. A. Yablon and J. R. Turner, *A Brontë Bibliography* (London, Conn., 1978)]

Winnifrith, T., *The Brontës and their Background: Romance and Reality* (London, 1973).

Kingsley

[See S. Harris, *Charles Kingsley: A Reference Guide* (to 1978; Boston, Mass., 1981)]

Jean Ingelow

Peters, M., *Jean Ingelow: Victorian Poetess* (Ipswich, 1972).

Cory

Carter, J. W., *William Johnson Cory 1823–1892* (Cambridge, 1959).

Allingham

[See S. A. Husni, *William Allingham: An Annotated Bibliography* (Beirut, 1984)]

Warner, A. J., *William Allingham: An Introduction* (Dublin, 1971).

MacDonald

[See J. M. Bulloch, *A Centennial Bibliography of G. MacDonald* (Aberdeen, 1925)]

Hein, R., *The Harmony Within: The Spiritual Vision of George Macdonald* (Michigan, 1982).
Holbrook, D. (ed.), *Phantastes*, with introd. (London, 1983).
Sadler, G. E. (ed.), *The Gifts of the Child Christ* (London, 1973).
Triggs, K., *George Macdonald* (Basingstoke, 1984).

Palgrave

Okachi, M. (ed.), *Oxford Lectures on Poetry* (Tokyo, 1973).

'Owen Meredith'

Raymond, E. N., *Victorian Viceroy: The Life of Robert, the first Earl of Lytton* (London, 1980).

L. Morris

Phillips, R. D., *Sir Lewis Morris* (Cardiff, 1981).

Thomson

[See L. Stevenson, 'James Thomson' in *Fav*]

Schaefer, W. D. (ed.), *'The Speedy Extinction of Evil and Misery'* (selected prose; Berkeley, 1967).
Thesing, W. B., *The London Muse: Victorian Poetic Responses to the City* (Athens, Ga., 1982).

Symonds

Peters, R. L. and D'A. Smith (edd.), *Gabriel: A Poem* (London, 1974).
Schueller, H. M. and R. L. Peters (edd.), *The Letters of John Addington Symonds* (Detroit, 1967–9).

O'Shaughnessy

Paden, W. D., *Arthur O'Shaughnessy: The Ancestry of a Victorian Poet* (Manchester, 1964).
Wieselhuber, F., *Die Faszination des Bösen in der viktorianischen Lyrik* (Heidelberg, 1976).

10. CARLYLE

[See G. B. Tennyson, 'Thomas Carlyle' in *DeL* and R. L. Tarr, *Thomas Carlyle: A Bibliography of English-Language Criticism 1824–1974* (Charlottesville, 1976)]

Behnken, E. M., *Thomas Carlyle: Calvinist without the Theology* (Columbia, Mo., 1978).
Campbell, I., *Thomas Carlyle* (Harlow, 1978).
Cate, G. A. (ed.), *The Correspondence of Thomas Carlyle and John Ruskin* (Stanford, 1982).
Clubbe, J. (ed.), *Two Reminiscences of Thomas Carlyle*, tr. from F. Althaus (Durham, NC, 1974).
—— (ed.), *Carlyle and His Contemporaries: Essays in Honor of C. R. Sanders* (Durham, NC, 1976).
Dale, P. A., *The Victorian Critic and the Idea of History: Carlyle, Arnold, Pater* (Cambridge, Mass., 1977).
Dibble, J. A., *The Pythia's Drunken Song: T. Carlyle's 'Sartor Resartus' and the Style Problem in German Idealist Philosophy* (The Hague, 1978).
Drescher, H. W. (ed.), *Thomas Carlyle 1981* (Frankfurt am Main, 1983).
Fielding, K. J. and R. L. Tarr (edd.), *Carlyle Past and Present: A Collection of New Essays* (London, 1976).
Goldberg, M. K. and J. P. Seigel (edd.), *Latter-Day Pamphlets* (Ottawa, 1983).
Harris, K. M., *Carlyle and Emerson: Their Long Debate* (Cambridge, Mass., 1978).
Kaplan, F., *Thomas Carlyle: A Biography* (Cambridge, 1983).
Krahé, P., *Thomas Carlyle, John Ruskin, Matthew Arnold: die weltanschauliche Krise und ihre literarische Verarbeitung* (Bonn, 1978).
Le Quesne, A. L., *Carlyle* (Oxford, 1982).
Rosenberg, J. D., *Carlyle and the Burden of History* (Oxford, 1985).
Sanders, C. R. (ed.), *The Letters of Thomas and Jane Welsh Carlyle* (Durham, NC, 1970–).
—— (ed.), *The Carlyle-Browning Correspondence and Relationship* (Manchester, 1975).
—— *Carlyle's Friendships, and Other Studies* (Durham, NC, 1977).
Sussmann, H. L., *Fact into Figure: Typology in Carlyle, Ruskin, and the Pre-Raphaelite Brotherhood* (Columbus, Ohio, 1979).
Vijn, J. P., *Carlyle and Jean Paul: Their Spiritual Optics* (Amsterdam, 1982).

11. NEWMAN

[See M. J. Svaglic and C. S. Dessain, 'John Henry Newman' in *DeL*; M. Dennigan, *The Works of J. H. Newman: A Checklist* (Dublin, 1974); V. F. Blehl, *John Henry Newman: A Bibliographical Catalogue of his Writings* (Charlottesville, 1978); J. R. Griffin, *Newman: A Bibliography of Secondary Studies* (Front Royal, Va., 1980)]

Bastable, J. D. (ed.), *Newman and Gladstone: Centennial Essays* (Dublin, 1978).

Chadwick, W. O., *Newman* (Oxford, 1983).

Davies, M. (ed.), *Newman against the Liberals: Twenty-Five Sermons Selected with a Preface* (Chawleigh, 1978).

Dessain, C. S., *John Henry Newman*, 3rd edn. (Oxford, 1980).

Hill, A. G. (ed.), *Loss and Gain* (Oxford, 1986).

Ker, I. T. (ed.), *The Idea of a University* (Oxford, 1976).

—— (ed.), *An Essay in Aid of a Grammar of Assent* (Oxford, 1985).

Lash, N. L. A., *Newman on Development: The Search for an Explanation in History* (London, 1979).

—— (ed.), *An Essay in Aid of a Grammar of Assent* (Notre Dame, Ia., 1979).

Martin, B. W., *John Henry Newman: His Life and Work* (London, 1982).

Sugg, J. (ed.), *A Packet of Letters: A Selection from the Correspondence of John Henry Newman, with Introduction* (Oxford, 1983).

Yearsley, L. H., *The Ideas of Newman: Christianity and Human Religiosity* (University Park, 1978).

12. RUSKIN

[See F. C. Townsend, 'John Ruskin' in *DeL* and K. H. Beetz, *John Ruskin: A Bibliography 1900–1974* (Metuchen, NJ, 1976)]

Abse, J., *John Ruskin: The Passionate Moralist* (London, 1980).

Anthony, P. D., *John Ruskin's Labour: A Study of Ruskin's Social Theory* (Cambridge, 1983).

Barnes, J., *Ruskin in Sheffield* (Sheffield, 1985).

Bell, Q. C. S., *Ruskin* (London, 1978).

Birch, D., *Ruskin's Myths* (Oxford, 1988).

Bradley, J. L. (ed.), *Ruskin: The Critical Heritage* (London, 1984).

—— and I. Ousby (edd.), *The Correspondence of John Ruskin and Charles Eliot Norton* (Cambridge, 1987).

Burd, V. A. (ed.), *John Ruskin and Rose La Touche: Her Unpublished Diaries of 1861 and 1867, Introduced and Edited* (Oxford, 1979).

Clegg, J., *Ruskin and Venice* (London, 1981).

Conner, P. R., *Savage Ruskin* (London, 1979).

Desylva, G. F., *John Ruskin's 'Modern Painters' i and ii: A Phenomenological Analysis* (Ann Arbor, 1981).

Evans, J. (ed.), *The Lamp of Beauty: Ruskin's Writings on Art, Selected and Edited*, 2nd edn. (Oxford, 1980).

Fellows, J., *The Failing Distance: The Autobiographical Impulse in John Ruskin* (Baltimore, 1975).

Fitch, R. E., *The Poison Sky: Myth and Apocalypse in Ruskin* (Athens, Ohio, 1982).

Fontaney, P., *Ruskin esthéticien: les années de formation* (Lille, 1980).

Hardman, M., *Ruskin and Bradford: An Experiment in Victorian Cultural History* (Manchester, 1986).

Hayman, J. (ed.), *Letters from the Continent 1858* (Toronto, 1982).

Helsinger, E. K., *Ruskin and the Art of the Beholder* (Cambridge, Mass., 1982).

Hewison, R. A. P., *John Ruskin: The Argument of the Eye* (Princeton, NJ, 1976).

—— *Ruskin and Venice* (London, 1978).

—— *Art and Society: Ruskin in Sheffield 1876* (London, 1981).

—— (ed.), *New Approaches to Ruskin: Thirteen Essays* (London, 1981).

—— (ed.), *The Ruskin Art Collection: Catalogue of the Rudimentary Series, Edited with an Introduction, Notes, and Appendix* (London, 1984).

Hilton, T., *John Ruskin* (New Haven, Conn., 1985–).

Hunt, J. D., *The Wider Sea: A Life of John Ruskin* (London, 1982).

—— and F. M. Holland (edd.), *The Ruskin Polygon: Essays on the Imagination of John Ruskin* (Manchester, 1982).

Kirchhoff, F., *John Ruskin* (Boston, Mass., 1984).

Landow, G. P., *John Ruskin* (Oxford, 1985).

Rhodes, R. E. (ed.), *Studies in Ruskin* (Athens, Ohio, 1982).

Spear, J. L., *Dreams of an English Eden: Ruskin and His Tradition in Social Criticism* (New York, 1984).

Stein, R. L., *The Ritual of Interpretation: The Fine Arts as Literature in Ruskin, Rossetti, and Pater* (Cambridge, Mass., 1975).

Talbot, F., *A Visit to Brantwood* (Bembridge, 1980).

Unrau, J. P., *Ruskin and St Mark's* (London, 1984).

Wihl, G., *Ruskin and the Rhetoric of Infallibility* (New Haven, Conn., 1985).

13. PATER

[See L. Evans, 'Walter Pater' in *DeL*; S. Wright, *A Bibliography of the Writings of Walter H. Pater* (New York, 1975); F. E. Court, *Walter Pater: An Annotated Bibliography of Writings about him* (to 1973; De Kalb, 1980)]

Beyer, A., *Walter Paters Beziehungen zur Französichen Literatur und Kultur* (Halle, 1973).

Conlon, J. J., *Walter Pater and the French Tradition* (Lewisburg, 1982).

Court, F. E., *Pater and His Early Critics* (Victoria, BC, 1980).

Dodd, P. (ed.), *Walter Pater: An Imaginative Sense of Fact* (London, 1981).

Downes, D. A., *The Temper of Victorian Belief: Studies in the Religious Novels of Pater, Kingsley, and Newman* (New York, 1972).

Hill, D. L. (ed.), *The Renaissance: Studies in Art and Poetry, the 1893 Text* (Berkeley, 1980).

Inman, B. J. A., *Walter Pater's Reading: A Bibliography of his Library Borrowings and Literary References 1858–1873* (New York, 1981).

Levey, M. V., *The Case of Walter Pater* (London, 1978).

McGrath, F. C., *The Sensible Spirit: W. Pater and the Modernist Paradigm* (Tampa, 1986).

Monsman, G. C., *Walter Pater* (London, 1977).

—— *Walter Pater's Art of Autobiography* (New Haven, Conn., 1980).

—— and I. Nadel (edd.), 'Essays in Marius', *English Literature in Transition* (Tempe, Ariz., 1984).

Phillips, A. (ed.), *The Renaissance: Studies in Art and Poetry* (Oxford, 1986).

Seiler, R. M. (ed.), *Walter Pater: The Critical Heritage* (London, 1980).

Small, I. (ed.), *The Aesthetes: A Sourcebook* (London, 1979).

—— (ed.), *Marius the Epicurean* (Oxford, 1986).

Uglow, J. (ed.), *Essays in Literature and Art* (London, 1973).

14. FOUR NOTABLE AUTHORS

Macaulay

[See J. Clive and T. Pinney, 'Thomas Babington Macaulay' in *DeL*]

Clive, J. and T. Pinney (edd.), *Selected Writings, with an Introduction* (Chicago, 1972).

Clive, J., *Thomas Babington Macaulay: The Shaping of a Historian* (New York, 1973).

Hamburger, J., *Macaulay and the Whig Tradition* (Chicago, 1976).

—— (ed.), *Napoleon and the Restoration of the Bourbons: The Completed Portions of Macaulay's Projected History of France* (London, 1977).

Millgate, E. J., *Macaulay* (London, 1973).

Pinney, T. (ed.), *The Letters of Thomas Babington Macaulay* (London, 1974–81).

—— (ed.), *The Selected Letters of Thomas Babington Macaulay* (Cambridge, 1982).

Young, C. K., *Macaulay* (Harlow, 1976).

Harriet Martineau

[See *NCBEL*]

Arbuckle, E. S. (ed.), *Harriet Martineau's Letters to Fanny Wedgwood* (Stanford, 1983).

Pichanick, V. K., *Harriet Martineau: The Woman and Her Work 1802–1876* (Ann Arbor, 1980).

Sanders, V., *Reason over Passion: Harriet Martineau and the Victorian Novel* (Brighton, 1986).

Thomas, G., *Harriet Martineau* (Boston, Mass., 1985).

Yates, G. G. (ed.), *Harriet Martineau on Women* (New Brunswick, 1985).

Mill

[See J. M. Robson, 'John Stuart Mill' in *DeL* and M. Laine, *Bibliography of Works on John Stuart Mill* (to 1978; Toronto, 1982)]

Berger, F. R., *Happiness, Justice and Freedom: The Moral and Political Philosophy of J. S. Mill* (Berkeley, 1984).

Garforth, F. W. (ed.), *John Stuart Mill's Theory of Education* (Oxford, 1979).

—— *Educative Democracy: John Stuart Mill on Education in Society* (Oxford, 1980).

Gray, J. N., *Mill on Liberty: A Defence* (London, 1983).

Hollander, S., *The Economics of John Stuart Mill* (Oxford, 1985).

Jong, W. R. de, *The Semantics of John Stuart Mill*, tr. H. D. Morton (Dordrecht, 1982).

Kamm, J. M., *John Stuart Mill in Love* (London, 1977).

Lively, J. and J. Rees (edd.), *Utilitarian Logic and Politics: James Mill's Essay on Government, Macaulay's Critique, and the Ensuing Debate, Selected and Introduced* (Oxford, 1978).

Martins, D. E., *John Stuart Mill and the Land Question* (Hull, 1981).

Robson, J. M. and J. Stillinger (edd.), *Autobiography and Literary Essays, Collected Works of John Stuart Mill*, vol. i (Toronto, 1981).

Semmel, B., *John Stuart Mill and the Pursuit of Virtue* (New Haven, Conn., 1984).

Soper, K. (ed.), *The Enfranchisement of Women and The Subjection of Women, with a New Introduction* (London, 1983).

Ten, C. L., *Mill on Liberty* (Oxford, 1980).

Thomas, W. E. S., *Mill* (Oxford, 1985).

Butler

[See *NCBEL* and W. G. Hammond, 'Samuel Butler: A Checklist of Works and Criticism' in *The Samuel Butler Newsletter* (Williamstown, Mass., 1980–1)]

Breuer, H.-P. and D. F. Howard (edd.), *Erewhon* (Newark, Del., 1981).

Breuer, H.-P. and R. E. Parsell (edd.), *The Notebooks of Samuel Butler* (Lanham, 1984–).

Hopkins, H. K. (ed.), *Samuel Butler and Miss E. M. A. Savage: Further Correspondence* (North Waltham, 1976).

Jeffers, T. L., *Samuel Butler Revalued* (University Park, 1981).

Johnstone, R. (ed.), *Samuel Butler on the Resurrection: Edited and Introduced* (Gerrard's Cross, 1980).

Mudford, P. (ed.), *Erewhon* (Harmondsworth, 1970).

Norrman, R. G., *Samuel Butler and the Meaning of Chiasmus* (Basingstoke, 1986).

Simonsen, K., *Erzahltechnik und Weltanschauung in Samuel Butlers Literarischen Werken* (Bern, 1974).

15.   OTHER PROSE WRITERS

[See 'Minor Prose', 'Philosophy' and 'Religion' in *NCBEL*]

Keble

[See R. W. Fulweiler, 'The Oxford Movement' and W. V. Harris, 'The Critics' in *DeL*; also Bibliography to Chap. 9, above]

Maurice

[See R. Helmstadter, 'The Victorian Churches' in *DeL*]

McClain, F. M., *F. D. Maurice: A Study* (Cambridge, Mass., 1982).
Styler, W. E. (ed.), *Learning and Working* (London, 1968).
Wolf, W. J., *An Abridgement of Maurice's 'Kingdom of Christ', Emended with an Introduction* (Lanham, 1983).

Gladstone

[See P. M. Long, *A Bibliography of Gladstone Publications at St Deiniol's Library* (Hawarden, 1979) and C. J. Dobson, *Gladstoniana: A Bibliography of Material Relating to W. E. Gladstone at St Deiniol's Library* (Hawarden, 1982)]

Feuchtwanger, E. J., *Gladstone* (London, 1975).
Foot, M. R. D. (ed.), *The Gladstone Diaries* (Oxford, 1968–   ).
Ramm, A., *Gladstone as Man of Letters* (Oxford, 1982).
Shannon, R. T., *Gladstone* (London, 1982–   ).

Smiles

Bull, G. (ed.), *Self-Help*, abridged, with introd. by Sir K. Joseph (Harmondsworth, 1986).

Spencer

Macrae, D. (ed.), *The Man versus the State* (Harmondsworth, 1969).
Peel, J. D. Y., *Herbert Spencer: The Evolution of a Sociologist* (London, 1971).
—— (ed.), *Herbert Spencer on Social Evolution: Selected Writings, Edited with an Introduction* (Chicago, 1972).
Turner, J. H., *Herbert Spencer: A Renewed Appreciation* (Beverly Hills, 1985).
Wiltshire, D. R., *The Social and Political Thought of Herbert Spencer* (Oxford, 1978).

Bagehot

[See W. V. Harris, 'Walter Bagehot' in *DeL*]

St John Stevas, N. (ed.), *The Collected Works of Walter Bagehot* (London, 1965–86).
Wheare, K. C., *Walter Bagehot* (London, 1974).

Dallas

[See W. V. Harris, 'Eneas Sweetland Dallas' in *DeL*]

Stephen

[See J. W. Bicknell, 'Leslie Stephen' in *DeL*]
Annan, N. G., *Leslie Stephen: The Godless Victorian* (London, 1984).

Morley

[See J. W. Bicknell, 'John Morley' in *DeL*]

Sidgwick

James, D. G., *Henry Sidgwick: Science and Faith in Victorian England* (London, 1970).
Schneewind, J. B., *Sidgwick's Ethics and Victorian Moral Philosophy* (Oxford, 1977).

Bradley

Manser, A. R., *Bradley's Logic* (Oxford, 1983).
—— and G. Stock (edd.), *The Philosophy of F. H. Bradley* (Oxford, 1984).
Sacchi, D., *Unità e Relazione: Studi sul Pensiero di F. H. Bradley* (Milan, 1981).
Vander Veer, G. L., *Bradley's Metaphysics and the Self* (New Haven, Conn., 1970).

16. HISTORY, BIOGRAPHY, AUTOBIOGRAPHY

[See 'History' in *NCBEL* and W. Matthews, *British Autobiography: An Annotated Bibliography of British Autobiographies ... before 1951* (Berkeley, 1955)]

General Studies

Cockshut, A. O. J., *Truth to Life: The Art of Biography in the Nineteenth Century* (London, 1974).
—— *The Art of Autobiography in 19th and 20th Century England* (New Haven, Conn., 1984).
Culler, A. D., *The Victorian Mirror of History* (New Haven, Conn., 1985).
Fleishman, A., *Figures of Autobiography: The Language of Self-Writing in Victorian and Modern England* (Berkeley, 1983).
Gay, P., *Style in History* (London, 1975).
Jann, R., *The Art and Science of Victorian History* (Columbus, Ohio, 1985).
Landow, G. P. (ed.), *Approaches to Victorian Autobiography* (Athens, Ohio, 1979).
Olney, J., *Metaphors of Self: The Meaning of Autobiography* (Princeton, NJ, 1972).

T. Arnold

Selchow, U., *Thomas Arnold: Versuch einer Neuwertung seiner Bedeutung als Theologe, Sozialkritiker und Headmaster der Public School in Rugby* (Hamburg, 1980).

Froude

[See R. Goetzman, *James Anthony Froude: A Bibliography of Studies* (New York, 1977)]

Clubbe, J. (ed.), *Froude's Life of Carlyle, Abridged and Edited* (London, 1979).

Buckle

Hanham, H. J. (ed.), *On Scotland and the Scotch Intellect* (selections from the *History*, with introd.; Chicago, 1970).

Maine

Feaver, G., *From Status to Contract: A Biography of Sir H. Maine 1822–1888* (London, 1969).

Kinglake

De Gaury, G., *Travelling Gent: The Life of A. Kinglake* (London, 1972).

Lecky

Curtis, L. P. (ed.), *A History of Ireland in the Eighteenth Century* (abridged, with introd.; Chicago, 1972).

Stubbs

Cornford, J. (ed.), *The Constitutional History of England* (abridged, with introd.; Chicago, 1979).

Freeman

Bratchel, M. E., *Edward Augustus Freeman and the Victorian Interpretation of the Norman Conquest* (Ilfracombe, 1969).

Seeley

Wormell, D. A., *Sir John Seeley and the Uses of History* (Cambridge, 1980).

Forster

Davies, J. A., *John Forster: A Literary Life* (Leicester, 1983).
Hoppé, A. J. (ed.), *The Life of Charles Dickens* (with notes; London, 1966).

Mrs Gaskell

[See R. L. Selig, *Elizabeth Gaskell: A Reference Guide* (Boston, Mass., 1977) and J. Welch, *Elizabeth Gaskell: An Annotated Bibliography 1929–1975* (New York, 1977)]

Brodetsky, T., *Elizabeth Gaskell* (Leamington Spa, 1986).
Chapple, J. A. V. and J. G. Sharps (edd.), *Elizabeth Gaskell: A Portrait in Letters* (Manchester, 1980).
Easson, A. W., *Elizabeth Gaskell* (London, 1979).
Gérin, W. (ed.), *The Life of Charlotte Brontë* (London, 1971).
—— *Elizabeth Gaskell: A Biography* (Oxford, 1976).
Stoneman, P., *Elizabeth Gaskell* (Brighton, 1987).

Gilchrist

Doyle-Davidson, W. A. G. (ed.), *Life of William Blake* (with new introd.; East Ardsley, Wakefield, 1973).
Gilchrist, H. H. (ed.), *Anne Gilchrist: Her Life and Writings*, 2nd edn. (London, 1887).

Pattison

Green, V. H. H. (ed.), *Love in a Cool Climate: The Letters of M. Pattison and M. Bradley 1879–1884* (Oxford, 1985).
Manton, J. (ed. with introd.), *Memoirs* (Fontwell, 1969).

Dundonald

Avila Martel, A. de, *Cochrane y la independencia del Pacifico* (Santiago de Chile, 1976).
Grimble, I., *The Sea Wolf: The Life of Admiral Cochrane* (London, 1978).
Thomas, D. S., *Cochrane: Britannia's Last Sea-King* (London, 1978).

Trollope

[See J. C. Olmsted and J. E. Welch, *The Reputation of Trollope: An Annotated Bibliography 1925–1975* (New York, 1978)]

Edwards, P. D. (gen. ed.), *Autobiography*, ed. M. Sadleir and F. Page (with introd. and notes; Oxford, 1980).
Terry, R. C. (ed.), *Trollope: Interviews and Recollections* (Basingstoke, 1987).

Darwin

[See R. B. Freeman, *The Works of Charles Darwin: An Annotated Bibliographical Handlist*, 2nd edn. (Folkestone, 1977)]

Barrett, E. H. and R. B. Freeman (edd.), *The Works of Charles Darwin* (London, 1986–   ).
Burkhardt, F. and S. Smith (edd.), *The Correspondence of Charles Darwin* (Cambridge, 1985–   ).
De Beer, G. (ed.), *Charles Darwin, T. H. Huxley: Autobiographies* (London, 1974).
Freeman, R. B., *Charles Darwin: A Companion* (Hamden, Conn., 1978).
Manier, E., *The Young Darwin and His Cultural Circle* (Dordrecht, 1978).
Ralling, C. (ed.), *The Voyage of Charles Darwin: His Autobiographical Writings Selected and Arranged* (London, 1978).

Huxley

[See J. W. Bicknell, 'Thomas Henry Huxley' in *DeL*]
De Beer, G. (ed.), *Charles Darwin, T. H. Huxley: Autobiographies* (London, 1974).

17. SCIENCE

General Studies

Cosslett, T., *The 'Scientific Movement' and Victorian Literature* (Brighton, 1982).
—— (ed.), *Science and Religion in the Nineteenth Century* (Cambridge, 1984).
Rupke, N., *The Great Chain of History: William Buckland and the English School of Geology 1814–1849* (Oxford, 1984).
Winsor, M. P., *Starfish, Jellyfish, and the Order of Life: Issues in Nineteenth-Century Science* (New Haven, Conn., 1976).

Lyell

Bailey, E. B., *Charles Lyell* (London, 1962).
Wilson, L. G. (ed.), *Sir Charles Lyell's Scientific Journals on the Species Question* (New Haven, Conn., 1970).

Somerville

Patterson, E. C., *Mary Somerville 1780–1872* (Oxford, 1979).
—— *Mary Somerville and the Cultivation of Science 1815–1840* (Boston, Mass., 1983).

Faraday

[See A. E. Jeffreys, *Michael Faraday: A List of His Lectures and Published Writings* (London, 1960)]

Agassi, J., *Faraday as a Natural Philosopher* (Chicago, 1971).
Bowers, B. P., *Michael Faraday and Electricity* (London, 1974).
Crookes, W. (ed.), *A Course of Six Lectures on the Chemical History of a Candle* (London, 1960).
Lehrs, E. L., *Spiritual Science, Electricity and Michael Faraday* (London, 1975).
Porter, G. and J. Friday (edd.), *Advice to Lecturers, Taken from the Writings of M. Faraday and L. Bragg* (London, 1974).
Williams, L. P. (ed.), *The Selected Correspondence of Michael Faraday* (Cambridge, 1971).

Miller

Rosie, G., *Hugh Miller: Outrage and Order: A Biography and Selected Writings* (Edinburgh, 1981).

Chambers

De Beer, G. (ed.), *Vestiges of the Natural History of Creation* (Leicester, 1969).
Millhauser, M., *Just Before Darwin: Robert Chambers and Vestiges* (Middletown, Conn., 1959).

Herschel

Buttmann, G., *The Shadow of the Telescope: A Biography of Herschel*, tr. B. E. J. Page, ed. D. S. Evans (Guildford, 1974).
Evans, D. S. (ed.), *Herschel at the Cape: Diaries and Correspondence of Sir John Herschel 1834–1838* (Cape Town, 1969).

P. H. Gosse

[See R. B. Freeman, *Philip Henry Gosse: A Bibliography* (Folkestone, 1980)]
Thwaite, A. B., *Edmund Gosse* (Oxford, 1985).

Darwin
[See Bibliography to Chap. 16, above]

Beer, G., *Darwin's Plots: Evolutionary Narrative in Darwin, George Eliot and Nineteenth-Century Fiction* (London, 1983).
Brent, P., *Charles Darwin: 'A Man of Enlarged Curiosity'* (London, 1981).
Ekman, P. (ed.), *Darwin and Facial Expression: A Century of Research in Review* (New York, 1973).
Gruber, H. E., *Darwin on Man: A Psychological Study of Scientific Creativity, together with Darwin's Early Unpublished Notebooks* (Chicago, 1974).
Irvine, W., *Apes, Angels, and Victorians: The Story of Darwin, Huxley, and Evolution* (New York, 1955).
Ospovat, D., *The Development of Darwin's Theory: Natural History, Natural Theology, and Natural Selection 1838–1859* (Cambridge, 1981).
Young, R. M., *Darwin's Metaphor: Nature's Place in Victorian Culture* (Cambridge, 1985).

Huxley
[See Bibliography to Chap. 16, above]

Gregorio, M. A. di, *T. H. Huxley's Place in Natural Science* (New Haven, Conn., 1984).
Paradis, J. G., *T. H. Huxley: Man's Place in Nature* (Lincoln, Nebr., 1978).

Galton

Forrest, D. W., *Francis Galton: The Life and Work of a Victorian Genius* (London, 1974).

18. TRAVEL

[See 'Travel' in *NCBEL* and J. Shattock, 'Travel Writing Victorian and Modern: A Review of Recent Research' in *The Art of Travel: Essays on Travel Writing*, ed. P. Dodd (London, 1982)]

Darwin

Keynes, R. D. (ed.), *The Beagle Record: Selections from the Original Pictorial Records and Written Accounts of the Voyage of H.M.S. Beagle* (Cambridge, 1979).
Moorehead, A., *Darwin and the Beagle* (Harmondsworth, 1979).

Borrow

Collie, M., *George Borrow: Eccentric* (Cambridge, 1982).
Williams, D., *A World of His Own: The Double Life of George Borrow* (Oxford, 1982).

Kinglake

[See Bibliography to Chap. 16, above]

Jewett, I. B. H., *Alexander W. Kinglake* (Boston, Mass., 1981).

Thackeray

[See J. S. Olmsted, *Thackeray and His Twentieth-Century Critics: An Annotated Bibliography 1900–1975* (New York, 1977)]

Carey, J., *Thackeray: Prodigal Genius* (London, 1977).
Ferris, I., *William Makepeace Thackeray* (Boston, Mass., 1983).
Monsarrat, A., *An Uneasy Victorian: Thackeray the Man* (London, 1980).
Peters, C., *Thackeray's Universe: Shifting Worlds of Imagination and Reality* (London, 1987).

Layard

Brackman, A. C., *The Luck of Nineveh* (London, 1981).
Saggs, H. W. F. (ed.), *Nineveh and Its Remains* (with introd. and notes; London, 1970).
Silverberg, R., *The Man Who Found Nineveh: The Story of A. H. Layard* (Tadworth, 1968).

Curzon

Fraser, I. H., *The Heir of Parham: Robert Curzon* (Alburgh, 1986).
Holland, M., *Robert Curzon: Traveller and Book Collector* (Manchester, 1983).

Wallace

Beddall, B. G., *Wallace and Bates in the Tropics: An Introduction to the Theory of Natural Selection* (New York, 1969).

Ellis, M. A. N., *Darwin's Moon: A Biography of A. R. Wallace* (London, 1966).
McKinney, H. L., *Wallace and Natural Selection* (New Haven, Conn., 1972).

Burton

[See N. M. Penzer, *An Annotated Bibliography of Sir Richard Francis Burton* (London, 1923)]
Brodie, F. M., *The Devil Drives: A Life of Sir Richard Burton* (London, 1967).
Burne, G. S., *Richard Francis Burton* (Boston, Mass., 1985).
Gournay, J. F., *L'appel du Proche-orient: Richard Francis Burton et son temps 1821–1890* (Lille, 1983).
Hastings, M. G. T., *Sir Richard Burton* (London, 1978).
Newbury, C. W. (ed.), *A Mission to Gelele, King of Dahome* (with introd. and notes; London, 1966).
Orrmont, A., *Fearless Adventurer: Sir Richard Burton* (London, 1972).
Waterfield, G. (ed.), *First Footsteps in East Africa—With Additional Chapters* (London, 1966).

Livingstone

[See J. A. Casada, *Dr David Livingstone and Sir Henry Morton Stanley: An Annotated Bibliography with Commentary* (New York, 1976)]
Ceserani, G. P., *The Travels of Livingstone*, tr. S. Wason, ed. D. Hamley (Harmondsworth, 1979).
Ransford, O. N., *David Livingstone: The Dark Interior* (London, 1978).

Speke

Maitland, A., *Speke* (London, 1971).

Palgrave

Allan, M., *Palgrave of Arabia: The Life of W. G. Palgrave 1826–1888* (London, 1972).

Macgregor

Ransome, A. (ed.), *The Voyage Alone in the Yawl Rob Roy* (with introd.; London, 1954).

Stanley

[See J. A. Casada, *Dr David Livingstone and Sir Henry Morton Stanley: An Annotated Bibliography with Commentary* (New York, 1976)]
Blashford-Snell, J. N., *In the Steps of Stanley* (London, 1975).
Hellinga, G., *Henry Morton Stanley: een individual-psychologische interpretatie* (with summary in English; Leiden, 1978).
Newson-Smith, S. (ed.), *The Story of Stanley and Livingstone Told in Their Own Words* (London, 1978).

Burnaby

Alexander, M., *The True Blue: The Life and Adventures of Colonel Fred Burnaby 1842–1885* (London, 1957).
Williams, D. (ed.), *A Ride to Khiva: Travels and Adventures in Central Asia, Abridged and Introduced* (London, 1972).

Stevenson

[See F. Bethke, *Three Victorian Travel Writers: A Bibliography of Criticism on Mrs Frances Trollope, Samuel Butler, and Robert Louis Stevenson* (Boston, Mass., 1977), and R. G. Swear-Ingen, *The Prose Writings of Robert Louis Stevenson: A Guide* (London, 1970)]

Calder J. (ed.), *The Works of Robert Louis Stevenson* (Edinburgh, 1980–   ).
Chastaing, P., *Avec Stevenson dans les Cévennes en 1878: quelques souvenirs et réflexions 100 ans après* (Paris, 1979).

Doughty

Tabachnick, S. E., *Charles Doughty* (Boston, Mass., 1981).

Jerome

[See R. G. Logan, *Jerome K. Jerome: A Concise Bibliography* (Walsall, 1971)]

Connolly, J., *Jerome K. Jerome: A Critical Biography* (London, 1982).
Green, M. (ed.), *The Other Jerome K. Jerome: Selected and Introduced* (London, 1984).

19. DRAMA

[See 'Drama' in *NCBEL* and L. W. Connolly and J. P. Wearing, *English Drama and Theatre 1800–1900: A Guide to Information Sources* (Detroit, 1978)]

General Studies

Baker, M., *The Rise of the Victorian Actor* (London, 1978).
Bingham, M., *Henry Irving and the Victorian Theatre* (London, 1978).
Booth, M. R. (ed.), *English Plays of the Nineteenth Century* (Oxford, 1967–76).
—— *Victorian Spectacular Theatre 1850–1910* (London, 1981).
Craik, T. W. (gen. ed.), *The Revels History of Drama in English*, vol. vii, *1880 to the Present Day*, ed. J. Hunt, K. Richards, and J. R. Taylor (London, 1978).
Hughes, A., *Henry Irving: Shakespearian* (Cambridge, 1981).
Leech, C. and T. W. Craik (gen. edd.), *The Revels History of Drama in English*, vol. vi, *1750–1880*, ed. M. R. Booth, R. Southern, F. and L.-L. Marker, and R. Davies (London, 1975).

Rees, T., *Theatre Lighting in the Age of Gas* (London, 1978).
Rowell, G., *Queen Victoria Goes to the Theatre* (London, 1978).
—— *The Victorian Theatre 1792–1914: A Survey*, 2nd edn. (Cambridge, 1979).
—— *Theatre in the Age of Irving* (Oxford, 1981).

Lytton

Campbell, J. L., *Edward Bulwer-Lytton* (Boston, Mass., 1986).
Fawkes, R., *Dion Boucicault: A Biography* (London, 1979).
Krause, D. (ed.), *The Dolmen Boucicault* (three plays; Dublin, 1984).
Thomson, P. (ed.), *Plays* (five, with introd. and notes; Cambridge, 1984).

Taylor

Banham, M. (ed.), *Plays by Tom Taylor* (four, incl. *The Ticket-of-Leave Man* (Cambridge, 1985).
Brown, J. R. (ed.), *The Ticket-of-Leave Man* (with introd. and notes; London, 1981).
Tolles, W., *Tom Taylor and the Victorian Drama* (New York, 1940).

Reade

Hammet, H. (ed.), *Plays* (three incl. *Masks and Faces* (Cambridge, 1986).
Smith, E. E., *Charles Reade* (London, 1976).

Hazlewood

[See R. L. Wolf, *Sensational Victorian: The Life and Fiction of M. E. Braddon* (New York, 1979)]

Robertson

Booth, M. R. (ed.), *Six Plays* (with introd.; Ashover, 1980).
Rault, A. (tr.), *La caste: Comédie* (Paris, 1974).
Tydeman, W. (ed.), *Plays by Tom Robertson* (four; Cambridge, 1982).

Gilbert

Cox-Ife, W., *W. S. Gilbert: Stage-Director* (London, 1981).
Rowell, G. (ed.), *Plays by W. S. Gilbert* (five; Cambridge, 1982).
Sutton, M. K., *W. S. Gilbert* (Boston, Mass., 1975).

Jones

Jackson, R. (ed.), *Plays* (three, incl. *The Silver King*; Cambridge, 1982).

Pinero

Lazenby, W. S., *Sir Arthur Wing Pinero* (New York, 1972).
Wearing, J. P. (ed.), *The Collected Letters of Sir Arthur Pinero* (Minneapolis, 1974).

20. CHILDREN'S BOOKS

[See 'Children's Books', in *NCBEL*; V. Haviland, *Children's Literature: A Guide to Reference Sources* (Washington, DC, 1966; First and Second Supplements, with assistance of M. N. Coughlan, Washington, DC, 1972, 1977); B. Alderson, 'General Book List', in F. J. H. Darton, *Children's Books in England: Five Centuries of Social Life*, 3rd edn. (Cambridge, 1982); G. J. Senick, *Children's Literature Review*, vol. iv (Detroit, 1982)]

General Studies

Avery, G., *Childhood's Pattern: A Study of the Heroes and Heroines of Children's Fiction 1770–1950* (London, 1975).
Bratton, J. S., *The Impact of Victorian Children's Fiction* (London, 1981).
Carpenter, H. and M. Prichard, *The Oxford Companion to Children's Literature* (Oxford, 1984).
Darton, F. J. H., *Children's Books in England* (see above).
Quigley, I., *The Heirs of Tom Brown: The English School Story* (London, 1982).
Salway, L. (ed.), *A Peculiar Gift: Nineteenth-Century Writings on Books for Children, Selected and Edited* (Harmondsworth, 1976).

Lear

Bibby, H. C., *The Art of the Limerick* (London, 1978).
Hark, I. R., *Edward Lear* (Boston, Mass., 1982).
Hyman, S. (ed.), *Edward Lear's Birds* (London, 1980).
Kelen, E., *Mr Nonsense: A Life of Edward Lear* (Nashville, Tenn., 1974).
Lehmann, J., *Edward Lear and His World* (London, 1977).
Liebert, H. W. (ed.), *Lear in the Original: Drawings and Limericks from his Book of Nonsense Drawing, with an Introduction and Notes* (New York, 1975).
Noakes, V., *Edward Lear: The Life of a Wanderer* (London, 1968).
—— *Edward Lear 1812–1888* (London, 1985).
Thorpe, A. (ed.), *The Birds of Edward Lear: A Selection of the Finest Bird Plates of the Artist, Edited and Introduced* (London, 1975).

Horne

[See Bibliography to Chap. 9, above]

Fisher, M. (ed.), *Memoirs of a London Doll* (with introd. and notes; London, 1967).

Yonge

[See M. Laski and K. Tillotson, 'Bibliography' in *A Chaplet for Charlotte Yonge*, ed. G. Battiscombe and M. Laski (London, 1965)]

Sandbach-Dahlström, C., *Be Good, Sweet Maid: C. Yonge's Domestic Fiction: A Study in Dogmatic Purpose and Fictional Form* (Stockholm, 1984).

Thackeray

[See Bibliography to Chap. 18, above]

Kingsley

[See Bibliography to Chap. 9, above]

Hughes

Little, J. E., *Thomas Hughes 1822–1896* (Uffington, 1972).
Matthews, J. P., *Thomas Hughes: 'Tom Brown's Schooldays'* (London, 1980).

Ballantyne

[See E. Quayle, *R. M. Ballantyne: A Bibliography of First Editions* (London, 1968))]
Quayle, E., *Ballantyne the Brave* (London, 1967).

Mrs Ewing

Avery, G., *Mrs Ewing* (London, 1961).
Blom, M. H. and T. E. Blom (edd.), *Canada Home: Fredericton Letters 1867–1869* (Vancouver, 1983).

'Carroll'

[See S. H. Williams and F. Madan, *The Lewis Carroll Handbook*, rev. edn., ed. R. L. Green and D. Crutch (Folkestone, 1979) and E. Guiliano, *Lewis Carroll: An Annotated International Bibliography 1960–1977* (Charlottesville, 1980]
Ash, R. (ed.), *Alice's Adventures Under Ground* (London, 1985).
Clark, A., *Lewis Carroll: A Biography* (London, 1979).
Cohen, M. N., *Lewis Carroll: Photographer of Children* (New York, 1979).
—— (ed.), with assistance from R. L. Green, *The Selected Letters of Lewis Carroll* (London, 1982).
Gasson, R. (ed.), *The Illustrated Lewis Carroll* (with introd.; London, 1978).
Green, R. L. (ed.), *Alice's Adventures in Wonderland* and *Through The Looking-Glass* (Oxford, 1983).
Guiliano, E. (ed.), *Lewis Carroll: A Celebration: Essays on the Occasion of the 150th Anniversary of the Birth of C. L. Dodgson* (New York, 1982).

MacDonald

[See Bibliography to Chap. 9, above]

Mrs Molesworth

Avery, G. (ed.), *My New Home* (with introd.; London, 1968).

Sewell

Chitty, S. E. R., *The Woman Who Wrote 'Black Beauty': A Life of Anna Sewell* (London, 1971).

Henty

[See R. L. Dartt, *G. A. Henty: A Bibliography* (Cedar Grove, 1971)]

Arnold, G., *Held Fast for England: G. A. Henty, Imperialist Boys' Writer* (London, 1980).

Thompson, J. C., *The Boy's Dumas, G. A. Henty: Aspects of Victorian Publishing* (Cheadle, 1975).

Burnett

Thwaite, A. B., *Waiting for the Party: The Life of Frances Hodgson Burnett 1849–1924* (London, 1974).

21. COMIC VERSE, PARODY, NONSENSE

General Studies

Collins, R. G. (ed.), *Nineteenth Century Literary Humor, Mosaic*, vol. ix (Winnipeg, 1976).

Henkle, R. B., *Comedy and Culture: England 1820–1900* (Princeton, NJ, 1980).

Huggett, E. (ed.), *Victorian England As Seen By 'Punch'* (London, 1978).

Sewell, E., *The Field of Nonsense* (London, 1952).

Barham

Browning, D. C. (ed.), *The Ingoldsby Legends* (London, 1960).

Aytoun

[See Bibliography to Chap. 9, above]

Lear

[See Bibliography to Chap. 20, above]

Thackeray

[See Bibliography to Chap. 18, above]

Calverley

Spear, H. D. (ed.), *The English Poems of Charles Stuart Calverley* (Leicester, 1974).

'Lewis Carroll'

[See Bibliography to Chap. 20, above]

Heath, P. (ed.), *The Philosopher's Alice* (London, 1974).

Wakeling, E., *The Logic of Lewis Carroll: A Study of Lewis Carroll's Contributions to Logic* (London, 1978).

Gilbert

[See Bibliography to Chap. 19, above]

Abrahams, D. C., *Lost Chords and Discords* (London, 1975).
Allen, R., *W. S. Gilbert: An Anniversary Survey and Exhibition Checklist, with Thirty-Five Illustrations* (Charlottesville, 1963).
—— (ed.), *The First Night Gilbert and Sullivan, containing Librettos of the Fourteen Operas, Exactly As Presented at their Première Performances* (London, 1975).
Ayre, L., *The Gilbert and Sullivan Companion* (London, 1986).
Baily, L. W. A., *Gilbert and Sullivan and their World* (London, 1973).
Bradley, I. C. (ed.), *The Annotated Gilbert and Sullivan* (Harmondsworth, 1982).
Eden, D., *Gilbert and Sullivan: The Creative Conflict* (Rutherford, 1986).
Ellis, J. (ed.), *The Bab Ballads* (Cambridge, Mass., 1970).
Goodman, A., *Gilbert and Sullivan at Law* (Rutherford, 1983).
Williamson, A., *Gilbert and Sullivan Opera: An Assessment* (London, 1982).
Wilson, R. J. and F. Lloyd, *Gilbert and Sullivan: The D'Oyly Carte Years* (London, 1984).

Swinburne

[See Bibliography to Chap. 7, above]

CHRONOLOGICAL TABLE

Arnold, D. (ed.), *The New Oxford Companion to Music* (Oxford, 1983).
Chapman, R. W. (ed.), *Annals of English Literature 1475–1950*, 2nd edn. (Oxford, 1961).
Craik, T. W. and C. Leech (gen. edd.), 'Chronological Table' in *The Revels History of Drama in English*, vols. vi–vii (See Bibliography to Chap. 19, above).
Drabble, M. (ed.), *The Oxford Companion to English Literature*, 5th edn. (Oxford, 1985).
Garland, H. and M. Garland (edd.), *The Oxford Companion to German Literature* (2nd edn., ed. M. Garland; Oxford, 1986).
Kennedy, M. (ed.), *The Oxford Dictionary of Music* (Oxford, 1985).
Osborne, H. (ed.), *The Oxford Companion to Art* (Oxford, 1970).
Reid, J. M. H. (ed.), *The Concise Oxford Dictionary of French Literature* (Oxford, 1976).
Williams, N., *Chronology of the Modern World 1763 to the Present Time*, rev. edn. (London, 1969).

Index

Main entries are in bold figures. An asterisk indicates a biographical footnote. Passages where a writer is alluded to are indexed under that writer's name, even when it does not appear in the text. The index excludes the Chronological Table and the Bibliography; and some incidental references have been omitted.